T0215169

Lecture Notes in Computer Science 8984

Commenced Publication in 1973
Founding and Former Series Editors:
Gerhard Goos, Juris Hartmanis, and Jan van Leeuwen

More information about this series at http://www.springer.com/series/7407

Martin Aher · Daniel Hole
Emil Jeřábek · Clemens Kupke (Eds.)

Logic, Language, and Computation

10th International Tbilisi Symposium
on Logic, Language, and Computation, TbiLLC 2013
Gudauri, Georgia, September 23–27, 2013
Revised Selected Papers

 Springer

Editors

Martin Aher
University of Tartu
Tartu
Estonia

Daniel Hole
Universität Stuttgart
Stuttgart
Germany

Emil Jeřábek
Institute of Mathematics, AS CR
Prague
Czech Republic

Clemens Kupke
University of Strathclyde
Glasgow
UK

ISSN 0302-9743   ISSN 1611-3349 (electronic)
Lecture Notes in Computer Science
ISBN 978-3-662-46905-7   ISBN 978-3-662-46906-4   (eBook)
DOI 10.1007/978-3-662-46906-4

Library of Congress Control Number: 2015937955

LNCS Sublibrary: SL1 – Theoretical Computer Science and General Issues

Springer Heidelberg New York Dordrecht London

Printed on acid-free paper

Springer-Verlag GmbH Berlin Heidelberg is part of Springer Science+Business Media
(www.springer.com)

Preface

The 10th International Tbilisi Symposium on Logic, Language, and Computation was held in Gudauri, Georgia, during September 23–27, 2013. The Symposium was organized by the Centre for Language, Logic, and Speech at the Tbilisi State University, the Georgian Academy of Sciences and the Institute for Logic, Language, and Computation (ILLC) of the University of Amsterdam. The conference series is centered around the interaction between logic, language, and computation. The contributions represent these three fields, and the symposia aim to foster interaction between them. The scientific program consisted of tutorials, invited and contributed talks, and two special sessions.

It is also worth mentioning that alongside their scientific merit, the Tbilisi symposia are renowned for their social atmosphere and heartwarming welcome by the Georgian hosts. The tenth symposium was no exception and we would like to extend our heartfelt thanks to the organizers, reviewers, and presenters who worked to bring it about.

The symposium offered three tutorials. Samson Abramsky gave a tutorial on contextual semantics, demonstrating how tools from computer science shed light on phenomena at the heart of quantum mechanics, namely non-locality, contextuality, and entanglement. The tutorial on aspect was given by Daniel Altshuler and he focused on the formal semantics of aspectual meaning from a crosslinguistic perspective. Rosalie Iemhoff gave tutorial on admissible rules, i.e., inference steps not explicitly mentioned in the axiomatization of theories, focusing on their nontrivial nature in intuitionistic and modal logic or Heyting arithmetic.

There were six invited talks given by Balder ten Cate, Agata Ciabattoni, Thomas Colcombet, Galit W. Sassoon, Alexandra Silva, and Sergei Tatevosov. Two workshops were organized at the event, the first on aspect, organized by Daniel Altshuler, Sergei Tatevosov, and Daniel Hole and the second on algebraic proof theory, organized by Agata Ciabattoni and Rosalie Iemhoff. Each included their own invited speakers: Roumyana Pancheva and Hans Kamp spoke about aspect and Matthias Baaz, Alessio Guglielmi, and Kazushige Terui gave talks on algebraic proof theory. This volume contains a selection of papers from both invited and contributed talks presented at the symposium. In what follows, we will briefly introduce the selected papers in logic, language, and computation. As many of the papers were interdisciplinary, they are presented in alphabetical order.

Martin Aher seeks to unravel puzzles involving deontic conflicts or, in other words, situations where each possible state of affairs lies contrary to some rule or another. The proposal is realized in a specific iteration of inquisitive semantics, called MadRis, which specifies both support and rejection conditions. The paper focuses on the Dr. Procrastinate puzzle where the desiderata are obtained by assigning each rule a unique violation-proposition, such that in a deontic conflict, no logical contradiction between rules occurs.

Philippe Balbiani and Çiğdem Gencer investigate admissibility and unifiability problems for contact logics. They prove that admissibility of weak rules is decidable for balanced and finitely axiomatized logics, that the unifiability problem for weak formulae is in NP for every logic and NP-complete for consistent logics, and that the unifiability problem for weak formulae can be reduced to theoremhood for consistent logics containing the formula C(1,1).

Kata Balogh's paper extends her prior work on focus that combines feature-based lexicalized tree-adjoining grammar (F-LTAG) and inquisitive semantics to account for the question-answer congruence of various narrow focus constructions. In the second part of the paper, Balogh demonstrates how to provide a uniform treatment of focusing and quantifier scope.

Marina Beridze, Liana Lortkipanidze, and David Nadaraia provide a detailed report on the construction of a Georgian dialect corpus. In the first part they discuss the representativeness in the corpus and problems related to morphological annotation. After that they give a detailed description of the database storing the computational lexicon.

The paper by Nick Bezhanishvili, Dion Coumans, Sam van Gool, and Dick de Jongh investigates the conjunction–implication fragment of intuitionistic propositional logic. Using duality for finite distributive lattices, they give a description of finitely generated universal models of this fragment, and up-sets of Kripke models definable by conjunction–implication formulas.

Cvetan Dunchev, Alexander Leitsch, Mikheil Rukhaia, and Daniel Weller study sequent calculi for first-order logic with induction rules, which often do not enjoy cut elimination. They present an alternative formalism for uniform description of infinite sequences of proofs replacing induction rules, and develop a cut-elimination method in this formalism, based on the CERES method.

Pushing forward the inquisitive semantics enterprise, Jeroen Groenendijk and Floris Roelofsen add a suppositional content type to the previously covered inquisitive and informative content types. The paper focuses on the case where rejecting the antecedent of a conditional sentences neither supports nor rejects it, but suppositionally dismisses it, providing a formal semantic account of this aspect of information exchange.

Paula Henk offers a new perspective on the arithmetical completeness of GL as the provability logic of Peano arithmetic. Her paper introduces several arithmetical accessibility relations that turn the collection of models of PA into a Kripke model, and shows that every finite GL-model is bisimilar to such an arithmetical Kripke model using a variant of Solovay's completeness proof.

Dick de Jongh and Zhiguang Zhao investigate the positive fragment of intuitionistic and minimal propositional and predicate logic. The authors first provide a characterization of the positive fragments of IPC/IQC in terms of so-called top models. Furthermore, they prove a uniform interpolation theorem for the positive fragments of IPC and MPC. Finally, they study conservative extensions of the positive fragment of IPC and IQC starting from the well-known result that Jankov's Logic KC is conservative over the positive fragment of IPC.

The joint paper by Gary Mar, Yuliya Manyakina, and Amanda Caffary lies at the intersection of logic and linguistics. They consider the similarities and differences between 'unless' and 'until' with the aim to propose a unified compositional account.

This is standardly considered unachievable in linguistics, and the authors seek to uncover the underlying source of the problems in Willard van Orman Quine's classic treatment of 'unless'.

Ralf Naumann and Wiebke Petersen describe a formalization of (a variant of) Löbner-Barsalou frame theory (LBFT) in terms of a dynamic frame theory that is based on both Dependence Logic and Dynamic Epistemic Logic. The focus of their work lies in particular on the interpretation of numerals and scalar quantifiers.

Alfred Ortmann presents evidence from Germanic and Mayan languages, which underpins the fourfold typology of nominal concepts derived from the binary features of uniqueness and relationality. His main findings are that recategorizations tend to be marked morphologically and that only phonologically 'strong' forms of definite articles are reliably semantically active. Overall, morphological marking in split article systems reflects conceptual markedness.

Katsuhiko Sano and Minghui Ma investigate Visser's basic propositional logic BPL. They provide an embedding of BPL into the modal logic wK4, based on which they present two alternative semantics for BPL: the proper successor semantics on Kripke frames and a topological semantics using the topological derivative operator.

The paper by Galit W. Sassoon considers challenging data on within-predicate and between-predicate comparisons where adjectives and nouns behave in opposite manner. In an interdisciplinary turn, Sassoon utilizes the psychological notion of a contrast set to account for both the behavior of nouns and adjectives in the above comparisons.

Kerstin Schwabe sets out to present a new analysis of German argument conditionals. Argument conditionals are conditional clauses which are anaphorically linked to a propositional *es*-argument in the embedding clause (*Max akzeptiert es, wenn Lea Geige spielt.* 'Max accepts it if Lea plays the violin'). Schwabe identifies two different implication types that occur in such conditional constructions and she discusses restrictions on predicate classes that embed argument conditionals.

In their contribution, Yulia Zinova and Hana Filip argue for a third–biaspectual–aspect category in Russian which complements the well-known perfective/imperfective partition. A new diagnostic is proposed which identifies positive cases of perfective aspect, thereby allowing us to establish the third biaspectual category with a clear behavioral criterion.

We would like to thank all of the above authors and the anonymous reviewers for their contribution to the volume. We are also very grateful to Maria Aloni, Johan van Benthem, Matthias Baaz, and Sebastian Löbner for their generous financial support to the conference through their respective research projects.

January 2015

Martin Aher
Daniel Hole
Emil Jeřábek
Clemens Kupke

Organization

Organizing Institutions

Centre for Language, Logic and Speech, Tbilisi State University,
Georgian Academy of Sciences,
Institute for Logic, Language and Computation, University of Amsterdam,
The Netherlands

Organizing Committee

Rusiko Asatiani	Tbilisi State University, Georgia
Anna Chutkerashvili	Tbilisi State University, Georgia
Paul Dekker	University of Amsterdam, The Netherlands
David Gabelaia	Tbilisi State University, Georgia
Marina Ivanishvili	Tbilisi State University, Georgia
Nino Javashvili	Tbilisi State University, Georgia
Ramaz Liparteliani	Tbilisi State University, Georgia
Liana Lortkipanidze	Tbilisi State University, Georgia
Peter van Ormondt	University of Amsterdam, The Netherlands
Khimuri Rukhaia	Tbilisi State University, Sokhumi State University, Georgia

Program Committee

Lev Beklemishev	Steklov Mathematical Institute, Moscow, Russia
Nick Bezhanishvili (Chair)	University of Amsterdam, The Netherlands
Dion Coumans	Radboud University Nijmegen, The Netherlands
Frans Groen	University of Amsterdam, The Netherlands
Wiebe van der Hoek	University of Liverpool, UK
Daniel Hole	University of Stuttgart, Germany
Clemens Kupke	University of Strathclyde, UK
Sebastian Loebner	Heinrich-Heine-University, Düsseldorf, Germany
Larry Moss	Indiana University, Bloomington, USA
Prakash Panangaden	McGill University, Montreal, Canada
Floris Roelofsen	University of Amsterdam, The Netherlands
Susan Rothstein	Bar-Ilan University, Tel Aviv, Israel
Luca Spada	University of Salerno, Italy

Standing Committee

Rusiko Asatiani	Tbilisi State University, Georgia
Matthias Baaz	Technische Universität Wien, Vienna, Austria
Guram Bezhanishvili	New Mexico State University, USA
Peter Bosch	University of Osnabrück, Germany
George Chikoidze	Georgian Technical University, Tbilisi, Georgia
Dick de Jongh (Chair)	University of Amsterdam, The Netherlands
Paul Dekker	University of Amsterdam, The Netherlands
Hans Kamp	University of Stuttgart, Germany
Manfred Krifka	Zentrum für Allgemeine Sprachwissenschaft, Berlin, Germany
Temur Kutsia	Johannes Kepler University, Linz, Austria
Sebastian Loebner	Heinrich-Heine-University, Düsseldorf, Germany
Barbara Partee	University of Massachusetts Amherst, USA

Tutorials

Samson Abramsky	University of Oxford, UK
Daniel Altshuler	Heinrich-Heine-University, Düsseldorf, Germany
Rosalie Iemhoff	Utrecht University, The Netherlands

Invited Speakers

Balder ten Cate	University of California, Santa Cruz, USA
Agata Ciabattoni	Technische Universität Wien, Vienna, Austria
Thomas Colcombet	Université Denis Diderot, Paris, France
Sergei Tatevosov	Moscow State University, Russia
Galit Sassoon	Bar Ilan University, Tel Aviv, Israel
Alexandra Silva	Radboud University Nijmegen, The Netherlands

Workshop Organizers

Agata Ciabattoni	Technische Universität Wien, Vienna, Austria
Daniel Altshuler	Heinrich-Heine-University, Düsseldorf, Germany
Daniel Hole	University of Stuttgart, Germany
Rosalie Iemhoff	Utrecht University, The Netherlands
Sergei Tatevosov	Moscow State University, Russia

Invited Speakers at Workshops

Matthias Baaz	Technische Universität Wien, Vienna, Austria
Alessio Guglielmi	University of Bath, UK

Hans Kamp	University of Texas, Austin, USA
Roumyana Pancheva	University of Southern California, Santa Cruz, USA
Kazushige Terui	Kyoto University, Japan

Contents

Research on Aspect: Reflections and New Frontiers

Daniel Altshuler[(⊠)]

Heinrich Heine Universität, Düsseldorf, Germany
daltshul@gmail.com

Abstract. The tutorial gave an overview of the way aspectual meaning has been analyzed in formal semantics. It focused on the way Klein (1994) influential analysis has been extended in recent years to account for the modal properties of aspectual operators. Based on the perfective aspect in Hindi and other languages, I showed that Kleinian extensions which do not view aspectual operators as being *partitive* with respect to events are inadequate. I explored some consequences of this conclusion and suggested that studying the interface between aspectual and adverbial meaning would allow us to address some of the most pressing issues.

Keywords: Aspect · Adverbs · Temporality · Modality · Semantics · Pragmatics · Discourse

1 The Neo-Kleinian Analysis of Aspect

Consider the sentences in (1), which differ in grammatical aspect—i.e. the progressive in (1)a, the perfective in (1)b and the perfect in (1)c. According to intuitions of native speakers, there is a difference in meaning between the three sentences. While it seems clear that (1)a differs from (1)b and (1)c in *not* entailing that Bill's letter writing culminated, it is difficult (perhaps impossible) to say what the difference between (1)b and (1)c is without further context (Reichenbach 1947/1966, p. 228).

(1) a. Bill was writing a letter to complain.
    b. Bill wrote a letter to complain.
    c. Bill had written a letter to complain.

When context is provided, viz. (2), not only do we see a clear difference between (1)b and (1)c, we observe yet another difference between (1)a and the other sentences. In (2) a, we understand that the events of Sue coming home and Bill writing a letter overlapped in time. In (2)b, however, the most salient interpretation is that Bill wrote a letter *after* Sue came home late, presumably in response to her lateness. Finally, in (2)c, we understand the reverse relationship: Bill's letter writing took place *prior* to Sue coming home.

(2) a. Sue came home late. Bill was writing a letter to complain.
    b. Sue came home late. Bill wrote a letter to complain.
    c. Sue came home late. Bill had written a letter to complain.

© Springer-Verlag Berlin Heidelberg 2015
M. Aher et al. (Eds.): TbiLLC 2013, LNCS 8984, pp. 1–9, 2015.
DOI: 10.1007/978-3-662-46906-4_1

There are two types of research programs which address the data above. The first is concerned with how grammatical aspect interacts with verbal meaning or aktionsart. This research program is important because it sheds light on how natural language is used to refer the completion (or lack thereof) of a given event. Another research program seeks to explain its effects on discourse structure. This research program is important because it sheds light not only on aspectual meaning, but also on discourse dynamics and the semantics/pragmatics interface.

Klein (1994) pioneered an analysis that attempts to synthesize these two research programs.[1] He argued that the semantic function of grammatical aspect is to relate a described eventuality to a topical time and the semantic function of tense is to relate the topical time to the speech time. This idea has been extremely influential. Virtually all recent conference presentations, journal articles, and dissertations on aspect cite it.[2] Klein's analysis has also given rise to influential work on the interaction between aspect and tense, adverbs, modals, mood and evidentials.[3] This work, which I will refer to as the "neo-Kleinian analysis of aspect", is summed up by the formulas below.[4] (3) makes Comrie's (1976, p. 4) intuition that the progressive portrays a situation "from [the] inside" precise: the time with respect to which we evaluate a progressive sentence is contained *within* the described event that warrants the assertion. (4) models Comrie's intuition that the perfective portrays the opposite relation, i.e. it portrays a situation "from [the] outside." (5) captures Reichenbach's 1947/1966 idea that the perfect describes a "past of a past" or, put differently, it portrays that the event is over by the topic time (Kratzer 1998).

(3)   PROGRESSIVE: $\lambda P \lambda t. \exists e[t \subseteq \tau(e) \wedge P(e)]$

(4)   PERFECTIVE: $\lambda P \lambda t. \exists e[\tau(e) \subseteq t \wedge P(e)]$

(5)   PERFECT: $\lambda P \lambda t. \exists e[\tau(e) < t \wedge P(e)]$

2   Problem with the Neo-Kleinian Analysis of Aspect

A problem with Klein's analysis is the existential quantification in (3). Applied to a telic description such as *write a letter*, (3) would incorrectly predict that a sentence like *John was writing a letter* entails culmination of the writing. Neo-Kleinians often acknowledge this shortcoming, usually called the *imperfective paradox* (Dowty 1979), and assume (often explicitly) that (3) could be enriched with a modal semantics.

---

[1] See also the seminal work by Moens and Steedman (1988) which was discussed in the tutorial.

[2] Klein's work is an extension of Reichenbach 1947/1966, which is also widely cited (see Kamp 1999/ 2013 for discussion). Work by Hans Kamp and colleagues (e.g. Kamp and Rohrer 1983, Kamp and Reyle 1993, Kamp et al. 2011) on the anaphoric properties aspect, as well as work by Comrie (1976) and Smith (1991) on the cross-linguistic properties of aspect also remain staples in current research on aspect.

[3] Here is a small sample of such work: Kratzer 1998, Demirdache and Uribe-Etxebarria 2000, Iatridou et al. 2001, Musan 2002, Paslawska, and von Stechow 2003, Gerö and von Stechow 2003, Grønn 2003, Matthewson 2006, Deo 2006, Hacquard 2006, Bittner 2008, Rothstein 2008, Bary 2009, Deal 2009, Thomas 2010, Altshuler 2012, 2014a, Rett and Murray 2013, Altshuler and Schwarzschild 2013.

[4] '$\subseteq$' stands for a subset relation; '$<$' is a precedence relation; 'τ' is a function from an event to its run time.

Bary (2009) takes this challenge head-on and builds on work by Gerö and von Stechow (2003) to propose the following modal extension of (3):

(6)   PROGRESSIVE: $\lambda P\lambda t.\forall w'[\text{Inert}_t(w^*)(w') \rightarrow \exists e[t \subset °\tau(e) \wedge P(w')(e)]]$

There are two key ingredients in (6). The first is the relation 'Inert$_t$(w*)(w')' which ensures that the world history w' is the same as the actual world w* until the end of the topic time t. The second is the relation 't $\subset °\tau(e)$', which ensures that t is contained within the run time of the event e, and t is not a final part of this run time. Given the universal quantification, this amounts to the following truth-conditions: a progressive sentence is true iff in every inertia world w' of w* at the topic time t there is an event e whose run time is a superinterval of t such that t is not a final part of this run time. Disregarding problems with inertia worlds (see, e.g. Landman 1992), (6) shows that, in principle, a neo-Kleninan analysis could be extended to deal with the imperfective paradox.

A possible worry for (6) is that it now appears that the semantics of the progressive is quite different from the perfective and the perfect in (4) and (5) respectively. Bary (2009, pp. 111–112) addresses this worry with respect to the perfective, showing that (4) could be extended in a parallel fashion:

(7)   PERFECTIVE: $\lambda P\lambda t\forall w'[\text{Inert}_t(w^*)(w') \rightarrow \exists e[\tau(e) \subseteq t \wedge P(w')(e)]]$

The crucial difference that we saw in (3) and (4) is preserved in (6) and (7): whereas the runtime of the P-event is a proper *superinterval* of the topic time t in (6), it is a *subinterval* in (7). This difference ensures that the universal quantification over inertia worlds—which plays a crucial role in (6)—is trivial in (7); (7) is truth-conditionally equivalent to (4).

While this is a good result for languages like English and Russian, where perfective of a telic VP always leads to a culmination entailment, it is not a good result for languages in which the perfective of a telic VP leads to the imperfective paradox analogous to (1)a.[5] For example, as shown in (8), the perfective *biskuT-ko khaa-yaa* in Hindi does not lead to the entailment that the cookie was finished (Singh 1998).

(8)   maayaa-ne biskuT-ko   **khaa-yaa** (par use   puuraa nahiin khaa-yaa)
      Maya-ERG cookie-ACC eat-PFV   but it-ACC finish not   eat-PFV
      '**Maya** ate the cookie (but did not finish it).'

(8) exemplifies what is often referred to as a *non-culminating accomplishment*—a kind of description that raises foundational questions about what it means to be *(im)perfective* (Demirdache and Martin 2015). The data in (9), however, provides an important clue:

---

[5] The *imperfective paradox* is therefore a misnomer. See Altshuler (2014b) for more discussion.

(9) #maayaa-ne biskuT-ko   **khaa-yaa** aur use ab tak khaa rahii   hai
     Maya-ERG   cookie-ACC eat-PFV   and it   still   eat PROG be.PRS
     Intended: 'Maya was eating the cookie, and is still eating it.'

As was first observed by Koenig and Muansuwan (2000) with respect to Thai, the perfective may lead to the imperfective paradox (viz. (8)), but it is *never* used to describe an event that was instantiated in the past and continued to develop until the speech time. That is, the perfective in (9) cannot be used in a way analogous to the progressive in, e.g. "Maya was eating the cookie and she still is."

In sum, we have aspectual forms of the kind illustrated below, in Fig. 1. There are imperfective forms like the English progressive, which lead to the imperfective paradox and are used to describe an event that was instantiated in the past and continued to develop until the speech time. We also have perfective forms like the Russian perfective, which do not lead to the imperfective paradox and are therefore never used to describe an event that was instantiated in the past and continued to develop until the speech time. Finally, we have perfective forms like in (8) and (9), which lead to the imperfective paradox but *cannot* be used to describe an event that was instantiated in the past and continued to develop until the speech time.

The c-form in Fig. 1 is not discussed by the neo-Kleinians and this is both surprising and unfortunate. It is surprising since many (if not most!) of the perfective forms in the world's languages are of this kind (Altshuler 2014b). It is unfortunate because it seems implausible that Klein's analysis could be extended to account for the distinction in a- and c-forms on the one hand, and b- and c-forms on the other, especially if one also wanted to preserve Bary's insight in (6)–(7). The implausibility of extending Klein's account to account for these different forms is highlighted by Grønn (2003) proposal to include a new aspectual operator into the Kleinian typology—one that imposes the overlap relation.[6] In order to account for the imperfective paradox, he suggests that "one could replace the imperfective condition e O t with a disjunction $t \subseteq e \lor e \subseteq t$. The modality could then be smuggled into the first disjunct" (*ibid,* 58). The issue, of course, is: how do you smuggle in the modality? Moreover, how does one make the modality fine grained enough to explain the difference between the a- and c-forms, which both lead to the imperfective paradox?

To the best of my knowledge, Koenig and Muansuwan 2000 were the first to address such questions. Working to explain the perfective in Thai, which could be classified as a c-form in Fig. 1 above, Koenig and Muansuwan proposed that the perfective imposes a maximality constraint: given a property of events P, a P-event must be the maximal subpart of the possible continuations that have the property P. A similar analysis was also proposed by Filip (2000, 2008) to account for the perfective in Slavic languages, and Altshuler (2014b) showed how this analysis could be implemented within Landman's (1992) modal semantics. Part of the tutorial was devoted to going through these analyses and motivating the hypothesis in (10):

---

[6] This builds on Smith's (1991) idea that there is an aspectual class, *neutral aspect*, whose meaning generalizes across the perfective/imperfective. See Csirmaz 2004 and Altshuler 2014b for more discussion.

Form	Is it ever used to describe an event that was instantiated in the past and continued to develop until the speech time?	Does it ever lead to the imperfective paradox?
a. English progressive	Yes	Yes
b. Russian perfective	No	No
c. Hindi perfective	No	Yes

Fig. 1. Contrasting aspectual forms

(10)   Hypothesis from Altshuler 2014b
  a.   An operator is *perfective* if it requires a *maximal stage* of an event in the extension of the VP that it combines with.

Due to space constraints, I will not discuss this hypothesis here. Instead, I'd like to highlight an implicit assumption in (10): aspectual operators are partitive with respect to events; they denote functions from a set of events denoted by a VP to a set of VP-event parts.

An important conclusion of the tutorial was that (11) is necessary if one wants to explain the contrasting perfective forms in languages like English/Slavic versus Hindi/Thai (viz. Fig. 1), while also having a theory of what it means to be *(im)perfective*.[7]

3   Moving Beyond the Neo-Kleinian Analysis of Aspect

In the tutorial, I suggested that if we want to maintain (10), as the data suggests we should, then we must move beyond the neo-Kleinian analysis. In particular, we need to: (a) define *event partitivity* (viz. discussion in the previous section) and (b) distinguish the way that eventualities are related to temporal coordinates provided by temporal adverbs and those provided by the tenses. In what follows, I briefly outline two puzzles that provide motivation for (b).

3.1   Present Perfect Puzzle

Klein (1992) notes that while past-oriented temporal adverbs like *yesterday* are not possible with the present perfect in English, they are possible in German:

(11)   *Yesterday Fritz has submitted his paper.
(12)   Gestern hat Fritz seine Arbeit eingereicht
       Yesterday has Fritz his paper submitted

While there are many proposals to explain the contrast above, the tutorial considered the following analysis by Kamp et al. (2013) the English perfect denotes a function from a

---

[7] In this way, I defended Bach's (1986, p. 12) original idea, formalized by Krifka (1992, p. 47). See also Moens and Steedman (1988) for similar ideas about partitivity over events. Cf. Bennett and Partee (1972) which propose a partitive analysis with respect to intervals (rather than events).

set of events E to a set of result states S of those events. Moreover, the perfect imposes two requirements: (a) there must be a result state in S that holds throughout the time provided by the tense, and (b) there must be an event complex that includes an event in E and a result state in S that is contained within the temporal coordinate provided by the adverb. Applying this analysis to (11), we derive a contradiction: (a) the result state of a paper submission holds throughout the time provided by the tense, i.e. the speech time, and (b) the paper-submission event, including the result state, takes place yesterday.

In contrast to (11), (12) is predicted to be good according to Kamp et al. (2013) because the German perfect requires a described event, not the entire event complex, to be contained within the temporal coordinate provided by the adverb. Therefore, no contradiction arises. The picture that emerges, then, is that all perfect operators relate results states to the temporal coordinate provided by the tense. They differ, however, in what event part is related to the temporal coordinate that is provided by temporal adverbs.

3.2 Russian Imperfective Puzzle

Altshuler (2012) notes a puzzle with respect to the interpretation of the imperfective aspect in flashback discourses such as (13) below. Here we see the imperfective in (13)b and (13)c. And although there is no order that the events described in (13)b and (13)c are understood to have occurred in, both are understood to precede the kissing event described in (13)a. Such is the case whether or not there is a temporal adverb in (13)b. If the adverb is there, then the flower-giving and the theater-inviting are understood to have taken place within the time denoted by *za nedelju do togo* ('a week before that')— i.e. during the week prior to the kissing event, which itself took place a week before the speech time.[8]

(13) a. *Nedelju nazad Marija po-celova-l-a Dudkina.*
Week ago Maria PFV-kissed-PST.3S-FEM Dudkin
'A week ago, Maria kissed Dudkin.'

   b. (*Za nedelju do togo*) *on* **dari-l** *ej cvety*
From week to that he give.IPF-PST.3S her flower
'A week before that he had given her flowers

   c. *i* **priglaša-l** *ee v teatr.*
and invite.IPF-PST.3S her to theater
and had invited her to the theater.'

What is puzzling about this discourse is that—assuming that the temporal adverb in (13)b contributes information about the topical time—we are led to the analysis that the Russian imperfective describes an event (e.g. giving flowers) that is contained *within* a topical time (viz. the perfective in (4)). However, given such an analysis of the Russian

---

[8] Although I focus on the episodic interpretation of (15b, c), an iterative interpretation is also possible, in which Dudkin gave flowers and invited Maria to the theater on several occasions. On such an interpretation, the iterations are still understood to have occurred during the week prior to the kissing event.

imperfective, one would be hard pressed to explain the aforementioned inferences in (13)b, c without the temporal adverb in (13)b.

Analogous to Kamp et al. (2013), Altshuler (2012) proposes to solve this puzzle by distinguishing the way that eventualities are related to temporal coordinates provided by temporal adverbs and those provided by the tenses. In particular, I proposed that an *event* described by the Russian imperfective is related to the temporal coordinate provided by the adverb, and a *result state* of that event is related to the temporal coordinate provided by the tense. The Russian imperfective differs from the German perfect in the type of relations that it imposes between these two coordinates, as well as in its modal properties.

4 Take-Home Message

The main take-home message of the first part of the tutorial was the idea that aspectual operators are *partitive* with respect to events. While this hypothesis is not new (see Footnote 8), it is important because it can explain cross-linguistic patterns that the neo-Kleinian analyses cannot. The take-home message of the second part of the tutorial was the idea that we need to distinguish the way that eventualities are related to temporal coordinates provided by temporal adverbs and those provided by the tenses. Evidence for this view came from the present perfect puzzle in Germanic and the imperfective in Russian.

References

Altshuler, D.: Aspectual meaning meets discourse coherence: a look at the Russian imperfective. J. Semant. **29**, 39–108 (2012)

Altshuler, D.: Discourse transparency and the meaning of temporal locating adverbs. Nat. Lang. Semant. **22**, 55–88 (2014a)

Altshuler, D.: A typology of partitive aspectual operators. Nat. Lang. Linguist. Theor. **32**, 735–775 (2014b)

Altshuler, D., Schwarzschild, R.: Correlating double access with cessation. In: Aloni, M., Franke, M., Roelofsen, F. (eds.) Proceedings of the 19th Amsterdam Colloquium, pp. 43–50 (2013)

Bach, E.: The algebra of events. Linguist. Philos. **9**, 5–16 (1986)

Bary, C.: Aspect in ancient Greek. a semantic analysis of the aorist and imperfective. Ph.D. dissertation, Radboud University, Nijmegen (2009)

Bennett, M., Partee, B.: Toward the Logic of Tense and Aspect in English. Indiana University Linguistics Club, Bloomington (1972)

Bittner, M.: Aspectual universals of temporal anaphora. In: Rothstein, S. (ed.) Theoretical and Cross-linguistic Approaches to the Semantics of Aspect, pp. 349–385. Benjamins, Amsterdam (2008)

Comrie, B.: Aspect. Cambridge University Press. Cambridge, MA (1976)

Csirmaz, A.: Perfective and imperfective in Hungarian: (invisible) differences. In: Blaho, S., Vicente, L., de Vos, M. (eds.) Proceedings of Console XII, Leiden (2004)

Deal, A.R.: Events in space. In: Friedman, T., Satoshi, I. (eds.) Proceedings of SALT XVIII, pp. 230–247. CLC Publications, Cornell (2009)

Demirdache, H., Uribe-Etxebarria, M.: The primitives of temporal relations. In: Martin, R., Michaels, D., Uriagereka, J. (eds.) Step by Step: Essays on Minimalist Syntax in Honor of Howard Lasnik. MIT Press, Cambridge (2000)

Demirdache, H., Martin, F.: Agent control over non-culminating events. In: Cifuentes Honrubia, C. (ed.) Aspect and Verbal Classes. Benjamins, Amsterdam (2015, under review)

Deo, A.: Tense and aspect in Indo-Aryan languages: variation and diachrony. Ph.D. dissertation, Stanford University (2006)

Dowty, D.: Word Meaning and Montague Grammar. Reidel, Dordrecht (1979)

Filip, H.: The quantization puzzle. In: Tenny, C., Pustejovsky, J. (eds.) Events as Grammatical Objects, from the Combined Perspectives of Lexical Semantics, Logical Semantics and Syntax, pp. 39–91. CSLI Press, Stanford (2000)

Filip, H.: Events and maximalization. In: Rothstein, S. (ed.) Theoretical and Crosslinguistic Approaches to the Semantics of Aspect, pp. 217–256. John Benjamins, Amsterdam (2008)

Gerö, E.C., von Stechow, A.: Tense in time: the greek perfect. In: Eckardt, R., von Heusinger, K., Schwarze, C. (eds.) Words in Time: Diachronic Semantics from Different Points of View, pp. 251–269. Mouton de Gruyter, Berlin (2003)

Grønn, A.: The semantics and pragmatics of the Russian factual imperfective. Ph.D. dissertation, University of Oslo, Oslo (2003)

Hacquard, V.: Aspects of modality. Ph.D. thesis, MIT, Cambridge (2006)

Iatridou, S., Anagnostopoulou, E., Izvorski, R.: Observations about the form and meaning of the perfect. In: Kenstowicz, M. (ed.) Ken Hale. A Life in Language. MIT Press, Cambridge (2001)

Kamp, H.: Deixis in discourse: Reichenbach on temporal reference. In: von Heusiger, K., ter Meulen, A. (eds.) Meaning and the dynamics of interpretation: Selected papers of Hans Kamp, pp. 105–159. Brill, Leiden (1999/2013)

Kamp, H., Rohrer, C.: Tense in texts. In: Baüerle, B., Schwarze, C., von Stechow, A. (eds.) Meaning, Use and Interpretation of Language, pp. 250–269. De Gruyter, Berlin (1983)

Kamp, H., Reyle, U.: From Discourse to Logic: Introduction to Model Theoretic Semantics of Natural Language, Formal Logic and Discourse Representation Theory. Kluwer, Dordrecht (1993)

Kamp, H., van Genabith, J., Reyle, U.: Discourse representation theory. In: Gabbay, D., Guenthner, F. (eds.) Handbook of Philosophical Logic. Kluwer, Dordrecht (2011)

Kamp, H., Reyle, U., Rossdeutscher, A.: Perfects as feature shifting operators. Manuscript. Stuttgart University (2013)

Klein, W.: The present perfect puzzle. Language **68**, 525–552 (1992)

Klein, W.: Time in Language. Routledge, London (1994)

Koenig, J.P., Muansuwan, N.: How to end without finishing: Thai semi-perfective markings. J. Semant. **17**, 147–184 (2000)

Kratzer, A.: More structural analogies between pronouns and tenses. In: Strolovitch, D., Lawson, A. (eds.) Proceedings of SALT, pp. 92–109. CLC, Ithaca (1998)

Krifka, M.: Thematic relations as links between nominal reference and temporal constitution. In: Sag, I.A., Szabolsci, A. (eds.) Lexical Matters, pp. 29–53. CSLI, Stanford (1992)

Landman, F.: The progressive. Nat. Lang. Semant. **1**, 1–32 (1992)

Matthewson, L.: Temporal semantics in a supposedly tenseless language. Linguist. Philos. **29**, 673–713 (2006)

Moens, M., Steedman, M.: Temporal ontology and temporal reference. Comput. Linguist. **14**, 15–28 (1988)

Musan, R.: The German Perfect: Its Semantic Composition and Its Interactions with Temporal Adverbials. Kluwer, Dordrecht (2002)

Paslawska, A., von Stechow, A.: Perfect readings in Russian. In: Alexiadou, A., Rathert, M., von Stechow, A. (eds.) Perfect Explorations, Interface Explorations, pp. 307–362. Mouton de Gruyter, Berlin (2003)

Reichenbach, H.: Elements of Symbolic Logic. Macmillan, New York (1947/1966)

Rett, J., Murray, S.: A semantic account of mirative evidentials. In: Proceedings of SALT 23, pp. 453–472 (2013)

Rothstein, B.: The Perfect Time Span on the Present Perfect in Swedish, German and English. Benjamins, Amsterdam (2008)

Singh, M.: On the semantics of the perfective aspect. Nat. Lang. Semant. **6**, 171–199 (1998)

Smith, C.: The Parameter of Aspect. Kluwer, Dordrecht (1991)

Thomas, G.: Temporal implicatures. Ph.D. thesis, MIT, Cambridge (2010)

Tutorial on Admissible Rules in Gudauri

Rosalie Iemhoff$^{(\boxtimes)}$

Department of Philosophy, Utrecht University,
Utrecht, The Netherlands
R.Iemhoff@uu.nl
http://www.phil.uu.nl/~iemhoff

Keywords: Logic · Admissible rules · Consequence relations

1 Introduction

Most theorems have more than one proof and most theories have more than one axiomatization. Certain proofs or axiomatizations are preferable to others because they are shorter or more transparent or for some other reason. Our aim is to describe or study the possible proofs of a theorem or the possible axiomatizations of a theory. As the former is a special instance of the latter, by considering a theory consisting of one theorem, it suffices to consider theories.

To describe the possible axiomatizations of a theory we first have to specify what we mean by a theory and what counts as an axiomatization of it. We assume that theories are given by consequence relations, and consider an arbitrary consequence relation to be an axiomatization of the theory if it has the same theorems as the consequence relation of the theory.

In [1] Avron argues convincingly that in general a logic is more than its set of theorems, meaning that there exist logics which have the same set of theorems but which nevertheless do not seem to be equal. For example, because the proofs of certain theorems differ with the logic. Then the question what counts as an axiomatization of a certain theory becomes more complex in that one wishes to axiomatize certain other characteristics of the theory, such as certain inference steps, rather than just its theorems.

In this paper, however, we restrict ourselves to the set of theorems as that part of a theory that an axiomatization has to capture. And as we will see, already in this case the variety of possible axiomatizations of a theory can be quite complicated and is in many cases not yet well-understood.

Thus our main aim is a description of the consequence relations that have the same theorems as a given consequence relation. As it turns out, admissible rules are the central notion here, where a rule is admissible in a theory if it can be added to a theory but no new theorems can be proved in the extension. Clearly, such extensions are axiomatizations of the original theory, which is why admissible rules are so important in this setting.

R. Iemhoff—Support by the Netherlands Organisation for Scientific Research under grant 639.032.918 is gratefully acknowledged.

M. Aher et al. (Eds.): TbiLLC 2013, LNCS 8984, pp. 10–17, 2015.
DOI: 10.1007/978-3-662-46906-4_2

The notion of admissibility, although sometimes under a different name, goes back to the 1930's, but a systematic study of the subject was first undertaken by Rybakov in the 1980's [24] and is continued by him and many others till today (see the bibliography for references). The first major results on this subject concerned the decidability of admissibility in certain intermediate and modal propositional logics, such as intuitionistic logic, modal logic K4, GL and S4. Later, the description of admissible rules in terms of bases was obtained for many of these logics and their fragments. Nowadays there are many aspects of admissibility that are studied. The work of Ghilardi [6] established a firm connection between admissibility and unification theory, and provided an algebraic approach to the issues discussed above. This algebraic approach to admissibility has flourished over the last decade and has been especially successful in the setting of substructural logics.

This paper is organized as follows. In Sect. 2 consequence relations and admissible rules are defined, and the main aim is formulated in these terms. Section 3 contains some of the main results in the area, a summary that, because of lack of space, is by no means complete. The paper ends with a brief discussion of topics that have been omitted in the main exposition. I thank Emil Jeřábek for useful comments on an earlier draft of this note.

2   Framework

To maintain a certain level of generality we assume that there is a language $\mathcal{L}$, which contains *propositional variables* or *atoms* $p, q, r, \ldots$, and possibly some connectives, constants or operators. There is a set of *expressions* $\mathcal{F}_\mathcal{L}$ in this language that at least contains the propositional variables. In this way, what we discuss below applies to various consequence relation, such as consequence relations for propositional intermediate and modal logics, to mention the main examples. But also consequence relations that are relations on sequents rather than formulas are captured by this approach. Although some of what we are going to say also applies to predicate logics, we restrict ourselves in this paper to propositional logics. *Substitutions* σ are maps from $\mathcal{F}_\mathcal{L}$ to $\mathcal{F}_\mathcal{L}$ that commute with all logical symbols in the language.

2.1   Consequence Relations

Multi-conclusion consequence relations are relations $\vdash$ between sets of expressions. We write $\Gamma \vdash \Delta$ if the pair (Γ, Δ) belongs to the relation. We also write Γ/Δ for the pair (Γ, Δ), and A, Γ for $\{A\} \cup \Gamma$, and Γ, Π for $\Gamma \cup \Pi$. A *finitary multi-conclusion structural consequence relation (mcr)* is a relation $\vdash$ between finite sets of expressions that satisfies, for all finite sets of expressions $\Gamma, \Gamma', \Delta, \Delta'$ and expressions A:

reflexivity $A \vdash A$,
weakening if $\Gamma \vdash \Delta$, then $\Gamma', \Gamma \vdash \Delta, \Delta'$,

transitivity if $\Gamma \vdash \Delta, A$ and $\Gamma', A \vdash \Delta'$, then $\Gamma', \Gamma \vdash \Delta, \Delta'$,
structurality if $\Gamma \vdash \Delta$, then $\sigma\Gamma \vdash \sigma\Delta$ for all substitutions σ.

A *finitary single-conclusion consequence relation (scr)* is a relation between finite sets of expressions and expressions satisfying the variants of the three properties above where there is a singleton to the right of $\vdash$, and $\Gamma \vdash \{A\}$ is replaced by $\Gamma \vdash A$. We often omit the word "finitary" in what follows, and when we speak about "consequence relations" we refer to both multi-conclusion and single-conclusion ones.

Although most logics we discuss can be represented via a single-conclusion consequence relation, the multi-conclusion analogue allows us to express certain properties more naturally, such as the disjunction property. It follows from Proposition 1 below that an intermediate logic has the disjunction property if and only if $\{p \vee q\}/\{p, q\}$ is admissible, and similarly for modal logic and the modal disjunction property, expressed by the admissibility of $\{\Box p \vee \Box q\}/\{p, q\}$.

The minimal single-conclusion and multi-conclusion consequence relations $\vdash_{\overline{m}}$ and $\vdash_{\overline{mm}}$ are defined as follows.

$$\Gamma \vdash_{\overline{m}} A \equiv_{def} A \in \Gamma \qquad \Gamma \vdash_{\overline{mm}} \Delta \equiv_{def} \Gamma \cap \Delta \neq \emptyset.$$

A is a *theorem* if $\emptyset \vdash A$, which we write as $\vdash A$. The set of all theorems of a consequence relation is denoted by $\mathsf{Th}(\vdash)$. Δ is a *multi-conclusion theorem* if $\vdash \Delta$, which is short for $\emptyset \vdash \Delta$. The set of all multi-conclusion theorems is denoted by $\mathsf{Thm}(\vdash)$. When we speak about consequence relations in general we use the word *theorem*, meaning *theorem* in case the relation is single-conclusion and *multi-conclusion theorem* in case the relation is multi-conclusion.

Given a logic L with set of theorems $\mathsf{Th}(\mathsf{L})$, there are in general many multi-conclusion consequence relations $\vdash$ such that $\mathsf{Th}(\vdash) = \mathsf{Th}(\mathsf{L})$. Natural examples are

$$\Gamma \vdash \Delta \equiv_{def} \Delta \cap \mathsf{Th}(\mathsf{L}) \neq \emptyset,$$

or, in case the language contains implication and conjunction,

$$\Gamma \vdash \Delta \equiv_{def} \exists A \in \Delta \, (\bigwedge \Gamma \to A) \in \mathsf{Th}(\vdash).$$

Both these consequence relations are *saturated*, meaning that

$$\Gamma \vdash \Delta \Rightarrow \exists A \in \Delta \, \Gamma \vdash A.$$

Clearly, every single-conclusion consequence relation is saturated. And if one starts with a single-conclusion consequence relation or logic and wishes to associate a saturated multi-conclusion consequence relation with it (meaning with the same theorems as the single-conclusion consequence relation or logic), then the two consequence relations given in the previous paragraph provide examples. In the next section we encounter multi-conclusion consequence relations that are no longer saturated, such as the admissibility relation.

2.2   Admissible and Derivable Rules

A *(multi-conclusion) rule* is an ordered pair of finite sets of expressions, written Γ/Δ or $\frac{\Gamma}{\Delta}$. It is *single-conclusion* if $|\Delta| = 1$, in which case we also write Γ/A for $\Gamma/\{A\}$. For $R = \Gamma/\Delta$ and a substitution σ, σR is short for $\sigma\Gamma/\sigma\Delta$, and similarly for sets of rules.

Given a multi-conclusion consequence relation $\vdash$ and a set of rules $\mathcal{R}$, $\vdash^{\mathcal{R}}$ is the smallest consequence relation extending $\vdash$ for which $\Gamma \vdash \Delta$ holds for all Γ/Δ in $\mathcal{R}$. Similarly for single-conclusion rules and single-conclusion consequence relations. In case of a single rule R we write $\vdash^{R}$ for $\vdash^{\{R\}}$. Given a consequence relation $\vdash$, a set of rules $\mathcal{R}$ is a *basis* for a consequence relation $\vdash' \supseteq \vdash$ or *axiomatizes* $\vdash'$ *over* $\vdash$ if $\vdash' = \vdash^{\mathcal{R}}$. A rule $R = \Gamma/\Delta$ is *derivable* if $\Gamma \vdash \Delta$. It is *admissible*, written $\Gamma \mathrel{\vdash\!\sim} \Delta$, if $\mathsf{Thm}(\vdash) = \mathsf{Thm}(\vdash^{R})$, and $\mathsf{Th}(\vdash) = \mathsf{Th}(\vdash^{R})$ in case $\vdash$ and R are single-conclusion. A set of rules is admissible if all of its members are.

As can be seen from the definition, a rule is admissible when one can add it to the consequence relation without obtaining new theorems, just (possibly) new derivations. This shows that admissibility solely depends on the theorems of a consequence relation, while derivability does not. The admissibility relation $\mathrel{\vdash\!\sim}$ itself is a consequence relation, namely the largest consequence relation with the same theorems as $\vdash$. Therefore, the main topic of this paper, the possible axiomatizations of a theory, can now be reformulated in exact terms as the admissible rules of consequence relations.

The following proposition provides the link between admissibility and unification.

Proposition 1. For every saturated consequence relation $\vdash$,

$$\Gamma \mathrel{\vdash\!\sim} \Delta \iff \forall\sigma : \forall A \in \Gamma\,(\vdash \sigma A) \implies \exists B \in \Delta\,(\vdash \sigma B).$$

Therefore every single-conclusion consequence relation satisfies

$$\Gamma \mathrel{\vdash\!\sim} A \iff \forall\sigma : \forall B \in \Gamma\,(\vdash \sigma B) \implies \vdash \sigma A.$$

In the literature admissibility is often defined via the equivalence above.

A single-conclusion consequence relation $\vdash$ is *structurally complete* [19] if all proper extensions in the same language have new theorems. It is not difficult to see that $\vdash$ is structurally complete if and only if it coincides with $\mathrel{\vdash\!\sim}$. Thus structural completeness means that there are no "hidden" principles of inference, no underivable admissible rules, all valid inferences are already captured by the consequence relation itself.

3   Results

Classical propositional logic as well as a certain formulation of classical predicate logic in which substitution is an explicit rule, are structurally complete [19,20]. Or, to be precise, for any rule Γ/A admissible in classical logic, $(\bigwedge\Gamma \to A)$ is a theorem of classical logic, and therefore Γ/A is derivable in any consequence relation for classical logic in which the deduction theorem holds. Nonderivable admissible rules appear as soon as one turns from classical logic to extensions such as modal logic or weaker logics such as intermediate logics. There do exist, though, some proper intermediate and modal logics that are structurally complete, Gödel-Dummett logic LC being an example [5].

3.1   Decidability

Rybakov proved numerous results on admissibility, most importantly the decidability of the admissibility relation of intuitionistic propositional logic IPC, the modal logics K4, GL, S4 and several other intermediate and modal logics [24]. He thereby answered a question by Harvey Friedman from 1975 about the decidability of admissibility in intuitionistic logic positively. Rybakov's method can be adapted to many other logics, as has been done in [2,18,25,26], where the decidability of admissibility in various temporal logics and minimal logic is established. Ghilardi constructed a transparent algorithm for deciding admissibility in IPC [7], and Metcalfe and the author developed proof systems for admissibility for several well-known intermediate and modal logics, from which decision algorithms can be obtained as well [11,12]. Jeřábek proved that the complexity of the admissibility relation is coNEXP-complete in many modal and intermediate logics such as K4, S4, GL and IPC [15], thus showing that in these logics checking admissibility is strictly more complex than checking derivability.

Derivability is a special case of admissibility, and therefore decidability of the latter implies the decidability of theoremhood in the former. That the other direction does not hold has been shown in [3], and later also in [34], where certain modal logics are shown to be instances of this phenomenon.

3.2   Bases

An explicit description of the admissible rules is a next step in the investigation of logics for which the admissibility relation is decidable. Even in the case that admissibility is undecidable it cannot be excluded that there exists a useful description of them, but until now the logics for which such an explicit description has been found all have a decidable admissibility relation.

Rybakov in [24] showed that various modal and intermediate logics, including IPC and K4, cannot have a finite basis for their admissible rules. This, of course, does not imply that these logics do not have an infinite basis that still can be described in a compact way. As we will see, they often do.

Roziére [23] was the first to provide a concrete basis for the admissible rules for a logic for which the problem is not trivial, by proving that the set V of the so-called *Visser rules* is a basis for the admissible rules of IPC. This result was not published and was independently but later obtained by the author, who, using techniques from [6], strengthened it by showing that in every intermediate logic in which these rules are admissible they form a basis [10]. This theorem has implications for several intermediate logics. It implies, for example, that the rules are a basis for the admissible rules in the logics of frames with exactly n maximal nodes. In particular, they are a basis for KC.

The Visser rules also appeared in the work of Visser [30,31], who proved that the admissible rules of IPC and Heyting Arithmetic are equal, and Skura [27], who used them in the context of refutation systems. Examples of intermediate logics in which not all Visser Rules are admissible are the Gabbay–de Jongh logics [9] and Medvedev logic, which is structurally complete [10,22,33].

Using similar techniques, Jeřábek provided bases for many transitive modal logics, including well-known logics such as K4, S4 and GL [14]. For modal logics below K4 much less is known about admissibility. Some partial answers can be found in [16,32].

As one would expect, admissibility is very sensitive to the language one uses. It has long been known that the implicational fragment of IPC is hereditarily structurally complete [21]. The same holds for the implication–conjunction and some other fragments of IPC [17,29]. In [17] Mints showed that any admissible underivable rule of IPC must contain both implication and disjunction. Interestingly, the implication–negation fragment of IPC is not structurally complete, as was first observed by Wroński. In [4] Cintula and Metcalfe proved that the so-called *Wroński Rules* are a basis for the admissible rules of this fragment. A nontrivial example of a logic for which the implication–negation fragment is structurally complete is relevant logic [28].

4   Furthermore

The above is but a brief summary of some of the highlights in the area of admissibility. I have mainly covered the topics that I have treated in my tutorial in beautiful Gudauri. Several equally important aspects of admissibility have been omitted due to lack of space. Over the last twenty years, admissibility has been studied in various other contexts than the ones mentioned above, such as substructural logics, canonical rules and predicate logic. Unification theory has been central in some of the results described above. Also, the algebraic view on admissibility has been explored and lead to various beautiful results. I hope that the exposition above has made the reader wish to know more about this field and that the bibliography may provide a guideline towards that aim.

References

1. Avron, A.: Simple consequence relations. Inf. Comput. **92**(1), 105–139 (1991)
2. Babenyshev, S., Rybakov, V.V.: Linear temporal logic LTL: basis for admissible rules. J. Log. Comput. **21**(2), 157–177 (2011)
3. Chagrov, A.: A decidable modal logic with undecidable admissibility problem. Algebra Log. **31**(1), 53–61 (1992). In Russian
4. Cintula, P., Metcalfe, G.: Admissible rules in the implication-negation fragment of intuitionistic logic. Ann. Pure Appl. Log. **162**(2), 162–171 (2010)
5. Dzik, W., Wroński, A.: Structural completeness of Gödel and Dummett's propositional calculi. Stud. Log. **32**, 69–73 (1973)

6. Ghilardi, S.: Unification in intuitionistic logic. J. Symb. Log. **64**(2), 859–880 (1999)
7. Ghilardi, S.: A resolution/tableaux algorithm for projective approximations in IPC. Log. J. IGPL **10**(3), 227–241 (2002)
8. Ghilardi, S.: Unification, finite duality and projectivity in varieties of Heyting algebras. Ann. Pure Appl. Log. **127**(1–3), 99–115 (2004)
9. Goudsmit, J.G., Iemhoff, R.: On unification and admissible rules in Gabbay-de Jongh logics. Ann. Pure Appl. Log. **165**(2), 652–672 (2014)
10. Iemhoff, R.: Intermediate logics and Visser's rules. Notre Dame J. Formal Log. **46**(1), 65–81 (2005)
11. Iemhoff, R., Metcalfe, G.: Proof theory for admissible rules. Ann. Pure Appl. Log. **159**(1–2), 171–186 (2009)
12. Iemhoff, R., Metcalfe, G.: Hypersequent systems for the admissible rules of modal and intermediate logics. In: Artemov, S., Nerode, A. (eds.) LFCS 2009. LNCS, vol. 5407, pp. 230–245. Springer, Heidelberg (2008)
13. Iemhoff, R., Rozière, P.: Unification in fragments of intermediate logics. J. Symb. Logic (to appear)
14. Jeřábek, E.: Admissible rules of modal logics. J. Log. Comput. **15**(4), 411–431 (2005)
15. Jeřábek, E.: Complexity of admissible rules. Arch. Math. Log. **46**, 73–92 (2007)
16. Jeřábek, E.: Blending margins: the modal logic K has nullary unification type. J. Logic Comput. (to appear)
17. Mints, G.: Derivability of admissible rules. In: Studies in Constructive Mathematics and Mathematical Logic. Zap. Nauchn. Sem. LOMI, part V, vol. 32, pp. 85–89. Nauka, Leningrad (1972)
18. Odintsov, S., Rybakov, V.V.: Unification and admissible rules for paraconsistent minimal Johansson's logic J and positive intuitionistic logic IPC$^+$. Ann. Pure Appl. Log. **164**(7–8), 771–784 (2013)
19. Pogorzelski, W.A.: Structural completeness of the propositional calculus. Bulletin de l'Académie Polonaise des Sciences, Série des sciences mathématiques, astronomiques et physiques **19**, 349–351 (1971)
20. Pogorzelski, W.A., Prucnal, T.: Structural completeness of the first-order predicate calculus. Zeitschrift für mathematische Logik und Grundlagen der Mathematik **21**(1), 315–320 (1975)
21. Prucnal, T.: On the structural completeness of some pure implicational propositional calculi. Stud. Log. **32**(1), 45–50 (1973)
22. Prucnal, T.: Structural completeness of Medvedev's propositional calculus. Rep. Math. Log. **6**, 103–105 (1976)
23. Rozière, P.: Règles admissibles en calcul propositionnel intuitionniste. Ph.D. thesis, Université Paris VII (1992)
24. Rybakov, V.: Admissibility of Logical Inference Rules. Elsevier, Amsterdam (1997)
25. Rybakov, V.: Rules admissible in transitive temporal logic T_{S4}, sufficient condition. Theoret. Comput. Sci. **411**(50), 4323–4332 (2010)
26. Rybakov, V.: Writing out unifiers in linear temporal logic. J. Log. Comput. **22**(5), 1199–1206 (2012)
27. Skura, R.: A complete syntactical characterization of the intuitionistic logic. Rep. Math. Log. **23**, 75–80 (1989)
28. Slaney, J., Meyer, R.: A structurally complete fragment of relevant logic. Notre Dame J. Formal Log. **33**(4), 561–566 (1992)
29. Słomczyńska, K.: Algebraic semantics for the $(\leftrightarrow, \neg\neg)$-fragment of IPC. Math. Log. Q. **58**(12), 29–37 (2012)

30. Visser, A.: Rules and arithmetics. Notre Dame J. Formal Log. **40**(1), 116–140 (1999)
31. Visser, A.: Substitutions of Σ_1^0-sentences: explorations between intuitionistic propositional logic and intuitionistic arithmetic. Ann. Pure Appl. Log. **114**(1–3), 227–271 (2002)
32. Williamson, T.: An alternative rule of disjunction in modal logic. Notre Dame J. Formal Log. **33**(1), 89–100 (1992)
33. Wojtylak, P.: On a problem of H. Friedman and its solution by T. Prucnal. Rep. Math. Log. **38**, 69–86 (2004)
34. Wolter, F., Zakharyaschev, M.: Undecidability of the unification and admissibility problems for modal and description logics. ACM Trans. Comput. Log. **9**(4), 1–20 (2008). Article 25

Deontic Conflicts and Multiple Violations

Martin Aher[✉]

Tartu University, Tartu, Estonia
martin.aher@gmail.com

Abstract. This paper presents a novel semantics for deontic modals which provides a uniform solution to prominent puzzles in the literature. The paper focuses on deontic conflicts, discussing them using the Dr. Procrastinate puzzle as an example. The focus lies on the Dr. Procrastinate puzzle as it combines an upward monotonicity puzzle with a conflict of obligations, allowing an explanation of the solutions to both types of puzzle in detail.

The semantics is an extension of radical inquisitive semantics, and it modifies Andersonian deontic modals as it introduces quantification over alternatives. The solution to deontic conflicts is made possible by the semantics allowing permission and prohibition statements to introduce multiple violations. Each rule is assigned a different violation, allowing for reasoning with rules also in cases where it is impossible to avoid violating all rules.

1 Introduction

This paper aims to unravel conflicts between deontic modal auxiliaries such as *may* and *must*. We will represent permission as $\Diamond \varphi$ and obligation as $\Box \varphi$ as is standard.

A deontic conflict is a situation in which every state of affairs results in the violation of a rule. For example, imagine a teenager whose mother and father are both cross with her. The mother thinks she spends too much time in her room and the father thinks she has stayed out too late. The two issue the following punitive rules.

(1)   a.   Mother: You must leave your room. $\Box p$
        b.   Father: You may not leave your room. $\neg \Diamond p$

The salient reading of the modals in (1) is deontic[1] - (1-a) says that, according to the rules which now apply to the teenager, if she does not leave her room, she breaks these rules, and (1-b) says that leaving the room breaks rules. Naturally,

---

I am grateful to Jeroen Groenendijk, Stefan Hinterwimmer, Floris Roelofsen, Mandy Simons, Carla Umbach, and Matthijs Westera for extensive discussion of the ideas presented here and closely related topics, to two anonymous reviewers for constructive criticism, and to the Estonian Research Council for their support.

[1] *May* and *must* can also receive, among others, epistemic readings. For a related treatment of epistemic modals, see [2].

© Springer-Verlag Berlin Heidelberg 2015
M. Aher et al. (Eds.): TbiLLC 2013, LNCS 8984, pp. 18–43, 2015.
DOI: 10.1007/978-3-662-46906-4_3

the two rules together are unfair, as she does not have any way to avoid displeasing both the mother and father. This situation is an example of a deontic conflict as all choices for the teenager result in a violation of some rule. Such deontic conflicts have been at the center of a number of prominent puzzles for standard deontic logic.

Standard modal logic (SML) [29] and theories that extend it, such as Kratzer semantics [23,24], express modals as quantification over possible worlds. Permission is represented as existential quantification and obligation (and thus prohibition) as universal quantification. Kratzer adds two contextual features for deontic modals. First, the *modal base*, which is a function f such that $f(w)$ represents the content of a body of laws in a world w. Secondly, an *ordering* on worlds according to how close they are to the ideal world.

Deontic conflicts such as the one in (1) are regrettably commonplace and their existence poses a problem for the standard account. In SML, (1-a) is the case when all accessible worlds are p worlds and (1-b) is the case when none of the accessible worlds are p worlds. Obviously, these statements cannot both be the case, so in each non-absurd state of evaluation, at least one of the rules in (1) will be predicted to be false. But that's counter-intuitive. The situation is a deontic conflict precisely because both of those rules hold simultaneously, leading to unavoidable trouble for the teenager.[2]

There are a number of well known puzzles for standard theories of deontic modals: puzzles which include deontic conflicts such as the *Dr. Procrastinate* puzzle,[3] other puzzles such as *Ross's paradox*,[4] the *free choice* puzzle[5] and the *conditional oughts* puzzle,[6] This paper will focus on the deontic conflicts and Dr. Procrastinate.

Jackson's Dr. Procrastinate puzzle focuses on an expert who, when asked to write a review, will not write it. This fact is represented by (2-a). As experts are expected to write reviews, intuitively, the obligation[7] in (2-b) holds. As not writing a review will delay the entire process of a review actually being written, (2-c) holds as well.

(2)   a.   Dr. Procrastinate will not write the review. $\neg q$
       b.   Dr. Procrastinate ought to accept the request and write
             the review. $\Box(p \land q)$
       c.   Dr. Procrastinate ought not to accept the request. $\Box \neg p$

---

[2] This simple version of a deontic conflict does not pose a problem for Kratzer semantics which also considers an ordering of worlds. See for example Lassiter [25, p. 151] for discussion on deontic conflicts which also cause problems for Kratzer semantics.

[3] See [19].

[4] See [27].

[5] See [20,30].

[6] See [19].

[7] In this paper, *ought* is used interchangeably with *must* because distinctions between the two do not play a role in the presented treatment.

In the literature on the puzzle it is agreed that there are two predictions to be made. First, one should not be able to infer (3) from (2-b) as that leads to an intuitive contradiction between (2-c) and (3).

(3)   Dr. Procrastinate ought to accept the request. $\Box p$

Intuitively, (2-b) and (2-c) coexisting is not absurd as both can be the case simultaneously. This is the case because the obligation in (2-b) requires one to bring about both p and q, and not p alone. In fact, accepting without writing is going to delay the entire process. Unfortunately, standard accounts of deontic modals are upward monotonic, which means that any entailment between propositions holds also when those propositions are embedded under a modal operator, so whenever $\varphi \models \psi$ then $O\varphi \models O\psi$. As standardly the entailment in (4-a) holds, so does the entailment in (4-b).

(4)   a. $p \wedge q \models p$
       b. $\Box(p \wedge q) \models \Box p$

According to the standard treatment of modals, the entailment in (4-b) holds, so whenever (2-b) holds, so does (3). Immediately, a solution suggests itself on how to avoid this part of the puzzle - the semantics for deontic modals should not be upward monotonic. This approach has been adopted by many recent authors, including Lassiter, Cariani and others. [11,25]. The treatment of deontic modals presented here is also non-monotonic, but the lack of upward monotonicity is motivated independently.

Looking ahead, we will consider the addition of multiple *violations* to the semantics, so that different deontic rules can refer to separate violations. By doing so, we wish to demonstrate that non-monotonicity is not a necessary component for solving the deontic conflict described in the story.

Regarding the deontic conflict part of the puzzle, despite the fact that Dr. Procrastinate will necessarily violate the obligation in (2-b), she could avoid violating the second obligation in (2-c). The semantics ought to also predict that her behaviour is more reproachable when she chooses to violate both obligations, i.e., to accept the request to write the review, despite (2-a) being the case. This fact does not concern monotonicity.

This paper will present the deontic semantics MADRIS,[8] which provides a uniform solution to these prominent puzzles of deontic modals. MADRIS stands for Modified Andersonian Deontic Radical Inquisitive Semantics as it is in the spirit of the current most prominent alternative to SML, which expresses modals as Andersonian [7] implications to violations.[9]

Anderson introduced a distinguished proposition v to stand for sentences of the kind "some rule has been violated." When some φ is obligatory, when you do not do φ then you have violated the obligation. This can be represented

---

[8] Based on Aher [1,3,4].

[9] Anderson introduced *relevant implication* instead of material implication, but a full discussion of this logic is outside of the scope of this paper.

as $\Box\varphi := \neg\varphi \to v$. Similarly, if some φ is permitted then it would be odd to find out that by doing φ you have incurred a violation. This intuition can be represented as $\Diamond\varphi := \varphi \to \neg v$.

A violation is not exactly a state of affairs or an unfortunate consequence but rather the observation that some rules have not been followed. Anderson [7, p.347] provides a useful analogy with chess to explain violations. According to the rules of chess, a pawn may move at most two squares at a time. So, playing e5 which moves the pawn three squares violates that rule. See the illustration on the following page.[10]

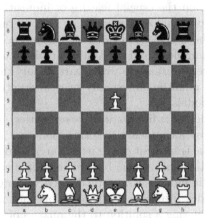

Naturally, nothing stops a player from lifting the pawn from e2 to e5, nor will a punishment necessarily follow. Yet, anyone that opens with e5 is not playing chess according to its rules. And v records the fact some rule is violated.

Anderson's treatment of deontic modals via material implication or relevant implication suffers from a number of puzzles besides *deontic conflicts*, most importantly, it does not account for the *strengthening the antecedent puzzle* [8]. We will demonstrate in Sect. 3.8 that MADRIS avoids the strengthening the antecedent puzzle.

Implication plays an important role in an Andersonian treatment of deontics, so for a modern treatment of implication, consider the conditional in (5).

(5)   If I agree with you, then we will both be wrong. $p \to q$

In the current prominent theory on conditionals by Kratzer [22,23], the antecedent becomes the restrictor of a modal operator in the consequent that's evaluated with respect to a modal base and an ordering source. If no modal is found in the consequent, it is assumed to be a covert epistemic necessity operator.[11] (5) is analyzed in Kratzer semantics with a covert necessity modal over the consequent *we will both be wrong* and (5) is the case when, after restricting the modal base for

---

[10] The image is taken from the popular online chess site chess.com.

[11] A reviewer pointed out that there's an alternative construal put forward by Frank [18], Kaufmann and Schwager [21] and Cariani, Kaufmann and Kaufmann [12] among others in which there's always a covert epistemic necessity operator over the consequent of a conditional.

this necessity modal to all worlds where antecedent, *I agree with you*, holds, the consequent, *it must be that we will both be wrong*, is the case as well.

In MADRIS, conditionals are designed to make similar predictions to Kratzer semantics[12] but there is the option to go with a stronger clause for negation than in Kratzer semantics, which is still weaker than classical negation for material implication. The treatment accounts for Ramsey's intuition that the conditional question *if p, then q?* has two contrary answers *if p, then q* and *if p, then not q*. This paper will illustrate the stronger clauses but is not committed to either the stronger or weaker negation of conditionals.

We will be focusing on the crucial feature of inquisitive semantics that its treatment of disjunction formalizes the intuition that *or* sentences serve to offer alternatives. This has been suggested in the literature as a solution to the *free choice* puzzle by, for example, Aloni [5]. Unlike previous accounts in which universal quantification over alternatives was a part of only the support-conditions of a sentence, we also quantify universally over alternatives in the rejection-conditions of deontic modals.

MADRIS is an extension of radical inquisitive semantics, and it modifies Andersonian deontic modals by introducing quantification over alternatives. This has a significant effect on the treatment of the negation of modals. In MADRIS, deontic modals are related to implications, but due to different negation conditions between the two, deontic modals cannot be defined via implication.

This account provides intuitive predictions for both modal sentences and their negations, while offering a solution to the puzzles of SML.[13]

2 Semantics

Consider a propositional language with negation ($\neg$), conjunction ($\wedge$) and implication ($\rightarrow$) as its basic connectives, to which we add a class of special atoms ($v_1, v_2, ...$) that state that a specific rule has been violated.

We introduce deontic sentential operators ($(\langle\!\langle v_1 \rangle\!\rangle \varphi, \langle\!\langle v_2 \rangle\!\rangle \varphi, ...)$), read as permission. We add a second deontic operator (*obligation*) standardly: $\boxed{v} \varphi := \neg \langle\!\langle v \rangle\!\rangle \neg\varphi$. The $v...v_n$ within the diamond and box symbols refers to the particular rule which grants the permission or sets an obligation. Depending on the rule, modals can refer to different violations, and we assume that each rule does generally refer to a different violation.

Disjunction is defined in the usual way: $\varphi \vee \psi := \neg(\neg\varphi \wedge \neg\psi)$. As in basic inquisitive semantics (See [13–15]), an interrogative sentential operator is introduced in the language by definition: $?\varphi := \varphi \vee \neg\varphi$, but it will not be utilized here.

---

[12] The treatment of conditionals will necessarily be brief. The radical framework, developed by Sano [28] and Groenendijk & Roelofsen [16], provides an intuitive basis for this treatment of deontic modals. The details of a suppositional extension can be found in [17].

[13] We are constrained to deontic modals. See work in progress on suppositional inquisitive semantics [2] on how to treat epistemic modals in a structurally similar manner.

A world is a binary valuation of the atomic sentences in the language, including the designated atoms that state that a specific rule has been violated. Let $\mathcal{A}$ be the set of atomic sentences. We represent a world w as a set which for each $a \in \mathcal{A}$ contains either a or $\bar{a}$, meaning that a holds in w, and that a doesn't hold in w, respectively. σ and τ are variables that range over states, which are sets of worlds, and we use ω to denote the set of all worlds, which corresponds to the ignorant state.

In our recursive semantics we define when a state supports ($\models^+$) and rejects ($\models^-$) a sentence.[14] We denote the set of states that supports a sentence by $[\varphi]^+$ and states that reject a sentence by $[\varphi]^-$. The recursive semantics that we will state guarantees that $[\varphi]^+$ and $[\varphi]^-$ are downward closed. i.e. if $\sigma \in [\varphi]^+$ and $\tau \subseteq \sigma$, then $\tau \in [\varphi]^+$ and same for $[\varphi]^-$. The meaning of a sentence is determined by the pair $\langle [\varphi]^+, [\varphi]^- \rangle$.

For the propositional case there are always one or more maximal supporting/rejecting states for a sentence called alternatives.

Definition 1. *Alternatives*

Support-alternatives: $\mathrm{ALT}[\varphi]^+ := \{\sigma \in [\varphi]^+ \mid \neg \exists \tau \in [\varphi]^+ : \tau \supset \sigma\}$
Rejection-alternatives: $\mathrm{ALT}[\varphi]^- := \{\sigma \in [\varphi]^- \mid \neg \exists \tau \in [\varphi]^- : \tau \supset \sigma\}$

The key notions of *inquisitiveness* and *informativeness* are defined standardly for inquisitive semantics (see, e.g., Ciardelli et al. [13, p. 9)]). But unlike in basic inquisitive semantics, a sentence φ can be inquisitive or informative both on the support-side and rejection-side, which is mirrored in the definition.

Definition 2. *Inquisitiveness and informativeness*

φ *is* **support-inquisitive** *iff at least two alternatives support* φ.
φ *is* **rejection-inquisitive** *iff at least two alternatives reject* φ.
φ *is* **inquisitive** *iff* φ *is support-inquisitive or rejection-inquisitive.*
φ *is* **support-informative**   *iff* $\bigcup[\varphi]^+ \neq \omega$.
φ *is* **rejection-informative**   *iff* $\bigcup[\varphi]^- \neq \omega$.
φ *is* **informative**   *iff* φ *is support-informative or rejection-informative.*

According to the clause for support-informativeness, a sentence φ is informative if the union of all its supporting states does not include all worlds, and likewise for rejection-informativeness.

When *the set of support-alternatives for* φ, $\mathrm{ALT}[\varphi]^+$, contains more than one element then φ is (support-) *inquisitive*, and when *the set of rejection-alternatives for* φ, $\mathrm{ALT}[\varphi]^-$, contains more than one element then φ is (rejection-) *inquisitive*. This plays a crucial role in explaining free choice phenomena concerning deontic modals.

---

[14] There is a further extension of the system [17] which distinguishes a third relation between states and sentences which concerns a state dismissing a supposition of a sentence. In the semantics presented here, when a state rejects p, it both supports and rejects $p \rightarrow q$, and $\Diamond p$. In the suppositional extension such states are characterized as neither supporting nor rejecting them, but as dismissing a supposition of theirs.

Since meanings are determined by the pair of supporting and rejecting states, entailment should also be stated relative to both components of meaning. Classically this would be a correct, but redundant formulation as the support and reject perspective on entailment would coincide.

Definition 3. *Entailment*

Support-entailment: $\varphi \models_+ \psi$ *iff* $[\varphi]^+ \subseteq [\psi]^+$
Rejection-entailment: $\varphi \models_- \psi$ *iff* $[\psi]^- \subseteq [\varphi]^-$
Entailment: $\varphi \models \psi$ *iff* φ *support-entails* ψ *and* φ *rejection-entails* ψ.

According to Definition 3, a sentence φ support-entails the sentence ψ if every state that supports φ also supports ψ, and likewise for rejection. The dual nature of entailment plays an important role in the explanation of various deontic puzzles.[15]

The recursive statement of the semantics is as follows.

Definition 4 (MADRIS).

Atomic sentences:
$\sigma \models^+ p$ *iff* $\forall w \in \sigma : p \in w$
$\sigma \models^- p$ *iff* $\forall w \in \sigma : \overline{p} \in w$

Negation:
$\sigma \models^+ \neg\varphi$ *iff* $\sigma \models^- \varphi$
$\sigma \models^- \neg\varphi$ *iff* $\sigma \models^+ \varphi$

Conjunction:
$\sigma \models^+ \varphi \wedge \psi$ *iff* $\sigma \models^+ \varphi$ *and* $\sigma \models^+ \psi$
$\sigma \models^- \varphi \wedge \psi$ *iff* $\sigma \models^- \varphi$ *or* $\sigma \models^- \psi$

Implication:
$\sigma \models^+ \varphi \rightarrow \psi$ *iff* $\forall \tau \in \mathrm{ALT}[\varphi]^+ : \tau \cap \sigma \models^+ \psi$
$\sigma \models^- \varphi \rightarrow \psi$ *iff* $\exists \tau \in \mathrm{ALT}[\varphi]^+ : \tau \cap \sigma \models^- \psi$

Deontic permission:
$\sigma \models^+ \otimes \varphi$ *iff* $\forall \tau \in \mathrm{ALT}[\varphi]^+ : \tau \cap \sigma \models^- v$
$\sigma \models^- \otimes \varphi$ *iff* $\forall \tau \in \mathrm{ALT}[\varphi]^+ : \tau \cap \sigma \models^+ v$

3   Illustrating the Semantics

The clauses of MADRIS are illustrated below with examples.[16]

---

[15] Equivalence is defined as mutual entailment.

[16] The natural language examples are for illustration only. The actual picture of positive and negative responses is naturally more complicated. See for example Brasoveanu et al. [10].

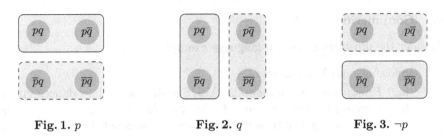

Fig. 1. p **Fig. 2.** q **Fig. 3.** $\neg p$

3.1   Atomic Sentences

Consider the natural language example in (6).

(6)   Sue sings.

    a.   *Positive response*:   Yes, Sue sings. p

    b.   *Negative response*:   No, Sue does not sing. $\neg p$

The treatment of atomic sentences is standard, but as is characteristic of the radical approach to inquisitive semantics, the semantics specifies both the support and rejection conditions for a sentence. According to clause 1 of Definition 4, an atomic sentence p is supported by a state σ if p holds in every world w in σ; and p is rejected in σ if p holds in no world w in σ.

This means that there is a unique maximal state σ that supports p, a unique element of $\mathrm{ALT}[p]^{+}$, which consists of all worlds where p holds; and a unique maximal state σ that rejects p, a unique element of $\mathrm{ALT}[p]^{-}$, which consists of all worlds where p does not hold. The fact that there is a single maximal state means that atoms are neither support-inquisitive nor rejection-inquisitive.

As the maximal supporting state does not include worlds where $\neg p$ holds, and the maximal rejecting state does not include worlds where p holds, p is both support informative and rejection informative. We will generally omit discussion of informativeness below, unless a sentence is not informative.

The meaning of the atomic sentences p and q is depicted in Figs. 1 and 2, respectively, where the circles correspond to worlds that concern only the value of these two atomic sentences. Maximal states that support a sentence are indicated by solid lines; maximal states that reject a sentence are indicated by dashed lines.

3.2   Negation

Negation is illustrated by the negative response to the atomic sentence in (6). According to clause 2 of Definition 4, negation flips between support and rejection, so that a sentence $\neg\varphi$ is supported by a state σ if σ rejects φ and conversely for the rejection of $\neg\varphi$. This means that $\neg\varphi$ is support-inquisitive when φ is rejection-inquisitive, and *vice versa*. Consider the simple example $\neg p$, whose meaning is depicted in Fig. 3.

3.3 Conjunction

Consider the illustrating natural language example in (7).

(7)   Sue sings and Mary dances.
    a.   *Primary positive response*:   Yes, Sue sings and Mary dances. $p \wedge q$
    b.   *Primary negative response 1*:   No, Sue does not sing. $\neg p$
    c.   *Primary negative response 2*:   No, Mary does not dance. $\neg q$

According to clause 3 of Definition 4, a state σ supports a conjunction $\varphi \wedge \psi$ if σ supports both φ and ψ; and σ rejects this conjunction if σ rejects φ or σ rejects ψ.

Consider the simple example $p \wedge q$. A state σ supports $p \wedge q$ if σ supports both p and q. This means that $\text{ALT}[p \wedge q]^+$ consists of a single element, the state that consists of all worlds where both p and q hold, and is thus not support-inquisitive.

A state σ rejects $p \wedge q$ if it rejects either p or it rejects q. As $\text{ALT}[p \wedge q]^-$ consists of two elements, a state consisting of all worlds where p does not hold and a state consisting of all worlds where q does not hold, $p \wedge q$ is rejection-inquisitive. The meaning of $p \wedge q$ is depicted in Fig. 4.

3.4 Disjunction

$\varphi \vee \psi$ is defined in the standard way as $\neg(\neg\varphi \wedge \neg\psi)$ and is illustrated by Fig. 5. As disjunction corresponds to the negation of conjunction, it is support-inquisitive but not rejection-inquisitive.

3.5 Implication

Implication directly utilizes the notion of alternatives as the universal quantification in the support clause and the existential quantification in the reject clause both concern the alternatives for the antecedent. According to clause 4 of Definition 4, a state σ supports $\varphi \rightarrow \psi$ if every alternative (i.e., maximal supporting state) for the antecedent φ, restricted to the information contained in σ, supports the consequent ψ. A state σ rejects $\varphi \rightarrow \psi$ only when some maximal supporting state for φ, restricted to the information contained in σ, rejects ψ. Consider the simple example $p \rightarrow q$, illustrated by the natural language example (8).

(8)   If Sue sings, then Pete plays the piano.
    a.   *Positive response*:
         Yes, if Sue sings, then Pete will play the piano. $p \rightarrow q$
    b.   *Negative response*:
         No, if Sue sings, then Pete won't play the piano. $p \rightarrow \neg q$

As explained above, there is only one maximal supporting state for an atomic sentence p, consisting of all worlds where p is the case. This means that the universal and existential quantification in the support and rejection clauses do not play a crucial role with this example. A state σ supports $p \rightarrow q$ if the maximal substate of σ where p is the case supports q. So, in all worlds in σ

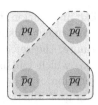

Fig. 4. $p \wedge q$ **Fig. 5.** $p \vee q$ **Fig. 6.** $p \rightarrow q$

where p is the case, q should be the case as well. A state σ rejects $p \rightarrow q$ if the maximal substate of σ where p is the case rejects q. So, in all the worlds in σ where p is the case, q should not be the case. Figure 6 shows the meaning of $p \rightarrow q$. The quantification over alternatives in the clauses comes into play when the antecedent or consequent is support-inquisitive. These effects are discussed in the Subsect. 3.7 which compares implication and deontic permission.

3.6 Violation-Based Deontic Modals

According to the clause for permission, the state σ supports a permission statement $\textcircled{v} \varphi$ if every maximal supporting state for the prejacent φ, restricted to the information contained in σ, rejects the violation v.

A state σ rejects $\textcircled{v} \varphi$ if every maximal supporting state for φ, restricted to the information contained in σ, supports v. So, a state that rejects permission for φ supports the statement that φ is prohibited.

Consider the simple exaple $\textcircled{v} p$ illustrated by example (9).

(9)   A country may establish a laboratory.

    a. *Positive response:*
       Yes, a country may establish a laboratory. $\textcircled{v} p$

    b. *Negative response:*
       No, a country may not establish a laboratory. $\neg \textcircled{v} q$

There is only one maximal supporting state for an atomic sentence p, consisting of all worlds where p is the case. The universal quantification in the support and rejection clause concerns only this state. A state σ supports $\textcircled{v} p$ if the maximal substate of σ where p is the case supports $\neg v$. So, in all worlds in σ where p is the case, the violation v must not be the case. A state σ rejects $\textcircled{v} p$ if the maximal substate of σ where p is the case supports v. So, in all worlds in σ where p is the case, the violation v should be the case as well. The simple example is structurally similar to implication and, in MADRIS when the antecedent/prejacent of $\textcircled{v} \varphi$ is not inquisitive, it can be expressed via implication.

Proposition 1 *If φ is not support-inquisitive, then $\textcircled{v} \varphi \equiv \varphi \rightarrow \neg v$.*

This holds e.g. when φ is the atom p. As is evident, we follow Anderson's intuition that the meaning of deontic operators is connected to implication.

Unlike implication, though, permission does not have an arbitrary sentence ψ as its consequent, instead, permission always refers to a specific violation v. Furthermore, the rejection clause for permission differs from the clause for implication, which will be discussed in Subsect. 3.7 where we compare modals and implication.

Figure 7 illustrates $\overset{\otimes}{\diamondsuit}p$, and the three deontic statuses: permission, prohibition and neutrality. For convenience, non-violation worlds ($\bar{v}$) are indicated in green and violation worlds (v) in red.[17] The illustrative picture allows one to determine the deontic status of a state of affairs by seeing whether worlds that support a state of affairs p are within, outside or both with respect to the maximal state that supports the deontic statement in the figure.

Permission. The state where p *is permitted* has no pv world in the maximal supporting state,[18] so looking at p worlds, $\neg v$ is also the case. The maximal state for $\overset{\otimes}{\diamondsuit}p$ is illustrated by using a continuous line in Fig. 7.

Prohibition. The state where p *is prohibited*, has no $p\bar{v}$ world. The state which supports $\neg\overset{\otimes}{\diamondsuit}p$ is illustrated by using a dashed line in Fig. 8.

Neutral. Both of these states are *deontically neutral towards* $\neg p$ as the maximal supporting states include both a $\bar{p}v$ and a $\bar{p}\bar{v}$ world.

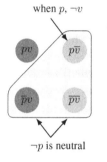

when $p, \neg v$

$\neg p$ is neutral

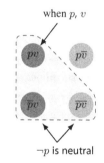

when p, v

$\neg p$ is neutral

Fig. 7. $[\overset{\otimes}{\diamondsuit}p\,]^{+}/[p \to \neg v]^{+}$ **Fig. 8.** $[\overset{\otimes}{\diamondsuit}p]^{-}/[p \to \neg v]^{-}$

3.7   Comparing Implication and Permission

The differences between implication and permission concern their rejection conditions and inquisitiveness. In the simple implication $p \to q$ quantification over the alternatives for the antecedent play no significant role due to the antecedent only having one maximal supporting state. This, however, is not the case for

---

[17] If you are reading this in gray-scale, violation worlds are darker and non-violation worlds are lighter.

[18] SML treats permission as weaker, so $\overset{\otimes}{\diamondsuit}p$ does not guarantee that when you bring about p, no violation occurs.

$(p \vee q) \to r$, where the antecedent is a support-inquisitive disjunction for which there are two maximal supporting states: the set of all worlds where p is the case and the set of all worlds where q is the case (see Fig. 5).

The natural language example in (10) illustrates $(p \vee q) \to r$.

(10)   If Sue sings or Mary dances, then Pete will play the piano. $(p \vee q) \to r$

    a.   *Primary positive response:*
        Yes, if Sue sings, Pete will play, and if Mary dances, he'll play too.
$$(p \to r) \wedge (q \to r)$$

    b.   *Primary negative responses:*
        No, if Sue sings Pete will not play. $p \to \neg r$
        No, if Mary dances, Pete will not play. $q \to \neg r$

For a state σ to support $(p \vee q) \to r$, what should hold is that for each of the two maximal supporting states for $p \vee q$, when σ is restricted to it, the resulting substate of σ supports r. So, in each world in σ where p is the case, r should also be the case; and in each world in σ where q is the case, r should also be the case.

For a state σ to reject $(p \vee q) \to r$, what should hold is that for one (or both) of the two maximal supporting states for $p \vee q$: the maximal supporting state for p and the maximal supporting state for q, when σ is restricted to it, the resulting substate of σ rejects r.

Consider $(p \to r) \wedge (q \to r)$. The first conjunct $p \to r$ is supported in σ if the maximal state where p is supported, restricted to σ, also supports r. Likewise for $q \to r$. According to the clause for conjunction, the state σ supports $(p \to r) \wedge (q \to r)$ if both conjuncts are supported. So both the maximal supporting states for p and for q, restricted to σ, also support r.

According to the rejection clause for conjunction, a state σ rejects $(p \to r) \wedge (q \to r)$ if it rejects either conjunct: $p \to r$ or $q \to r$. A state σ rejects $p \to r$ if all maximal supporting states for p, restricted to σ, reject r. Likewise for $q \to r$.

This means that $(p \vee q) \to r$ is supported and rejected in the same states as $(p \to r) \wedge (q \to r)$ and hence that the two sentences are equivalent.

Proposition 2 $(p \vee q) \to r \equiv (p \to r) \wedge (q \to r)$

Classically this equivalence also holds and neither of the sentences is support-inquisitive. The maximal supporting state for $(p \vee q) \to r$ is illustrated in Fig. 9. MADRIS also produces the result that both sentences are rejection-inquisitive. As we discussed with regard to $p \wedge q$ above, illustrated by Fig. 4, this conjunction is rejected when either p or q is rejected. The conjunction between $p \to r$ and $q \to r$ should also be rejected when either conjunct is rejected. MADRIS obtains this result as illustrated by Fig. 10 showing the two maximal rejecting states for $(p \vee q) \to r$.[19]

---

[19] A comparison of Figs. 9 and 16 also shows that $(p \vee q) \to r$ and $(p \wedge q) \to \neg r$ are consistent with each other. This is also the case in Kratzer semantics if it's combined with an alternative-based treatment of disjunction. See for example Alonso-Ovalle [6].

Fig. 9. $[(p \vee q) \rightarrow r]^+$

Fig. 10. $[(p \vee q) \rightarrow r]^-$

In MADRIS the free choice effect of $\overset{\textcircled{v}}{\diamond}(p \vee q)$ receives a straightforward semantic treatment, as $\overset{\textcircled{v}}{\diamond}\varphi$ is support-equivalent to $\varphi \rightarrow \neg v$.

Proposition 3 $[\overset{\textcircled{v}}{\diamond}(p \vee q)]^+ \equiv [(p \vee q) \rightarrow \neg v]^+ \equiv [(p \rightarrow \neg v) \wedge (q \rightarrow \neg v)]^+$

The solution to the free choice problem in MADRIS has been extensively discussed in earlier work,[20] so it is not repeated here. But it is helpful to use free choice examples to illustrate the difference between the behaviour of implication and permission under negation.

According to an Andersonian analysis of permission as an implication, $\neg\overset{\textcircled{v}}{\diamond}(p \vee q)$ is support-inquisitive, but intuitively it is not.

(11)   A country may not establish a research center or a laboratory. $\neg\overset{\textcircled{v}}{\diamond}(p \vee q)$

The salient reading of (11) says that both disjuncts are prohibited. We refer to this as the *no choice* reading, in that choosing to establish either a research center or a laboratory will break the rule in (11). This is because the drafters of a law or rule establish which permissions and obligations hold, which leaves no room for inquisitiveness. This leads to the standard non-inquisitiveness intuition regarding the interpretation of *free choice* examples and their negation (see example (11)): $\neg\overset{\textcircled{v}}{\diamond}(p \vee q) \equiv \boxed{v}(\neg p \wedge \neg q)$, which the semantics predicts.

Unlike implication, both the support and reject clause for permission has universal quantification scoping over the prejacent, guaranteeing that even with an inquisitive prejacent φ, $\overset{\textcircled{v}}{\diamond}\varphi$ is not rejection-inquisitive. For a state σ to support $\neg\overset{\textcircled{v}}{\diamond}(p \vee q)$, what should hold is that for each of the two maximal supporting states for $p \vee q$, p and q, restricting σ to them results in a substate of σ which supports v. So, in each world in σ where p is the case, v should also be the case, and in each world in σ where q is the case, v should also be the case. This results in a single maximal rejecting state illustrated in Fig. 11. As we saw earlier, due to the existential quantifier in the rejection clause for implication, when the antecedent is support-inquisitive, an implication is rejection-inquisitive. As illustrated by Fig. 12, $[(p \vee q) \rightarrow \neg v]^-$ contains two maximal rejecting states.

---

[20] See [4], especially for discussion on how to also attain disjunctive readings under permission.

One rejecting state corresponds to $[p \rightarrow v]^+$ and is shaped like an 'L' while the other rejecting state corresponds to $[q \rightarrow v]^+$ and is rectangle-shaped. Due to not being rejection-inquisitive, $[\diamondsuit (p \vee q)]^-$ is stronger than $[(p \vee q) \rightarrow \neg v]^-$.[21] The only way modals can be inquisitive is when an inquisitive connective scopes over modals.

Fig. 11. $[\diamondsuit (p \vee q)]^-$

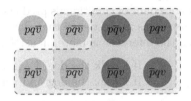

Fig. 12. $[(p \vee q) \rightarrow \neg v]^-$

3.8   Strengthening the Antecedent

Besides deontic conflicts, an Andersonian treatment of deontic modals standardly suffers from the *strengthening the antecedent* puzzle. The modified Andersonian treatment of modals allows MADRIS to avoid this puzzle.

Andersonian modals which reduce deontic modals to implication inherit the properties of implication; for example, material implication is downward monotonic (DM). The property of DM shown in (12).

(12)   An operator is DM iff $\psi \models \varphi$ implies $O\varphi \models O\psi$.

Downward monotonicity is generally regarded an unwanted property of deontic modals due to the strengthening the antecedent puzzle that we will discuss presently.

Strengthening the antecedent is a puzzle for material implication and other DM implications. The problem lies in the fact that in a material implication account an implication entails the implication where the antecedent has been strengthened with a conjunct: (14).

In the following, we will distinguish between the clauses in MADRIS and material implication by representing the latter with $\rightarrow_m$. In propositional logic, a conjunction entails its conjuncts:

(13) $p \wedge q \models p$

We will make use of this entailment as in (14), the antecedent of the premise is p and the antecedent of the conclusion is $p \wedge q$.

(14) $p \rightarrow_m r \models p \wedge q \rightarrow_m r$

---

[21] Stronger is understood through entailment: $[\diamondsuit (p \vee q)]^- \models [(p \vee q) \rightarrow \neg v]^-$.

As discussed by Lewis [26, p.80] and others, the entailment in (14) leads to counter-intuitive examples such as (15).

(15)   a.   If I strike a match, it will light.
        b.   Hence, if I strike a match and the match is wet, it will light.

Intuitively, we can accept (15-a) without accepting (15-b), but a material implication account of condtionals predicts that when (15-a) is the case, (15-b) cannot be false. This is not to say that there do not exist natural language examples in which the inference is more plausible. Consider (16).

(16)   a.   If I walk the dog, I will get some fresh air.
        b.   If I walk the dog and whistle, I will get some fresh air.

Intuitively, we accept both (16-a) and (16-b). In fact, we can add any arbitrary conjunct in (16-b), such as whistling, because it does not change the outcome. But the existence of examples such as (15) demonstrates that the plausibility of the inference in (16) cannot be a general inference rule for implication.

Strengthening the antecedent is also relevant for deontic modals. Recall that Anderson defined a permission utterance as relevant implication from the prejacent to the negation of a violation v. Anderson used relevant implication but we will adopt material implication for brevity's sake. If the modal is defined using material implication, then whenever (17-a) holds, (17-b) holds as well.

(17)   a. $p \rightarrow_m \neg v$
        b. $(p \wedge q) \rightarrow_m \neg v$

This leads to examples such as the following.

(18)   a.   You may walk the dog.
        b.   You may walk the dog and kill the president.

Intuitively, no-one would accept that when permission is granted to walk the dog, this also grants permission to kill the president. So, strengthening the antecedent should not to be valid for neither implication nor modals in MADRIS. Because (13) holds, if MADRIS modals were DM, whenever (18-a) is the case, so would be (18-b).

In MADRIS, strengthening the antecedent is not valid for implication or modals, which means deontic modals are not DM in MADRIS. We will demonstrate how strengthening the antecedent fails in MADRIS. The modal and implication case are parallel.

Consider the maximal supporting and rejecting states for the premise and conclusion in (18-a). A state σ supports $p \rightarrow r$ if the maximal supporting state for p, restricted to σ, supports r. Such a state cannot contain worlds where p and q hold, but r does not, nor worlds where p holds but q and r do not. On the other hand, a state σ supports $(p \wedge q) \rightarrow r$ if the maximal supporting state for $p \wedge q$, restricted to σ, supports r. The only worlds incompatible with such a state are those where both p and q hold but r does not. We thus conclude that every state that supports $p \rightarrow r$ also supports $(p \wedge q) \rightarrow r$ so that $p \rightarrow r$ support-entails $(p \wedge q) \rightarrow r$.

This fact is illustrated in Figs. 13 and 14.

Fig. 13. $[p \rightarrow r]^+$

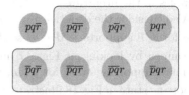

Fig. 14. $[(p \wedge q) \rightarrow r]^+$

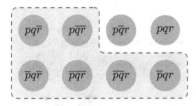

Fig. 15. $[p \rightarrow r]^-$

Fig. 16. $[(p \wedge q) \rightarrow r]^-$

The support-entailment explains the intuitiveness of the inference in (16). When the additional information in the second conjunct does not have an effect on the implication, we do end up at only worlds in which $(p \wedge q) \rightarrow r$ also holds.

It is only when we begin to consider how one might reject the two sentences that the we see a difference. Recall that entailment looks at both supporting and rejecting states, such that when φ entails ψ, every state that supports φ must also support ψ and every rejecting state for ψ must be a rejecting state for φ.

Consider the maximal rejecting state for $(p \wedge q) \rightarrow r$ compared to the maximal rejecting state for $p \rightarrow r$. A state σ rejects $(p \wedge q) \rightarrow r$ if the maximal supporting state for $p \wedge q$, restricted to σ, rejects r. As we are interested only in worlds where both conjuncts hold, the only worlds that annot be in the state are those where p, q and r hold. So it is possible to reject $(p \wedge q) \rightarrow r$ with relatively little information.

Conversely, a state rejects $p \rightarrow r$ if the maximal supporting state for p, restricted to σ, rejects r. Such a state cannot include both worlds where p, q and r hold and also worlds where p and r hold but q does not hold. As we can see in Figs. 15 and 16, the maximal rejecting state for $(p \wedge q) \rightarrow r$ is not a rejecting state for $p \rightarrow r$.

As $(p \wedge q) \rightarrow r$ only concerns the situation in which both p and q are the case, it does not provide as much information regarding when r follows as $p \rightarrow r$ which also concerns itself with $p\overline{q}$ worlds. This means that $p \rightarrow r$ does not rejection-entail $(p \wedge q) \rightarrow r$.

Recall that entailment requires both support-entailment and rejection-entailment. As $p \rightarrow r$ does not rejection-entail $(p \wedge q) \rightarrow r$, it also does not entail it.

Due to the weaker rejection-conditions of the conclusion, strengthening the antecedent is not a valid inference pattern, which explains the counter-intuitive examples in the literature.

Also consider the deontic case. As with implication, the maximal supporting state for $\diamondsuit^{v} p$ supports $\diamondsuit^{v}(p \wedge q)$ so $\diamondsuit^{v} p$ support-entails $\diamondsuit^{v}(p \wedge q)$. This can be determined by looking at Figs. 17 and 18. A state σ supports $\diamondsuit^{v}(p \wedge q)$ if the maximal supporting state for $p \wedge q$, restricted to σ, rejects v. As the maximal supporting state in Fig. 18 illustrates, the only world incompatible with $\diamondsuit^{v}(p \wedge q)$ is the one where p, q and v all hold. This world is also incompatible with $\diamondsuit^{v} p$ because a state σ supports $\diamondsuit^{v} p$ if the maximal supporting state for p, restricted to σ, rejects v. So, for $\diamondsuit^{v} p$ is incompatible with all p worlds where v is the case. So the world where p and v are the case but q isn't is also incompatible with $\diamondsuit^{v} p$.

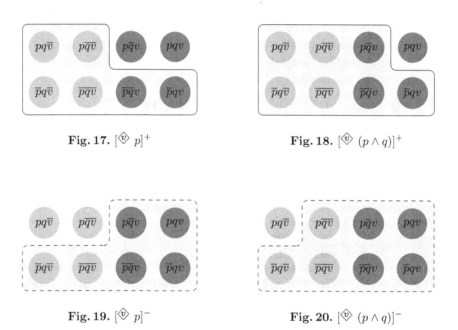

Fig. 17. $[\diamondsuit^{v} p]^{+}$ Fig. 18. $[\diamondsuit^{v}(p \wedge q)]^{+}$

Fig. 19. $[\diamondsuit^{v} p]^{-}$ Fig. 20. $[\diamondsuit^{v}(p \wedge q)]^{-}$

From this we can conclude that $\diamondsuit^{v}(p \wedge q)$ grants less permission than $\diamondsuit^{v} p$. It only grants permission for those situations in which both p and q are the case, and does not say whether a violation is incurred or not in those worlds where q is not the case. So it does not grant permission for cases where someone brings about p without bringing about q. In this sense, $\diamondsuit^{v}(p \wedge q)$ is a weaker permission statement than $\diamondsuit^{v} p$ that does grant permission to bring about p without bringing about q.

On the other hand, as we can see in Figs. 19 and 20, the maximal rejecting state for $\diamondsuit^{v}(p \wedge q)$ is not a rejecting state for $\diamondsuit^{v} p$ as it includes the world where p is the case but q and v are not the case.

$\diamondsuit^{v} (p \wedge q)$ is weaker than $\diamondsuit^{v} p$ as it only concerns the situation in which both p and q are the case. As such, for a state to reject $\diamondsuit^{v} (p \wedge q)$, the state cannot be such that it includes the worlds where both p and q are the case and no violation is incurred.

The world where p holds but q and v do not does not concern the conjunction example. Yet, the inclusion of this world does not satisfy the requirements for a state to reject $\diamondsuit^{v} p$. For a state to reject $\diamondsuit^{v} p$, when p is the case, a violation must occur. A state with the world where p is the case, but a violation does not occur, is not a rejecting state for $\diamondsuit^{v} p$. This means that $\diamondsuit^{v} p$ does not rejection-entail $\diamondsuit^{v} (p \wedge q)$, and then it also does not entail it.

MADRIS provides a semantic solution to the puzzle of strengthening the antecedent for implication and deontic modals in parallel fashion.[22] So MADRIS correctly predicts that deontic modals are not DM.

3.9   Multiple Violations

The semantics allows the designation of v_1, v_2, *etc* for each specific violation. Unlike Anderson's original conceptualization, now v_n stands for "rule$_n$ has been violated" where n indexes each rule to a specific violation. Violations can be reasoned about in the same manner as any other information but there is no guarantee that every set of rules allows one to avoid all violations as there exist inherently conflicted sets of rules. Multiple violations will allow one to still determine the state with least violations.

Consider again the deontic conflict in (1), but this time we distinguish the two deontic statements by mother and father as two separate rules.

(19)   a.   Mother: You must leave your room. $\qquad\qquad\qquad \boxed{v1} p$

 b.   Father: You may not leave your room. $\qquad\qquad\quad \neg \diamondsuit^{v2} p$

This distinction is sufficient for MADRIS to provide the tools required to state that each alternative for the teenager results in a violation. Furthermore, MADRIS allows for a more fine-grained analysis of such a *deontic conflict* through the introduction of multiple violations.

One way to conceptualize multiple violations is to differentiate deontic authorities. We will not use this conceptualization but it is useful to consider it briefly to see its shortcomings.

In the above example, mother and father can be taken to represent different deontic authorities: each provides rules they enforce largely independently of the other. We could then say that there exists a violation for mother: v_1 and a violation for father: v_2.

What the analysis gains from such a treatment is that we can now differentiate between different consequences of the inevitable breaking of the rules.

---

[22] Strengthening the antecedent also doesn't hold for obligation for the same reason as it does not hold for implication and permission, but we do not have the space to go through the calculations here.

The teenager can reason from the fact that mother's violation results in a stern look ($v_1 \rightarrow q$) and father's violation results in a more severe punishment ($v_2 \rightarrow r$) that, wishing to avoid r, it is advantageous to stay in the room ($\neg p$), even though doing so also violates a rule.

But such a conceptualization is problematic as rules set by one authority, for example by mother, can be inconsistent and deontic conflicts can still occur. For reasons of forgetfulness, malice, etc. people create situations of *deontic conflicts*. So, it could easily be the case that mother uttered both (19-a) and (19-b) in which case the conceptualization does not allow us to reason about the consequences of choosing p and $\neg p$ in the same manner as before.

It is possible to reason that some rules are more important to follow than others, even when they come from the same authority. A single law can specify that the violation of one article is followed by a harsher punishment than another. Consider different degrees of murder: manslaughter receives fewer years in prison than murder even though the violations are considered from the perspective of one authority - the state.

So, as is generally accepted in law, it is more plausible to assume that each rule has its own violation associated with it, such that the statement (19-a) being distinct from (19-b) would be the basis for associating (19-a) with v_1 and (19-b) with v_2.

A standard example of this in legal discourse, illustrated in (20), is a case when a court deems someone guilty of violating one article of a law, but judges that the defendant did not violate other articles of the same law.[23]

(20)   a.   The jury finds the defendant in violation of article 1.
        b.   The jury find the defendant not in violation of article 2.

Were the conceptualization of multiple violations authority-based, the judgment would be inconsistent: the defendant both incurs and does not incur the same violation. But this is not plausible.[24]

Returning to the deontic conflict in (19), v_1 refers to the rule (19-a) and v_2 refers to the rule (19-b), so when the teenager chooses to leave the room, $\neg p$ holds, and via rule $\neg \langle v_2 \rangle p$, v_2 holds as well. This violation says that the rule in (19-b) has been violated.

Further Work on Suppositions. A prevalent intuition regarding deontic statements says that sentences such as $\langle v \rangle p$ should not provide information regarding whether p or $\neg p$ is the case. This intuition is straightforwardly accounted for in MADRIS but it reappears with regard to certain deontic conflicts. Consider the conjunction in (21) on the assumption that both permission statements refer to the same violation.

---

[23] This example is a simplification of a World Trade Organization panel report from case DSU 344. For further details see [4, p. 104].

[24] This is not to say that further work should not focus on more fine-grained conceptualizations.

(21) $\diamondsuit p \wedge \neg \diamondsuit p$

    a. $\diamondsuit p$

    b. $\neg \diamondsuit p$

The conjunction in (21) is supported by a state σ if both conjuncts, (21-a) and (21-b) are supported in the state. The first conjunct is supported by a state σ if the maximal supporting state for p, restricted to σ, supports $\neg v$. The second conjunct, (21-b), is supported by a state σ if the maximal supporting state for p, restricted to σ, supports v. The conjunction is supported by σ only if there exist no worlds that support p, i.e., the prejacent is not the case.

It is problematic that the conjunction of two permission statements, neither of which alone provides information regarding whether p or $\neg p$ is the case, provides the information that $\neg p$ is the case. This is because both $\diamondsuit p$ and $\neg \diamondsuit p$ share the same prejacent p but the conjuncts provide contrary deontic information. The first states that no violation is incurred, and the other than a violation is incurred, which makes the two statements intuitively inconsistent.

MADRIS does not yet have the tools to account for this type of an inconsistency, as it allows the prejacent to be vacuously supported by the empty state. The maximal supporting state for (21) where the prejacent p is rejected is illustrated in Fig. 21. Intuitively, this is a case of supposition failure as the supposition that the prejacent p is the case fails in all cases.

Fig. 21. $[\diamondsuit p \wedge \neg \diamondsuit p]^{+}$

Not all deontic conflicts result in supposition failure. This paper focuses on the majority of deontic conflicts which can be intuitively avoided in case the permission and violation statements refer to different violations. But where such interpretations are infelicitous, and we have to assume that both deontic statements refer to the same violation, a deontic conflict results in supposition failure.

Groenendijk and Roelofsen have recently developed an extension of radical inquisitive semantics called suppositional inquisitive semantics [17] which adds suppositional content as a third component of meaning next to informative and inquisitive.[25] In the extension, the rejection of the antecedent of a conditional or the rejection of the prejacent of a modal no longer vacuously supports the implication or modal statement as a whole. To more accurately account for

---

[25] Such an approach is not to be confused with work on presuppositions which, as far as the author is aware, is an entirely disconnected phenomenon.

examples such as (21), ongoing work extends suppositional inquisitive semantics in the spirit of MADRIS to also account for such cases.[26]

4 Solving Puzzles

Alongside deontic conflicts as a whole, this paper demonstrates how introducing multiple violations solves the Dr. Procrastinate puzzle that combines an upward monotonicity puzzle with a deontic conflict. This puzzle allows us to demonstrate the finer workings of this non-monotonic semantics for deontic modals with multiple violations.

4.1 Dr. Procrastinate

Recall the Dr. Procrastinate puzzle in example (2) repeated here as (22).

(22) a. Dr. Procrastinate will not write the review. $\neg q$
      b. Dr. Procrastinate ought to accept and write the review. $\boxed{v}\,(p \wedge q)$
      c. Dr. Procrastinate ought not to accept. $\boxed{v}\,\neg p$

According to the literature, there are two predictions to make: i) the conjunction of (22-b) and (22-c) is not intuitively absurd as they can be the case simultaneously; ii) we know that Dr. Procrastinate will violate the obligation in (22-b) but could avoid violating the second violation in (22-c), so if Dr. Procrastinate accepts, despite the fact that she will not finish writing the review, the semantics should predict that her behaviour is more reproachable than when she does not accept.

Upward Monotonicity. A standard approach to the puzzle concerns upward monotonicity as (22-b) is generally represented by an embedded conjunction. In SML and Kratzer semantics obligation is upward monotonic, so the embedded conjunction $\boxed{v}\,(p \wedge q)$ in (22-b) entails the embedded conjunct $\boxed{v}\,p$, which contradicts $\boxed{v}\,\neg p$ in (22-c).

For the sake of argument, assume that the obligations in (22-b) and (22-c) refer to the same violation. MADRIS captures that the obligations in (22-b) and (22-c) are not contradictory because the semantics is not upward monotonic.

Recall that because MADRIS specifies both support and rejection conditions, entailment also concerns both support and rejection such that for φ to entail ψ every state which supports φ must also support ψ and, also, every state which rejects ψ must also reject φ. This two-fold requirement is classically the case, but with the specified rejection conditions for permission and obligation, it makes the semantics non-monotonic.

Consider $\boxed{v}\,(p \wedge q)$ and $\boxed{v}\,p$. For $\boxed{v}\,(p \wedge q)$ to entail $\boxed{v}\,p$, the definition of entailment specifies two conditions: a) every state which supports $\boxed{v}\,p$ must also support $\boxed{v}\,(p \wedge q)$, and b) every state which rejects $\boxed{v}\,p$ must also reject $\boxed{v}\,(p \wedge q)$.

---

[26] See [2].

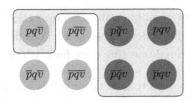

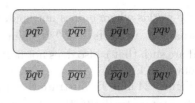

Fig. 22. $[\boxed{v}\,(p \wedge q)]^{+}$ **Fig. 23.** $[\boxed{v}\,p]^{+}$

Consider requirement (a) first. Figure 22 shows the maximal supporting state for $\boxed{v}\,(p \wedge q)$. A state σ supports $\boxed{v}\,(p \wedge q)$ if every rejection-alternative for $(p \wedge q)$, restricted to σ, supports v. ALT$[p \wedge q]^{-}$ consists of two elements, one consisting of all the worlds where p does not hold, and the other consisting of all the worlds where q does not hold. Due to universal quantification over these alternatives, σ supports $\boxed{v}\,(p \wedge q)$ when all worlds in σ where either p or q does not hold are such that v does hold.

Figure 23 shows the maximal supporting state for $\boxed{v}\,p$. A state σ supports $\boxed{v}\,p$ if every alternative for $\neg p$, restricted to σ, supports v. ALT$[p]^{-}$ consists of a single element consisting of all the worlds where p does not hold, so σ supports $\boxed{v}\,p$ when all worlds in σ where p does not hold are such that v does hold.

As Figs. 22 and 23 illustrate, every state which supports $\boxed{v}\,(p \wedge q)$ also supports $\boxed{v}\,p$, so $\boxed{v}\,(p \wedge q)$ support-entails $\boxed{v}\,p$. To determine whether entailment also holds, we also need to consider rejection-entailment.

Consider the rejection-entailment requirement that every state which rejects $\boxed{v}\,p$ must also reject $\boxed{v}\,(p \wedge q)$. A state σ rejects $\boxed{v}\,p$ if every alternative for $\neg p$, restricted to σ, rejects v. ALT$[p]^{-}$ consists of a single element consisting of all the worlds where p does not hold, so σ supports $\boxed{v}\,p$ when all worlds in σ where p does not hold are such that v does not hold. The maximal rejecting state for $\boxed{v}\,p$ is shown on Fig. 24.

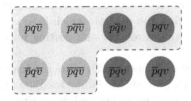

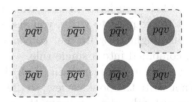

Fig. 24. $[\boxed{v}\,p]^{-}$ **Fig. 25.** $[\boxed{v}\,(p \wedge q)]^{-}$

Also consider that a state σ rejects $\boxed{v}\,(p \wedge q)$ if every rejection-alternative for $(p \wedge q)$, restricted to σ, rejects v. ALT$[p \wedge q]^{-}$ consists of two elements, one consisting of all the worlds where p does not hold, and the other consisting of all the worlds where q does not hold. Due to universal quantification over these alternatives, σ rejects $\boxed{v}\,(p \wedge q)$ when all worlds in σ where either p or q does not hold are such that v also does not hold. The maximal rejecting state for $\boxed{v}\,(p \wedge q)$ is shown on Fig. 25.

Figures 24 and 25 illustrate that the maximal rejecting state for $\boxed{v}\,p$ is not a rejecting state for $\boxed{v}\,(p \wedge q)$ as it contains the world $\{p\bar{q}v\}$ which is not contained in the maximal rejecting state for $\boxed{v}\,(p \wedge q)$. Using this world, one can easily provide a counterexample.

Consider the state $\{p\bar{q}v, \overline{pqv}\}$ in which *not writing the review* can lead to a violation. The state rejects $\boxed{v}\,p$ because in the only world in the state where p does not hold, v does not hold. But the state does not reject $\boxed{v}\,(p \wedge q)$ because in the world $p\bar{q}v$ where q does not hold, v does hold. As demonstrably every state which rejects $\boxed{v}\,p$ does not reject $\boxed{v}\,(p \wedge q)$, then $\boxed{v}\,(p \wedge q)$ does not rejection-entail $\boxed{v}\,p$ and thus, it also does not entail it. This also demonstrates that MADRIS is non-monotonic.

The non-monotonicity of MADRIS arises from the rejection conditions specified in the semantics and motivated independently of the puzzle. Yet, non-monotonicity alone is insufficient to account for the second intuition in the Dr. Procrastinate puzzle. Introducing multiple violations accounts for both the intuition that (22-b) does not contradict (22-c) and also for the second intuition.

Reasoning with Multiple Violations. The second intuition which needs to be covered concerns the possibility that Dr. Procrastinate can avoid making the situation worse by fulfilling (22-c), despite violating (22-b). To allow reasoning in such a *contrary to duty* situation, the obligations will need to refer to different violations. Introducing multiple violations provides a basic way to quantitatively compare better and worse states by determining states with less violations.[27]

(23)   a.   Dr. Procrastinate ought to accept and write the review. $\boxed{v1}\,(p \wedge q)$
       b.   Dr. Procrastinate ought not to accept. $\boxed{v2}\,\neg p$

(23-a) can be dubbed the *expert rule* as it says that when you are an expert in your field you have an obligation to accept requests to write reviews. If you accept the request to write, you also ought to fulfill the request, which is to say that one ought to write. For convenience, accepting a request and writing have been combined into a single rule.

The *procrastinate rule* in (23-b) is also necessary because Dr. Procrastinate will not write the book review, so (22-a) holds. Despite always failing to abide by the expert rule, she can make things even worse by accepting and not writing. The rule in (23-b) says that if you will not fulfill the request, you ought not to accept it. In this case, not accepting the request delays the entire reviewing process. As this ought to be avoided, the rule in (23-b) holds.

---

[27] More involved scenarios will likely require a more fine-grained approach which compares violations.

In what follows, v_1 says that the expert rule has been violated, and v_2 says that the procrastinate rule has been violated.

Intersecting (23-a), (23-b) and (22-a) and the maximal supporting state is shown in Fig. 26. The worlds factively eliminated by $\neg q$ are left gray. Green worlds contain no violations, orange worlds only one and red worlds two violations.

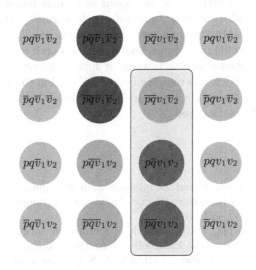

Fig. 26. $(\boxed{v_1}\,(p \wedge q)) \wedge (\boxed{v_2}\,\neg p) \wedge (\neg q)$ (Color figure online)

The maximal supporting state for the story contains three worlds, so the representation of the situation in MADRIS is not absurd. Each of the worlds is a v_1 world, which correctly captures the intuition that as long as Dr. Procrastinate does not write the review, she is doing something wrong, i.e., she incurs a violation of the expert rule.

Furthermore, only one p world remains and in that world v_2 occurs which says that Dr. Procrastinate is also in violation of the procrastinate rule. This means that MADRIS predicts that in case Dr. Procrastinate does accept to write a review, despite not writing it, then she will incur a second violation on top of v_1. Yet, the two remaining $\neg p$ worlds differ in that one is a v_2 world and the other is a $\neg v_2$ world (coloured orange because it contains only one violation). When both a violation and a non-violation follows $\neg p$, we say that this state is deontically neutral with respect to $\neg p$. Thus, Dr. Procrastinate - barring additional information - can avoid the second violation by not accepting to write the review. And this is the second intuition for the semantics to capture.

5   Conclusions

MADRIS is an alternative semantics for deontic modals that provides a uniform semantic solution to puzzles of standard modal logic and Kratzer semantics.

MADRIS utilizes the radical inquisitive semantics account of conditionals and provides a strong treatment of deontic permission. This non-monotonic semantics for modals was developed to provide an intuitive account of the *free choice effect* and monotonicity puzzles. The modification of the Andersonian treatment of deontic modals by introducing quantification over alternatives, and especially universal quantification in the rejection-clause for permission, MADRIS also makes intuitive predictions concerning the behaviour of modals under negation.

Furthermore, *deontic conflicts* and *contrary to duty* situations are common in deontic contexts. MADRIS allows one to reason with multiple violations that not only avoid the problematic inferences in puzzles such as *Dr. Procrastinate* but also give an intuitive characterizations of such situations.

The work in this article has recently been developed in the framework of suppositional inquisitive semantics which adds suppositional content to the semantics. For further information, see [2].

References

1. Aher, M.: Deontic contexts and the interpretation of disjunction in legal discourse. Canadian Journal of Linguistics/Revue Canadienne de Linguistique **58**(1), 13–42 (2013). http://bit.ly/15FfFdB
2. Aher, M., Groenendijk, J.A.G.: Searching for directions: epistemic and deontic modals in InqS. Presented at the Tenth International Tbilisi Symposium on Language, Logic and Computation (TbiLLC), 26 September 2013 (2014). http://bit.ly/1pA0kin
3. Aher, M.: Free Choice in Deontic Inquisitive Semantics (DIS). In: Aloni, M., Kimmelman, V., Roelofsen, F., Sassoon, G.W., Schulz, K., Westera, M. (eds.) Logic, Language and Meaning. LNCS, vol. 7218, pp. 22–31. Springer, Heidelberg (2012). http://bit.ly/UzirsR
4. Aher, M.: Modals in legal language. Ph.D. thesis, University of Osnabrück (2013). http://bit.ly/1ca9Ru4
5. Aloni, M.: Free choice, modals, and imperatives. Nat. Lang. Semant. **15**, 65–94 (2007). http://bit.ly/Zdh8k9
6. Alonso-Ovalle, L.: Disjunction in alternative semantics. Ph.D. thesis, University of Massachusetts, Amherst (2006)
7. Anderson, A.R.: Some nasty problems in the formal logic of ethics. Nous **1**, 345–360 (1967). http://bit.ly/NcSlZG
8. Asher, N., Bonevac, D.: Free choice permission is strong permission. Synthese **145**(3), 303–323 (2005). http://bit.ly/RswjTm
9. Barker, C.: Free choice permission as resource-sensitive reasoning. Semant. Pragmat. **3**, 1–38 (2010). http://bit.ly/16goZPL
10. Brasoveanu, A., Farkas, D., Roelofsen, F.: N-words and sentential negation: evidence from polarity particles and VP ellipsis. Semant. Pragmat. **6**, 1–33 (2013). http://bit.ly/11wY2e0
11. Cariani, F.: Ought and resolution semantics. Noûs (2011). doi:10.1111/j.1468-0068.2011.00839.x. http://bit.ly/LRCsJQ
12. Cariani, F., Kaufmann, M., Kaufmann, S.: Deliberative modality under epistemic uncertainty. Linguist. Philos. **36**(3), 225–259 (2011)

13. Ciardelli, I., Groenendijk, J.A.G., Roelofsen, F.: Inquisitive Semantics: NASSLLI 2012 lecture notes (2012) Unpublished manuscript. http://bit.ly/V6uWy6
14. Ciardelli, I., Roelofsen, F.: Inquisitive logic. J. Philos. Log. **40**(1), 55–94 (2011). http://bit.ly/NlCcRF
15. Groenendijk, J.A.G., Roelofsen, F.: Inquisitive Semantics and Pragmatics. Presented at the Stanford workshop on Language, Communication and Rational Agency, 30–31 May 2009. http://bit.ly/MoWgAx
16. Groenendijk, J.A.G., Roelofsen, F.: Radical Inquisitive Semantics. presented first at Osnabrueck University Institute of Cognitive Science Colloquium on the 13th of January 2010. Unpublished http://bit.ly/NFO9zn
17. Groenendijk, J.A.G., Roelofsen, F.: Suppositional Inquisitive Semantics. In: Proceedings of the Tenth International Tbilisi Symposium on Language, Logic and Computation (2014). Submitted
18. Frank, A.: Context dependence in modal constructions. Ph.D. thesis, University of Stuttgart (1996)
19. Jackson, F.: On the semantics and logic of obligation. Mind, New Series **94**(374), 177–195 (1985). http://bit.ly/OQSwx9
20. Kamp, H.: Free choice permission. In: Aristotelian Society Proceedings N.S 74, pp. 57–74 (1973). http://bit.ly/Rb1cxb
21. Kaufmann, S., Schwager, M.: A unified analysis of conditional imperatives. In: Cormany, E., Ito, S., Lutz, D. (eds.) Proceedings of semantics and linguistic theory(SALT), vol. 19, pp. 239–259 (2011). eLanguage
22. Kratzer, A.: Conditional necessity and possibility. In: Bäuerle, R., Egli, U., von Stechow, A. (eds.) Semantics from Different Points of View, vol. 6, pp. 117–147. Springer, Heidelberg (1979)
23. Kratzer, A.: Modals and Conditionals: New and Revised Perspectives. Oxford studies in Theoretical Linguistics. Oxford University Press, Oxford (2012)
24. Kratzer, A.: What "Must" and "Can" must and can mean. Linguist. Philos. **1**, 337–355 (1977). http://bit.ly/ZhvZtR
25. Lassiter, D.: Measurement and modality: the scalar basis of modal semantics. Ph.D Dissertation, Department of Linguistics, New York University (2011). http://bit.ly/OYyCji
26. Lewis, D.: Counterfactuals. Basil Blackwell, Oxford (1973)
27. Ross, A.: Imperatives and logic. Theoria **7**, 53–71 (1941). Reprinted in Philosophy of Science 11(1), 30–46 (1944). http://bit.ly/QPYk73
28. Sano, K.: A Note on Support and Rejection for Radical Inquisitive Semantics (2010). Unpublished manuscript
29. von Wright, G.H.: Deontic logic. Mind, New Series **60**(237), 1–15 (1951)
30. Zimmermann, T.E.: Free choice disjunction and epistemic possibility. Nat. Lang. Seman. **8**, 255–290 (2000)

Admissibility and Unifiability in Contact Logics

Philippe Balbiani[1]([⊠]) and Çiğdem Gencer[2]

[1] Institut de Recherche En Informatique de Toulouse, CNRS — Université de Toulouse, 118 Route de Narbonne, 31062 Toulouse Cedex 9, France
Philippe.Balbiani@irit.fr
[2] Department of Mathematics and Computer Science, Faculty of Science and Letters, Istanbul Kültür University, Ataköy Campus, 34156 Bakırköy-Istanbul, Turkey
c.gencer@iku.edu.tr

Abstract. Contact logics are logics for reasoning about the contact relations between regular subsets in a topological space. Admissible inference rules can be used to improve the performance of any algorithm that handles provability within the context of contact logics. The decision problem of unifiability can be seen as a special case of the decision problem of admissibility. In this paper, we examine the decidability of admissibility problems and unifiability problems in contact logics.

Keywords: Contact logics · Admissibility · Unifiability · Decidability

1 Introduction

The decision problem of unifiability in a logical system L can be formulated as follows: given a formula $\phi(X_1, \ldots, X_n)$, determine whether there exists formulas $\psi_1, \ldots, \psi_n$ such that $\phi(\psi_1, \ldots, \psi_n) \in L$. The research on unifiability was motivated by a more general decision problem, the admissibility problem: given an inference rule "from $\{\phi_1(X_1, \ldots, X_n), \ldots, \phi_m(X_1, \ldots, X_n)\}$, infer $\psi(X_1, \ldots, X_n)$", determine whether for all formulas $\chi_1, \ldots, \chi_n$, if $\{\phi_1(\chi_1, \ldots, \chi_n), \ldots, \phi_m(\chi_1, \ldots, \chi_n)\} \subseteq L$, then $\psi(\chi_1, \ldots, \chi_n) \in L$. In 1984, Rybakov [15] proved that there exists a decision procedure for determining whether a given inference rule is admissible in intuitionistic propositional logic. See also [16]. Later on, Ghilardi [11,12] proved that intuitionistic propositional logic has a finitary unification type and extended this result to various extensions of $K4$. See also [9,10] where decision procedures for unifiability in extensions of $K4$ are suggested.

Contact logics are logics for reasoning about the contact relations between regular subsets in a topological space [5,17]. They are based on the primitive notion of regular regions and on the Boolean operations (empty region, complement of a region and union of two regions) that allow to obtain new regular regions from given ones. In contact logics, formulas are built from simple formulas of the form $C(a, b)$ and $a \equiv b$ — where a and b are terms in a Boolean language — using the Boolean constructs $\bot$, $\neg$ and $\vee$, the intuitive reading of $C(a, b)$ and $a \equiv b$ being "the regular regions denoted by a and b are in contact"

M. Aher et al. (Eds.): TbiLLC 2013, LNCS 8984, pp. 44–60, 2015.
DOI: 10.1007/978-3-662-46906-4_4

and "the regular regions denoted by a and b are equal". The main semantics of contact logics are the contact algebras of the regular subsets in a topological space [6–8]. But contact logics have also received a relational semantics that allow to use methods from modal logic for studying them [4].

In this setting, one important issue is the mechanization of reasoning in contact logics. Since admissible inference rules can be used to improve the performance of any algorithm that handles provability, it becomes natural to consider admissibility and unifiability within the context of contact logics. In this paper, we will examine variants of contact logics. The central result in this paper is the proof that the admissibility problem and the unifiability problem are decidable in these variants. In Sect. 2, we present the syntax and the semantics of these variants. Section 3 is about their axiomatization/completeness and their decidability/complexity. In Sects. 4–6, we define the admissibility problem and we study its decidability. Section 7 is about the unifiability problem and its decidability. See [16] for details about admissibility and unifiability and [17] for details about contact logics.

2 Syntax and Semantics of Contact Logics

In this section, we present the syntax and the semantics of contact logics. We adopt the standard rules for omission of the parentheses.

2.1 Syntax

To start with syntax, let us first consider a countable set AT of atomic terms (with typical members denoted x, y, etc.) and a countable set AF of atomic formulas (with typical members denoted X, Y, etc.). The terms (denoted a, b, etc.) are inductively defined as follows:

- $a ::= x \mid 0 \mid -a \mid (a \sqcup b)$.

The other Boolean constructs for terms (1, $\sqcap$, etc.) are defined as usual. We will use the following notations:

- a^0 for $-a$,
- a^1 for a.

Reading terms as regions, the constructs 0, $-$ and $\sqcup$ should be regarded as the empty region, the complement operation and the union operation. For all positive integers n and for all $(\epsilon_1, \ldots, \epsilon_n) \in \{0,1\}^n$, formulas of the form $x_1^{\epsilon_1} \sqcap \ldots \sqcap x_n^{\epsilon_n}$ will be called monoms. In the sequel, we use $a(x_1, \ldots, x_n)$ to denote a term a whose atomic terms form a subset of $\{x_1, \ldots, x_n\}$. Considering $a(x_1, \ldots, x_n)$ as a formula in classical propositional logic, let $mon(a(x_1, \ldots, x_n))$ be the set of all monoms of the form $x_1^{\epsilon_1} \sqcap \ldots \sqcap x_n^{\epsilon_n}$ inconsistent with $-a(x_1, \ldots, x_n)$, that is to say $mon(a(x_1, \ldots, x_n)) = \{x_1^{\epsilon_1} \sqcap \ldots \sqcap x_n^{\epsilon_n} : (\epsilon_1, \ldots, \epsilon_n) \in \{0,1\}^n$ and $a(x_1, \ldots, x_n)$ is a tautological consequence of $x_1^{\epsilon_1} \sqcap \ldots \sqcap x_n^{\epsilon_n}\}$. The formulas (denoted ϕ, ψ, etc.) are inductively defined as follows:

– $\phi ::= X \mid \bot \mid \neg\phi \mid (\phi \vee \psi) \mid C(a, b) \mid a \equiv b$.

The other Boolean constructs for formulas ($\top$, $\wedge$, etc.) are defined as usual. We will use the following notations:

– $\bar{C}(a, b)$ for $\neg C(a, b)$,
– $a \not\equiv b$ for $\neg a \equiv b$,
– $a \leq b$ for $a \sqcap -b \equiv 0$.

Reading formulas as properties about regions, the constructs C and $\equiv$ should be regarded as the contact relation and the equality relation. Sets of formulas will be denoted Γ, Δ, etc. Formulas and sets of formulas are also called "expressions" (denoted α, β, etc.). We shall say that an expression α is weak iff no atomic formula occurs in α. In the sequel, we use $\alpha(x_1, \ldots, x_n)$ to denote a weak expression α whose atomic terms form a subset of $\{x_1, \ldots, x_n\}$. A substitution is a function s assigning to each atomic term x a term $s(x)$ and to each atomic formula X a formula $s(X)$. As usual, s induces a homomorphism $s(\cdot)$ assigning to each term a a term $s(a)$ and to each expression α an expression $s(\alpha)$.

2.2   Semantics

Now, for the semantics. In [5,17], the language of contact logics is interpreted either in relational structures, or in topological structures. In both cases, terms are interpreted by sets of points. The main difference between the two kinds of structures is the following: in relational structures, two regions are in contact when at least one point of the first region is related to at least one point of the second region whereas in topological structures, two regions are in contact when their topological closures have a nonempty intersection. The two semantics have been proved to be equivalent [5,17]. In this paper, we only consider the relational semantics. A frame is a relational structure $\mathcal{F} = (W, R)$ where W is a non-empty set of points and R is a binary relation on W. A valuation based on $\mathcal{F}$ is a function V assigning to each atomic term x a subset $V(x)$ of W. V induces a function $(\cdot)^V$ assigning to each term a a subset $(a)^V$ of W such that

– $(x)^V = V(x)$,
– $(0)^V = \emptyset$,
– $(-a)^V = W \setminus (a)^V$,
– $(a \sqcup b)^V = (a)^V \cup (b)^V$.

As a result,

– $(a^0)^V = W \setminus (a)^V$,
– $(a^1)^V = (a)^V$.

We shall say that V is balanced iff for all terms a, either $(a)^V = \emptyset$, or $(a)^V = W$, or $(a)^V$ is infinite and coinfinite. An interpretation is a subset I of AF. A model is a structure $\mathcal{M} = (W, R, V, I)$ where $\mathcal{F} = (W, R)$ is a frame, V is a valuation based on $\mathcal{F}$ and I is an interpretation. The satisfiability of a formula ϕ in $\mathcal{M}$, in symbols $\mathcal{M} \models \phi$, is defined as follows:

- $\mathcal{M} \models X$ iff $X \in I$,
- $\mathcal{M} \not\models \bot$,
- $\mathcal{M} \models \neg\phi$ iff $\mathcal{M} \not\models \phi$,
- $\mathcal{M} \models \phi \vee \psi$ iff either $\mathcal{M} \models \phi$, or $\mathcal{M} \models \psi$,
- $\mathcal{M} \models C(a,b)$ iff $((a)^V \times (b)^V) \cap R \neq \emptyset$,
- $\mathcal{M} \models a \equiv b$ iff $(a)^V = (b)^V$.

As a result,

- $\mathcal{M} \models \bar{C}(a,b)$ iff $((a)^V \times (b)^V) \cap R = \emptyset$,
- $\mathcal{M} \models a \not\equiv b$ iff $(a)^V \neq (b)^V$,
- $\mathcal{M} \models a \leq b$ iff $(a)^V \subseteq (b)^V$.

Let $\mathcal{F}$ be a frame. A formula ϕ is valid in $\mathcal{F}$, in symbols $\mathcal{F} \models \phi$, iff for all models $\mathcal{M}$ based on $\mathcal{F}$, $\mathcal{M} \models \phi$. A set Γ of formulas is valid in $\mathcal{F}$, in symbols $\mathcal{F} \models \Gamma$, iff for all formulas $\phi \in \Gamma$, $\mathcal{F} \models \phi$. Let CF be a class of frames. A formula ϕ is valid in CF, in symbols $CF \models \phi$, iff for all frames $\mathcal{F}$ in CF, $\mathcal{F} \models \phi$. Let CF_0 be the class of all frames. Obviously,

Proposition 1. *The following formulas are valid in CF_0:*

- $C(x,y) \to x \not\equiv 0$,
- $C(x,y) \to y \not\equiv 0$,
- $C(x,y) \wedge x \leq z \to C(z,y)$,
- $C(x,y) \wedge y \leq z \to C(x,z)$,
- $C(x \sqcup y, z) \to C(x,z) \vee C(y,z)$,
- $C(x, y \sqcup z) \to C(x,y) \vee C(x,z)$.

In this paper, we will consider the following classes of frames:

- the class CF_r of all reflexive frames,
- the class CF_s of all symmetrical frames.

Obviously,

Proposition 2. *The following formula is valid in CF_r:*

- $x \not\equiv 0 \to C(x,x)$.

The following formula is valid in CF_s:

- $C(x,y) \to C(y,x)$.

3 Axiomatization and Decidability of Contact Logics

In this section, we present the axiomatization and the decidability of contact logics. From now on, formulas will also be called "axioms" and pairs of the form (Γ, ϕ) where Γ is a finite set of formulas and ϕ is a formula will also be called "inference rules". When an axiom or an inference rule contains no occurrence of atomic formulas, it is qualified as "weak". An axiomatic system consists of a collection of axioms and a collection of inference rules. Let λ_0 be the axiomatic system consisting of

- a complete set of axioms for Classical Propositional Calculus (i.e. $X \to (Y \to X)$, $(X \to (Y \to Z)) \to ((X \to Y) \to (X \to Z))$, etc.),
- a complete set of axioms for non-degenerate Boolean algebras (i.e. $x \sqcup (y \sqcup z) \equiv (x \sqcup y) \sqcup z$, $x \sqcup y \equiv y \sqcup x$, etc.),
- the following axioms:
  - $C(x,y) \to x \not\equiv 0$,
  - $C(x,y) \to y \not\equiv 0$,
  - $C(x,y) \wedge x \leq z \to C(z,y)$,
  - $C(x,y) \wedge y \leq z \to C(x,z)$,
  - $C(x \sqcup y, z) \to C(x,z) \vee C(y,z)$,
  - $C(x, y \sqcup z) \to C(x,y) \vee C(x,z)$,
- the inference rule of modus ponens (i.e. $(\{X, X \to Y\}, Y)$).

We will consider extensions of λ_0 — denoted λ, μ, etc. — by either adding new axioms, or adding new inference rules. The extension of λ_0 with a set A of axioms will be denoted $\lambda_0(A)$. The extension of λ_0 with a single axiom ϕ will be denoted $\lambda_0(\phi)$. In this paper, we will consider the following extensions of λ_0:

- $\lambda_r = \lambda_0(x \not\equiv 0 \to C(x,x))$,
- $\lambda_s = \lambda_0(C(x,y) \to C(y,x))$.

The extension of λ_0 with a single inference rule (Γ, ϕ) will be denoted $\lambda_0 + (\Gamma, \phi)$. A formula ϕ is said to be derivable in an extension λ of λ_0 from a finite set Γ of formulas, in symbols $\Gamma \vdash_\lambda \phi$, iff there exists a finite sequence $\phi_0, \ldots, \phi_m$ of formulas such that $\phi_m = \phi$ and for all nonnegative integers i, if $i \leq m$, then at least one of the following conditions holds:

- $\phi_i \in \Gamma$,
- there exists an axiom ψ in λ and there exists a substitution s such that $\phi_i = s(\psi)$,
- there exists an inference rule (Δ, ψ) in λ and there exists a substitution s such that $\phi_i = s(\psi)$ and $\{\phi_0, \ldots, \phi_{i-1}\} \supseteq s(\Delta)$.

The finite sequence $\phi_0, \ldots, \phi_m$ is called "derivation of ϕ in λ from Γ". The propositions below contain facts which can be found in most elementary logic texts.

Proposition 3. *Let Γ be a finite set of formulas and ϕ be a formula. If $\Gamma \vdash_\lambda \phi$, then for all substitutions s, $s(\Gamma) \vdash_\lambda s(\phi)$.*

Proposition 4. *Let Γ be a finite set of formulas and ϕ, ψ be formulas. The following conditions are equivalent:*

- $\Gamma \cup \{\phi\} \vdash_\lambda \psi$,
- $\Gamma \vdash_\lambda \phi \to \psi$.

A formula ϕ is said to be provable in λ, in symbols $\vdash_\lambda \phi$, iff $\emptyset \vdash_\lambda \phi$. In this case, every derivation of ϕ in λ from $\emptyset$ is called "proof of ϕ in λ". The provable formulas of λ will be called "theorems of λ". We will denote by $Th(\lambda)$ the set of all theorems of λ. We shall say that λ is consistent iff $\bot \notin Th(\lambda)$. We will denote by $CF(\lambda)$ the class of all frames $\mathcal{F}$ such that $\mathcal{F} \models Th(\lambda)$ and we will denote by $CF_{fin}(\lambda)$ the class of all finite frames $\mathcal{F}$ such that $\mathcal{F} \models Th(\lambda)$. We shall say that λ is balanced iff for all formulas ϕ, the following conditions are equivalent:

- $\phi \notin Th(\lambda)$,
- there exists a countable frame $\mathcal{F} \in CF(\lambda)$, there exists a balanced valuation V on $\mathcal{F}$ and there exists an interpretation I such that $(\mathcal{F}, V, I) \not\models \phi$.

λ_0 itself is balanced, but also most extensions of λ_0 considered in [5,17] like λ_r and λ_s are balanced. In [5,17], one can also find the facts contained in the following

Proposition 5. *Let ϕ be a formula. The following conditions are equivalent:*

- $\phi \in Th(\lambda_0)$,
- $CF_0 \models \phi$.

Proposition 6. *Let ϕ be a formula. The following conditions are equivalent:*

- $\phi \in Th(\lambda_r)$,
- $CF_r \models \phi$.

The following conditions are equivalent:

- $\phi \in Th(\lambda_s)$,
- $CF_s \models \phi$.

More generally,

Proposition 7. *Let ϕ be a formula. If there exists a finite set A of axioms such that $\lambda = \lambda_0(A)$, then the following conditions are equivalent:*

- $\phi \in Th(\lambda)$,
- $CF(\lambda) \models \phi$,
- $CF_{fin}(\lambda) \models \phi$.

A consequence of Proposition 7 is the following

Proposition 8. *If there exists a finite set A of axioms such that $\lambda = \lambda_0(A)$, then $Th(\lambda)$ is decidable.*

Later on, we will use Propositions 3–8 without explicit reference.

4 Admissibility: Definitions

Let λ be an extension of λ_0. An inference rule (Γ, ϕ) is said to be admissible in λ iff for all substitutions s, if $s(\Gamma) \subseteq Th(\lambda)$, then $s(\phi) \in Th(\lambda)$. The next proposition indicates that inference rules admissible in λ do not increase $Th(\lambda)$ when added to λ.

Proposition 9. *Let (Γ, ϕ) be an inference rule. If (Γ, ϕ) is admissible in λ, then $Th(\lambda + (\Gamma, \phi)) = Th(\lambda)$.*

Proof. Suppose (Γ, ϕ) is admissible in λ. If $Th(\lambda + (\Gamma, \phi)) \neq Th(\lambda)$, then obviously, there exists a formula ψ such that $\psi \in Th(\lambda + (\Gamma, \phi))$ and $\psi \notin Th(\lambda)$. Hence, there exists a proof $\psi_0, \ldots, \psi_m$ of ψ in $\lambda + (\Gamma, \phi)$. Since (Γ, ϕ) is admissible in λ, each use of (Γ, ϕ) in $\psi_0, \ldots, \psi_m$ can be replaced by a corresponding proof in λ. Thus, there exists a proof of ψ in λ. Therefore, $\psi \in Th(\lambda)$: a contradiction.

Inference rules that are admissible in λ can be used to improve the performance of any algorithm that handles λ-provability. In this respect, the following decision problem, called "admissibility problem in λ", in symbols $ADM(\lambda)$, is of the utmost importance:

– input: an inference rule (Γ, ϕ),
– output: determine whether (Γ, ϕ) is admissible in λ.

Applicability of inference rules that are admissible in λ to ameliorate algorithms for λ-provability incites us to study the decidability of $ADM(\lambda)$. To start this study, let us first define the notion of derivability in λ. We shall say that an inference rule (Γ, ϕ) is derivable in λ iff $\Gamma \vdash_\lambda \phi$. It happens that derivability is a special case of admissibility.

Proposition 10. *Let (Γ, ϕ) be an inference rule. If (Γ, ϕ) is derivable in λ, then (Γ, ϕ) is admissible in λ.*

Proof. Suppose (Γ, ϕ) is derivable in λ. If (Γ, ϕ) is not admissible in λ, then there exists a substitution s such that $s(\Gamma) \subseteq Th(\lambda)$ and $s(\phi) \notin Th(\lambda)$. Since (Γ, ϕ) is derivable in λ, $\Gamma \vdash_\lambda \phi$. Hence, $s(\Gamma) \vdash_\lambda s(\phi)$. Thus, there exists a derivation $\phi_0, \ldots, \phi_m$ of $s(\phi)$ in λ from $s(\Gamma)$. Since $s(\Gamma) \subseteq Th(\lambda)$, each use of $s(\Gamma)$ in $\phi_0, \ldots, \phi_m$ can be replaced by a corresponding proof in λ. Therefore, there exists a proof of $s(\phi)$ in λ. Consequently, $s(\phi) \in Th(\lambda)$: a contradiction.

Nevertheless, in the general case, it may happen that derivability and admissibility in such-or-such contact logic do not coincide. It suffices, for instance, to consider the inference rule $(\{C(x, y)\}, C(y, x))$. Since for all substitutions s, $s(C(x, y)) \notin Th(\lambda_0)$, $(\{C(x, y)\}, C(y, x))$ is admissible in λ_0. Since $C(x, y) \rightarrow C(y, x) \notin Th(\lambda_0)$, $(\{C(x, y)\}, C(y, x))$ is not derivable in λ_0. As a result, the following decision problem, called "derivability problem in λ", in symbols $DER(\lambda)$, has its importance:

– input: an inference rule (Γ, ϕ),
– output: determine whether (Γ, ϕ) is derivable in λ.

Obviously,

Proposition 11. *If there exists a finite set A of axioms such that $\lambda = \lambda_0(A)$, then $DER(\lambda)$ is decidable.*

We shall say that λ is structurally complete iff for all inference rules (Γ, ϕ), if (Γ, ϕ) is admissible in λ, (Γ, ϕ) is derivable in λ. By Propositions 10 and 11,

Proposition 12. *If λ is structurally complete and there exists a finite set A of axioms such that $\lambda = \lambda_0(A)$, then $ADM(\lambda)$ is decidable.*

Now, we intend to extend Proposition 12 to structurally incomplete extensions of λ_0. However, in this paper, we will only be able to study the decidability of the following decision problem, called "weak admissibility problem in λ", in symbols $wADM(\lambda)$:

- input: a weak inference rule (Γ, ϕ),
- output: determine whether (Γ, ϕ) is admissible in λ.

We end this section with the following

Proposition 13. *Let $(\Gamma(x_1, \ldots, x_n), \phi(x_1, \ldots, x_n))$ be a weak inference rule. The following conditions are equivalent:*

- *$(\Gamma(x_1, \ldots, x_n), \phi(x_1, \ldots, x_n))$ is not admissible in λ,*
- *there exists terms $a_1, \ldots, a_n$ such that $\Gamma(a_1, \ldots, a_n) \subseteq Th(\lambda)$ and $\phi(a_1, \ldots, a_n) \notin Th(\lambda)$.*

Proof. ($\Rightarrow$) Suppose $(\Gamma(x_1, \ldots, x_n), \phi(x_1, \ldots, x_n))$ is not admissible in λ. Hence, there exists a substitution s such that $s(\Gamma(x_1, \ldots, x_n)) \subseteq Th(\lambda)$ and $s(\phi(x_1, \ldots, x_n)) \notin Th(\lambda)$. Let $a_1, \ldots, a_n$ be terms such that for all positive integers i, if $i \leq n$, then $a_i = s(x_i)$. Since $s(\Gamma(x_1, \ldots, x_n)) \subseteq Th(\lambda)$ and $s(\phi(x_1, \ldots, x_n)) \notin Th(\lambda)$, $\Gamma(a_1, \ldots, a_n) \subseteq Th(\lambda)$ and $\phi(a_1, \ldots, a_n) \notin Th(\lambda)$.
($\Leftarrow$) Suppose there exists terms $a_1, \ldots, a_n$ such that $\Gamma(a_1, \ldots, a_n) \subseteq Th(\lambda)$ and $\phi(a_1, \ldots, a_n) \notin Th(\lambda)$. Let s be a substitution such that for all positive integers i, if $i \leq n$, then $s(x_i) = a_i$. Since $\Gamma(a_1, \ldots, a_n) \subseteq Th(\lambda)$ and $\phi(a_1, \ldots, a_n) \notin Th(\lambda)$, $s(\Gamma(x_1, \ldots, x_n)) \subseteq Th(\lambda)$ and $s(\phi(x_1, \ldots, x_n)) \notin Th(\lambda)$. Hence, $(\Gamma(x_1, \ldots, x_n), \phi(x_1, \ldots, x_n))$ is not admissible in λ.

5   Admissibility: Useful Lemmas

Let λ be an extension of λ_0. The decidability of $wADM(\lambda)$ is difficult to establish and we defer proving it till next section. In the meantime, we present useful lemmas. Let n be a nonnegative integer. Let Φ_n be the set of all weak formulas with atomic terms in $x_1, \ldots, x_n$. We define on Φ_n the equivalence relation $\equiv_\lambda^n$ as follows:

- $\phi(x_1, \ldots, x_n) \equiv_\lambda^n \psi(x_1, \ldots, x_n)$ iff $\phi(x_1, \ldots, x_n) \leftrightarrow \psi(x_1, \ldots, x_n) \in Th(\lambda)$.

Obviously, considered as formulas in classical propositional logic, the terms $a(x_1, \ldots, x_n)$ and $b(x_1, \ldots, x_n)$ are equivalent iff $mon(a(x_1, \ldots, x_n)) = mon (b(x_1, \ldots, x_n))$. Hence, there exists exactly 2^{2^n} pairwise non-equivalent terms in $x_1, \ldots, x_n$. Since each weak formula $\phi(x_1, \ldots, x_n)$ in Φ_n is a Boolean combination of elementary formulas of the form $C(a(x_1, \ldots, x_n), b(x_1, \ldots, x_n))$ or of the form $a(x_1, \ldots, x_n) \equiv b(x_1, \ldots, x_n)$,

Lemma 1. $\equiv_\lambda^n$ *has finitely many equivalence classes on* Φ_n.

Let A_n be the set of all n-tuples of terms. Note that n-tuples of terms in A_n may contain occurrences of atomic terms distinct from $x_1, \ldots, x_n$. Given $(a_1, \ldots, a_n) \in A_n$, a frame $\mathcal{F} \in CF(\lambda)$ and a valuation V on $\mathcal{F}$, let

- $\Phi_{(a_1,\ldots,a_n)}^{\mathcal{F},V}$ be the set of all C-free weak formulas $\phi(x_1, \ldots, x_n)$ such that $(\mathcal{F}, V) \models \phi(a_1, \ldots, a_n)$.

Consider a complete list $\phi_1(x_1, \ldots, x_n), \ldots, \phi_k(x_1, \ldots, x_n)$ in $\Phi_{(a_1,\ldots,a_n)}^{\mathcal{F},V}$ of representatives for each equivalence class on $\Phi_{(a_1,\ldots,a_n)}^{\mathcal{F},V}$ modulo $\equiv_\lambda^n$ and define

- $\phi_{(a_1,\ldots,a_n)}^{\mathcal{F},V}(x_1, \ldots, x_n) = \phi_1(x_1, \ldots, x_n) \wedge \ldots \wedge \phi_k(x_1, \ldots, x_n)$.

Obviously,

Lemma 2. $(\mathcal{F}, V) \models \phi_{(a_1,\ldots,a_n)}^{\mathcal{F},V}(a_1, \ldots, a_n)$.

Hence, $\phi_{(a_1,\ldots,a_n)}^{\mathcal{F},V}(x_1, \ldots, x_n)$ is in $\Phi_{(a_1,\ldots,a_n)}^{\mathcal{F},V}$. Let

- $\Phi_{a_1,\ldots,a_n} = \{\phi_{(a_1,\ldots,a_n)}^{\mathcal{F},V}(x_1, \ldots, x_n) \colon \mathcal{F} \in CF(\lambda)$ and V is a valuation on $\mathcal{F}\}$.

Consider a complete list $\psi_1(x_1, \ldots, x_n), \ldots, \psi_l(x_1, \ldots, x_n)$ in $\Phi_{(a_1,\ldots,a_n)}$ of representatives for each equivalence class on $\Phi_{(a_1,\ldots,a_n)}$ modulo $\equiv_\lambda^n$ and define

- $\psi_{(a_1,\ldots,a_n)}(x_1, \ldots, x_n) = \psi_1(x_1, \ldots, x_n) \vee \ldots \vee \psi_l(x_1, \ldots, x_n)$.

We have the

Lemma 3. $\psi_{(a_1,\ldots,a_n)}(a_1, \ldots, a_n) \in Th(\lambda)$.

Proof. Suppose $\psi_{(a_1,\ldots,a_n)}(a_1, \ldots, a_n) \notin Th(\lambda)$. Thus, there exists a frame $\mathcal{F} \in CF(\lambda)$ and there exists a valuation V on $\mathcal{F}$ such that $(\mathcal{F}, V) \not\models \psi_{(a_1,\ldots,a_n)}(a_1, \ldots, a_n)$. Let i be a positive integer such that $1 \le i \le l$ and $\phi_{(a_1,\ldots,a_n)}^{\mathcal{F},V}(x_1, \ldots, x_n)$ is equivalent to $\psi_i(x_1, \ldots, x_n)$ modulo $\equiv_\lambda^n$. Since $\mathcal{F} \models Th(\lambda)$ and, by Lemma 2, $(\mathcal{F}, V) \models \phi_{(a_1,\ldots,a_n)}^{\mathcal{F},V}(a_1, \ldots, a_n)$, $(\mathcal{F}, V) \models \psi_i(a_1, \ldots, a_n)$. Therefore, $(\mathcal{F}, V) \models \psi_{(a_1,\ldots,a_n)}(a_1, \ldots, a_n)$: a contradiction.

Moreover,

Lemma 4. *For all C-free weak formulas $\phi(x_1, \ldots, x_n)$, the following conditions are equivalent:*

- $\phi(a_1, \ldots, a_n) \in Th(\lambda)$,
- $\psi_{(a_1,\ldots,a_n)}(x_1, \ldots, x_n) \to \phi(x_1, \ldots, x_n) \in Th(\lambda)$.

Proof. ($\Rightarrow$) Suppose $\phi(a_1, \ldots, a_n) \in Th(\lambda)$. If $\psi_{(a_1,\ldots,a_n)}(x_1, \ldots, x_n) \to \phi(x_1, \ldots, x_n) \notin Th(\lambda)$, then there exists a frame $\mathcal{F} \in CF(\lambda)$ and there exists a valuation V on $\mathcal{F}$ such that $(\mathcal{F}, V) \not\models \psi_{(a_1,\ldots,a_n)}(x_1, \ldots, x_n) \to \phi(x_1, \ldots, x_n)$. Hence, $(\mathcal{F}, V) \models \psi_{(a_1,\ldots,a_n)}(x_1, \ldots, x_n)$ and $(\mathcal{F}, V) \not\models \phi(x_1, \ldots, x_n)$. Thus, there exists a positive integer i such that $i \leq l$ and $(\mathcal{F}, V) \models \psi_i(x_1, \ldots, x_n)$. Let $\mathcal{F}' \in CF(\lambda)$ be a frame and V' be a valuation on $\mathcal{F}'$ such that $\phi_{(a_1, \ldots, a_n)}^{\mathcal{F}', V'}(x_1, \ldots, x_n)$ is equivalent to $\psi_i(x_1, \ldots, x_n)$ modulo $\equiv_\lambda^n$. Since $(\mathcal{F}, V) \models Th(\lambda)$ and $(\mathcal{F}, V) \models \psi_i(x_1, \ldots, x_n)$, $(\mathcal{F}, V) \models \phi_{(a_1, \ldots, a_n)}^{\mathcal{F}', V'}(x_1, \ldots, x_n)$. Therefore, for all C-free weak formulas $\theta(x_1, \ldots, x_n)$, if $(\mathcal{F}', V') \models \theta(a_1, \ldots, a_n)$, then $(\mathcal{F}, V) \models \theta(x_1, \ldots, x_n)$. Since $\mathcal{F}' \models Th(\lambda)$ and $\phi(a_1, \ldots, a_n) \in Th(\lambda)$, $(\mathcal{F}', V') \models \phi(a_1, \ldots, a_n)$. Since for all C-free weak formulas $\theta(x_1, \ldots, x_n)$, if $(\mathcal{F}', V') \models \theta(a_1, \ldots, a_n)$, then $(\mathcal{F}, V) \models \theta(x_1, \ldots, x_n)$, $(\mathcal{F}, V) \models \phi(x_1, \ldots, x_n)$: a contradiction.

($\Leftarrow$) Suppose $\psi_{(a_1, \ldots, a_n)}(x_1, \ldots, x_n) \rightarrow \phi(x_1, \ldots, x_n) \in Th(\lambda)$. Consequently, $\psi_{(a_1, \ldots, a_n)}(a_1, \ldots, a_n) \rightarrow \phi(a_1, \ldots, a_n) \in Th(\lambda)$. By Lemma 3, $\psi_{(a_1, \ldots, a_n)}(a_1, \ldots, a_n) \in Th(\lambda)$. Since $\psi_{(a_1, \ldots, a_n)}(a_1, \ldots, a_n) \rightarrow \phi(a_1, \ldots, a_n) \in Th(\lambda)$, $\phi(a_1, \ldots, a_n) \in Th(\lambda)$.

We define on A_n the equivalence relation $\cong_\lambda^n$ as follows:

- $(a_1, \ldots, a_n) \cong_\lambda^n (b_1, \ldots, b_n)$ iff for all weak formulas $\phi(x_1, \ldots, x_n)$ in Φ_n, $\phi(a_1, \ldots, a_n) \in Th(\lambda)$ iff $\phi(b_1, \ldots, b_n) \in Th(\lambda)$.

By Lemma 1,

Lemma 5. $\cong_\lambda^n$ *has finitely many equivalence classes on* A_n.

It is of interest to consider the equivalence relation $\cong_\lambda^n$, seeing that, according to our definitions,

Lemma 6. *If* $(a_1, \ldots, a_n) \cong_\lambda^n (b_1, \ldots, b_n)$, *then for all weak inference rules* $(\Gamma(x_1, \ldots, x_n), \phi(x_1, \ldots, x_n))$, *the following conditions are equivalent:*

- $\Gamma(a_1, \ldots, a_n) \subseteq Th(\lambda)$ *and* $\phi(a_1, \ldots, a_n) \notin Th(\lambda)$,
- $\Gamma(b_1, \ldots, b_n) \subseteq Th(\lambda)$ *and* $\phi(b_1, \ldots, b_n) \notin Th(\lambda)$.

Now, we define on A_n the equivalence relation $\simeq_\lambda^n$ as follows:

- $(a_1, \ldots, a_n) \simeq_\lambda^n (b_1, \ldots, b_n)$ iff for all C-free weak formulas $\phi(x_1, \ldots, x_n)$ in Φ_n, $\phi(a_1, \ldots, a_n) \in Th(\lambda)$ iff $\phi(b_1, \ldots, b_n) \in Th(\lambda)$.

Obviously,

Lemma 7. *If* $(a_1, \ldots, a_n) \cong_\lambda^n (b_1, \ldots, b_n)$, *then* $(a_1, \ldots, a_n) \simeq_\lambda^n (b_1, \ldots, b_n)$.

Moreover, by Lemma 1,

Lemma 8. $\simeq_\lambda^n$ *has finitely many equivalence classes on* A_n.

The key things to note about the equivalence relations $\cong_\lambda^n$ and $\simeq_\lambda^n$ are contained in the following lemmas.

Lemma 9. *The following conditions are equivalent:*

- $(a_1, \ldots, a_n) \simeq_\lambda^n (b_1, \ldots, b_n)$,
- $\psi_{(a_1, \ldots, a_n)}(x_1, \ldots, x_n) \leftrightarrow \psi_{(b_1, \ldots, b_n)}(x_1, \ldots, x_n) \in Th(\lambda)$.

Proof. ($\Rightarrow$) Suppose $(a_1, \ldots, a_n) \simeq_\lambda^n (b_1, \ldots, b_n)$. If $\psi_{(a_1,\ldots,a_n)}(x_1,\ldots,x_n) \leftrightarrow \psi_{(b_1,\ldots,b_n)}(x_1,\ldots,x_n) \notin Th(\lambda)$, then either $\psi_{(a_1,\ldots,a_n)}(x_1, \ldots, x_n) \to \psi_{(b_1,\ldots,b_n)}(x_1, \ldots, x_n) \notin Th(\lambda)$, or $\psi_{(b_1,\ldots,b_n)}(x_1,\ldots,x_n) \to \psi_{(a_1,\ldots,a_n)}(x_1,\ldots, x_n) \notin Th(\lambda)$. Without loss of generality, let us assume that $\psi_{(a_1,\ldots,a_n)}(x_1,\ldots,x_n) \to \psi_{(b_1,\ldots,b_n)}(x_1,\ldots,x_n) \notin Th(\lambda)$. By Lemma 4, $\psi_{(b_1,\ldots,b_n)}(a_1,\ldots,a_n) \notin Th(\lambda)$. Since $(a_1,\ldots,a_n) \simeq_\lambda^n (b_1,\ldots,b_n)$, $\psi_{(b_1,\ldots,b_n)}(b_1,\ldots,b_n) \notin Th(\lambda)$. By Lemma 3, $\psi_{(b_1,\ldots,b_n)}(b_1,\ldots,b_n) \in Th(\lambda)$: a contradiction.
($\Leftarrow$) Suppose $\psi_{(a_1,\ldots,a_n)}(x_1,\ldots,x_n) \leftrightarrow \psi_{(b_1,\ldots,b_n)}(x_1,\ldots,x_n) \in Th(\lambda)$. Hence, for all C-free weak formulas $\phi(x_1,\ldots,x_n)$, $\psi_{(a_1,\ldots,a_n)}(x_1,\ldots,x_n) \to \phi(x_1,\ldots, x_n) \in Th(\lambda)$ iff $\psi_{(b_1,\ldots,b_n)}(x_1,\ldots,x_n) \to \phi(x_1,\ldots,x_n) \in Th(\lambda)$. By Lemma 4, for all C-free weak formulas $\phi(x_1,\ldots,x_n)$, $\phi(a_1,\ldots,a_n) \in Th(\lambda)$ iff $\phi(b_1,\ldots,b_n) \in Th(\lambda)$. Thus, $(a_1,\ldots,a_n) \simeq_\lambda^n (b_1,\ldots,b_n)$.

Lemma 10. *If λ is balanced and $(a_1,\ldots,a_n) \simeq_\lambda^n (b_1,\ldots,b_n)$, then $(a_1,\ldots,a_n) \cong_\lambda^n (b_1,\ldots,b_n)$.*

Proof. Suppose λ is balanced and $(a_1,\ldots,a_n) \simeq_\lambda^n (b_1,\ldots,b_n)$. If $(a_1,\ldots,a_n) \not\cong_\lambda^n (b_1,\ldots,b_n)$, then there exists a weak formula $\phi(x_1,\ldots,x_n)$ in Φ_n such that $\phi(a_1,\ldots,a_n) \in Th(\lambda)$ not-iff $\phi(b_1,\ldots,b_n) \in Th(\lambda)$. Without loss of generality, let us assume that $\phi(a_1,\ldots,a_n) \in Th(\lambda)$ and $\phi(b_1,\ldots,b_n) \notin Th(\lambda)$. Since λ is balanced, there exists a countable frame $\mathcal{F} \in CF(\lambda)$ and there exists a balanced valuation V on $\mathcal{F}$ such that $(\mathcal{F}, V) \not\models \phi(b_1,\ldots,b_n)$. By Lemma 2, $(\mathcal{F}, V) \models \phi_{(b_1,\ldots,b_n)}^{\mathcal{F},V}(b_1,\ldots,b_n)$. Since $\mathcal{F} \models Th(\lambda)$, $\neg\phi_{(b_1,\ldots,b_n)}^{\mathcal{F},V}(b_1,\ldots,b_n) \notin Th(\lambda)$. Since $(a_1,\ldots,a_n) \simeq_\lambda^n (b_1,\ldots,b_n)$, $\neg\phi_{(b_1,\ldots,b_n)}^{\mathcal{F},V}(a_1,\ldots,a_n) \notin Th(\lambda)$. Since λ is balanced, there exists a countable frame $\mathcal{F}' \in CF(\lambda)$ and there exists a balanced valuation V' on $\mathcal{F}'$ such that $(\mathcal{F}', V') \models \phi_{(b_1,\ldots,b_n)}^{\mathcal{F},V}(a_1,\ldots,a_n)$. Suppose $\mathcal{F} = (W, R)$ and $\mathcal{F}' = (W', R')$. Now, consider $(\epsilon_1,\ldots,\epsilon_n) \in \{0,1\}^n$. If $(b_1^{\epsilon_1} \sqcap \ldots \sqcap b_n^{\epsilon_n})^V = \emptyset$, then $(\mathcal{F}, V) \models b_1^{\epsilon_1} \sqcap \ldots \sqcap b_n^{\epsilon_n} \equiv 0$. Hence, $\phi_{(b_1,\ldots,b_n)}^{\mathcal{F},V}(x_1,\ldots,x_n) \to x_1^{\epsilon_1} \sqcap \ldots \sqcap x_n^{\epsilon_n} \equiv 0 \in Th(\lambda)$. Since $\mathcal{F}' \models Th(\lambda)$ and $(\mathcal{F}', V') \models \phi_{(b_1,\ldots,b_n)}^{\mathcal{F},V}(a_1,\ldots,a_n)$, $(\mathcal{F}', V') \models a_1^{\epsilon_1} \sqcap \ldots \sqcap a_n^{\epsilon_n} \equiv 0$. Thus, $(a_1^{\epsilon_1} \sqcap \ldots \sqcap a_n^{\epsilon_n})^{V'} = \emptyset$. Similarly, the reader may easily verify that if $(b_1^{\epsilon_1} \sqcap \ldots \sqcap b_n^{\epsilon_n})^V = W$, then $(a_1^{\epsilon_1} \sqcap \ldots \sqcap a_n^{\epsilon_n})^{V'} = W'$ and if $(b_1^{\epsilon_1} \sqcap \ldots \sqcap b_n^{\epsilon_n})^V$ is infinite and coinfinite, then $(a_1^{\epsilon_1} \sqcap \ldots \sqcap a_n^{\epsilon_n})^{V'}$ is infinite and coinfinite. In all cases, there exists a bijection $f_{(\epsilon_1,\ldots,\epsilon_n)}$ from $(b_1^{\epsilon_1} \sqcap \ldots \sqcap b_n^{\epsilon_n})^V$ to $(a_1^{\epsilon_1} \sqcap \ldots \sqcap a_n^{\epsilon_n})^{V'}$. Let f be the union of all $f_{(\epsilon_1,\ldots,\epsilon_n)}$ when $(\epsilon_1,\ldots,\epsilon_n)$ describes $\{0,1\}^n$. The reader may easily verify that f is a bijection from W to W' such that for all $u \in W$ and for all $(\epsilon_1,\ldots,\epsilon_n) \in \{0,1\}^n$, $u \in (b_1^{\epsilon_1} \sqcap \ldots \sqcap b_n^{\epsilon_n})^V$ iff $f(u) \in (a_1^{\epsilon_1} \sqcap \ldots \sqcap a_n^{\epsilon_n})^{V'}$. Let R'_f be the binary relation on W' defined by $u'R'_f v'$ iff $f^{-1}(u')Rf^{-1}(v')$. We define $\mathcal{F}'_f = (W', R'_f)$. Obviously, f is an isomorphism from $\mathcal{F}$ to $\mathcal{F}'_f$. Since $\mathcal{F} \models Th(\lambda)$, $\mathcal{F}'_f \models Th(\lambda)$. Since $\phi(a_1,\ldots,a_n) \in Th(\lambda)$, $(\mathcal{F}'_f, V') \models \phi(a_1,\ldots,a_n)$. Therefore, $(\mathcal{F}, V) \models \phi(b_1,\ldots,b_n)$: a contradiction.

6   Admissibility: Decidability

Let λ be an extension of λ_0. By Proposition 13 and Lemmas 5–8 and 10, $wADM(\lambda)$ would be decidable if λ is balanced, $Th(\lambda)$ is decidable and a complete set of representatives for each class on A_n modulo $\simeq_\lambda^n$ could be computed. Let k be a nonnegative integer. Given $(a_1(z_1,\ldots,z_k),\ldots,a_n(z_1,\ldots,z_k)) \in A_n$, we define on $\{0,1\}^k$ the equivalence relation $\sim_{(a_1,\ldots,a_n)}^k$ as follows:

- $(\epsilon_1,\ldots,\epsilon_k) \sim_{(a_1,\ldots,a_n)}^k (\epsilon_1',\ldots,\epsilon_k')$ iff for all positive integers i, if $i \leq n$, then $z_1^{\epsilon_1} \sqcap \ldots \sqcap z_k^{\epsilon_k} \in mon(a_i(z_1,\ldots,z_k))$ iff $z_1^{\epsilon_1'} \sqcap \ldots \sqcap z_k^{\epsilon_k'} \in mon(a_i(z_1,\ldots,z_k))$.

Obviously,

Lemma 11. $\sim_{(a_1,\ldots,a_n)}^k$ has at most 2^n equivalence classes on $\{0,1\}^k$.

Hence, there exists a one-to-one function f assigning to each equivalence class $\mid (\epsilon_1,\ldots,\epsilon_k) \mid_{\sim_{(a_1,\ldots,a_n)}^k}$ an n-tuple $f(\mid (\epsilon_1,\ldots,\epsilon_k) \mid_{\sim_{(a_1,\ldots,a_n)}^k}) \in \{0,1\}^n$. By means of the one-to-one function f, for all positive integers i, if $i \leq n$, then we define the term $b_i(x_1,\ldots,x_n)$ as follows:

- $b_i(x_1,\ldots,x_n) = \bigsqcup \{x_1^{\epsilon_1'} \sqcap \ldots \sqcap x_n^{\epsilon_n'} : z_1^{\epsilon_1} \sqcap \ldots \sqcap z_k^{\epsilon_k} \in mon(a_i(z_1,\ldots,z_k))$ and $f(\mid (\epsilon_1,\ldots,\epsilon_k) \mid_{\sim_{(a_1,\ldots,a_n)}^k}) = (\epsilon_1',\ldots,\epsilon_n')\}$.

Given a nonempty set W, the reader may easily verify the following

Lemma 12.
- for all valuations V on W, there exists a valuation V' on W such that for all positive integers i, if $i \leq n$, then $(a_i(z_1,\ldots,z_k))^V = (b_i(x_1,\ldots,x_n))^{V'}$,
- for all valuations V on W, there exists a valuation V' on W such that for all positive integers i, if $i \leq n$, then $(b_i(x_1,\ldots,x_n))^V = (a_i(z_1,\ldots,z_k))^{V'}$.

The key thing to note about the terms $b_i(x_1,\ldots,x_n),\ldots,b_i(x_1,\ldots,x_n)$ is contained in the following

Lemma 13. $(a_1(z_1,\ldots,z_k),\ldots,a_n(z_1,\ldots,z_k)) \simeq_\lambda^n (b_1(x_1,\ldots,x_n),\ldots,b_n(x_1,\ldots,x_n))$.

Proof. Suppose $(a_1(z_1,\ldots,z_k),\ldots,a_n(z_1,\ldots,z_k)) \not\simeq_\lambda^n (b_1(x_1,\ldots,x_n),\ldots,b_n(x_1,\ldots,x_n))$. Hence, there exists a C-free weak formula $\phi(y_1,\ldots,y_n)$ in Φ_n such that $\phi(a_1(z_1,\ldots,z_k),\ldots,a_n(z_1,\ldots,z_k)) \in Th(\lambda)$ not-iff $\phi(b_1(x_1,\ldots,x_n),\ldots,b_n(x_1,\ldots,x_n)) \in Th(\lambda)$. Thus, we have to consider the following two cases.
Case $\phi(a_1(z_1,\ldots,z_k),\ldots,a_n(z_1,\ldots,z_k)) \in Th(\lambda)$ **and** $\phi(b_1(x_1,\ldots,x_n),\ldots,b_n(x_1,\ldots,x_n)) \notin Th(\lambda)$. Hence, there exists a frame $\mathcal{F} \in CF(\lambda)$ and there exists a valuation V on $\mathcal{F}$ such that $(\mathcal{F},V) \not\models \phi(b_1(x_1,\ldots,x_n),\ldots,b_n(x_1,\ldots,x_n))$. By Lemma 12, there exists a valuation V' on $\mathcal{F}$ such that for all positive integers i, if $i \leq n$, then $(b_i(x_1,\ldots,x_n))^V = (a_i(z_1,\ldots,z_k))^{V'}$. Since $(\mathcal{F},V) \not\models \phi(b_1(x_1,\ldots,x_n),\ldots,b_n(x_1,\ldots,x_n))$, $(\mathcal{F},V') \not\models \phi(a_1(z_1,\ldots,z_k),\ldots,a_n(z_1,\ldots,z_k))$. Thus, $\mathcal{F} \not\models \phi(a_1(z_1,\ldots,z_k),\ldots,a_n(z_1,\ldots,z_k))$. Since $\mathcal{F} \in CF(\lambda)$, $\phi(a_1(z_1,\ldots,z_k),\ldots,a_n(z_1,\ldots,z_k)) \notin Th(\lambda)$: a contradiction.
Case $\phi(a_1(z_1,\ldots,z_k),\ldots,a_n(z_1,\ldots,z_k)) \notin Th(\lambda)$ **and** $\phi(b_1(x_1,\ldots,x_n),\ldots,b_n(x_1,\ldots,x_n)) \in Th(\lambda)$. Similar to the case $\phi(a_1(z_1,\ldots,z_k),\ldots,a_n(z_1,\ldots,z_k)) \in Th(\lambda)$ and $\phi(b_1(x_1,\ldots,x_n),\ldots,b_n(x_1,\ldots,x_n)) \notin Th(\lambda)$.

By means of the lemmas presented above, let us prove the following

Proposition 14. *A complete set of representatives for each class on A_n modulo $\simeq_\lambda^n$ can be computed.*

Proof. By Lemma 13, the set of all n-tuples of terms on $\{x_1, \ldots, x_n\}$ constitutes a complete set of representatives for each class on A_n modulo $\simeq_\lambda^n$. Since there exists exactly 2^{2^n} pairwise non-equivalent terms of the form $b(x_1, \ldots, x_n)$, a complete set of representatives for each class on A_n modulo $\simeq_\lambda^n$ can be computed.

As a result,

Proposition 15. *If λ is balanced and there exists a finite set A of axioms such that $\lambda = \lambda_0(A)$, then $wADM(\lambda)$ is decidable.*

Proof. Suppose λ is balanced and there exists a finite set A of axioms such that $\lambda = \lambda_0(A)$. We define an algorithm taking as input a weak inference rule $(\Gamma(x_1, \ldots, x_n), \phi(x_1, \ldots, x_n))$ and returning the value *true* iff $(\Gamma(x_1, \ldots, x_n), \phi(x_1, \ldots, x_n))$ is admissible in λ as follows:

- compute a complete set $\{(a_1^1, \ldots, a_n^1), \ldots, (a_1^N, \ldots, a_n^N)\}$ of representatives for each class on A_n modulo $\simeq_\lambda^n$;
- if there exists a positive integer k such that $k \leq N$, $\Gamma(a_1^k, \ldots, a_n^k) \subseteq Th(\lambda)$ and $\phi(a_1^k, \ldots, a_n^k) \notin Th(\lambda)$ then return *false* else return *true*.

By Propositions 13 and 14 and Lemmas 5–8 and 10, this algorithm is sound and complete with respect to $wADM(\lambda)$ and can be executed.

However, the exact complexity of $wADM(\lambda)$ is not known.

7   Unifiability

Let λ be an extension of λ_0. A formula ϕ is said to be unifiable in λ iff there exists a substitution s such that $s(\phi) \in Th(\lambda)$. It happens that if λ is consistent, then unifiability is a special case of admissibility.

Proposition 16. *Let ϕ be a formula. If λ is consistent, then the following conditions are equivalent:*

- *ϕ is unifiable in λ,*
- *$(\{\phi\}, \bot)$ is not admissible in λ.*

Proof. Suppose λ is consistent.
($\Rightarrow$) Suppose ϕ is unifiable in λ. If $(\{\phi\}, \bot)$ is admissible in λ, then for all substitutions s, if $s(\phi) \in Th(\lambda)$, then $\bot \in Th(\lambda)$. Since λ is consistent, $\bot \notin Th(\lambda)$. Since for all substitutions s, if $s(\phi) \in Th(\lambda)$, then $\bot \in Th(\lambda)$, for all substitutions s, $s(\phi) \notin Th(\lambda)$. Hence, ϕ is not unifiable in λ: a contradiction.
($\Leftarrow$) Suppose $(\{\phi\}, \bot)$ is not admissible in λ. Hence, there exists a substitution s such that $s(\phi) \in Th(\lambda)$. Thus, ϕ is unifiable in λ.

Now, let us consider the following decision problem, called "weak unifiability problem in λ", in symbols $wUNI(\lambda)$:

- input: a weak formula ϕ,
- output: determine whether ϕ is unifiable in λ.

Lemma 14. *For all weak formulas $\phi(x_1, \ldots, x_n)$, the following conditions are equivalent:*

- ϕ *is unifiable in λ,*
- *there exists $(\epsilon_1, \ldots, \epsilon_n) \in \{0, 1\}^n$ such that $\phi(\epsilon_1, \ldots, \epsilon_n) \in Th(\lambda)$.*

Proof. ($\Rightarrow$) Suppose $\phi(x_1, \ldots, x_n)$ is unifiable in λ. Hence, there exists a substitution s such that $s(\phi(x_1, \ldots, x_n)) \in Th(\lambda)$. Let t be a ground substitution. Since $s(\phi(x_1, \ldots, x_n)) \in Th(\lambda)$, $t(s(\phi(x_1, \ldots, x_n))) \in Th(\lambda)$. Let $(\epsilon_1, \ldots, \epsilon_n) \in \{0, 1\}^n$ be obtained from $(t(s(x_1)), \ldots, t(s(x_n)))$ by applying ordinary reasoning in nondegenerate Boolean algebras. Since $t(s(\phi(x_1, \ldots, x_n))) \in Th(\lambda)$, $\phi(\epsilon_1, \ldots, \epsilon_n) \in Th(\lambda)$.
($\Leftarrow$) Suppose there exists $(\epsilon_1, \ldots, \epsilon_n) \in \{0, 1\}^n$ such that $\phi(\epsilon_1, \ldots, \epsilon_n) \in Th(\lambda)$. Let s be a substitution such that for all positive integers i, if $i \leq n$, then $s(x_i) = \epsilon_i$. Since $\phi(\epsilon_1, \ldots, \epsilon_n) \in Th(\lambda)$, $s(\phi(x_1, \ldots, x_n)) \in Th(\lambda)$. Thus, ϕ is unifiable in λ.

Hence, it is easy to check that when $Th(\lambda)$ is decidable, $wUNI(\lambda)$ is decidable. Now, remark that for all weak formulas $\phi(x_1, \ldots, x_n)$ and for all $(\epsilon_1, \ldots, \epsilon_n) \in \{0, 1\}^n$, $\phi(\epsilon_1, \ldots, \epsilon_n)$ is equivalent modulo $\equiv_\lambda^n$ to one of the following elementary formulas: $\bot, \top, C(1, 1), \bar{C}(1, 1)$. Moreover, even when $Th(\lambda)$ is undecidable, the elementary formula in $\{\bot, \top, C(1, 1), \bar{C}(1, 1)\}$ that is equivalent modulo $\equiv_\lambda^n$ to $\phi(\epsilon_1, \ldots, \epsilon_n)$ in λ can be computed. As a result, in all cases, i.e. whatever is the decidability status of $Th(\lambda)$,

Proposition 17. $wUNI(\lambda)$ *is decidable.*

Remark that the elementary formula in $\{\bot, \top, C(1, 1), \bar{C}(1, 1)\}$ that is equivalent modulo $\equiv_\lambda^n$ to $\phi(\epsilon_1, \ldots, \epsilon_n)$ in λ can be computed in linear time. As a result,

Proposition 18. $wUNI(\lambda)$ *is in NP.*

It happens that if λ is consistent, then the satisfiability problem in Boolean Logic is reducible to $wUNI(\lambda)$.

Proposition 19. *Let $a(x_1, \ldots, x_n)$ be a term. If λ is consistent, then the following conditions are equivalent:*

- $a(x_1, \ldots, x_n)$ *is satisfiable in Boolean Logic,*
- $a(x_1, \ldots, x_n) \equiv 1$ *is unifiable in λ.*

Proof. Suppose λ is consistent.
($\Rightarrow$) Suppose $a(x_1, \ldots, x_n)$ is satisfiable in Boolean Logic. Hence, there exists $(\epsilon_1, \ldots, \epsilon_n) \in \{0, 1\}^n$ such that $a(\epsilon_1, \ldots, \epsilon_n)$ is equivalent to 1 in Boolean Logic.

Thus, $a(\epsilon_1, \ldots, \epsilon_n) \equiv 1 \in Th(\lambda)$. Let s be a substitution such that for all positive integers i, if $i \leq n$, then $s(x_i) = \epsilon_i$. Since $a(\epsilon_1, \ldots, \epsilon_n) \equiv 1 \in Th(\lambda)$, $s(a(x_1, \ldots, x_n) \equiv 1) \in Th(\lambda)$. Therefore, $a(x_1, \ldots, x_n) \equiv 1$ is unifiable in λ.

($\Leftarrow$) Suppose $a(x_1, \ldots, x_n) \equiv 1$ is unifiable in λ. Hence, there exists a substitution s such that $s(a(x_1, \ldots, x_n) \equiv 1) \in Th(\lambda)$. Let t be a ground substitution. Since $s(a(x_1, \ldots, x_n) \equiv 1) \in Th(\lambda)$, $t(s(a(x_1, \ldots, x_n) \equiv 1)) \in Th(\lambda)$. Let $(\epsilon_1, \ldots, \epsilon_n) \in \{0, 1\}^n$ be obtained from $(t(s(x_1)), \ldots, t(s(x_n)))$ by applying ordinary reasoning in Boolean Logic. If $a(x_1, \ldots, x_n)$ is not satisfiable in Boolean Logic, then $a(\epsilon_1, \ldots, \epsilon_n)$ is equivalent to 0 in Boolean Logic. Since λ is consistent, $\bot \notin Th(\lambda)$. Thus, there exists a frame $\mathcal{F} \in CF(\lambda)$. Let V be a valuation on $\mathcal{F}$ such that for all positive integers i, if $i \leq n$, then

- if $t(s(x_i))$ is equivalent to 0 in Boolean Logic, then $V(x_i) = \emptyset$,
- if $t(s(x_i))$ is equivalent to 1 in Boolean Logic, then $V(x_i) = W$.

Therefore, for all positive integers i, if $i \leq n$, then $V(x_i) = (t(s(x_i)))^V$. Since $a(\epsilon_1, \ldots, \epsilon_n)$ is equivalent to 0 in Boolean Logic, $(\mathcal{F}, V) \not\models t(s(a(x_1, \ldots, x_n) \equiv 1))$. Since $\mathcal{F} \in CF(\lambda)$, $t(s(a(x_1, \ldots, x_n) \equiv 1)) \notin Th(\lambda)$ a contradiction.

As a result,

Proposition 20. *If λ is consistent, then $wUNI(\lambda)$ is NP-hard.*

Now, we give a syntactic result for unifiability and non-unifiability of a weak formula in λ.

Proposition 21. *Let $\phi(x_1, \ldots, x_n)$ be a weak formula. If λ is consistent and $C(1, 1) \in Th(\lambda)$, then the following conditions are equivalent:*

- *$\phi(x_1, \ldots, x_n)$ is not unifiable in λ,*
- *$\phi(x_1, \ldots, x_n) \to \bigvee \{x_i \not\equiv 0 \wedge x_i \not\equiv 1 \colon 1 \leq i \leq n\} \in Th(\lambda)$.*

Proof. Suppose λ is consistent and $C(1, 1) \in Th(\lambda)$.

($\Rightarrow$) Suppose $\phi(x_1, \ldots, x_n)$ is not unifiable in λ. If $\phi(x_1, \ldots, x_n) \to \bigvee \{x_i \not\equiv 0 \wedge x_i \not\equiv 1 \colon 1 \leq i \leq n\} \notin Th(\lambda)$, then there exists a frame $\mathcal{F} \in CF(\lambda)$ and there exists a valuation V on $\mathcal{F}$ such that $(\mathcal{F}, V) \not\models \phi(x_1, \ldots, x_n) \to \bigvee \{x_i \not\equiv 0 \wedge x_i \not\equiv 1 \colon 1 \leq i \leq n\}$. Hence, $(\mathcal{F}, V) \models \phi(x_1, \ldots, x_n)$ and $(\mathcal{F}, V) \not\models \bigvee \{x_i \not\equiv 0 \wedge x_i \not\equiv 1 \colon 1 \leq i \leq n\}$. Suppose $\mathcal{F} = (W, R)$. Thus, for all positive integers i, if $i \leq n$, then either $V(x_i) = \emptyset$, or $V(x_i) = W$. Let s be a substitution such that for all positive integers i, if $i \leq n$, then

- if $V(x_i) = \emptyset$, then $s(x_i) = 0$,
- if $V(x_i) = W$, then $s(x_i) = 1$.

Therefore, for all positive integers i, if $i \leq n$, then $V(x_i) = (s(x_i))^V$ Since $(\mathcal{F}, V) \models \phi(x_1, \ldots, x_n)$, $(\mathcal{F}, V) \models \phi(s(x_1), \ldots, s(x_n))$. Since for all positive integers i, if $i \leq n$, then $s(x_i)$ is either equal to 0, or equal to 1, $\phi(s(x_1), \ldots, s(x_n))$ is equivalent modulo $\equiv_\lambda^n$ to an elementary formula in $\{\bot, \top, C(1, 1), \bar{C}(1, 1)\}$. Since $\mathcal{F} \models Th(\lambda)$, $C(1, 1) \in Th(\lambda)$ and $(\mathcal{F}, V) \models \phi(s(x_1), \ldots, s(x_n))$, $\phi(s(x_1), \ldots,$

$s(x_n))$ is equivalent modulo $\equiv_\lambda^n$ to $\top$. Consequently, $\phi(x_1, \ldots, x_n)$ is unifiable in λ: a contradiction.

($\Leftarrow$) Suppose $\phi(x_1, \ldots, x_n) \to \bigvee\{x_i \not\equiv 0 \wedge x_i \not\equiv 1 : 1 \leq i \leq n\} \in Th(\lambda)$. If $\phi(x_1, \ldots, x_n)$ is unifiable in λ, then by Lemma 14, there exists $(\epsilon_1, \ldots, \epsilon_n) \in \{0, 1\}^n$ such that $\phi(\epsilon_1, \ldots, \epsilon_n) \in Th(\lambda)$. Let s be a substitution such that for all positive integers i, if $i \leq n$, then $s(x_i) = \epsilon_i$. Since $\phi(x_1, \ldots, x_n) \to \bigvee\{x_i \not\equiv 0 \wedge x_i \not\equiv 1 : 1 \leq i \leq n\} \in Th(\lambda)$, $s(\phi(x_1, \ldots, x_n)) \to \bigvee\{s(x_i) \not\equiv 0 \wedge s(x_i) \not\equiv 1 : 1 \leq i \leq n\} \in Th(\lambda)$. Since for all positive integers i, if $i \leq n$, then $s(x_i) = \epsilon_i$, $\phi(\epsilon_1, \ldots, \epsilon_n) \to \bigvee\{\epsilon_i \not\equiv 0 \wedge \epsilon_i \not\equiv 1 : 1 \leq i \leq n\} \in Th(\lambda)$. Since $\phi(\epsilon_1, \ldots, \epsilon_n) \in Th(\lambda)$, $\bigvee\{\epsilon_i \not\equiv 0 \wedge \epsilon_i \not\equiv 1 : 1 \leq i \leq n\} \in Th(\lambda)$. Since $(\epsilon_1, \ldots, \epsilon_n) \in \{0, 1\}^n$, $\bigwedge\{\epsilon_i \equiv 0 \vee \epsilon_i \equiv 1 : 1 \leq i \leq n\} \in Th(\lambda)$. Since $\bigvee\{\epsilon_i \not\equiv 0 \wedge \epsilon_i \not\equiv 1 : 1 \leq i \leq n\} \in Th(\lambda)$, λ is not consistent: a contradiction.

8 Conclusion

Admissibility problems and unifiability problems are decidable in many modal logics [1–3,13,14], but modal logics for which they become undecidable are known [18]. Nevertheless, very little is known about these problems in some of the most important modal logics considered in Computer Science and Artificial Intelligence. For example, the decidability and the complexity of the unification problem for the following modal logics remains open: modal logic K, multi-modal variants of K, sub-Boolean modal logics.

In this paper, we have examined variants of contact logics. The central result in this paper is the proof that the weak admissibility problem and the weak unifiability problem are decidable in these variants.

Much remains to be done. For example, λ being a consistent extension of λ_0, Propositions 16 and 20 imply that $wADM(\lambda)$ is $coNP$-hard, but the exact complexity of $wADM(\lambda)$ is not known. One may also consider the admissibility problem $ADM(\lambda)$ defined in Sect. 4 and the following unifiability problem: given a formula ϕ, determine whether ϕ is unifiable in λ. Finally, there is also the related question of the unification type of λ. Our conjecture is that the unification type of most extensions of λ_0 considered in [5,17] is finitary.

Acknowledgements. We would like to thank the referees for the feedback we have obtained from them in the revision process of the present paper. Special thanks are also due to Yannick Chevalier and Tinko Tinchev for their extensive remarks concerning Lemma 12.

References

1. Baader, F., Ghilardi, S.: Unification in modal and description logics. Logic J. IGPL **19**, 705–730 (2011)
2. Baader, F., Morawska, B.: Unification in the description logic $\mathcal{EL}$. In: Treinen, R. (ed.) RTA 2009. LNCS, vol. 5595, pp. 350–364. Springer, Heidelberg (2009)

3. Babenyshev, S., Rybakov, V.: Unification in linear temporal logic LTL. Ann. Pure Appl. Logic **162**, 991–1000 (2011)
4. Balbiani, P., Tinchev, T.: Boolean logics with relations. J. Logic Algebraic Program. **79**, 707–721 (2010)
5. Balbiani, P., Tinchev, T., Vakarelov, D.: Modal logics for region-based theories of space. Fundamenta Informaticæ **81**, 29–82 (2007)
6. Dimov, G., Vakarelov, D.: Contact algebras and region-based theory of space: a proximity approach – I. Fundamenta Informaticæ **74**, 209–249 (2006)
7. Dimov, G., Vakarelov, D.: Contact algebras and region-based theory of space: proximity approach – II. Fundamenta Informaticæ **74**, 251–282 (2006)
8. Düntsch, I., Winter, M.: A representation theorem for Boolean contact algebras. Theoret. Comput. Sci. **347**, 498–512 (2005)
9. Gencer, Ç.: Description of modal logics inheriting admissible rules for $K4$. Logic J. IGPL **10**, 401–411 (2002)
10. Gencer, Ç., de Jongh, D.: Unifiability in extensions of $K4$. Logic J. IGPL **17**, 159–172 (2009)
11. Ghilardi, S.: Unification in intuitionistic logic. J. Symbolic Logic **64**, 859–880 (1999)
12. Ghilardi, S.: Best solving modal equations. Ann. Pure Appl. Logic **102**, 183–198 (2000)
13. Iemhoff, R., Metcalfe, G.: Proof theory for admissible rules. Ann. Pure Appl. Logic **159**, 171–186 (2009)
14. Jeřábek, E.: Admissible rules of Łukasiewicz logic. J. Logic Comput. **20**, 425–447 (2010)
15. Rybakov, V.: A criterion for admissibility of rules in the model system $S4$ and the intuitionistic logic. Algebra Logic **23**, 369–384 (1984)
16. Rybakov, V.: Admissibility of Logical Inference Rules. Elsevier, Amsterdam (1997)
17. Vakarelov, D.: Region-based theory of space: algebras of regions, representation theory, and logics. In: Gabbay, D.M., Zakharyaschev, M., Goncharov, S.S. (eds.) Mathematical Problems from Applied Logic II. Logics for the XXIst Century, pp. 267–348. Springer, New York (2007)
18. Wolter, F., Zakharyaschev, M.: Undecidability of the unification and admissibility problems for modal and description logics. ACM Trans. Comput. Logic **9**, 25:1–25:20 (2008)

F-LTAG Semantics for Issues Around Focusing

Kata Balogh[(✉)]

Institut für Sprache und Information,
Heinrich-Heine-Universität Düsseldorf, Düsseldorf, Germany
Katalin.Balogh@hhu.de

This paper proposes an analysis in a Feature-based Lexicalized Tree-Adjoining Grammar (F-LTAG) [9,18] for deriving the semantic representations of various narrow focus constructions. Te paper presents an extension of the F-LTAG analysis by Balogh [3] based on the syntax-semantics approach by Kallmeyer & Romero [11] and the semantic-pragmatic analysis of focus by Balogh [2].

The main aim of the current paper is to broaden the coverage of the focus approach in F-LTAG as introduced by Balogh [3] that proposes the basics of an analysis of the syntax-semantics interface of various narrow focus constructions. The semantic representations in the current paper – as before – are given using the logical language of basic Inquisitive Semantics (InqB) by Ciardelli, Groenendijk and Roelofsen [5], such that these representations can further be interpreted according to its semantics and pragmatics. The choice for the logical system of InqB – as opposed to, e.g., Alternative Semantics [16].[1] or the Structured Meanings Account [12] – is not for a principled reason, but convenient for the following motivation. One of the main claims in favor of the system of InqB is, that its semantics and dialogue management system offers an elegant way to analyze various discourse-related phenomena involving focus, such as: focusing in answers, question-answer relations, contrast in denial and specification by focusing. Therefore the use of the framework of InqB offers an elegant way to broaden the analysis by a dialogue management system. The current paper is addressing the compositional derivation of semantic representations from a computational linguistic point of view, hence the paper does not deal with general logical or formal semantic issues of the used semantic framework (Inquisitive Semantics).

1 Background

The analysis proposed in this paper offers a compositional way to calculate the semantic representations for different focus constructions in a uniform way. The core framework of the analysis is a Feature-based Lexicalized Tree-Adjoining Grammar (F-LTAG), that is a TAG where each elementary tree is anchored by a lexical item – LTAG [9] – and furthermore each node in a tree is annotated with feature structures [18]. For the semantic component I adapt the F-LTAG account based on unification following Kallmeyer & Joshi [10] and Kallmeyer & Romero [11]. The semantic representations are given using flat semantic representations

---

[1] See e.g. Babko-Malaya [1].

© Springer-Verlag Berlin Heidelberg 2015
M. Aher et al. (Eds.): TbiLLC 2013, LNCS 8984, pp. 61–81, 2015.
DOI: 10.1007/978-3-662-46906-4_5

where the logical formulas mirror the logical expressions of basic Inquisitive Semantics (InqB). Integrating the logical language of InqB into the semantic representations serves the broader purpose of integrating the current analysis with a component of semantic-pragmatic interpretation and discourse modeling (e.g. modeling question-answer relations).

1.1   Basic LTAG

In the formalism of Lexicalized Tree-Adjoining Grammar (LTAG) the derivation of a sentence is carried out by operations on trees, beginning with a set of elementary trees that consist of two disjoint sets: the set of initial trees and the set of auxiliary trees. In LTAG there are two operations on trees: *substitution* and *adjunction*. Substitution is the replacement of a non-terminal leaf node by another tree. Adjunction is the replacement of an internal node by another tree. The trees to adjoin are auxiliary trees with a special node, the footnote, marked by *. In the auxiliary tree (the trees to adjoin) the root node and the footnode must have the same label. Every non-terminal leaf that is not a footnote is a substitution node, in the trees marked by ↓ for readability reasons.

Substitution: *Adjunction:*

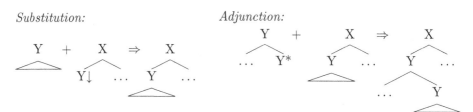

In feature based tree-adjoining grammar (F-TAG) each node is annotated with two feature structures: the *top* and the *bottom features*. The top features of a node give the relation of the node to the tree above it, while the bottom features give the relation to the tree below it. At the end of the derivation – on the final derived tree – top and bottom features are unified for all nodes.

At substitution in F-TAG the top features of the root of the tree to substitute unify with the top features of the substitution node. Substitution nodes have only top features. At adjunction the top features of the root of the auxiliary tree unify with the top features of the target node, and the bottom features of the footnode of the auxiliary tree unify with the bottom features of the target node.

F-TA Gsubstitution: *F-TA Gadjunction:*

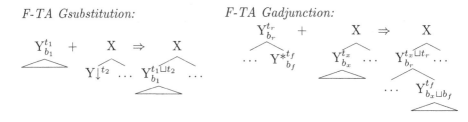

1.2   F-LTAG Semantics

In the semantic component of F-LTAG in [10,11], elementary trees come with features on each node and a (flat) semantic representation, the latter consisting of a set of labelled propositions and a set of scope constraints. The feature structures, labelled proposition propositions and scope constraints contain meta-variables of individuals, propositions or situations, all of them given by boxed numbers, hereby linking the feature structures to a semantic representation. By substitution and adjunction of the trees, feature structures get unified and the meta-variables get identified. Also the semantic representation of the resulting tree is calculated by taking the union of the representations of the participating trees. For an illustration of the F-LTAG semantics see Example 1, the derivation of the question *Who walks?* assigning the semantic representation as $?\exists x.walk(x)$ using the language of InqB. To prevent confusion with the 'classical' first-order logical system, let me provide a schematic explanation of the semantic representation here. According the to system of InqB, the expression $?\exists x.walk(x)$ is equivalent to the disjunction $\exists x.walk(x) \vee \neg\exists x.walk(x)$ and leads to the set of *possibilities* (= sets of worlds) $\bigcup_{d\in D} walk(d) \cup \neg walk(d)$ (see more details in the next section). The example here differs from [11] in two crucial ways: (i) it uses the logical language of InqB in the semantic representations, and (ii) for the wh-scope two new features – WHMAX and WHMIN – are introduced.

Example 1. Who walks?

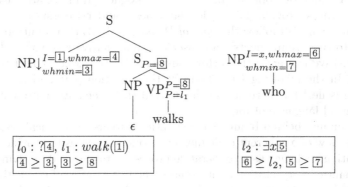

The elementary tree of *walks* comes with a semantic representation consisting of two propositions: l_0 contributes the question-operator applied to a proposition given here as the meta-variable ④. The proposition l_1 says, that the predicate *walk* is applied to the individual variable ① that is contributed by the NP-tree substituted to the given position: given by $I = ①$ on the feature structure of the substitution node. Here, two special features are introduced: WHMAX and WHMIN. These features are inspired by the idea of a separate wh-scope window for wh-quantificational elements from Romero, Kallmeyer & Babko-Malaya [14] and by the MAXS and MINS features from Kallmeyer & Romero [11] that indicate the *scope window* of a given quantificational phrase. The features MAXS and MINS determine the upper scope boundary and lower scope boundary of quantificational NPs like *someone* or *everyone*, hereby creating a scope-window. WHMAX and WHMIN similarly indicate the scope window for wh-elements and focused constituents. Separating these two different scope windows is motivated by the different scope properties of these elements and has the advantage to account for, e.g., focusing in questions or quantified NPs in focus. Next to the propositions l_0 and l_1, the scope constrains $4 \geq 3$, $3 \geq 8$ are given that determine the scope relations between the given propositions.[2] The scope constrains are defined between the propositional meta-variables and the propositional labels.

The NP-tree of the wh-phrase gets substituted into the S-tree of *walks* resulting in the equations $1 = x$, $4 = 6$, $3 = 7$ and since nothing is adjoined at the VP node[3], we have $8 = l_1$. After these equations the combination of the semantic representations results in:

$$l_0 : ?\boxed{4}, \; l_1 : walk(x), \; l_2 : \exists x \boxed{5}$$
$$\boxed{4} \geq \boxed{3}, \boxed{3} \geq l_1, \boxed{4} \geq l_2, \boxed{5} \geq \boxed{3}$$

The only possible plugging (see e.g. [4]) is: $4 \mapsto l_2$, $5 \mapsto l_1$, $3 \mapsto l_1$, determined by the scope constraints $4 \geq 3$, $3 \geq l_1$, $4 \geq l_2$, $5 \geq 3$. This plugging derives the semantic representation as $?\exists x.walks(x)$.

1.3   Basic Inquisitive Semantics

In the following analysis I adapt several ideas of basic Inquisitive Semantics [5], a logical semantic approach of linguistic dialogue and information exchange, where utterances provide data (informativeness) and raise issues (inquisitiveness). In my analysis I follow the *Fact of Division* in InqB that all utterances are divided into two "components": an *assertion* (informative content) and a *question* (inquisitive content), the latter considered as the issue behind the given utterance. In the following I use INFC for the assertion part and INQC for the underlying issue.[4] Furthermore, in the derived (flat) semantic representations I use the logical language of InqB.[5]

The main aim behind Inquisitive Semantics is to create a logical system that models the flow of a coherent dialogue. The principal goal is to provide a model of information exchange as a cooperative process of raising and resolving issues. In the semantic interpretation of utterances, the main source of inquisitiveness is *disjunction* [6,13]. The disjunction of two propositions is naturally interpreted as providing the information that one of the two propositions is true and also raising the issue *which one* of them is true. Hence the disjunction $p \lor q$ provides two

---

[2] $4 \geq 3$ requires, that the proposition that 4 stands for is either equal to or scopes over the proposition that 3 stands for.

[3] To keep the examples easier, none of the following examples contain adjunction at the VP node, so in later examples I will skip the P features at the VP and S nodes.

[4] In earlier versions of Inquisitive Semantics [7] these two notions were referred to as the Theme (question) and the Rheme (assertion).

[5] Note, that certain details are different – e.g., the representation of proper names – between the InqB representation and a flat semantic representation. This technical detail will not be discussed any further in this paper.

Possibilities: p is true or q is true, while eliminating the option that both of them are false. Similarly, questions also lead to possibilities of whom the questioner wants to know which one holds. Take, for example, the polar question *Is it raining?* $(?p)$ identified by the set of two propositions/possibilities *it is raining* (p) and *it is not raining* $(\neg p)$. Since the questioner is interested whether p or $\neg p$ is the case, the question $?p$ can be defined as the disjunction of its two possibilities: $p \vee \neg p$. Also in general, questions in InqB are defined in terms of disjunction. In the logical language of InqB '?' is the interrogative operator, and $?\phi$ is an abbreviation of $\phi \vee \neg \phi$.

In (basic) Inquisitive Semantics, the core concept defines the meaning of expressions is that of a *proposition* (note, that the notion of *proposition* in InqB is different from the classical formal semantic notion of *proposition*). A *proposition* is a downward closed set of information states, where information states are defined as sets of possible worlds ($s \subseteq \omega$, ω being the set of all possible worlds) as illustrated in Fig. 1 (i)–(v) below. Special states are the *ignorant state* (iv), when $s = \omega$ and the *inconsistent state* (v) when $s = \emptyset$.

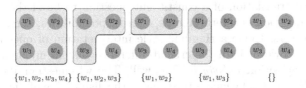

$\{w_1, w_2, w_3, w_4\}$ $\{w_1, w_2, w_3\}$ $\{w_1, w_2\}$ $\{w_1, w_3\}$ $\{\}$

Fig. 1. Information states in InqB

The *proposition* expressed by ϕ is referred to as $[\phi]$. As an illustration see Figs. 1 and 2 below, where p, q are the two proposition letters in the language. The set of worlds, $\omega = \{w_1, w_2, w_3, w_4\}$ where the valuations are $p(w_1) = p(w_2) = 1, p(w_3) = p(w_4) = 0, q(w_1) = q(w_3) = 1, q(w_2) = q(w_4) = 0$.

p q $p \vee q$

Fig. 2. *Propositions* in InqB

The informative content of a proposition A is the union of the sets of possible worlds by $\bigcup A$, referred to as $\mathsf{info}(A)$. In terms of *inquisitiveness* and *informativeness* a proposition A is informative in a given state s if its informative content is a proper subset of s ($\mathsf{info}(A) \subset s$) and A is inquisitive in s if its informative content is not an element of A ($\mathsf{info}(A) \neq A$). In terms of information updates, this means that an informative utterance eliminates some worlds (or provides information), while an inquisitive utterance introduces new issues.

Based on *inquisitivity* and *informativity* three meaningful sentence types can be defined: (a) *questions* that are inquisitive and not informative, (b) *assertions* that are informative and not inquisitive and (c) *hybrids* that are both informative and inquisitive. Such a hybrid type is the proposition $p \vee q$, that provides the information that $\neg p \wedge \neg q$ is not the case, while it raises the issue which one of p or q is true, thus it gives two possibilities. The question $?(p \vee q)$ is not informative, it does not exclude anything, it only raises the issue whether p or q or $\neg p \wedge \neg q$ is the case (three possibilities).[6] Similarly to $p \vee q$ the predicate logical expression $\exists x.\phi$ also provides the information that $\neg\exists x.\phi$ is not the case and additionally it raises the issue which individuals are ϕ. It leads to several possibilities depending on the number of individuals in the domain. Take, for example, the proposition $\exists x.P(x)$ and a small domain of three individuals $D = \{a, b, c\}$. The existential expression $\exists x.P(x)$ then excludes the option that none of a, b, c is P, and raises the issue which one is P. Relative to the given domain D, this expression leads to the set of three possibilities: $P(a), P(b), P(c)$. Following this line, I assume the standard logical translation of a constituent question to be of the form $?\exists x.\phi$. A constituent question is interpreted as a set of possibilities, corresponding to its possible answers. I give a Hamblin-style interpretation of questions as sets of propositions, however with the crucial difference that in my analysis the set contains the proposition *nobody is P* as well. The wh-question *Who walks?* is translated as $?\exists x.walk(x)$ which is the same as the disjunction of the propositions (possibilities) $walk(d_1) \vee walk(d_2) \vee ... \vee walk(d_n) \vee \neg\exists x.walk(x)$ relative to the given domain of individuals.

Following the Fact of Division in Inquisitive Semantics, Balogh [2] proposes an analysis of sentences containing focused constituents claiming that focusing leads to a special question-assertion (or theme-rheme with the old terminology) division. Note, that in this approach the sentences themselves are not split into two parts, but the way is defined how to signal the inherent issue (question) of the utterance and the information it provides (assertion). The question/issue behind the utterance is always inquisitive, introducing two or more possibilities. In order to derive the special division of a focused sentence Balogh [2] defines the *Rule of Division* by focusing. The rule is presented here with a slight terminology change following the new version of InqB.

Definition 1. Rule of Division
Let α be an utterance in natural language, α' the translation of α in the language of InqB, $\mathbf{c_F}$ the constituents with focus marking and $\natural$ the operation: if $\varphi = ?\psi$ then $\varphi^\natural = \psi$, otherwise $\varphi^\natural = \varphi$.

Every utterance α is divided into a question, INQC(α) and an assertion INFC (α) where INQC(α) $= ?\exists\boldsymbol{x}(\alpha'[\mathbf{c_F}'/\boldsymbol{x}])^\natural$ and INFC(α) $= \alpha'$

---

[6] Note, that $?\phi$ is not a separate category in the syntax of the logical language, but it is defined in terms of disjunction as given above.

This definition correctly derives the question-assertion (or theme-rheme) division of various narrow focus constructions, that further gets interpreted in the system of InqB. The representation of focusing has to provide different structures for the different (narrow) focus constructions. Consider the basic cases of a sentence with a transitive verb: (i) none of the arguments is focused, (ii) the subject is focused or (iii) the object is focused, or (iv) both the subject and the object are focused. Applying the Rule of Division above, all these sentences lead to different question-assertion divisions, where the issues behind (the INQCs) are different depending on the focus structure, while the information content (INFC) is the same in all sentences.

(1)   Pim likes Sam.
      ⤳ translates as $\varphi = like(p, s)$
      ⤳ INQC: $?like(p, s)$ + INFC: $like(p, s)$

      PIM$_F$ likes Sam.
      ⤳ translates as $\varphi = like(p_F, s)$
      ⤳ INQC: $?\exists x.like(x, s)$ + INFC: $like(p, s)$

      Pim likes SAM$_F$.
      ⤳ translates as $\varphi = like(p, s_F)$
      ⤳ INQC: $?\exists y.like(p, y)$ + INFC: $like(p, s)$

      PIM$_F$ likes SAM$_F$.
      ⤳ translates as $\varphi = like(p_F, s_F)$
      ⤳ INQC: $?\exists x \exists y.like(x, y)$ + INFC: $like(p, s)$

Notice the close analogy/similarity with Rooth's [15, 16] Alternative Semantics. What figures the domain of alternatives in Rooth's account appears here as a choice question. The proposal of Balogh [2] provides a context-based analysis of focusing with special attention to question-answer congruence, exhaustivity, contrast in denials, and specification. However, the system does not offer a compositional analysis at the syntax-semantics interface. As can be seen in Definition 1, focus marking of constituents get directly translated in the logical language as ϕ_F not referring to the syntactic structure and the contribution of the focused constituent. In the following I propose an analysis aiming to fill this gap by providing the intended semantics representations (question-assertion divisions) compositionally on the basis of the syntactic structure of the given sentence.

2   F-LTAG Semantics for Focusing

Following InqB, in my F-LTAG analysis the semantic representations of utterances all consist of two components: one that represents the inquisitive content (question/issue) and one that represents the informative content (assertion). According to this, each S-tree comes with a semantic representation, such as the following:

$$\left\langle \begin{array}{l} \boxed{l_0 : ?\boxed{i},\ l_1 : R^n(\boxed{t_1}, ..., \boxed{t_n})} \\ \boxed{\{\boxed{i} \geq \boxed{j}, \boxed{j} \geq l_1, ...\}} \\ \boxed{l_1 : R^n(\boxed{t_1}, ..., \boxed{t_n})} \\ \boxed{\{\text{constraints}\}} \end{array} \right\rangle$$

In this two-dimensional representation the above part is the representation of the question/issue (INQC), while the below one is the representation of the assertion (INFC). Defined in this way all S-trees come with a semantic representation, where the (INQC) will lead to a question – the *issue behind* the sentence –, and the (INFC) leads to a proposition – the *semantic content* of the sentence. Take, for example, the sentence *Pim likes Sam* that is built up from three elementary trees, the S-tree of the verb and the two NP-trees of the two arguments.

Example 2. Pim likes Sam

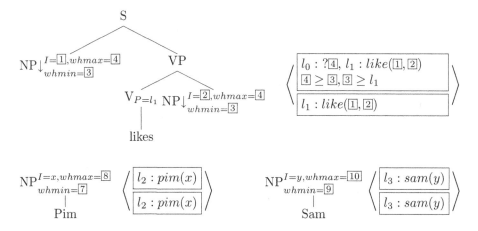

By substituting the NP-tree in the S-tree the features on the nodes get unified (thus $\boxed{1} = x, \boxed{2} = y$) and the corresponding semantic representations are combined, resulting in the semantic representation of the sentence as:

$$\left\langle \begin{array}{l} \boxed{l_0 : ?\boxed{4},\ l_1 : like(x,y),\ l_2 : pim(x),\ l_3 : sam(y)\ \ \ \boxed{4} \geq \boxed{3}, \boxed{3} \geq l_1} \\ \boxed{l_1 : like(x,y),\ l_2 : pim(x),\ l_3 : sam(y)} \end{array} \right\rangle$$

There is one way of plugging possible here: $\boxed{4} \mapsto l_1, \boxed{3} \mapsto l_1$, deriving the semantic representation of the given sentence as the following, where the inquisitive content (INQC) corresponds to the question *Does Pim like Sam?* and the informative content (INFC) corresponds to the proposition *Pim likes Sam.*

$$\left\langle \begin{array}{l} \boxed{?like(x,y),\ pim(x),\ sam(y)} \\ \boxed{like(x,y),\ pim(x),\ sam(y)} \end{array} \right\rangle$$

2.1   Subject/Object Focus

Sentences consisting of a transitive verb have the possibilities of narrow focus: either the subject or the object (or both) can be focused. First, look at the sentences in (1) with single focus. The analysis derives the INFC as the proposition *Pim likes Sam* for both, while the different focus structures lead to two different INQCs corresponding to the inherent questions: *Who likes Sam?* and *Whom does Pim like?* respectively.

In the analysis of PIM_F *likes Sam* with narrow focus on the subject, we take the S-tree of *likes* as above and substitute two NP-trees: for the non-focused object the tree for *Sam* as in Example 2, while for the focused subject we take the tree for *Pim* with a special semantics:

Example 3. Focused subject

$$\mathrm{NP}^{I=x, whmax=\boxed{8}, foc=+}_{whmin=\boxed{7}}$$
$$\mid$$
$$\mathrm{Pim}$$

$$\left\langle \begin{array}{|l|} \hline l_2 : \exists x\boxed{11}, \\ \boxed{8} \geq l_2, \boxed{11} \geq \boxed{7} \\ \hline l_2 : pim(x) \\ \hline \end{array} \right\rangle$$

The semantic representation of the focused NP contributes a special INQC as an existential expression.[7] The substitutions of the two NPs carried out and the respective meta-variables unified: $\boxed{1} = x, \boxed{2} = y, \boxed{8} = \boxed{4}, \boxed{7} = \boxed{3}$, that leads to the semantics:

$$\left\langle \begin{array}{|l|} \hline l_0 :?\boxed{4}, \; l_1 : like(x,y), \; l_2 : \exists x\boxed{11}, \; l_3 : sam(y) \\ \boxed{4} \geq \boxed{3}, \boxed{3} \geq l_1, \boxed{4} \geq l_2, \boxed{11} \geq \boxed{3} \\ \hline l_1 : like(x,y), \; l_2 : pim(x), \; l_3 : sam(y) \\ \hline \end{array} \right\rangle$$

Again, one way of plugging is possible here: $\boxed{4} \mapsto l_2, \boxed{11} \mapsto l_1, \boxed{3} \mapsto l_1$ providing the twofold semantic representation corresponding to the question *Who likes Sam?* as the INQC and the proposition *Pim likes Sam* as the INFC.

$$\left\langle \begin{array}{|l|} \hline ?\exists x.like(x,y), sam(y) \\ \hline like(x,y), pim(x), sam(y) \\ \hline \end{array} \right\rangle$$

The analysis of *Pim likes SAM_F* is similar, we take the same S-tree, for the non-focused subject we substitute the tree for *Pim* as before (Example 2) and for the focused object we substitute the tree for *Sam* as:

---

[7] Note, that the language of InqB is used, where $\exists x.\phi$ leads to a set of possibilities.

Example 4. Focused object

$$\mathrm{NP}^{l=y,whmax=\boxed{10},foc=+}_{whmin=\boxed{9}}$$
$$\Big|$$
$$\mathrm{Sam}$$
$$\left\langle \begin{array}{|l|} \hline l_3 : \exists y\boxed{12} \\ \boxed{10} \geq l_3, \boxed{12} \geq \boxed{9} \\ \hline l_3 : sam(y) \\ \hline \end{array} \right\rangle$$

The two substitutions here lead to the semantic representations before and after plugging:

$$\left\langle \begin{array}{|l|} \hline l_0 :?\boxed{4},\, l_1 : like(x,y),\, l_2 : pim(x),\, l_3 : \exists y\boxed{12} \\ \boxed{4} \geq \boxed{3}, \boxed{3} \geq l_1, \boxed{4} \geq l_3, \boxed{12} \geq \boxed{3} \\ \hline l_1 : like(x,y),\, l_2 : pim(x),\, l_3 : sam(y) \\ \hline \end{array} \right\rangle$$

$$\left\langle \begin{array}{|l|} \hline ?\exists y.like(x,y), pim(x) \\ \hline like(x,y), pim(x), sam(y) \\ \hline \end{array} \right\rangle$$

Similarly to the previous example, the resulting representation corresponds to the question *Whom does Pim like?* as the INQC and to the proposition *Pim likes Sam* as the INFC.

2.2   Multiple Focus and Focus in Questions

After showing the basic cases, let us now turn to more complex examples such as multiple focus. In sentences containing a transitive verb, not only single focusing is possible, but also both arguments can be focused at the same time: $PIM_F likes SAM_F$. The INFC of this sentence is again the proposition *Pim likes Sam*, while the INQC is the multiple wh-question *Who likes whom?* The analysis derives the correct division, by substituting the NP-trees of the focused arguments (see Examples 3 and 4) into the S-tree of *likes* (see Example 2). The substitutions of the focused subject and object lead to the semantic representation:

$$\left\langle \begin{array}{|l|} \hline l_0 :?\boxed{4},\, l_1 : like(x,y),\, l_2 : \exists x\boxed{11},\, l_3 : \exists y\boxed{12} \\ \boxed{4} \geq \boxed{3}, \boxed{3} \geq l_1, \boxed{4} \geq l_2,\, \boxed{11} \geq \boxed{3}, \boxed{4} \geq l_3, \boxed{12} \geq \boxed{3} \\ \hline l_1 : like(x,y),\, l_2 : pim(x),\, l_3 : sam(y) \\ \hline \end{array} \right\rangle$$

Here, two different pluggings are possible: (i) $\boxed{4} \mapsto l_2, \boxed{11} \mapsto l_3, \boxed{12} \mapsto l_1$ and (ii) $\boxed{4} \mapsto l_3, \boxed{12} \mapsto l_2, \boxed{11} \mapsto l_1$, yielding two semantic representations, where the representations of the INQC are slightly different: at plugging (i) $?\exists x\exists y.like(x,y)$ and at (ii) $?\exists y\exists x.like(x,y)$. These two representations are logically equivalent, both corresponding to the question *Who likes whom?*

The analysis proposed above also gives a straightforward derivation of a special construction, when an argument is focused within a wh-question as, e.g. *Who likes SAM$_F$?* In the derivation of *Who likes SAM$_F$?* we take the S-tree of *likes* (Example 5) and substitute the elementary trees of the wh-phrase *who* (see Example 1) and the focused object *Sam* (see Example 4):

Example 5.

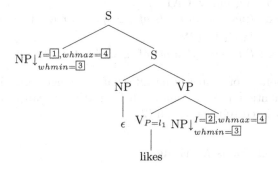

After all substitutions are carried out and all pluggings are resolved we get the intended representation of *Who likes SAM$_F$?* as:

$$\left\langle \begin{array}{|l|} \hline ?\exists x \exists y.like(x,y) \\ \hline ?\exists x.like(x,y) \wedge sam(y) \\ \hline \end{array} \right\rangle$$

3   Focused NPs with Determiners and Adjectives

In Sect. 2 different focus structures were shown, however, all examples contained proper names. In this section I propose an extension of the analysis to compound NPs involving determiners and adjectives.

(2)   a. [Two young BOYS]^F blew out the fire.
          answering: *Who blew out the fire?*

      b. Pim saw [a grumpy CAT]^F.
          answering: *What did Pim see?*

      c. Pim saw a [GRUMPY]^F cat.
          answering: *What (kind of) cat did Pim see?*

These examples raise various new issues for the analysis. First of all we must account for focus marking [8,17] within an NP, and secondly we must derive compositionally the correct issue behind it, depending on the question-contribution of the NP with focus marking. As a starting point we derive the semantic representation of the examples in (2), where pitch accent on the noun head leads to focus marking of the whole NP, while pitch accent on the adjective does not focus mark the whole functional projection. Note, however, that the same placement of the pitch accent can lead to different interpretations, used in different contexts.

For a more comprehensive analysis, also including examples in (3) below, we have to deal with the information structure of a sentence and discourse coherence: what is "given/retrievable" and "non-given/not-retrievable" information.

(3)   a. Pim saw a grumpy [CAT]^F.
          context: *Pim saw all kinds of grumpy animals. What did he see?*
        b. Pim saw [a GRUMPY cat]^F.
          context: *Pim saw all kinds of cats. What did he see?*

Such a component of representing information structure, givenness and its effect on the semantic representation is left for further research. The analysis of this paper is restricted to the cases in (2).

3.1   NP Internal Focus Marking

In this section I will discuss the issue how to analyze the relation between the placement of the pitch accent and the marking of the focused constituent in F-LTAG. For this we need to introduce two features FOC and PITCH that stand for focus marking and the placement of the pitch accent respectively. The value of the pitch accent is passed to the FOC feature that appears on higher nodes in the elementary tree of the noun phrase. In Sect. 2, the proposal of the analysis of narrow focus constructions was introduced, deriving a two-fold semantics of utterances representing the INQC (underlying issue) and the INFC (information content). Focus-marked (FOC = +) constituents contribute a special semantics to the INQC of the sentence meaning, yielding the corresponding wh-question. The elementary tree of a focus-marked constituent comes with a different semantic representation as their non-focused counterpart. Focus marking is signaled within the feature structure of the given elementary tree by the feature FOC with possible values + and − for focused and non-focused occurrences. Following Selkirk's [17] Focus Projection principle, the same accenting can receive different focus marking, hence different focus interpretations. Selkirk's focus marking principles suggest, that pitch accent on the object noun can lead to a narrow focus interpretation or to a broad (VP) focus interpretation.

(4)   a. Pim saw [a CAT]^F.   b. Pim [saw a CAT]^F.

In both sentences the NP-tree of the object is built from the tree of the common noun and the tree of the determiner. In the tree of the noun the N-node has the PITCH feature signaling the placement of the pitch accent on the common noun. The value of the pitch accent is then passed to the FOC feature that appears on several nodes of the elementary tree of the NP (◇ marking the node for the lexical anchor).

$$\text{NP}^{foc=\boxed{1}}_{foc=\boxed{1}}$$
$$|$$
$$\text{N}_\diamond{}^{foc=\boxed{1}}_{foc=\boxed{1},pitch=\boxed{1}}$$

Pitch accent on the noun is represented by $pitch = +$ on the N-node, that focus-marks the N-head and the whole NP by passing up its value.

Example 6. NP internal focus marking

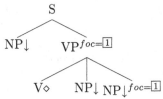

After adjunction of the determiner (if no more adjunction's take place), the top and bottom features unify, and thus the meta-variables are identified: $\boxed{1} = \boxed{2}$ and $\boxed{1} = +$. As a result, the whole NP is focus-marked by $foc = +$. As for the broad focus interpretation, the $+$ value of the FOC feature can be optionally passed up from the rightmost NP argument to the higher VP node marking the possible focus projection. This is not possible from the subject position (or from the not right-most argument), the focused NP in that position gets narrow focus interpretation.

$$S$$
$$\overbrace{\qquad\qquad}$$
$$\text{NP}{\downarrow} \qquad \text{VP}^{foc=\boxed{1}}$$
$$\overbrace{\qquad\qquad}$$
$$\text{V}_\diamond \quad \text{NP}{\downarrow} \ \text{NP}{\downarrow}^{foc=\boxed{1}}$$

Example 6 shows how the value of the FOC feature is passed to the maximal projection of the noun phrase, marking the whole NP as the focus of the sentence. This raises the issue how we can deal with NPs containing adjectives like *a grumpy cat* where either the noun or the adjective gets the pitch accent. In case the noun is accented – *a grumpy CAT* –, it passes the focus marking to its maximal projection, and the whole noun phrase will be in focus. In case the adjective is accented – *a GRUMPY cat* – the default interpretation is where only the adjective is focus marked, and not the whole NP.

The syntax of the NP *a grumpy cat* is illustrated below in Example 7. Three different focus markings are derived: (a) without pitch accent, (b) accent on the noun head: *a grumpy CAT*, and (c) accent on the adjective: *a GRUMPY cat.*

Example 7. Derivation of a grumpy cat

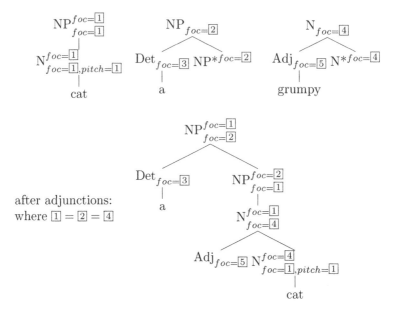

after adjunctions:
where $\boxed{1} = \boxed{2} = \boxed{4}$

Pitch accent on the noun head and non-accented determiner and adjective leads to focus marking on the whole NP, while non-accented noun-head with non-accented determiner and accented or non-accented adjective give $foc = -$ on the maximal projection.

Example 8. Focus marking in a grumpy CAT versus a GRUMPY cat

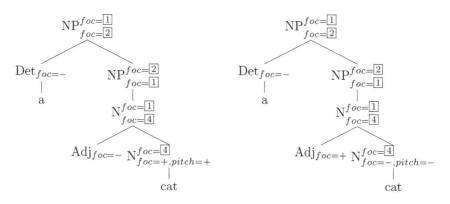

3.2   F-LTAG Semantics of Focused NPs

Within the NP each part contributes something to the INQC and the INFC of the whole. Example 9 illustrates the derivation of the semantic representation of an indefinite NP without focusing. Using two-dimensional semantic representations this example derives the semantic contribution without focusing, hence in all semantic contributions INQC = INFC. For an easier read of the examples, only the most relevant features are displayed. Not all of the FOC features are displayed here, they are according to the examples in Sect. 3.1.

Example 9. Indefinite NP *a grumpy cat* without focus

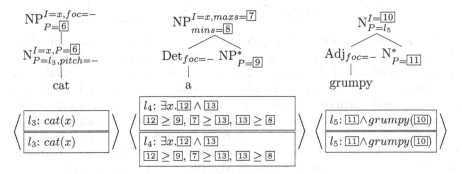

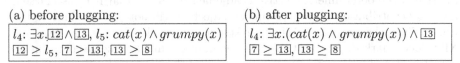

The tree of the determiner is adjoined at the NP-node of the tree of the noun, while the tree of the adjective is adjoined at the N-node of the tree of the noun. After the adjunctions, the following equations hold: $\boxed{9} = \boxed{6}$, $\boxed{10} = x$, $\boxed{11} = l_3$ and $\boxed{6} = l_5$. The resulting representation of the INQC-contribution of the NP *a grumpy cat* before and after plugging ($\boxed{12} \mapsto l_5$) are the following.

(a) before plugging:

l_4: $\exists x.\boxed{12} \wedge \boxed{13}$, l_5: $cat(x) \wedge grumpy(x)$
$\boxed{12} \geq l_5$, $\boxed{7} \geq \boxed{13}$, $\boxed{13} \geq \boxed{8}$

(b) after plugging:

l_4: $\exists x.(cat(x) \wedge grumpy(x)) \wedge \boxed{13}$
$\boxed{7} \geq \boxed{13}$, $\boxed{13} \geq \boxed{8}$

In case, we have a pitch accent on the N-head, the maximal projection is focus marked, that leads to a different semantic representation. In such cases, the INQC-contribution of the NP is $\exists x.\boxed{5}$ (similarly as shown in Sect. 2.1). However, by simply combining the semantic representations in Example 10 the achievement of the intended semantic representation for the maximal projection is problematic.

Example 10.

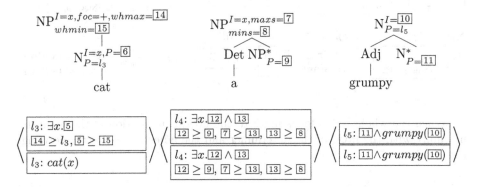

Carrying out the adjunctions and the composition of the semantic contributions, the INFC-contribution is derived correctly as before, while for the representation of the INQC it gives the following, unwanted result.

$$
\text{INQC}_{NP}: \quad \boxed{\begin{array}{l} l_4: \exists x. \exists x. \boxed{5} \wedge \boxed{13},\ l_5: \boxed{11} \wedge grumpy(x) \\ \boxed{12} \geq l_5,\ \boxed{7} \geq \boxed{13},\ \boxed{13} \geq \boxed{8} \end{array}}
$$

As the example sentences in (2) show, in case the whole NP is focus marked, the underlying wh-question is the one where the NP is replaced by the corresponding wh-phrase. This suggests, that in such cases the INQC-contribution of the determiner and the adjunct should be discarded, not adding information to the INQC-contribution of the whole NP. To capture this, we need to express the following generalization: (a) in case the determiner/adjective is itself not marked for focusing (*foc=−*) and adjoined to an NP-tree where the root node is marked for focusing (*foc=+*), then the INQC-contribution of the determiner/adjunct is discarded; (b) in case the determiner/adjective is not focus-marked (*foc=−*) and adjoined to an NP-tree where the root node is neither marked for focusing (*foc=−*), then the INQC-contribution of the determiner/adjective is adding information to the whole.

As before, the non-focused parts contribute the same information to the theme and the theme of the whole, thus the semantic representation of the non focused determiner and adjective is as shown in Example 9: INQC=INFC. When the tree of the determiner/adjective is adjoined to an NP that is focus-marked, the INQC-contribution of the determiner/adjective will not add anything to the whole. Since the appearance of this restriction depends on whether the whole NP is focus marked (*foc=+* at the root node), discarding the theme contribution must be driven by the semantic representation of the NP-tree. I suggest, that the INQC-contribution of a focused NP tree is marked for being "complete" (C!), such that it blocks unification with the theme-contribution of the adjoining auxiliary trees (the trees of the determiner and the adjective).

Example 11. Blocking unification of theme contributions

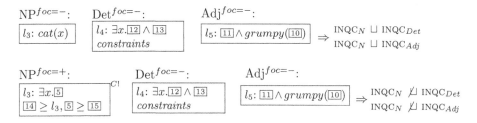

When the whole NP is focus marked, the INQC-contribution of the noun do not unify with the INQC of the determiner and the adjective, correctly deriving the division as:

$$\left\langle \quad \boxed{\begin{array}{l} l_3: \exists x.\boxed{5} \\ \boxed{14} \geq l_3, \boxed{5} \geq \boxed{15} \\ \hline l_4: \exists x.cat(x) \wedge grumpy(x) \wedge \boxed{13} \\ \boxed{7} \geq \boxed{13}, \boxed{13} \geq \boxed{8} \end{array}} \quad \right\rangle$$

As shown is example (2c) before, in the NP *a grumpy cat* we can also use pitch accent on the adjective, marking it as focus: *a* GRUMPY^F *cat*. In such cases only the adjective is focused, and the focus marking feature do not percolate up to the maximal projection. The contributing trees and their semantic representations are as in Example 9, except for the adjective, that is now focus marked:

Example 12. Focused adjective

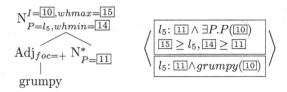

Here, no blocking applies, since the root node of the noun-tree is not focus marked ($foc = -$).

$NP^{foc=-}$:

$$\boxed{l_3: cat(x)}$$

$Det^{foc=-}$:

$$\boxed{\begin{array}{l} l_4: \exists x.\boxed{12} \wedge \boxed{13} \\ \boxed{12} \geq \boxed{9}, \boxed{7} \geq \boxed{13}, \boxed{13} \geq \boxed{8} \end{array}}$$

$Adj^{foc=+}$:

$$\boxed{\begin{array}{l} l_5: \boxed{11} \wedge \exists P.P(\boxed{10}) \\ \boxed{15} \geq l_5, \boxed{14} \geq \boxed{11} \end{array}}$$

Carrying out the adjunctions leads to the unifications: $\boxed{6} = \boxed{9} = l_5, \boxed{10} = x, \boxed{11} = l_3$ and finally – after plugging ($\boxed{12} \mapsto l_5$) – to the semantic representation of the noun phrase as expected. The expression $\exists P.P(x)$ standing for the possibilities of x is P, x is P' etc. depending on a contextually given set of predicates.

$$\boxed{\begin{array}{l} l_4: \exists x.cat(x) \wedge \exists P.P(x) \wedge \boxed{13} \\ \boxed{7} \geq \boxed{13}, \boxed{13} \geq \boxed{8} \end{array}}$$

3.3   Further Research: Focus and Quantifier Scope

In Sect. 1.2 a special scope window was introduced for focused constituents and questions, given by the new features WHMAX and WHMIN. These features follow the idea of MAXS and MINS from Kallmeyer & Romero [11]. Differentiating the two scope windows opens a new issue for direct further research: the relation between focus and quantifier scope. In case we have both a quantificational NP and a focused constituent in the sentence, the distinction of the two scope windows gets relevant. It offers a way to account for the effects of the concurrence of focused and quantified NPs, and well as quantified NPs in focus.

First, I illustrate the F-LTAG derivation of different scope orders as introduced by Kallmeyer & Romero [11]. Consider the sentence *A dog chased every cat*, that has two interpretations, regarding which quantifier has wider scope. As already shown in Sect. 1.1, the mechanism derives an underspecified semantic representation for this sentence, where two pluggings are possible, that lead to the two different readings.

Example 13. Scope ambiguity

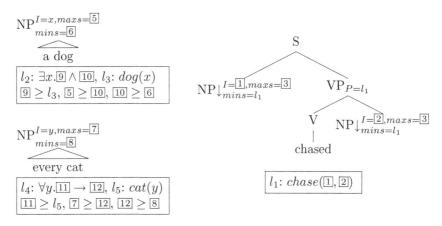

After substituting the two NP trees the semantic representations are combined, features get unified and meta-variables get their values: $\boxed{1} = x$, $\boxed{2} = y$, $\boxed{3} = \boxed{5} = \boxed{7}$, $l_1 = \boxed{6} = \boxed{8}$, resulting in the following semantic representation of the sentence:

$$l_1: chase(x,y), l_2: \exists x.\boxed{9} \wedge \boxed{10}, l_3: dog(x), l_4: \forall y.\boxed{11} \rightarrow \boxed{12}, l_5: cat(y)$$
$$\boxed{9} \geq l_3, \boxed{3} \geq \boxed{10}, \boxed{10} \geq l_1, \boxed{11} \geq l_5, \boxed{3} \geq \boxed{12}, \boxed{12} \geq l_1$$

The above semantic representation is still underspecified, hence the scope order of the quantifiers is still undefined. Following the given scope constraints, there are two different pluggings possible here: (i) $\boxed{9} \mapsto l_3$, $\boxed{11} \mapsto l_5$, $\boxed{12} \mapsto l_2$, $\boxed{10} \mapsto l_1$ resulting in $\forall y.cat(y) \rightarrow \exists x.dog(x) \wedge chase(x,y)$; and (ii) $\boxed{9} \mapsto l_3$, $\boxed{11} \mapsto l_5$, $\boxed{10} \mapsto l_4$, $\boxed{12} \mapsto l_1$ resulting in $\exists x.dog(x) \wedge \forall y.cat(y) \rightarrow chase(x,y)$.

In the F-LTAG analysis of focusing, I introduced the scope window for focus and questions by the features WHMAX/WHMIN inspired by the MAXS/MINS features from Kallmeyer & Romero [11]. The distinction of two different scope windows allows us to correctly derive the INQC of the sentence containing quantified NPs or other scope taking constituents, e.g., in *A dog chased every cat*.

Example 14. Different scope windows

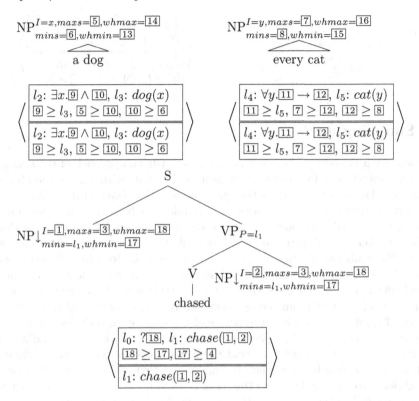

After substitution of the NP-trees and the combination/unification of the semantic representations, the following representation of the INQC is derived:

$$l_0: ?\boxed{18},\ l_1: chase(x,y),\ l_2: \exists x.\boxed{9} \wedge \boxed{10},\ l_3: dog(x),\ l_4: \forall y.\boxed{11} \rightarrow \boxed{12},\ l_5: cat(y)$$
$$\boxed{18} \geq \boxed{17}, \boxed{17} \geq l_1, \boxed{9} \geq l_3, \boxed{3} \geq \boxed{10}, \boxed{10} \geq l_1, \boxed{11} \geq l_5, \boxed{3} \geq \boxed{12}, \boxed{12} \geq l_1$$

Here, different pluggings are possible, deriving possible INQCs of the sentence *A dog chased every cat*. The scope constraints allow the pluggings: (i) $\boxed{18} \mapsto l_2$, $\boxed{10} \mapsto l_4$, $\boxed{12} \mapsto l_1$, $\boxed{9} \mapsto l_3$, $\boxed{11} \mapsto l_5$ and (ii) $\boxed{18} \mapsto l_4$, $\boxed{10} \mapsto l_1$, $\boxed{12} \mapsto l_2$, $\boxed{9} \mapsto l_3$, $\boxed{11} \mapsto l_5$ deriving the possible INQCs as $?\exists x.dog(x) \wedge \forall y.cat(y) \rightarrow chase(x,y)$ and $?\forall y.cat(y) \rightarrow \exists x.dog(x) \wedge chase(x,y)$ respectively.

By differentiating the two scope windows, we can also correctly derive the semantic representation of a sentence in which one of the quantified NP is in focus. Take, for example, the sentence *[A DOG]^F chased every cat* where the theme or underlying question is *Who chased every cat?* Having two different scope windows we can account for the fact, that in the underlying question no inverse scope is possible. The wh-phrase takes scope, namely the widest scope, but this is due to a different scope window as the scope taking of quantifiers. The wh-phrase will always take the widest scope, not allowing of an interpretation with inverse scope order.

Example 15. Quantified NP in focus

$$\text{NP}^{I=x,maxs=\boxed{5},whmax=\boxed{14}}_{mins=\boxed{6},whmin=\boxed{13}}$$

$\overbrace{\text{a dog}}$

$$\left\langle \begin{array}{l} \boxed{l_2: \exists x.\boxed{19}} \\ \boxed{\boxed{14} \geq l_2,\ \boxed{19} \geq \boxed{13}} \\ \boxed{l_2: \exists x.\boxed{9} \wedge \boxed{10},\ l_3: dog(x)} \\ \boxed{\boxed{9} \geq l_3,\ \boxed{5} \geq \boxed{10},\ \boxed{10} \geq \boxed{6}} \end{array} \right\rangle$$

4   Summing up

The approach introduced here is a proposal towards an approach of the syntax-semantics interface of focus constructions using F-LTAG with a unification based semantics. The analysis derives the question-assertion (INQC/INFC) division of different (narrow) focus constructions, extended to NPs with a richer inner structure. The analysis of focused NPs in the current paper follows the core ideas of the F-LTAG analysis proposed by Balogh [3]. This analysis provides an extension to the syntax-semantics interface of Kallmeyer & Romero [11] and determines the semantic representations of narrow focus constructions as assumed in Balogh [2] on the basis of the syntactic structures of the sentences in a straightforward, intuitive and compositional way. The advantage of this analysis is that different accenting/focus structure of the same word order bear the same information content (INFC), while the different focus structures lead to different inherent issues (INQC) indicating that these sentences are felicitous in different contexts. Consequently, they relate to four different wh-questions, which offers a straightforward way to deal with the basic cases of question-answer congruence.

This paper further broadened the coverage of the analysis by extending it to NPs with determiners and adjectives and to closely related issues like focus marking, focus projection and the relation with quantifier scope. The F-LTAG analysis of the relation of accent placement and focus is proposed, which is required to deal with, among others, NP internal focus marking. Another issue addressed here is the investigation of the relation of focusing and quantifier scope. The semantic component of LTAG as introduced by Kallmeyer & Romero [11] offers an elegant analysis of scope ambiguities. In their analysis scope windows are introduced for quantificational NPs by the features MAXS and MINS signalling the maximal and minimal scope sides. To offer a uniform analysis of the similarities and differences of these scope sides, this paper introduces the features WHMAX and WHMIN as the scope window for focus and questions. The distinction of the two different scope windows gives the possibility to deal with the relation of focusing and quantifier scope, which is left for subsequent work.

References

1. Babko-Malaya, O.: LTAG semantics of focus. In: Han, C.-H., Sarkar, A. (eds.) Proceedings of the TAG+7: Seventh International Workshop on Tree Adjoining Grammar and Related Formalisms, Vancouver, BC, Canada (2004)

2. Balogh, K.: Theme with variations. A context-based analysis of focus. Ph.D. thesis, ILLC, University of Amsterdam, Amsterdam (2009)
3. Balogh, K.: Representing focus in LTAG. In: Han, C.-H., Satta, G. (eds.) Proceedings of the 11th International Workshop on Tree Adjoining Grammars and Related Formalisms, Inria, Paris (2012)
4. Bos, J.: Predicate logic unplugged. In: Dekker, P., Stokhof, M. (eds.) Proceedings of the Tenth Amsterdam Colloquium. University of Amsterdam (1996)
5. Ciardelli, I., Groenendijk, J., Roelofsen, F.: Inquisitive semantics. Lecture notes for a graduate course at NASSLLI, June 18–22, 2012, Austin, USA (2012)
6. Groenendijk, Jeroen: Inquisitive semantics: two possibilities for disjunction. In: Bosch, Peter, Gabelaia, David, Lang, Jérôme (eds.) TbiLLC 2007. LNCS, vol. 5422, pp. 80–94. Springer, Heidelberg (2009)
7. Groenendijk, J., Roelofsen, F.: Inquisitive semantics and pragmatics. In: Larrazabal, J.M., Zubeldia, L. (eds.) SPR 2009. Proceedings of the ILCLI International Workshop on Semantics, Pragmatics and Rhetoric, Universidad del País Vasco, Donostia, Spain (2009)
8. Jackendoff, R.S.: Semantic Interpretation in Generative Grammar. MIT Press, Cambridge (1972)
9. Joshi, A.K., Schabes, Y.: Tree-adjoining grammars. In: Rozenberg, G., Salomaa, A. (eds.) Handbook of Formal Languages, pp. 69–123. Springer, Heidelberg (1997)
10. Kallmeyer, L., Joshi, A.K.: Factoring predicate argument and scope semantics: underspecified semantics with LTAG. Res. Lang. Comput. 1(1–2), 3–58 (2003)
11. Kallmeyer, L., Romero, M.: Scope and situation binding in LTAG using semantic unification. Res. Lang. Comput. 6(1), 3–52 (2008)
12. Krifka, M.: The semantics of questions and the focusation of answers. In: Chungmin, L., Gordon, M., Büring, D. (eds.) Topic and Focus: A Cross-Linguistic Perspective. Kluwer Academic Publishers, Dordrecht (2004)
13. Mascarenhas, S.: Inquisitive semantics and logic. Master thesis, University of Amsterdam (2009)
14. Romero, M., Kallmeyer, L., Babko-Malaya, O.: LTAG semantics for questions. In: Han, C.-H., Sarkar, A. (eds.) Proceedings of TAG+7: Seventh International Workshop on Tree Adjoining Grammar and Related Formalisms, Vancouver, BC, Canada (2004)
15. Rooth, M.: Association with focus. Ph.D. thesis, University of Massachusetts, Amherst (1985)
16. Rooth, M.: A theory of focus interpretation. Nat. Lang. Seman. 1(1), 75–116 (1992)
17. Selkirk, E.: Sentence prosody: intonation, stress, and phrasing. In: Glodsmith, J.A. (ed.) The Handbook of Phonological Theory. Blackwell Publishing, Cambridge (1996)
18. Vijay-Shanker, K., Joshi, A.K.: Feature structure based tree adjoining grammars. In: Proceedings of the COLING, pp. 714–719 (1988)

Dialect Dictionaries in the Georgian Dialect Corpus

Marina Beridze[✉], Liana Lortkipanidze, and David Nadaraia

Arnold Chikobava Institute of Linguistics, Tbilisi, Georgia
marine.beridze@gmail.com, l_lordkipanidze@yahoo.com,
dnad@itex.ge

Abstract. The Georgian Dialect Corpus – GDC (http://mygeorgia.ge/gdc) serves as a source to document and study the regional varieties of the Georgian language. The first steps in terms of the Georgian dialect data collection were taken by Prof. Iost Gippert within his research projects [TITUS, ARMAZI].

The Corpus design strategy on one hand is based on an international corpus linguistics practice and on the other hand on the traditions of the Georgian dialectology and dialectography. The Georgian linguistic and cultural characteristics are being considered in the Corpus design.

The dialect dictionaries are incorporated in the corpus for two reasons: (a) to achieve a high level of representativeness and (b) to use the POS markers of the dictionary lemmas for the morphological annotation of the Corpus. The present paper deals with the practical tasks how these dictionaries complement the dialect lexical fund and how the part of speech markers of the dictionaries are applied in the process of morphological annotation.

1   Introduction

The Kartvelian language family consists of three Georgian languages (Georgian, Zan and Svan) and its numerous dialects. The classification of the Georgian dialects is based on ethnic-geographic and the linguistic principles. The dialect names coincide the names of the region it is spread. According to various classifications there are 16–17 Georgian dialects overall, out of which several dialects are spread outside Georgia, they are:

- Fereydanian – spread in Iran, near Isfahan, in particular, in Fereydunshahr and about 10 villages nearby. The dialect is spoken by 300 000 Georgians – the descendants of internally displaced Georgians to Iran 400 years ago;
- Ingilo – Spoken by the Georgian population in Hereti, originally belonged to Georgia, now is Azerbaijan. The population are both Christian (Kakhetian region) and Muslim (Zaqatala) Georgians that speak the Georgian language, in particular, Ingilo dialect.
- The Georgian language spoken by Georgians in Turkey that covers both the Georgian dialects that are spread in originally Georgian regions that now belongs to Turkey (Taoian, Klarj and Imerkhevian), as well as, the dialects of internally displaced Georgians, particularly, the language spoken by Adjarian immigrants.

© Springer-Verlag Berlin Heidelberg 2015
M. Aher et al. (Eds.): TbiLLC 2013, LNCS 8984, pp. 82–96, 2015.
DOI: 10.1007/978-3-662-46906-4_6

The variety of the Georgian dialect represents the development of the Georgian language itself. The diversity is represented by the complex phonetic, grammatical and lexical system. The main characteristics of the literary/standard Georgian and between the dialects are:

The Sound composition that varies from one dialect to another, and in general, there are over 20 sounds in dialect system that are different from the standard/literary Georgian.

The variation of grammatical features (different morphological inventory, different usage of the common morphological inventory (affixes)), different grammatical categories: duality of number (in Khevsurian dialect); the fourth group of the Georgian verb (Imeretian Dialect) there are three overall in standard Georgian etc.

Morphological variants as a result of complex phonetic variations (such as case markers, verb stem markers, root morphemes etc.)

Excessive number of grammatical homonyms in dialects

Distinct syntax features (e.g. Ergative case in intransitive verbs, indirect structures etc.)

Distinct lexical funds

New word senses in common lexical fund, polysemy

Distinct collocations

New features due to foreign language influence etc. (These issues and related examples are widely discussed in [1].

The above mentioned features enable us to make further classifications in closely related dialects. For instance, some researchers group mountainous (Mtiuletian-Gudamakrian, Khevsurian, Pshavian, Tush, Mokhevian) and South-Western dialects (Samtskhetian-Javakhetian, Imerkhevian, Klarj, Taoian, Adjarian) together. These dialects share some common features, but at the same time there is significant difference between them.

The Georgian Dialect Corpus is being created within the framework of the project – the Linguistic Portrait of Georgia. The corpus can be queried at: http://mygeorgia.ge/gdc/.

The size of the GDC:

- Word: 1 453 261
- Lemma: 301 203,
- Context: 199861
- Text: 3017
- The texts are recorded from 2703 informants in 812 villages in Georgia, Iran and Azerbaijan.

The oldest data is recorded in the beginning of the XX century and the recent text data in 2012. The working team of the GDC is in charge of the whole process, the data collection, including field activities and incorporating the obtained data into the corpus. It is worth mentioning that the team takes into consideration of the representativeness during the data collection process.

Currently, the corpus incorporates 17 subsystems of the Georgian language, as well as the samples of Laz dialects of Zan Language. The words and word phrases can be queried via the corpus interface; the search pattern also provides access to the full texts of the corpus.

We are adding text data to the Corpus and working on the morphological annotation, thus, the corpus can be queried in terms of its meta-textual (not linguistic) features such as:

- Language and dialect
- The place of recording
- The speaker (informant)
- Thematic and chronological features of the texts
- Text type (narrative, poetry, speech).

We plan to add other (not linguistic) query types to the corpus, such as:

- The title of the text
- The recorder of the text
- The publication (if the text is in printed/paper format)
- Information about the informant, his/her family members (if there is a case of mixed marriage or co-occurrence other dialect)
- Information about the informants or his/her family member immigration (if relevant)
- Time and type of immigration (mass or individual); settlement type (contact or non-contact, compact or non-compact) etc.

After the morphological annotation is completed, the corpus can be queried by parts of speech and grammatical categories:

As mentioned above, currently, we work in two directions, in particular:

- Adding new text data into the corpus
- Developing morphological annotation of the corpus.

We made a decision to incorporate the dialect dictionaries in the corpus for two reasons: first, to supplement the lexical data of the corpus by adding dictionary entries and dictionary examples, and secondly, to use the part of speech markers of the dictionary lemmas in the process of morphological annotation of the corpus.

2   The Representativeness in the GDC and the Dialect Dictionaries

The representativeness is one of the main challenges and should be taken into consideration in the design of a corpus. When discussing the related works with this regard, it is worth to mention Biber and his works [2], but not all corpus linguists implement his plans in their corpus, according to G. Leech "A seminal article by Biber (1993) has frequently been cited, but no attempt (to my knowledge) has been made to implement Biber's plan for building a representative corpus" [3].

It is obvious that there are no universal rules for representativeness, but they vary greatly from one type of corpus to another, e.g. there are different requirements for representativeness in general and specialized corpora [4]. For instance, National corpora focus on more genre and register diversities aiming at creating micro-model of a given language.

The dialect corpus, in general, can be classified as a specialized corpus and it deals with the representativeness differently [5].

Our approach for dialect data collection and documentation aims to create a valuable source for scientific research, as well as to represent the language model [6].

The concept of the representativeness in the GDC is based on the hitsorical and cultural reality of Georgia and thus, defining its role and place in national science and cultural paradigm. The main challenges in this direction are to fully represent the following:

- Lexical data
- Linguistic means
- Dialect and inter-dialect strata
- Age, gender, social varieties
- Specialized, folklore variations
- Variations due to immigrations
- Peculiarities due to chronological factors
- Small marginal group speeches (Georgian Hebrews).

The content of the corpus is widely discussed in several other publications [7, 8], however we will briefly refer it in this paper. The corpus data covers:

- The dialect texts published since the 1920s
- The audio data recorded since the 1960s
- The video and audio data recorded since the 1990s
- The dialect component of ethnographic encyclopedic data collected in 1935, and
- Non textual data – dictionaries, in particular, dictionary examples.

All the corpus related works, such as data collection and their further linguistic processing is being performed by the working team of the Georgian Dialect Corpus.

The meta-information in the corpus can be queried in whole corpus, as well as in individual sub corpora. The corpus interface allows limiting the search results, e.g. it can query in separate thematic, type or geographic features.

The GDC represents all dialect data, but it is obvious that not all data will be proportionally represented in the corpus. Such as, the language of Georgian Hebrews is only in 12 fascicles recorded in 1937 (words: 27481, word-forms: 8881). Today, a small number of this segment is fully assimilated, and we were not able to record the speech of Georgian Hebrews in Israel at this stage, but we have conducted several fruitful expeditions in Iran, Azerbaijan and Turkey, thus, the dialects represented in these regions are widely covered in the corpus.

It is worth mentioning concerning the genre and thematic variation of the text data of the corpus, we focus on spontaneous speech in the process of recording by manipulating different topics; the lexicographic questionnaires and encyclopedic data represent the different fields, and as mentioned above, we included dialect dictionaries in the corpus.

The dialect dictionary examples are incorporated in the corpus in such a way that a dictionary entry serves as a keyword in the corpus. We have made this decision for several reasons; firstly, it is based on the Georgian dialect tradition, certain number of data of collective expeditions are represented in studies and in dictionary examples, and secondly, the most of these dialect dictionaries were compiled by the researchers who were speakers of these dialects and belonged to this particular cultural, social and industrial area. Thus, the information preserved in these dictionaries is very valuable and supplements the lexical fund of the Georgian dialects.

3   The Dictionaries and the Problem Related to Morphological Annotation of the Corpus

The morphological analysis concept for the GDC is based on the principles of literary (standard) language analysis. Annotation is carried out using the material of the separate dialects in order to avoid grammatical homonymy among the dialects.

The Georgian language is of complex, inflectional and agglutinative nature. Vast amount of flexions categories of verbs, nouns, adjectives and numerals should be described to build up the computer model of Georgian morphology. For example, we can meet 66 (as for dialects, even more) members in the flexions paradigm of only one verb lexeme, and in the paradigm of declension of the noun, given all possible prepositions and particles, the number of forms can rise up to 200.

We apply morphological analysis based on the computational lexicon to ensure its high level. This lexicon is structured using the lists of lemmas and affixes which are interrelated through the identifiers, corresponding to the patterns of representation of the morphotactics. Modeling the morphotactical interrelations of the lemmas and affixes in the system is carried out with help of the Georgian language morphological generator algorithm which we have already described earlier.

We have been working on the Georgian language morphological analyzer since 2003.

The Georgian automatic explanatory-combinatorial dictionary is compiled, representing definition, morphological, syntactic and semantic fields of words. The morphological computational lexicon (**GeoTrans**), enclosing about 100 000 basic (modern Georgian literary) language lexemes is incorporated in the program application of this dictionary. Functioning of this application depends on the morphological generator, which in its turn depends on morphotactics data of each unit in the computational lexicon. The morphological generator is designed to generate a separate lexeme as well as its paradigm. For the unknown word forms not described in the lexicon, the system provides one or some potential patterns of word formation.

The computational lexicon enables the dictionaries of the basic language and of its dialects to be created and supplemented/enriched with new lexemes within it. In fact, this system represents a formal model of accumulating knowledge of language. It is invariant with regard to the language and it enables adding a new language without changes in the interface and program code. It becomes possible to carry out annotation of the Georgian dialect corpus semi-automatically, using **GeoTransTools** (program instruments of the morphological analyzer), realized through the system.

In our earlier works we have thoroughly discussed the concept of the morphological analyzer of the Georgian literary language [9, 10]. In this article we are representing some general schemes and consider some issues related to creating the dialect module of the analyzer.

4 Descriptions of the Database Tables of the Computational Lexicon

The architecture of the computational lexicons of the morphological analyzer rests upon the relational databases. Figure 1 represents the interrelations between them.

The basic language computation lexicon is maintained in the tables of the relational databases: (1) The table of the lemmas from the basic language dictionary - **Baz_LemVoc**, (2) The database table of the affixes of the lexemes formation – **BazAfix** and (3) The database table of the identifiers of the word formation rules of the basic language – **Baz_MoFlID**.

Now we are going to describe each table of the relational databases of the computational lexicon separately:

(1) **Baz_LemVoc** – All lemmas from the basic language computational lexicon are maintained in the table of lemmas of the basic language dictionary and each lexicon entry contains lemma characteristics (see Fig. 1), as follows:

N – lemma identifier;
Word – lemma;
Word_V – variation of a lemma;

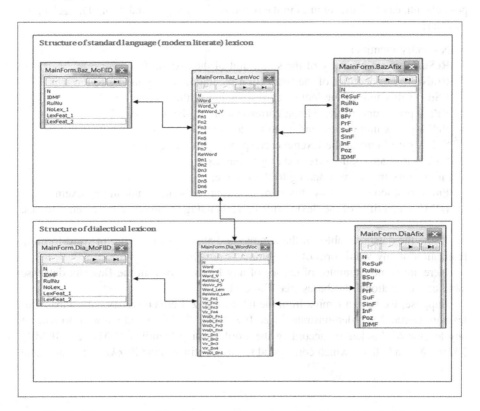

Fig. 1. The structure of the databases of the computational morphological lexicon

(The future form of a verb that at the same time is a lemma can be often represented by two parallel lexemes – with or without the preverb. To compactly record such a situation, a marker of the lemma variation is introduced _ **Word_V**).

ReWord_V – inversive entry of the lemma variation (e.g.: for lemma çero it will be oreç). Inversive entries of lemmas and affixes facilitate the search for lemmas and affixes in the databases based on endings. This speeds up the process of morphological analysis considerably;

Fn1-Fn7 – identifiers of the lemma formatting paradigm. One lemma can have more than one marker and it can simultaneously belong to many lexemes, e.g. da 'sister/and' (noun and conjunction), asi 'a hundred' (is a numeral and a noun); sakidi 'hanging/hanger' (an adjective and a participle); gverdçit'eli (red-sided/ Gverdtciteli) (an adjective and a proper noun) etc. Those markers are related to **RulNu** fields of **BazAfix** and **Baz_MoFlID** database tables;

ReWord – inversive entry of the lemma;
Dn1-Dn7 – the identifiers of the word-forming patterns consistent with the lemma.

(2) **BazAfix** – the database table of the affixes of the lexemes formation maintains all possible affixes of all the lemmas in the dictionary (see Fig. 1 and Table 1). Each entry contains:

N – entry identifier;
ReSuF – inversive entry of the suffix unit of the lexeme;
RulNu – the identifier of the word-form paradigm corresponding to the affix;
BSu – suffix unit of the lemma corresponding to the lexeme;
BPr – prefix unit of the lemma corresponding to the lexeme;
PrF – prefix unit corresponding to the lexeme;
SuF – suffix unit of the lexeme corresponding to the lexeme;
SinF – loss affix unit corresponding to the lexeme;
InF – infix unit corresponding to the lexeme;
Poz – position of the loss affix corresponding to the infix unit in the lexeme;
IDMF – identifier of the flexion rule corresponding to the set of the lexeme affixes.

Using the database tables of the lemmas and affixes the identifier of word-forming realization of any word form of any lemma is possible.

Here are some examples of entries of any lexeme given in the **BazAfix** database table of the relational databases (see Table 1).

Suppose, we have a lemma from the table of **Baz_LemVoc** relational databases of lexicon, çarmoačens 'demonstrates' (see Fig. 1 and Table 1.) and we want to receive any lexeme of this lemma according the word-forming identifier **IDMF**, e.g. IDMF_ 33259. We find affixes which correspond to this identifier in the **BazAfix** database table

Table 1. The entries in the table of the relational databases - BazAfix on the examples of lexemes and their corresponding lemmas.

#	Lexeme	Lemma	Entry in the **BazAfix** Table of the Dictionary Relational Databases									
			ReS uF	Bsu	BPr	PrF	SuF	SinF	InF	RulNu	IDMF	Poz
1	*daçere*	*(da)çers*	*-e*	*-s*	*(da) -*	*(da) -*	*-e*	*#*	*#*	*vz01.2*	*IDMF_ 62060*	*0*
2	*çarmogveĉina*	*çarmoaĉens*	*- ani*	*-ens*	*#*	*#*	*ina*	*-a-*	*-gve-*	*v0a1.19*	*IDMF_ 33259*	*2*
3	*çeros*	*(da)çers*	*-so*	*-s*	*(da) -*	*#*	*-os*	*#*	*#*	*vz01.2*	*IDMF_ 62060*	*0*
4	*çeros*	*çero*	*-s*	*#*	*#*	*#*	*-s*	*#*	*#*	*n3.2*	*IDMF_ 751*	*0*
5	*kravs*	*šekravs*	*-s*	*-s*	*-še*	*#*	*-s*	*#*	*#*	*va- va1.17*	*IDMF_ 71218*	*0*
6	*kravs*	*kravi*	*-s*	*-i*	*#*	*#*	*-s*	*#*	*#*	*nuk1.2*	*IDMF_ 57*	*0*
7	*da*	*da*	*#*	*-a*	*#*	*#*	*-a*	*#*	*#*	*na2.1*	*IDMF_ 71238*	*0*
8	*da*	*da*	*#*	*#*	*#*	*#*	*#*	*#*	*#*	*conj1.6*	*IDMF_ 31159*	*0*
9	*unda*	*unda*	*#*	*#*	*#*	*#*	*#*	*#*	*#*	*part1.8*	*IDMF_ 31159*	*0*
10	*unda*	*endomeba*	*-a*	*-omeba*	*en-*	*u-*	*-a*	*#*	*#*	*vr01.1*	*IDMF_ 84328*	*0*
11	*çargvedgina*	*çaradgens*	*-ani*	*-ens*	*#*	*#*	*-ina*	*-a-*	*-gve-*	*v0a1.15*	*IDMF_ 81688*	*3*

and also, the position of the loss affix/infix in the lexeme. Then we conduct operations in the following order:

- Basic suffix unit **Bsu** -ens cut from the lemma, in this step we will have çarmoaĉ;
- In the position **Poz** - 2 (it is regarded from the end of the word-form) from the received form will be extracted the string SinF –a- (in this case this is a letter) and we will have çarmoĉ;
- In the same position **Poz** – 2 of the received word-form inserts the string **InF** –gve - and we will have - çarmogveĉ;
- The resulted word-form adds concatenation **SuF** -ina and we have çarmogveĉina;
- By the end of the received word-form will be concatenated **SuF** -ina and we will have çarmogveĉina;
- **#** _ denotes zero affix and naturally, its presence in the affix field implies that no operation can be conducted. In the given example such cases are:
- **BPr** - # - the affix which must be extracted from the beginning of the resulted word-form
- **PrF** - # - the affix which must be added to the beginning of the resulted word-form.
- i.e. finally we have the lexeme - çarmogveĉina 'if we have demonstrated'.

The entries from the Table 1 for the lexemes, *daçere* 'you write' and **çarmogvečina** 'if we have demonstrated' with the characteristic data we noted, mean the following:

Lexeme – lexeme *daçere* 'write';
Lemma – *lemma* of word-form *daçere* 'write' – *(da)çers* = *çers/daçers* 'will write'. Entries in the fields of the relational databases table BazAfix:
ReSuF – -e;
BSu – -s;
BPr – *(da)-* = *da-/#;*
PrF – *(da)-* = *da-/#* preverb is given in the parenthesis. It attaches to verb to denote future tense forms. It is the case where one identifier corresponds to two forms *çers/daçers* 'wtites/will write' _ V fut 3p sg and at the same time the verb form without a preverb is homonymous to the verb form of the present tense singular, III person (*çers* 'writes' _ V prs 3p sg *çers* _ V fut perf 3p sg);
SuF – -e;
SinF – *#*;
InF – *#*;
RulNu – *vz01.2*;
IDMF – *IDMF_62060*;
Poz – 0
Lexeme – lexeme *çarmogvečina*
Lemma – lemma of word-form *çarmogvečina* 'if we have demonstrated' – *çarmoačens* 'demonstrates'. That is the case, where one identifier corresponds to one entry in the database and there is no homonym in the present forms. Entries from the fields of the relational databases **BazAfix** table:
ReSuF – *ani*;
BSu – *ens;*
BPr – *#;*
PrF – *#;*
SuF – *ina;*
SinF – *a;*
InF – *gve;*
RulNu – *v0a1.19;*
IDMF – IDMF_ 33259;
Poz – 2.

In **BazAfix** table of the relational databases of the dictionary, homonymic lexemes have one common dictionary entry with different markers of the flexion paradigm. Such markers in the Table 1 (provided above) are *da* 'sister/and' and *unda* 'wants/must'. In the examples numbered 3–4, 5–6 and 7–8 are shown the entries of homonymic lexemes, which have common lexemes and different lemmas.

(3) **Baz_MoFlID** – in the table of the relational databases lexicon of the identifiers of the word forming rules of the basic language, all set of the grammemes which correspond to all possible morphological phenomenon, are maintained, such as: "V impf 3p sg, N Nom pl" and others (see Fig. 1 and Table 2). Each entry of the table of relational database lexicon contains:

N – entry identifier;
IDMF – the identifier of the flexion rule corresponding to the set of the word-form affixes of the lexeme;
RulNu – the identifier of the word-form paradigm corresponding to the affix;
NoLex_1 – the number of the lexeme in the flexion paradigm, corresponding to the identifiers: IDMF and RulNu;
LexFeat_1 – the marker of the characteristic of lexeme of the set of grammemes, which corresponds to the identifiers: **IDMF**, **RulNu** and **NoLex_1**, in Georgian;
LexFeat_2 –the name of the set of the lexeme characteristic grammemes, which corresponds to the identifiers: **IDMF**, **RulNu** and **NoLex_1**, in Georgian.

5   Description of the Dialectic Morphological Analyzer Module

The dialectic computational lexicon is the new component, added to the Georgian language morphological analyzer and is now in the process of developing. By its means modification process of the GeoTrans into the multi-system analyzer is ongoing. The computational lexicon of the Georgian dialectic analyzer maintains in the tables of the databases: (1) the lexemes databases table of the dialectic computational lexicon – **Dia_WordVoc**, (2) the table of the set of word forming affixes of the dialect dictionary – **DiaAfix** and (3) the table of the identifiers of the dialect dictionary relational databases – **Dia_MoFlID**. In order to better understand the algorithm of the dialect module of the morphological analyzer we represent some tables: (see Fig. 1 and Table 3).

(1) **Dia_MoFlID** – Every entry of the databases table of the dialectic computational lexicon contain:
N – unique identifier of the lexeme;
Word – Lexeme. Providing first lexemes and not the lemmas to the dialectic dictionary, is conditioned by the fact that quite often in the articles of the existing dialect dictionaries lemma is not used as a basic word. Such forms in the analyzer are considered hypothetic lemmas (we call the forms hypothetic if they are not evidenced in the available dialect texts and dictionaries) such lemma in accordance of the literary analyzer is given part of speech marker which is also hypothetic. Such examples are given in the fourth and fifth lines of the Table 3, for the lexemes *magizgni* and *magigni* (both correspond to the possessive case of the literary pronoun *e.g.* 'that', with the suffix - *magisgan* – 'because of that';
Word_V – phonetic variation of the lexeme;
ReWord_V – inverse entry of the lexeme's phonetic variation;
WoVir_PS – the of part of speech marker of the hypothetic lexeme, coinciding with the marker of the corresponding literary lemma part speech marker;
Word_Lem – the lemma corresponding to the lexeme;
ReWord_Lem – inverse entry of the lemma corresponding to the lexeme;

Table 2. Entries in the table Baz_MoFlID of the relational databases of the dictionary on the examples of the lexemes and their corresponding lemmas.

Lexeme	Lemma	Entry in the **Baz_MoFlID** table of the relational databases of the dictionary				
		IDMF	RulNu	NoLex_1	LexFeat_1	LexFeat_2
daçere	(da)çers	IDMF_62060	vz01.2	38	V PluPerf Pl 1	zmna çqvetili mx. r. III
çarmogv ečina	çarmoače ns	IDMF_ 33259	v0a1.19	44	V PluPerf Pl 1	zmna II t'urmeobit'i mr. r. I
çeros	(da)çers	IDMF_62060	vz01.2	27	Imp 3p Sg	zmna bržanebit'I mx. r.
çeros	çero	IDMF_751	n3.2	7	N Dat Sg	arsebit'i saxeli mx. r. mic'
kravs	šekravs	IDMF_71218	vava1.17	5	V Prs 3p Sg	zmna açmqo mx. r. III
kravs	kravi	IDMF_57	nuk1.2	7	N Dat Sg	arsebit'i saxeli mx. r. mic'
unda	unda	IDMF_ 31159	part1.8	1	Part	naçilaki
unda	endome-ba	IDMF_ 84328	vr01.1	3	V Prs 3p Sg	zmna açmqo mx. r. IIII
da	da	IDMF_71238	na2.1	1	N Nom Sg	arsebit'i saxeli mx. r. mic'
da	da	IDMF_ 31159	conj1.6	1	Cj	kavširi
çargved-gina	çarad-gens	IDMF_ 81688	v0a1.15	44	V II_Rezul 3p Sg	zmna II t'urmeobit'i mr. r. I

Table 3. The entries in the databases table of dialects - Dia_WordVoc on the examples of the lexemes.

Lexeme in the corpus	lemma from Baz_LemVoc	The entries in the databases table **Dia_WordVoc**				
		Word	Word_V	WoVir_PS	Word_Lem	Vir_Fn1	WoDi_Fn1
gūrbina	*gaurbens*	*(ga)urbens*	*gaurbens*		*gūrbens*	*v0a1.23*	*Di_v0a1.23*
georbina	gairbens	(ga)irbens	gairbens		*georbens*	*v0a1.19*	*Di_v0a1.19*
gaotoãnian	*gatoãnis*	*(ga)toãnis*	*gatoãnis*		*gaotoãnis*	*viz1.20*	*D_viz1.20*
magizgni	*eg*	*magizgni*		Pron –Gan			
magigni	*eg*	*magigni*		Pron –Gan			

Vir_Fn1-Vir_Fn4 – the identifiers of the flexion paradigm which correspond to the hypothetic lemma;

WoDi_Fn1-WoDi_Fn4 – the identifiers of the dialect flexion paradigm which correspond to the lemma;

Vir_Dn1-Vir_Dn4 – the identifiers of the derivative word forming paradigm which correspond to the hypothetic lemma;

WoDi_Dn1 – WoDi_Dn4 – the identifiers of the dialect derivative word forming paradigm which correspond to the lemma.

(2) **DiaAfix** – the database table of the word forming affixes complex. Each entry contains:

N – entry identifier;

ReSuF – inversive entry of the suffix unit corresponding to the dialect lexeme;

RulNu – the identifier of the word-form paradigm corresponding to the dialect affix;

BSu – the suffix unit of the lemma corresponding to the dialect lexeme;

BPr – the prefix unit of the lemma corresponding to the dialect lexeme;

PrF — the prefix unit corresponding to the dialect lexeme;

SuF – – the suffix unit of the dialect lexeme;

SinF – loss affix which corresponds to the dialect lexeme;

InF – infix unit corresponding to the dialect lexeme;

Poz – loss affix/position of the infix unit which corresponds to the dialect lexeme;

IDMF – the identifier of the flexion rule corresponding to the set of the word-form affixes of the dialect lexeme.

(3) **Dia_MoFlID** – the database table of the identifiers of the word forming rules. Each entry of the table contains:

N – entry identifier;

IDMF – the identifier of the flexion rule corresponding to the set of the word-form affixes of the dialect lexeme;

RulNu – the identifier of the word forming pattern corresponding to the dialect affix;

NoLex_1 – the number of the lexeme in the flexion paradigm corresponding to dialectic identifiers **IDMF** and **RulNu**;

LexFeat_1 – the name of the set of the lexeme characteristics corresponding to the dialect identifiers **IDMF**, **RulNu** and **NoLex_1**;

LexFeat_2 – the marker of the name of the lexeme characteristics corresponding to the dialect identifiers: **IDMF**, **RulNu** and **NoLex_1**.

The procedure of compiling the dictionary for a dialect includes 4 stages:

(1) Supplementing the dictionary of lemmas (basic forms) with help of the existing (if such) dictionaries;
(2) Morphological annotation based on the literary (standard) and dialectic dictionaries;
(3) Uniting all unrecognized word forms into clusters, to which then, the hypothetic information will correspond and refer, coming from the lexeme pattern, concerning part of speech, lemma and other characteristics.
(4) Assessing the best hypothesis and supplement new lemmas and rules of word formation to the dictionary of the morphological analyzer of the given dialect.

In order to select the dialectic texts automatically, besides enriching the dictionary with lexemes, it became necessary to consider new derivative and inflectional variations, which, as mentioned above, triggers diverse grammar, phonetic and other processes in the dialects.

6   Program Algorithm for Morphological Analysis

The programs for morphological analyses of the literary language and the dialects are realized as separate utilities in the system. In both cases the algorithm of analysis of the provided word form are the same:

(1) All the variations of the hypothetic lemma are searched. All the lexemes having identical root ending ("tail") are grammatically analyzed. The lemma will restore from the word form under analysis in accordance with database table of affixes (**BazAfix/DiaAfix**) and all the ending variations will be considered.
(2) For each variation of the received lemmas beginning from the longest, the corresponding lemma is searched in the dictionary of the lemmas (**LemVoc/DiaWordVoc**).
(3) For each variation of the found lemma according database table of affixes, (**BazAfix/DiaAfix**), the word forming pattern marker **RulNu** and the marker of the set of word forming affixes **IDMF**, in the database table of identifiers (**Baz_MoFlID/Dia_MoFlId**) the abbreviation of the name of the set of lexeme characteristics LexFeat_1 is searched for and refers to the word form under analysis. Optionally, it is possible to refer directly the name of the set in Georgian (see example 1).
(4) If the variation of the lemma does not consider any "nearest" dictionary lemma, it means that the word under analysis is not provided in the dictionary as a given lemma. In that case according to the given variation of the lemma, the ending and the lexeme which corresponds the "nearest" lemma in the dictionary, the hypothetic lexeme is generated - the pattern of word forming for an unknown word. In case such generating is successful, (if it fully coincides with the analyzed one) this hypothesis is delivered to the morphological analyzer of the lexeme.

(5) The successful variations of the analysis will be saved as:

the word-form: {lemma 1, distinguish variation 1}
{lemma 2, Distinguish variation 2}
{lemma 3, Distinguish variation 3}
And so on.

Furthermore the addition of the lemmas in the dialect dictionary happens according the following pattern:

(1) If the lemma and the marker of its characteristics are hypothetic and at the same time in the dialect dictionary there occurs the same lemma and the marker of the same characteristics for another lemma, then the possibility of this hypothesis is very close to the truth, and this increases the size of so called calculator of "productivity".
(2) If even a single variation of the analysis can be found among the lexemes of the same size, we move to point 4 with the successful result. If we have no successful points then the required length of the "tail" decreases with one. If even after that the required length of the "tail" becomes less than two, then we go to point 5 with rejection and if not – then we go to point 3.
(3) As it is very rare in the dialects to have possibility of generating the full paradigm out of the acknowledged forms, generated paradigms are unified and filtered based on their productivity and the paradigm of the highest level productivity is selected.
(4) Successful result, procedure complete.
(5) Unsuccessful result, complete procedure.

We describe the process of morphological annotation of the Upper Imeretian collection of the GDC based on the Upper Imeretian Dictionary [11]. The annotation is based on **GeoTrans** (see [12]), an automated morphological dictionary of Standard Georgian. At the present experimental stage of the morphological annotation of the GDC, the following has been achieved:

- Formatting of the dictionary: development of the digital version of the dictionary and creation of a list of lemmas (totally 5671 lemmas)
- Automated selection and part-of-speech tagging of the forms from the list of lemmas of the dialect dictionary, coinciding with those of the standard. Totally 784 such lemmas were detected; a list of homonyms was identified, totaling 27 items. After this process, 4860 'unknown' entries in the list of lemmas were manually attached to part-of-speech tag.
- By means of the marked lists, the knowledge base of the automated morphological dictionary of Standard Georgian was enriched. This implies that a subsystem for morphological modeling of a given dialect variety was added to **GeoTrans**. In this system, each dialect form will be tagged in accordance with a respective part of speech and, frequently, marked in accordance with an inflectional pattern by means of which word forms are lemmatized.
- At the next stage, the **GeoTrans** standard language analyzer enabled us **to select the lemmas** from the textual data of the corpus, **coinciding with those of the standard language**, amounting to 3331 lemmas.
- The GeoTrans dialect analyzer specific dialect **lemmas** were selected and tagged, 472 lemmas in total.

- By means of the standard language analyzer, all the **word forms** underwent complete morphological analyses, coinciding with those of the standard, which amounted to 9285 forms. Here too, homonymous (528) and non-homonymous (8757) forms will be similarly distinguished.
- Following that, by means of *lemmas and standard inflectional patterns*, lemmatization was performed and dialect (specific) word forms were morphologically tagged.

7   Conclusion

Equipping dialect dictionaries with morphological information and in such a way enriching the morphological knowledge base by means of the automated standard analyzer is an optimistic perspective for the automation of dialect corpus analysis. The concept of morphological annotation of the GDC envisages a differentiated approach to text data: to present dialect (specific) vocabulary, vocabulary common with the standard language, inflectional and derivational patterns common with the standard language, dialect-specific inflectional and derivational patterns as separate 'regions' and then, to undertake the annotation strategy respectively.

References

1. Jorbenadze, B.: The Kartvelian Languages and Dialects. Mecniereba, Tbilisi (1991)
2. Biber, D.: Representativeness in corpus design. Lit. Linguist. Comput. **8**, 243–257 (1993)
3. Leech, G.: The Importance of Reference Corpora, Lancaster University. http://www.uzei. com/modulos/usuariosFtp/conexion/archivos59A.pdf
4. Sinclair, J.: Preliminary recommendations on corpus typology. In: EAG–TCWG–CTYP/P, Version of May (1996)
5. Leech, G.: New resources, or just better old ones? The Holy Grail of representativeness. In: Hundt, M., Nesselehauf, N., Biewer, C. (eds.) Corpus Linguistics and the Web, pp. 133–149. Rodopi, Amsterdam (2007)
6. Kryuchkova, O.U., Goldyn, V.E.: Textual dialect corpuses as a model of traditional rural communication. In: Papers of the International Conference on Computational Linguistics, Dialogue-2008, pp. 268–273, Moscow (2008)
7. Beridze, M., Nadaraia, D.: Dictionary as a textual component of a corpus (Georgian Dialect Corpus). In: Proceedings of the International Conference "Corpus Linguistics-2011", pp. 92–97, St. Petersburg (2011)
8. Beridze, M., Nadaraia, D.: The corpus of georgian dialects. In: Fifth International Conference: NLP, Corpus Linguistics, Corpus Based Grammar Research, Slovakia, Bratislava (2009)
9. Lortkipanidze L.: Record and reproduction of morphological functions. In: Proceedings of the 5th Tbilisi Symposium on Language, Logic and Computation. ILLC, University of Amsterdam CLLS, Tbilisi State University, pp. 105–111 (2003)
10. Lortkipanidze L.: Interactive system for compilation of multilingual concordancers. In: Conference abstracts of the 6th International Contrastive Linguistics Conference (ICLC6), Berlin (2010)
11. Dzotsenidze, Q.: Upper Imeretian Dictionary, Tbilisi (1974)
12. Lortkipanidze, L.: Software Tools for Morphological Annotation of Corpus. In: Proceedings of the International Conference "Corpus Linguistics – 2011". St. Petersburg, pp. 243–248. (2011)

Duality and Universal Models for the Meet-Implication Fragment of IPC

Nick Bezhanishvili[1]($\boxtimes$), Dion Coumans[2], Samuel J. van Gool[2,3], and Dick de Jongh[1]

[1] ILLC, Faculty of Science, University of Amsterdam,
Science Park 107, 1098 XG Amsterdam, The Netherlands
n.bezhanishvili@uva.nl
[2] IMAPP, Faculty of Science, Radboud University Nijmegen,
P. O. Box 9010, 6500 GL Nijmegen, The Netherlands
[3] Mathematical Institute, University of Bern,
Sidlerstrasse 5, 3012 Bern, Switzerland

Abstract. In this paper we investigate the fragment of intuitionistic logic which only uses conjunction (meet) and implication, using finite duality for distributive lattices and universal models. We give a description of the finitely generated universal models of this fragment and give a complete characterization of the up-sets of Kripke models of intuitionistic logic which can be defined by meet-implication-formulas. We use these results to derive a new version of subframe formulas for intuitionistic logic and to show that the uniform interpolants of meet-implication-formulas are not necessarily uniform interpolants in the full intuitionistic logic.

Keywords: Duality · Universal models · Intuitionistic logic · Heyting algebras · Free algebras · Implicative semilattices · Definability · Interpolation

1 Introduction

Heyting algebras are the algebraic models of intuitionistic propositional logic, IPC. In this paper we will be concerned with the syntactic fragment of IPC consisting of the formulas which only use the connectives of conjunction ($\wedge$) and implication ($\rightarrow$), but no disjunction ($\vee$) or falsum ($\bot$). The algebraic structures corresponding to this fragment are called implicative semilattices[1]. A result due to Diego [1] says that the variety of implicative semilattices is locally finite, i.e., finitely generated algebras are finite, or equivalently, the finitely generated free algebras are finite. In logic terms, this theorem can be expressed as saying that there are only finitely many equivalence classes of $(\wedge, \rightarrow)$-formulas in IPC.

One of the key results in this paper is a dual characterization of a $(\wedge, \rightarrow)$-subalgebra of a given Heyting algebra generated by a finite set of elements (Theorem 26). This theorem leads to Diego's theorem and a characterization of the

---

[1] In less recent literature, these are also called Brouwerian semilattices.

© Springer-Verlag Berlin Heidelberg 2015
M. Aher et al. (Eds.): TbiLLC 2013, LNCS 8984, pp. 97–116, 2015.
DOI: 10.1007/978-3-662-46906-4_7

n-universal models of the $(\wedge, \rightarrow)$-fragment of IPC (Theorem 27) as submodels of the universal model, in the same spirit as the proof by Renardel de Lavalette et al. in [2]. The first characterization of this model was obtained by Köhler [3] using his duality for finite implicative meet-semilattices. Our slightly different approach in this paper also enables us to obtain new results about the $(\wedge, \rightarrow)$-fragment of IPC. In particular, in Theorem 29, we give a full characterization of the up-sets of a Kripke model which can be defined by $(\wedge, \rightarrow)$-formulas. Since our characterization in particular applies to the n-universal model of IPC, this may be considered as a first step towards solving the complicated problem of characterizing the up-sets of the n-universal models which are definable by intuitionistic formulas (also see our more detailed remarks in Sect. 5). Building on this result, we use the de Jongh formulas for IPC to construct formulas that play an analogous role in the $(\wedge, \rightarrow)$-fragment. Finally, we use the characterization of $(\wedge, \rightarrow)$-definable subsets of the n-universal models of IPC to show that a uniform interpolant of a $(\wedge, \rightarrow)$-formula in intuitionistic logic may not be equivalent to a $(\wedge, \rightarrow)$-formula.

A word on methodology. The two essential ingredients to our proofs are, on the one hand, Birkhoff duality for finite distributive lattices and, on the other hand, the theory of n-universal models for IPC [4,5]. Our methods in this paper are directly inspired by the theory of duality for $(\wedge, \rightarrow)$-homomorphisms as developed in [3,6–8], and also by the observations about the relation between the n-universal models and duality for Heyting algebras in [9]. However, we made an effort to write this paper in such a way to be as self-contained as possible, and in particular we do not require the reader to be familiar with any of these results. In particular, we give a brief introduction to duality for finite distributive lattices and its connection to Kripke semantics for IPC in Sect. 2, and we do not need to go into the intricacies of duality for implicative meet-semilattices, instead opting to give direct proofs of the duality-theoretic facts that we need.

The paper is organized as follows: in Sect. 2 we present the necessary preliminaries about IPC and Heyting algebras in the context of duality for distributive lattices; in Sect. 3 we study the meet-implication fragment of IPC and prove our main theorems mentioned above; in Sect. 4 we apply these results to $(\wedge, \rightarrow)$-de Jongh formulas and analyze semantically the uniform interpolation in the $(\wedge, \rightarrow)$-fragment of IPC. In Sect. 5 we summarize our results and give suggestions on where to go from here.

2   Algebra, Semantics and Duality

We briefly outline the contents of this section. In Subsect. 2.1, we recall the definitions and basic facts about adjunctions between partially ordered sets, Heyting algebras, and implicative meet-semilattices. Subsect. 2.2 contains the preliminaries about duality theory that we will need in this paper. In Subsect. 2.3 we show how to define the usual Kripke semantics for IPC via duality, and in Subsect. 2.4 we recall how the universal and canonical models for IPC are related to free finitely generated Heyting algebras via duality.

2.1   Adjunction, Heyting Algebras, Implicative Meet-Semilattices

Since the notion of adjunction is crucial to logic in general, and in particular to intuitionistic logic, we recall some basic facts about it right away. An adjunction can be understood as an invertible rule that ties two logical connectives or terms. The typical example in intuitionistic logic is the adjunction between $\wedge$ and $\rightarrow$, which can be expressed by saying that the following (invertible) rule is derivable in IPC.

$$\frac{p \wedge q \vdash r}{p \vdash q \rightarrow r} \qquad\qquad (1)$$

Recall that an *adjunction* between partially ordered sets A and B is a pair of functions $f : A \leftrightarrows B : g$ such that, for all $a \in A$ and $b \in B$, $f(a) \leq b$ if, and only if, $a \leq g(b)$; notation: $f \dashv g$. In this case, we say that f is *lower adjoint* to g and g is *upper adjoint* to f. Note that the derivability of rule (1) in IPC says exactly that, for any ψ, the function $\varphi \mapsto \varphi \wedge \psi$ on the Lindenbaum algebra for IPC (cf. Example 3(b) below) is lower adjoint to the function $\chi \mapsto \psi \rightarrow \chi$. The following general facts about adjunctions are well-known and will be used repeatedly in this paper.

Proposition 1. *Let A and B be partially ordered sets and let $f : A \leftrightarrows B : g$ be an adjunction. The following properties hold:*

1. *If f is surjective, then $fg = \mathrm{id}_B$, and therefore g is injective and the image of g is $\{a \in A \mid gf(a) \leq a\}$;*
2. *The function f preserves any joins (suprema) which exist in A and the function g preserves any meets (infima) which exist in B;*
3. *For any $b \in B$, $g(b)$ is the maximum of $\{a \in A \mid f(a) \leq b\}$. In particular, the fact that g is upper adjoint to f uniquely determines g.*

Moreover, if C and D are complete lattices and $f : C \rightarrow D$ is a function which preserves arbitrary joins, then f has an upper adjoint.

Proof. Straightforward; cf., e.g., [10, 7.23–7.34]. □

Recall that a tuple $(A, \wedge, \vee, \rightarrow, 0, 1)$ is a *Heyting algebra* if $(A, \wedge, \vee, 0, 1)$ is a bounded lattice, and the operation $\rightarrow$ is upper adjoint to $\wedge$, i.e., for any $a, b, c \in A$,

$$a \wedge b \leq c \iff a \leq b \rightarrow c. \qquad\qquad (2)$$

The equation (2) says that $b \rightarrow c$ is the maximum of $\{a \in A \mid a \wedge b \leq c\}$; therefore, a lattice admits at most one "Heyting implication", i.e., an operation $\rightarrow$ such that it becomes a Heyting algebra. The lattices underlying Heyting algebras are always distributive (in fact, for any $a \in A$, the function $b \mapsto a \wedge b$ preserves any join that exists in A, since it is a lower adjoint). All finite distributive lattices admit a Heyting implication. A *Heyting homomorphism* is a map between Heyting algebras that preserves each of the operations. An implicative meet-semilattice is a "Heyting algebra without disjunction". More precisely, an *implicative meet-semilattice* is a tuple $(A, \wedge, \rightarrow)$ such that $(A, \wedge)$ is a semilattice, and condition (2) holds. We will write $(\wedge, \rightarrow)$-homomorphism to abbreviate "homomorphism of implicative meet-semilattices". Note that any implicative meet-semilattice has a largest element, 1, which is preserved by any $(\wedge, \rightarrow)$-homomorphism. Also note that finite implicative meet-semilattices are distributive lattices, but $(\wedge, \rightarrow)$-homomorphisms do not necessarily preserve joins. However, *surjective* $(\wedge, \rightarrow)$-homomorphisms do preserve join (cf. [3, Lemma 2.4 and the remark thereafter]):

Lemma 2. *If $f : A \rightarrow B$ is a surjective $(\wedge, \rightarrow)$-homomorphism between Heyting algebras, then f is join-preserving.*

Proof. First of all, we have $0_B = f(a)$ for some $a \in A$, and $0_A \leq a$, so that $f(0_A) = 0_B$. Now let $a, a' \in A$. Pick $c \in A$ such that $f(c) = f(a) \vee f(a')$. Now

$$
\begin{aligned}
f(a \vee a') \rightarrow (f(a) \vee f(a')) &= f(a \vee a') \rightarrow f(c) \\
&= f((a \vee a') \rightarrow c) \\
&= f((a \rightarrow c) \wedge (a' \rightarrow c)) \\
&= (f(a) \rightarrow f(c)) \wedge (f(a') \rightarrow f(c)) \\
&= (f(a) \vee f(a')) \rightarrow f(c) = 1,
\end{aligned}
$$

so $f(a \vee a') \leq f(a) \vee f(a')$. The other inequality holds because f is order-preserving. $\qquad\square$

Example 3. (a) An important example of a Heyting algebra is the collection of upward closed sets ('up-sets') of a partially ordered set $(X, \leq)$, ordered by inclusion; we denote this Heyting algebra by $\mathcal{U}(X)$. The Heyting implication of two up-sets U and V is given by the formula

$$U \rightarrow V = (\downarrow(U \cap V^c))^c, \tag{3}$$

that is, a point x is in $U \rightarrow V$ if, and only if, for all $y \geq x$, $y \in U$ implies $y \in V$. The reader who is familiar with models for IPC will recognize the similarity between this condition and the interpretation of a formula $\varphi \rightarrow \psi$ in a model; we will recall the precise connection between the two in 2.3 below.

(b) Another example of a Heyting algebra, of a more logical nature, is that of the Lindenbaum algebra for IPC; we briefly recall the definition. Fix a set of propositional variables P and consider the collection $F(P)$ of all propositional formulas whose variables are in P. Define a pre-order $\preceq$ on $F(P)$ by saying, for $\varphi, \psi \in F(P)$, that $\varphi \preceq \psi$ if, and only if, ψ is provable from φ in IPC. The Lindenbaum algebra is defined as the quotient of $F(P)$ by the congruence relation $\approx := (\preceq) \cap (\preceq)^{-1}$. The Lindenbaum algebra is the free Heyting algebra over the set P, i.e., any function from P to a Heyting algebra H lifts uniquely to a Heyting homomorphism from the Lindenbaum algebra over P to H. We will denote the free Heyting algebra over P by $F_{HA}(P)$. Note that the same construction can be applied to the $(\wedge, \vee)$- and $(\wedge, \rightarrow)$-fragments of IPC to yield the free distributive lattice $F_{DL}(P)$ and the free implicative meet-semilattice $F_{\wedge, \rightarrow}(P)$, respectively. $\qquad\square$

2.2 Duality

We briefly recall the facts about duality that we will need. Let D be a distributive lattice. We recall the definition of the *dual poset*, D_*, of D. The points of D_* are the prime filters of D, i.e., up-sets $F \subseteq D$ which contain finite meets of their subsets and have the property that if $a \vee b \in F$, then $a \in F$ or $b \in F$. The partial order on D_* is the inclusion of prime filters. The map $\eta : D \to \mathcal{U}(D_*)$ which sends $d \in D$ to $\{F \in D_* \mid d \in F\}$ is (assuming the axiom of choice) an embedding of distributive lattices, which is called the *canonical extension* of D. If D is finite, then η is an isomorphism, so that any finite distributive lattice is isomorphic to the lattice of up-sets of its dual poset. The assignments $X \mapsto \mathcal{U}(X)$ and $D \mapsto D_*$ between finite posets and finite distributive lattices extend to a dual equivalence, or duality, of categories: homomorphisms from a distributive lattice D to a distributive lattice E are in a natural bijective correspondence with order-preserving maps from E_* to D_*. A homomorphism $h : D \to E$ is sent to the map $h_* : E_* \to D_*$ which sends $F \in E_*$ to $h^{-1}(F)$, and an order-preserving map $f : X \to Y$ is sent to the homomorphism $f^* : \mathcal{U}(Y) \to \mathcal{U}(X)$ which sends an up-set U of Y to $f^{-1}(U)$.

If X and Y are posets, it is natural to ask which order-preserving maps $f : X \to Y$ are such that their dual $f^{-1} : \mathcal{U}(Y) \to \mathcal{U}(X)$ is a Heyting homomorphism. It turns out that these are the *p-morphisms*, i.e., the order-preserving maps which in addition satisfy the condition: for any $x \in X$, $y \in Y$, if $f(x) \leq y$, then there exists $x' \geq x$ such that $f(x') = y$.

To end this subsection, we recall how duality yields a straight-forward description of the free finitely generated[2] distributive lattice, $F_{DL}(P)$. In any category of algebras, the free algebra over a set P is the P-fold coproduct of the one-generated free algebra. Therefore, since duality transforms coproducts into products, the dual space $F_{DL}(P)_*$ is the P-fold power of the poset $F_{DL}(\{p\})_*$, the dual of the one-generated free algebra. Note that $F_{DL}(\{p\})$ is the three-element chain $\{0 \leq p \leq 1\}$, so its dual is the two-element poset $2 = \{0, 1\}$. Since finite products in the category of finite posets are simply given by equipping the Cartesian product with the pointwise order, it follows that $F_{DL}(P)_* = 2^P$. Therefore, the free distributive lattice over a finite set P is the lattice of up-sets of 2^P; in a formula, $F_{DL}(P) = \mathcal{U}(2^P)$.

2.3 Semantics via Duality

Notation. Throughout the rest of this paper, we fix a finite set of propositional variables $P = \{p_1, \ldots, p_n\}$. We denote the free algebras over P by $F_{HA}(n)$, $F_{DL}(n)$, etc.

In this paper, a *frame* is a poset $(M, \leq)$. A *model* is a triple $(M, \leq, c)$, where $(M, \leq)$ is a poset and c, the *colouring*, is an order-preserving function from M

---

[2] Essentially the same argument as the one sketched in this paragraph can be used to give a description of an arbitrary, not necessarily finitely generated, free distributive lattice, but we will not need this in what follows.

to 2^n. The colouring c yields, via duality, a distributive lattice homomorphism $c^* : \mathcal{U}(2^n) \to \mathcal{U}(M)$. As noted at the end of 2.2, $\mathcal{U}(2^n)$ is the free distributive lattice over the set of generators n. By the universal property of the free Heyting algebra, the lattice homomorphism c^* has a unique extension to a Heyting homomorphism, v, from the free n-generated Heyting algebra to the Heyting algebra $\mathcal{U}(M)$, as in diagram (4).

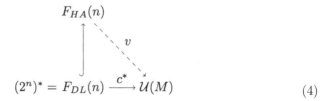

$$(2^n)^* = F_{DL}(n) \xrightarrow{c^*} \mathcal{U}(M) \tag{4}$$

A point x in a model M is said to *satisfy* a formula φ if, and only if, $x \in v(\varphi)$; we employ the usual notation: $M, x \models \varphi$. Note that, as an alternative to the above algebraic description, one may equivalently define the satisfaction relation for models by induction on the complexity of formulas; see e.g. [5, Definition 2.1.8]. A model is said to satisfy φ if every point of the model satisfies φ. A *p-morphism* f from a model M to a model N is a p-morphism between the underlying frames of M and N which in addition satisfies, for any $x \in M$, $c_N(f(x)) = c_M(x)$. From the above definitions, it is clear that p-morphisms preserve truth, i.e., $M, x \models \varphi$ if, and only if, $N, f(x) \models \varphi$, for any formula φ. A *generated submodel* of M is a submodel M' such that the inclusion $f : M' \hookrightarrow M$ is a p-morphism, or equivalently, such that M' is an up-set of M. We say M' is a *p-morphic image* of M if there exists a surjective p-morphism $f : M \twoheadrightarrow M'$.

Recall that a *general frame* is a tuple $(M, \leq, A)$, where $(M, \leq)$ is a poset and A is a subalgebra of the Heyting algebra of up-sets of M. The elements of the algebra A are called the *admissible sets* of the general frame. An important subclass of the class of general frames consists of the $(M, \leq, A)$ for which $(M, \leq)$ is the dual poset of the Heyting algebra A; these are precisely the *descriptive* general frames.[3]

An *admissible colouring* on a general frame $(M, \leq, A)$ is a colouring $c : M \to 2^n$ with the additional property that, for each $1 \leq i \leq n$, the set $\{x \in M \mid c(x)_i = 1\}$ is admissible. By the latter description and duality, admissible colourings c on a descriptive frame $(M, \leq, A)$ correspond to homomorphisms $c^* : F_{DL}(n) \to A$. Note that, in this case, the semantics map v defined in (4) also maps into A, since A is a sub-Heyting-algebra of $\mathcal{U}(M)$.

We finally recall a few definitions and observations about so-called "borders" in Kripke models, that we will need in what follows.

Definition 4. *Let M be a Kripke model.*

1. *If A is an up-set in a Kripke frame $(M, \leq)$, then a* border point *of A is a maximal element of the complement of A, i.e., a point u which is not in A, while all its proper successors are in A.*

---

[3] For an equivalent characterization of descriptive general frames as the 'compact refined' general frames, cf. e.g. [5, Definition 2.3.2, Theorem 2.4.2].

2. If φ is a propositional formula, then a point u is called a φ-border point if u is a border point of $v(\varphi)$, the subset of M where φ holds.
3. We say that M is a model with borders, or that M has borders, if, for every $x \in M$ such that $x \not\models p$, there is a p-border point u above x.

Proposition 5.   1. Every image-finite model has borders.
2. Every descriptive model has borders.

Proof. Item (1) is straightforward. For the proof of (2) see, e.g., [5, Theorem 2.3.24].   □

2.4   Canonical and Universal Models

The dual poset of the free n-generated Heyting algebra, $F_{HA}(n)$, is called the *canonical frame* and is denoted by $C(n)$. In logic terms, points in the canonical frame are so-called "theories with the disjunction property". The canonical frame carries a natural colouring c, which is the dual of the inclusion $F_{DL}(n) \hookrightarrow F_{HA}(n)$. Concretely, $c(x)_i = 1$ if, and only if, the variable p_i is an element of x. The model thus defined is called the *canonical model*, and is also denoted by $C(n)$.[4]

Note that, by the embedding $\eta : F_{HA}(n) \hookrightarrow \mathcal{U}(C(n))$, any element φ of $F_{HA}(n)$ defines an up-set $\eta(\varphi) = \{x \in C(n) \mid \varphi \in x\}$ of $C(n)$. Since η is in particular a Heyting homomorphism that extends c^*, it is equal to the semantics map v for $C(n)$ defined in (4). Concretely, this means that, for any $x \in C(n)$ and $\varphi \in F_{HA}(n)$, we have $C(n), x \models \varphi$ if, and only if, $\varphi \in x$; this fact is often referred to as the *truth lemma*.

Let $\widehat{F_{HA}}(n)$ be the profinite completion of $F_{HA}(n)$; recall from [11, Theorem 4.7] that $\widehat{F_{HA}}(n)$ is the Heyting algebra of up-sets of $C(n)_{\text{fin}} := \{x \in C(n) \mid \uparrow x \text{ is finite}\}$, the image-finite[5] part of $C(n)$. The generated submodel $C(n)_{\text{fin}}$ of $C(n)$ is known as the *universal model* and denoted by $U(n)$.

Lemma 6.   The map $v : F_{HA}(n) \to \mathcal{U}(U(n))$ is injective.

Proof. Cf., e.g., [5, Theorem 3.2.20].   □

Importantly, the universal model can be described by an inductive top-down construction, as follows.

Theorem 7.   The universal model $U(n)$ is the unique image-finite model satisfying all of the following conditions:

1. there are 2^n maximal points with mutually distinct colours in $U(n)$;
2. for any $x \in U(n)$ and $c' < c(x)$, there is a unique point $x' \in U(n)$ with $c(x') = c'$ and $\uparrow x' = \{x'\} \cup \uparrow x$;

---

[4] The canonical frame and model are also known as the Henkin frame and model.
[5] Recall that a model M is called *image-finite* if, for each $w \in M$, the set of successors of w is finite.

3. *for any finite antichain $S \subseteq U(n)$ and $c' \leq \min\{c(x) \mid x \in S\}$, there is a unique point $x' \in U(n)$ with $c(x') = c'$ and $\uparrow x' = \{x'\} \cup \bigcup_{x \in S} \uparrow x$.*

Proof. Cf., e.g., [5, Sect. 3.2].   □

The following important fact states a 'universal property' for the universal model. Following the usual terminology (cf., e.g., [5, Sect. 3.1]), the *depth* of a point w in a frame M is the maximal length of a chain in the generated subframe $\uparrow w$. We say that a frame M has *finite depth* $\leq m$ if every chain in M has size at most m.

Proposition 8. *If M is a model on n variables of finite depth $\leq m$, then there exists a unique p-morphism $f : M \rightarrow U(n)$. Moreover, the image of f has depth $\leq m$.*

Proof. [6] We prove the statement by induction on m. First let M be a model of depth 0. In this case, there is clearly a unique p-morphism from M to $U(n)$, namely the one which sends each point in M to the unique maximal point in $U(n)$ of the same colour. Now let M be a model of depth $m + 1$, for $m \geq 0$. Let $x \in M$ be arbitrary; we will define $f(x) \in U(n)$. Note that, for every $y > x$, the submodel $M_y := \uparrow y$ generated by y has depth $\leq m$. Thus, for each $y > x$, let $f_y : M_y \rightarrow U(n)$ be the unique p-morphism; the image of f_y has depth $\leq m$ by the induction hypothesis. Therefore, the set $S := \bigcup_{y > x} \text{im}(f_y)$ has depth $\leq m$ in $U(n)$. If S is empty, then x is maximal, and we define $f(x)$ to be the unique maximal point of $U(n)$ that has the same colour as x. Otherwise, S has finitely many minimal points, $s_0, \ldots, s_k$, say. Pick points $y_0, \ldots, y_k$ in M such that $s_i \in \text{im}(f_{y_i})$. If $k = 0$ and $c(y_0) = c(x)$, then we define $f(x) := s_0$. Otherwise, by Theorem 7, there is a unique point s in $U(n)$ whose immediate successors are $s_0, \ldots, s_k$ such that $c(s) = c(x)$; we define $f(x) := s$. It is straightforward to check that f defined in this manner is the unique p-morphism from M to $U(n)$, and clearly the image of f has depth $\leq m + 1$.   □

Remark 9. Two points x and x' in a model M of finite depth are bisimilar if, and only if, the unique p-morphism f in Proposition 8 sends them to the same point of $U(n)$.

Definition 10 (De Jongh Formulas). *We define formulas φ_w, ψ_w and θ_w, for each $w \in U(n)$, by induction on the depth of w. Let $w \in U(n)$. Let I_w denote the (finite) set of immediate successors of w. By recursion, we assume that the formulas $\varphi_{w'}$, $\psi_{w'}$ and $\theta_{w'}$ have been defined for each $w' \in I_w$. We define:*

$$\theta_w := \bigvee_{w' \in I_w} \varphi_{w'}, \tag{5}$$

$$\varphi_w := \bigwedge_{p \in T_w} p \wedge \bigwedge_{q \in B_w} (q \rightarrow \theta_w) \wedge \bigwedge_{w' \in I_w} (\psi_{w'} \rightarrow \theta_w), \tag{6}$$

$$\psi_w := \varphi_w \rightarrow \theta_w, \tag{7}$$

---

[6] This fact is well-known, cf. e.g. [6, p. 428]. We briefly recall the proof here. Also cf., e.g., [12, Theorem 3.2.3], for more details. Note, however, that we do not assume here that M is finite, only that M has finite depth.

where T_w is the set of propositional variables p which are true in w, B_w is the set of propositional variables q such that w is a q-border point.[7]

Note that the above definition includes the case where w is a maximal point, i.e., $k = 0$. Also note that the syntactic shape of our definition of φ_w is slightly different from the usual definition (e.g. [5, Definition 3.3.1]), but easily seen to be equivalent using the fact that $(\bigvee_{i=1}^{m} \alpha_i) \to \beta$ is equivalent in IPC to $\bigwedge_{i=1}^{m}(\alpha_i \to \beta)$, for any formulas $\alpha_1, \ldots, \alpha_m$ and β. The following theorem shows which subsets of the universal model are defined by De Jongh formulas.

Theorem 11. *For each $w \in U(n)$, we have $v(\theta_w) = (\uparrow w) \setminus \{w\}$, $v(\varphi_w) = \uparrow w$, and $v(\psi_w) = U(n) \setminus \downarrow w$.*

Proof. By induction on the depth of w, cf., e.g., [5, Theorem 3.3.2]. □

Note that the de Jongh formula ψ_w has the following property: a frame G refutes ψ_w iff there is a generated subframe of G p-morphically mapped onto the subframe of $U(n)$ generated by w. In this way, de Jongh formulas correspond to the so-called Jankov or splitting formulas, see [5, Sect. 3.3] for the details.

3   Separated Points and the Meet-Implication Fragment

In this section we use a duality for Heyting algebras and $(\wedge, \to)$-homomorphisms for characterizing n-universal models of the $(\wedge, \to)$-fragment of IPC (Theorem 27) and for characterizing $(\wedge, \to)$-definable up-sets of n-universal models of IPC (Theorem 29). The main technical contribution is the characterization of the dual model of the $(\wedge, \to)$-subalgebra of a Heyting algebra generated by a finite set of generators (Theorem 26). Our proofs rely on discrete duality and do not use topology. They can be extended to Priestley [13] and Esakia [14] dualities by adding topology, but we will not use this (explicitly) in this paper. In the study of the meet-implication fragment, the following notion of 'separated point' in a model will be crucial.[8]

Definition 12. *Let M be a model. A point $x \in M$ is* separated *if, and only if, there exists a propositional variable q for which x is a q-border point.*

The following easy lemma will be used frequently in what follows.

Lemma 13. *Let $f : M \to N$ be a p-morphism between models. If x is a separated point in M, then $f(x)$ is separated in N.*

Proof. Let $x \in M$ be a separated point. Choose q such that x is a q-border point. We claim that $f(x)$ is a q-border point in N, and therefore separated. Indeed, $N, f(x) \not\models q$ since f preserves colourings. Also, if $y' > f(x)$, then since f is a p-morphism we may pick $x' > x$ such that $f(x') = y'$. Since $x' > x$, we have that $M, x' \models q$ since x is a q-border point, so q also holds in $y = f(x')$, since f preserves colourings. □

---

[7] We use the usual convention that $\bigvee \emptyset = \bot$ and $\bigwedge \emptyset = \top$.

[8] This notion has it roots in [2]. Our 'separated' points are precisely those points which are 'not inductive and not full' in the terminology of [2, Definition 5].

The following alternative characterization of separated points relates them to the $(\wedge, \rightarrow)$-fragment.

Lemma 14. *Let x be a point in a model M. The following are equivalent:*

1. *the point x is separated;*
2. *there exists a $(\wedge, \rightarrow)$-formula φ such that x is a φ-border point.*

Proof. It is clear that (1) implies (2). For (2) implies (1), we prove the contrapositive. Suppose that x is not separated. We prove the negation of (2), i.e., x is not a φ-border point for any $(\wedge, \rightarrow)$-formula φ, by induction on complexity of φ. For φ a propositional variable, this is true by assumption. For $\varphi = \psi \wedge \chi$, note that $v(\varphi)^c = v(\psi)^c \cup v(\chi)^c$. From this equality, it follows that if x were a φ-border point, it would already be either a ψ-border point or a χ-border point, which contradicts the induction hypothesis. For $\varphi = \psi \rightarrow \chi$, suppose that x is a φ-border point. We will prove that x is also a χ-border point, which again contradicts the induction hypothesis. By maximality of x, all $y > x$ satisfy $\psi \rightarrow \chi$. However, x does not satisfy $\psi \rightarrow \chi$, so we must have that $x \in v(\psi) \cap v(\chi)^c$. Since $v(\psi)$ is an up-set, we conclude that, for all $y > x$, $y \in v(\psi)$, and therefore $y \in v(\chi)$. Hence, x is a χ-border point, as required.   □

For a model M, we denote by M^s the submodel consisting of the separated points of M. That is, the order and colouring on M^s are the restrictions of the corresponding structures on M. (Note that the model M^s is a submodel, but almost never a *generated* submodel, i.e. an up-set, of M!)

Lemma 15. *Let M be a model on n variables. The submodel M^s has finite depth $\leq n$.*

Proof. Let C be a chain in M^s. For any $x, y \in M^s$, if $x < y$, then $c(x) < c(y)$, since x is separated and $y > x$ in M. Therefore, $\{c(x) \mid x \in C\}$ is a chain in the poset $(2^n, \leq)$, so that it must have size $\leq n$. Hence, C has size at most n.   □

Definition 16 (The Model $M_{\wedge,\rightarrow}$). *Let M be a model and M^s its submodel of separated points. Let $f : M^s \rightarrow U(n)$ be the unique p-morphism which exists by Lemma 15 and Proposition 8. Define $M_{\wedge,\rightarrow} := \mathrm{im}(f)$ to be the generated submodel of $U(n)$ consisting of those points in the image of f, as in the following diagram.*

$$
\begin{array}{ccc}
 & U(n) & \\
f \nearrow & & \uparrow \\
M \supseteq M^s & \twoheadrightarrow & M_{\wedge,\rightarrow}
\end{array} \qquad (8)
$$

The above definition can in particular be applied to $U(n)$ itself. The following proposition characterizes the points in the generated submodel $U(n)_{\wedge,\rightarrow}$ of $U(n)$.

Proposition 17. *Let $n \geq 1$. The generated submodel $U(n)_{\wedge,\rightarrow}$ consists exactly of those points $x \in U(n)$ such that for all $y \geq x$, y is separated.*

Proof. Write $S := \{x \in U(n) \mid$ for all $y \in U(n)$, if $y \geq x$, then y is separated$\}$. Note that S is a generated submodel of $U(n)$, and also of $U(n)^s$. Let f be as in Definition 16. By definition, $U(n)_{\wedge,\rightarrow} = \mathrm{im}(f)$. We show that $S = \mathrm{im}(f)$. If $x' \in U(n)^s$, then $f(x') \in S$: for any $y \in U(n)$ with $y \geq x$, there exists $y' \in U(n)^s$ such that $f(y') = y$. By Lemma 13, y is separated. For the converse, note that the restriction, g, of f to the generated submodel S is still a p-morphism, since S is a generated submodel of $U(n)^s$. Also, the inclusion map $i : S \rightarrow U(n)$ is a p-morphism, since S is a generated submodel of $U(n)$. Therefore, by the uniqueness part of Proposition 8, we must have $i = g$. Thus, if x is in S, then $x = i(x) = g(x) = f(x)$. In particular, x is in $\mathrm{im}(f)$. $\square$

Lemma 18. *For any model M, $M_{\wedge,\rightarrow}$ is contained in $U(n)_{\wedge,\rightarrow}$. In particular, $M_{\wedge,\rightarrow}$ is a generated submodel of $U(n)$ of depth $\leq n$, and thereby a finite model.*

Proof. Since $M_{\wedge,\rightarrow}$ is the image of a p-morphism, it is a generated submodel, and all its points are separated, so by Proposition 17, every point of $M_{\wedge,\rightarrow}$ is in $U(n)_{\wedge,\rightarrow}$. The 'in particular'-part follows from Lemma 15. $\square$

In Theorem 26 below, we will show that, for any model with borders M, the model $M_{\wedge,\rightarrow}$ is dual to the $(\wedge,\rightarrow)$-subalgebra of A that is generated by the admissible up-sets $v(p_1), \ldots, v(p_n)$. We need two lemmas, Lemmas 19 and 20.

Lemma 19. *Let $f : H \rightarrow K$ be a function between Heyting algebras with an upper adjoint $g : K \rightarrow H$. Then f preserves binary meets if, and only if, for all $a \in H$, $b \in K$, the equality $a \rightarrow g(b) = g(f(a) \rightarrow b)$ holds. In particular, if f is surjective and preserves binary meets, then g preserves Heyting implication.*

Proof. Let $a \in H$ be arbitrary. Consider the following two diagrams.

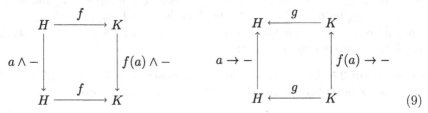

A way to express the assertion that f preserves binary meets is that, for all $a \in H$, the left diagram in (9) commutes. By uniqueness of adjoints, the left diagram in (9) commutes if, and only if, the right diagram in (9) commutes.

The 'in particular'-part now follows since, if f is surjective, then $b' = fg(b')$ for any $b' \in K$ (Proposition 1). $\square$

Lemma 19 and its proof are very similar to, and were in fact directly inspired by, the *Frobenius condition* in [15, Definition p.157] and the remark following it; we leave further exploration of the precise connection to future research.

The following lemma now provides the key connection between the construction of M^s and the $(\wedge,\rightarrow)$-fragment.

Lemma 20. *Let M be a model with borders. Consider the following diagram:*

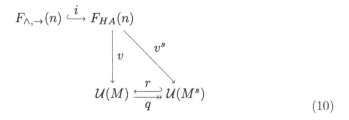

$$(10)$$

where i is the natural inclusion, v and v^s are the valuation maps of M and M^s, respectively, q is the lattice homomorphism dual to the inclusion $M^s \hookrightarrow M$, and r is its upper adjoint. Then r is a $(\wedge, \rightarrow)$-homomorphism, and

$$r \circ v^s \circ i = v \circ i. \qquad (11)$$

Remark 21. Note that, by Proposition 1, the function r sends an up-set V of M^s to the up-set $\{x \in M \mid \forall y \geq x \, (y \in M^s \Rightarrow y \in V)\}$ of M. Therefore, the equality (11) says precisely that, for any $(\wedge, \rightarrow)$-formula φ and $x \in M$, we have

$$M, x \models \varphi \iff \forall y \geq x \, (y \in M^s \Rightarrow M^s, y \models \varphi). \qquad (12)$$

In this sense, Lemma 20 is an algebraic rendering of the crucial ingredient to [2, Proof of Theorem.1]. The proof we give here is different in spirit.

Proof (of Lemma 20). Note that r is $\wedge$-preserving since it is an upper adjoint, and r is $\rightarrow$-preserving by Lemma 19. Therefore, both $v \circ i$ and $r \circ v^s \circ i$ are $(\wedge, \rightarrow)$-homomorphisms. Hence, to prove (11), it suffices to prove that $v \circ i$ and $r \circ v^s \circ i$ are equal on propositional variables. Let p be any propositional variable. We have that $vi(p) \leq rqvi(p) = rv^s i(p)$, because r is upper adjoint to q and $v^s(p) = qv(p)$ by definition of v^s. On the other hand, suppose that $x \notin vi(p)$. Since M is a model with borders, pick $y \in \max(v(p)^c)$ such that $y \geq x$. Then $y \in M^s$, so $x \notin rqvi(p)$, as required. $\qquad \square$

Proposition 22. *Let M be a model with borders and let M^s and $f : M^s \rightarrow M_{\wedge, \rightarrow}$ be as in Definition 16. For any $w \in M^s$ and $(\wedge, \rightarrow)$-formula φ, we have*

$$M, w \models \varphi \iff M_{\wedge, \rightarrow}, f(w) \models \varphi. \qquad (13)$$

Proof. Immediate from Definition 16 and the equivalence in (12). $\qquad \square$

The above considerations in particular allow us to prove the following theorem, originally due to Diego [1].

Theorem 23 (Diego). *For any n, $F_{\wedge, \rightarrow}(n)$ embeds as a $(\wedge, \rightarrow)$-subalgebra into $\mathcal{U}(U(n)_{\wedge, \rightarrow})$. In particular, $F_{\wedge, \rightarrow}(n)$ is finite and therefore, the variety of implicative meet-semilattices is locally finite.*

Proof. Let $h : F_{\wedge,\to}(n) \to \mathcal{U}(U(n)_{\wedge,\to})$ be the extension of the assignment $p_i \mapsto p_i$ to a $(\wedge, \to)$-homomorphism. We show that h is injective. Suppose that $\varphi \neq \psi$ in $F_{\wedge,\to}(n)$. By Lemma 6, we have $v^{U(n)}(i(\varphi)) \neq v^{U(n)}(i(\psi))$. By Lemma 20, applied to $U(n)$, we have $v^s(i(\varphi)) \neq v^s(i(\psi))$, since r is injective. This means that there exists $x \in U(n)^s$ such that $U(n)^s, x \models \varphi$ and $U(n)^s, x \not\models \psi$. Hence, since $f : U(n)^s \to U(n)$ is a p-morphism, we obtain $f(x) \in h(\varphi)$ and $f(x) \notin h(\psi)$, so $h(\varphi) \neq h(\psi)$, as required. The 'in particular'-part now follows, since by Lemma 18, $U(n)_{\wedge,\to}$ is finite. $\qquad\square$

It follows from Theorem 23 that $F_{\wedge,\to}(n)$ is a finite Heyting algebra for each n, in which the binary supremum is given by

$$\varphi \veebar \psi = \bigwedge\{\chi \in F_{\wedge,\to}(n) \mid \varphi \leq \chi \text{ and } \psi \leq \chi\}, \tag{14}$$

and the bottom element $\underline{\bot}$ is given by $p_1 \wedge \cdots \wedge p_n$.

Definition 24. *For each intuitionistic formula φ, let $s(\varphi)$ denote the formula obtained from φ by replacing each occurrence of a disjunction $\vee$ by $\veebar$, and replacing each occurrence of $\bot$ by $\underline{\bot}$.*

Algebraically, the above definition is the unique Heyting algebra homomorphism $s : F_{HA}(n) \to F_{\wedge,\to}(n)$ extending the assignment $p_i \mapsto p_i$. This means that if φ is provable in IPC, $s(\varphi)$ is also provable in IPC. In particular, if φ implies ψ in IPC, then $s(\varphi \to \psi) = s(\varphi) \to s(\psi)$ is also provable in IPC. This means that $s(\varphi)$ implies $s(\psi)$.

Theorem 25. *Every up-set of $U(n)_{\wedge,\to}$ is definable by a $(\wedge,\to)$-formula.*

Proof. Let U be an up-set of $U(n)_{\wedge,\to}$. Recall that $U(n)_{\wedge,\to}$ is a finite generated submodel of $U(n)$, by Lemma 18. We denote by $\min(U)$ the finite set of minimal points of U. It follows from Theorem 11 that U is defined by the disjunction $\varphi_U := \bigvee_{u \in \min(U)} \varphi_u$ of de Jongh formulas. We also have the $(\wedge, \to)$-formula $s(\varphi_U)$ defined as in Definition 24. To prove the theorem, it therefore suffices to prove the following claim.

Claim. The up-set of $U(n)_{\wedge,\to}$ defined by $s(\varphi_U)$ is equal to U.

Proof of Claim. By induction on the partial order of inclusion of up-sets of $U(n)_{\wedge,\to}$. For the base case, $U = \emptyset$, note that $\min(\emptyset) = \emptyset$, so that $s(\varphi_\emptyset) = s(\bot) = p_1 \wedge \cdots \wedge p_n$, which indeed defines the empty subset of $U(n)_{\wedge,\to}$, since no separated point makes all propositional variables true.

Now suppose that U is a non-empty up-set in $U(n)_{\wedge,\to}$. The induction hypothesis is that, for all proper subsets $V \subsetneq U$, the formula $s(\varphi_V)$ defines V.

We distinguish two cases: (1) U has a one minimal point; (2) U has more than one minimal point.

(1) Let w be the minimum of U. By the induction hypothesis, for every $w' \in I_w$, $s(\varphi_{w'})$ defines $\uparrow w'$ in $U(n)_{\wedge,\to}$. Therefore, the formula $s(\psi_{w'}) = s(\varphi_{w'}) \to s(\theta_{w'})$ defines $(\downarrow w')^c$ in $U(n)_{\wedge,\to}$. Thus, $s(\psi_{w'})$ and $\psi_{w'}$ define the same

up-set in $U(n)_{\wedge,\rightarrow}$. Moreover, the induction hypothesis also implies that $s(\theta_w) = s(\varphi_{\uparrow I_w})$ defines $\uparrow I_w$ in $U(n)_{\wedge,\rightarrow}$. Thus, the formulas $s(\theta_w)$ and θ_w define the same subset of $U(n)_{\wedge,\rightarrow}$. It follows that a point $x \in U(n)_{\wedge,\rightarrow}$ satisfies $s(\varphi_w)$ if, and only if, x satisfies φ_w. By Theorem 11, the latter holds if, and only if, $x \geq w$. Thus, $s(\varphi_w)$ defines $\uparrow w = U$.

(2) Note first that, if $u \in U$, then $u \geq w$ for some $w \in \min(U)$. Therefore, $u \models s(\varphi_w)$, using case (1). Since φ_w implies φ_U in IPC, we have that $s(\varphi_w)$ implies $s(\varphi_U)$. Hence, $u \models s(\varphi_U)$. It remains to show that there is no border point u of U which satisfies $s(\varphi_U)$. Let u be a border point of U. We write B for the up-set $\uparrow I_u$, which is a subset of U since u is a border point of U. We will distinguish two sub-cases: (a) $B = U$, and (b) $B \subsetneq U$.

(a) $B = U$. Then, in particular, $I_u = \min(B) = \min(U)$. Since u is separated, choose a propositional variable q so that u is a q-border point. Then every point $w \in \min(U) = I_u$ satisfies q, so φ_U implies q in IPC, so $s(\varphi_U)$ implies $s(q) = q$ in IPC. Since u does not satisfy q, u also does not satisfy $s(\varphi_U)$.

(b) $B \subsetneq U$. Applying the induction hypothesis to B, we see that $s(\varphi_B) = \bigvee_{u' \in I_u} s(\varphi_{u'})$ defines B. It follows from this that u does not satisfy $s(\psi_u)$, since u certainly satisfies $s(\varphi_u)$, using the induction hypothesis again. An easy application of Theorem 11 shows that, for every $w \in \min(U)$, φ_w implies ψ_u in IPC, since $w \not\leq u$. Hence, $s(\varphi_w)$ implies $s(\psi_u)$, for every $w \in I_u$. Therefore, $s(\varphi_U)$ implies $s(\psi_u)$. However, u does not satisfy $s(\psi_u)$, so u does not satisfy $s(\varphi_U)$. $\square$

Let M be a model with borders. In diagram (15) below we show how the valuation of formulas in the models M and M^s, as in diagram (10), is related to the unique map $f : M^s \rightarrow U(n)$ that was used in the diagram (8).

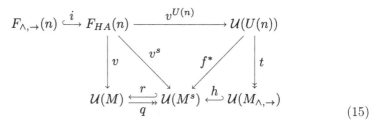

$$(15)$$

In the above diagram, the left part of the diagram is defined as in (10), $v^{U(n)}$ denotes the natural valuation on $U(n)$, and the triangle $f^* = h \circ t$ is the dual of the triangle in (8).

Theorem 26. *Let M be a model with borders. Denote by B be the $(\wedge, \rightarrow)$-subalgebra of $\mathcal{U}(M)$ that is generated by $v(p_1), \ldots, v(p_n)$. Then B is equal to the image of the composite rh. In particular, B isomorphic to the implicative meet-semilattice $\mathcal{U}(M_{\wedge,\rightarrow})$.*

Proof. Chasing the diagram (15), we have:

$$vi = rv^s i = rf^* v^{U(n)} i = rhtv^{U(n)} i, \qquad (16)$$

where we use Lemma 20 and the fact that $v^s = f^* v^{U(n)}$, since f is a p-morphism of models. Note that $B = \text{im}(vi)$, so we need to show that $\text{im}(rh) = \text{im}(vi)$. For the inclusion "$\subseteq$", let $U \in \mathcal{U}(M_{\wedge, \to})$, and $V := rh(U)$; we prove that $V \in \text{im}(vi)$. Since U is an up-set in $U(n)_{\wedge, \to}$ by Lemma 18, Theorem 25 implies that there is a $(\wedge, \to)$-formula φ such that $v^{U(n)} i(\varphi) \cap U(n)_{\wedge, \to} = U$. Therefore, since $U \subseteq M_{\wedge, \to}$, we have $t v^{U(n)} i(\varphi) = v^{U(n)} i(\varphi) \cap M_{\wedge, \to} = U$. Thus, $V = rh(U) = rht v^{U(n)} i(\varphi) = vi(\varphi)$, using (16), so $V \in \text{im}(vi)$.

For the inclusion "$\supseteq$", note first that $\text{im}(rh)$ contains $v(p_1), \ldots, v(p_n)$. It thus remains to show that $\text{im}(rh)$ is a $(\wedge, \to)$-subalgebra of $\mathcal{U}(M)$, or equivalently, that rh preserves $\wedge$ and $\to$. Since r is an upper adjoint and h is sa Heyting homomorphism, rh preserves $\wedge$. Moreover, using Lemma 19 and the fact that $qr = \text{id}$, we have, for any $U, V \in \mathcal{U}(M_{\wedge, \to})$, that

$$rh(U) \to rh(V) = r(qrh(U) \to h(V)) = r(h(U) \to h(V)) = rh(U \to V),$$

where the last step uses that h is a Heyting homomorphism. $\square$

We now use this theorem to prove three facts about the $(\wedge, \to)$-fragment of IPC. The first is a strong form of Diego's theorem.

Corollary 27. *For any n, $F_{\wedge, \to}(n) \cong \mathcal{U}(U(n)_{\wedge, \to})$.*

Proof. Apply Theorem 26 to the model $U(n)$. Using Lemma 6, the map $v^{U(n)} i : F_{\wedge, \to}(n) \to \mathcal{U}(U(n))$ is injective, so $F_{\wedge, \to}(n)$ is isomorphic to the image of $v^{U(n)} i$. The image of $v^{U(n)} i$ is the subalgebra generated by $v(p_1), \ldots, v(p_n)$, which, by Theorem 26 is isomorphic to $\mathcal{U}(U(n))_{\wedge, \to}$. $\square$

Theorem 28. *For any $\varphi \in F_{HA}(n)$ and any model M and $x \in M^s$, we have:*

$$M^s, x \models \varphi \iff M^s, x \models s(\varphi).$$

Proof. Recall that s is the unique Heyting homomorphism $F_{HA}(n) \to F_{\wedge, \to}(n)$ such that $s(p) = p$ for all propositional variables p. Note that si is the identity on $F_{\wedge, \to}(n)$, so s is surjective. Also note that $t v^{U(n)} i$ is surjective, as we showed in the proof of the inclusion "$\subseteq$" of Theorem 26. We conclude that $t v^{U(n)} is$ is a surjective $(\wedge, \to)$-preserving map, and therefore it is a Heyting homomorphism by Lemma 2. Now, $ht v^{U(n)} is$ is also a Heyting homomorphism and $ht v^{U(n)} is(p) = ht v^{U(n)}(p) = v^s(p)$. By uniqueness of the map v^s, we conclude that $ht v^{U(n)} is = v^s$. Thus, for any $x \in M^s$, we have

$$x \in v^s(\varphi) \iff x \in ht v^{U(n)} is(\varphi) \iff x \in f^* v^{U(n)} is(\varphi) \iff x \in v^s is(\varphi),$$

as required. $\square$

Theorem 29. *Let M be a model with borders. Let $U \subseteq M$ be an up-set. The following are equivalent:*

1. There exists a $(\wedge, \to)$-formula φ such that $v(\varphi) = U$;

2. *For all $x \in M$, if, for all $z \in M^s$ such that $z \geq x$, there exists $y \in U \cap M^s$ bisimilar to z in M^s, then $x \in U$;*
3. *For all $x \in M$,*
   (a) if all separated points above x are in U, then $x \in U$, and
   (b) if $x \in M^s$ and there exists $x' \in U \cap M^s$ which is bisimilar to x in M^s, then $x \in U$.

Proof. By Theorem 26(1), the up-sets which are definable by a $(\wedge, \rightarrow)$-formula are precisely the up-sets in the image of rh. Let $h^\flat$ denote the lower adjoint of h, which is given explicitly by sending $S \in \mathcal{U}(M^s)$ to $f(S) \in \mathcal{U}(M_{\wedge,\rightarrow})$. By Proposition 1(1), applied to the adjunction $h^\flat q \dashv rh$, an up-set U is in $\text{im}(rh)$ if, and only if, $rhh^\flat q(U) \subseteq U$. Writing out the definitions of r, h, $h^\flat$ and q, we see that this condition is equivalent to:

$$\forall x \in M, \text{ if } \left(\forall z \in M^s \text{ if } z \geq x \text{ then } z \in f^{-1}(f(U \cap M^s))\right) \text{ then } x \in U.$$

This condition is in turn equivalent to (2), using Remark 9. If (2) holds, then (3a) is clear. For (3b), suppose x is separated and there exists $x' \in U \cap M^s$ which is bisimilar to x in M^s. By bisimilarity, for any $z \in M^s$ with $z \geq x$, there exists $y \in M^s$ with $y \geq x'$ and y bisimilar to z in M^s. Moreover, since U is an up-set containing x', we have $y \in U$. Using (2), we conclude that $x \in U$. Now assume (3) and let $x \in M$ be a point such that for all $z \in M^s$ with $z \geq x$, there exists $y \in U \cap M^s$ bisimilar to z in M^s. If z is any separated point above x, then it follows from applying (3b) to z that $z \in U$. Therefore, by (3a), $x \in U$.   □

4   Subframe Formulas and Uniform Interpolation

In this section we will apply the results obtained in the previous section to show that $(\wedge, \rightarrow)$-versions of de Jongh formulas correspond to subframe formulas in just the same way as de Jongh formulas correspond to Jankov formulas (Theorem 31). We will also use the characterization of $(\wedge, \rightarrow)$-definable up-sets of $U(n)$ to prove that uniform interpolants in the $(\wedge, \rightarrow)$-fragment of IPC are not always given by the IPC-uniform interpolants (Example 34).

We need an auxiliary lemma before proving the main theorem of this section.

Lemma 30. *For each finite rooted frame F, there exist $n \in \omega$ and a colouring $c : F \rightarrow 2^n$ such that $M = (F, c)$ is isomorphic to a generated submodel of $U(n)_{\wedge,\rightarrow}$.*

Proof. Let $n := |F|$ and enumerate the points of F as $x_1, \ldots, x_n$. Define $c(x_i)_j$, the jth coordinate of the colour of the point x_i, to be 1 if $x_i \geq x_j$, and 0 otherwise. All points in $M = (F, c)$ have distinct colours, and are in particular separated, so $M = M^s$. Let f be the unique p-morphism from $M = M^s$ to $U(n)$ from Proposition 8, its image is $M_{\wedge,\rightarrow}$. Recall from Lemma 18 that $M_{\wedge,\rightarrow}$ is a submodel of $U(n)^s$. Let g be the unique p-morphism from $U(n)^s$ onto $U(n)_{\wedge,\rightarrow}$. Since the composite $gf : M \rightarrow U(n)_{\wedge,\rightarrow}$ preserves colours, it is injective, and it is therefore an isomorphism onto a generated submodel of $U(n)_{\wedge,\rightarrow}$.   □

Theorem 31. *Let F be a finite rooted frame and let $M = (F, c)$ be the model on F defined in the proof of Lemma 30. There exists a $(\wedge, \rightarrow)$-formula $\beta(F)$ such that for any descriptive model N we have*

$$N \not\models \beta(F) \quad \Longleftrightarrow \quad M \text{ is a p-morphic image of } N^s.$$

Proof. By Lemma 30, M is isomorphic to a generated submodel of $U(n)_{\wedge, \rightarrow}$. Without loss of generality, we will assume in the rest of this proof that M actually *is* a generated submodel of $U(n)_{\wedge, \rightarrow}$. Since the model M is rooted, there exists $w \in U(n)_{\wedge, \rightarrow}$ such that $M = \uparrow w$. We define $\beta(F) := s(\psi_w) = s(\varphi_w) \rightarrow s(\theta_w)$ and prove that $\beta(F)$ satisfies the required property.

First note that, as follows from the proof of Theorem 25, $s(\varphi_w)$ defines the up-set of $U(n)_{\wedge, \rightarrow}$ generated by w and $s(\theta_w)$ defines the up-set of $U(n)_{\wedge, \rightarrow}$ generated by the set of proper successors of w. Therefore, w is the only point of $U(n)_{\wedge, \rightarrow}$ that satisfies $s(\varphi_w)$ and refutes $s(\theta_w)$.

Let $v \in N$ be such that $N, v \not\models \beta(F)$. Since N is descriptive, we can find a successor u of v such that $N, u \models s(\varphi_w)$, $N, u \not\models s(\theta_w)$ and every proper successor of u satisfies $s(\theta_w)$ (see, e.g., [5, Theorem 2.3.24]). By Lemma 14, this implies that $u \in N^s$. Let $f : N^s \rightarrow U(n)_{\wedge, \rightarrow}$ be the unique p-morphism as in Proposition 8. Because $u \in N^s$, $s(\varphi_w)$ is a $(\wedge, \rightarrow)$-formula and $N, u \models s(\varphi_w)$, Proposition 22 entails that $U(n)_{\wedge, \rightarrow}, f(u) \models s(\varphi_w)$. By the same argument we also have that $U(n)_{\wedge, \rightarrow}, f(u) \not\models s(\theta_w)$. Thus, we obtain that $U(n)_{\wedge, \rightarrow}, f(u) \models s(\varphi_w)$ and $U(n)_{\wedge, \rightarrow}, f(u) \not\models s(\theta_w)$. We have shown in the previous paragraph that this implies $f(u) = w$. Therefore, as f is a p-morphism, we obtain that F is a p-morphic image of N^s.

For the other direction, let $f : N^s \rightarrow M$ be a surjective p-morphism. Since f is surjective, pick $u \in N^s$ such that $f(u) = w$. As w satisfies $s(\varphi_w)$ and refutes $s(\theta_w)$, and both are $(\wedge, \rightarrow)$-formulas, the same argument as above gives that $N, u \models s(\varphi_w)$ and $N, u \not\models s(\theta_w)$. Hence, $N \not\models \beta(F)$. □

The formula $\beta(F)$ defined in Theorem 31 is called the *subframe formula* of F.

Recall that, for any formula φ in n variables, we say a Heyting algebra A *validates the equation* $\varphi \approx 1$, notation $A \models \varphi \approx 1$, if $\overline{v}(\varphi) = 1$ under each assignment $v : \{p_1, \ldots, p_n\} \rightarrow A$. If there is an assignment v under which $\overline{v}(\varphi) \neq 1$, we say that A *refutes the equation* $\varphi \approx 1$.

Corollary 32. *Let F be a finite rooted frame and A its Heyting algebra of up-sets. Then for each Heyting algebra B we have*

$$B \not\models \beta(F) \approx 1 \quad \Longleftrightarrow \quad \text{there is a } (\wedge, \rightarrow)\text{-embedding } A \hookrightarrow B$$

Proof. It follows from the proof of Theorem 31 that the model (F, c) refutes $\beta(F)$. This means that, in the Heyting algebra $A = \mathcal{U}(F)$, the formula $\beta(F)$ does not evaluate to 1 under the assignment $v : p_i \mapsto c^*(p_i)$. Suppose that there is a $(\wedge, \rightarrow)$-embedding $i : A \hookrightarrow B$. Since $\beta(F)$ is a $(\wedge, \rightarrow)$-formula, under the assignment $i \circ v$, the formula $\beta(F)$ does not evaluate to 1 in B. Conversely, suppose that $B \not\models \beta(F) \approx 1$, under an assignment v. Let G be the descriptive

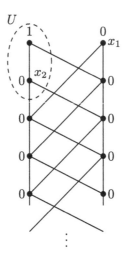

Fig. 1. The 1-universal model, $U(1)$, also known as the Rieger-Nishimura ladder, with $U(1)^s = \{x_1, x_2\}$ and $U = v(\neg\neg p)$.

frame with B as its algebra of admissible up-sets. The assignment v yields an admissible colouring c' on G with the property that $N = (G, c') \not\models \beta(F)$. By Theorem 31, this implies in particular that F is a p-morphic image of N^s. It now follows from Theorem 26 that A is $(\wedge, \rightarrow)$-embedded into B.   □

Remark 33. Subframe formulas axiomatize a large class of logics having the finite model property [6, Chap. 11]. The frames of these logics are closed under taking subframes. Alternatively varieties of Heyting algebras corresponding to these logics are closed under $(\wedge, \rightarrow)$-subalgebras. There exist many different ways to define subframe formulas for intuionistic logic: model-theoretic [6, Chap. 11], algebraic [8,16], and via the so-called NNIL formulas [17]. Theorem 31 gives a new way to define subframe formulas. The proof of this theorem shows that the same way de Jongh formulas for intuitionistic logic correspond to Jankov formulas [5], de Jongh formulas for the $(\wedge, \rightarrow)$-fragment of intuitionistic logic correspond to subframe formulas. This provides a different perspective on the interaction of de Jongh-type formulas and frame-based formulas such as Jankov formulas, subframe formulas etc.

We finish this section by applying the results of this paper to show that the uniform IPC-interpolant, as defined by Pitts [18], of a meet-implication formula is not necessarily equivalent to a meet-implication formula.

Example 34. As can be readily checked, the uniform interpolant of the formula $p \rightarrow (q \rightarrow p)$ in IPC with respect to the variable p is the formula $\neg\neg p$. We will use the characterization in Theorem 29 to prove that $\neg\neg p$ is not equivalent to a $(\wedge, \rightarrow)$-formula. Namely, if there were a $(\wedge, \rightarrow)$-formula φ equivalent to $\neg\neg p$, then in particular the up-set U defined by the formula $\neg\neg p$ in the 1-universal model of IPC (see Fig. 1 below) would be $(\wedge, \rightarrow)$-definable. It thus suffices to show that

U is not $(\wedge, \rightarrow)$-definable. To see this, note that $U(1)^s = \max v(p)^c = \{x_1, x_2\}$, and these two points are bisimilar in $U(1)^s$. Since $x_2 \in U$ but $x_1 \notin U$, U does not satisfy (3b) in Theorem 29, and is therefore not $(\wedge, \rightarrow)$-definable.

We now also prove that the least $(\wedge, \rightarrow)$-definable up-set of $U(1)$ containing U is $U(1)$ itself. Indeed, let W be a $(\wedge, \rightarrow)$-definable up-set which contains U. Then, by the above, x_1 belongs to W. It then easily follows from (3a) in Theorem 29 that every colour 0 point of $U(1)$ must also belong to W. Thus, $W = U(1)$. This argument shows, via semantics, that the $(\wedge, \rightarrow)$-formula which is a uniform interpolant of $p \rightarrow (q \rightarrow p)$ is $\top$. We refer to [19] for more details on uniform interpolation in fragments of intuitionistic logic. □

5 Conclusions and Future Work

In this paper we studied the $(\wedge, \rightarrow)$-fragment of intuitionistic logic via methods of duality theory. We gave an alternative proof of Diego's theorem and characterized $(\wedge, \rightarrow)$-definable up-sets of the n-universal model of intuitionistic logic, using duality as our main tool. Interestingly, we were able to directly use finite duality for distributive lattices and adjunction properties such as the Frobenius property (Lemma 19), without resorting to any of the existing dualities for implicative meet-semilattices. We expect that the techniques developed in Sect. 3 could be extended to the infinite setting in order to give a unified account of the different dualities that exist in the literature for implicative meet-semilattices, e.g., [3,7] and [8]. We leave this as an interesting question for future work.

The characterization of $(\wedge, \rightarrow)$-definable up-sets that we gave in Theorem 29 can be considered as a first step towards solving the complicated problem of characterizing all IPC-definable up-sets of n-universal models. This problem is linked to the following interesting question. In [20] free Heyting algebras are described from free distributive lattices via step-by-step approximations of the operation $\rightarrow$. In [21], the authors explained how the construction in [20] can be understood via (finite) duality for distributive lattices. This begs the question whether one can use duality for implicative meet-semilattices to build free Heyting algebras, starting from free implicative meet-semilattices and approximating the operation of disjunction, $\vee$, step-by-step. The results of this paper can be considered as the first (or actually zeroth) step of such a step-by-step construction.

Finally, we note that [22] and [23] study n-universal models in other fragments of intuitionistic logic. We leave it to future work to investigate how the duality methods of this paper relate to the methods developed in [22] and [23].

Acknowledgements. We are thankful to Mai Gehrke for many inspiring discussions on this paper. We also thank the referees for many useful suggestions. The first listed author would also like to acknowledge the support of the Rustaveli Science Foundation of Georgia under grant FR/489/5-105/11.

References

1. Diego, A.: Sur les algèbres de Hilbert (transl. from the Spanish original by L. Iturrioz). Collection de Logique Mathématique, vol. Série A 21. Gauthier-Villars, Paris (1966)
2. Renardel de Lavalette, G.R., Hendriks, A., de Jongh, D.H.J.: Intuitionistic implication without disjunction. J. Logic Comput. **22**, 375–404 (2012)
3. Köhler, P.: Brouwerian semilattices. Trans. Amer. Math. Soc. **268**, 103–126 (1981)
4. de Jongh, D.: Investigations on the intuitionistic propositional Calculus. Ph.D. thesis, University of Wisconsin (1968)
5. Bezhanishvili, N.: Lattices of Intermediate and Cylindric Modal Logics. ILLC Dissertation Series, ILLC, vol. 2006-2. University of Amsterdam, Amsterdam (2006)
6. Chagrov, A., Zakharyaschev, M.: Modal Lc. In: Oxford Logic Guides, vol. 35. Clarendon Press, Oxford (1997)
7. Bezhanishvili, G., Jansana, R.: Esakia style duality for implicative semilattices. Appl. Categ. Struct. **21**, 181–208 (2013)
8. Bezhanishvili, G., Bezhanishvili, N.: An algebraic approach to canonical formulas: intuitionistic case. Rev. Symb. Log. **2**, 517–549 (2009)
9. Gehrke, M.: Canonical extensions, Esakia spaces, and universal models. In: Bezhanishvili, G. (ed.) Leo Esakia on Duality in Modal and Intuitionistic Logics. Trends in Logic: Outstanding Contributions. Springer, New York (2013). http://www.liafa.univ-paris-diderot.fr/mgehrke/Ge12.pdf
10. Davey, B.A., Priestley, H.A.: Introduction to Lattices and Order, 2nd edn. Cambridge University Press, Cambridge (2002)
11. Bezhanishvili, G., Gehrke, M., Mines, R., Morandi, P.J.: Profinite completions and canonical extensions of Heyting algebras. Order **23**, 143–161 (2006)
12. Yang, F.: Intuitionistic Subframe Formulas, $NNIL$-formulas, and n-universal Models, vol. 2008-12, Master of Logic Thesis Series. ILLC, University of Amsterdam (2008)
13. Priestley, H.A.: Representation of distributive lattices by means of ordered Stone spaces. Bull. London Math. Soc. **2**, 186–190 (1970)
14. Esakia, L.L.: Topological Kripke models. Sov. Math. Dokl. **15**, 147–151 (1974)
15. Pitts, A.M.: Amalgamation and interpolation in the category of Heyting algebras. J. Pure and Appl. Algebra **29**, 155–165 (1983)
16. Bezhanishvili, G., Ghilardi, S.: An algebraic approach to subframe logics. Intuitionistic case. Ann. Pure Appl. Logic **147**, 84–100 (2007)
17. Visser, A., de Jongh, D., van Benthem, J., de Lavalette, G.R.: NNIL a study in intuitionistic logic. In: Ponse, A., de Rijke, M., Venema, Y. (eds.) Modal Logics and Process Algebra: A Bisimulation Perspective, pp. 289–326 (1995)
18. Pitts, A.M.: On an interpretation of second order quantification in first order intuitionistic propositional logic. J. Symbolic Log. **57**, 33–52 (1992)
19. de Jongh, D., Zhao, Z.: Positive formulas in intuitionistic and minimal logic. In: Aher, M., Hole, D., Jerabek, E., Kupke, C. (eds.) Logic, Language, and Computation. LNCS, vol. 8984, pp. xx–yy. Springer, Heidelberg (2014)
20. Ghilardi, S.: Free Heyting algebras as bi-Heyting algebras. C. R. Math. Acad. Sci. Soc. R. Canada **XVI**, 240–244 (1992)
21. Bezhanishvili, N., Gehrke, M.: Finitely generated free Heyting algebras via Birkhoff duality and coalgebra. Log. Methods Comput. Sci. **7**, 1–24 (2011)
22. Hendriks, A.: Computations in Propositional Logic, vol. 1996-01, ILLC Dissertation Series. ILLC, University of Amsterdam (1996)
23. Tzimoulis, A., Zhao, Z.: The universal model for the negation-free fragment of IPC. Report X-2013-01, ILLC, University of Amsterdam (2013)

Cut-Elimination and Proof Schemata

Cvetan Dunchev[1], Alexander Leitsch[1], Mikheil Rukhaia[2(✉)],
and Daniel Weller[3]

[1] Institute of Computer Languages, Vienna University of Technology,
Vienna, Austria
{cdunchev,leitsch}@logic.at
[2] Vekua Institute of Applied Mathematics, Tbilisi State University,
Tbilisi, Georgia
mrukhaia@logic.at
[3] Institute of Discrete Mathematics and Geometry, Vienna University
of Technology, Vienna, Austria
weller@logic.at

Abstract. By Gentzen's famous Hauptsatz (the cut-elimination theorem) every proof in sequent calculus for first-order logic with cuts can be transformed into a cut-free proof; cut-free proofs are analytic and consist entirely of syntactic material of the end-sequent (the proven theorem). But in systems with induction rules, cut-elimination is either impossible or does not produce proofs with the subformula property. One way to overcome this problem is to formulate induction proofs as infinite sequences of proofs in a uniform way and to develop a method, which yields a uniform description of the corresponding cut-free proofs. We present such a formalism, as an alternative to systems with induction rules, and define a corresponding cut-elimination method (based on the CERES-method for first-order logic). The basic tools of proof theory, such as sequent- and resolution calculi are enriched with inductive definitions and schemata of terms, formulas, proofs, etc. We define a class of inductive proofs which can be transformed into this formalism and subjected to schematic cut-elimination.

1 Introduction

Cut-elimination was originally introduced by G. Gentzen as a theoretical tool from which results like decidability and consistency could be proven. Cut-free proofs are computationally explicit objects from which interesting information such as Herbrand disjunctions and interpolants can be easily extracted. When viewing formal proofs as a model for mathematical proofs, cut-elimination corresponds to the removal of lemmas, which leads to interesting applications (see, e.g. [4,5]).

For such applications to mathematical proofs, the cut-elimination method CERES (cut-elimination by resolution) was developed in [6]. It essentially reduces cut-elimination for a proof π to a theorem proving problem: the refutation of the *characteristic clause set* $\mathrm{CL}(\pi)$. Given a resolution refutation ρ of $\mathrm{CL}(\pi)$, an essentially cut-free proof can be constructed by a proof-theoretic transformation.

This work was supported by the project I383 of the Austrian Science Fund.

M. Aher et al. (Eds.): TbiLLC 2013, LNCS 8984, pp. 117–136, 2015.
DOI: 10.1007/978-3-662-46906-4_8

It is well-known that cut-elimination in a standard calculus of arithmetic with an induction rule is impossible in general [18]. In the inductive calculi defined in [9,14,15] cut-elimination works but does not produce analytic proofs, i.e. proofs with the subformula property. The aim of this paper is the development of a schematic calculus (representing a class of inductive proofs) admitting cut-elimination providing *analytic proofs*. Instead of proving a sequent $S\colon \Gamma \vdash \forall x.\, A(x)$ with induction we consider the infinite sequence $S_n\colon \Gamma \vdash A(n)$ and proofs φ_n of S_n. Each of these proofs φ_n is an ordinary LK-proof and enjoys cut-elimination resulting in an analytic proof. One could hope that, with a sufficiently nice finite description of the infinite sequence φ_n, a finite description of a sequence of corresponding cut-free proofs comes within reach. The subject of this paper is to find appropriate finite representations of such proof sequences and to develop a formalism to represent sequences of corresponding cut-free proofs as well as the induced Herbrand disjunctions. It turned out that, to this aim, the method CERES is more suitable than the traditional reductive method: in [5] Fürstenberg's proof of the infinitude of primes was formalized as a proof schema and then analyzed by the CERES method. It turned out that the schema of resolution refutations of (the schemata of) the characteristic clause sets defines a substitution schema representing Euclid's construction of primes. In fact, the schema of characteristic clause sets (which is much more compact and shorter than the proof schema itself) encodes the main information provided by cut-elimination – the instantiations of quantifiers; this information is revealed by the resolution refutations. The analysis of Fürstenberg's proof was mainly performed purely mathematically (i.e. on the meta level) and the resolution schema was defined and proven correct by hand. Therefore a higher degree of mechanization appears desirable. As a full automation of CERES in proof schemata is unrealistic we concentrate on subclasses of schemata (representing specific types of inductive proofs) and develop formalisms which serve as tools for partial mechanization of cut-elimination in schemata and as a basis for proving formally the correctness of the result.

Because of lack of space, many proofs are just sketches; for full details we refer to [12,16].

1.1   Related Work

In [15] a reductive cut-elimination method was given for intuitionistic proof systems with induction. Although the language they consider is first-order, they allow higher-order quantification on terms (but not on predicates). We do not allow quantification over schematic variables, but just on instances of them (which are variables of type ι).

Another approach is to avoid the explicit use of an induction rule by so-called cyclic proofs. In [8] a cyclic proof system is presented and it is shown that this system subsumes the use of the induction rule. The problem of cut-elimination for cyclic proofs is still open [9].

In this paper we define a proof system similar to the cyclic proofs of [8]. There are some major differences between the two systems: instead of using a trace condition and a notion of companion node, we will have a notion of *proof link* with associated primitive recursive proof definitions. In cyclic proofs, only predicate symbols are divided into ordinary and inductive sets, i.e. no inductively defined terms are allowed. Finally, cyclic proofs subsume full induction, while in our system we can have only simple inductions. Every proof from our system can be transformed into a proof from the system given in [8].

2   Notations and Definitions

We work in a two-sorted setting with the sort ω, intended to represent the natural numbers, and the sort ι, intended to represent an arbitrary first-order domain. Our language consists of countable sets of *variables* of both sorts, and sorted n-ary function and predicate symbols, i.e. we associate with every n-ary function f a tuple of sorts $(\tau_1, \ldots, \tau_n, \tau)$ with the intended interpretation $f\colon \tau_1 \times \cdots \times \tau_n \to \tau$, and analogously for predicate symbols.

Terms are built from variables and function symbols in the usual inductive fashion. We assume the constant function symbols $0\colon \omega$ and $s\colon \omega \to \omega$ (zero and successor) to be present (if $t\colon \omega$ we will often write $t+1$ instead of $s(t)$). By $V(t)$ we denote the set of variables of a term t.

Formulas are built inductively from atoms using the logical connectives $\neg$, $\wedge$, $\vee$, $\Rightarrow$, $\forall$ and $\exists$ as usual. A variable occurrence in a formula is called *bound* if it is in the scope of $\forall$ or $\exists$ connectives, otherwise it is called *free*. The notions of interpretation, satisfiability and validity of formulas are defined in the usual classical sense.

Sequents are expressions of the form $\Gamma \vdash \Delta$, where Γ and Δ are multisets of formulas. Sequents containing only atomic formulas are called *clauses*. We define some simple operations on sequents: let $S\colon \Gamma \vdash \Delta$ and $S'\colon \Pi \vdash \Lambda$ be sequents; we define $S \circ S'$ (the merge of S and S') as $\Gamma, \Pi \vdash \Delta, \Lambda$. Let $\mathcal{S}$ and $\mathcal{S}'$ be sets of sequents then $\mathcal{S} \times \mathcal{S}' = \{S \circ S' \mid S \in \mathcal{S}, S' \in \mathcal{S}'\}$.

Let $\mathcal{E}$ be a finite set of equations. We consider an extension of the sequent calculus LK (defined as usual) by an equality rule $\mathcal{E}$, which makes the notation of mathematical proofs more ractical, and by the induction rule ind:

$$\frac{S[t]}{S[t']}\mathcal{E} \qquad \frac{\Gamma \vdash \Delta, A(0) \quad A(k), \Pi \vdash \Lambda, A(s(k))}{\Gamma, \Pi \vdash \Delta, \Lambda, A(t)}\text{ind}$$

For the $\mathcal{E}$ rule, we require that $\mathcal{E} \models t = t'$, and for ind, k is a variable of sort ω, not occurring in $\Gamma, \Pi, \Delta, \Lambda$ and t is a term of sort ω. We denote this calculus by LKIE. Note that, without restrictions on the $\mathcal{E}$ rule, its applicability is undecidable in general. However, in our paper, the equational theories consist of equations which can be oriented to terminating and confluent rewrite systems and thus are decidable. The system LKIE $\setminus \{\text{ind}\}$ is denoted by LKE.

A *proof* is a tree where the nodes are labeled by sequent occurrences and edges are labeled by rules in the usual way. A proof of S is a proof with root node S. Let $\mathcal{A}$ be a set of sequents; a proof φ of S from $\mathcal{A}$ is a proof of S where all leaves of φ belong to $\mathcal{A}$. If not stated otherwise $\mathcal{A}$ is defined as the set of sequents of the form $A \vdash A$ for atomic formulas A over the underlying syntax.

A proof φ is called *cut-free* if the cut rule does not occur in φ. φ is called an *atomic cut normal form* if all cuts are on atomic formulas only. Finally, proofs are endowed with an *ancestor relation* on occurrences of formulas in a natural way (for a precise definition see [6]).

2.1　A Motivating Example

Now we turn our attention to the issue of cut-elimination in the presence of induction. Let us consider the equational theory $\mathcal{E} = \{f_I(0, x) = x, f_I(s(n), x) = f(f_I(n, x))\}$ and the sequent S:

$$\forall x(P(x) \Rightarrow P(f(x))) \vdash \forall n((P(f_I(n, c)) \Rightarrow P(g(n, c))) \Rightarrow (P(c) \Rightarrow P(g(n, c))))$$

Obviously, S is not valid in pure first-order logic (under the theory $\mathcal{E}$) and thus cannot be proven without induction. That means that there exists no proof of S in LKE. In fact we need the following inductive lemma: $\forall x(P(x) \Rightarrow P(f(x))) \vdash \forall n \forall x(P(x) \Rightarrow P(f_I(n, x)))$.

A proof ψ of this inductive lemma in LKIE could be:

$$
\dfrac{
\dfrac{
\dfrac{
\dfrac{
\dfrac{P(f_I(0, u)) \vdash P(f_I(0, u))}{P(u) \vdash P(f_I(0, u))}\mathcal{E}
}{\vdash P(u) \Rightarrow P(f_I(0, u))}{\Rightarrow_r}
}{\vdash \forall x(P(x) \Rightarrow P(f_I(0, x)))}{\forall_r}
\quad
\dfrac{\boxed{\,\psi_r\,}\qquad \Gamma, \forall x(P(x) \Rightarrow P(f_I(\alpha, x))) \vdash \forall x(P(x) \Rightarrow P(f_I(s(\alpha), x)))}{}
}{\forall x(P(x) \Rightarrow P(f(x))) \vdash \forall x(P(x) \Rightarrow P(f_I(\gamma, x)))}\text{ind}
}{\forall x(P(x) \Rightarrow P(f(x))) \vdash \forall n \forall x(P(x) \Rightarrow P(f_I(n, x)))}{\forall_r}
$$

where $\Gamma = \forall x(P(x) \Rightarrow P(f(x)))$ and ψ_r is a simple cut-free first-order proof. Now we can define a proof φ of the sequent S

$$
\dfrac{\boxed{\,\psi\,}\qquad\qquad \boxed{\,\varphi_r\,}}{
\dfrac{\forall x(P(x) \Rightarrow P(f(x))) \vdash C \qquad C \vdash \forall n((P(f_I(n, c)) \Rightarrow P(g(n, c))) \Rightarrow (P(c) \Rightarrow P(g(n, c))))}{\forall x(P(x) \Rightarrow P(f(x))) \vdash \forall n((P(f_I(n, c)) \Rightarrow P(g(n, c))) \Rightarrow (P(c) \Rightarrow P(g(n, c))))}}\text{cut}
$$

where C denotes $\forall n \forall x(P(x) \Rightarrow P(f_I(n, x)))$ and φ_r is a simple cut-free first-order proof.

In the attempt of performing reductive cut-elimination a la Gentzen, we locate the place in the proof, where $\forall n$ is introduced. In φ_r, $\forall n \forall x(P(x) \Rightarrow P(f_I(n, x)))$ is obtained from $\forall x(P(x) \Rightarrow P(f_I(\beta, x)))$ by $\forall_l$ (where β is an eigenvariable introduced by $\forall_r$). In the proof ψ we may delete the $\forall_r$ inference yielding the cut-formula and replace γ by β. But in the attempt to eliminate $\forall x(P(x) \Rightarrow P(f_I(\beta, x)))$ in ψ we get stuck, as we cannot "cross" the ind rule. Neither can the indrule be eliminated as β is variable. In fact, if we had instead $\forall x(P(x) \Rightarrow P(f_I(t, x)))$ for a closed term t over $\{0, s, +, *\}$ we could prove $\vdash t = \bar{n}$ from the axioms of Peano arithmetic and also

$$\forall x(P(x) \Rightarrow P(f(x))) \vdash \forall x(P(x) \Rightarrow P(f_I(\bar{n}, x)))$$

without induction (by iterated cuts) and cut-elimination would proceed.

This problem, however, is neither rooted in the specific form of ψ nor the ind rule. In fact, there exists no cut-free proof of S in LKIE. In fact, by the subformula property, the conclusion of the induction rule must be the sequent

$$\forall x(P(x) \Rightarrow P(f(x)) \vdash (P(f_I(\alpha,c)) \Rightarrow P(g(\alpha,c))) \Rightarrow (P(c) \Rightarrow P(g(\alpha,c)))$$

for some variable α. But this is impossible, as the corresponding induction step (the right premise of the induction rule) would be the sequent

$$\forall x(P(x) \Rightarrow P(f(x)), (P(f_I(\beta,c)) \Rightarrow P(g(\beta,c))) \Rightarrow (P(c) \Rightarrow P(g(\beta,c)))$$
$$\vdash$$
$$(P(f_I(s(\beta),c)) \Rightarrow P(g(s(\beta),c))) \Rightarrow (P(c) \Rightarrow P(g(s(\beta),c)))$$

which is not valid and thus not derivable in LKE. In order to prove the end-sequent an inductive lemma is needed; something which implies $\forall n \forall x(P(x) \Rightarrow P(f_I(n,x)))$ and cannot be eliminated.

While there are no cut-free proofs of S in LKIE, the sequents S_n:

$$\forall x(P(x) \Rightarrow P(f(x))) \vdash ((P(f_I(\bar{n},c)) \Rightarrow P(g(\bar{n},c))) \Rightarrow (P(c) \Rightarrow P(g(\bar{n},c))))$$

do have such proofs in LKE for all numerals $\bar{n}$; indeed, they can be proven without induction. But instead of a unique proof φ of S we get an infinite sequence of proofs φ_n of S_n, which have cut-free versions φ'_n. This kind of "infinitary" cut-elimination only makes sense if there exists a *uniform* representation of the sequence of proofs φ'_n. In the next sections we develop a formalism that has the potential of producing such a uniform representation, thus paving the way for cut-elimination in the presence of induction.

3   Schematic Language

In order to give a systematic treatment of cut-elimination in the presence of induction along the lines of the previous section, we start by defining a *schematic first-order language*, an extension of the language described in [1,2] to first-order logic. This formal language will allow us to specify an (infinite) set of first-order formulas by a finite term. Towards this, we assume that our function symbols are partitioned into *constant function symbols* and *defined function symbols*. The first set will contain the usual uninterpreted function symbols and the second will allow primitive recursively defined functions in the language. Additionally we introduce *schematic variable symbols* of type $\omega \rightarrow \iota$ and build *schematic variables* from schematic variable symbols and terms of type ω, which will be used to describe infinite sequences of distinct variables. By $\bar{}$ we denote sequences of terms of appropriate type.

For every defined function symbol f, we assume that its type is $\omega \times \tau_1 \times \cdots \times \tau_n \rightarrow \tau$ (with $n \geq 0$), and we assume given two rewrite rules

$$f(0,\bar{x}) \rightarrow t_0 \quad \text{and} \quad f(s(y),\bar{x}) \rightarrow t[f(y,\bar{x})]$$

where $t[\cdot]$ is a context, $V(t_0) \subseteq \{x_1, \ldots, x_n\}$, $V(t[f(y, \overline{x})]) \subseteq \{y, x_1, \ldots, x_n\}$, and t_0, t are terms not containing f; if a defined function symbol g occurs in t_0 or t then $g \prec f$. We assume that these rewrite rules are primitive recursive, i.e. that $\prec$ is irreflexive. To denote that an expression t rewrites to an expression t' (in arbitrarily many steps), we write $t \twoheadrightarrow t'$. It is obvious that, in our term language, the primitive recursive functions can be expressed.

Theorem 3.1. *The unification problem of terms is undecidable.*

Proof. Immediate since multiplication can be represented in our settings. For the details see [12,16,17]. □

Analogously to function symbols, we assume that the predicate symbols are partitioned into *constant predicate symbols* and *defined predicate symbols*, assuming as above, rewrite rules and an irreflexive order $\prec$ for the latter, to build *formula schemata*. In our setting, it is important to clarify how to interpret multiple occurrences of the same bound variable. For an occurrence of a bound variable x, we consider the lowermost (in the bottom-growing formula-tree) quantifier that binds x to be associated to that occurrence.

Proposition 3.1. *Let A be a formula. Then every rewrite sequence starting at A terminates, and A has a unique normal form.*

Proof. Trivial, since all definitions are primitive recursive. □

4 Schematic Proofs

Towards defining a notion of *proof schema*, we need to introduce some notations: Let $S(\overline{x})$ be a sequent with the vector of free variables $\overline{x}$, then by $S(\overline{t})$ we denote $S(\overline{x})$ where $\overline{x}$ is replaced by $\overline{t}$ respectively, where $\overline{t}$ is a vector terms of appropriate type. We assume a countably infinite set of *proof symbols* denoted by φ, ψ, φ_i, ψ_j. If φ is a proof symbol and $S(\overline{x})$ a sequent, then the expression $\dfrac{\varphi(\overline{t})}{S(\overline{t})}$ is called a *proof link*. For a variable $k \colon \omega$, proof links such that $V(a_1) \subseteq \{k\}$ are called *k-proof links*.

Definition 4.1. *The sequent calculus* LKS *consists of the rules of* LKE, *where proof links may appear at the leaves of a proof, and where $\mathcal{E}$ is the set of rewrite rules (interpreted as equations) for the defined function and predicate symbols.*

Note that LK-proofs are also LKS-proofs and we call them *normal* LKS-*proofs*.

Definition 4.2 (Proof Schemata). *Let ψ be a proof symbol and $S(n, \overline{x})$ be a sequent such that $n \colon \omega$. Then a proof schema pair for ψ is a pair of* LKS-*proofs $(\pi, \nu(k))$ with end-sequents $S(0, \overline{x})$ and $S(k+1, \overline{x})$ respectively, such that π may not contain proof links and $\nu(k)$ may contain only proof links of the form $\dfrac{\psi(k, \overline{t})}{S(k, \overline{t})}$ and we say that it is a* proof link *to ψ. We call $S(n, \overline{x})$ the end-sequent of ψ,*

and assume an identification between formula occurrences in the end-sequents of
π *and* $\nu(k)$ *so that we can speak of occurrences in the end-sequent of* ψ.

   Finally, a proof schema Ψ *is a tuple of proof schema pairs for* $\psi_1, \ldots, \psi_\alpha$,
written as $\langle \psi_1, \ldots, \psi_\alpha \rangle$, *such that the* LKS-*proofs for* ψ_β *may also contain*
k-proof links to ψ_γ *for* $1 \leq \beta < \gamma \leq \alpha$. *We also say that the end-sequent of*
ψ_1 *is* the end-sequent *of* Ψ.

According to the definition above, proof schemata naturally represent infinite
sequences of (first-order) proofs. Towards stating this fact formally as a soundness result we need a notion of evaluation of proof schemata.

Definition 4.3 (Evaluation of Proof Schemata). *Let* Ψ *be a proof schema.*
We define the rewrite rules for proof links in Ψ

$$\frac{\psi(0, \overline{x})}{S(0, \overline{x})} \to \pi \quad \text{and} \quad \frac{\psi(k+1, \overline{x})}{S(k+1, \overline{x})} \to \nu(k)$$

for all proof schema pairs $(\pi, \nu(k))$ *for* ψ. *Now for* $\gamma \in \mathbb{N}$ *we define* $\psi \downarrow_\gamma$ *as*
a normal form of $\dfrac{\psi(\gamma, \overline{x})}{S(\gamma, \overline{x})}$ *under the rewrite system just given extended by the*
rewrite rules for defined function and predicate symbols. Further, we define $\Psi \downarrow_\gamma =$
$\psi_1 \downarrow_\gamma$.

Proposition 4.1 (Soundness of Proof Schemata). *Let* Ψ *be a proof schema*
with end-sequent $S(n, \overline{x})$, *and let* $\gamma \in \mathbb{N}$. *Then there exists an* LK-*proof of*
$S(\gamma, \overline{x}) \downarrow$.

Proof. By induction on γ, using Definition 4.3 it is easy to see that the proposition holds for a proof schema containing only one proof symbol. Then the result
follows by induction on the number of proof symbols in Ψ.   □

Corollary 4.1. *The sequent calculus* LKS *is sound.*

   Let π be an LKIE-proof. If all induction rules in π are of the following form:

$$\frac{\Gamma \vdash \Delta, A(0) \quad A(k), \Pi \vdash \Lambda, A(k+1)}{\Gamma, \Pi \vdash \Delta, \Lambda, A(t)} \text{ind}$$

where $k \colon \omega$ and $V(t) \subseteq \{k\}$, then π is called *k-simple*.

Proposition 4.2. *Let* π *be a k-simple* LKIE-*proof of a sequent* S. *Then there*
exists a proof schema with end-sequent S.

Proof. Inductively introduce for each ind rule in π a new proof symbol and
replace the ind rule with the corresponding proof link. Then extract a proof
schema pair $(\pi_\beta, \nu_\beta(k))$ out of ind, taking its left premise as π_β; $\nu_\beta(k)$ is constructed via cut on the corresponding proof link and on the right premise of the
ind rule. If necessary add weakening and contraction rules at the end of π_β and
$\nu_\beta(k)$ respectively to match the end-sequent.   □

Example 4.1. The proof ψ of the inductive lemma given in Sect. 2.1 is k-simple, thus it can be transformed to a proof schema pair of the sequent $S_\psi(n) = \forall x(P(x) \Rightarrow P(f(x))) \vdash \forall x(P(x) \Rightarrow P(f_I(n,x)))$. For the defined function symbol f_I, we assume as rewrite rules (oriented versions of) the equalities given in Sect. 2.1. Then we define a proof schema pair $\psi = (\pi_1, \nu_1(k))$; π_1 is:

$$\cfrac{\cfrac{\cfrac{\cfrac{\cfrac{P(f_I(0,u(0))) \vdash P(f_I(0,u(0)))}{P(u(0)) \vdash P(f_I(0,u(0)))}\mathcal{E}}{\vdash P(u(0)) \Rightarrow P(f_I(0,u(0)))}\Rightarrow_r}{\vdash \forall x(P(x) \Rightarrow P(f_I(0,x)))}\forall_r}{\forall x(P(x) \Rightarrow P(f(x))) \vdash \forall x(P(x) \Rightarrow P(f_I(0,x)))}\mathsf{w_I}$$

where u is a schematic variable (hence $u(0)$ can be regarded as an eigenvariable); $\nu_1(k)$ is:

$$\cfrac{\cfrac{\psi(k)}{\forall x(P(x) \Rightarrow P(f(x))) \vdash \forall x(P(x) \Rightarrow P(f_I(k,x)))} \qquad \overbrace{\diagdown(1)\diagup}}{\forall x(P(x) \Rightarrow P(f(x))) \vdash \forall x(P(x) \Rightarrow P(f_I(s(k),x)))}\mathsf{cut, c_I}$$

where (1) is (letting $Q[z]$ be $P(f_I(z,u(s(k))))$)

$$\cfrac{\cfrac{P(u(s(k))) \vdash P(u(s(k)))}{\cfrac{\cfrac{Q[k] \vdash Q[k] \quad \cfrac{Q[s(k)] \vdash Q[s(k)]}{P(f(f_I(k,u(s(k))))) \vdash Q[s(k)]}\mathcal{E}}{Q[k] \Rightarrow P(f(f_I(k,u(s(k))))), Q[k] \vdash Q[s(k)]}\Rightarrow_I}{\forall x(P(x) \Rightarrow P(f(x))), Q[k] \vdash Q[s(k)]}\forall_I}}{\cfrac{P(u(s(k))), \forall x(P(x) \Rightarrow P(f(x))), P(u(s(k))) \Rightarrow Q[k] \vdash Q[s(k)]}{\cfrac{\forall x(P(x) \Rightarrow P(f(x))), P(u(s(k))) \Rightarrow Q[k] \vdash P(u(s(k))) \Rightarrow Q[s(k)]}{\cfrac{\forall x(P(x) \Rightarrow P(f(x))), \forall x(P(x) \Rightarrow P(f_I(k,x))) \vdash P(u(s(k))) \Rightarrow Q[s(k)])}{\forall x(P(x) \Rightarrow P(f(x))), \forall x(P(x) \Rightarrow P(f_I(k,x))) \vdash \forall x(P(x) \Rightarrow P(f_I(s(k),x)))}\forall_r}\forall_I}\Rightarrow_r}\Rightarrow_I}$$

Now, we can define a proof schema $\Psi = \langle \varphi, \psi \rangle$ of $P(c), \forall x(P(x) \Rightarrow P(f(x))) \vdash P(f_I(n,c))$, where φ is associated with the pair $(\pi, \nu(k))$; π is a trivial cut-free proof similar to π_1 above and $\nu(k)$ is:

$$\cfrac{\cfrac{\psi(s(k))}{\forall x(P(x) \Rightarrow P(f(x))) \vdash \forall x(P(x) \Rightarrow P(f_I(s(k),x)))} \qquad \overbrace{\diagdown(2)\diagup}}{P(c), \forall x(P(x) \Rightarrow P(f(x))) \vdash P(f_I(s(k),c))}\mathsf{cut}$$

where (2) is a simple proof of $P(c), \forall x(P(x) \Rightarrow P(f_I(s(k),x))) \vdash P(f_I(s(k),c))$.

5   The Resolution Calculus RS

Here we define the schematic resolution calculus RS, which is more general than that introduced in [3]. We define the calculus as a term algebra. Such kind of definition is not new and it was investigated for example in [10,13].

We extend our language by introducing *clause variables*, denoted by X, Y, and *clause-set variables*, denoted by $\mathcal{X}, \mathcal{Y}$. Substitutions are defined as usual, by mapping variables to the terms of corresponding type. Our aim is to develop a framework for specifying schemata of clause sets and their resolution refutations, which is vital to the CERES-method. Our first step is to define clause schemata.

Example 5.1. Let us assume we want to specify the infinite sequence of clauses

$$D_\gamma \colon Q(x_0, y_0) \vdash P(x_0, y_0), \dots, P(x_0, f^\gamma(y_\gamma)), R(x_0, z).$$

for $\gamma \in \omega$. In this sequence of clauses neither the lengths of the clauses nor the number of variables in the clauses is bounded. To handle the infinite sequence of variables we use schematic variables of type $\omega \to \iota$ (see Sect. 3) and for the increasing length an inductive definition based on the merge of clauses.

Definition 5.1 (Clause Schema). *Let a be an arithmetic term, $\overline{u}$ a sequence of schematic variables and $\overline{X}$ a sequence of clause variables. Then $c(a, \overline{u}, \overline{X})$ is a clause schema w.r.t. the rewrite system $\mathcal{R}$:*

$$c(0, \overline{u}, \overline{X}) \to C \circ \overline{X} \quad and \quad c(k+1, \overline{u}, \overline{X}) \to c(k, \overline{u}, \overline{X}) \circ D$$

where C is a clause with $V(C) \subseteq \{\overline{u}\}$ and D is a clause with $V(D) \subseteq \{k, \overline{u}\}$. Clauses and clause variables are clause schemata w.r.t. the empty rewrite system.

We introduce a *clause substitution* to be a mapping from clause variables to clauses. Let $C_1, \dots, C_\alpha$ be clauses not containing variables of type ω different from $n \colon \omega$ and $\gamma \in \mathbb{N}$, then $\theta = [X_1/C_1, \dots, X_\alpha/C_\alpha]$ is a clause substitution. $c(n, \overline{u}, \overline{X})\theta[n/\gamma]$ then denotes the normal form (under $\mathcal{R}$) under the assignment of n to γ after the application of θ.

Example 5.2. We show now how to specify the sequence of clauses in Example 5.1 in the formalism of Definition 5.1. Let $x, y \colon \omega \to \iota$ be two schematic variables, X a clause variable and f_I be the defined function symbol from Sect. 2.1. Then the rewrite rules

$$c(0, x, y, X) \to \;\vdash P(x(0), y(0)) \circ X,$$
$$c(k+1, x, y, X) \to c(k, x, y, X) \circ \vdash P(x(0), f_I(k+1, y(k+1)))$$

together with the substitution $\theta \colon [X/Q(x(0), y(0)) \vdash R(x(0), z)]$ (for $z \colon \iota$) specify the sequence D_γ in Example 5.1. Indeed, $c(n, x, y, X)\theta[n/\gamma] = D_\gamma$ for all $\gamma \in \omega$.

Clause schemata define infinite sequences of clauses. Our next step consists in describing infinite sequences of *clause sets*. This is achieved by defining recursive structure based on so called *clause-set terms*.

Example 5.3. Sets of clauses can be described via union and merge operators which play a major role in the specification of characteristic clause sets in CERES. Let $\mathcal{C} \times \mathcal{D} = \{C \circ D \mid C \in \mathcal{C}, D \in \mathcal{D}\}$ be the merge of clause sets $\mathcal{C}$ and $\mathcal{D}$, $\oplus$ an operator representing union and $\otimes$ another one representing $\times$. Then the clause set

$$\{P(x) \vdash Q(x);\; P(x), Q(x) \vdash;\; \vdash P(x), Q(x);\; Q(x) \vdash P(x)\}$$

can be represented by the term $(\{P(x) \vdash\} \oplus \{\vdash P(x)\}) \otimes (\{\vdash Q(x)\} \oplus \{Q(x) \vdash\})$.

Definition 5.2 (Clause-Set Term). *Clause-set terms are defined inductively using binary symbols $\oplus$ and $\otimes$ (which semantically correspond to conjunctions and disjunctions respectively) in the following way:*
- *Clause sets and clause-set variables are clause-set terms.*
- *If Θ_1 and Θ_2 are clause-set terms, then so are $\Theta_1 \oplus \Theta_2$ and $\Theta_1 \otimes \Theta_2$.*

Definition 5.3. *Let Θ be a clause-set term not containing variables other than of type ι. Then the set of clauses $|\Theta|$ assigned to Θ is defined as $|\mathcal{C}| = \mathcal{C}$ for clause sets $\mathcal{C}$, $|\Theta_1 \otimes \Theta_2| = |\Theta_1| \times |\Theta_2|$, and $|\Theta_1 \oplus \Theta_2| = |\Theta_1| \cup |\Theta_2|$.*

Example 5.4. Let $\mathcal{D}_\gamma$ (for $\gamma \in \omega$) be the set of clauses $\{P(u_i) \vdash P(u_i) \mid i = 0, \ldots, \gamma\} \cup \{P(f^{i-1}(u_i)) \vdash P(f^i(u_i)) \mid i = 1, \ldots, \gamma\} \cup \{\vdash P(c); P(f^\gamma(c)) \vdash\}$ for $\gamma \in \omega$. We see that the number of clauses in the sets, the number of variables, and the term depths increase with increasing γ. Below we will define a formalism for specifying such sequences of clause sets.

Definition 5.4. *Let Θ be a clause-set term, $\mathcal{X}_1, \ldots, \mathcal{X}_\alpha$ clause-set variables and $\mathcal{C}_1, \ldots, \mathcal{C}_\alpha$ objects of appropriate type. Then $\Theta[\mathcal{X}_1/\mathcal{C}_1, \ldots, \mathcal{X}_\alpha/\mathcal{C}_\alpha]$ is called a clause-set term over $\{\mathcal{C}_1, \ldots, \mathcal{C}_\alpha\}$.*

Note that, according to the definition above, every ordinary clause-set term is also a clause-set term over any set $\{\mathcal{C}_1, \ldots, \mathcal{C}_\alpha\}$)

Definition 5.5 (Clause-Set Schema). *A clause-set schema $\mathcal{C}(n)$ is a structure $(\mathcal{C}_1, \ldots, \mathcal{C}_\alpha)$ together with a set of rewrite rules $\mathcal{R} = \mathcal{R}_1 \cup \ldots \cup \mathcal{R}_\alpha$, where the $\mathcal{R}_i$ (for $1 \leq i \leq \alpha$) are pairs of rewrite rules*

$$\mathcal{C}_i(0, \overline{u}_i, \overline{X}_i, \overline{\mathcal{X}}_i) \to \Theta_i' \qquad and \qquad \mathcal{C}_i(k+1, \overline{u}_i, \overline{X}_i, \overline{\mathcal{X}}_i) \to \Theta_i$$

where Θ_α' is a clause-set term and the other Θ_i' and Θ_i are clause-set terms over terms in $\mathcal{C}_1, \ldots, \mathcal{C}_\alpha$, such that $V(\Theta_i') \subseteq \{\overline{u}_i, \overline{X}_i, \overline{\mathcal{X}}_i\}$ and $V(\Theta_i) \subseteq \{k, \overline{u}_i, \overline{X}_i, \overline{\mathcal{X}}_i\}$.
    Furthermore, we assume that $\mathcal{C}_i(\gamma, \overline{u}_i, \overline{X}_i, \overline{\mathcal{X}}_i)$ is strongly normalizing for all $\gamma \in \mathbb{N}$.

Note that the above definition is more liberal than the definitions of proof schemata and the schematic language: there, the rewrite rules representing the definitions of the symbols are required to be primitive recursive, and are therefore strongly normalizing. Here, we allow any "well-formed", i.e. strongly normalizing, definition. We will make use of this more liberal definition in Definition 6.1, where a class of clause-set schemata is defined in a mutually recursive way.
    We define a *clause-set substitution* as a mapping from clause-set variables to clause-set terms. Let ϑ be a clause-set substitution, θ be a clause substitution and $\gamma \in \mathbb{N}$, then $\mathcal{C}(\gamma) \downarrow$ denotes a clause set $|\mathcal{C}|$ where $\mathcal{C}$ is a normal form of $\mathcal{C}_1(n, \overline{u}_1, \overline{X}_1, \overline{\mathcal{X}}_1)\vartheta\theta[n/\gamma]$ w.r.t. $\mathcal{R}$ extended with the rewrite rules for defined function and predicate symbols.

Example 5.5. Let $\mathcal{D}_\gamma$ be the sequence of clause sets specified in Example 5.4. The following rewrite system (using no clause variables and clause set variables, but the schematic variable u) specifies $\mathcal{D}_\gamma$:

$$\mathcal{C}_1(0, u) \to \{\vdash\},$$
$$\mathcal{C}_1(k+1, u) \to \mathcal{C}_2(k+1, u) \oplus (\{\vdash P(c)\} \oplus \{P(f_I(k+1, c)) \vdash\}),$$
$$\mathcal{C}_2(0, u) \to \{P(f_I(0, u(0))) \vdash P(f_I(0, u(0)))\},$$
$$\mathcal{C}_2(k+1, u) \to \mathcal{C}_2(k, u) \oplus (\{P(u(k+1)) \vdash P(u(k+1))\} \oplus$$
$$(\{P(f_I(k, u(k+1))) \vdash\} \otimes \{\vdash P(f_I(k+1, u(k+1)))\})).$$

Indeed, the normal form of $\mathcal{C}_1(n, u)[n/\gamma]$ is just $\mathcal{D}_\gamma$ for $\gamma \in \omega$.

Definition 5.6. *A clause-set schema* $\mathcal{C}(n)$ *is unsatisfiable iff for all* $\gamma \in \mathbb{N}$, $\mathcal{C}(\gamma)\downarrow$ *is unsatisfiable.*

The clause-set schema defined in Example 5.5 is unsatisfiable because, for every γ, $\mathcal{D}_\gamma$ is an unsatisfiable set of clauses.

Analogously to clause-set schemata, we define a resolution proof schema as a recursive structure based on *resolution terms*.

Definition 5.7 (Resolution Term). *Clause schemata are resolution terms; if* ρ_1 *and* ρ_2 *are resolution terms, then* r$(\rho_1; \rho_2; P)$ *is a resolution term, where* P *is an atom formula schema.*

r$(\rho_1; \rho_2; P)$ expresses the result obtained by resolving the clauses derived by ρ_1 and ρ_2, where P is the resolved atom (still without specification of the most general unifier).

We define a notion of resolution proof schema in the spirit of LKS-proof schemata.

Definition 5.8 (Resolution Proof Schema). *A resolution proof schema* $R(n)$ *is a structure* $(\varrho_1, \ldots, \varrho_\alpha)$ *together with a set of rewrite rules* $\mathcal{R} = \mathcal{R}_1 \cup \ldots \cup \mathcal{R}_\alpha$, *where the* $\mathcal{R}_i$ *(for* $1 \le i \le \alpha$) *are pairs of rewrite rules*

$$\varrho_i(0, \overline{u}_i, \overline{X}_i) \to \rho_i' \qquad and \qquad \varrho_i(k+1, \overline{u}_i, \overline{X}_i) \to \rho_i$$

where ρ_i' *is a resolution term over terms of the form* $\varrho_j(a_j, \overline{t}_j, \overline{C}_j)$, *and* ρ_i *is a resolution term over terms of the form* $\varrho_j(a_j, \overline{t}_j, \overline{C}_j)$ *and* $\varrho_i(k, \overline{t}_i, \overline{C}_i)$ *for* $1 \le i < j \le \alpha$.

To evaluate resolution proof schemata we need a stronger notion of substitution, which will unify schematic variables with term schemata. The idea is to specify a global unifier for the whole schema instead of single unifiers for resolution steps.

Definition 5.9 (Substitution Schema). *Let* $u_1, \ldots, u_\alpha$ *be schematic variable symbols of type* $\omega \to \iota$ *and* $t_1, \ldots, t_\alpha$ *be term schemata containing only* k *as arithmetic variable. Then a substitution schema is an expression of the form* $[u_1/\lambda k.t_1, \ldots, u_\alpha/\lambda k.t_\alpha]$.

The intended semantics of a substitution schema is that for all $\gamma \in \mathbb{N}$ we have a substitution $[u_1(\gamma)/t_1 \downarrow_\gamma, \ldots, u_\alpha(\gamma)/t_\alpha \downarrow_\gamma]$.

Let $R(n) = (\varrho_1, \ldots, \varrho_\alpha)$ be a resolution proof schema, θ be a clause substitution, ϑ be a substitution schema and $\gamma \in \mathbb{N}$, then $R(\gamma) \downarrow$ denotes a resolution term which is normal form of $\varrho_1(n, \overline{u}_1, \overline{X}_1)\theta\vartheta[n/\gamma]$ w.r.t. $\mathcal{R}$ extended with rewrite rules for defined function and predicate symbols.

It remains to define the notion of a resolution refutation schema of a clause-set schema.

Definition 5.10 (Resolvent). *Let $C: \Gamma \vdash \Delta$ and $D: \Pi \vdash \Lambda$ be clauses not containing arithmetic variables and let P be an atom. Then the clause $\operatorname{res}(C, D, P) = \Gamma, \Pi \backslash P \vdash \Delta \backslash P, \Lambda$ is called* the resolvent of C and D on P, *where $\Pi \backslash P$ (resp. $\Delta \backslash P$) denotes the multi-set of atoms in Π (resp. Δ) after removal of all occurrences of P. In case P does not occur in Δ and Π, $\operatorname{res}(C, D, P)$ is called a pseudo-resolvent.*

Note that even if $\operatorname{res}(C, D, P)$ is a pseudo-resolvent, inferring it from C and D is sound in any case. Let C be a clause and σ be a substitution. Then $C\sigma$ is called an *instance* of C. Let $\mathcal{C}, \mathcal{D}$ be sets of clauses such that all $C \in \mathcal{C}$ are instances of clauses in $\mathcal{D}$. Then $\mathcal{C}$ is called an *instantiation* of $\mathcal{D}$.

Definition 5.11 (Resolution Deduction). *If C is a clause then C is a resolution deduction with end-sequent C. If ρ_1 and ρ_2 are resolution deductions with end-sequents respectively C_1 and C_2, such that for an atom P there is a resolvent $\operatorname{res}(C_1, C_2, P) = D$, then $\rho = \mathsf{r}(\rho_1, \rho_2, P)$ is a resolution deduction with end-sequent D. Let $\mathcal{C}$ be a set of clauses. If the set of all clauses occurring in ρ is an instantiation of $\mathcal{C}$, then ρ is called a resolution deduction from $\mathcal{C}$ and if $D = \vdash$ then ρ is called a resolution refutation of $\mathcal{C}$.*

Note that resolution terms, containing only ordinary clauses and atoms, represent resolution deductions iff under evaluation of r by res, we obtain a consistent structure of resolvents.

Definition 5.12 (Refutation Schema). *A resolution proof schema $R(n)$ is called a* resolution deduction schema *from a clause-set schema $\mathcal{C}(n)$ if there exist a clause substitution and a substitution schema such that for every $\gamma \in \mathbb{N}$, $R(\gamma) \downarrow$ is a resolution deduction from $\mathcal{C}(\gamma) \downarrow$.*

Furthermore, if for all $\gamma \in \mathbb{N}$, $R(\gamma) \downarrow$ is a resolution refutation of $\mathcal{C}(\gamma) \downarrow$, then $R(n)$ is called a resolution refutation schema *of $\mathcal{C}(n)$.*

Example 5.6. Consider the clause set schema defined in Example 5.5 specifying the sequence of clause sets $(\mathcal{D}_\gamma)_{\gamma \in \omega}$. We define resolution refutations of $\mathcal{D}_\gamma$ informally in the following way: Start with the clause $\vdash P(c)$ in $\mathcal{D}_\gamma$. Assume inductively that you have already derived $\vdash P(f^{\gamma-1}(c))$ from $\mathcal{D}_\gamma$ for $\gamma > 0$; then by resolving with the clause $P(u_1) \vdash P(f(u_1))$ (which is in $\mathcal{D}_\gamma$) you obtain $\vdash P(f^\gamma(c))$. In the final step you resolve $\vdash P(f^\gamma(c))$ with $P(f^\gamma(c)) \vdash$ (which is in $\mathcal{D}_\gamma$) to obtain $\vdash$.

For the formal specification by rewrite rules we use the schematic variable u and two symbols ϱ_1, ϱ_2:

$$\varrho_1(0, u) \to \vdash,$$
$$\varrho_1(k+1, u) \to r(\varrho_2(k+1, u); \; [P(f_I(k+1, c)) \vdash]; \; P(f_I(k+1, c))),$$
$$\varrho_2(0, u) \to \vdash P(c),$$
$$\varrho_2(k+1, u) \to r(\varrho_2(k, u); \; [P(u(k+1)) \vdash P(f(u(k+1)))]; \; P(f_I(k, c))).$$

Note that, for computation of a global substitution for unification, we have renamed $P(u(1)) \vdash P(f(u_1))$ for every new application of the clause. The required substitution schema θ is $[u/\lambda k. f_I(\mathrm{pre}(k), c)]$ for $\mathrm{pre}(0) \to 0$ and $\mathrm{pre}(k+1) \to k$, formalizing the predecessor function. Then $\varrho(n, u)\theta[n/\gamma]$ is a resolution refutation of $\mathcal{D}_\gamma$.

We illustrate the specification for $\gamma = 2$: It is easy to verify that, on $\varrho(2, u)$, the rewrite system produces the resolution term

$$r(\; r(\; r([\vdash P(c)]; \; [P(u(1)) \vdash P(f(u(1)))]; \; P(c));$$
$$[P(u(2)) \vdash P(f(u(2)))]; \; P(f(c)));$$
$$[P(f(f(c))) \vdash]; \; P(f(f(c)))).$$

after application of θ this term becomes

$$r(r(r(\vdash P(c); \; [P(c) \vdash P(f(c))]; \; P(c)); \; [P(f(c)) \vdash P(f(f(c)))]; \; P(f(c)));$$
$$[P(f(f(c))) \vdash]; \; P(f(f(c)))).$$

which specifies the refutation of $\mathcal{D}_2$ defined informally above. Its representation by a sequence of clauses would be

$$[\vdash P(c)], \; [P(c) \vdash P(f(c))], \; [\vdash P(f(c))], \; [P(f(c)) \vdash P(f(f(c)))],$$
$$[\vdash P(f(f(c)))], \; [P(f(f(c))) \vdash], \; [\vdash].$$

Proposition 5.1. *If R is a resolution refutation schema of a clause-set schema $\mathcal{C}$ then $\mathcal{C}$ is unsatisfiable.*

Proof. By Definition 5.12 we obtain, under the chosen substitution schema, a resolution refutation of $\mathcal{C}(\gamma)$ for all γ. But by Definition 5.6 this means, under the assumption of soundness of ordinary resolution, that the clause-set $\mathcal{C}$ is unsatisfiable. $\qquad\square$

Corollary 5.1. *The resolution calculus RS is sound.* $\qquad\square$

Completeness does not hold for RS, since unsatisfiability of schemata is a property which is not semi-decidable even for propositional schemata (see [2]).

6 A Cut-Elimination Method for LKS

In this section we consider the problem of cut-elimination for proof schemata. Note that (trivially) for every $\gamma \in \mathbb{N}$ we can obtain a cut-free proof of $S(\gamma)$ by computing $\Psi\!\downarrow_\gamma$, which contains cuts, and then applying a usual cut-elimination algorithm. What we are interested in here is rather a *schematic* description of all the cut-free proofs for a parameter n. It is not possible to obtain such a description by naively applying Gentzen-style cut-elimination to the LKS-proofs in Ψ, since it is not clear how to handle the case

$$\frac{\psi_1(a_1) \qquad \psi_2(a_2)}{\dfrac{\Gamma \vdash \Delta, C \quad C, \Pi \vdash \Lambda}{\Gamma, \Pi \vdash \Delta, \Lambda}}\text{cut}$$

as this would require "moving the cut through a proof link". This is not a problem of our calculi in particular, but a general one for such kind of proofs (see [8]). In this paper, we will go a different route: we define an extension of the CERESmethod, which is based on a *global* analysis of the proof schema. It will eventually yield the desired schematic description of the sequence of cut-free proofs.

6.1   The Characteristic Term

At the heart of the CERESmethod lies the *characteristic clause set*, which describes the cuts in a proof. The connection between cut-elimination and the characteristic clause set is that any resolution refutation of the characteristic clause set can be used as a skeleton of a proof containing only atomic cuts.

The characteristic clause set can either be defined directly as in [6], or it can be obtained via a transformation from a *characteristic term* as in [7]. We use the latter approach here; the reason for this will be explained later.

Our main aim is to extend the usual inductive definition of the characteristic term to the case of proof links. This will give rise to a notion of *schematic characteristic term*. The usual definition of the characteristic term depends upon the cut-status of the formula occurrences in a proof (i.e. whether a given formula occurrence is a cut-ancestor, or not). But a formula occurrence in a proof schema gives rise to many formula occurrences in its evaluation, some of which will be cut-ancestors, and some will not. Therefore we need some machinery to track the cut-status of formula occurrences through proof links. Hence we call a set Ω of formula occurrences from the end-sequent of an LKS-proof π a *configuration for* π. We are interested of those configurations which keep track of all cut-ancestors in a proof schema Ψ as well as the propagation of the cut-ancestors through the proof links. A configuration Ω for π is called *relevant w.r.t. a proof schema* Ψ if π is a proof in Ψ and there is a $\gamma \in \mathbb{N}$ such that π induces a subproof π' of $\Psi\!\downarrow_\gamma$ such that the occurrences in Ω correspond to cut-ancestors in π'. Note that the set of relevant cut-configurations can be computed given a proof schema Ψ.

Next, we will represent the characteristic term of a proof link in our object language: For all proof symbols ψ and configurations Ω we assume a unique symbol $\mathrm{cl}^{\psi,\Omega}$ called *clause-set symbol*. The intended semantics of $\mathrm{cl}^{\psi,\Omega}(a)$ is "the characteristic clause set of $\psi(a)$, with the configuration Ω".

Definition 6.1 (Characteristic Term). *Let π be an LKS-proof and Ω a configuration. In the following, by $\Gamma_\Omega, \Delta_\Omega$ and Γ_C, Δ_C we will denote multisets of formulas of Ω- and cut-ancestors respectively. Let r be an inference in π. We define the clause-set term $\Theta_\mathsf{r}^{\pi,\Omega}$ inductively:*

– *if* r *is an axiom of the form* $\Gamma_\Omega, \Gamma_C, \Gamma \vdash \Delta_\Omega, \Delta_C, \Delta$, *then* $\Theta_r^{\pi,\Omega} = [\Gamma_\Omega, \Gamma_C \vdash \Delta_\Omega, \Delta_C]$

– *if* r *is a proof link of the form* $\dfrac{\psi(a,\overline{u})}{\Gamma_\Omega, \Gamma_C, \Gamma \vdash \Delta_\Omega, \Delta_C, \Delta}$ *then define* Ω' *as the set of formula occurrences from* $\Gamma_\Omega, \Gamma_C \vdash \Delta_\Omega, \Delta_C$ *and* $\Theta_r^{\pi,\Omega} = cl^{\psi,\Omega'}(a,\overline{u})$.

– *if* r *is a unary rule with immediate predecessor* r′, *then* $\Theta_r^{\pi,\Omega} = \Theta_{r'}^{\pi,\Omega}$.

– *if* r *is a binary rule with immediate predecessors* r_1, r_2, *then*

  • *if the auxiliary formulas of* r *are* Ω- *or cut-ancestors, then* $\Theta_r^{\pi,\Omega} = \Theta_{r_1}^{\pi,\Omega} \oplus \Theta_{r_2}^{\pi,\Omega}$,

  • *otherwise* $\Theta_r^{\pi,\Omega} = \Theta_{r_1}^{\pi,\Omega} \otimes \Theta_{r_2}^{\pi,\Omega}$.

  Finally, define $\Theta^{\pi,\Omega} = \Theta_{r_0}^{\pi,\Omega}$, *where* r_0 *is the last inference of* π, *and* $\Theta^\pi = \Theta^{\pi,\emptyset}$. Θ^π *is called the characteristic term of* π.

We say that a clause-set term is *normal* if it does not contain clause-set symbols and defined function and predicate symbols.

Definition 6.2 (Characteristic Term Schema). *Let* $\Psi = \langle \psi_1, \ldots, \psi_\alpha \rangle$ *be a proof schema. We define the rewrite rules for clause-set symbols for all proof symbols* ψ_β *and configurations* Ω:

$$cl^{\psi_\beta,\Omega}(0,\overline{u}) \rightarrow \Theta^{\pi_\beta,\Omega} \qquad and \qquad cl^{\psi_\beta,\Omega}(k+1,\overline{u}) \rightarrow \Theta^{\nu_\beta(k),\Omega}$$

where $1 \le \beta \le \alpha$. *Next, let* $\gamma \in \mathbb{N}$ *and let* $cl^{\psi_\beta,\Omega} \downarrow_\gamma$ *be a normal form of* $cl^{\psi_\beta,\Omega}(\gamma,\overline{u})$ *under the rewrite system just given extended by rewrite rules for defined function and predicate symbols. Then define* $\Theta^{\psi_\beta,\Omega} = cl^{\psi_\beta,\Omega}$ *and* $\Theta^{\Psi,\Omega} = \Theta^{\psi_1,\Omega}$ *and finally the* characteristic term schema $\Theta^\Psi = \Theta^{\Psi,\emptyset}$.

The definition above explains why we chose to define the characteristic clause set via the characteristic term: the clause-set term is closed under the rewrite rules we have given for the clause-set symbols, while the notion of clause set is not (a clause will in general become a formula when subjected to the rewrite rules). We say that a clause-set symbol $cl^{\psi,\Omega}$ depends on a clause-set symbol $cl^{\varphi,\Omega'}$, if a term $\Theta^{\psi,\Omega}$ contains $cl^{\varphi,\Omega'}$. We assume that the dependency relation is transitive and reflexive.

The following proposition shows that the definition of the characteristic term schema satisfies the requirement of Definition 5.5.

Proposition 6.1. *Let* Ψ *be a proof schema and* Θ^Ψ *be a characteristic term schema of* Ψ. *Then* Θ^Ψ *is strongly normalizing.*

Proof. If the dependency relation on the clause-set symbols occurring in Θ^Ψ is acyclic, then the result is trivial. Otherwise, note that according to the definition of proof schemata, only clause-set symbols for the same proof symbol can depend on each other. But then, again by Definition 4.2, the parameter is strictly decreasing. Thus the rewrite rules are strongly normalizing. □

Example 6.1. Let us consider the proof schema Ψ of the sequent $S(n)$, defined in Example 4.1. If we compute the characteristic terms for all possible configurations, this would result in a clause set with redundant clauses, having broader search space. In order to prune significantly the search space, we make use of the notion of relevant configurations. In this example there is only one relevant configuration, namely $\Omega = \{\forall x(P(x) \Rightarrow P(f_I(k,x)))\}$, which contains the cut-ancestor for φ which is propagated through the proof link to ψ. The $\emptyset$ configuration for φ is also considered as relevant and should be taken into account. The characteristic term schema of Ψ then is $(\mathrm{cl}^{\varphi,\emptyset}, \mathrm{cl}^{\psi,\Omega})$ with the rewrite system as given in Example 5.5 with $\mathcal{C}_1 = \mathrm{cl}^{\varphi,\emptyset}$ and $\mathcal{C}_2 = \mathrm{cl}^{\psi,\Omega}$.

Next we show that the notion of characteristic term is well-defined and that evaluation and extraction of characteristic terms commute. The later property will be used to derive results on schematic characteristic clause sets from standard results on (non-schematic) CERES. The following propositions are easily proved by double induction on the parameter and on the number of proof symbols in the proof schema.

Proposition 6.2. *Let Ψ be a proof schema and Ω be a configuration, then $\Theta^{\psi_\beta,\Omega}\downarrow_\gamma$ is a normal clause-set term for all $1 \leq \beta \leq \alpha$ and $\gamma \in \mathbb{N}$. Hence $\Theta^{\Psi}\downarrow_\gamma$ is a normal clause-set term.* □

Proposition 6.3. *Let Ψ be a proof schema, Ω be a configuration and $\gamma \in \mathbb{N}$. Then $\Theta^{\Psi\downarrow_\gamma,\Omega} = \Theta^{\Psi,\Omega}\downarrow_\gamma$.* □

From the characteristic term we finally define the notion of characteristic clause set. For a normal LKS-proof π and configuration Ω, $\mathrm{CL}(\pi,\Omega) = |\Theta^{\pi,\Omega}|$. We define the *standard characteristic clause set* $\mathrm{CL}(\pi) = \mathrm{CL}(\pi,\emptyset)$ and the *schematic characteristic clause set* $\mathrm{CL}(\Psi)\downarrow_\gamma = |\Theta^{\Psi}\downarrow_\gamma|$.

Example 6.2. For the characteristic term schema from Example 6.1 we have $\mathrm{CL}(\Psi)\downarrow_0 = \{\vdash\}$ and $\mathrm{CL}(\Psi)\downarrow_\gamma = \mathcal{D}_\gamma$ for $\gamma > 0$ and $\mathcal{D}_\gamma$ from Example 5.4.

Finally, we prove that the schematic characteristic clause set is always unsatisfiable.

Proposition 6.4. *Let π be a normal LKS-proof. Then $\mathrm{CL}(\pi)$ is unsatisfiable.*

Proof. By the identification of normal LKS-proofs with LK-proofs, the result follows from Proposition 3.2 in [6]. □

Proposition 6.5. *For a proof schema Ψ, $\mathrm{CL}(\Psi)\downarrow_\gamma$ is unsatisfiable for all $\gamma \in \mathbb{N}$.*

Proof. By Proposition 6.3 $\mathrm{CL}(\Psi)\downarrow_\gamma = \mathrm{CL}(\Psi\downarrow_\gamma)$ which is unsatisfiable by Proposition 6.4. □

6.2   Atomic Cut Normal Form Schema

We are ready to produce a description of cut-free proofs, which is called Atomic Cut Normal Form Schema, shortly ACNF schema.

Definition 6.3 (ACNF Schema). *Let Ψ be a proof schema with end-sequent $S(n)$, and R be a resolution refutation schema of the schematic characteristic clause set* $\mathrm{CL}(\Psi)$. *Let ϑ be the substitution schema corresponding to R. Then the pair (R, ϑ) is an ACNF schema of Ψ.*

Example 6.3. An ACNF schema of the proof schema Ψ is given in Example 5.6 since $D_\gamma = \mathrm{CL}(\Psi)\!\downarrow_\gamma$.

6.3   Herbrand Systems

By the Herbrand-Gentzen Theorem we will denote the following well-known result.

Theorem 6.1. *Let π be an* LKE*-proof of a closed formula*

$$\psi : \exists x_1 \cdots \exists x_\alpha F(x_1, \ldots, x_\alpha)$$

with $F(x_1, \ldots, x_\alpha)$ quantifier-free such that π contains only quantifier-free cuts. Then there exist terms $t_{1,1}, \ldots, t_{1,\alpha}, \ldots, t_{\iota,1}, \ldots, t_{\iota,\alpha}$ such that $F(t_{1,1}, \ldots, t_{1,\alpha}) \vee \cdots \vee F(t_{\iota,1}, \ldots, t_{\iota,\alpha})$ is LKE*-provable, and the sum of the sizes of the $t_{\lambda,\kappa}$ is bounded by the size of π.*

This result is of both theoretical and practical importance: theoretically, it gives the precise relation between propositional and first-order provability, and practically it can be used to present the content of a first-order proof to a human in a way that abstracts from the propositional content of the proof. Note that the assumption of quantifier-free cuts is necessary for the complexity bound stated in the theorem.

Definition 6.4. *Let $\psi(n) = \exists x_1 \cdots \exists x_\alpha F(n, x_1, \ldots, x_\alpha)$ with $F(n, x_1, \ldots, x_\alpha)$ quantifier-free and $n : \omega$ the only free variable of $\psi(n)$. Then a* Herbrand system *for $\psi(n)$ is a rewrite system R (containing the list constructors and a function symbol w) such that for all $\beta \in \mathbb{N}$, the normal form of $w(\beta)$ w.r.t. R is a list of lists of terms $t_{\gamma,\delta}$ (of length ι) such that $F(\beta, t_{1,1}, \ldots, t_{1,\alpha}) \vee \cdots \vee F(\beta, t_{\iota,1}, \ldots, t_{\iota,\alpha})$ is* LKE*-provable.*

We will prove a generalization of the Herbrand-Gentzen Theorem for ACNF schemata: given a Herbrand system H and an ACNF schema (R, θ) of Ψ, consider the functions $h : \beta \mapsto |w(\beta)|$ and $a : \beta \mapsto |R(\beta)\!\downarrow| \, ||\Psi(\beta)\!\downarrow| \, |$ (where $|\cdot|$ denotes symbolic size) bounding the complexity of normal forms of the schematic data structures. We will show how to extract a Herbrand system from an ACNF schema such that h is bounded by a (modulo a constant). This shows that the ACNF schema already contains all the first-order information of the cut-free proof — and that information can be accessed without reference to the usual Gentzen-style cut-reduction rules. This indicates that in the analysis of concrete proof schemata via CERES, it will suffice to analyze the Herbrand system extracted from an ACNF schema.

Theorem 6.2. *Let* $\psi(n) = \exists x_1 \cdots \exists x_\alpha F(n, x_1, \ldots, x_\alpha)$, Ψ *be a proof schema with end-sequent* $\vdash \psi(n)$, *and* (R, θ) *an ACNF schema of* Ψ. *Then there exists a Herbrand system* H *for* $\psi(n)$ *such that for all* $\beta \in \mathbb{N}$, $|w(\beta) \downarrow| \leq 2|R(\beta) \downarrow\ ||\Psi(\beta) \downarrow|$.

Proof. We sketch the construction of H. H contains the rewrite rules for the defined function symbols, a constant ϵ (the empty list), and a binary function symbol list (list constructor). For all function symbols f, we add rewrite rules $f(\text{list}(x, y)) \to \text{list}(f(x), f(y))$ and $f(\epsilon) \to \epsilon$. A list of terms $t_1, \ldots, t_\lambda$ is encoded in R as the term $\text{list}(t_1, \text{list}(t_2, \ldots (\text{list}(t_\lambda, \epsilon) \cdots)$. Furthermore, R contains binary function symbols prepend and merge with rewrite rules ensuring that prepend prepends a list to another, and merge takes two lists $l_1, \ldots, l_\lambda$ and $l'_1, \ldots, l'_\lambda$ and returns the list $\text{prepend}(l_1, l'_1), \ldots, \text{prepend}(l_\lambda, l'_\lambda)$. We proceed by structural induction on the proofs in Ψ, adding (for every cut-configuration Ω) a function symbol $w^{S,\Omega}$ and appropriate rewrite rules for every sequent $S(n)$ in Ψ such that $w^{S,\Omega}(\beta)$ normalizes to the list of witnesses of ψ induced by the sequent in $\Psi(\beta) \downarrow$ that corresponds to $S(n)$ in case Ω is the correct cut-configuration for that sequent (i.e. we formalize the proof of the Herbrand-Gentzen theorem as a rewrite system, ignoring witnesses of cut-ancestors). In this construction, the (schematic) variables in Ψ are considered as function symbols. For R, we add rewrite rules to collect the instances of the clauses; this requires an additional parameter since a variable not depending on k may be instantiated by a term depending on k. Finally, if $\theta = [x_1/\lambda k.t_1, \ldots, x_\alpha/\lambda k.t_\alpha]$, we add the rewrite rules $x_\iota(k) \to t_\iota$.

    This yields the desired rewrite system: According to the CERES method for first-order logic, $\Psi(\beta) \downarrow$ and $R(\beta) \downarrow$ can be combined to a cut-free proof of size $|R(\beta) \downarrow\ ||\Psi(\beta) \downarrow|$. By construction, $w(\beta) \downarrow$ contains the witnesses contained in that proof, the size of which is bounded by $|R(\beta) \downarrow\ ||\Psi(\beta) \downarrow|$ by construction, and additionally some spurious witnesses (corresponding to clauses that have not been used in the refutation) the size of which is bounded by $|R(\beta) \downarrow\ ||\Psi(\beta) \downarrow|$ as well. $\square$

Example 6.4. Continuing Example 6.3 (remembering also the definition of Ψ in Example 4.1), we describe the Herbrand system H extracted from the ACNF schema given there. The following rules are obtained from H after applying some simplifications combining the many rewrite rules introduced by the structural induction into bigger, simpler rules. The first group of rules is induced by the $\forall_l$ inferences operating on end-sequent ancestors in Ψ:

$$w^{\varphi, \emptyset}(0, j) \to \text{list}(\epsilon, \epsilon)$$
$$w^{\varphi, \emptyset}(k + 1, j) \to \text{merge}(w^{\psi, \Omega}(k + 1, j), \text{list}(\epsilon, \epsilon))$$
$$w^{\psi, \Omega}(0, j) \to \text{list}(\epsilon, \epsilon)$$
$$w^{\psi, \Omega}(k + 1, j) \to \text{merge}(w^{\psi, \Omega}(k, j), \text{list}(f_I(k, u(s(k), j)), \epsilon))$$

The second group of rules is induced by θ and the fact that $u(1)$ is instantiated in R by a term containing the parameter k (necessitating a second argument place).

$$x(k) \rightarrow f_I(\text{pre}(k), c)$$
$$u(1, k+1) \rightarrow \text{list}(x(k+1), u(1, k))$$
$$u(1, 0) \rightarrow \epsilon$$

The rewrite rule $w(k) \rightarrow w^{\varphi, \emptyset}(k, k)$ is always added. H furthermore contains the rewrite rules for pre, f_I as given earlier, and rewrite rules for merge, prepend as discussed above. A simple computation yields the witnesses for $\beta = 2$:

$$w(2) \rightarrow w^{\varphi, \emptyset}(2, 2) \rightarrow \text{merge}(w^{\psi, \Omega}(2, 2), \text{list}(\epsilon, \epsilon))$$
$$w^{\psi, \Omega}(2, 2) \rightarrow \text{merge}(w^{\psi, \Omega}(1, 2), \text{list}(f(u(2, 2)), \epsilon))$$
$$w^{\psi, \Omega}(1, 2) \rightarrow \text{merge}(w^{\psi, \Omega}(0, 2), \text{list}(f_I(0, u(1, 2)), \epsilon))$$
$$\rightarrow \text{merge}(\text{list}(\epsilon, \epsilon), \text{list}(x(2), \text{list}(x(1), \epsilon)))$$
$$\rightarrow \text{list}(x(2), \text{list}(x(1), \epsilon))$$

Eventually yielding $w(2) \rightarrow \text{list}(f(u(2, 2)), \text{list}(f(c), \text{list}(c, \epsilon)))$, i.e. the witnesses $f(c), c$ and the spurious witness $f(u(2, 2))$ corresponding to an unused clause.

7   Open Problems

The current results can be considered as a first step of performing cut-elimination in inductive proofs. Currently our formalism admits just one parameter and thus is not capable of modeling nested inductions. Hence a generalization of the method to several parameters is highly desirable. While the construction of the schematic characteristic clause sets is fully mechanizable (and already implemented under the GAPT framework[1], see [11]), a fully automated construction of schematic resolution refutations is impossible even in principle. However, for practical proof analysis of nontrivial proofs an interactive use of the schematic resolution calculus and a formal verification of the obtained proofs would be vital. The current schematic resolution method is very strong and the task of determining the schematic most general unifiers is not mechanizable. It would be useful to search for weaker systems admitting a higher degree of automation which are still capable of formalizing relevant problems. Nevertheless, we believe that (the current implementation of) the method can also serve as a tool for a semi-automated development of proof schemata by mathematicians.

References

1. Aravantinos, V., Caferra, R., Peltier, N.: A schemata calculus for propositional logic. In: Giese, M., Waaler, A. (eds.) TABLEAUX 2009. LNCS (LNAI), vol. 5607, pp. 32–46. Springer, Heidelberg (2009)

---

[1] General Architecture for Proof Theory framework, http://www.logic.at/gapt.

2. Aravantinos, V., Caferra, R., Peltier, N.: Decidability and undecidability results for propositional schemata. J. Artif. Intell. Res. **40**, 599–656 (2011)
3. Aravantinos, V., Echenim, M., Peltier, N.: A resolution calculus for first-order schemata. Fundamenta Informaticae **125**(2), 101–133 (2013)
4. Baaz, M., Hetzl, S., Leitsch, A., Richter, C., Spohr, H.: Cut-elimination: experiments with CERES. In: Baader, F., Voronkov, A. (eds.) LPAR 2004. LNCS (LNAI), vol. 3452, pp. 481–495. Springer, Heidelberg (2005)
5. Baaz, M., Hetzl, S., Leitsch, A., Richter, C., Spohr, H.: CERES: an analysis of fürstenberg's proof of the infinity of primes. Theoret. Comput. Sci. **403**, 160–175 (2008)
6. Baaz, M., Leitsch, A.: Cut-elimination and redundancy-elimination by resolution. J. Symbolic Comput. **29**(2), 149–176 (2000)
7. Baaz, M., Leitsch, A.: Towards a clausal analysis of cut-elimination. J. Symbolic Comput. **41**(3–4), 381–410 (2006)
8. Brotherston, J.: Cyclic proofs for first-order logic with inductive definitions. In: Beckert, B. (ed.) TABLEAUX 2005. LNCS (LNAI), vol. 3702, pp. 78–92. Springer, Heidelberg (2005)
9. Brotherston, J., Simpson, A.: Sequent calculi for induction and infinite descent. J. Log. Comput. **21**(6), 1177–1216 (2011)
10. Ciabattoni, A., Leitsch, A.: Towards an algorithmic construction of cut-elimination procedures. Math. Struct. Comput. Sci. **18**, 81–105 (2008)
11. Dunchev, C.: Automation of Cut-Elimination in Proof Schemata. Ph.D. thesis, Vienna University of Technology (2012)
12. Dunchev, C., Leitsch, A., Rukhaia, M., Weller, D.: CERES for First-Order Schemata. Technical report, Vienna University of Technology (2012). http://arxiv.org/abs/1303.4257
13. Fontaine, P., Merz, S., Paleo, B.W.: Exploring and exploiting algebraic and graphical properties of resolution. In: SMT 2010. Edinburgh (2010)
14. Martin-Löf, P.: Hauptsatz for the Intuitionistic Theory of Iterated Inductive Definitions. In: Proceedings of the Second Scandinavian Logic Symposium, vol. 63 of Studies in Logic and the Foundations of Mathematics, pp. 179–216 (1971)
15. McDowell, R., Miller, D.: Cut-elimination for a logic with definitions and induction. Theoret. Comput. Sci. **232**(1–2), 91–119 (2000)
16. Rukhaia, M.: CERES in Proof Schemata. Ph.D. thesis, Vienna University of Technology (2012)
17. Salzer, G.: On the Relationship between Cycle Unification and the Unification of Infinite Sets of Terms. In: Baader, F., Snyder, W. (eds.) UNIF 1993, Mass, Boston (1993)
18. Takeuti, G.: Proof Theory, 2nd edn. North Holland, Amsterdam (1987)

Towards a Suppositional Inquisitive Semantics

Jeroen Groenendijk and Floris Roelofsen[(✉)]

Institute for Logic, Language, and Computation, University of Amsterdam,
Amsterdam, The Netherlands
floris.roelofsen@gmail.com

Abstract. One of the primary usages of language is to exchange information. This can be done directly, as in *Will Susan sing? No, she won't,* but it is also often done in a less direct way, as in *If Pete plays the piano, will Susan sing? No, if Pete plays the piano, Susan won't sing.* In the latter type of exchange, both participants make a certain *supposition,* and exchange information under the assumption that this supposition holds. This paper develops a semantic framework for the analysis of this kind of information exchange. Building on earlier work in inquisitive semantics, it introduces a notion of meaning that captures informative, inquisitive, and suppositional content, and discusses how such meanings may be assigned in a natural way to sentences in a propositional language. The focus is on conditionals, which are the only kind of sentences in a propositional language that introduce non-trivial suppositional content.

1 Towards a More Fine-Grained Notion of Meaning

Traditionally, the meaning of a sentence is identified with its informative content, and the informative content of a sentence is taken to be determined by its truth conditions. Thus, the proposition expressed by a sentence is construed as a set of possible worlds, those worlds in which the sentence is true, and this set of worlds is taken to determine the effect that is achieved when the sentence is uttered in a conversation. Namely, when the sentence is uttered, the speaker is taken to *propose an update of the common ground* of the conversation (Stalnaker 1978). The common ground of a conversation is the body of information that has been publicly established in the conversation so far. It is modeled as a set of possible worlds, namely those worlds that are compatible with the established information. When a speaker utters a sentence, she is taken to propose to update the common ground by restricting it to those worlds in which the uttered sentence is true, i.e., those worlds that are contained in the proposition expressed by the sentence. If accepted by the other conversational participants, this update ensures that the new common ground contains the information that the uttered sentence is true.

We are very grateful to Martin Aher, Ivano Ciardelli, Katsuhiko Sano, and Matthijs Westera for extensive discussion of the ideas presented here and closely related topics, to two anonymous reviewers for useful feedback, and to the Netherlands Organisation for Scientific Research (NWO) for financial support.

M. Aher et al. (Eds.): TbiLLC 2013, LNCS 8984, pp. 137–156, 2015.
DOI: 10.1007/978-3-662-46906-4_9

This basic picture of sentence meaning and the effect of an utterance in conversation has proven very useful, but it also has some inherent limitations. Perhaps most importantly, it is completely centred on informative content and truth conditions. Evidently, there are many meaningful sentences in natural language that cannot be thought of as being true or false. Questions are a prominent case in point. For instance, the meaning of the question *Is Susan singing?* clearly cannot be taken to reside in its truth conditions. So in order to deal with such sentences, the basic picture sketched above needs to be generalized. One way to do this has been articulated in recent work on inquisitive semantics (e.g. Ciardelli 2012; 2013). The basic idea is that a speaker who utters *Is Susan singing?* still proposes to update the common ground of the conversation; however, she does not propose one particular update, but rather offers a choice: one way to comply with her proposal would be to restrict the common ground to worlds where Susan is singing, but another way to comply with her proposal, equally acceptable, would be to restrict the common ground to worlds where Susan is not singing. So the basic Stalnakerian picture of the effect of an utterance in terms of issuing a proposal to update the common ground of the conversation can be generalized appropriately, in such a way that it applies to declarative and interrogative sentences in a uniform way.

What about the basic truth conditional notion of sentence meaning? How could this be suitably generalized? The simplest approach that has been explored in inquisitive semantics is to move from truth conditions to *support conditions.* The idea is that the meaning of a sentence should determine precisely which pieces of information support the proposal that a speaker makes in uttering the sentence. This notion of meaning is adopted in the most basic implementation of inquisitive semantics, InqB.[1] Clearly, the support based notion of meaning is directly tied to the idea that the conversational effect of an utterance is a proposal to update the common ground in one or more ways. The latter—let's call it the *proposal picture of conversation*—is one of the main tenets of the inquisitive semantics framework in general, not just of the particular system InqB. The support based notion of meaning, on the other hand, is specific to InqB. It ties in well with the proposal picture of conversation, but there may well be other notions of meaning that also tie in well with this picture.

The goal of this paper is to develop such a notion of meaning, which is more fine-grained than the InqB notion. Motivation for such a more fine-grained notion comes from the basic observation that proposals may not only be *supported* by a given piece of information; they may also be *rejected* or *dismissed*. To illustrate, consider (1a), and the two responses to it in (1b) and (1c):

(1)   a.   If Pete plays the piano, Susan will sing.
       b.   No, if Pete plays the piano, Susan won't sing.
       c.   Pete won't play the piano.

---

[1] See Ciardelli (2009); Groenendijk and Roelofsen (2009); Ciardelli and Roelofsen (2011) for early expositions of InqB, and Roelofsen (2013); Ciardelli et al. (2013) for a more recent perspective and comparison with earlier work on the semantics of questions (e.g., Hamblin 1973; Karttunen 1977; Groenendijk and Stokhof 1984).

Intuitively, both (1b) and (1c) are pertinent responses; they address the proposal that (1a) expresses. However, rather than supporting the proposal, (1b) rejects it, while (1c) dismisses a supposition of it and thereby renders it void.

We will consider what it means in general to reject a proposal or to dismiss a supposition of it, and how these notions are related to each other, as well as to support. We will define a semantics for a propositional language, which specifies recursively for every sentence (i) which information states (or equivalently, which pieces of information) support it, (ii) which information states reject it, and (iii) which information states dismiss a supposition of it. We refer to this system as InqS. We will argue that the more fine-grained notion of meaning adopted in InqS considerably broadens the empirical scope of InqB, especially in the domain of conditionals. In Aher 2014 it is shown that the framework developed here allows for a novel treatment of epistemic and deontic modals as well, with interesting connections to the treatment of conditionals presented here.[2]

The paper is organized as follows. Section 2 reviews the background and motivation for InqS in more detail; Sect. 3 presents the system itself, identifying its basic logical properties and discussing some illustrative examples; and finally, Sect. 4 summarizes and concludes.

2   Background and Motivation

2.1   Support and Persistence

In a support based semantics, the basic idea is that one knows the meaning of a sentence just in case one knows which information states—or equivalently, which pieces of information—support the given sentence, and which don't. For instance, an information state s, modeled as a set of possible worlds, supports an atomic declarative sentence p just in case every world in s makes p true; it supports $\neg p$ if every world in s makes p false; and finally, it supports the interrogative sentence $?p$ just in case it supports either p or $\neg p$.

---

[2] One way to reject the proposal expressed by (1a), not listed above, is as follows:
(i) No, if Pete plays the piano, Susan might not sing.
This response involves the epistemic modal *might*. Accounting for such responses is beyond the scope of the current paper, but not beyond the scope of InqS in general. Indeed, the InqS analysis of epistemic modals presented in Aher 2014 naturally characterizes (i) as a rejecting response to (1a), and also clearly brings out the difference between (i) and (1b). Namely, (i) rejects (1a) in a *defeasible* way, subject to possible retraction when additional information becomes available, while (1b) rejects (1a) indefeasibly. Or, phrased in terms of conversational attitudes, (i) signals that the addressee is *unwilling* to accept the proposal expressed by (1a), while (1b) signals that she is really *unable* to do so.

There is a rich psycholinguistic literature on the denial of conditional statements (see, e.g., Handley 2006; Espino and Byrne 2012; Égré and Politzer 2013, and references therein), but the distinction between defeasible and indefeasible rejection has, to the best of our knowledge, not been brought to attention previously.

Given such a support-based semantics, we can think of a speaker who utters a sentence φ as proposing to enhance the common ground of the conversation, modeled as an information state, in such a way that it *comes to support* φ. Thus, in uttering p a speaker proposes to enhance the common ground in such a way that it comes to support p, and in uttering $?p$ a speaker proposes to enhance the common ground in such a way that it comes to support either p or $\neg p$.

Prima facie it is natural to assume that support is *persistent*, that is, if an information state s supports a sentence φ, then it is natural to assume that every more informed information state $t \subset s$ will also support φ. In other words, information growth cannot lead to retraction of support. This assumption is indeed made in InqB, and it determines to a large extent how the system behaves.

2.2   Support for Conditionals

Let us now zoom in on conditional sentences, which is where we would like to argue that a more refined picture is ultimately needed. Consider again the conditional statement in (1a), repeated in (2) below, and the corresponding conditional question in (3):

(2)   If Pete plays the piano, Susan will sing. $p \to q$

(3)   If Pete plays the piano, will Susan sing? $p \to ?q$

The meanings of these sentences in InqB can be depicted as follows:

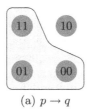 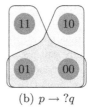

(a) $p \to q$ (b) $p \to ?q$

In these figures, 11 is a world where p and q are both true, 10 a world where p is true but q is false, etcetera. We have only depicted the *maximal* states that support each sentence. Since support is persistent, all substates of these maximal supporting states also support the given sentences.

In general, in InqB a state s is taken to support a conditional sentence $\varphi \to \psi$ just in case every state $t \subseteq s$ that supports φ also supports ψ. For instance, the state $s = \{11, 01, 00\}$ supports $p \to q$, because any substate $t \subseteq s$ that supports p (there are only two such states, namely $\{11\}$ and $\emptyset$) also support q. Similarly, one can verify that the states $\{11, 01, 00\}$ and $\{11, 01, 00\}$ both support $p \to ?q$.

For convenience, we will henceforth use $|\varphi|$ to denote the state consisting of all worlds where φ is classically true. So the states $\{11, 01, 00\}$ and $\{10, 01, 00\}$ can be denoted more perspicuously as $|p \to q|$ and $|p \to \neg q|$, respectively.

2.3   Support and Reject

The support conditions for a sentence φ capture an essential aspect of the proposal that is made in uttering φ, namely what is needed to compliantly settle this proposal. However, besides compliantly settling a given proposal, conversational participants may react in different ways as well. In particular, they may *reject* the proposal. What does it mean exactly to reject the proposal made in uttering φ? And can this, perhaps indirectly, be explicated in terms of the support conditions for φ as well?

At first sight, this seems quite feasible indeed. Suppose that a speaker A utters a sentence φ, and a responder B reacts with ψ. A proposes to enhance the common ground to a state that supports φ, while B proposes to enhance the common ground to a state that supports ψ. Then we could say that B *rejects* A's initial proposal just in case any state s that supports ψ is such that no consistent substate $t \subseteq s$ supports φ. After all, if this is the case, then any way of satisfying B's counterproposal leads to a common ground which does not support φ and which cannot be further enhanced in any way such that it comes to support φ while remaining consistent.

For many basic cases, this characterization of rejection in terms of support seems adequate. For instance, if A utters an atomic sentence p and B responds with $\neg p$, then according to the given characterization, B rejects A's initial proposal, which accords with pre-theoretical intuitions.

However, in the case of conditionals, the given characterization is problematic. Intuitively, the proposal expressed by (2) above can be rejected with (4).

(4)   No, if Pete plays the piano, Susan won't sing. $p \rightarrow \neg q$

However, there is a consistent state that supports both (2) and (4), namely $|\neg p|$. So according to the above characterization, (4) does not reject (2).

This example illustrates something quite fundamental: in general, reject conditions cannot be derived from support conditions. Thus, a semantics that aims to provide a comprehensive characterization of the proposals that speakers make when uttering sentences in conversation, needs to specify both support- and reject-conditions (and perhaps more). InqB, which is only concerned with support, has been extended in previous work to a semantics that specifies reject conditions as well, with the aim to deal with the type of phenomena discussed here. The resulting framework is referred to as *radical inquisitive semantics*, InqR for short (Groenendijk and Roelofsen 2010; Sano 2012; Aher 2013).[3]

---

[3] The need to specify both support and reject conditions is independent from the need to have a notion of meaning that embodies inquisitive content. There is a lot of work addressing the first issue while leaving inquisitive content out of the picture, e.g., work on *data semantics* (Veltman 1985), *game-theoretic semantics* and *independence friendly logic* (Hintikka and Sandu 1997; Hodges 1997), *dependence logic* (Väänänen 2007), and *truth-maker semantics* (Fraassen 1969; Fine 2012).

2.4   Dismissing a Supposition

The semantics to be developed in the present paper further extends the InqR framework, providing yet a more comprehensive characterization of the proposals that speakers make when uttering sentences in conversation. This further refinement is motivated by the observation that, besides compliant support and full-fledged rejection, there is, as we saw already in the introduction, yet another way to react to the conditionals in(2) and(3):

(5)   Pete won't play the piano. $\neg p$

Suppose that A utters (2) or (3) and that B reacts with (5). One natural way to think about this response is as one that *dismisses a supposition* that A was making, namely the supposition 'that Pete will play the piano'.

Clearly, the suppositions that a speaker makes in issuing a certain proposal, and responses that dismiss such suppositions, cannot be characterized purely in terms of the support conditions for that sentence.

2.5   From Radical to Suppositional

At first sight it may seem that suppositional phenomena *can* be captured if we have both support- and reject-conditions at our disposal. Indeed, an attempt to do so has been articulated in work on InqR (see in particular Groenendijk and Roelofsen 2010, Sect. 3). There, states that dismiss a supposition of a sentence φ are characterized as states that can be obtained by intersecting a state that supports φ with a state that rejects φ. Within the broader conceptual framework of InqR, such states can be thought of as ones that reject the *question behind* φ. If correct, this connection between support, rejection, and suppositional dismissal would show that there is no need to further refine the semantic machinery of InqR in order to deal with suppositional phenomena.

This characterization works fine for simple cases like $\neg p$ in response to $p \rightarrow q$. Namely, $|\neg p|$ can be obtained as the intersection of $|p \rightarrow q|$ and $|p \rightarrow \neg q|$, which support and reject $p \rightarrow q$, respectively. So $\neg p$ is correctly predicted to dismiss a supposition of the conditional. However, the predictions for more complex cases are not always satisfactory. Consider, for instance, a conditional with a disjunctive antecedent, and a response rejecting just one of the disjuncts:

(6)   a.   If Pete or Bill plays the piano, Susan will sing. $(p \vee q) \rightarrow r$
         b.   Well, Pete won't play the piano. $\neg p$

Under the strategy under consideration, InqR fails to predict that (6b) dismisses a supposition of (6a). Any state s that supports $(p \vee q) \rightarrow r$ has to support both $p \rightarrow r$ and $q \rightarrow r$. Then s cannot contain a world w where q holds, and p and r do not hold. But this world is included in $|\neg p|$. So, $|\neg p|$ cannot be obtained as the intersection of a state that supports $(p \vee q) \rightarrow r$ and a state that rejects it.

In order to avoid this and other problematic predictions when characterizing suppositional dismissal in terms of support and rejection, we will develop a semantics in which all three notions are characterized separately.

3   Suppositional Inquisitive Semantics

We will consider a propositional language $\mathcal{L}$, based on a finite set of atomic sentences $\mathcal{P}$. Complex sentences are built up using the usual connectives, $\neg$, $\wedge$, $\vee$, and $\rightarrow$, as well as an additional operator, ?. As in InqB, $?\varphi$ is defined as an abbreviation of $\varphi \vee \neg\varphi$ (the rationale behind this will become clear later).

The basic ingredients of the semantics that we will develop for this language are *possible worlds*, which we take to be functions mapping every atomic sentence in $\mathcal{P}$ to a truth value, 1 or 0, and *information states*, which are sets of possible worlds. For brevity, we will often simply talk about worlds and states instead of possible worlds and information states. w will denote the set of all worlds.

The semantics consists in a simultaneous recursive definition of three notions:

$$s \models^+ \varphi \qquad s \text{ supports } \varphi$$
$$s \models^- \varphi \qquad s \text{ rejects } \varphi$$
$$s \models^\circ \varphi \qquad s \text{ dismisses a supposition of } \varphi$$

In terms of these three semantic notions we can define corresponding *logical relations of responsehood* along the following lines:[4]

ψ supports (rejects, dismisses a supposition of) φ iff every state that supports ψ, supports (rejects, dismisses a supposition of) φ.

We will denote the set of all states that support a sentence φ as $[\varphi]^+$, and similarly for $[\varphi]^-$ and $[\varphi]^\circ$. The triple $\langle [\varphi]^+, [\varphi]^-, [\varphi]^\circ \rangle$ is called the *proposition* expressed by φ, and is denoted as $[\varphi]$. If two sentences φ and ψ express exactly the same proposition, they are said to be *equivalent*, notation $\varphi \equiv \psi$.

Before turning to the semantics proper, we first introduce some auxiliary notions which will be helpful in articulating and explaining the system.

3.1   Informative Content and Alternatives

In uttering a sentence φ, a speaker proposes to establish a common ground that supports φ. Now suppose that w is a world that is not included in any state that supports φ. Then, any way of compliantly settling the given proposal will lead to a common ground that does not contain w. Thus, in uttering φ, a speaker proposes to exclude any world that is not in $\bigcup[\varphi]^+$ as a candidate for the actual world. In other words, she provides the information that the actual world must be contained in $\bigcup[\varphi]^+$. For this reason, we will refer to $\bigcup[\varphi]^+$ as the *informative content* of φ, and denote it as $\mathsf{info}(\varphi)$.

---

[4] In terms of the three basic semantic notions, a whole range of derived semantic notions can be defined, which can be used in the same way to define additional logical responsehood relations. One case in point is the notion of a state s *suppositionally dismissing a sentence* φ, which holds when s dismisses a supposition of φ, and no substate of s supports or rejects φ. For lack of space, a proper discussion of these logical responsehood relations has to be left for another occasion.

Definition 1 (Informative Content). $\mathsf{info}(\varphi) := \bigcup [\varphi]^+$

Among the states that support a sentence φ, some are easier to reach than others. Suppose for instance, that s and t are two states that support φ, and that $t \subset s$. Establishing either s or t as the new common ground would be sufficient to compliantly settle the proposal expressed by φ. However, it is easier to establish s then it is to establish t, because this would require the elimination of fewer possible worlds, i.e., it would require less information.

From this perspective, those states that support φ and are not contained in any other state that supports φ have a special status. They are the *weakest*, least informed states supporting φ. We will refer to such states as the *support-alternatives* for φ, and denote the set of all support-alternatives for φ as $\mathsf{alt}^+(\varphi)$. Similarly, we will refer to the weakest states that reject φ as the *reject-alternatives* for φ, and denote the sets of all these states as $\mathsf{alt}^-(\varphi)$. We will sometimes refer to support-alternatives simply as *alternatives*.

Definition 2 (Alternatives)

- $\mathsf{alt}^+(\varphi) := \{s \mid s \models^+ \varphi \text{ and there is no } t \text{ supsets such that } t \models^+ \varphi\}$
- $\mathsf{alt}^-(\varphi) := \{s \mid s \models^- \varphi \text{ and there is no } t \supset s \text{ such that } t \models^- \varphi\}$

In our current setting, where we consider a propositional language based on a finite set of atomic sentences, the set of all possible worlds is finite, and therefore the set of all states is also finite. This means that infinite sequences of states $s_0 \subset s_1 \subset s_2 \subset \dots$ supporting a certain sentence do not exist. As a result, every state that supports a sentence φ is included in a support-alternative for φ, and similarly for states that reject φ.

Fact 1 (Alternatives)

- *Every $s \in [\varphi]^+$ is contained in some $\alpha \in \mathsf{alt}^+(\varphi)$*
- *Every $s \in [\varphi]^-$ is contained in some $\alpha \in \mathsf{alt}^-(\varphi)$*

We will rely on this fact in formulating and explaining the semantics, in particular the clause for implication, because certain notions become more transparent when explicated in terms of alternatives. We will also show how the semantics can be lifted to the more general setting where the set of possible worlds is infinite and the existence of alternatives cannot be guaranteed.

3.2   Informative, Inquisitive, and Suppositional Sentences

We will say that a sentence φ is *informative* just in case (i) it has the potential to provide information, i.e., $\mathsf{info}(\varphi) \neq \omega$, and (ii) it can be rejected, i.e., $[\varphi]^- \neq \emptyset$. We will say that φ is *inquisitive* just in case (i) there is at least one state that supports φ, and (ii) in order to establish such a state as the new common ground it does not suffice for other conversational participants to simply accept $\mathsf{info}(\varphi)$. The latter holds if and only if $\mathsf{info}(\varphi)$ does not support φ, i.e., $\mathsf{info}(\varphi) \notin [\varphi]^+$. Finally, we will say that φ is *suppositional* just in case there is at least one consistent state that dismisses a supposition of φ, which means that $[\varphi]^\circ \neq \{\emptyset\}$.

Definition 3 (Informative, Inquisitive and Suppositional Sentences)

- φ is *informative* iff $[\varphi]^- \neq \emptyset$ and $\mathsf{info}(\varphi) \neq \omega$
- φ is *inquisitive* iff $[\varphi]^+ \neq \emptyset$ and $\mathsf{info}(\varphi) \notin [\varphi]^+$
- φ is *suppositional* iff $[\varphi]^\circ \neq \{\emptyset\}$

If there are two or more alternatives for a sentence, then that sentence has to be inquisitive. After all, if φ is not inquisitive, then $\mathsf{info}(\varphi)$, which amounts to $\bigcup[\varphi]^+$, supports φ. But this means that $\bigcup[\varphi]^+$ is the unique alternative for φ, which contradicts the assumption that there are two or more alternatives for φ.

Vice versa, if φ is inquisitive, i.e., if $\bigcup[\varphi]^+ \notin [\varphi]^+$, then, given our assumption that there are finitely many possible worlds, there must be at least two states $s, t \in [\varphi]^+$ such that $s \cup t \notin [\varphi]^+$. But then, by Fact 1, there must be at least two support-alternatives for φ, one containing s, one containing t, and neither of them containing $s \cup t$. So there is a straightforward connection between inquisitiveness and the number of support-alternatives for a sentence.

Fact 2 (Alternatives and Inquisitiveness)

- φ is *inquisitive* iff $\mathsf{alt}^+(\varphi)$ has two or more elements.

With these basic notions and facts in place, we now turn to the clauses of InqS.

3.3   InqS: The Boolean Fragment

We first consider the Boolean fragment of our language, which we denote as $\mathcal{L}_B$. After considering $\mathcal{L}_B$, we will turn to implication. As the reader may expect, the clause for implication will be more intricate than those for the Boolean connectives, and several aspects of it will deserve some careful consideration.

The clauses for $\mathcal{L}_B$ are given in Definition 4 below. After laying out the definition, we will describe informally what each of the clauses amounts to.

Definition 4 (Atomic Sentences and Boolean Connectives)

1. $s \models^+ p$ iff $s \neq \emptyset$ and $s \subseteq |p|$
   $s \models^- p$ iff $s \neq \emptyset$ and $s \cap |p| = \emptyset$
   $s \models^\circ p$ iff $s = \emptyset$

2. $s \models^+ \neg\varphi$ iff $s \models^- \varphi$
   $s \models^- \neg\varphi$ iff $s \models^+ \varphi$
   $s \models^\circ \neg\varphi$ iff $s \models^\circ \varphi$

3. $s \models^+ \varphi \wedge \psi$ iff $s \models^+ \varphi$ and $s \models^+ \psi$
   $s \models^- \varphi \wedge \psi$ iff $s \models^- \varphi$ or $s \models^- \psi$
   $s \models^\circ \varphi \wedge \psi$ iff $s \models^\circ \varphi$ or $s \models^\circ \psi$

4. $s \models^+ \varphi \vee \psi$ iff $s \models^+ \varphi$ or $s \models^+ \psi$
   $s \models^- \varphi \vee \psi$ iff $s \models^- \varphi$ and $s \models^- \psi$
   $s \models^\circ \varphi \vee \psi$ iff $s \models^\circ \varphi$ or $s \models^\circ \psi$

Atomic Sentences. A state s supports an atomic sentence p just in case s is consistent and p is true in all worlds in s. Similarly, s rejects p just in case s is consistent and p is false in all worlds in s. Finally, s dismisses a supposition of p if s is inconsistent. The idea behind the latter clause is that in uttering p, a speaker makes the trivial supposition that p may or may not be the case—a supposition that is dismissed only by the absurd, inconsistent state.

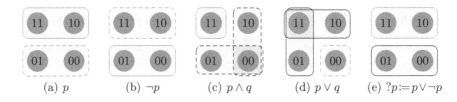

(a) p (b) $\neg p$ (c) $p \wedge q$ (d) $p \vee q$ (e) $?p := p \vee \neg p$

Fig. 1. The propositions expressed by some basic sentences.

Negation. A state s supports $\neg\varphi$ just in case it rejects φ. Vice versa, it rejects $\neg\varphi$ just in case it supports φ. Finally, it dismisses a supposition of $\neg\varphi$ just in case it dismisses a supposition of φ. Thus, $\neg\varphi$ straightforwardly inherits the suppositional content of φ. Notice that, as in classical logic, $\neg\neg\varphi \equiv \varphi$ for any φ.

Conjunction. A state s supports $\varphi \wedge \psi$ just in case it supports both φ and ψ, and it rejects $\varphi \wedge \psi$ just in case it rejects either φ or ψ. Finally, s dismisses a supposition of $\varphi \wedge \psi$ just in case it dismisses a supposition of φ or dismisses a supposition of ψ. Thus, $\varphi \wedge \psi$ inherits the suppositional content of φ and ψ in a straightforward, cumulative way.

Disjunction. A state s supports $\varphi \vee \psi$ just in case it supports either φ or ψ, and it rejects $\varphi \vee \psi$ just in case it rejects both φ and ψ. Finally, s dismisses a supposition of $\varphi \vee \psi$ just in case it dismisses a supposition of φ or dismisses a supposition of ψ. Thus, again, $\varphi \vee \psi$ inherits the suppositional content of φ and ψ in a straightforward, cumulative way.

Propositions expressed by sentences in $\mathcal{L}_B$ can be visualized in a perspicuous way. This is done in Fig. 1 for some simple sentences. In this figure, as before, 11 is a world where both p and q are true, 10 a world where p is true and q is false, etcetera. The support- and reject-alternatives for each sentence are depicted with solid and dashed borders, respectively. Notice in particular that Fig. 1(d) and Fig. 1(e) immediately reveal that $p \vee q$ and $?p$ are inquisitive, since there are two support-alternatives for these sentences.

Some Logical Properties. The Boolean connectives satisfy De Morgan's laws:

$$\varphi \wedge \psi \equiv \neg(\neg\varphi \vee \neg\psi)$$
$$\varphi \vee \psi \equiv \neg(\neg\varphi \wedge \neg\psi)$$

Moreover, it can be shown that for every sentence $\varphi \in \mathcal{L}_B$, the informative content of φ in InqS, i.e., $\bigcup[\varphi]^+$, coincides precisely with the proposition that φ expresses in classical propositional logic (CPL). So, as far as $\mathcal{L}_B$ is concerned, InqS is a conservative refinement of classical logic. That is, the two fully agree on the informative content of every sentence in the language; only, while classical logic *identifies* the meaning of a sentence with its informative content, InqS has a more fine-grained notion of meaning.

Fact 3 (Conservative Refinement of CPL). *For any $\varphi \in \mathcal{L}_B$, $\mathsf{info}(\varphi) = |\varphi|$*

The *inconsistent* state, $\emptyset$, never supports or rejects a sentence in $\mathcal{L}_B$, but always suppositionally dismisses it.

Fact 4 (Inconsistency). *For any $\varphi \in \mathcal{L}_B$: $\emptyset \not\models^+ \varphi$, $\emptyset \not\models^- \varphi$, and $\emptyset \models^\circ \varphi$.*

Moreover, the inconsistent state is the *only* state that suppositionally dismisses any sentence in $\mathcal{L}_B$. In other words, no sentence in $\mathcal{L}_B$ is suppositional.

Fact 5 (No Suppositionality). *For any $\varphi \in \mathcal{L}_B$, $[\varphi]^\circ = \{\emptyset\}$.*

Recall that in InqB support is persistent, i.e., information grows never leads to retraction of support. It follows from Fact 4 that in InqS support and rejection are not fully persistent: any state that supports or rejects a sentence φ has a substate, namely $\emptyset$, which no longer supports/rejects φ. However, in the Boolean fragment of InqS, support and rejection *are* persistent *modulo inconsistency*. That is, if s supports φ then any *consistent* substate of s still supports φ. And similarly for rejection.

Fact 6 (Persistence Modulo Inconsistency). *For any $\varphi \in \mathcal{L}_B$, $\star \in \{+, -\}$, if $s \models^\star \varphi$ and $s \supseteq t \neq \emptyset$, then $t \models^\star \varphi$.*

A state never supports and rejects a sentence at the same time.

Fact 7 (Support and Rejection are Mutually Exclusive). *For any $\varphi \in \mathcal{L}_B$, $[\varphi]^+ \cap [\varphi]^- = \emptyset$.*

Finally, it follows from Facts 6 and 7 that in the Boolean fragment support and rejection are incompatible in a stronger sense as well: a state that supports a sentence φ can never have any *overlap* with a state that rejects φ.

Fact 8 (Support and Rejection do not Overlap). *For any $\varphi \in \mathcal{L}_B$, if $s \models^+ \varphi$ and $t \models^- \varphi$, then $s \cap t = \emptyset$.*

3.4 Implication

We now turn to implication, which typically introduces non-trivial suppositional content. The initial idea is that, for a state s to either support or reject an implication $\varphi \rightarrow \psi$, it is a necessary requirement that the antecedent φ be *supposable* in s. If this is not the case, then s suppositionally dismisses the implication, and does not support or reject it.

The key question, then, is what it means exactly for φ to be supposable in s. To answer this question, we will consider a number of concrete examples. We will start with the simplest case, and gradually consider more complex ones. As we proceed, our notion of supposability and the semantics for implication that is defined in terms of it will become more and more refined. Consider first an implication with an atomic antecedent and an atomic consequent:

(7) $p \to r$

It would be natural to say that p is supposable in a state s iff the single support-alternative for p, $|p|$, is consistent with s, i.e., $s \cap |p| \neq \emptyset$. Furthermore, it would be natural to say that if this condition is met, s supports the implication iff $s \cap |p|$ supports r, and s rejects the implication iff $s \cap |p|$ rejects r. However, this characterization of supposability only applies if there is a *unique* support-alternative for the antecedent. To see how it may be generalized, let us consider an example in which there are *two* support-alternatives for the antecedent:

(8) $(p \vee q) \to r$

To deal with such cases, as well as the simpler cases where there is a single support-alternative for the antecedent, it seems reasonable to say that, in general, the antecedent is supposable in s iff *every* support-alternative for it is consistent with s:

(9) φ is supposable in s, notation $s \lhd \varphi$, iff $\forall \alpha \in \mathsf{alt}^+(\varphi) : s \cap \alpha \neq \emptyset$

With this characterization of supposability in place, we may formulate the clauses for implication as follows:

$$s \models^+ \varphi \to \psi \quad \text{iff} \quad s \lhd \varphi \text{ and } \forall \alpha \in \mathsf{alt}^+(\varphi): s \cap \alpha \models^+ \psi$$
$$s \models^- \varphi \to \psi \quad \text{iff} \quad s \lhd \varphi \text{ and } \exists \alpha \in \mathsf{alt}^+(\varphi): s \cap \alpha \models^- \psi$$
$$s \models^\circ \varphi \to \psi \quad \text{iff} \quad s \ntriangleleft \varphi$$

However, this formulation of the clauses is problematic in several ways. One problem is that the given conditions for rejecting an implication are too stringent. To see this, consider the following state:

(10) $s := |\neg p \wedge (q \to \neg r)|$

This state is inconsistent with one of the support-alternatives for the antecedent of (8), namely $|p|$. However, it is consistent with the other support-alternative, $|q|$, and if we intersect it with this alternative we get at the state $|\neg p \wedge \neg r|$, which rejects the consequent of the implication, r. So, on the one hand, not every support-alternative for the antecedent is consistent with s, and we want our semantics to capture this by characterizing s as dismissing a supposition of the implication; on the other hand, however, one of the support-alternatives for the antecedent *is* consistent with s, and restricting s to this alternative leads to rejection of the consequent. We want our semantics to capture this as well, by characterizing s as a state that rejects the implication as a whole (besides dismissing a supposition of it).

The general upshot of this example is that the idea that we started out with, namely that supposability of the antecedent as a whole is a necessary requirement for a state to support or reject an implication, is not exactly on the right track. In particular, it is too stringent in the case of rejection.

Rather than considering the supposability of the antecedent as a whole, it seems more suitable to consider the supposability of each support-alternative for the antecedent separately. Let us say, for now, that an alternative α is supposable in a state s just in case the two are consistent with each other:

(11)   An alternative α is supposable in a state s, notation $s \lhd \alpha$, iff $s \cap \alpha \neq \emptyset$.

Then we arrive at the following revised formulation of the clauses for implication:

$$s \models^+ \varphi \to \psi \quad \text{iff} \quad \forall \alpha \in \text{alt}[\varphi]^+: s \lhd \alpha \text{ and } s \cap \alpha \models^+ \psi$$

$$s \models^- \varphi \to \psi \quad \text{iff} \quad \exists \alpha \in \text{alt}[\varphi]^+: s \lhd \alpha \text{ and } s \cap \alpha \models^- \psi$$

$$s \models^\circ \varphi \to \psi \quad \text{iff} \quad \exists \alpha \in \text{alt}[\varphi]^+: s \not\lhd \alpha$$

This formulation, however, still needs further refinement. First, consider a case in which there are no support-alternatives for the antecedent at all:

(12) $(p \wedge \neg p) \to r$

According to the clauses above, this implication is trivially supported by any state, because the clause for support quantifies universally over the support-alternatives for the antecedent, which in this case do not exist. On the other hand, according to the given clauses, there is no state that dismisses a supposition of the implication, because this requires inconsistency with some support-alternative for the antecedent, of which there are none. We want exactly the oppositive result: no state should support this implication, and every state should dismiss a supposition of it. Thus, the clauses should be adapted: support should require a non-empty set of support-alternatives for the antecedent, while dismissal of a supposition should occur if this set is empty. This leads us to the formulation below. For uniformity, we have adapted the rejection clause as well, although this is strictly speaking redundant; the new, redundant part of the clause is displayed in gray.

$$s \models^+ \varphi \to \psi \quad \text{iff} \quad \text{alt}^+(\varphi) \neq \emptyset \text{ and } \forall \alpha \in \text{alt}^+(\varphi): s \lhd \alpha \text{ and } s \cap \alpha \models^+ \psi$$

$$s \models^- \varphi \to \psi \quad \text{iff} \quad \text{alt}^+(\varphi) \neq \emptyset \text{ and } \exists \alpha \in \text{alt}^+(\varphi): s \lhd \alpha \text{ and } s \cap \alpha \models^- \psi$$

$$s \models^\circ \varphi \to \psi \quad \text{iff} \quad \text{alt}^+(\varphi) = \emptyset \text{ or } \exists \alpha \in \text{alt}^+(\varphi): s \not\lhd \alpha$$

This formulation is appropriate as long as φ and ψ are non-suppositional, i.e., as long as they do not contain any implications themselves. However, to deal with nested implications, some further refinements are needed.

First consider a case where the *consequent* is suppositional, which will be relatively easy to accommodate.

(13) $p \to (q \to r)$

Consider the following state:

(14) $s := |p \to \neg q|$

The semantics should predict that this state dismisses a supposition of (13), because if we restrict it to the unique support-alternative for the antecedent, $|p|$, we arrive at the state $|\neg q|$, and this state dismisses a supposition of the consequent, $q \rightarrow r$. However, this is not captured by the clause for dismissal given above, which requires that there is a support-alternative for the antecedent that is inconsistent with s. This is clearly not the case here. So the clause needs to be adapted, and there is a natural way to do so: in order for s to dismiss a supposition of $\varphi \rightarrow \psi$ it should be the case that $\text{alt}^+(\varphi)$ is empty, or that it contains an alternative that is not supposable in s, or that it contains an alternative α which is such that $s \cap \alpha$ dismisses a supposition of the consequent. Notice that, w.r.t. the previous formulation, the first two conditions are old, and the third one is newly added. Moreover, notice that whenever the consequent of the implication is non-suppositional, the second and the third requirement coincide, demanding that $s \cap \alpha$ be consistent. Leaving the support and reject clauses unchanged, we arrive at the following formulation:

$$s \models^+ \varphi \rightarrow \psi \quad \text{iff} \quad \text{alt}^+(\varphi) \neq \emptyset \text{ and } \forall \alpha \in \text{alt}^+(\varphi): s \lhd \alpha \text{ and } s \cap \alpha \models^+ \psi$$

$$s \models^- \varphi \rightarrow \psi \quad \text{iff} \quad \text{alt}^+(\varphi) \neq \emptyset \text{ and } \exists \alpha \in \text{alt}^+(\varphi): s \lhd \alpha \text{ and } s \cap \alpha \models^- \psi$$

$$s \models^\circ \varphi \rightarrow \psi \quad \text{iff} \quad \text{alt}^+(\varphi) = \emptyset \text{ or } \exists \alpha \in \text{alt}^+(\varphi): s \ntriangleleft \alpha \text{ or } s \cap \alpha \models^\circ \psi$$

There is one more amendment to make, in order to deal with cases where the antecedent of the implication is itself suppositional. We will do this in two steps, again first considering the simplest case and then a more complex one. Consider first:

(15) $(p \rightarrow q) \rightarrow r$

Suppose that our state of evaluation is the following:

(16) $s := |\neg p \wedge r|$

According to the clauses as formulated above, this state supports the implication in (15), because there is a single support-alternative for the antecedent, $\alpha := |p \rightarrow q|$, which is consistent with s, and the intersection of s with α amounts to s itself, which supports the consequent, r. Moreover, the clauses do not characterize s as a state that dismisses a supposition of (15), because $s \cap \alpha$ is consistent and does not dismiss a supposition of the consequent.

Again, we want precisely the opposite result: s should be characterized as dismissing a supposition of the implication, and not as supporting it. The culprit for this is our notion of supposability of support-alternatives. According to (11), a support-alternative α for a sentence φ is supposable in a state s iff $s \cap \alpha \neq \emptyset$. However, even if $s \cap \alpha \neq \emptyset$, it may be the case that $s \cap \alpha$ no longer supports φ. This is indeed the case in the example above where $\alpha := |p \rightarrow q|$ is the unique support-alternative for the antecedent, $p \rightarrow q$, and $s \cap \alpha$ no longer supports $p \rightarrow q$. For this reason, α should not be characterized as supposable in s.

Our notion of supposability should be made sensitive to this. That is, we should not just require that $s \cap \alpha$ is consistent, but rather that in going from α to $s \cap \alpha$, support of φ is preserved:

(17)   A support-alternative α for a sentence φ is supposable in a state s, notation $s \lhd \alpha$, iff $s \cap \alpha \models^+ \varphi$.

With this refined notion of supposability in place, the clauses for implication can remain as they were formulated above. Examples like (15), with a suppositional, but non-inquisitive antecedent, are now suitably dealt with.

The final, most complex case to consider is one in which the antecedent is both suppositional and inquisitive, which means that it has multiple support-alternatives. Take the following example:

(18) $((p \rightarrow q) \vee l) \rightarrow r$

Notice that the antecedent is a disjunction, whose first disjunct is suppositional. Consider a state that dismisses the first disjunct, but supports the second, and moreover, supports the consequent of the implication:

(19) $s := |\neg p \wedge l \wedge r|$

According to the clauses as formulated above, this state supports the implication in (18). Let us see why this is the case. First, there are two support-alternatives for the antecedent, $|p \rightarrow q|$ and $|l|$. Intersecting s with either of these alternatives simply yields s, which supports the antecedent, so both support-alternatives for the antecedent are supposable. Moreover, the intersection of s with either of the support-alternatives for the antecedent also supports the consequent, r. Therefore, s supports the implication as a whole as well.

The clauses also characterize s as a state that does not dismiss any supposition of the implication in (18). This is because the intersection of s with either of the two support-alternatives for the antecedent is just s, and as we already saw, s supports the antecedent.

These are not the right results: we want the semantics to characterize s as a state that dismisses a supposition of the implication, and does not support it. The culprit for this is again our notion of supposability of support-alternatives. The idea was that a support-alternative α for φ is supposable in s iff in going from α to $s \cap \alpha$, *support of φ is preserved*. Formally, we require that $s \cap \alpha$ should still support φ.

But now look at the example again. There are two support-alternatives for the antecedent, corresponding to the two disjuncts, $|p \rightarrow q|$ and $|l|$. Let us focus on the first. Intersecting s with this alternative simply yields s, which supports the antecedent of the implication. Crucially, however, this is because it supports the *second* disjunct, l. It does not support the first disjunct, the one that corresponds to the support-alternative that we are considering. And, upon closer examination, there is a clear sense in which support is not fully *preserved* in going from $|p \rightarrow q|$ to s. Namely, there are states between $|p \rightarrow q|$ and s, such as $|\neg p|$, which do not support the antecedent. Only when we further strengthen these states in such a way that they come to support the second disjunct, do they come to support the antecedent as a whole. From this perspective, it is not right to say that support is preserved in going from $|p \rightarrow q|$ to s. It is true that we have support at s, but only after it was lost somewhere along the way. These considerations lead to the following, definitive, characterization of supposability of support-alternatives.[5]

Definition 5 (Supposability of Support-Alternatives). *A support–alternative α for a sentence φ is supposable in a state s, notation $s \lhd \alpha$, iff for every state t between α and $s \cap \alpha$, i.e., every t such that $\alpha \supseteq t \supseteq (s \cap \alpha)$, we have that $t \models^+ \varphi$.*

With this refined notion of supposability in place, the clauses for implication can remain as formulated above. We restate them here in an official definition.[6]

Definition 6 (Implication)

$$s \models^+ \varphi \to \psi \quad \textit{iff} \quad \mathsf{alt}^+(\varphi) \neq \emptyset \ \textit{and} \ \forall \alpha \in \mathsf{alt}^+(\varphi)\colon s \lhd \alpha \ \textit{and} \ s \cap \alpha \models^+ \psi$$

$$s \models^- \varphi \to \psi \quad \textit{iff} \quad \mathsf{alt}^+(\varphi) \neq \emptyset \ \textit{and} \ \exists \alpha \in \mathsf{alt}^+(\varphi)\colon s \lhd \alpha \ \textit{and} \ s \cap \alpha \ ! \models^- \psi$$

$$s \models^\circ \varphi \to \psi \quad \textit{iff} \quad \mathsf{alt}^+(\varphi) = \emptyset \ \textit{or} \ \ \exists \alpha \in \mathsf{alt}^+(\varphi)\colon s \not\lhd \alpha \ \textit{or} \ \ s \cap \alpha \models^\circ \psi$$

This completes our suppositional semantics for the full propositional language $\mathcal{L}$.

Depicting Propositions. The propositions expressed by simple conditional sentences can again be visualized. Figure 2 does this for the most basic case, $p \to q$. Figure 2(a) depicts the maximal state supporting $p \to q$, i.e., $|p \to q|$, as well as its maximal substate that *no longer* supports $p \to q$, i.e., $|\neg p|$. Any

---

[5] This notion of supposability preserves a key property of the simple notion of supposability in terms of consistency, namely that for every support-alternative α of any sentence φ, there is a unique 'turning point' state s, such that α is supposable in any superstate of s and no longer supposable in any substate of s. For this to obtain, it is crucial that the notion requires support to be preserved in all states between α and $s \cap \alpha$, and not just in $s \cap \alpha$.

[6] Recall from our discussion in Sect. 3.1 that the fact that we are considering a propositional language based on a finite set of atomic sentences is crucial in ensuring that every state that supports a sentence is contained in an alternative for that sentence, which in turn justifies our formulation of the clauses for implication in terms of alternatives. However, this cannot always be ensured. For instance, if we consider a first-order language with an infinite domain of interpretation, the existence of alternatives can no longer be guaranteed (Ciardelli 2009). Fortunately, there is a way to formulate the clauses for implication that does not make reference to alternatives, and which in the current setting is equivalent to the clauses as formulated in Definition. 6:

$$s \models^+ \varphi \to \psi \ \text{iff} \ [\varphi]^+ \neq \emptyset \ \text{and} \ \forall t \in [\varphi]^+ \exists u \supseteq t \in [\varphi]^+\colon s \lhd u \ \text{and} \ s \cap u \models^+ \psi$$

$$s \models^- \varphi \to \psi \ \text{iff} \ [\varphi]^+ \neq \emptyset \ \text{and} \ \exists t \in [\varphi]^+ \forall u \supseteq t \in [\varphi]^+\colon s \lhd u \ \text{and} \ s \cap u \models^- \psi$$

$$s \models^\circ \varphi \to \psi \ \text{iff} \ [\varphi]^+ = \emptyset \ \text{or} \ \ \exists t \in [\varphi]^+ \forall u \supseteq t \in [\varphi]^+\colon s \not\lhd u \ \text{or} \ \ s \cap u \models^\circ \psi$$

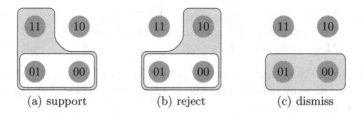

Fig. 2. States that support, reject, and dismiss a supposition of $p \to q$.

substate of $|p \to q|$ that is not completely contained in $|\neg p|$ still supports $p \to q$. Similarly, Fig. 2(b) depicts the maximal state rejecting $p \to q$, i.e., $|p \to \neg q|$, as well as its maximal substate that no longer rejects $p \to q$, i.e., $|\neg p|$. Finally, Fig. 2(c) depicts the maximal state that dismisses a supposition of $p \to q$, i.e., again $|\neg p|$.

Some Logical Properties. Recall again that in InqB support is fully persistent, and that in the Boolean fragment of InqS support and reject are persistent modulo inconsistency (Fact 6). In the full fragment of InqS this feature is lost. For instance, the information state $|p \to q|$ supports the sentence $p \to q$, but the state $|\neg p|$, which is a substate of $|p \to q|$, does not support $p \to q$; rather, it dismisses a supposition of it. Similarly for rejection: $|p \to \neg q|$ rejects $p \to q$, but $|\neg p|$, which is a substate of $|p \to \neg q|$, does not reject $p \to q$. Instead, as noted above, $|\neg p|$ dismisses a supposition of the implication. Thus, unlike in InqB, information growth can lead to suppositional dismissal, and thereby also to retraction of support or rejection, even if consistency is preserved.

However, a weaker form of persistency is still maintained in InqS, namely persistency *modulo suppositional dismissal*. That is, if a state s supports a sentence φ, then any more informed state $t \subseteq s$ either still supports φ, or dismisses a supposition of φ. And similarly for rejection. Finally, dismissal of a supposition is fully persistent. If a state s dismisses a supposition of φ, then so does any more informed state $t \subseteq s$. Information growth cannot lead to retraction of dismissal.

Fact 9 (Persistence Modulo Suppositional Dismissal). *For any* φ, $\star \in \{+, -, \circ\}$, *if* $s \models^\star \varphi$ *and* $t \subseteq s$, *then* $t \models^\star \varphi$ *or* $t \models^\circ \varphi$.

Fact 4 extends from the Boolean fragment of InqS to the full system: the inconsistent state never supports or rejects a sentence but always suppositionally dismisses it. The same goes for Fact 7: a state never supports and rejects a sentence at the same time. However, the full system does not exclude the possibility that a state either supports or rejects a sentence and at the same time also dismisses a supposition of it. To see that this option should indeed be left open, consider the following examples:

(20)   a.   Maria will go if Peter goes, or if Frank goes. $(p \to r) \vee (q \to r)$
         b.   Well, Peter isn't going, but indeed,
                if Frank goes, Maria will go as well. $\neg p \wedge (q \to r)$

(21)   a.   Maria will go if Peter goes, and if Frank goes. $(p \to r) \wedge (q \to r)$
        b.   Well no, Peter isn't going, and if Frank goes,
              Maria definitely won't. $\neg p \wedge (q \to \neg r)$

The response in (20b) supports (20a), but at the same time it also dismisses a supposition of it. Similarly, the response in (21b) rejects (21a), but again, it also dismisses a supposition of it.

Facts 4 and 9 together imply that the three components of a proposition in InqS jointly form a non-empty set of states S that is *downward closed*, i.e., for any $s \in S$ and $t \subseteq s$ we have that $t \in S$ as well.

Fact 10. *For any φ, $[\varphi]^+ \cup [\varphi]^- \cup [\varphi]^\circ$ is non-empty and downward closed.*

In InqB, propositions are defined precisely as non-empty, downward closed sets of states. So, while InqS offers a more fine-grained notion of meaning than InqB in that it distinguishes three different meaning components, if we put these three meaning components together, we always obtain the same kind of semantic object that we had already in InqB. Thus, InqS is a refinement of InqB, but at the same time it retains one of its core features.

We saw in Sect. 3.3 that the Boolean fragment of InqS preserves many central features of CPL. As soon as implication is taken into consideration, however, InqS diverges more radically from CPL. In particular, Facts 3 (conservative refinement), 5 (no suppositionality), and 8 (no overlap) no longer hold, which can all be shown with a single example: $\neg(p \to q)$. We have that $\mathsf{info}(\neg(p \to q)) = |p \to \neg q|$ which differs from the proposition expressed by $\neg(p \to q)$ in CPL. Furthermore, $\neg(p \to q)$ is suppositional, and it has supporting and rejecting states that overlap, for instance $|p \to \neg q|$ and $|p \to q|$, respectively.

One 'classical' property that InqS *does* preserve, even when implication is taken into consideration, is that whenever a state s supports a sentence φ, then no substate $t \subseteq s$ rejects φ, and vice versa, whenever s rejects φ, no substate $t \subseteq s$ supports φ. In the terminology of Veltman (1985), this means that every sentence in our language is *stable*.

Fact 11 (Stability). *For any $\varphi \in \mathcal{L}$ and any state s:*

- *If s supports φ then no $t \subseteq s$ rejects φ*
- *If s rejects φ then no $t \subseteq s$ supports φ*

Veltman introduced the notion of stability in his work on *data semantics*, which, like InqS, is concerned in particular with conditionals and epistemic modals. Veltman emphasizes that in data semantics, both conditionals and epistemic modals are typically unstable, unlike sentences that do not contain modals or conditionals. In InqS, it is still the case that sentences involving epistemic modals are typically unstable (see Aher 2014). However, all sentences in the propositional language considered here, including conditionals, are stable.

Finally, recall that we defined $?\varphi$ as an abbreviation of $\varphi \vee \neg\varphi$. Having spelled out the clauses for all the basic connectives in our system, we can now derive the interpretation of $?\varphi$ as well. First, a state supports $?\varphi$ iff it supports either

φ or $\neg\varphi$. So $[?\varphi]^+ = [\varphi]^+ \cup [\neg\varphi]^+ = [\varphi]^+ \cup [\varphi]^-$. Second, a state rejects $?\varphi$ iff it rejects both φ and $\neg\varphi$. But to reject $\neg\varphi$ is to support φ. Thus, in order to reject $?\varphi$, a state would have to support φ and reject φ at the same time, which is impossible. So, for any φ, $[?\varphi]^-$ will be empty. Finally, a state dismisses a supposition of $?\varphi$ iff it dismisses a supposition of φ or of $\neg\varphi$, and the latter occurs just in case the state dimisses a supposition of φ itself. So, $[?\varphi]^\circ = [\varphi]^\circ$.

Fact 12. *For any φ,* $[?\varphi] = \langle [\varphi]^+ \cup [\varphi]^-, \emptyset, [\varphi]^\circ \rangle$

Now let us return to our initial motivating examples, repeated below:

(22) a. If Pete plays the piano, will Susan sing? $p \rightarrow ?q$
     b. Yes, if Pete plays the piano, Susan will sing. $p \rightarrow q$
     c. No, if Pete plays the piano, Susan won't sing. $p \rightarrow \neg q$
     d. Pete won't play the piano. $\neg p$

As desired, our semantics predicts that (22b) and (22c) support (22a); that (22b) and (22c) reject each other; and that (22d) neither supports nor rejects any of (22a), (22b), and (22c), but dismisses a supposition of all three of them.[7] These examples are iconic for the issues that we set out to address. But, as we saw along the way, the semantics deals with many more complex cases as well.

4   Conclusion

Our starting point in this paper was the general perspective on meaning that is taken in inquisitive semantics, which is that sentences express proposals to update the common ground of the conversation in one or more ways. There are several ways in which a conversational participant may respond to such proposals, depending on her information state. The most basic inquisitive semantics framework, InqB, characterizes which states support a given proposal. Radical inquisitive semantics, InqR, also characterizes independently which states reject a given proposal. The suppositional inquisitive semantics developed in the present paper, InqS, further distinguishes states that dismiss a supposition of a given proposal. We have thus arrived at a more and more fine-grained formal characterization of proposals, and thereby at a more and more fine-grained characterization of meaning. We have argued that this is necessary for a better account of information exchange through conversation, in particular when the exchange involves conditional questions and assertions. Elsewhere, we argue that the framework developed here also offers new insights into the semantics of epistemic and deontic modals (Aher 2014).

---

[7] Sentence (22d) not only dismisses a supposition of the other three sentences, but it *suppositionally dismisses* them, given the way this notion was defined in footnote 4.

References

Aher, M.: Modals in Legal Discourse. Ph.D. thesis, University of Osnabrück (2013)

Aher, M., Groenendijk, J., Roelofsen, F.: Epistemic and deontic modals in suppositional inquisitive semantics (2014, in preparation)

Ciardelli, I.: Inquisitive semantics and intermediate logics. Master thesis, University of Amsterdam (2009)

Ciardelli, I., Roelofsen, F.: Inquisitive logic. J. Philos. Logic **40**(1), 55–94 (2011)

Ciardelli, I., Groenendijk, J., Roelofse, F.: Inquisitive semantics. NASSLLI lecture notes (2012). www.illc.uva.nl/inquisitivesemantics

Ciardelli, I., Groenendijk, J., Roelofsen, F.: Inquisitive semantics: a new notion of meaning. Lang. Linguist. Compass **7**(9), 459–476 (2013)

Égré, P., Politzer, G.: On the negation of indicative conditionals. In: Aloni, M., Franke, M., Roelofsen, F. (eds.) Proceedings of the Nineteenth Amsterdam Colloquium, pp.10–18 (2013)

O, E., Byrne, R.M.J.: It is not the case that if you understand a conditional you know how to negate it. J. Cogn. Psychol. **24**(3), 329–334 (2012). doi:10.1080/20445911.2011.639759

Fine, K.: Counterfactuals without possible worlds. J. Philos. **109**(3), 221–246 (2012)

Groenendijk, J., Roelofsen, F.: Inquisitive semantics and pragmatics. Presented at the Workshop on Language, Communication, and Rational Agency at Stanford (2009). www.illc.uva.nl/inquisitivesemantics

Groenendijk, J., Roelofsen, F.: Radical inquisitive semantics. Presented at the Sixth International Symposium on Logic, Cognition, and Communication (2010). www.illc.uva.nl/inquisitivesemantics

Groenendijk, J., Stokhof, M.: Studies on the Semantics of Questions and the Pragmatics of Answers. Ph.D. thesis, University of Amsterdam (1984)

Hamblin, C.L.: Questions in montague english. Found. Lang. **10**, 41–53 (1973)

Handley, S., Evans, J., Thompson, V.: The negated conditional: A litmus test for the suppositional conditional? J. Exp. Psychol. Learn. Mem. Cogn. **32**(3), 559–569 (2006). doi:10.1037/0278-7393.32.3.559

Hintikka, J., Sandu, G.: Game-theoretical semantics. In: Van Benthem, J., ter Meulen, A. (eds.) Handbook of Logic and Language, pp. 361–410. Elsevier, Amsterdam (1997)

Hodges, W.: Compositional semantics for a language of imperfect information. Logic J. IGPL **5**(4), 539–563 (1997)

Karttunen, L.: Syntax and semantics of questions. Linguist. Philos. **1**, 3–44 (1977)

Roelofsen, F.: Algebraic foundations for the semantic treatment of inquisitive content. Synthese **190**(1), 79–102 (2013). doi:10.1007/s11229-013-0282-4

Sano, K.: An impossibility theorem in radical inquisitive semantics. In: Workshop on Relating Particles to Evidence and Inference, Goettingen (2012)

Stalnaker, R.: Assertion. Syntax Semant. **9**, 315–332 (1978)

Väänänen, J.: Dependence Logic: A New Approach to Independence Friendly Logic. Cambridge University Press, Cambridge (2007)

van Fraassen, B.: Facts and tautological entailments. J. Philos. **66**(15), 477–487 (1969)

Veltman, F.: Logics for Conditionals. Ph.D. thesis, University of Amsterdam (1985)

Kripke Models Built from Models of Arithmetic

Paula Henk[✉]

Institute for Logic, Language and Computation (ILLC),
University of Amsterdam, Amsterdam, The Netherlands
P.Henk@uva.nl

Abstract. We introduce three relations between models of Peano Arithmetic (PA), each of which is characterized as an arithmetical accessibility relation. A relation R is said to be an *arithmetical accessibility relation* if for any model $\mathcal{M}$ of PA, $\mathcal{M} \vDash \mathsf{Pr}_\pi(\varphi)$ iff $\mathcal{M}' \vDash \varphi$ for all $\mathcal{M}'$ with $\mathcal{M} \; R \; \mathcal{M}'$, where $\mathsf{Pr}_\pi(x)$ is an intensionally correct provability predicate of PA. The existence of arithmetical accessibility relations yields a new perspective on the arithmetical completeness of GL. We show that any finite Kripke model for the provability logic GL is bisimilar to some "arithmetical" Kripke model whose domain consists of models of PA and whose accessibility relation is an arithmetical accessibility relation. This yields a new interpretation of the modal operators in the context of PA: an arithmetical assertion φ is consistent (possible, $\Diamond\varphi$) if it holds in some arithmetically accessible model, and provable (necessary, $\Box\varphi$) if it holds in all arithmetically accessible models.

Keywords: Arithmetic · Modal logic · Provability logic · Internal models

1 Introduction

The modal system GL bears a special relation to Peano Arithmetic[1](PA). Interpreting the modality $\Box$ as an (intensionally correct) provability predicate of PA, GL captures exactly what is provable in PA, in propositional terms, about provability in itself. The fascinating proof is due to Robert Solovay.

The goal of this article is to reveal a new aspect of the relation between GL and PA. We do this by constructing a big arithmetical Kripke model whose nodes are models of PA. The accessibility relation is chosen so as to guarantee that for any world $\mathcal{M}$, the (arithmetical) sentence φ is in the extension of the provability predicate (of PA) in $\mathcal{M}$ if and only if φ holds in all worlds accessible from $\mathcal{M}$. In other words, it does not matter whether we look at $\mathcal{M}$ as a model of PA, or as a world in the Kripke model (seeing the provability predicate as a modality). We show that any Kripke model for GL is bisimilar to some big arithmetical Kripke model of this kind.

---

[1] Here, PA can be replaced by any recursively enumerable Σ_1-sound theory containing Elementary Arithmetic (EA).

© Springer-Verlag Berlin Heidelberg 2015
M. Aher et al. (Eds.): TbiLLC 2013, LNCS 8984, pp. 157–174, 2015.
DOI: 10.1007/978-3-662-46906-4_10

In order to construct such an arithmetical Kripke frame, we need to find a suitable accessibility relation; we call such a relation an *arithmetical accessibility relation*. In order to appreciate the existence of arithmetical accessibility relations, we shall make a detour to set theory. In [4], Hamkins presents a (set–theoretic) forcing interpretation of modal logic. In this context, $\Diamond \varphi$ is interpreted as: "φ holds in some forcing extension", and $\Box \varphi$ as: "φ holds in all forcing extensions" (where φ is a statement in the language of set theory). Hamkins and Löwe [5] prove that if ZFC is consistent, then the principles of forcing provable in ZFC are exactly those derivable in the modal system S4.2.

Although Hamkins and Löwe say that they want to do for forceability what Solovay did for provability, the situation is not entirely symmetric. Forcing is a relation between models of set theory – a ground model has some access to the truths of its forcing extension –, and hence it is natural to view it as an accessibility relation in a Kripke model. The interpretation of the modal operators in set theory is thereby in tune with their usual modal logical meanings: $\Diamond \varphi$ means that φ holds in some successor (i.e. forcing extension), and $\Box \varphi$ that φ holds in all successors (forcing extensions). As a result, one can imagine the collection of all models of set theory, related by forcing, as an enormous Kripke model, where the valuation is given by first–order satisfiability.

Provability, on the other hand, is not a relation between models of PA. Also, whereas the usual interpretation of $\Box \varphi$ in modal logic involves universal quantification (over all accessible worlds), the interpretation of $\Box \varphi$ in PA is an *existential* sentence: there exists a proof of φ. Similarly, in the context of PA, the interpretation of $\Diamond \varphi$ switches from existential to universal: φ is consistent, i.e. all proofs are not proofs of $\neg \varphi$. It is therefore natural to ask whether there is a relation between models of PA that is the analogue of forcing in the context of ZFC.

We shall answer this question positively, by providing three examples of arithmetical accessibility relations. This allows one to view the collection of all models of PA, related by such an arithmetical accessibility relation, as a big Kripke model. We also get a new interpretation of the modal operators in the context of PA. The traditional meaning of $\Box \varphi$ – "there exists a proof of φ" – is equivalent to an interpretation of $\Box \varphi$ as: "φ holds in all arithmetically accessible models". Similarly, the traditional meaning of $\Diamond \varphi$ – "φ is consistent" – is equivalent to an interpretation of $\Diamond \varphi$ as: "φ holds in some arithmetically accessible model".

An important precursor of our work is [11], where several examples of arithmetical accessibility relations are given. While some basic ideas were already present there, our approach is slightly different. Furthermore, many details which were only sketched in [11] are subject to a more thorough treatment here.

The next section contains the preliminaries. Our examples of arithmetical accessibility relations are introduced in Sects. 3 and 4 establishes that any finite Kripke model for GL is bisimilar to some arithmetical Kripke model. The arithmetical completeness of GL is an easy consequence[2] of this. Finally, in Sect. 5 we

---

[2] Our proof of Solovay's Theorem is not "new"– the construction of the bisimulation makes crucial use of the most important ingredients of the original proof. Solovay's Theorem will thus remain among the important theorems in mathematical logic which have "essentially" only one proof (see [3]).

shall make some general observations concerning the structure of the arithmetical Kripke frames.

2 Preliminaries

This section sketches the basic notions and preliminaries. Section 2.1 deals with arithmetic, Sect. 2.2 with modal logic, in particular the system GL, and Sect. 2.3 introduces the notion of an internal model.

2.1 Arithmetic

We work in a first–order language with $\neg, \to$ and $\forall$ as primitive connectives; the connectives $\wedge, \vee, \leftrightarrow$ and $\exists$ are assumed to be defined in the usual way. We assume a Hilbert–style axiomatization of first–order logic, with modus ponens as the only rule of inference. Our official signature Σ of arithmetic is relational; it includes:

- a binary relation symbol E (equality)
- a unary relation symbol Z (being equal to zero)
- a binary relation symbol S ($\mathsf{S}xy$ being interpreted as: $x + 1 = y$)
- a ternary relation symbol A ($\mathsf{A}xyz$ being interpreted as: $x + y = z$)
- a ternary relation symbol M ($\mathsf{M}xyz$ being interpreted as: $x \times y = z$).

We also use Σ to refer to the language of arithmetic, i.e. the first–order language based on the signature of arithmetic. We shall use lower case Greek letters for the sentences and formulas of Σ.

The theory of Peano Arithmetic (PA) is a first–order theory in the language of arithmetic. It contains axioms stating that E is a congruence relation, the basic facts about the relations $\mathsf{Z}, \mathsf{S}, \mathsf{A}$ and M (for example that $\mathsf{Z}x$ implies $\neg \mathsf{S}yx$ for all y), as well as a functionality axiom – with respect to E – for each of the above relations. Finally, the axioms of PA include induction for all formulas in the language Σ of arithmetic.

All first–order models considered in this article are models of PA, or expansions of models of PA. From now on, the word "model" will refer to such a model. We use $\Sigma_{\mathcal{M}}$ to refer to the signature of $\mathcal{M}$. If $\Sigma_{\mathcal{M}} = \Sigma_{\mathcal{M}'}$, we write $\mathcal{M} \equiv \mathcal{M}'$ to mean that $\mathcal{M}$ and $\mathcal{M}'$ are elementarily equivalent, i.e. that for every sentence φ of $\Sigma_{\mathcal{M}}$, $\mathcal{M} \vDash \varphi \Leftrightarrow \mathcal{M}' \vDash \varphi$. We write $\mathcal{M} \cong \mathcal{M}'$ if $\mathcal{M}$ and $\mathcal{M}'$ are isomorphic. If φ is a formula whose free variables are among $x_0, \ldots, x_n$, and $m_0, \ldots, m_k$ is a sequence of elements of $\mathcal{M}$, with $n \leq k$, we write $\mathcal{M} \vDash \varphi[m_1, \ldots, m_k]$ to mean that $\mathcal{M}$ satisfies φ when x_j is interpreted as m_j.

In practice, we shall often speak of the formulas of Σ as containing terms built up from the constant symbol 0, a unary function symbol S, and binary function symbols $+$ and $\times$. Such formulas can be transformed into proper formulas of Σ by the well–known term–unwinding algorithm[3]. We define for each natural number n a term $\overline{n}$ of our unofficial language by letting $\overline{0} = 0$, and $\overline{n+1} = \mathsf{S}\overline{n}$. We shall often also write n instead of $\overline{n}$, and $x = y$ instead of $\mathsf{E}xy$.

---

[3] The details of the algorithm are worked out in [10].

We assume as given some standard coding of the syntactical objects of Σ. If φ is a formula, we write $\ulcorner\varphi\urcorner$ for the code of φ, and similarly for terms. We shall often identify a formula with its code, thus writing for example $\varphi(\psi)$ instead of $\varphi(\ulcorner\psi\urcorner)$.

We also assume as given intensionally correct[4] formulas of Σ that express relations between syntactical objects (of Σ and its expansions) and operations on them. We use self–explanatory notation for such formulas; for example, the formula form expresses the property of being (the code of) a formula, and the formula var the property of being (the code of) a variable. We write $\forall\varphi \in \mathsf{form}\, \alpha(\varphi)$ instead of $\forall x\,(\mathsf{form}(x) \to \alpha(x))$, and similarly for other syntactical objects such as variables or sentences.

Throughout this article, λ denotes a formula that expresses the property of being an axiom of first–order logic, and π denotes a formula that expresses the property of being an axiom of PA. Both λ and π can be taken to be Δ_1. Given λ and π, the proof predicate Prf_π of PA is constructed in the usual way, and is thus an intensionally correct representation of the relation

$$\{(n, p) \mid p \text{ codes a PA-proof of the formula with code } n\}. \tag{1}$$

The provability predicate Pr_π is obtained by letting: $\mathsf{Pr}_\pi(x) := \exists y\,\mathsf{Prf}_\pi(x, y)$. We shall often omit the subscript, writing simply Pr for Pr_π. We write $\mathsf{Con}(\varphi)$ for the sentence $\neg\mathsf{Pr}(\neg\varphi)$, and Con for $\mathsf{Con}(\top)$. The following hold:

1. $\vdash_{\mathsf{PA}} \varphi \Rightarrow \vdash_{\mathsf{PA}} \mathsf{Pr}(\varphi)$
2. $\vdash_{\mathsf{PA}} \forall\varphi, \psi \in \mathsf{form}\, (\mathsf{Pr}(\mathsf{impl}(\varphi, \psi)) \to (\mathsf{Pr}(\varphi) \to \mathsf{Pr}(\psi)))$
3. $\vdash_{\mathsf{PA}} \forall\varphi \in \mathsf{form}\, (\mathsf{Pr}(\varphi) \to \mathsf{Pr}(\mathsf{Pr}(\varphi)))$.

In 2, impl represents the function computing the code of $\varphi \to \psi$, given as input the codes of φ and ψ. Item 1, together with the versions of 2 and 3 where the universal quantifiers are only required to range over the codes of standard sentences, are referred to as the *Hilbert–Bernays–Löb derivability conditions*.

The following theorem (Theorem 4.6.v in [2]) states that inside PA, properties of theorems of PA can be proven by induction on the complexity of PA–proofs.

Theorem 1. *Let α be a formula of Σ. Then*

$$\vdash_{\mathsf{PA}} \forall\varphi \in \mathsf{form}\, [(\pi(\varphi) \to \alpha(\varphi)) \wedge (\lambda(\varphi) \to \alpha(\varphi))]$$
$$\wedge\, \forall\varphi, \psi \in \mathsf{form}\, [\alpha(\varphi) \wedge \alpha(\mathsf{impl}(\varphi, \psi)) \to \alpha(\psi)]$$
$$\to\, \forall\varphi \in \mathsf{form}\, (\mathsf{Pr}(\varphi) \to \alpha(\varphi)).$$

---

[4] By this, we mean that the definitions of these relations and operations in PA mimic the corresponding "informal" recursive definitions, and that the relevant recursion equations are provable in PA. In contrast, for a formula to be *extensionally* correct, it is only required to have the right extension in the standard model, or in other words to behave as intended with respect to the codes of standard sentences and terms. The concept of extensional correctness is found in the literature under various names, for example *binumerability* [2,7] or *representability* [1]. There exist formulas which are extensionally correct with respect to a property but fail to express this property in an intensionally correct way – see p. 68 of [2] for an example.

Remark 1. The proof uses the induction axiom for the formula α. When working in an expansion $\mathcal{M}$ of a model of PA, Theorem 1 can be applied with a formula α of the signature $\Sigma_\mathcal{M}$ given that induction holds in $\mathcal{M}$ for α.

2.2   Modal Logic

We denote by $\mathcal{L}_\Box$ the language of propositional modal logic. We use upper case Latin letters for the formulas of $\mathcal{L}_\Box$.

Definition 1 (Kripke Model). *A Kripke frame is a tuple $\langle W, R \rangle$ with $W \neq \emptyset$ and $R \subseteq W \times W$. A Kripke model is a triple $M = \langle W, R, \Vdash \rangle$, where $\langle W, R \rangle$ is a Kripke frame, and $\Vdash$ is a forcing relation on W satisfying the usual clauses for the connectives, and $w \Vdash \Box A$ if for all y with wRy, $y \Vdash A$.*

As usual, we use $\Diamond A$ as an abbreviation for $\neg\Box\neg A$. We write $\langle W, R \rangle \Vdash A$ in case for all models $\langle W, R, \Vdash \rangle$ and for all $w \in W$, $w \Vdash A$.

Definition 2 (Bismulation). *Let $M = \langle W, R, V \rangle$ and $M' = \langle W', R', V' \rangle$ be Kripke models. A binary relation $Z \subseteq W \times W'$ is a bisimulation between M and M' if the following conditions are satisfied:*

- *(at) If wZw', then w and w' satisfy the same propositional letters*
- *(back) If wZw' and wRv, then there exists v' in M' with $w'R'v'$ and vZv'*
- *(forth) If wZw' and $w'R'v'$, then there exists v in M with wRv and vZv'.*

When Z is a bisimulation between M and M', and wZw', we say that w and w' are bisimilar. The following theorem states that satisfiability of modal formulas is invariant under bisimulations.

Theorem 2. *Let M and M' be Kripke models, and let w, w' be nodes of M and M' respectively. If w is bisimilar to w', then for every modal formula A, we have that $M, w \Vdash A$ iff $M', w' \Vdash A$.*

We now introduce the modal system GL, named after Gödel and Löb, and also known as provability logic.

Definition 3 (Provability Logic GL). *The axioms of GL are all tautologies of propositional logic, and*

1. $\Box(A \to B) \to (\Box A \to \Box B)$
2. $\Box(\Box A \to A) \to \Box A$.

The rules of GL are modus ponens, and necessitation: $\vdash_{GL} A \Rightarrow \vdash_{GL} \Box A$.

In other words, GL is K plus Löb's axiom $\Box(\Box A \to A) \to \Box A$. GL is known to be sound and complete with respect to transitive irreflexive finite trees.

Theorem 3 (Modal Completeness of GL). *Let $\mathcal{K}$ be the class of frames that are transitive irreflexive finite trees. Then $\vdash_{GL} A \Leftrightarrow \forall F [F \in \mathcal{K} \Rightarrow F \Vdash A]$.*

The notion of an arithmetical realization below will be used to translate formulas of $\mathcal{L}_\square$ to sentences of the language of arithmetic.

Definition 4 (Arithmetical Realization). *A realization $*$ is a function from the propositional letters of $\mathcal{L}_\square$ to sentences of Σ. The domain of $*$ is extended to all $\mathcal{L}_\square$-formulas by requiring:*

1. $(\bot)^* = \bot$
2. $(A \to B)^* = A^* \to B^*$
3. $(\square A)^* := \mathsf{Pr}(\ulcorner A^* \urcorner)$.

Definition 5 (Provability Logic). *A modal formula A is a provability principle of* PA *if for all realizations $*$, $\vdash_{PA} A^*$. The provability logic of* PA, $\mathrm{PrL}(PA)$, *is the set of all provability principles of* PA, *or a logic that generates it.*

The following theorem states that GL is arithmetically sound and complete, i.e. it is the provability logic of PA.

Theorem 4. $\mathrm{PrL}(PA) = GL$.

Proof Sketch. For the direction $GL \subseteq \mathrm{PrL}(PA)$ (arithmetical soundness), one has to check that the axioms of GL are provable in PA under all realizations. This follows from the Hilbert–Bernays–Löb derivability conditions introduced in Sect. 2.1 (to see that Löb's Theorem is provable under all realizations, one also uses the Gödel–Carnap Fixed Point Lemma).

The proof of $\mathrm{PrL}(PA) \subseteq GL$ (arithmetical completeness) was proven by Robert Solovay in [9]. Given a modal formula A with $\nvdash_{GL} A$, we need a realization $*$ with $\nvdash_{PA} A^*$. The idea of Solovay's proof is to simulate in PA a Kripke model $M = \langle \{1, \dots, n\}, R, V \rangle$ for GL, with $M, 1 \nVdash A$ (M exists by Theorem 3). This is done by constructing sentences $\sigma_0, \dots, \sigma_n$ of the language of arithmetic such that, intuitively, σ_i corresponds to the node i of M (the sentence σ_0 is used as an auxilliary). We will refer to the sentences $\sigma_0 \dots, \sigma_n$ as the *Solovay sentences*. The arithmetical realization $*$ is defined as: $p^* := \bigvee_{i:M,i \Vdash p} \sigma_i$. The Kripke model M is then simulated in PA in the sense that for all $A \in \mathcal{L}_\square$,

$$M, i \Vdash A \quad \Rightarrow \quad \vdash_{PA} \sigma_i \to A^* \tag{2}$$

The proof of (2) uses the following properties of the Solovay sentences:

1. $\vdash_{PA} \sigma_i \to \neg\sigma_j$ if $i \neq j$
2. $\vdash_{PA} \sigma_i \to \mathsf{Con}(\sigma_j)$ if iRj, or if $i = 0$ and $j \neq 1$
3. $\vdash_{PA} \sigma_i \to \mathsf{Pr}(\bigvee_{j:iRj} \sigma_j)$ for $i \geq 1$.

Furthermore, we have that for all $0 \leq i \leq n$, the sentence σ_i is independent from PA. We shall use the above properties in Sect. 4 to prove that any finite GL–model is bisimilar to some arithmetical Kripke model, obtaining the arithmetical completeness of GL as a corollary.

2.3   Internal Models

Roughly speaking, a model $\mathcal{M}'$ is an *internal model* of a model $\mathcal{M}$ (or: internal to $\mathcal{M}$) if the domain of $\mathcal{M}'$ is definable in $\mathcal{M}$, and the interpretations of the atomic formulas of $\Sigma_{\mathcal{M}'}$ are given by formulas of $\Sigma_{\mathcal{M}}$.

Definition 6 (Relative Translation). *Let Θ be a signature. A relative translation from Σ to Θ is a tuple $j = \langle \delta, \tau \rangle$, where δ is a Θ–formula with one free variable, and τ a mapping from relation symbols R of Σ to formulas R^τ of Θ, where the number of free variables of R^τ is equal to the arity of R. We extend τ to a translation τ^* from all formulas of Σ to formulas of Θ by requiring:*

1. $(Rx_0 \ldots x_n)^{\tau^*} = R^\tau x_0 \ldots x_n$ for an $n+1$–ary relation symbol R
2. $(\varphi \to \psi)^{\tau^*} = \varphi^{\tau^*} \to \psi^{\tau^*}$
3. $\bot^{\tau^*} = \bot$
4. $(\forall x\, \varphi)^{\tau^*} = \forall x\, (\delta(x) \to \varphi^{\tau^*})$.

We will, par abus de langage, confuse τ and τ^* from now on. If j is a relative translation, we refer to the components of j by δ_j and τ_j. We only consider cases where the language of the internal model is the language of arithmetic; the above definition can of course also be formulated for the more general case.

Definition 7 (Internal Model). *Let $\mathcal{M}$ be a model, and let $j = \langle \delta, \tau \rangle$ be a relative translation from Σ to $\Sigma_{\mathcal{M}}$. We say that j defines an internal model of $\mathcal{M}$ if $\mathcal{M} \vDash \varphi^{\tau_j}$ for every axiom φ of PA. If a relative translation j defines an internal model of $\mathcal{M}$, we denote by $\mathcal{M}^j$ the following model:*

- *$\mathcal{M}^j := \{a \in \mathcal{M} \mid \mathcal{M} \vDash \delta_j(a)\} / \sim$, where $a \sim b :\Leftrightarrow \mathcal{M} \vDash \mathsf{E}^{\tau_j}[a,b]$*
- *If $\mathbf{a}, \mathbf{b} \in \mathcal{M}^j$, let $\mathcal{M}^j \vDash \mathsf{Sab} :\Leftrightarrow \mathcal{M} \vDash \mathsf{S}^{\tau_j}[a,b]$ for some $a \in \mathbf{a}$, $b \in \mathbf{b}$, and similarly for other atomic formulas.*

Note that if j defines an internal model of $\mathcal{M}$ then – by our choice of axioms of PA – we have that in $\mathcal{M}$, E^{τ_j} is a congruence relation, and the relations defined by the formulas Z^{τ_j}, S^{τ_j}, A^{τ_j}, and M^{τ_j} are functional relative to E^{τ_j}.

We say that $\mathcal{M}'$ is an internal model of $\mathcal{M}$, and write $\mathcal{M} \triangleright \mathcal{M}'$, if some relative translation j to $\Sigma_{\mathcal{M}}$ defines an internal model of $\mathcal{M}$, and $\mathcal{M}'$ is (modulo isomorphism) this internal model, i.e. $\mathcal{M}' \cong \mathcal{M}^j$. In this context, we shall often refer to $\mathcal{M}$ as the *external model*. The following theorem is a well–known basic fact about the internal model relation.

Theorem 5. *Let $\mathcal{M}$ be a model, and suppose that a relative translation j from Σ to $\Sigma_{\mathcal{M}}$ defines an internal model of $\mathcal{M}$. Then for any formula $\varphi(x_0, \ldots, x_n)$ of the language Σ of arithmetic,*

$$\mathcal{M}^j \vDash \varphi[\mathbf{a_0}, \ldots, \mathbf{a_n}] \Leftrightarrow \mathcal{M} \vDash \varphi^{\tau_j}[a_0, \ldots, a_n] \text{ for } a_0 \in \mathbf{a_0}, \ldots, a_n \in \mathbf{a_n}. \qquad (3)$$

In particular, $\mathcal{M}^j \vDash \varphi \Leftrightarrow \mathcal{M} \vDash \varphi^{\tau_j}$ for any sentence φ of Σ.

Proof. By induction on the complexity of $\varphi(x_0, \ldots, x_n)$.

Note that if j defines an internal model of $\mathcal{M}$ (as in Definition 7) then it follows by Theorem 5 that $\mathcal{M}^j \vDash \varphi$ for every axiom φ of PA. Hence $\mathcal{M} \triangleright \mathcal{M}'$ implies that $\mathcal{M}'$ is a model of PA.

3   t–Internal and t–Associated Models

We introduce three arithmetical accessibility relations between models of PA, all of which are based on the t–*internal model relation*. Roughly speaking, an internal model $\mathcal{M}'$ of $\mathcal{M}$ is a t–*internal* to $\mathcal{M}$ if $\mathcal{M}$ has a truth–predicate for sentences of $\Sigma_{\mathcal{M}'}$, and furthermore the axioms of PA (including the nonstandard ones) are in the extension of the truth predicate. We shall generalize this relation by allowing the truth predicate to be definable in $\mathcal{M}$ with parameters, or definable in a certain expansion of $\mathcal{M}$.

3.1   Definitions

Before defining the t–internal model relation, it is useful to mention a technicality. Suppose that j defines an internal model of $\mathcal{M}$. As suggested above, we want to require that $\mathcal{M}$ has a truth predicate tr for the internal model $\mathcal{M}^j$. Thus for any sentence φ of the language of $\mathcal{M}^j$,

$$\mathcal{M} \vDash \varphi^{\tau_j} \leftrightarrow \mathsf{tr}(\varphi). \tag{4}$$

But we shall require something even stronger, namely we want the truth predicate to be well-behaved with respect to the boolean connectives and the quantifiers, so that (4) can be proved by an induction on the complexity of φ. For instance, to express that tr behaves as expected with respect to the atomic formulas, we would like to say (in $\mathcal{M}$), that whenever $m \in \mathcal{M}^j$, then $\mathsf{Z}^\tau[m]$ if and only if the code of $\mathsf{Z}m$ is in the extension of tr. However, a truth predicate should apply to codes of *sentences*. Hence when inside the truth predicate, we want to associate to m (the code of) some constant naming it.

A simple way to achieve this is to stipulate that m is the code of its own name, and in general that elements of $\mathcal{M}^j$ are codes of their own names. This means that inside $\mathcal{M}$ we are working with the language $\Sigma \cup \{c_m \mid m \in \mathcal{M}^j\}$, where for all $m \in \mathcal{M}^j$, $\ulcorner c_m \urcorner = m$. To avoid ambiguities that this could potentially lead to[5], we additionally assume the domain of $\mathcal{M}^j$ (as given by δ_j) to be disjoint from the set of codes of terms of Σ (in $\mathcal{M}$). This can always be arranged without high costs in complexity, for example by making the range of the domain function to consist of even numbers, and the range of the coding function to be a subset of the odd numbers. The fact that this setup excludes the possibility of $\mathcal{M}$ and $\mathcal{M}^j$ sharing the same domain need not concern us here — we think of models modulo isomorphism, and thus the internal model relation is still allowed to be, for example, reflexive.

---

[5] To see how such ambiguities can arise, suppose (in $\mathcal{M}$) that 17 is in the extension of δ_j, but also that 17 is the code of the constant 0. Suppose also that we use sequences to code syntactical objects; for example the code of the sentence $\mathsf{Z}c$ (where c is a constant) is the number $\langle \ulcorner \mathsf{Z} \urcorner, \ulcorner c \urcorner \rangle$ (where $\langle m, n \rangle$ is the code of the pair (m, n)). The number $\langle \mathsf{Z}, 17 \rangle$ can then either be parsed as coding the sentence $\mathsf{Z}0$ of the language Σ, or the sentence $\mathsf{Z}c_{17}$ of the language $\Sigma \cup \{c_m \mid m \in \mathcal{M}^j\}$.

We refer to the language $\Sigma \cup \{c_m \mid m \in \mathcal{M}^j\}$ as Σ_{δ_j}. The formulas representing syntactical objects of this language in $\mathcal{M}$ are distinguished by the subscript δ_j. Thus the formula sent_{δ_j} expresses the property of being a sentence of the language $\Sigma \cup \{c_m \mid m \in \mathcal{M}^j\}$.

We introduce some notation to make our definition of the t–internal model relation more readable. Let $\mathsf{sbst}_1(x, y)$ be a formula of Σ that is an intensionally correct representation of the primitive recursive function Sbst_1 with:

$$
\mathrm{Sbst}_1(m, n) = \begin{cases} \ulcorner [t/v_0]\varphi \urcorner & \text{if } n = \ulcorner \varphi \urcorner,\, m = \ulcorner t \urcorner,\, \text{and } t \text{ is free for } v_0 \text{ in } \varphi \\ 0 & \text{otherwise} \end{cases}
$$

In particular, we have for any formula φ and for any term t,

$$
\vdash_{\mathsf{PA}} \mathsf{sbst}_1(\ulcorner t \urcorner, \ulcorner \varphi \urcorner) = \overline{\mathrm{Sbst}_1(\ulcorner t \urcorner, \ulcorner \varphi \urcorner)}. \tag{5}
$$

Let $\mathcal{M}$ be a model, and let $j = \langle \delta, \tau \rangle$ be a relative translation to $\Sigma_{\mathcal{M}}$. Fix in $\mathcal{M}$ (the code of) a (possibly nonstandard) formula φ of the language Σ_δ, with at most v_0 free. We shall use

$$
\mathsf{tr}(\varphi(x)) \tag{6}
$$

as shorthand for $\mathsf{tr}\,(\mathsf{sbst}_1(x, \varphi))$. For example, taking Zv_0 as φ, $\mathsf{tr}(Zx)$ stands for $\mathsf{tr}(\mathsf{sbst}_1(x, Zv_0))$. Note that if x is in the extension of δ, it is the code of the constant c_x, and hence $\mathsf{sbst}_1(x, \ulcorner Zv_0 \urcorner)$ is the code of the Σ_δ–sentence Zc_x. Thus in this case $\mathsf{tr}(Zx)$ is $\mathsf{tr}(Zc_x)$.

More generally, if φ is a formula all of whose free variables are among $v_0, \ldots, v_n$, we write $\mathsf{tr}(\varphi(x_0, \ldots, x_n))$ as shorthand for

$$
\mathsf{tr}\,(\mathsf{sbst}_n(x_0, \ldots, x_n, \varphi)), \tag{7}
$$

where sbst_n is an intensionally correct representation of the function corresponding to the simultaneous substitution of n terms in a formula. We write $\mathsf{form}_\delta(v_0)$ for the set of formulas of Σ_δ with at most v_0 free.

Definition 8 (t–Internal Model). *Let $\mathcal{M}$ be a model, and $j = \langle \delta, \tau \rangle$ a relative translation from Σ to $\Sigma_{\mathcal{M}}$. We say that j defines a t–internal model of $\mathcal{M}$ if there is a formula tr of the signature $\Sigma_{\mathcal{M}}$ with one free variable, such that the following sentences are satisfied in $\mathcal{M}$:*

1. $\forall x, y\, (\delta(x) \wedge \delta(y) \to ((Sxy)^\tau \leftrightarrow \mathsf{tr}(Sxy)))$, *similarly for other atomic formulas*
2. $\forall \varphi \in \mathsf{sent}_\delta, \forall \psi \in \mathsf{sent}_\delta\, (\mathsf{tr}(\varphi \to \psi) \leftrightarrow (\mathsf{tr}(\varphi) \to \mathsf{tr}(\psi)))$
3. $\forall \varphi \in \mathsf{sent}_\delta\, (\mathsf{tr}(\neg \varphi) \leftrightarrow \neg \mathsf{tr}(\varphi))$
4. $\forall \varphi \in \mathsf{form}_\delta(v_0), \forall u \in \mathsf{var}\, \{\mathsf{tr}\,([u/v_0]\forall u\, \varphi) \leftrightarrow \forall x\, (\delta(x) \to \mathsf{tr}(\varphi(x)))\}$
5. $\forall \varphi \in \mathsf{sent}\, (\pi(\varphi) \to \mathsf{tr}(\varphi))$.

We refer to the formula tr as the *truth predicate* (for the internal model), and write tr_j for the truth predicate that comes with a relative translation j as in Definition 8. The next theorem states that tr_j is indeed a well–behaved truth predicate – modulo the translation τ_j – for the language of the internal model.

Theorem 6. *Suppose that j defines a* t*–internal model of $\mathcal{M}$, and let φ be a formula of Σ whose free variables are among $v_0, \ldots, v_n$. Then the following sentence*[6] *is satisfied in $\mathcal{M}$:*

$$\delta_j(x_0) \wedge \ldots \wedge \delta_j(x_n) \to (\varphi^{\tau_j}(x_0, \ldots, x_n) \leftrightarrow \mathsf{tr}_j(\varphi(x_0, \ldots, x_n))). \qquad (8)$$

In particular, $\mathcal{M} \vDash \varphi^{\tau_j} \leftrightarrow \mathsf{tr}_j(\varphi)$ for any sentence φ of Σ.

Proof. For readability, we shall drop the subscript j from δ, τ, and tr. The proof is by (external) induction on the complexity of φ. The base cases hold by Definition 8. The inductive cases for $\to$ and $\neg$ follow easily by using that tr and τ commute with the propositional connectives. We treat the universal case, assuming $n = 0$ for simplicity. Let φ be the formula $\forall y\, \psi(v_0, y)$. Argue in $\mathcal{M}$:

$$\delta(x) \wedge \delta(y) \to \{\psi^\tau(x, y) \leftrightarrow \mathsf{tr}(\psi(x, y))\}$$
$$\to \delta(x) \to \{\forall y\, (\delta(y) \to \psi^\tau(x, y)) \leftrightarrow \forall y\, (\delta(y) \to \mathsf{tr}(\psi(x, y)))\}$$
$$\leftrightarrow \delta(x) \to \{(\forall y\, \psi(x, y))^\tau \leftrightarrow \mathsf{tr}(\forall y\, \psi(x, y))\},$$

where the first line is the induction assumption, the second follows by logic, and the third line follows by the properties of τ and tr.

Suppose that j defines a t–internal model of $\mathcal{M}$. Using Theorems 5 and 6 of Definition 8, it is easy to see that $\mathcal{M} \vDash \varphi^{\tau_j}$ for every axiom φ of PA. Hence, in particular j defines an internal model of $\mathcal{M}$. We say that $\mathcal{M}'$ is a t–internal model of $\mathcal{M}$, and write $\mathcal{M} \rhd_t \mathcal{M}'$, if some relative translation j defines a t–internal model of $\mathcal{M}$, and $\mathcal{M}' \cong \mathcal{M}^j$ (where $\mathcal{M}^j$ is as in Definition 7).

Allowing the truth predicate to contain parameters from the external model yields the notion of a t–internal model with parameters.

Definition 9 (t –Internal Model with Parameters). *Let $\mathcal{M}$ be a model, and $j = \langle \delta, \tau \rangle$ a relative translation to $\Sigma_{\mathcal{M}}$. We say that j defines a t–internal model of $\mathcal{M}$ with parameters if there is a formula tr of the signature $\Sigma_{\mathcal{M}}$ with two free variables, and some*[7] *$m \in \mathcal{M}$ such that 1–5 of Definition 8 are satisfied in $\mathcal{M}$, if the remaining free variable in tr is interpreted as*[8] *m.*

It is clear that an analogue of Theorem 6 holds for the case where j defines a t–internal model of $\mathcal{M}$ with parameters. Hence if j defines a t–internal model of $\mathcal{M}$ with parameters, it also defines an internal model of $\mathcal{M}$ (note that if φ is an axiom of PA, then φ and also φ^{τ_j} are sentences, whence $\mathcal{M} \vDash \varphi^{\tau_j}[m]$ iff $\mathcal{M} \vDash \varphi^{\tau_j}$). We say that $\mathcal{M}'$ is a t–internal model of $\mathcal{M}$ with parameters, and write $\mathcal{M} \rhd_{\mathsf{tpar}} \mathcal{M}'$, if some relative translation j defines a t–internal model of $\mathcal{M}$ with parameters, and $\mathcal{M}' \cong \mathcal{M}^j$.

---

[6] The free variables are assumed to be bound by universal quantifiers.

[7] Due to the availability of coding, allowing one parameter is as strong as allowing an arbitrary finite number of parameters.

[8] For example, for 5 we require that $\mathcal{M} \vDash \forall \varphi \in \mathsf{sent}\, (\pi(\varphi) \to \mathsf{tr}(\varphi, y))[m]$.

The definition of our final example of an arithmetical accessibility relation uses the notion of an inductive expansion. A model $\mathcal{M}^+$ is said to be an *inductive expansion* of a model $\mathcal{M}$ in case $\mathcal{M}^+$ is an expansion of $\mathcal{M}$ (i.e. $\mathcal{M}$ and $\mathcal{M}^+$ have the same domain, $\Sigma_\mathcal{M} \subseteq \Sigma_{\mathcal{M}^+}$, and the interpretation of $\Sigma_\mathcal{M}$ is the same in $\mathcal{M}$ and in $\mathcal{M}^+$), and furthermore $\mathcal{M}^+$ satisfies the induction axioms in the language $\Sigma_{\mathcal{M}^+}$. Allowing the truth predicate to be definable in some inductive expansion of the external model yields the notion of a t–associated model.

Definition 10 (t–Associated Model). *Let $\mathcal{M}$ be a model, and $j = \langle \delta, \tau \rangle$ a relative translation from Σ to $\Sigma_\mathcal{M}$. We say that j defines a t –associated model of $\mathcal{M}$ if there is some inductive expansion $\mathcal{M}^+$ of $\mathcal{M}$, and some formula tr of $\Sigma_{\mathcal{M}^+}$ with one free variable such that 1–5 of Definition 8 hold in $\mathcal{M}^+$.*

Note that if j defines a t–associated model of $\mathcal{M}$ and $\mathcal{M}^+$ is an inductive expansion of $\mathcal{M}$ as in Definition 10, then j defines a t–internal model of $\mathcal{M}^+$. Hence by Theorem 6, $\mathcal{M}^+ \vDash \varphi^{\tau_j} \leftrightarrow \mathrm{tr}_j(\varphi)$ for any sentence φ of Σ. Furthermore since for all φ, φ^{τ_j} is a sentence of $\Sigma_\mathcal{M}$, we have that $\mathcal{M}^+ \vDash \varphi^{\tau_j}$ iff $\mathcal{M} \vDash \varphi^{\tau_j}$. Hence by 5 of Definition 8, $\mathcal{M} \vDash \varphi^{\tau_j}$ for every axiom φ of PA, and thus in particular j defines an internal model of $\mathcal{M}$. We say that $\mathcal{M}'$ is a t–associated model of $\mathcal{M}$, and write $\mathcal{M} \blacktriangleright_t \mathcal{M}'$, if some relative translation j defines a t–associated model of $\mathcal{M}$, and $\mathcal{M}' \cong \mathcal{M}^j$.

Remark 2. If $\mathcal{M}'$ is a t–associated model of $\mathcal{M}$, then the interpretations of the atomic formulas of $\Sigma_{\mathcal{M}'}$ are given by formulas of $\Sigma_\mathcal{M}$, and some inductive expansion $\mathcal{M}^+$ of $\mathcal{M}$ has a truth predicate for $\mathcal{M}'$. For the purposes of this article (in particular for proving Theorem 7 below), we could also have chosen a more general definition, where the interpretations of the atomic formulas of $\Sigma_{\mathcal{M}'}$ are only required to be given by formulas of $\mathcal{M}^+$. Equivalently, we could postulate that the interpretations of the atomic formulas are only defined by the truth predicate in the first place. For example, Z^τ would be the formula $\mathrm{tr}(\mathsf{sbst}_1(x, \mathsf{Zv_0}))$.

As an overview of the relations between models introduced so far, we note that the following implications are easily seen to hold:

$$\mathcal{M} \rhd_t \mathcal{M}' \Rightarrow \mathcal{M} \rhd_{\mathsf{tpar}} \mathcal{M}' \Rightarrow \mathcal{M} \blacktriangleright_t \mathcal{M}' \Rightarrow \mathcal{M} \rhd \mathcal{M}' \qquad (9)$$

We will see in Sect. 5 that the reverse implications fail. As we go from right to left above, the external model is required to have more and more strength in comparison to the internal one.

3.2   Arithmetical Accessibility Relations

In this section, we use the term "worlds" to refer to models of PA whose signature is the signature Σ of arithmetic. A relation R between worlds is said to be an *arithmetical accessibility relation* if for any sentence φ of the language of arithmetic, and for any world $\mathcal{M}$, $\mathcal{M} \vDash \mathrm{Pr}_\pi(\varphi)$ iff $\mathcal{M}' \vDash \varphi$ for all worlds $\mathcal{M}'$ with $\mathcal{M} \, R \, \mathcal{M}'$. We will show that each of the relations $\rhd_t$, $\rhd_{\mathsf{tpar}}$ and $\blacktriangleright_t$ between worlds is an arithmetical accessibility relation.

Theorem 7. *Let $\mathcal{M}$ be a world, and $R \in \{\rhd_t, \rhd_{\mathsf{tpar}}, \blacktriangleright_t\}$. For any sentence φ of the language of arithmetic,*

$$\mathcal{M} \vDash \mathsf{Pr}(\varphi) \Leftrightarrow \text{ for all worlds } \mathcal{M}' \text{ with } \mathcal{M} \, R \, \mathcal{M}', \ \mathcal{M}' \vDash \varphi. \tag{10}$$

Proof. Fix a sentence φ of the language of arithmetic. We give here the general structure of the proof; the essential ingredients are provided by Theorems 8 and 9 below.

For the direction from left to right, suppose that $\mathcal{M} \vDash \mathsf{Pr}(\varphi)$, and let $\mathcal{M}'$ be such that $\mathcal{M} \, R \, \mathcal{M}'$. Since both $\mathcal{M} \rhd_t \mathcal{M}'$ and $\mathcal{M} \rhd_{\mathsf{tpar}} \mathcal{M}'$ imply $\mathcal{M} \blacktriangleright_t \mathcal{M}'$, it suffices to prove the claim for $\blacktriangleright_t$, i.e. it suffices to show that if $\mathcal{M} \blacktriangleright_t \mathcal{M}'$, then $\mathcal{M}' \vDash \varphi$. So suppose that $\mathcal{M} \blacktriangleright_t \mathcal{M}'$, let j be a relative translation that defines a t–associated model of $\mathcal{M}$ with $\mathcal{M}^j \cong \mathcal{M}'$, and let $\mathcal{M}^+$ be an inductive expansion of $\mathcal{M}$ with the truth predicate. Since $\mathcal{M} \vDash \mathsf{Pr}(\varphi)$ by assumption, also $\mathcal{M}^+ \vDash \mathsf{Pr}(\varphi)$, and hence by Theorem 8 below, $\mathcal{M}^+ \vDash \mathsf{tr}_j(\varphi)$. By Theorem 6 this implies $\mathcal{M}^+ \vDash \varphi^{\tau_j}$, and thus also $\mathcal{M} \vDash \varphi^{\tau_j}$. By Theorem 5 it follows that $\mathcal{M}^j \vDash \varphi$, and thus also $\mathcal{M}' \vDash \varphi$.

For the other direction, assume that $\mathcal{M} \vDash \neg\mathsf{Pr}(\varphi)$. Since $\mathcal{M} \rhd_t \mathcal{M}'$ implies both $\mathcal{M} \rhd_{\mathsf{tpar}} \mathcal{M}'$ and $\mathcal{M} \blacktriangleright_t \mathcal{M}'$, it now suffices to show the claim for $\rhd_t$, i.e. that there is some $\mathcal{M}'$ with $\mathcal{M} \rhd_t \mathcal{M}'$ and $\mathcal{M}' \vDash \neg\varphi$. Theorem 9 below provides a model $\mathcal{M}'$ with the required properties.

It is part of the definition of a t–associated model that some inductive expansion of the external model "knows" that all axioms of PA are true in the internal model. According to the following theorem, it is even the case that any such inductive expansion "knows" every *theorem* of PA to be true in the internal model. The reason for this is that the inductive expansion has sufficient amount of induction available for proving, by an internal induction on the complexity of a PA–proof, that the property of being true extends from axioms to theorems.

Theorem 8. *Suppose that j defines a t–associated model of $\mathcal{M}$, and let $\mathcal{M}^+$ be an inductive expansion of $\mathcal{M}$ with the truth predicate tr_j. Then*

$$\mathcal{M}^+ \vDash \forall\varphi \in \mathsf{sent}\,(\mathsf{Pr}_\pi(\varphi) \to \mathsf{tr}_j(\varphi)). \tag{11}$$

Proof Sketch. As usual in such cases, we need to prove the following stronger claim concerning formulas:

$$\mathcal{M}^+ \vDash \forall\varphi \in \mathsf{form}\,(\mathsf{Pr}_\pi(\varphi) \to \forall\mathsf{a} \in \mathsf{as}_{\delta_j}\,\mathsf{tr}_j(\varphi[\mathsf{a}])). \tag{12}$$

where a is an assignment from the variables of Σ to elements in the extension of δ_j, and $\varphi[\mathsf{a}]$ denotes the *sentence*[9] of the language Σ_{δ_j} obtained by simultaneously substituting the constant $c_{\mathsf{a}(v_i)}$ for v_i.

For readability, we shall drop the subscript j from δ and tr. Since induction holds in $\mathcal{M}^+$ by assumption, we can use Theorem 1 to prove the statement, taking as $\alpha(\varphi)$ the formula $\forall\mathsf{a} \in \mathsf{as}_{\delta_j}\,\mathsf{tr}_j(\varphi[\mathsf{a}])$. Thus it suffices to show that the following sentences are satisfied in $\mathcal{M}^+$:

---

[9] Remember that elements of the internal model are assumed to function simultaneously as codes of their own names.

1. $\forall \varphi, \psi \in$ form $\{\forall a \in as_\delta \, tr((\varphi \to \psi)[a]) \land \forall a \in as_\delta \, tr(\varphi[a]) \to \forall a \in as_\delta \, tr(\psi[a])\}$
2. $\forall \varphi \in$ form$(\pi(\varphi) \to \forall a \in as_\delta \, tr(\varphi[a]))$
3. $\forall \varphi \in$ form$(\lambda(\varphi) \to \forall a \in as_\delta \, tr(\varphi[a]))$.

Modulo some facts[10] concerning the assignments in as_δ that we assume to hold in $\mathcal{M}^+$, 1 and 2 are consequences of 2 and 5 of Definition 8 respectively. For 3, we have to show (in $\mathcal{M}^+$) that whenever a formula φ is an axiom of first–order logic, then φ is true under every assignment in as_δ. We show this by an internal subsidiary induction on the structure of φ, using the fact that tr commutes with the propositional connectives and the quantifiers (together with the above mentioned facts concerning the assignments in as_δ). Note that here again we essentially use the fact that $\mathcal{M}^+$ is an *inductive* expansion of $\mathcal{M}$.

Theorem 9 (Arithmetized Completeness). *Let $\mathcal{M} \vDash$ PA, and $\mathcal{M} \vDash$ Con(φ). Then there exists some $\mathcal{M}'$ with $\mathcal{M} \rhd_t \mathcal{M}'$ and $\mathcal{M}' \vDash \varphi$.*

Proof Sketch. It is a well–known fact that if $\mathcal{M} \vDash$ Con(φ), then $\mathcal{M}$ has an internal model where φ is true. The proof is by formalizing the Completeness Theorem for first–order logic[11] in PA. By examining the proof, one can see that the internal model constructed in this process is actually a t–internal model. The (definable) formula representing the Henkin set in $\mathcal{M}$ can be seen as a truth predicate, and furthermore it defines a model of PA $+ \varphi$ in $\mathcal{M}$ as required in Definition 8.

4   A New Perspective on Solovay's Theorem

Arithmetical accessibility relations can be used to construct big arithmetical Kripke frames whose nodes are models of PA with signature Σ. We shall show that any GL–model is bisimilar to a Kripke model based on such a Kripke frame, obtaining the arithmetical completeness of GL as a corollary.

Definition 11 (Arithmetical Kripke Frame). *An arithmetical Kripke frame is a structure $\mathcal{F}_{big} = \langle W_{big}, R_{big} \rangle$, where W_{big} is the collection of worlds modulo isomorphism, and $R_{big} \in \{\rhd_t, \rhd_{tpar}, \blacktriangleright_t\}$.*

Remark 3. An alternative but completely legitimate option is to work with arithmetical Kripke frames whose nodes are complete theories (in the language of PA) extending PA. The definitions in the previous section can be adjusted so as to define a relation between complete theories, and also the arguments leading to Theorem 7 would work analogously as in the case of models. We have chosen the model–theoretic approach since this yields a more natural definition of our triplet of arithmetical accessibility relations, in particular of the relation $\blacktriangleright_{tpar}$ where the truth predicate is allowed to contain parameters from the external model. Another option would be to take as W_{big} the collection of all models

---

[10] For example, it should hold in $\mathcal{M}^+$ that if φ is a *sentence* of the language Σ_δ, then tr(φ) if and only if $\forall a \in as_\delta \, tr(\varphi[a])$.

[11] This was first noted in [12], and more carefully articulated in [2].

of PA modulo *elementary equivalence*. In fact, the two alternative options are equivalent in the sense that the resulting arithmetical Kripke frames are isomorphic — to every complete theory corresponds a class of elementary equivalent models and vice versa.

Although $\mathcal{F}_{\text{big}}$ is a Kripke frame, it is not a GL–frame. As we will see in Sect. 5 below, R_{big} fails to be conversely well-founded in all of the three cases (taking $\mathcal{F}_{\text{big}}$ with $\blacktriangleright_{\text{t}}$, $\mathcal{F}_{\text{big}}$ even contains a reflexive point).

Given an arithmetical realization $*$, the forcing relation $\Vdash^*$ on $\mathcal{F}_{\text{big}}$ is defined as follows:

$$\mathcal{M} \Vdash^* p :\Leftrightarrow \mathcal{M} \vDash p^*, \tag{13}$$

i.e. the propositional letter $p \in \mathcal{L}_\square$ is forced at node $\mathcal{M}$ if and only if the arithmetical sentence p^* is satisfied in $\mathcal{M}$ (seen as a first–order model of PA). Let $\mathfrak{M}^*_{\text{big}}$ denote the resulting Kripke model. As an immediate consequence of Theorem 7, we have for every sentence $A \in \mathcal{L}_\square$ and for every $\mathcal{M} \in W_{\text{big}}$,

$$\mathfrak{M}^*_{\text{big}}, \mathcal{M} \Vdash^* A \Leftrightarrow \mathcal{M} \vDash A^*. \tag{14}$$

This means that the forcing of modal formulas is independent, modulo the realization $*$, of whether $\mathcal{M}$ is seen as a node in the Kripke model $\mathfrak{M}^*_{\text{big}}$, or as a first–order model of PA.

Let $M = \langle \{1, \ldots, n\}, R, \Vdash \rangle$ be a Kripke model for GL, and let $*$ be the Solovay realization corresponding to M, i.e. $p^* := \bigvee_{i:M,i\Vdash p} \sigma_i$, where $\sigma_0, \ldots, \sigma_n$ are the Solovay sentences. Remember from Sect. 2.2 that the Solovay sentences are constructed in such a way that the following hold:

1. $\vdash_{\text{PA}} \sigma_i \to \neg\sigma_j$ if $i \neq j$
2. $\vdash_{\text{PA}} \sigma_i \to \text{Con}(\sigma_j)$ if iRj, or if $i = 0$ and $j = 1$
3. $\vdash_{\text{PA}} \sigma_i \to \text{Pr}(\bigvee_{j:iRj} \sigma_j)$ for $i \geq 1$
4. $\nvdash_{\text{PA}} \sigma_i$ and $\nvdash_{\text{PA}} \neg\sigma_i$ for all i.

The following theorem states that $\mathfrak{M}^*_{\text{big}}$ is bisimilar to M.

Theorem 10. *Fix a* GL*-model* $M = \langle \{1, \ldots, n\}, R, \Vdash \rangle$*. Let* $\sigma_0, \cdots, \sigma_n$ *be the corresponding Solovay sentences, and* $p^* := \bigvee_{i:M,i\Vdash p} \sigma_i$*, for any propositional letter* p *of* $\mathcal{L}_\square$*. The relation* $Z : W \times W_{\text{big}}$ *defined as:* $(i, \mathcal{M}) \in Z :\Leftrightarrow \mathcal{M} \vDash \sigma_i$ *for* $i \geq 1$ *is a bisimulation between* M *and* $\mathfrak{M}^*_{\text{big}}$*. Furthermore, for every node* i *of* M *there is some node* $\mathcal{M}$ *of* $\mathfrak{M}^*_{\text{big}}$ *such that* $(i, \mathcal{M}) \in Z$*.*

Proof. Since for all i, σ_i is independent from PA, we have for all σ_i some model $\mathcal{M}$ with $\mathcal{M} \vDash \sigma_i$, and thus for all i there is some $\mathcal{M}$ such that $(i, \mathcal{M}) \in Z$. Note also that any model where σ_0 is true is not in the range of Z. We will now verify that Z is a bisimulation.

To see that if $(i, \mathcal{M}) \in Z$ then i and $\mathcal{M}$ satisfy the same propositional letters suppose first that $M, i \Vdash p$. Then by definition of $*$, we have σ_i as a disjunct of p^*. By definition of Z, we have that $\mathcal{M} \vDash \sigma_i$, hence $\mathcal{M} \vDash p^*$, and thus by definition of $\Vdash^*$ it is the case that $\mathfrak{M}_{\text{big}}, \mathcal{M} \Vdash^* p$. If on the other hand $M, i \nVdash p$, then $p^* = \sigma_{j_1} \vee \cdots \vee \sigma_{j_m}$, where $i \neq j_k$ for all k. By property 1 of the Solovay sentences, we find that $\vdash_{\mathsf{PA}} \sigma_i \to \neg \sigma_{j_k}$ for all k, whence $\vdash_{\mathsf{PA}} \sigma_i \to \neg p^*$ and thus $\mathcal{M} \vDash \neg p^*$. By definition of $\Vdash^*$, we have that $\mathfrak{M}_{\mathsf{big}}, \mathcal{M} \nVdash^* p$.

To verify the *back*-condition of the bisimulation, suppose that $(i, \mathcal{M}) \in Z$ and iRj. By the assumption that $(i, \mathcal{M}) \in Z$, we have that $\mathcal{M} \vDash \sigma_i$. By property 2 of the Solovay sentences and the assumption that iRj, we have $\vdash_{\mathsf{PA}} \sigma_i \to \mathsf{Con}(\sigma_j)$, and thus $\mathcal{M} \vDash \mathsf{Con}(\sigma_j)$. By Theorem 7 there is some $\mathcal{M}'$ with $\mathcal{M} \, R_{\mathsf{big}} \, \mathcal{M}'$ and $\mathcal{M}' \vDash \sigma_j$. By definition of Z, this means that $(j, \mathcal{M}') \in Z$.

Finally, to verify the *forth*–condition suppose that $(i, \mathcal{M}) \in Z$ and let $\mathcal{M}'$ be such that $\mathcal{M} \, R_{\mathsf{big}} \, \mathcal{M}'$. Since $(i, \mathcal{M}) \in Z$, we have that $\mathcal{M} \vDash \sigma_i$. By property 3 of the Solovay sentences, $\vdash_{\mathsf{PA}} \sigma_i \to \mathsf{Pr}(\bigvee_{j:iRj} \sigma_j)$, and so $\mathcal{M} \vDash \mathsf{Pr}(\bigvee_{j:iRj} \sigma_j)$. By Theorem 7, this implies $\mathcal{M}' \vDash \bigvee_{j:iRj} \sigma_j$, i.e. there is some j with iRj and $\mathcal{M}' \vDash \sigma_j$, i.e. with $(j, \mathcal{M}') \in Z$ as required.

Corollary 1 (Arithmetical Completeness of GL). $\mathrm{PrL}(\mathsf{PA}) \subseteq \mathsf{GL}$

Proof. If $\mathsf{GL} \nvdash A$ for some $A \in \mathcal{L}_\square$, then by modal completeness of GL there is a GL–model M with $M = \langle \{1, \ldots, n\}, R, \Vdash \rangle$, and $M, 1 \nVdash A$. Let $*$ be the Solovay realization corresponding to M, and let Z be the bisimulation from Theorem 10. Let $\mathcal{M} \in W_{\mathsf{big}}$ be such that $(1, \mathcal{M}) \in Z$, i.e. $\mathcal{M} \vDash \sigma_1$. Since Z is a bisimulation, we have $\mathfrak{M}^*_{\mathsf{big}}, \mathcal{M} \nVdash^* A$ by Theorem 2. By (14), this implies $\mathcal{M} \nvDash A^*$. Since $\mathcal{M}$ is a model of PA, this means that $\nvdash_{\mathsf{PA}} A^*$ as required.

5 Properties of Arithmetical Kripke Frames

This section contains some observations concerning the structure of the big arithmetical Kripke frames. We also provide separating examples for the different relations between models of PA introduced in this paper.

First, it is not difficult to see that the relations $\rhd_t$ and $\rhd_{\mathsf{tpar}}$ are transitive. Since the definition of a t–associated model postulates a truth predicate in some inductive *expansion*, the transitivity of $\blacktriangleright_t$ is at least not obvious.

However, different from GL–frames, the big Kripke frames are not conversely well–founded. This follows from the fact that there exists a sequence of consistent theories $\{T_n\}_{n \in \omega}$ such that $T_n \vdash \mathsf{Con}(T_{n+1})$ for all n. This was proven independently by Feferman and Friedman, as an answer to a question posed by Gaifman (see [8]). By Theorem 9, we get a sequence of models $\{\mathcal{M}_i\}_{i \in \omega}$ with $\mathcal{M}_i \vDash T_i$ and $\mathcal{M}_i \rhd_t \mathcal{M}_{i+1}$ for all i. Since $\mathcal{M} \rhd_t \mathcal{M}'$ implies $\mathcal{M} \rhd_{\mathsf{tpar}} \mathcal{M}'$ and $\mathcal{M} \blacktriangleright_t \mathcal{M}'$, this yields an infinite ascending chain in all our arithmetical Kripke models.

The following lemma shows that taking $\rhd_t$ for R_{big}, the big arithmetical frame is irreflexive. Indeed, if a world $\mathcal{M}$ sees a world $\mathcal{M}'$ in this frame, $\mathcal{M}$ and $\mathcal{M}'$ cannot even satisfy the same sentences of PA.

Proposition 1. *If $\mathcal{M} \rhd_t \mathcal{M}'$, then $\mathcal{M} \not\equiv \mathcal{M}'$.*

Proof. The proof of Proposition 1 proceeds by a modified liar–argument. Suppose that j defines a t–internal model of $\mathcal{M}$. By the Gödel–Carnap Fixed Point Lemma, let γ be a sentence of the language Σ such that

$$\mathcal{M} \vDash \gamma \leftrightarrow \neg\mathsf{tr}(\gamma). \tag{15}$$

By Theorem 6, we also have $\mathcal{M} \vDash \gamma^{\tau_j} \leftrightarrow \mathsf{tr}(\gamma)$. Using Theorem 5,

$$\mathcal{M}^j \vDash \gamma \Leftrightarrow \mathcal{M} \vDash \gamma^{\tau_j} \Leftrightarrow \mathcal{M} \vDash \mathsf{tr}(\gamma) \Leftrightarrow \mathcal{M} \nvDash \gamma, \tag{16}$$

whence clearly $\mathcal{M} \not\equiv \mathcal{M}^j$, and thus also $\mathcal{M} \not\equiv \mathcal{M}'$ whenever $\mathcal{M} \rhd_t \mathcal{M}'$.

In contrast, there are elementary equivalent models $\mathcal{M}$ and $\mathcal{M}'$ such that $\mathcal{M}'$ is a t–internal model of $\mathcal{M}$ with parameters.

Proposition 2. *There are worlds $\mathcal{M}$ and $\mathcal{M}'$ with $\mathcal{M} \equiv \mathcal{M}'$ and $\mathcal{M} \rhd_{\mathsf{tpar}} \mathcal{M}'$.*

Proof. Let $\mathcal{N}$ be the standard model, and let Σ_c be the signature $\Sigma \cup \{c\}$, where c is a constant. One can use a standard compactness argument to show that the theory

$$T := \mathsf{Th}_\Sigma(\mathcal{N}) \cup \{\varphi \in c \mid \mathcal{N} \vDash \varphi\} + \mathsf{Con}\{\varphi \mid \varphi \in c\} \tag{17}$$

in the language Σ_c has a model $\mathcal{M}^+$. Since $\mathcal{M} \vDash \mathsf{Con}\{\varphi \mid \varphi \in c\}$, we can use the arithmetized Henkin construction to find a t–internal model $\mathcal{M}'$ of $\mathcal{M}^+$ with $\mathcal{M}' \vDash \varphi$ for all $\varphi \in c$. Let $\mathcal{M}$ be the reduct of $\mathcal{M}^+$ to Σ, and note that $\mathcal{M} \rhd_{\mathsf{tpar}} \mathcal{M}'$ (since the construction of $\mathcal{M}'$ inside $\mathcal{M}$ uses $c^\mathcal{M}$ as a parameter). Since c contains the codes of all true sentences and since $\mathcal{M}$ is a model of $\mathsf{Th}_\Sigma(\mathcal{N})$, we have that $\mathcal{M} \equiv \mathcal{M}'$.

Note that Propositions 1 and 2 provide a separating example for the relations $\rhd_{\mathsf{tpar}}$ and $\rhd_t$.

Remark 4. As pointed out in Remark 3, we could have chosen as W_{big} the collection of models of PA modulo *elementary equivalence*. In that case, $\langle W_{\mathsf{big}}, \rhd_{\mathsf{tpar}}\rangle$ would thus contain a reflexive point, whereas $\langle W_{\mathsf{big}}, \rhd_t\rangle$ would not.

We now provide a separating example for the relations $\blacktriangleright_t$ and $\rhd_{\mathsf{tpar}}$, and see that the frame $\langle W_{\mathsf{big}}, \blacktriangleright_t\rangle$ contains a reflexive point.

Proposition 3. *Let $\mathcal{N}$ be the standard model. Then $\mathcal{N} \rhd_{\mathsf{tpar}} \mathcal{N}$.*

Proof. Note that all elements of $\mathcal{N}$ are definable, and thus $\mathcal{N} \rhd_{\mathsf{tpar}} \mathcal{M}$ implies $\mathcal{N} \rhd_t \mathcal{M}$ for all $\mathcal{M}$. In particular $\mathcal{N} \rhd_{\mathsf{tpar}} \mathcal{N}$ would imply $\mathcal{N} \rhd_t \mathcal{N}$, which is excluded by Proposition 1.

To complete the separating example, we need to show that $\mathcal{N} \blacktriangleright_t \mathcal{N}$, where $\mathcal{N}$ is the standard model. This follows from the fact that $\mathcal{N}$ has a full inductive satisfaction class. Explaining the notion of a full inductive satisfaction class and its relation to the t–associated model relation is beyond the scope of this paper, the reader is referred to [6] for more information.

Finally, we provide a separating example for $\rhd$, the internal model relation, and $\blacktriangleright_t$. Let $\mathcal{M}$ be any model with $\mathcal{M} \vDash \mathsf{Pr}(\bot)$. It is clear that $\mathcal{M} \rhd \mathcal{M}$. However there is no inductive expansion $\mathcal{M}^+$ that has a truth predicate for $\mathcal{M}$ satisfying 1–5 of Definition 8. If $\mathcal{M}^+$ were such an expansion, then by Theorem 8, $\mathcal{M}^+ \vDash \mathsf{Pr}(\bot) \to \mathsf{tr}(\bot)$, but also by assumption $\mathcal{M}^+ \vDash \mathsf{Pr}(\bot)$, and so $\mathcal{M}^+ \vDash \mathsf{tr}(\bot)$ which is a contradiction. Thus $\mathcal{M} \not\blacktriangleright_t \mathcal{M}$.

We have now delivered our promise of Sect. 3.1, namely to show that all the implications in

$$\mathcal{M} \rhd_t \mathcal{M}' \Rightarrow \mathcal{M} \rhd_{\mathsf{tpar}} \mathcal{M}' \Rightarrow \mathcal{M} \blacktriangleright_t \mathcal{M}' \Rightarrow \mathcal{M} \rhd \mathcal{M}' \tag{18}$$

are irreversible.

6   Conclusion

We have established three examples of arithmetical accessibility relations between models of PA. We have shown how, as a result, one can see the collection of models of PA, related by one of these relations, as a big Kripke model where the forcing of modal formulas coincides with the local satisfiability of first–order sentences (modulo an arithmetical realization). We showed how this insight can be used to gain a new, model–theoretic perspective on Solovay's proof of arithmetical completeness of the modal logic GL. Finally, we have seen that the properties of the big arithmetical Kripke model are dependent on the exact choice of the accessibility relation as well as the domain of the Kripke model. We conclude with some open questions.

Question 1. The arguments of this article go through if we replace PA with a Σ_1–sound theory containing $\mathsf{I}\Sigma_2$. However, Solovay's Theorem holds for all Σ_1–sound theories containing EA. Can we make our arguments work for theories weaker than $\mathsf{I}\Sigma_2$? (Σ_2–induction is used in the standard proof of the Arithmetized Completeness Theorem).

Question 2. What is the relation between the big arithmetical frames and the canonical model for GL?

Question 3. What is the modal logic of the arithmetical Kripke model if the accessibility relation is replaced by some other relation between models of PA? Some possibilities are: the internal model relation where we demand a truth predicate for the internal model (but do not require that the axioms of PA are in the extension of the truth predicate), the internal model relation, and the end-extension relation. A difference from the t–internal model relation is that these relations need not be definable by an arithmetical formula.

Acknowledgements. I thank Albert Visser who provided the insight and expertise needed to write this paper. I am grateful to Dick de Jongh for useful discussions, and for comments on several drafts of the article.

References

1. Cooper, S.B.: Computability Theory. CRC Mathematics Series. Chapman & Hall, London (2004)
2. Feferman, S.: Arithmetization of metamathematics in a general setting. Fundam. Math. **49**, 35–92 (1960)
3. Foundations of Mathematics mailing list. http://cs.nyu.edu/pipermail/fom/2009-August/013996.html
4. Hamkins, J.D.: A simple maximality principle. J. Symb. Log. **68**, 527–550 (2003)
5. Hamkins, J.D., Löwe, B.: The modal logic of forcing. Trans. Am. Math. Soc. **360**, 1793–1817 (2008)
6. Kaye, R.: Models of Peano Arithmetic. Oxford Logic Guides. Oxford University Press, New York (1991)
7. Lindström, P.: Aspects of Incompleteness. Lecture Notes in Logic. ASL/A K Peters, Natick, Massachusetts (2002)
8. Smoryński, C.: Nonstandard models and related developments. In: Harrington, L.A., Morley, M.D., Scedrov, A. (eds.) Harvey Friedman's Research on the Foundations of Mathematics. Studies in logic and the foundations of mathematics, pp. 179–229. North-Holland, Amsterdam/New York/Oxford (1985)
9. Solovay, R.M.: Provability interpretations of modal logic. Israel J. Math. **25**, 287–304 (1976)
10. Visser, A.: An inside view of EXP. J. Symb. Log. **57**, 131–165 (1992)
11. Visser, A.: An overview of interpretability logic. Adv. Modal Log. **1**, 307–359 (1998)
12. Wang, H.: A arithmetical models for formal systems. Methodos **3**, 217–232 (1951)

Positive Formulas in Intuitionistic and Minimal Logic

Dick de Jongh[1]([⊠]) and Zhiguang Zhao[2]

[1] ILLC, University of Amsterdam, Amsterdam, The Netherlands
d.h.j.dejongh@uva.nl
[2] Delft University of Technology, Delft, The Netherlands
zhaozhiguang23@gmail.com

Abstract. In this article we investigate the positive, i.e. $\neg, \bot$-free formulas of intuitionistic propositional and predicate logic, IPC and IQC, and minimal logic, MPC and MQC. For each formula φ of IQC we define the positive formula φ^+ that represents the positive content of φ. The formulas φ and φ^+ exhibit the same behavior on top models, models with a largest world that makes all atomic sentences true. We characterize the positive formulas of IPC and IQC as the formulas that are immune to the operation of turning a model into a top model. With the +-operation on formulas we show, using the uniform interpolation theorem for IPC, that both the positive fragment of IPC and MPC respect a revised version of uniform interpolation. In propositional logic the well-known theorem that KC is conservative over the positive fragment of IPC is shown to generalize to many logics with positive axioms. In first-order logic, we show that IQC + DNS (double negation shift) + KC is conservative over the positive fragment of IQC and similar results as for IPC.

Keywords: Intuitionistic logic · Minimal logic · Jankov's logic · Intermediate logics · Positive formulas · Interpolation · Conservativity

1 Introduction

In this paper we discuss the formulas in intuitionistic logic containing no negation or $\bot$. For propositional logic IPC this is the fragment $[\wedge, \vee, \rightarrow]$. Smaller fragments not containing both $\vee$ and $\rightarrow$ have been extensively studied. By Diego's theorem [4] they are locally finite, i.e. they do contain only finitely many equivalence classes of formulas in a fixed finite number of variables. For a discussion of the history of these studies see [15]. The fragment $[\wedge, \vee, \rightarrow]$, which we call the positive fragment, does not have this property. It has been little studied as a fragment. Its interest is to start with that it has a very close relationship to minimal logic, the logic resulting when the ex falso principle is deleted from intuitionistic logic. In fact, one can see minimal propositional logic as this fragment with one designated propositional variable (the contradiction), and this is not different in first order logic. The ex falso principle has been criticized from the start, for example by Kolmogorov [13] in the earliest partial formalization of intuitionistic

© Springer-Verlag Berlin Heidelberg 2015
M. Aher et al. (Eds.): TbiLLC 2013, LNCS 8984, pp. 175–189, 2015.
DOI: 10.1007/978-3-662-46906-4_11

logic. Heyting, however, did accept the principle in his basic papers [10], and from then on it has been accepted as a principle of intuitionistic logic. After this, Johansson, not supporting the ex falso principle, introduced minimal logic in [12]. Some proponents of intuitionistic mathematics (Griss [9], van Danzig) favored the idea of dropping negation altogether: negationless mathematics, but they had few followers. Brouwer himself thought formulas with negation to be indispensable in intuitionistic mathematics [1].

It is worth mentioning that in the pure arithmetic (of natural numbers), formalized in Heyting Arithmetic HA it makes no difference whether one accepts the ex falso principle or introduces negation, since in HA from $0 = 1$ all arithmetic sentences are derivable without the use of either (see e.g. [16], Vol. I, Proposition 3.2, p. 126). In analysis this is still true as long as one has only equations between numerical terms as atomic formulas, but no longer so when one e.g. has set variables with undecidable atomic formulas $X(t)$. A final striking fact is that first order intuitionistic logic without $\bot$ can be proved to be complete for so-called Beth-models by constructive methods whereas this is not the case for full first order logic (see [16], Vol. II, p. 685, which uses a proof by H. Friedman in an unpublished manuscript). In any case, it is good to start with logic to see how the positive fragment fits into the full logic. For that purpose we define in this paper a +-operation on the formulas of intuitionistic logic which we claim represents their positive content. This operation turns out be very useful in studying various properties of positive formulas in the framework of the full logic.

Minimal propositional logic MPC and minimal predicate logic MQC are obtained from the positive fragment, i.e. the $\neg, \bot$-free fragment, of intuitionistic propositional logic IPC and intuitionistic predicate logic IQC by adding a weaker negation: $\neg \varphi$ is defined as $\varphi \to f$, where the special propositional variable f is interpreted as the contradiction. Therefore, the language of minimal logic is the $\neg, \bot$-free fragment of intuitionistic logic plus f. Variable f has no specific properties, the Hilbert type system for MQC is as IQC's but without $f \to \varphi$. An alternative formulation of minimal logic, in fact the original one, in a language containing $\neg$ instead of f can be given by adding to a Hilbert type axiom system for the positive fragment the axiom $(p \to q) \to ((p \to \neg q) \to \neg p)$ (see [12]).

For the semantics of minimal logic, f is interpreted as an ordinary propositional variable, so we get the semantics of the $[\vee, \wedge, \to]$-fragment of IPC (resp. the $[\vee, \wedge, \to, \forall, \exists]$-fragment of IQC), with an additional propositional variable f.

The content of this article is the following:

In Sect. 2 we recall the syntax and semantics of intuitionistic and minimal logic. In Sect. 3 we introduce the top-model property and the +-operation on formulas, and show that the top-model property characterizes the positive formulas of IPC and IQC. We then use this property in Sect. 4 to show that the positive fragment of IPC has a revised form of uniform interpolation and that this transfers to MPC. In Sect. 5 we discuss the behavior of positive formulas in some extensions of IPC and IQC, taking as a starting point the theorem that Jankov's Logic KC has the same positive fragment as IPC.

2 Syntax and Semantics of MPC

In this section we recall the syntax as well as the derivation systems of IPC, IQC, MPC and MQC, and their Kripke semantics. For more details, see [2] and [17].

2.1 Syntax

The propositional language $\mathcal{L}_I(P)$ of IPC consists of a countable or finite set P of propositional variables p_0, p_1, p_2, ..., propositional constants $\bot, \top$ and binary connectives $\wedge, \vee, \rightarrow$. A first order language $\mathcal{L}_I(Q)$ of IQC consists of a countable or finite set Q of predicate letters and individual constants[1], propositional constants $\bot, \top$, binary connectives $\wedge, \vee, \rightarrow$ and quantifiers $\forall$ and $\exists$. In both cases $\neg\varphi$ is defined as $\varphi \rightarrow \bot$, although in practice it is often convenient to view formulas as containing both $\neg$ and $\bot$. The *positive fragment* $\mathcal{L}_I^+(P)$ of IPC consists of the formulas of $\mathcal{L}_I(P)$ that do not contain $\neg$ or $\bot$, similarly for a language $\mathcal{L}_I(Q)$.

The propositional language $\mathcal{L}_M(P)$ of MPC (resp. first order language $\mathcal{L}_M(Q)$ of MQC) consists of the formulas of the positive fragment to which the special propositional variable f is added. We may drop the indices I and M and write $\mathcal{L}(P)$ etc. if the distinction is irrelevant.

We take the axioms of IPC as in [2]. The axioms for MPC are the same except that $\bot \rightarrow \varphi$ is left out. So, derivations in MPC are the same as in IPC except that no $\bot$ or $\neg$ occurs, instead f may have occurrences. To add predicate-logical axioms to obtain IQC and MQC we use the approach of Enderton [5] to classical logic with universally quantified axioms and modus ponens as the only rule. In this paper we will both proof-theoretically and semantically be only interested in sentences.

For the discussion of uniform interpolation in Sect. 4 we introduce the following notation: For any formula φ and any sequence $\boldsymbol{p} = (p_1, \ldots, p_n)$ of propositional variables (here p_i can be f, but cannot be $\bot, \top$), $\varphi(\boldsymbol{p})$ is a formula with only propositional variables in $\boldsymbol{p}$.

2.2 Kripke Semantics

In this part we give the Kripke semantics of our systems.

Definition 1. *A propositional Kripke frame is a pair $\mathfrak{F} = (W, R)$ where W is a non-empty set and R is a partial order on it.*

A propositional Kripke model is a triple $\mathfrak{M} = (W, R, V)$ where (W, R) is a Kripke frame and V is a valuation $V : P \cup \{f\} \rightarrow \mathscr{P}(W)$ (where $\mathscr{P}(W)$ is the powerset of W) such that for any $q \in P \cup \{f\}$, $V(q)$ is an upset: for any $w, w' \in W$, $w \in V(q)$ and wRw' imply $w' \in V(q)$.

To be able to treat propositional and predicate logic uniformly we define first-order models in a similar way. For a language $\mathcal{L}(Q)$, we write At_Q or At for the set of atomic sentences.

---

[1] We do not consider identity and functional symbols, but our results will surely hold for the extension with such symbols.

Definition 2. *A predicate Kripke frame for a language* $\mathcal{L}(Q)$ *is a triple* $\mathfrak{F} = (W, R, \{D_w \mid w \in W\})$ *where* W *is a non-empty set,* R *is a partial order on* W, *and* $\{D_w \mid w \in W\}$ *a set of non-empty domains such that for any* $w, w' \in W$, wRw' *implies* $D_w \subseteq D_{w'}$.

A predicate Kripke model for a language $\mathcal{L}(Q)$ *is a quadruple* $\mathfrak{M} = (W, R, \{D_w \mid w \in W\}, V)$ *where* $(W, R, \{D_w \mid w \in W\})$ *is a Kripke frame and* V *is a valuation* $V : At \cup \{f\} \to \mathscr{P}(W)$ *such that for any* $Ad_1 \ldots d_k$ *in* At, $V(Ad_1 \ldots d_k) \subseteq \{w \in W \mid (d_1, \ldots, d_k) \in (D_w)^k\}$, *and* $w, w' \in W$, $w \in V(Ad_1 \ldots d_k)$ *and* wRw' *imply* $w' \in V(Ad_1 \ldots d_k)$, *similarly for* f.

For propositional formulas, the satisfaction relation is defined as usual with clauses for $p, f, \perp, \top, \vee, \wedge, \to$, where the semantics of f is the same as for the other propositional variables. For predicate logic only sentences will be evaluated with clauses for $\forall, \exists$ as e.g. in van Dalen [19]. In the first order case $w \models \varphi$ (and hence $w \not\models \varphi$) is only defined if the individual constants in φ are in D_w. If we define V on P or At and omit the clause for f, then we get the Kripke semantics of IPC or IQC; if we omit the clause for $\perp$, then we get the Kripke semantics of MPC or MQC. We use $\models_I$ and $\models_M$ to distinguish the satisfaction relation of IQC and MQC, and omit the index when it is not important or clear from the context.

For IQC, we have the following completeness theorem (see e.g. [2]):

Theorem 1 (Strong Completeness of IQC)
For any set of IQC*-sentences* Γ *and* φ, $\Gamma \vdash_{\mathsf{IQC}} \varphi$ *iff* $\Gamma \models_I \varphi$.

By a standard Henkin type completeness proof, we have that MQC is strongly complete with respect to Kripke models, i.e. for any Γ and φ, $\Gamma \vdash_{\mathsf{MQC}} \varphi$ iff $\Gamma \models_M \varphi$. The proof procedure is essentially the same as the proof for IQC with respect to Kripke frames, just leave out $\perp$ and the accompanying condition that the members of the model have to be consistent sets (which of course they are).

Theorem 2 (Strong Completeness of MQC)
For any MQC*-formulas* Γ *and* φ, $\Gamma \vdash_{\mathsf{MQC}} \varphi$ *iff* $\Gamma \models_M \varphi$.

By a completeness-via-canonicity proof using adequate sets, we have the finite model property for IPC (again see [2]) and thereby for MPC:

Theorem 3 (Finite Model Property of MPC)
For any MPC*-formula* φ, *if* $\not\vdash_{\mathsf{MPC}} \varphi$, *then there is a rooted finite Kripke model* $\mathfrak{M}$ *falsifying* φ.

By the completeness theorem for MQC and IQC, since the semantic behavior of MQC in the language $\mathcal{L}_{\mathsf{M}}(Q)$ is exactly the same as that of IQC in the language $\mathcal{L}_I(Q \cup \{f\})$ without $\perp$ (i.e. the positive $[\vee, \wedge, \to, \top, \forall, \exists]$-fragment $\mathcal{L}_I^+(Q \cup \{f\})$ of $\mathcal{L}_I(Q \cup \{f\})$), we can regard MQC as the positive fragment of IQC, and we have the following lemma:

Lemma 1. *For any sentences* Γ *and* φ *in* $\mathcal{L}_{\mathsf{M}}(Q) = \mathcal{L}_I^+(Q \cup (\{f\}))$, $\Gamma \vdash_{\mathsf{MQC}} \varphi$ *iff* $\Gamma \vdash_{\mathsf{IQC}} \varphi$.

This allows us to write $\vdash \varphi$ if the index does not matter.

For intermediate logics we sometimes need descriptive frames.

Definition 3. *A* general frame *is a triple* $\mathfrak{F} = \langle W, R, \mathcal{P} \rangle$, *where* $\langle W, R \rangle$ *is a Kripke frame and* $\mathcal{P}$ *is a family of upward closed sets containing* $\emptyset$ *and closed under* $\cap$, $\cup$ *and the following operation* $\supset$: *for every* $X, Y \subseteq W$,

$$X \supset Y = \{x \in W \mid \forall y \in W (xRy \wedge y \in X \to y \in Y)\}$$

Elements of the set $\mathcal{P}$ *are called* admissible sets.

Definition 4. *A* general frame $\mathfrak{F} = \langle W, R, \mathcal{P} \rangle$ *is called* refined *if for any* $x, y \in W$,

$$\forall X \in \mathcal{P} \, (x \in X \to y \in X) \Rightarrow xRy.$$

$\mathfrak{F}$ *is called* compact, *if for any family* $\mathcal{Z} \subseteq \mathcal{P} \cup \{W \setminus X \mid X \in \mathcal{P}\}$ *with the finite intersection property,* $\bigcap(\mathcal{Z}) \neq \emptyset$.

Definition 5. *A* general frame $\mathfrak{F}$ *is called a* descriptive frame *iff it is* refined *and* compact.

Intermediate propositional logics are complete with respect to descriptive frames (see [2]):

Theorem 4. *If* L *is an intermediate propositional logic, then, for all formulas* φ, $\vdash_L \varphi$ *iff* φ *is valid in all descriptive frames* $\mathfrak{F}$ *that satisfy* L.

3   The Top-Model Property

We give a characterization of the $\neg, \bot$-free formulas of IPC by means of the following property:

Definition 6 (Top-Model Property)

1. *A propositional or predicate Kripke model* $\mathfrak{M} = (W, R, V)$ *is a* top model *if it has a largest point* t, *the* top *of the model, in which all formulas in* P *or* At *are satisfied.*
2. *Any model* $\mathfrak{M} = (W, R, V)$ *can be turned into its top model* $\mathfrak{M}^+ = (W^+, R^+, V^+)$ *by adding a node* t *at the top of the model, connecting all worlds* w *to* t, *and making all atomic sentences true in* t. *In case of first order logic,* $D_t = \bigcup_{w \in W} D_w$.
3. *A formula* φ *has the* top-model property, *if for all Kripke models* $\mathfrak{M} = (W, R, V)$, *all* $w \in W$, $\mathfrak{M}, w \models \varphi$ *iff* $\mathfrak{M}^+, w \models \varphi$.

Analogously to 1,2 of the above definition we talk about *top frames*.

Lemma 2. *Let* t *be the top of any top model, and let* φ *be a positive formula without free variables. Then* $t \models \varphi$.

Proof. Trivial, by induction on the length of φ. $\qquad\square$

For the top-model property we have the following theorem. It was first proved in [18,21] (see also [15]). We write $\varphi \sim \psi$ for $\vdash \varphi \leftrightarrow \psi$.

Theorem 5.   *1. Every formula in $\mathcal{L}_I^+(P)$, $\mathcal{L}_I^+(Q)$, $\mathcal{L}_M(P)$ and $\mathcal{L}_M(Q)$ has the top-model property, and so has $\bot$.*
2. For any formula φ in $\mathcal{L}_I(P)$, there exists a procedure to produce a formula φ^+ in $\mathcal{L}_I^+(P)$ or $\varphi^+ =\bot$ such that for any top model $\mathfrak{M}$ and any node w in $\mathfrak{M}$, we have $\mathfrak{M}, w \models \varphi \leftrightarrow \varphi^+$.
3. For any formula φ in $\mathcal{L}_I(Q)$, there exists a procedure to produce a formula φ^+ in $\mathcal{L}_I^+(Q)$ or $\varphi^+ =\bot$ such that for any top model $\mathfrak{M}$ and any node w in $\mathfrak{M}$, we have $\mathfrak{M}, w \models \varphi \leftrightarrow \varphi^+$.
4. For any set of formulas Γ in $\mathcal{L}_I(P)$ or $\mathcal{L}_I(Q)$, any top model $\mathfrak{M}$ and any node w in $\mathfrak{M}$, we have $\mathfrak{M}, w \models \Gamma$ iff $\mathfrak{M}, w \models \Gamma^+$, where $\Gamma^+ = \{\gamma^+ \mid \gamma \in \Gamma\}$.

Proof. 1. By induction on the length of the formula φ. We just give the inductive steps for $\rightarrow$ and $\forall$. Let t denote the top element of $\mathfrak{M}$.

- $\mathfrak{M}, w \models \psi \rightarrow \chi \iff$ in all w' such that wRw', if $\mathfrak{M}, w' \models \psi$ then $\mathfrak{M}, w' \models \chi$
  $\iff_{IH}$ in all $w' \in W\backslash\{t\}$ such that wRw', if $\mathfrak{M}^+, w' \models \psi$ then $\mathfrak{M}^+, w' \models \chi$
  [Now note that since φ is positive, and χ is a subformula of φ, it must be the case that χ is positive. Therefore, by Lemma 2, $t \models \chi$] $\iff$ in all $w' \in W$ such that wRw', if $\mathfrak{M}^+, w' \models \psi$ then $\mathfrak{M}^+, w' \models \chi \iff \mathfrak{M}^+, w \models \psi \rightarrow \chi$.
- $\mathfrak{M}, w \models \forall z \psi(z) \iff$ if wRw' then $\mathfrak{M}, w' \models \psi(d)$ for all $d \in D_{w'}$ [Now note that by Lemma 2, $t \models \psi(d)$ for all $d \in D_t$.] $\iff_{IH}$ if wRw' then $\mathfrak{M}^+, w' \models \psi(d)$ for all $d \in D_{w'} \iff \mathfrak{M}^+, w \models \forall z \psi(z)$.

2 and 3. We obtain φ^+ from φ in stages. That is, $\varphi = \varphi^0 \dashrightarrow \varphi^1 \dashrightarrow \cdots \dashrightarrow \varphi^n = \varphi^+$. Each stage m starts off with φ^m and produces φ^{m+1}. The procedure starts at $n = 0$.

Stage $2n$. Remove all $\top$ and $\bot$ using the following equivalences:

Remove$\bot$	Remove$\top$
$\bot \wedge \varphi \sim \varphi \wedge \bot \sim \bot$	$\top \wedge \varphi \sim \varphi \wedge \top \sim \varphi$
$\bot \vee \varphi \sim \varphi \vee \bot \sim \varphi$	$\top \vee \varphi \sim \varphi \vee \top \sim \top$
$\bot \rightarrow \varphi \sim \top$	$\top \rightarrow \varphi \sim \varphi$
$\varphi \rightarrow \bot \sim \neg\varphi$	$\varphi \rightarrow \top \sim \top$
$\neg\bot \sim \top$	$\neg\top \sim \bot$

This procedure may produce a formula φ^{2n+1} containing neither $\top$ nor $\bot$. However, it is also possible that it ends by producing $\top$ or $\bot$. In the latter two cases, the theorem is trivial, since in any model $\mathfrak{M}$ and any world w, $\mathfrak{M}, w \models \top$ and $\mathfrak{M}, w \not\models \bot$, and therefore $\iff$ holds. So, in the remainder of this proof we assume that not $\varphi^{2n+1} = \bot$ and not $\varphi^{2n+1} = \top$. Note the special feature of the procedure: a new negation may be produced.

Stage $2n + 1$. Consider the first $\neg$ in φ^{2n+1} such that $\neg\psi$ is a subformula of φ^{2n+1} and ψ is positive: that is, ψ does not contain $\neg, \bot$. This can be done since all $\bot$ were removed in the previous stage. Replace $\neg\psi$ by $\bot$. This results in $\varphi^{2n+2} = \varphi^{2n+1}[\bot/\neg\psi]$, which contains less symbols than φ^{2n+1}.

The even stages use logical equivalences, so by definition $\mathfrak{M}^+, w \models \varphi^{2n} \iff \mathfrak{M}^+, w \models \varphi^{2n+1}$ (valuations on $\mathfrak{M}^+$ are preserved), since for equivalent formulas this holds for any model.

Next, it has to be shown that also the odd stages preserve valuations on $\mathfrak{M}^+$, that is: $\mathfrak{M}^+, w \models \varphi^{2n+1} \iff \mathfrak{M}^+, w \models \varphi^{2n+2} = \varphi^{2n+1}[\bot/\neg\psi]$ for all $n \in \mathbb{N}$. Let $\psi = \psi(x_1, \ldots, x_k)$ and $d_1, \ldots, d_k \in D_w$. Consider the valuation of $\psi(d_1, \ldots, d_k)$ in top world t. We have chosen ψ positive. Therefore, by Lemma 2, $t \models \psi(d_1, \ldots, d_k)$. By definition of $\mathfrak{M}^+$, wRt for all $w \in W$, so for all $w \in W$, there is a w' such that wRw' and $w' \models \psi(d_1, \ldots, d_k)$ (namely $w' = t$). Therefore, for all $w \in W$, it must be the case that $\mathfrak{M}^+, w \not\models \neg\psi(d_1, \ldots, d_k)$. It can be concluded by a trivial induction that φ^{2n+1} is equivalent to $\varphi^{2n+1}[\bot/\neg\psi]$.

The described procedure will come to an end, since all steps reduce the number of symbols in the formula. Therefore, there is a final stage, say stage m, which produces a φ^{m+1} that no longer contains $\bot$ or $\neg$. Now define $\varphi^{m+1} = \varphi^+$. Since both the odd and even stages preserve valuations on $\mathfrak{M}^+$, we know that $\mathfrak{M}^+, w \models \varphi^{n-1} \iff \mathfrak{M}^+, w \models \varphi^n$ for all n. By induction, this implies that $\mathfrak{M}^+, w \models \varphi \iff \mathfrak{M}^+, w \models \varphi^+$.

4 follows immediately from 2 and 3.   □

And this theorem leads to the following characterization.

Theorem 6. *A formula φ of* IPC *or* IQC *has the top-model property iff φ is equivalent to a $\neg, \bot$-free formula (in fact to φ^+) or to $\bot$.*

Proof. The direction from right to left is Theorem 5.1, so let us prove the other direction and assume that φ has the top-model property, but is not equivalent to φ^+. Then there is a model $\mathfrak{M}$ with a world w so that φ and φ^+ have different truth values in $\mathfrak{M}, w$. Then, because both have the top-model property, φ and φ^+ have different truth values in $\mathfrak{M}^+, w$ as well. But that contradicts the fact given by Theorem 5 that φ and φ^+ behave identically on top models.   □

Theorem 7. *1. If $\vdash_{\mathsf{IPC}} \varphi$, then $\vdash_{\mathsf{IPC}} \varphi^+$. If $\vdash_{\mathsf{IQC}} \varphi$, then $\vdash_{\mathsf{IQC}} \varphi^+$.*

2. Not always $\vdash_{\mathsf{IPC}} \varphi \to \varphi^+$ and not always $\vdash_{\mathsf{IPC}} \varphi^+ \to \varphi$.

3. If $\varphi(\psi_1, \ldots, \psi_k)$ arises from the simultaneous substitution of $\psi_1, \ldots, \psi_k$ for $p_1, \ldots, p_k$ in $\varphi(p_1, \ldots, p_k)$, then $(\varphi(\psi_1, \ldots, \psi_k))^+ = (\varphi(\psi_1^+, \ldots, \psi_k^+))^+$.

4. If $\vdash_{\mathsf{IPC}} \varphi \to \psi$, then $\vdash_{\mathsf{IPC}} \varphi^+ \to \psi^+$. If $\vdash_{\mathsf{IQC}} \varphi \to \psi$, then $\vdash_{\mathsf{IQC}} \varphi^+ \to \psi^+$.

5. φ^+ is unique up to provable equivalence.

6. If $\vdash_{\mathsf{IPC}} \varphi \to \psi$ and ψ is positive, then $\vdash_{\mathsf{IPC}} \varphi^+ \to \psi$. If $\vdash_{\mathsf{IQC}} \varphi \to \psi$ and ψ is positive, then $\vdash_{\mathsf{IQC}} \varphi^+ \to \psi$. If $\vdash_{\mathsf{IPC}} \psi \to \varphi$ and ψ is positive, then $\vdash_{\mathsf{IPC}} \psi \to \varphi^+$. If $\vdash_{\mathsf{IQC}} \psi \to \varphi$ and ψ is positive, then $\vdash_{\mathsf{IQC}} \psi \to \varphi^+$.

7. If $\Gamma \vdash_{\mathsf{IPC}} \varphi$ and φ is positive, then $\Gamma^+ \vdash_{\mathsf{IPC}} \varphi$, where $\Gamma^+ = \{\gamma^+ \mid \gamma \in \Gamma\}$.

Proof. 1. Assume not $\vdash_{\mathsf{IPC}} \varphi^+$. Then $\mathfrak{M}, w$ exist such that $\mathfrak{M}, w \nvDash \varphi^+$. By Theorem 5.1 also $\mathfrak{M}^+, w \nvDash \varphi^+$. But then by Theorem 5.2, $\mathfrak{M}^+, w \nvDash \varphi$, so not $\vdash_{\mathsf{IPC}} \varphi$. Same for IQC.

2. For $\varphi = p \vee \neg p$, $\varphi^+ = p$, so $\nvdash_{\mathsf{IPC}} \varphi \to \varphi^+$. For $\varphi = \neg\neg p$, $\varphi^+ = \top$, so $\nvdash_{\mathsf{IPC}} \varphi^+ \to \varphi$.

3. By the fact that the construction of the $+$-formula in Theorem 5 is inside-out. We can construct $(\varphi(\psi_1, \ldots, \psi_k))^+$ by first applying the $+$-operation to the formulas $\psi_1, \ldots, \psi_k$ in $\varphi(\psi_1, \ldots, \psi_k)$ to obtain $\varphi(\psi_1^+, \ldots, \psi_k^+)$, and then continue to work on the remainder to obtain $(\varphi(\psi_1^+, \ldots, \psi_k^+))^+$.

4. Suppose $\vdash_{\mathsf{IPC}} \varphi \to \psi$ and $\nvdash_{\mathsf{IPC}} \varphi^+ \to \psi^+$, then by the completeness of IPC, there is a rooted model $\mathfrak{M}$ with root w such that $\mathfrak{M}, w \vDash \varphi^+$ and $\mathfrak{M}, w \nvDash \psi^+$. By Theorem 5.1, $\mathfrak{M}^+, w \vDash \varphi^+$ and $\mathfrak{M}^+, w \nvDash \psi^+$. By Theorem 5.2, $\mathfrak{M}^+, w \vDash \varphi$ and $\mathfrak{M}^+, w \nvDash \psi$, a contradiction to $\vdash_{\mathsf{IPC}} \varphi \to \psi$. For IQC, the proof is similar.

5. Immediate from 4.

6. From 4.

7. Similar to 4, where the strong completeness is used. $\qquad\qquad\square$

Items 5 and 6 give us the right to say that φ^+ represents the positive content of φ. Item 3 will be used to obtain results on positive formulas proved by intermediate logics in Sect. 5.

We finally sketch another approach to get to Theorem 7.1 the advantage of which is that it can be transformed into a full proof-theoretic proof. We do not fully execute this here because of lack of space. The first step is the next theorem for which we provide here only a semantic proof.

Theorem 8. *If $\varphi(p_1, \ldots, p_k)$ is positive and $\vdash_{\mathsf{IPC}} \neg\neg(p_1 \wedge \cdots \wedge p_k) \to \varphi$, then $\vdash_{\mathsf{IPC}} \varphi$.*

Proof. Asume, φ positive, $\nvdash_{\mathsf{IPC}} \varphi$. Then for some model $\mathfrak{M}$ with root r, $\mathfrak{M}, r \nvDash \varphi$. Hence, by Theorem 5.1, $\mathfrak{M}^+, r \nvDash \varphi$. But also, $\mathfrak{M}^+, r \vDash \neg\neg(p_1 \wedge \cdots \wedge p_k)$, so $\mathfrak{M}^+, r \nvDash \neg\neg(p_1 \wedge \cdots \wedge p_k) \to \varphi$, and finally, $\nvdash_{\mathsf{IPC}} \neg\neg(p_1 \wedge \cdots \wedge p_k) \to \varphi$. $\qquad\square$

The next step (which replaces Lemma 2 in this approach) is trivial:

Lemma 3. *If $\psi(p_1, \ldots, p_k)$ is positive, then $\vdash_{\mathsf{IPC}} \neg\neg(p_1 \wedge \cdots \wedge p_k) \to \neg\neg\psi$.*

After this one proceeds to prove Theorem 7.1 as follows. If $\vdash_{\mathsf{IPC}} \varphi$, then also $\vdash_{\mathsf{IPC}} \neg\neg(p_1 \wedge \cdots \wedge p_k) \to \varphi$, after which $\vdash_{\mathsf{IPC}} \neg\neg(p_1 \wedge \cdots \wedge p_k) \to \varphi^+$ follows, since under the assumption $\neg\neg(p_1 \wedge \cdots \wedge p_k)$, φ and φ^+ are equivalent by the same procedure as used in the proof of Theorem 5.2, using the just stated lemma on the way when we replace $\neg\psi$ by $\bot$. Finally, we can conclude $\vdash \varphi^+$ by Theorem 8. For first order logic this approach works as well when one replaces $\neg\neg(p_1 \wedge \cdots \wedge p_k)$ by $\neg\neg\forall \boldsymbol{x}(A_1 \wedge \cdots \wedge A_k)$.

4 Uniform Interpolation

In this section we prove a revised version of the uniform interpolation theorem for the positive fragment of IPC and for MPC, using the uniform interpolation theorem of IPC and the top-model property.

First of all we state the uniform interpolation theorem of IPC. We formulate the theorem for formulas $\varphi(\boldsymbol{p}, q)$ and $\psi(\boldsymbol{p}, r)$ with one variable q and r in addition to the common ones $\boldsymbol{p}$; the more general case with $\boldsymbol{q}$ and $\boldsymbol{r}$ then follows by repeated application.

Theorem 9 (Uniform Interpolation Theorem of IPC)

1. *For any formula $\varphi(\boldsymbol{p}, q)$ in which q is not a member of $\boldsymbol{p}$, there is a formula $\chi(\boldsymbol{p})$, the* uniform post-interpolant *for $\varphi(\boldsymbol{p}, q)$, such that*
   (a) $\vdash_{\mathsf{IPC}} \varphi(\boldsymbol{p}, q) \to \chi(\boldsymbol{p})$,
   (b) *For any $\psi(\boldsymbol{p}, \boldsymbol{r})$ where $\boldsymbol{r}$ and $\boldsymbol{p}, q$ are disjoint, if $\vdash_{\mathsf{IPC}} \varphi(\boldsymbol{p}, q) \to \psi(\boldsymbol{p}, \boldsymbol{r})$, then $\vdash_{\mathsf{IPC}} \chi(\boldsymbol{p}) \to \psi(\boldsymbol{p}, \boldsymbol{r})$.*
2. *For any formula $\psi(\boldsymbol{p}, r)$ in which r is not a member of $\boldsymbol{p}$, there is a formula $\chi(\boldsymbol{p})$, the* uniform pre-interpolant *for $\psi(\boldsymbol{p}, r)$, such that*
   (a) $\vdash_{\mathsf{IPC}} \chi(\boldsymbol{p}) \to \psi(\boldsymbol{p}, r)$,
   (b) *For any $\varphi(\boldsymbol{p}, \boldsymbol{q})$ where $\boldsymbol{q}$ and $\boldsymbol{p}, r$ are disjoint, if $\vdash_{\mathsf{IPC}} \varphi(\boldsymbol{p}, \boldsymbol{q}) \to \psi(\boldsymbol{p}, r)$, then $\vdash_{\mathsf{IPC}} \varphi(\boldsymbol{p}, \boldsymbol{q}) \to \chi(\boldsymbol{p})$.*

This theorem is proved in [14] by a proof-theoretical method and in [8] by the bisimulation quantifier method. In accordance with the latter we write $\exists q\, \varphi(\boldsymbol{p}, q)$ for the post-interpolant and $\forall r\, \psi(\boldsymbol{p}, r)$ for the pre-interpolant.

For the positive fragment, we first treat the post-interpolant. There is a complication in the case of the pre-interpolant.

Theorem 10 (Uniform Interpolation Theorem for the positive fragment of IPC, post-interpolant)

   For any positive formula $\varphi(\boldsymbol{p}, q)$ in which q is not a member of $\boldsymbol{p}$, there is a positive formula $\theta(\boldsymbol{p})$ such that

1. $\vdash_{\mathsf{IPC}} \varphi(\boldsymbol{p}, q) \to \theta(\boldsymbol{p})$,
2. *For any positive $\psi(\boldsymbol{p}, \boldsymbol{r})$ where $\boldsymbol{r}$ and $\boldsymbol{p}, q$ are disjoint, if $\vdash_{\mathsf{IPC}} \varphi(\boldsymbol{p}, q) \to \psi(\boldsymbol{p}, \boldsymbol{r})$, then $\vdash_{\mathsf{IPC}} \theta(\boldsymbol{p}) \to \psi(\boldsymbol{p}, \boldsymbol{r})$. Moreover, $\theta(\boldsymbol{p})$ is $(\exists q\, \varphi)^+$, where $\exists q\, \varphi$ is the uniform post-interpolant for φ in full IPC.*

Proof. 1. By Theorem 9.1(a), $\vdash_{\mathsf{IPC}} \varphi(\boldsymbol{p}, q) \to \exists q\, \varphi(\boldsymbol{p}, q)$. As $\varphi(\boldsymbol{p}, q)$ is positive, by Theorem 7.6, $\vdash_{\mathsf{IPC}} \varphi(\boldsymbol{p}, q) \to (\exists q\, \varphi(\boldsymbol{p}, q))^+$. Note that, since $\varphi(\boldsymbol{p}, q)$ is satisfiable (it is positive!), $(\exists q\, \varphi(\boldsymbol{p}, q))^+$ cannot be $\bot$ and hence is positive.
   2. By Theorem 9.1(b), $\vdash_{\mathsf{IPC}} \exists q\, \varphi(\boldsymbol{p}, q) \to \psi(\boldsymbol{p}, \boldsymbol{r})$. As $\psi(\boldsymbol{p}, \boldsymbol{r})$ is positive, by Theorem 7.6, $\vdash_{\mathsf{IPC}} (\exists q\, \varphi(\boldsymbol{p}, q))^+ \to \psi(\boldsymbol{p}, \boldsymbol{r})$. □

This result is not trivial. The post-interpolant of $(p \to q) \to p$ in full IPC is $\neg\neg p$. In the positive fragment it is $(\neg\neg p)^+ = \top$.

For the pre-interpolant the situation is more complex. For example, $\forall r.\, p \to r$ is $\neg p$ and that is (up to equivalence) the only formula in p without r to imply $p \to r$, and therefore no pre-interpolant for $p \to r$ exists in the positive fragment. Actually, this is not a real surprise since in classical propositional logic the situation is the same. However, in a way this is the only failure of the theorem; pre-interpolants exist as long as we just consider positive formulas that are implied by at least one positive one not containing the quantified variables.

Theorem 11. (Uniform Interpolation Theorem for the positive fragment of IPC, pre-interpolant)

For any positive formula $\psi(\boldsymbol{p}, r)$ in which r is not in $\boldsymbol{p}$, one of the following two cases holds:

1. *There is a positive formula $\theta(\boldsymbol{p})$, the uniform pre-interpolant for $\psi(\boldsymbol{p}, r)$, such that*
   (a) $\vdash_{\mathsf{IPC}} \theta(\boldsymbol{p}) \to \psi(\boldsymbol{p}, r)$,
   (b) *For any $\varphi(\boldsymbol{p}, \boldsymbol{q})$ where $\boldsymbol{q}$ and $\boldsymbol{p}, r$ are disjoint, if $\vdash_{\mathsf{IPC}} \varphi(\boldsymbol{p}, \boldsymbol{q}) \to \psi(\boldsymbol{p}, r)$, then $\vdash_{\mathsf{IPC}} \varphi(\boldsymbol{p}, \boldsymbol{q}) \to \theta(\boldsymbol{p})$. Moreover, $\theta(\boldsymbol{p})$ is $(\forall r\, \psi)^+$.*
2. *For any positive $\theta(\boldsymbol{p}, \boldsymbol{q})$ where $\boldsymbol{q}$ and $\boldsymbol{p}, r$ are disjoint, $\nvdash_{\mathsf{IPC}} \theta(\boldsymbol{p}, \boldsymbol{q}) \to \psi(\boldsymbol{p}, r)$.*

Proof. 1(a). By Theorem 9.2(a), $\vdash_{\mathsf{IPC}} \forall r\, \psi(\boldsymbol{p}, r) \to \psi(\boldsymbol{p}, r)$. As $\psi(\boldsymbol{p}, r)$ is positive, by Theorem 7.6, $\vdash_{\mathsf{IPC}} (\forall r\, \psi(\boldsymbol{p}, r))^+ \to \psi(\boldsymbol{p}, r)$. The case that $(\forall r\, \psi(\boldsymbol{p}, r))^+ = \bot$ will be treated under 2. In the other cases, we are done.

1(b). By Theorem 9.2(b), $\vdash_{\mathsf{IPC}} \varphi(\boldsymbol{p}, \boldsymbol{q}) \to \forall r\, \psi(\boldsymbol{p}, r)$. As $\varphi(\boldsymbol{p}, \boldsymbol{q})$ is positive, by Theorem 7.6, $\vdash_{\mathsf{IPC}} \varphi(\boldsymbol{p}, \boldsymbol{q}) \to (\forall r\, \psi(\boldsymbol{p}, r))^+$.

2.   If $\vdash_{\mathsf{IPC}} \theta(\boldsymbol{p}, \boldsymbol{q}) \to \psi(\boldsymbol{p}, r)$, then, by 1(b), $\vdash_{\mathsf{IPC}} \theta(\boldsymbol{p}, \boldsymbol{q}) \to (\forall r\, \psi(\boldsymbol{p}, r))^+$. This means that, if $(\forall r\, \psi(\boldsymbol{p}, r))^+ = \bot$, $\theta(\boldsymbol{p}, \boldsymbol{q})$ cannot be positive, since positive formulas are satisfiable. □

Again, the result is not trivial. The pre-interpolant of $((p \to q) \to p) \to p$ in the full logic is $\neg\neg p \to p$. In the positive fragment it is $(\neg\neg p \to p)^+ = p$. Uniform interpolation for MPC immediately follows.

Corollary 1 (Uniform Interpolation Theorem for MPC)

1. *For any formula $\varphi(\boldsymbol{p}, \boldsymbol{q})$ of MPC in which q is not a member of $\boldsymbol{p}$, and $\boldsymbol{p}, q$ may contain f, $\vdash_{\mathsf{MPC}} \varphi(\boldsymbol{p}, \boldsymbol{q}) \to (\exists q\, \varphi(\boldsymbol{p}, \boldsymbol{q}))^+$, and for any positive $\psi(\boldsymbol{p}, \boldsymbol{r})$ where $\boldsymbol{r}$ and $\boldsymbol{p}, q$ are disjoint, if $\vdash_{\mathsf{MPC}} \varphi(\boldsymbol{p}, \boldsymbol{q}) \to \psi(\boldsymbol{p}, \boldsymbol{r})$, then $\vdash_{\mathsf{MPC}} (\exists q\, \varphi(\boldsymbol{p}, \boldsymbol{q}))^+ \to \psi(\boldsymbol{p}, \boldsymbol{r})$.*
2. *For MPC-formula $\psi(\boldsymbol{p}, r)$ in which r is not a member of $\boldsymbol{p}$ one of the following two cases holds:*
   (a) *$(\forall r\varphi(\boldsymbol{p}, r))^+$ is an MPC-formula, $\vdash_{\mathsf{MPC}} (\forall r\, \varphi(\boldsymbol{p}, r))^+ \to \psi(\boldsymbol{p}, r)$, and for any $\varphi(\boldsymbol{p}, \boldsymbol{q})$ where $\boldsymbol{q}$ and $\boldsymbol{p}, r$ are disjoint, if $\vdash_{\mathsf{MPC}} \varphi(\boldsymbol{p}, \boldsymbol{q}) \to \psi(\boldsymbol{p}, r)$, then $\vdash_{\mathsf{MPC}} \varphi(\boldsymbol{p}, \boldsymbol{q}) \to (\forall r\, \psi(\boldsymbol{p}, r))^+$.*
   (b) *For any MPC-formula $\varphi(\boldsymbol{p}, \boldsymbol{q})$ where $\boldsymbol{q}$ and $\boldsymbol{p}, r$ are disjoint, $\nvdash_{\mathsf{MPC}} \varphi(\boldsymbol{p}, \boldsymbol{q}) \to \psi(\boldsymbol{p}, r)$.*

This means that in MPC the uniform post-interpolant exists for any formula, and the uniform pre-interpolant exists for any formula that is implied by at least one formula with the right variables. The result stands if instead of the formulation of the syntax with the additional variable f one chooses to formulate MPC with $\neg$. In itself this is not remarkable, but there is a stark contrast with full IPC, in which as we have seen, uniform interpolants of positive formulas may need $\neg$.

We do not obtain uniform interpolation for the positive fragment of IQC since it does not even hold for IQC itself (see e.g. [20]). But simple interpolation for the positive fragment of IQC immediately follows from the usual proofs of simple interpolation in IQC itself.

5   Relationship with KC and Other Logics

5.1   Propositional Case

We consider intermediate propositional and predicate logics, logics between IPC and classical logic. We assume they are given by axiomatizations plus the rules of substitution and modus ponens. We first show that to derive positive formulas just positive substitutions in the axioms and the +-operation nearly suffice. This is the basic theorem of this section.

Theorem 12. *If L is an intermediate logic, φ is positive and $L \vdash \varphi$, then there are axioms $\alpha_0(p_0, \ldots, p_{n_0}), \ldots, \alpha_k(p_0, \ldots, p_{n_k})$ of L and formulas $\psi_{00}, \ldots, \psi_{0n_0}, \ldots, \psi_{k0}, \ldots, \psi_{kn_k}$, which are positive or $\bot$, such that φ is derivable in IPC, resp. IQC, from $(\alpha_0(\psi_{00}, \ldots, \psi_{0n_0}))^+, \ldots, (\alpha_k(\psi_{k0}, \ldots, \psi_{kn_k}))^+$.*

Proof. If $L \vdash \varphi$, then there are axioms $\alpha_0(p_0, \ldots, p_{n_0}), \ldots, \alpha_k(p_0, \ldots, p_{n_k})$ of L and formulas $\theta_{00}, \ldots, \theta_{0n_0}, \ldots, \theta_{k0}, \ldots, \theta_{kn_k}$ such that φ is derivable in IPC or IQC from $\alpha_0(\theta_{00}, \ldots, \theta_{0n_0}), \ldots, \alpha_k(\theta_{k0}, \ldots, \theta_{kn_k})$. By Theorem 7.7, φ is derivable in IPC or IQC from $(\alpha_0(\theta_{00}, \ldots, \theta_{0n_0}))^+, \ldots, (\alpha_k(\theta_{k0}, \ldots, \theta_{kn_k}))^+$. Then, by Theorem 7.3, φ is derivable in IPC or IQC from $(\alpha_0(\theta_{00}^+, \ldots, \theta_{0n_0}^+))^+, \ldots, (\alpha_k(\theta_{k0}^+, \ldots, \theta_{kn_k}^+))^+$. Now $\psi_{00}, \ldots, \psi_{0n_0}, \ldots, \psi_{k0}, \ldots, \psi_{kn_k}$ can be taken to be $\theta_{00}^+, \ldots, \theta_{0n_0}^+, \ldots, \theta_{k0}^+, \ldots, \theta_{kn_k}^+$. $\quad\square$

The reader should note that in the above proof the formulas $(\alpha_0(\theta_{00}^+, \ldots, \theta_{0n_0}^+))^+, \ldots, (\alpha_k(\theta_{k0}^+, \ldots, \theta_{kn_k}^+))^+$ may not be derivable in L itself. Nevertheless, the theorem turns out to be very useful.

It is well-known that KC is conservative over the positive fragment of IPC (see [2]). This now follows directly.

Theorem 13. *If φ is positive, then $\vdash_{\mathsf{IPC}} \varphi \iff \vdash_{\mathsf{KC}} \varphi$.*

Proof. Let us just prove the non-trivial direction. Assume $\vdash_{\mathsf{KC}} \varphi$ and φ is positive. Then, by Theorem 12, φ is a consequence in IPC of some formulas of the form $(\neg\psi \vee \neg\neg\psi)^+$ with ψ positive or $\bot$. Since $(\neg\psi \vee \neg\neg\psi)^+ \sim \bot \vee \top \sim \top$ or $\sim \top \vee \bot \sim \top$ (depending on whether ψ is positive or $\bot$) , this implies that $\vdash_{\mathsf{IPC}} \varphi$. $\quad\square$

An immediate consequence is:

Corollary 2. *If φ and ψ are positive and $\vdash_{\mathsf{KC}} \varphi \vee \psi$, then $\vdash_{\mathsf{KC}} \varphi$ or $\vdash_{\mathsf{KC}} \psi$.*

By a slightly more complicated argument, using that KC can be axiomatized by $\neg p \vee \neg\neg p$ for all atoms p, uniform interpolation for KC follows.

Theorem 13 can be generalized in three directions. In the first place, Jankov's Theorem [11] states that KC is the strongest intermediate logic with this property. A frame-theoretic proof was given in [3], followed by a simpler approach in [18]. Secondly, there are generalizations to predicate logic, which we will discuss in the next subsection. Finally, as discussed to a certain extent in [3], the corollary can be strengthened by considering the relationship of KC with other intermediate logics. It turns out that for many such logics Theorem 13 generalizes. So, we turn to the question for which intermediate logics L, KC $+L$ is conservative over L with respect to positive formulas. The next example shows that this is not so for all such logics.

Example 1. $BD_2 + KC$ is not conservative over the positive fragment of BD_2, the logic of the frames bounded to depth 2 (see [2])[2].

Proof. The logic BD_2 is often axiomatized by $p \vee (p \rightarrow q \vee \neg q)$, but can be axiomatized positively e.g. by $((p \rightarrow (((q \rightarrow r) \rightarrow q) \rightarrow q)) \rightarrow p) \rightarrow p$. $BD_2 + KC$ contains LC, Dummett's logic. This logic is axiomatized by the positive formula $(p \rightarrow q) \vee (q \rightarrow p)$ (expressing linearity of frames), which is not provable in BD_2.   □

Definition 7. *An intermediate logic L has the $+$-property, if, whenever $\vdash_L \varphi$, also $\vdash_L \varphi^+$.*

Theorem 14. *If L is an intermediate propositional logic axiomatized over IPC that has the $+$-property and φ is positive, then $\vdash_{IPC+L} \varphi$ iff $\vdash_{KC+L} \varphi$.*

Proof. Assume $\vdash_{KC+L} \varphi$ and φ is positive. Then, by Theorem 12, φ is a consequence in IPC from some formulas of the form $(\neg\psi \vee \neg\neg\psi)^+$ and some formulas $\alpha_0^+, \ldots, \alpha_k^+$, where $\alpha_0, \ldots, \alpha_k$ are L-axioms. The formulas $(\neg\psi \vee \neg\neg\psi)^+$ can be treated as in the proof of Theorem 13. The L-axioms are provable in L, and by the $+$-property, so are their $+$-formulas.   □

Theorem 15. *If L is an intermediate propositional logic that is complete with respect to a class of frames that is closed under the operation that turns a frame into its top frame, then L has the $+$-property.*

Proof. Repeat the proof of Theorem 7.1.   □

The last two theorems immediately lead to

Theorem 16. *If L is an intermediate propositional logic that is complete with respect to a class of frames that is closed under the operation that turns a frame into its top frame, then, for positive φ, $\vdash_{IPC+L} \varphi$ iff $\vdash_{KC+L} \varphi$.*

To give a semantic characterization of the $+$-property of logics we need descriptive frames. First we give a lemma.

Lemma 4. *If $\mathfrak{F} = \langle W, R, \mathcal{P} \rangle$ is a descriptive frame, then so is $\mathfrak{F}^+ = \langle W \cup \{t\}, R^+, \mathcal{P}^+ \rangle$, if $\mathcal{P}^+ = \{X \cup \{t\} \mid X \in \mathcal{P}\} \cup \{\emptyset\}$.*

Proof. Straightforward.   □

A semantic characterization of the $+$-operation for intermediate logics can then be given as follows (simultaneously strengthening Theorem 15).

---

[2] A Kripke frame is of depth n if the largest chain contains n nodes.

Theorem 17. *An intermediate logic L has the $+$-property iff, for each descriptive frame $\mathfrak{F}$ of L, $\mathfrak{F}^+$ is a descriptive L-frame as well.*

Proof. $\Leftarrow$: Again like Theorem 7.1.

$\Rightarrow$: Assume $\mathfrak{F}$ is a descriptive L-frame, but $\mathfrak{F}^+$ is not. Then, for some φ, $\vdash_L \varphi$ but there exists a model $\mathfrak{N}$ on $\mathfrak{F}^+$ that falsifies φ. If this is not a top model, then some propositional variables are false in the top node. This means that they are false in the whole model and can be replaced by $\perp$ without influencing the truth value of any relevant formula. So, the formula $\varphi^\perp$ resulting from the substitution of $\perp$ for the propositional variables in question is still falsified. Moreover, $\varphi^\perp$ is provable in L as well.

So, w.l.o.g. we can assume that $\mathfrak{N}$ is a top model $\mathfrak{M}^+$ falsifying φ. Then $\mathfrak{M}^+$ falsifies φ^+ as well, and hence also $\mathfrak{M}$ falsifies φ^+. But that means that $\nvdash_L \varphi^+$, and hence that L does not have the $+$-property. $\qquad\qquad\square$

Unfortunately, the theorem has not yet been of much practical value to determine for which logics L, $\mathsf{IPC}+L$ and $\mathsf{KC}+L$ prove the same positive formulas. But it does enable us to see that the $+$-property is not necessary.

Example 2. The finite Gödel-Dummett logics LC_n with linear orders of length n as their characteristic frames, extend KC, and therefore satisfy $\mathsf{LC}_n \vdash \varphi \Leftrightarrow \mathsf{KC}+\mathsf{LC}_n \vdash \varphi$ for even all formulas. But by Theorem 17, they lack the $+$-property because, clearly, their class of frames is not closed under the $+$-operation.

We could conclude here by applying Theorem 15 that the tree logics T_n of [6] do satisfy the $+$-property, but we prefer to give a more satisfying proof applicable to first-order logic in the next section.

5.2   First Order Case

Let QKC be IQC plus KC. Theorem 13 can be directly, with the same proof, generalized to

Theorem 18. *If φ is positive, then $\vdash_\mathsf{IQC} \varphi$ iff $\vdash_\mathsf{QKC} \varphi$.*

This can further be strengthened by adding DNS (Double Negation Shift), axiomatized by $\forall x \,\neg\neg Ax \to \neg\neg \forall x\, Ax$, to QKC. Just as QKC the logic DNS is always valid on top models, and, in the proof of Theorem 13, applying the $+$-operation in the same way turns this axiom into $\top$ when a positive formula or $\perp$ is substituted for Ax. So, we get

Theorem 19. *If φ is positive, then $\vdash_\mathsf{IQC} \varphi \Longleftrightarrow \vdash_{\mathsf{QKC}+\mathsf{DNS}} \varphi$.*

In predicate logic we have of course the same propositional intermediate logics with positive axioms to strengthen IQC. Let us take a look at the T_n.

Lemma 5. $\mathsf{IQC} + \mathsf{T}_n$ *has the $+$-property.*

Proof. We can apply Theorem 12. It is easy to check that the form of the $\mathsf{T_n}$-axioms, $\bigwedge_{i=0}^{n}((p_i \to \bigvee_{j \neq i} p_j) \to \bigvee_{j \neq i} p_j) \to \bigvee_{i=0}^{n} p_i$, is such that substitution of $\perp$ for an atom in one of these axioms gives a formula provable in IPC itself. $\square$

We can now immediately conclude:

Corollary 3. $\mathsf{QKC + T_n}$ *is conservative over the positive fragment of* $\mathsf{IQC + T_n}$.

Proof. Assisted by the proof of the last lemma we can follow the line of the proof of Theorem 13. $\square$

There is another very important logic with positive axioms, the logic CD, axiomatized by $\forall x(A \vee B(x)) \to A \vee \forall x\, B(x)$ and known to be complete with respect to Kripke models with constant domains (see [7]). Results apply here because, if $\mathfrak{M} \models \mathsf{CD}$, then $\mathfrak{M}^{+} \models \mathsf{CD}$, since the domain of the top point is the union of all the domains of $\mathfrak{M}$, and thus the same domain as the other worlds of $\mathfrak{M}$.

Corollary 4. *Assume* φ *is positive. Then* $\vdash_{\mathsf{IQC+CD}} \varphi \iff \vdash_{\mathsf{QKC+CD+DNS}} \varphi$.

The same results as for $\mathsf{IQC + CD}$ hold for the logic axiomatized by $\forall x, y$ $(Px \to Py)$, the logic for constant domains consisting of a single element. Actually, this is not an intermediate logic of course, it is not contained in classical logic, and more properly called a superintuitionistic logic.

Acknowledgement. We thank Albert Visser, Nick Bezhanishvili, Rosalie Iemhoff, Grisha Mints and Anne Troelstra for informative discussions on the subject. We thank the referees for their corrections and Linde Frölke for her preparatory work.

References

1. Brouwer, L.E.J.: Essentieel negatieve eigenschappen. Indag. Math. **10**, 322–323 (1948)
2. Chagrov, A.V., Zakharyaschev, M.: Modal Logic. Oxford Logic Guides. Clarendon Press, Oxford (1997)
3. de Jongh, D., Yang, F.: Jankov's theorems for intermediate logics in the setting of universal models. In: Bezhanishvili, N., Löbner, S., Schwabe, K., Spada, L. (eds.) TbiLLC 2009. LNCS, vol. 6618, pp. 53–76. Springer, Heidelberg (2011)
4. Diego, A.: Sur les Algèbres de Hilbert, vol. 21. E. Nauwelaerts, Gauthier-Villars, Louvain (1966)
5. Enderton, H.B.: A Mathematical Introduction to Logic. Harcourt/Academic Press, Burlington (2001)
6. Gabbay, D.M., de Jongh, D.H.J.: A sequence of decidable finitely axiomatizable: intermediate logics with the disjunction property. J. Symbolic Logic **39**(1), 67–78 (1974)
7. Gabbay, D.M., Shehtman, V., Skvortsov, D.: Quantification in Nonclassical Logic I. Studies in Logic and the Foundations of Mathematics. Clarendon Press, Oxford (2009)
8. Ghilardi, S., Zawadowski, M.W.: Undefinability of propositional quantifiers in the modal system S4. Stud. Logica. **55**(2), 259–271 (1995)

9. Griss, G.F.C.: Negationless intuitionistic mathematics I. Indag. Math. **8**, 675–681 (1946)
10. Heyting, A.: Die formalen Regeln der intuitionistischen Logik, pp. 42–56 (1930)
11. Jankov, V.A.: Calculus of the weak law of the excluded middle (in russian). Izv. Akad. Nauk SSSR Ser. Mat. **32**(5), 1044–1051 (1968)
12. Johansson, I.: Der Minimalkalkül Ein Reduzierter Intuitionistischer Formalismus. Compos. Math. **4**, 119–136 (1937)
13. Kolmogorov, A.: Zur Deutung der intuitionistischen Logik. Math. Z. **35**(1), 58–65 (1932)
14. Pitts, A.M.: On an interpretation of second order quantification in first order intuitionistic propositional logic. J. Symb. Logic **57**, 33–52 (1992)
15. Renardel de Lavalette, G.R., Hendriks, A., de Jongh, D.: Intuitionistic implication without disjunction. J. Log. Comput. **22**(3), 375–404 (2012)
16. Troelstra, A., van Dalen, D.: Constructivism in Mathematics, vols. 2. North-Holland, Amsterdam (1988)
17. Troelstra, A.S., Schwichtenberg, H.: Basic Proof Theory. Cambridge Tracts in Theoretical Computer Science. Cambridge University Press, Cambridge (2000)
18. Tzimoulis, A., Zhao, Z.: The Universal Model for the Negation-free Fragment of IPC. Technical Notes (X) Series X-2013-01, ILLC, University of Amsterdam (2013)
19. van Dalen, D.: Logic and Structure. Universitext. Springer, London (2012)
20. Visser, A.: Uniform interpolation and layered bisimulation. In: Hájek, P. (ed.) Proceedings of Gödel 1996: Logical Foundations of Mathematics, Computer Science and Physics - Kurt Gödel's Legacy, Brno, Czech Republic. Lecture Notes Logic, vol. 6, pp. 139–164. Springer Verlag, Berlin (1996)
21. Zhao, Z.: An Investigation of Jankov's Logic (2012) (Unpublished paper)

Unless and *Until:* A Compositional Analysis

Gary Mar[1](✉), Yuliya Manyakina[2], and Amanda Caffary[3]

[1] Department of Philosophy, Stony Brook University, Stony Brook, NY, USA
gary.mar@stonybrook.edu
[2] Department of Linguistics, McGill University, Montréal, Canada
yuliya.manyakina@mail.mcgill.ca
[3] Department of Linguistics, Stony Brook University, Stony Brook, NY, USA
amanda.caffary@gmail.com

> *Until and unless you discover that money is the root of all good,*
> *you ask for your own destruction.*
>
> —Ayn Rand, *Atlas Shrugged*

Abstract. The analyses of *unless* and *until* lie at the intersection of logic and linguistics. They crop up in papers about tense connectives [1], quantification [15], anaphora [7], polarity and duality [17,18] and in classical theorems of tense logic [10]. *Unless* and *until* are morphologically similar, and in some contexts, they even appear to be 'interchangeable'. In this paper we give compositional analyses showing the interrelatedness of these two connectives. In addition, we use this case study to draw some broader methodological points. The *locus classicus* on the logic of *unless* is Quine's *Elementary Logic* [20] where he sets forth three methodological dogmas. We dub these Quine's *Three Dogmas of Linguistic Negativism* and argue that these three dogmas not only give a misleading account of the interplay between logic and linguistics but that rejecting them leads to discovering a unified compositional analysis.

Keywords: Unless · Until · Quine's dogmas · Quantifier restriction · Modal tense operators · Punctual and durative until

1 Introduction

The proper analysis of *unless* lies at the intersection of logic and linguistics. It crops up, for example, in papers about tense connectives [1], quantification [15], and anaphora [7].[1] Chandler [1] and von Fintel [4] argue that *unless* should not be treated as a truth-functional connective. Rather, due to the non-equivalence of (1-a) and (1-b), Chandler argues that *unless* should be regarded as a tense connective when it connects sentences describing events that occur at different times:

---

[1] Here and throughout the paper we use colored fonts to make our analyses more perspicuous. Our convention is that occurrences of *unless* and *if* are *blue*, occurrences of quantifiers and later occurrences of *until* and *temporal* particles or operators are *green*, *negative elements* are *red*, and other colors such as *orange* and *purple* highlight other features.

© Springer-Verlag Berlin Heidelberg 2015
M. Aher et al. (Eds.): TbiLLC 2013, LNCS 8984, pp. 190–209, 2015.
DOI: 10.1007/978-3-662-46906-4_12

(1)   a.   Willard will die *unless* he is operated on;
       b.   Willard will be operated on *unless* he dies.

Furthermore, *unless* interacts with anaphoric reference in such constructions as

(2)   Peter doesn't own a donkey, *unless* he is hiding *it* well,

where the pronoun '*it*' appears to refer to a (possibly) non-existent donkey.

Not only do *unless* and *until* appear to be morphologically similar, but, in some contexts, they even appear 'interchangeable':[2,3]

(3)   I will not leave *unless/until* you have a replacement.

To our knowledge, no one has combined *unless* and *until* in a formal compositional analysis, which is a goal of this paper.

Our goal, however, is not simply to give a compositional analysis. We wish to use this case study to draw some broader *methodological* lessons about the intersection of logic and linguistics. The *locus classicus* of the logician's discussion of *unless* is Quine's *Elementary Logic* [20], in which Quine sets forth, or at least implicitly assumes, three methodological principles. We dub these 'Quine's three dogmas of linguistic negativism' alluding to Quine's famous "Two Dogmas of Empiricism"[21].[4] Whether or not our particular, provisional, analysis can withstand all counterexamples, we wish to argue that Quine's methodological dogmas, like Quine's famous attack on the dogmas of logical empiricism,

---

[2] Although they *appear* interchangeable, there are differences. *Unless* supports inferences of uncertainty whereas *until* need not. If I say, "I'll stay *unless* you have a replacement", this often implies that I'm uncertain whether you have a replacement or not. However, if I say, "I won't leave *until* you have a replacement" it might be the case that I know you will have a replacement in the near future and that I'm postponing my leaving until that happens.

[3] Similar linguistic phenomena occur in other languages (e.g., Russian):

(i)   Ja budu žit' na Long Islande **esli** ja **ne/poka**   ja **ne**   najdu kvartiru   v
       I   will   live on Long Island   if   I   NEG/until I   NEG find   apartment in
       gorode
       city
       "I will live on Long Island, *unless/until* I find an apartment in the city."
       (Russian)

The translation for *unless* in Russian is literally *if not*, drawing a suggestive cross-linguistic parallel.

[4] The terminology of 'negativism' is adapted from Hao Wang's [22] characterization of Quine's philosophical views as *logical* negativism. Not only are Quine's theses largely negative—the rejection of analyticity, the indeterminacy of translation, the view that modal logic is 'conceived in sin'—but also they have been negative in their influence. "... [Both] Carnap and Quine have inadequate conceptions of logic and apply logic in philosophy in misleading manners, which do not do justice to logic in its more developed state and, through the conspicuity of their work, give to philosophers the wrong ideas about logic." [22]

have hindered more than helped the development of a more constructive and collaborative view of the interplay between logic and linguistics. It turns out, in fact, that questioning Quine's three dogmas leads to a unified, systematic, and perhaps even elegant compositional analysis of *unless* and *until*.

The structure of our paper is *philosophical*, but the arguments, for the most part, appeal to linguistic intuitions and data. In Sect. 1 we set forth the *question* to be investigated. Next in Sect. 2, we consider *objections* to our position—objections are not set forth as *opinions* or alternative *positions*, but as *arguments*. In Sect. 3, we present our proposal analyzing *unless* in terms of *if not*, where the negation expresses exceptional circumstances introduced by the relevant situations introduced by *if*. In Sect. 4, we formally characterize our proposal to extend this analysis of *unless* to *until* using temporal modal operators and temporal particles. In Sect. 5 we compare and contrast our proposal with other influential accounts, and then in Sect. 6 we summarize our conclusions and views about the relation between logic and linguistics.

2   Three Objections

Any compositional analysis of *unless* as *if not* (which is tautologically equivalent to the logician's inclusive *or*) or as *if and only if not* (which is tautologically equivalent to the logician's exclusive *or*) faces at least three objections.[5]

2.1   Objection 1: An Analysis of *Unless* as *If Not* is Logically Redundant

Quine [20] has already argued that *unless* is correctly paraphrased by the logician's *or*, and the logician's *or* is tautologically equivalent to *if not*. Therefore, so the objection goes, our analysis of *unless* as equivalent to *if not* is logically redundant. For Quine the following are all intuitively equivalent:

(4)   a.   Smith will sell *unless* he hears from you;
         b.   *Either* Smith hears from you *or* he will sell;
         c.   *If* Smith does *not* hear from you, he will sell.

Quine notes that *unless* appears to share the ambiguity of the inclusive and exclusive senses of *or*, and he counts this as evidence for the correctness of his analysis. In Quine's example above, *or* is inclusive: it could be the case that Smith hears from you, but still sells to the highest bidder because your offer is not enough. Quine's recommendation is, that "it will be convenient to dodge the existing ambiguity of usage by agreeing in general to understand *unless* in the inclusive sense." [20]

---

[5] We are grateful for a reviewer for calling our attention to the myth of *vel* and *aut* at http://plato.stanford.edu/entries/disjunction/#MytVelAut. Commutativity holds for the logician's *or* in either the inclusive or exclusive senses.

2.2   Objection 2: An Analysis of *Unless* as *If Not* Fails to Explain Negative Polarity and Negative Affixation

Negative Polarity Items (NPIs) are lexical items that appear in negative contexts. An environment with *if not* licenses NPIs, such as *any*, but an environment with *unless* does not.

(5)   a.   *If* you do*n't* do *anything*, you'll never get anywhere;

      b.   * *Unless* you do *anything*, you'll never get anywhere.[6]

    Thus, an analysis of *unless* as *if not* fails to explain why morphologically incorporated negative prefixes (negative affixation), such as *un-*, do not license NPIs.

2.3   Objection 3: Analyzing *Until* in terms of *Unless* Fails to Distinguish Processes and Propositions

Any analysis which proposes building a compositional analysis of *until* from *unless* using temporal particles and parameters cannot possibly succeed because *unless* connects sentences that express propositions or states of affairs whereas until connects descriptions of processes, activities or states.

    Consider the following:

(6)   a.   The baby did*n't* sleep *until* 2 a.m.;

      b.   *The baby did*n't* sleep *unless* (it is) 2 a.m.;

      c.   ?*If* (it is) *not* 2 a.m., then the baby did*n't* sleep.

Quine famously objected to modal logic as "conceived in sin", the sin of confusing *use* and *mention*: how can *implies*, which connects names of statements, be analyzed in terms of *if... then...* which connects *statements*. In a similar fashion, one might object that since *unless* connects propositions but *until* connects descriptions of *processes, events* or *states*, the latter cannot be analyzed in terms of the former. Löbner [16] puts this point succinctly: events do not possess a negation as a contrary—"a storm is an event, but there are no non-storms."

    These three objections appear to question the *need* for a compositional alternative to Quine's analysis of *unless* and to provide a conclusive case against the very *possibility* of analyzing *until* in terms of *unless*.

3   Our Proposal

Despite these seemingly powerful objections, we shall argue that

1. *unless*, while not simply *replaceable* by *if not*, is better analyzed *compositionally* in terms of the logical contributions of *if* and *not*, rather than by the logician's *or*;[7]

---

[6] In this paper we use the following linguistic conventions: * = ungrammatical, ? = questionable/degraded, # = infelicitous.

[7] Section 3.7 expands on the notion that *unless* is not simply *replaceable* by *if not*.

2. the NPI and Negative Affixation objections strengthen, rather than weaken, our argument;
3. there is an elegant compositional analysis of *until* in terms of *unless* using *temporal frame semantics* with *tense operators* and temporal particles.

3.1 Quine's Three Dogmas of Linguistic Negativism

Consider again the *locus classicus* of the logician's analysis of *unless*, Quine's *Elementary Logic* [20], which we quote in three sections:

> 'Unless' thus seems to answer to 'or'; and it seems even to share the ambiguity of 'or', as between the inclusive and the exclusive sense. In either sense, 'unless' can be eliminated in favor of conjunction and denial; for we have seen (Sect. 5) how to eliminate 'or' in either of its senses. But in practicing with examples it will be convenient, as in the case of 'or' (cf. Sect. 5), to dodge the existing ambiguity of usage by agreeing in general to understand 'unless' in the inclusive sense.
>
> Between 'unless' and 'or' there is doubtless a rhetorical difference, such as was observed between 'but' and 'and'. Perhaps we tend to prefer 'unless' to 'or' when we feel that the first of the two component statements deserves more emphasis than the second, or that the first component is more likely to be true than the second.
>
> [One should ignore] a minor grammatical difference between 'unless' and 'or' as applied to futures...In logical analysis...it is simplest to sweep away any special problems of tense by pretending that differences of time are recorded solely through explicit mention of epochs. [20]

In these passages, Quine lays down methodological *dicta*, which we shall call Quine's *Three Dogmas of Linguistic Negativism*. Quine's First Dogma is a plea for preferential treatment: he recommends that we "dodge the existing ambiguity of usage by agreeing in general to understand 'unless' in the inclusive sense." Quine's Second Dogma is to relegate differences with respect to topic to rhetoric: he claims that differences between 'unless' and 'or' can attributed to "a rhetorical difference, such as was observed between 'but' and 'and'." Finally, Quine's Third Dogma recommends we adopt the pretense of tenselessness: he recommends that we ignore "a minor grammatical difference between 'unless' and 'or' as applied to futures...". "In logical analysis," Quine proclaims, "it is simplest to sweep away any special problems of tense by pretending that differences of time are recorded solely through explicit mention of epochs." We wish to show that rejecting each of Quine's dogmas can lead to the discovery of a more accurate, and systematically unified, analysis of *unless* and *until*.

Quine's analysis of *unless* seems to be based on an *assumption* that comes naturally to logicians, but which is anathema to linguists—namely, the assumption that simple chains of natural equivalences of propositional logic preserve linguistic meaning.[8] Quine's argument appears to be something like the following. Suppose you are deciding whether to make an offer on Smith's house, and the broker tells you,

(7)   Smith will sell *unless* he hears from you.

Now the above statement in (7) can be paraphrased by

(8)   *If* Smith does *not* hear from you, he will sell.

But the latter is *tautologically equivalent*, by *contraposition* (CP) to

(9)   *If* Smith wo*n't* sell, then Smith did hear from you,

which, in turn, is *tautologically equivalent* by *conditional/disjunction* (CDJ) to:

(10)   Smith will sell *or* he hears from you.

Therefore, Quine concludes, *unless* is equivalent to the logician's *or*. We shall dub this argument 'Quine's Quagmire' not only because of the dubious assumptions upon which it is based but also because these assumptions commit Quine to a quagmire of deviant (#) and questionable (?) paraphrases. The first tautological equivalence preserves linguistic meaning:

(11)   a.   *Unless* Smith hears from you, he will sell;
       b.   = *If* Smith does *not* hear from you, he will sell;

but the following do not:

(12)   a.   ?*Either* Smith will sell *or* he hears from you;
       b.   #*If* Smith will *not* sell, then Smith hears from you;
       c.   ?Smith will sell *or* he hears from you;
       d.   *Smith hears from you *unless* he will sell.[9,10]

Questioning the validity of Quine's Quagmire blocks a *false prediction* of Quine's analysis, namely, the commutativity of *unless*:

(13)   a.   I wont leave *unless* you have a replacement;
       b.   ≠ ?You have a replacement *unless* I won't leave.

Our analysis will explain when and why *unless* statements fail to commute.

---

[8] This restriction to "simple chains of natural equivalences" is to avoid unwanted implications, for instance, that "all tautologies say that same thing."

[9] Quine's dogmas also commit him to the dubious claim that 'P *unless* Q' is equivalent to '*not*-P *only if* Q', which yields the (even more) deviant paraphrase: #Smith does *not* hear from you *only if* he will sell.

[10] Here and subsequently the natural deduction system and theorems refer to Kalish, Montague and Mar [9]. The practice of placing two spaces at the end of displayed sentences before including punctuation marks, which integrate the displays into the text follows, is the convention of Kalish and Montague.

3.2   Argument 1: Non-Commutativity

Our first argument against Quine's analysis—and our reply to the redundancy objection—is simple: the logician's inclusive *or* and exclusive *or* are both commutative but *unless* is typically non-commutative.

This reply dodges Quine's dogma of preferential treatment. Quine's prescription to prefer the inclusive *or* over the exclusive *or* as a paraphrase of *unless* is moot: neither alternative explains why *unless* is non-commutative.

(14)   a.   Smith will sell *unless* he hears from you;
        b.   ≠ *Smith hears from you *unless* he will sell;

(15)   a.   Mary will arrive at 10:30 a.m. *unless* the plane is late;
        b.   ≠ ?The plane is late *unless* Mary will arrive at 10:30 a.m..

An analysis due to Geis gives a persuasive explanation of when and why *contraposition* fails [5]. Consider the following intuitively equivalent paraphrases:

(16)   a.   I wo*n't* leave *unless* you have someone to take my place;
        b.   = *If* you do*n't* have someone to take my place, I wo*n't* leave;
        c.   = I will leave *only if* you have someone to take my place.

According to Quine's dictum, *if* is a sign of the antecedent whereas *only if* is a sign of the consequent. If Quine's dictum is valid, then the third paraphrase should be equivalent to:

(17)   ?*If* I *will* leave, *then* you have someone to take my place.

Contrary to Quine's dictum, the correct analysis of *only if* is compositional: *if* introduces the antecedent, whereas *only* is a sign of negation distributed over the antecedent and consequent. This analysis yields, not Quine's questionable paraphrase in (17), but its *contrapositive* in (16-b).

The correct paraphrases in (16-b) and (16-c) of (16-a) state that a *necessary* condition for my leaving is that you have a suitable replacement. The questionable paraphrase in (17) incorrectly suggests either that my leaving is a *sufficient* condition for your having a replacement or that my leaving makes it necessary that there's someone to take my place.

According to analyses of *if* as a quantification, or domain, restrictor (cf. [4,5,13,14]), the *if* clause in English sentences quantifies over an implicit restricted range of contextually relevant cases. Whereas the logician's truth-functional conditional is restricted to actual cases, conditional clauses in English restrict quantifiers to range over a set of relevant set of possibilities: *if* in English means something like "in (all relevant) cases in which". Quantificational restriction explains why the logician's rule of contraposition fails to preserve equivalence in English.

The *topic*, or range of relevant circumstances introduced by *if*, in the conditional in (16-b) is different from the topic of its contrapositive (17): the former conditional is about *my giving you the time to find a suitable replacement*, whereas the latter contrapositive is about *your having someone waiting to take my job if I leave.* What is essential for our proposal is that our compositional analysis of *unless* as *if not* gives a domain restricting role to if which is lacking in the case of *or.* Our analysis casts doubt on Quine's second dogma: the shift in topic is not merely *rhetorical* but *logical,* affecting the validity of such logical transformations as CP and CDJ.

The suggestive occurrence of *less* in *unless* provides further evidence for our compositional analysis. The OED entry for *unless* states that *unless* derives from a contraction of *under lesser cases,* or according to other etymologies *on a less condition (than).* So the *un-* in *unless* comes from the preposition *on,* rather than an explicitly negative prefix. On the other hand, *on a lesser or lower condition* contains the lingering presence of a negative.[11] This intriguing historical fact about (a *diachronic* version of) English supports our attempt to understand the semantics of *unless* by deriving it from *if not.* Our emphasis on a shift in *topic* picked out by restrictive role of *if* is historically embedded in the distinction between a *lesser* condition and the *greater* or main condition. This domain restricting role for *if* is required not only to capture the distinction between necessary and sufficient conditions but also to explain why and when CP and CDJ fail to preserve linguistic equivalence in English.[12]

Quine's third dogma, the pretense of tenselessness, continues to generate questionable paraphrases:

(18)   a.   *Unless* Smith hears from you, he will sell;
         b.   *Smith hears from you *unless* he will sell;
         c.   ?*If* Smith will *not* sell, then Smith hears from you.

From an intuitive causal/temporal point of view, the tenses in (18-b) and (18-c) are backward: they appear to assert that your failing to call Smith *now* or in the *near future* is either a necessary condition or a causal consequence of Smith's failing to sell in the *future.* This violates our intuitive conception of time: an event in the future cannot cause what is happening now. Now, Quine admits that it is more natural to alter the verb tenses in the second questionable paraphrase as follows:

(19)   *If* Smith did*n't* sell, then he *(must have) heard* from you.

Here we have changed the tense of the *antecedent* from the *future* to the *past* and the tense of the *consequent* from the *present* to the *past* or *past perfect* tense.

Rather than subscribing to Quine's third dogma of "sweep[ing] away any special problems of tense," our analysis will focus on how *tense* and *temporal*

---

[11] It turns out that this observation of ours was made independently and, more insightfully, by von Fintel [4].

[12] Within the realm of mathematics the relevant cases are intuitively 'universal' and 'timeless', and so the logician's classical transformations preserve equivalence of all of the following: (i) *If* a natural number is evenly divisible by 2, *then* it is even; (ii) *If* a natural number is *not* even, *then* it is *not* evenly divisible by 2; (iii) *Unless* a natural number is even, it is *not* evenly divisible by 2; (iv) A natural number is evenly divisible by 2 *only if* it is even.

particles interact with other elements of meaning to arrive at a compositional account of *until* from our compositional account of *unless*.

To summarize, Quine's Quagmire depends on the fallacious assumption that the logician's equivalences always preserve linguistic meaning. This natural, but false, assumption leads Quine to dismiss, through his dogmas, other elements of linguistic meaning that may affect the validity of these transformations. In contrast, by adopting Geis's analysis of *if* as specifying *the relevant cases in which* the consequent condition holds, we can explain why 'P *unless* Q' is not accurately paraphrased by 'P *or* Q'. Quine's paraphrase loses the non-commutativity of *unless* imposed by *if*. Our analysis of *unless* as *if not*, in contrast, can explain the non-commutativity of *unless* in terms of the failure of contraposition. The antecedent condition introduced by if ranges over, or restricts, the relevant cases or *lesser conditions* under which the condition expressed in the consequent (the *topic* of the conditional) may or may not obtain.

Combining our analysis of *unless* as *if not* together with Geis's explanation of the failure of contraposition therefore gives an explanation for when and why commutativity, which holds for the logician's *or* in either the inclusive or exclusive senses, often fails for *unless*.[13]

3.3   Argument 2: Failed Predictions About Factoring

Quine's analysis of *unless* as the logicians '∨' gives false predictions about factoring. In particular, it predicts that the sentence in (20) is equivalent to (21):

(20)   I will go to the party, *unless* John does *or* Mary does*n't*,

(21)   (G ∨ J ∨ ∼M)

The latter (21) may be translated as

(22)   I go to the party, *or* John goes to the party, *or* Mary does*n't* go to the party,

---

[13] Our analysis may even be useful to explain some occurrences of a non-commuting *or*. Consider the famous declaration by the American patriot Patrick Henry: "Give me liberty *or* give me death" (we are indebted to Gillon [7] for this example). Whether or not this declaration was intended as inclusive or exclusive (perhaps Henry invites the liberty of death if he can't have the liberty in life), Henry's defiant disjunction is not intuitively equivalent to: "Give me death *or* give me liberty". Our analysis suggests that non-commuting occurrences of *or* can be paraphrased by a fronted *unless*:

i.   *Unless* you give me liberty, give me death;
ii.   *If* you do*n't* give me liberty, then give me death.

Then the exceptional cases of the non-commutativity of *or* can be explained by the non-commutativity of the fronted *unless* which, in turn, is explained by the failure of contraposition: the cases in which Patrick Henry is *not granted his liberty* are different from the cases in which *he is not given death*.

which is clearly not equivalent to the original sentence. Instead, the original sentence is equivalent to:

(23)   I will go to the party *unless* John goes, *and* I will go to the party *unless* Mary does*n't*.

Our paraphrase in (23) can be symbolized and translated, respectively, by:

(24) $(\sim J \rightarrow G) \wedge (M \rightarrow G)$

(25)   I will go to the party *if* John does*n't* go, *and* I will go to the party *if* Mary does go.

Our analysis, in fact, allows us to demonstrate that (26-a)-(26-c) are equivalent, using the theorem in (27):

(26)   a.   I will go to the party, *unless* John does *or* Mary does*n't*;
      b.   I will go the party *if* John does*n't*, *and* I will go to the party *if* Mary does go;
      c.   *Unless* John goes to the party, I will go, *and unless* Mary does*n't* go, I will go.

(27)   T50 $[(P \rightarrow R) \wedge (Q \rightarrow R)] \leftrightarrow [P \vee Q \rightarrow R]$

3.4   Argument 3: NPI Phenomena

Our compositional analysis of *unless* as *if not* is strengthened, rather than weakened, by NPI phenomena. To remind the reader, NPIs are lexical items that appear in negative contexts. The issue with treating *unless* as equivalent to *if not* is that to *if not* licenses NPIs, such as *any*, but to *unless* does not.

A systematic account of how *unless* interacts with NPIs can explained using the Quantifier Confinement Laws (QC) for the antecedent of a conditional together with linguistic rules governing the scope of *any* and *all* when interacting with other operators such as negation. This strengthens our analysis by using, compositionally, the QC laws governing *if* in the analysis of *unless* as *if not*.

Here the behavior of *any* with respect to *unless* is similar to the behavior with *any* in the antecedent of a conditional. *Any*, unlike *all*, takes wide scope when interacting with *not*, and the apparent interchangeability of *any* and *some* in the presence of negation in the context of the antecedent of a conditional is also explained by the QC Laws:

(28)   T221 $\forall x (Fx \rightarrow P) \leftrightarrow (\exists x Fx \rightarrow P)$

(29)   T222 $\exists x (Fx \rightarrow P) \leftrightarrow (\forall x Fx \rightarrow P)$

The attachment behavior of *-not* is compositionally promiscuous in the following paraphrases. Note in particular the difference between (30-b) and (30-c):

(30)   a.   *Unless* you're with us, you're against us;
      b.   = *If-not* (you're with us), then you're against us;

    c.   = *If not*-(you're with us), then you're against us;
    d.   = *If* (you're *not* with us), then you're against us.

The Positive Polarity Item (PPI) *all* promotes promiscuity:[14]

(31)   a.   *Unless* you're with us on *all* of the issues, you're against us;
        b.   = *If-not* (you're with us on *all* of the issues), you're against us;
        c.   = *If not*-(you're with us on *all* of the issues), you're against us;
        d.   = *If* (you're *not* with us on *some* issue), you're against us.

However, this promiscuity is confined in the presence of NPIs, such as *any*:

(32)   a.   ? *Unless* you're with us on *any* of the issues, you're against us;
        b.   ≠ *If-not* (you're with us on *any* of the issues), you're against us;
        c.   = *If not*-(you're with us on *some* of the issues), you're against us;
        d.   = *Unless* you're with us on *some* of the issues, you're against us.

Here the non-equivalence of the two displayed sentences arises from the fact that *any* is typically represented by a universal quantifier with *wide* scope. In the first sentence, *unless* blocks the wide scope reading of *any*, thus creating an ungrammatical reading with *any* in an NPI context. The second sentence allows for the wide scope reading, making *any* interchangeable with *some*.

3.5   Argument 4: Negative Affixation and Contrariness

Our analysis is not negatively affected by Negative Affixation phenomena. To remind the reader, the problem is that morphologically incorporated negative prefixes, such as *un-*, do not license NPIs.

    The problem with negative affixation does not arise because *unless* is analyzed in terms of *if not*. Rather, the problem arises because *unhappy* (a contrary state of happiness) does not mean the same as *not happy* (the contradictory of the state of affairs of being happy).

(33)   a.   ?Assad is *unhappy* with *any* of Obama's demands *unless* they had Putin's prior approval
        b.   Assad is *not happy* with *any* of Obama's demands *unless* they had Putin's prior approval
        c.   = *If* they did *not* have Putin's prior approval, Assad is *not happy* with *any* of Obama's demands.

Affixing negation to the predicate to create *unhappy* eliminates a reading in which negation has wider scope. This occurs in the following:

(34)   a.   Assad is *not happier* than Putin with *any* of Obama's demands;
        b.   *Assad is *unhappier* than Putin with *any* of Obama's demands.

---

[14] PPIs, in contrast to NPIs, appear in affirmative or positive contexts; they do not require negation in order to be licensed.

Note that all of the following combinations are possible:

(35)   Assad is (*unhappy/not happy*) with (*all, some, most, a few*) of Obama's
         demands.

3.6   Argument 5: Successful Factoring with *Until* and *Unless*

Unless can sometimes be replaced by, or factored with, *until*, indicating that
our compositional analysis is not precluded by distinguishing the categories of
propositions and processes, states of affairs and states.

Quine's charge is that modal logic was "conceived in sin" because it confused
use and *mention*: *entails* connects *names* of propositions, whereas the material conditional connects *propositions* themselves [21]. Fear of violating Quinean
dicta hampered logical research into modal logics for nearly a decade. When logicians were able to cast off the chains of Quine's dogmatism, analyses combining
modal operators and propositional connectives were not only possible, but also
plausible, and hence more unified theoretically. Similarly, the charge that *unless*
and *until* must connect totally disjoint categories of linguistic entities prevents
us from seeing that they can factor the very same sentences.[15]

(36)   *Until* and *unless* you realize that money is the root of all good, you ask
         for your own destruction.

(37)   *Unless* and *until* you have someone to take my place I won't leave.

To summarize our arguments, we have shown that Quine's analysis of *unless* as
the logician's inclusive *or* does not render our analysis redundant since ours,
unlike Quine's, can explain why and when *unless* fails to commute. Moreover,
Quine's analysis yields false predictions about factoring. NPIs strengthen our
analysis insofar as an explanation of duality of QC laws in the antecedent of a
conditional can be invoked to explain the linguistic differences between *any* and
all and the apparent equivalence of *any* and *some*. Negative affixation problems,
explained by the difference between negation as a predicate forming operator
and a propositional operator, do not pose any special problems for our analysis.
Finally, the parallel use of *unless* and *until* in factoring holds out the possibility
of a compositional analysis, to which we turn in Sect. 4.

3.7   A Note on "Replaceability"

It should be noted that our proposal is not that *unless* can be simply replaced
by *if not*. The examples due to Geis [5] clearly show that this cannot be done.

---

[15] Important differences remain. Löbner [16] notes that propositions connected by
unless are typically complete or perfective states of affairs, whereas *until* typically
connects *incomplete* or *imperfective* processes or phases of states of affairs. Furthermore, he notes that the complement clause that accompanies *unless*, unlike that of
until, typically has a negative polarity [16]. These observations, in our view, should
not deter, but be invitations for deeper, compositional analyses.

(38)   a.   I would prefer it *if* you did*n't* call me immediately.

      b.   *I would prefer it *unless* you call me immediately.

Our analysis, while differing it its details from Geis's, uses his semantic strategies of treating *if* as a restrictor and *not* as an exceptive [5].

Geis argues that there is a difference between *unless* by *if not* when conjoined as exceptive clauses, in cases of anaphoric reference with phrases such as *in such cases*, and when combined with counterfactuals [5].

(39)   a.   I won't leave *unless* you have a replacement *and unless* you ask me to stay.

      b.   I won't leave *if* you do*n't* have a replacement *and if* you do*n't* ask me to stay.

Geis marks (39-a) ungrammatical, but we disagree. Geis claims that *unless* in (39-a) implies the *uniqueness* of the exceptional circumstances introduced by the *unless* clause. However, this explanation cannot be correct. Suppose my demands for not leaving include both that you get a *replacement* for my menial job and ask me to stay in a lucrative way (i.e., by giving me a raise). Moreover, in certain cases there seems nothing grammatically wrong, or deviant, with the following conjoined and disjoined *unless* clauses, calling into question Geis's attribution of ungrammaticality to (39-a).[16]

Thus far, we have refuted various arguments *against* the possibility of analyzing *unless* in terms of *if* and *not*. We have illustrated how we intend to analyze *unless* in terms of *if not*, where the negation expresses exceptional circumstances introduced by the relevant situations introduced by *if*. Our proposal is not that *unless* can simply be replaced by *if not*. Rather, we have shown that analyzing *unless* in compositional terms of *if* and *not* can explain much of the previously anomalous semantic behaviors of *unless*.[17]

The third objection was that any proposal to build a compositional analysis of *until* from *unless* is doomed to fail. We face this challenge in the next section.

---

[16] There is nothing grammatically wrong with the following conjoined and disjoined *unless* clauses: (i) Rosemary can't sleep *unless* she has her pillow *and unless* it is quiet; (ii) Rosemary can't sleep *unless* she has her pillow *or unless* it is quiet; (iii) Rosemary can't sleep *if* she does*n't* have her pillow *and* (*if*) it is*n't* completely quiet; (iv) Rosemary can't sleep *if* she does*n't* have her pillow *or* (*if*) it is*n't* completely quiet.

    Note the optionality of *if* in the second clause in examples (iii) and (iv). Here, the equivalences among (i) and (iii) and (ii) and (iv) can be explained by our analysis and the following pair of propositional theorems: T50 $(P \rightarrow Q) \wedge (P \rightarrow R) \leftrightarrow (P \vee Q \rightarrow R)$; T60 $(P \rightarrow Q) \vee (P \rightarrow R) \leftrightarrow (P \wedge Q \rightarrow R)$.

[17] Here we rely on the work of others (cf. Geis [5], von Fintel [4], Kratzer [13,14]) who have substantial proposals on how to to treat *if* as a quantifier domain restrictor and *if-not* as a specifying exceptions to those restrictions.

4   A Compositional Analysis of *Until*

Consider the proverbial saying:

(40)   The game's not over *until* the fat lady sings.

The meaning of this saying is that one should not presume to know the outcome of an event until that event is over. The saying can be paraphrased as:

(41)   a.   *Unless* the fat lady *has already* sung, the game's *not yet* over;
        b.   *If* the fat lady has*n't* sung *yet*, then the game's *still not* over.

The temporal particle *already* relates the present time to the time in the past whereas *yet* relates the present time to the time in the future at which the event referred to in the proposition the *fat lady sings* is completed.

A variation of Quine's original example also admits of a paraphrase relating *unless* and *until.*

(42)   Smith didn't sell the house *until* last Thursday.

Suppose there is question whether you called Smith in time to place a qualifying bid on the house. The *time in question* is then the time at which you called Smith. Then from the above statement, we could legitimately infer that:

(43)   a.   *Unless* the time in question was already *last* Thursday, Smith had*n't* yet sold the house;
        b.   *If* the time in question was*n't yet* last Thursday, then Smith had*n't* sold the house *yet*
        c.   *If* the time in question was*n't* Thursday *yet*, then Smith *still* had*n't* sold the house.

Using these ideas, we can now motivate our compositional analysis of *until* in terms of *unless.*

Temporal language exhibits a logical structure that is modal. A *minimal tense logic* can be obtained from the Kripke frame semantics for the normal modal logic **K** by adding temporal operators and tense axioms.

First, we introduce a pair of temporal operators with respect to the future and a pair with respect to the past.

(44)   a.   □ It *will always* [i.e., in *all* futures] be the case that
        b.   ◊ It *will* [i.e., in *some* future] be the case that
        c.   ■ It *has always been* [i.e., in *all* pasts] the case that
        d.   ♦ It *was once* [i.e., in *some* past] the case that

Only one member of each pair is required since the standard laws of duality or laws of modal negation hold for these modal operators:

(45) $\sim \blacklozenge \varphi \Leftrightarrow \blacksquare \sim \varphi$

(46) $\square \sim \varphi \Leftrightarrow \sim \lozenge \varphi$

For purposes of translating and symbolizing it will be useful to have all four operators.

Secondly, we may state the semantics for the temporal operators. A model $\mathbf{M}$ for *tense logic* consists of $(\mathbf{T}, <, \alpha)$, where $\mathbf{T}$ is a set of times, $<$ is an ordering relation over times (where '$<$' is read "*is earlier than*", and its converse '$>$' is read "*is later than*"), and α is the actual present. Then the standard clauses for the operators come in two valences—future and past:

(47)   a. $M, \alpha \models \Box \varphi \Leftrightarrow \forall t \in T \ (\alpha < t \Rightarrow M, t \models \varphi)$
       b. $M, \alpha \models \Diamond \varphi \Leftrightarrow \exists t \in T \ (\alpha < t \ \& \ M, t \models \varphi)$

(48)   a. $M, \alpha \models \blacksquare \varphi \Leftrightarrow \forall t \in T \ (\alpha > t \Rightarrow M, t \models \varphi)$
       b. $M, \alpha \models \blacklozenge \varphi \Leftrightarrow \exists t \in T \ (\alpha > t \ \& \ M, t \models \varphi)$

One valence is simply the *converse* of the other with respect to the ordering relation '$<$'.

Finally, we obtain tense logic by adding two axioms interrelating the past and future valences of the temporal operators. The axioms for minimal tense logic have the form of the famous Brouwersche axiom of modal logic with alternating valences:

(49)   a. $(B\Box \blacklozenge) \ \varphi \to \Box \blacklozenge \varphi$
       b. $(B\blacksquare \Diamond) \ \varphi \to \blacksquare \Diamond \varphi$

Using this modal apparatus of tense logic, let's consider again a previous example:

(50)   I won't leave *until* you have a replacement.

We have the following intuitively equivalent paraphrases:

(51)   a.   I wo*n't* leave *until* you have a replacement;
       b.   = I will *not* leave *until* you have a replacement;
       c.   = *If-it is not the case that* you have a replacement *yet, then* I *will not* leave *yet*;

Now what does it mean to say that *your having a replacement* is *not-yet*? It means that *your having a replacement* is *not (yet) true* in *some past*. What does it mean to say that *I will not leave*? It means that *my not leaving* is *true* in *all futures*. We can symbolize the above using the temporal operators and a natural scheme of abbreviation:

(52)   a.   *If it is not the case that it was the case that* R, *then it will always be the case that not* L
       b. $(\sim \blacklozenge R \to \Box \sim L)$
       c. $\Box \sim L$ *unless* $\blacklozenge R$

We may summarize our compositional analysis as follows:

(53) $\sim \Diamond L$ *until* R $:= \Box \sim L$ *unless* $\blacklozenge R$

Using Kripke modal frame semantics for tense logic, we may summarize our compositional analysis of *until* in terms of *unless* as follows:

(54)　a.　$\sim$Q *until* P　$\Leftrightarrow \Box \sim$Q *unless* $\blacklozenge$P

　　　b.　　　　　　　$\Leftrightarrow$ *if-not* $\blacklozenge$P *then* $\Box \sim$Q

　　　c.　　　　　　　$\Leftrightarrow$ M, $\alpha \models (\sim\blacklozenge$P $\rightarrow \Box\sim$Q$)$

This last equivalence can be paraphrased by: '$\sim$Q *until* P' is the case if, and only if, at the *actual present* α, *in every future* (with respect to α) $\sim$Q holds *unless* P held at *some past.*

5　Comparison with Other Accounts

5.1　Kamp (1968)

Our compositional analysis of *until* is different from the analysis in Kamp's Theorem, which states that on continuous linear orders, every first-order statement with one free variable is definable in terms of *until* and *since* [10]. According to Kamp's analysis, the semantic clause for *until* is an existential generalization over a conjunction:

(55)　M, $\alpha \models$ P *until* Q　$:=$

　　　$\exists t \in$ T $[\alpha < t$ & M, $t \models$ P & $\forall x \in$ T $(\alpha < x < t \Rightarrow$ M, $x \models$ Q$)]$

To see more clearly the critical difference between Kamp's analysis and ours, let's call the sentence Q following connective *until* the *concedent* (a cross between *concluding* and *antecedent* conditions). Then Kamp's analysis requires that the *concedent* will at some time in the future be realized whereas our analysis does not. Ordinary language does not require Kamp's implication.

Recall Adlai Stevenson's famous rhetorical reply during the 1962 Cuban missile crisis. The Russian representative was refusing to answer a question about whether the Soviets were installing missiles in Cuba, and Stevenson responded:

(56)　"I am prepared to wait for my answer *until* Hell freezes over."

According to Kamp's analysis, the above statement implies that there is a time in the future when Hell does, in fact, freeze over. Stevenson's statement has no such implication. On the contrary, assuming that Hell never freezes over, our analysis gives the correct conversational implication, according to which Stevenson is stating he is prepared to wait forever or as long as it takes.

5.2　Karttunen (1974)

Karttunen's analysis of *until* is built upon a distinction between *punctual* and *durative until* (distinguished notationally by UNTIL^P and UNTIL^D) [11]. UNTIL^P connects event descriptions of accomplishments or achievements (e.g., falling asleep, waking up, or breaking an enchantment) located at a point in time, whereas *durative* UNTIL^D connects event descriptions of states or activities (e.g., sleeping, waking from sleep, or living happily ever after) that endure over a time interval. A key linguistic difference is that UNTIL^P is *polarity sensitive* whereas UNTIL^D is not [11].

Consider the following:

(57)   a.   Sleeping Beauty did *not* wake up *until* Prince Charming kissed her.
       b.   Sleeping Beauty slept *until* Prince Charming kissed her.

Sentence (57-a) connects the *punctual* commencement of *Sleeping Beauty's waking up* after a point in time at which *Prince Charming kissed her*, whereas sentence (57-b) states that the *durative* state of *Sleeping Beauty's being asleep* occurred during the interval of time before *she was kissed by Prince Charming*.

According to Karttunen's analysis, '$\sim$ Q UNTIL^P t', has the logical form of '$\sim$ (Q BEFORE t)' [11]. Karttunen claims that UNTIL^P creates a negative polarity context for Q and triggers the presupposition that the event Q occurs at some time related to the point in time t expressed in UNTIL^P clause. This presupposition that the event Q actually occurs cannot be cancelled in the way conversational implicatures typically can. Karttunen claims that former does in fact semantically imply that Sleeping Beauty woke up *after* Prince Charming kissed her. The corresponding implication for *durative* UNTIL^D does not hold. This implicature is merely *conversational* because it can be cancelled:

(58)   Sleeping Beauty slept *until* Prince Charming kissed her; *in fact, she slept for another hundred years.*

A salient linguistic difference between UNTIL^P and UNTIL^D is that the former appears to be acceptable only in the context of *negation*, whereas the latter is acceptable in both positive and negative contexts.

(59)   a.   *Sleeping Beauty woke up *until* Prince Charming kissed her.
       b.   Sleeping Beauty did *not* sleep *until* Prince Charming kissed her.

Notice that (59-b) is ambiguous between Sleeping Beauty's *not falling asleep until* Prince Charming kissed her and Sleeping Beauty's *not being in a continuous state of sleep until* Prince Charming kissed her.

(60)   a.   Sleeping Beauty did *not* sleep (fall asleep) UNTIL^P Prince Charming kissed her.
       b.   Sleeping Beauty did *not* sleep (sleep continuously) UNTIL^D Prince Charming kissed her.

There is a debate whether this ambiguity is *lexical* (cf. [2, 11]) or *scopal* ([8, 12, 19]).

Our analysis has certain theoretical advantages over Karttunen's account. First, his account must *stipulate* that the event Q occurs at some time related to the point in time t expressed in the UNTIL^P clause. When the storyteller says that Sleeping Beauty did *not* wake up *until* Prince Charming kissed her, this does not imply that Sleeping Beauty never woke up prior to Prince Charming's kissing her, but this proposition refers to the relevant event of sleeping relative to the reference point of Prince Charming's kissing her (i.e., the sleeping due to the enchantment which was broken by Prince Charming's kiss). This quantificational relevance restrictor is already present in our analysis of *if* as involving quantification over the relevant cases and meaning something like '*in cases in which*'.

Secondly, Kartunnen's account *stipulates* that UNTIL^P triggers the presupposition that the event Q occurs at some time related to the point in time t expressed in the UNTIL^P clause, whereas UNTIL^D does not. We can explain this presupposition by analyzing UNTIL^P in terms of *exclusive unless*.[18]

Thirdly, we mentioned the debate whether the ambiguity of sentences such as "Sleeping Beauty did not sleep until Prince Charming kissed her" is *lexical* ([2,11]) or *scopal* ([8,12,19]). In our view *both* lexical and scopal ambiguities are present. The difference between (61-a) and (61-b) is explained in terms of the *scopal* ambiguity between (61-c) and (61-d), respectively:

(61)   a.   Sleeping Beauty was *still not* sleeping.
      b.   Sleeping Beauty was *not still* sleeping.
      c.   *It is still the case that not*-Sleeping Beauty is sleeping.
      d.   *It is not the case that* (*still*-Sleeping Beauty is sleeping).

Finally, if our above account of NPIs has been successful, we can use the logically distinctive behavior of negation when it has scope *over a conditional* compared to its behavior when *confined* to the *antecedent* of a conditional to account for the existence of NPIs within UNTIL^P. However, we do not have the time to develop this line of thought here and leave this for future endeavors.

6   Concluding Remarks

We have shown that the similarity between *unless* and *until* is more than merely morphological. According to our compositional analysis, we can obtain an analysis of the latter in terms of the former by adding modal tense operators and an array of temporal particles. This discovery was aided and abetted by the explicit rejection of all three of Quine's dogmas of linguistic negativism. Although there is more work to be done, our compositional analysis is *elegant*: it has a pleasing simplicity and symmetry.

Our case study recommends a less *prescriptive* and *coercive* approach than Quine's in favor of one that is a more *descriptive* and *collaborative*. In the case of logic in the second half of the 20th century, Quinean dogmas had a decidedly

---

[18] According to our analysis of the punctual sense of *until*, we do not need to stipulate *ad hoc* that after Prince Charming kissed her, Sleeping Beauty woke up because this will be a logical consequence of analyzing *until* in terms of an exclusive *unless*:
$\sim$Q UNTIL^P P $\Leftrightarrow \Box \sim$Q *unless-exclusive* $\blacklozenge$P
        $\Leftrightarrow$ *iff-not* $\blacklozenge$P *then* $\Box \sim$Q
        $\Leftrightarrow$ [*if-not* $\blacklozenge$P *then* $\Box \sim$Q] *and* [*if* $\blacklozenge$P *then* $\sim\Box \sim$Q]
        $\Leftrightarrow$ [*if-not* $\blacklozenge$P *then* $\Box \sim$Q] *and* [*if* $\blacklozenge$P *then* $\Diamond$Q]

negative influence on the flourishing of logical and linguistic research into such theoretically fruitful areas as modal logic and propositional attitudes. In our study we have argued that Quine's linguistic negativism has had a similar negative influence, forcing semantics to conform to the Procrustean bed of canonical first-order logic. This unduly prescriptive approach ignores that linguistics can be a fountainhead for discovering new elements of meaning that widen the scope, and renew the vigor, of logical research. Logic without linguistics is empty; linguistics without logic is blind.

We hope that our compositional and collaborative approach to *unless* and *until*, exploring and exploiting the rich interplay of resources from logic and linguistics, has produced an account that is more correct, formally elegant, and theoretically unified than has previously been offered.

Acknowledgements. We wish to thank Sebastian Löbner, Hans Kamp, Revantha Ramanayake, Richard Larson, Thomas Graf, Jiwon Yun, Chris Collins, Paola Cepeda and John Foulks for helpful discussion. We also thank Alan Bale and Luis Alonso-Ovalle for pointing out some important resources, and we especially thank the reviewers of the TbiLLC proceedings for constructive critique. We express our gratitude for the hospitality of Rusiko Asatiani, Matthias Baaz, Nick Bezhanishvili, David Gabelaia and the organizers of the Tenth International Tbilisi Symposium on Language, Logic and Computation and the Georgian Academy of Sciences and Institute for Logic, Language and Computation (ILLC) of the University of Amsterdam. Any shortcomings or errors are our own responsibility.

References

1. Chandler, M.: The logic of 'unless'. Philoso. Stud. Intern. J. Philos. Anal. Tradit **41**, 383–405 (1982)
2. Condoravdi, C.: Punctual until as a scalar NPI. In: Hanson, K., Inkelas, S. (eds.) The Nature of the Word, pp. 631–654. MIT Press, Cambridge (2002)
3. Filip, H.: Events and maximalization: the case of telicity and perfectivity. In: Rothstein, S. (ed.) Theoretical and Crosslinguistic Approaches to the Semantics of Aspect, pp. 217–256. John Benjamins, Amsterdam (2008)
4. von Fintel, K.: Restrictions on quantifier domains. PhD Dissertation, University of Massachusetts (1994)
5. Geis, M.: If and unless. In: Kachru, B., Lees, R., Malkiel, Y., Petrangeli, A., Saporta, S. (eds.) Issues in Linguistics: Papers in Honor of Henry and Renee Kahane, pp. 231–253. University of Illinois Press, Urbana (1973)
6. Giannakidou, A.: Until, aspect, and negation: a novel argument for two untils. In: Jackson, B. (ed.) SALT XII, pp. 84–103. Cornell University, Ithaca (2002)
7. Gillon, B.: Anaphora and some non-commutative uses of or. J. Pragmat. **28**, 373–381 (1997)
8. Heinämäki, O.: Semantics of English temporal connectives, PhD Dissertation, University of Indiana at Bloomington (1974)
9. Kalish, D., Montague, R., Mar, G.: Logic: Techniques of Formal Reasoning, 2nd edn. Oxford University Press, New York (1980)
10. Kamp, H.: Tense Logic and the theory of linear order. Ph.D. Dissertation, UCLA (1968)

11. Karttunen, L.: Until, in Papers from the Tenth Regional Meeting of the Chicago Linguistics Society. CLS, Chicago (1974)
12. Klima, E.S.: Negation in English. In: Fodor, J., Katz, J. (eds.) The Structure of Language, pp. 357–374. Prentice Hall, New Jersey (1964)
13. Kratzer, A.: Conditionals. Chicago Linguist. Soc. **22**(2), 1–15 (1986)
14. Kratzer, A.: Modals and Conditionals. New and Revised Perspectives. Oxford University Press, Oxford (2012)
15. Leslie, S.-J.: "If", "unless", and quantification. In: Stainton, R.J., Viger, C. (eds.) Compositionality, Context and Semantic Values: Essays in Honour of Ernie Lepore. Studies in Linguistics and Philosophy (SLAP), vol. 85, pp. 3–30. Springer, Dordrecht (2009)
16. Löbner, S.: German schon - erst - noch: an Integrated analysis. Linguist. Philoso. **12**, 167–212 (1989)
17. Löbner, S.: Polarity in natural language: predication, quantification, and negation in particular and characterizing sentences. Linguist. Philoso. **23**, 213–308 (2000)
18. Löbner, S.: Dual oppositions in lexical meaning. In: Maienborn, C., von Heusinger, K., Portner, P. (eds.) Semantics: An International Handbook of Language and Meaning. de Gruyter Mouton, Berlin (2011)
19. Mittwoch, A.: Negative Sentences with until. In: Chicago Linguistics Society, vol. 13, pp. 410–417 (1977)
20. Quine, W.V.O.: Elementary Logic. Harvard University Press, Cambridge (1941)
21. Quine, W.V.O.: Two dogmas of empiricism. Philos. Rev. **60**, 20–43 (1951)
22. Wang, H.: Beyond Analytic Philosophy: Doing Justice to What We Know. MIT Press Bradford Books, Boston (1988)

Frame Theory, Dependence Logic and Strategies

Ralf Naumann and Wiebke Petersen[✉]

Institut für Sprache und Information, Heinrich Heine Universität,
Düsseldorf, Germany
petersen@phil.uni-duesseldorf.de

Abstract. We present a formalization of the Löbner-Barsalou frame theory (LBFT) in Dependence Logic with explicit strategies. In its present formalization, [Pet07], frames are defined as a particular kind of typed feature structures. On this approach, the semantic value of a lexical item is reduced to its contribution to the truth conditions of sentences in which it occurs. This reduction does neither account for dynamic phenomena nor for results from neuroscience which show that meaning cannot be reduced to truth conditions. In order to overcome these shortcomings, we develop a dynamic frame theory which is based both on Dependence Logic [Vää07] and Dynamic Epistemic Logic ([vB11]). The semantic phenomenon with respect to which this framework is tested are numerical expressions like 'two' or 'at least two'. They are interpreted as strategies which change the input information state to which they are applied.

Keywords: Dependence logic · Dynamic epistemic logic · Dynamic semantics · Numerals · Scalar quantifiers

1 Introduction

In the last two decades, there has been a growing interest in combining ideas from cognitive science, neuroscience (neurophysiology and neuroimaging), formal linguistics and computer science, using advanced tools from mathematical logic. A major reason for this trend can be seen in improved empirical methods of testing linguistic theories with respect to their empirical and cognitive adequacy: (i) How are sentences (or expressions occurring in them) processed in the brain? and (ii) How is semantic knowledge about the meanings of words acquired in the process of language learning? In this paper we will focus on one particular linguistic phenomenon: bare numerals like 'two' or 'three' and so-called scalar expressions like 'at least', 'at most', 'more than', 'less than', and 'exactly', which can be used to modify bare numerals.

(1)   a.   John read (at least / at most / exactly) two books.
       b.   Mary drank (less than /more than) three cups of coffee.

The research was supported by the German Science Foundation (DFG) funding the Collaborative Research Center 991.

M. Aher et al. (Eds.): TbiLLC 2013, LNCS 8984, pp. 210–233, 2015.
DOI: 10.1007/978-3-662-46906-4_13

There are at least two reasons for choosing this particular topic. First, it has received much attention in recent years, not only from linguists but also from cognitive and neuroscientists. Second, and even more importantly, the theoretical analyses and empirical results presented in those studies provide ample evidence for the fact that these expressions cannot be analyzed in such a way that their meaning is reduced to the contribution they make to the truth conditions of sentences in which they occur.

There is no general agreement what exactly this additional, non-truth-functional meaning component should be. We will show that in order to answer this question one has to take up ideas from different conceptual and theoretical frameworks. In particular, we will argue for the following interdependent theses: (i) In principle, there is no difference between linguistic and non-linguistic meaning (Situation Theory), (ii) The meaning of a linguistic expressions is its *context change potential* (Dynamic Semantics, Update Semantics); (iii) The meanings of linguistic expressions are closely related to how the information (or belief) state of an agent changes when processing an utterance containing this expression (Dynamic Epistemic Logic) and (iv) The meanings of linguistic expressions are closely related to the notions of a strategy from game theory and that of a plan from cognitive science and philosophy.

2   Bare Numerals and Scalar Quantifiers

2.1   Bare Numerals

There are two different semantic analyses of bare numerals like 'two'. According to the first one, the set-theoretical condition imposed by 'two' is the same as that for 'at least two' (2). This is, following [Hor89], the so-called 'one-sided' analysis.

(2) $[[two]] = \{\langle P, Q \rangle : |P \cap Q| \geq 2\}$

On this analysis, bare numerals form a scale such that the following inferences are true with respect to this scale.

(3)   a.   Joe has four children → John has three {two, one} children.
       b.   John doesn't have three children. → John doesn't have {five, six, ...} children.

The 'exactly' interpretation arises if an implicature with respect to such a scale is used. Evidence for this semantic analysis comes from the fact that such an implicature can be canceled.

(4)   a.   Pat has three children and possibly four.
       b.   Pat has three or even four children.
       c.   Pat doesn't have three children. → Pat has less than three children.

By contrast, on a 'two-sided' analysis, the set-theoretic condition is $\{\langle P, Q \rangle : |P \cap Q| = 2\}$. If the meaning of an expression is reduced to its truth-conditions (or its contribution to the truth-conditions of sentences), 'two' and 'at least two' have the same meaning on a one-sided analysis. By contrast, given the same assumption, 'two' should be equivalent to 'exactly two' on a two-sided analysis. Both analyses face empirical problems. The most important of these problems is that bare numerals give rise to different interpretations, depending on the context in which they occur ([Mus04, Car98], [Sza10, 145ff.]).

(5)   A: How many mistakes did you make?
       B: I made three mistakes.

The preferred interpretation of 'three' in (5) is 'exactly three'. Similarly, on a predicative or a collective use, a bare numeral gets an 'exactly'-reading.

(6)   Those are two dogs.
       (false if the speaker is pointing at three dogs)

(7)   Two dogs (together) pulled the sled to the barn.
       (false if the collective agent of the event consisted of three dogs, or of two dogs and a sheep)

By contrast, if a bare numeral is used distributively, the preferred interpretation of 'three' is 'at least three' (8). E.g., (8a) is true even if there are more than two dogs which barked.

(8)   a.   Two dogs were hungry. They barked.
       b.   You need to make three mistakes to be allowed to take the test again.

Finally, a bare numeral can also receive an 'at most' interpretation, witness (9), the preferred interpretation of which is that the addressee passes the test if (s)he makes *at most* three mistakes.

(9)   You can make three mistakes and still pass the test.

2.2   Scalar Quantifiers

If the meaning of a (modified) generalized quantifier is defined solely in terms of its truth conditions, which, in turn, are defined purely set-theoretically, the pairs in (10) and (11) are semantically equivalent.

(10)   a.   John read at least three books.
        b.   John read more than two books.

(11)   a.   John read at most three books.
        b.   John read fewer than four books.

This view of defining the meaning of scalar quantifiers has been criticized both for empirical reasons and from the perspective of language acquisition.

Language Acquisition. [Mus04] conducted different experiments with 5-year old, preschooler children in order to assess their semantic competence with

Table 1. Results of an experiment on comparing the availability of readings for bare numerals for children aged five [Mus04]

Context / group	exactly n	at least n	at most n
Adult	100 %	95 %	97,5 %
Child	100 %	80 %	83,5 %

Table 2. Results of an experiment on comparing the semantic knowledge of children aged five for modified bare numerals [Mus04]

Context / group	exactly n	at least n	at most n	more than n
Adult	100 %	100 %	95,5 %	-
Child	100 %	50 %	54,1 %	88 %

respect to bare numerals like 'two' and modified bare numerals like 'at least two' or 'exactly two'. The aim of the first two experiments was to access the ability of those children to differentiate between an 'exactly' and a non-'exactly' interpretation of bare numerals. The findings are given in Table 1 (percentage indicates the acceptance rates).

The main finding of this experiment is that preschoolers aged 5 can assign numerals the full range of interpretations available in the adult grammar (i.e. 'exactly n', 'at least n' and 'at most n') ([Mus04, 30]). The second experiment aimed at comparing the children's semantic knowledge of bare numerals that are modified with 'exactly', 'at least', 'at most' or 'more than', Table 2.

[Mus04] draws the following consequences from this experiment: (i) Children aged 5 know what 'exactly n' and 'more than n' mean but they are clueless about the meaning of phrases like 'at least n' and 'at most n'; (ii) Children do not disregard the modifier expression, witness the high acceptance rate for the comparative 'more than' and (iii) Although children have implicit knowledge of the fact that bare numerals can have exact and non-exact interpretations, they do not yet know the meaning of the expressions corresponding to the non-exact interpretations of bare numerals.

[GKC+10] tested the semantic knowledge of 11-year-old children with respect to modified bare numerals, also including 'fewer than', which was absent from the study carried out in [Mus04]. The results in descending order indicate the percentage of correct answers: (i) 'exactly' (100 %), (ii) 'more than' (97 %), (iii) 'at least' (88 %), (iv) 'fewer than' (77 %), 'at most' (43 %). This experiment shows that in contrast to 5-year-old children, 11-year-old children do very well with 'at least' (88 %), but they still have significant difficulties in understanding 'at most' (43 %). [GKC+10, 143] comment: 'While five-year-olds have serious trouble with superlative quantifiers, they are quite good with 'more than'. By the time they are 11, children are essentially perfect with 'more than', still struggling with 'at most', and fairly good with 'at least' and 'fewer than'. [PM03] showed 5-year-old children a scenario in which (exactly) three horses jumped over a fence. At the end of the story, a puppet described what happened by uttering (12a).

(12)   a.   Two of the horses jumped over the fence.
        b.   Exactly three horses jumped over the fence.

The comment (12a) of the puppet was consistently rejected by the children. They argued that *three* and not just *two* horses jumped over the fence, i.e. 'two' is not interpreted as 'at least two'. The result of this experiment therefore shows that given a particular scenario, children are able to determine a unique interpretation for a bare numeral.

The 'namely'-Construction. In contrast to comparative scalar modifiers superlative scalar modifiers followed by the 'namely'-construction allow a specific or referential reading, conveying the information that the speaker has a particular set of persons in mind, (13) ([GN07, 534]).

(13)   a.   I will invite at least two people, namely Jack and Jill.
        b.   ?I will invite more than one person, namely Jack and Jill.
        c.   *I will invite more / fewer than two people, namely Jack and Jill.

3   A Frame-Based Analysis of Bare Numerals and Scalar Modifiers

3.1   Frames, Feature Structures and Teams

The discussion of the data in Sect. 2 has shown that bare numerals allow different interpretations and that veridical visual observations are interpreted in a unique way, leaving no way for epistemic uncertainty.[1] Using a dynamic framework, in which meanings are context change potentials, we can give the following possible analysis of the above data: (i) linguistic inputs like utterances or speech acts involving bare numerals update the information state of an agent in a non-deterministic way because (s)he cannot epistemically distinguish between the different interpretations receiving only this input, and (ii) for a veridical observation, the exact number can be exactly determined (provided it is not too large). To make this idea precise, consider the following example taken from [vB11, 45f.].

Throwing a Party: You know that (i) John comes if Mary or Ann does, (b) Ann comes if Mary does not come, (c) If Ann comes, John does not.

The question is what information can be deduced from this set of premises? Using first-order reasoning, one gets:

> By (c), if Ann comes, John does not come. But by (a), if Ann comes, John comes. This is a contradiction, so Ann does not come. But then, by (b), Mary comes. So, by (a) once more, John must come. Indeed a party {John, Mary} satisfies all three premises.

---

[1] Of course, this need in general not to be true for arbitrary observations. Here we refer to the circumstances under which the children and the adults observed the scene where three horses jumped over a fence.

As noted in [vB11, 46], the premises can equally be seen from a dynamic perspective on which they are taken as information events, like observations or utterances by others, which change the information state an agent is in. At the beginning, no information is available to the agent so that all eight options of inviting three different persons are possible.

(14) $\{MAJ, MA\neg J, M\neg AJ, M\neg A\neg J, \neg MAJ, \neg MA\neg J, \neg M\neg AJ, \neg M\neg A\neg J\}$

The three premises are formally taken as *updating* this initial information state the agent is in. A possible sequence of updates is given in (15).

(15)   (M or A) → J, new state : $\{MAJ, M\neg AJ, \neg MAJ, \neg M\neg AJ, \neg M\neg A\neg J\}$
          not-M → A, new state : $\{MAJ, M\neg AJ, \neg MAJ\}$
          A → not-J, new state : $\{M\neg AJ\}$

Applying this type of reasoning to the sentence 'Three horses jumped over the fence, involving the bare numeral 'three', one arrives at the following sequence of deliberations. Only getting this information, the agent doesn't know whether 'three' has to be interpreted as 'at most three' (L), 'exactly three' (E) or 'at least three' (M).[2] Thus, at least theoretically, there are eight options, (16).

(16) $\{MEL, ME\neg L, M\neg EL, \neg MEL, M\neg E\neg L, \neg ME\neg L, \neg M\neg EL,$
          $\neg M\neg E\neg L\}$

Given that 5-year-old preschoolers can already distinguish between the three principle cases in the sense that they know that in a given context exactly one option is true, he or she applies the four rules in (17), reducing the eight options in (16) to the three given in (18).[3]

(17)   a. $E \to \neg(M \vee L)$
          b. $M \to \neg(E \vee L)$
          c. $L \to \neg(M \vee E)$
          d. $E \vee L \vee M$

(18) $\{\neg M\neg EL, M\neg E\neg L, \neg ME\neg L\}$

The scenario presenting three horses jumping over a fence is an observation made by the child that triggers an update of its current information state. This observation corresponds to E in (16). Together with the additional premise (17a), the new, updated, information state of the child is (19a), which is expressed by the sentence (19b). By contrast, this observation falsifies (19c) because it is not in accordance with the observation made by the child.

(19)   a. $\{\neg ME\neg L\}$
          b.   Exactly three horses jumped over the fence.
          c.   Two of the horses jumped over the fence.

---

[2] Though using his knowledge that bare numerals are often used with an 'at least' interpretation when used distributively, this may be the preferred assumption.

[3] This follows from the example in (12) as well as the examples from Musolino's first two experiments.

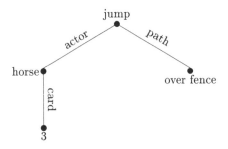

Fig. 1. Barsalou-Löbner frame

In the frame theory of [Pet07], one way of representing an event of type 'Three horses jumping over the fence' is given in Fig. 1.

However, such a frame or feature structure only models *one* possible option of how the current information state of an agent can be updated upon hearing the utterance 'Three horses jumped over a fence'. It does not capture the agent's epistemic uncertainty about the fact that 'three' can have three different readings.

In our approach, this problem is solved by using a different form of representation that resembles the tabular form in database theory. Consider Table 3 ($\oplus$ is the operation which maps a sum-object in a Link-style representation to its set of atoms).

Table 3. A frame for the event of three horses jumping over a fence

	type	path	actor
e_1	jumping	f	$h_1 \oplus h_2 \oplus h_3$
e_2	jumping	f	$h_1 \oplus h_2 \oplus h_3 \oplus h_4$
e_3	jumping	f	$h_1 \oplus h_2 \oplus h_3 \oplus h_4 \oplus h_5$
e_4	jumping	f	$h_1 \oplus h_2$
e_5	jumping	f	h_1

This table can be taken as a set of events with each event being a finite mapping s from a domain $\mathrm{dom}(s)$ to the universe U of a model M. Elements of $\mathrm{dom}(s)$ are called features or attributes. They can be properties of objects like colour or profession, but they can also represent properties of events like their type and thematic relations like actor. One way of interpreting this table is the following. It is split into three (sub-)tables such that each subtable matches one of the three possible readings allowed by 'three'.

The set of events in Table 4 (left) corresponds to the reading 'Exactly three horses jumped over the fence'. The subtable consisting of e_1, e_2 and e_3 (Table 4, middle) represents the reading that at least three horses jumped over the fence (assuming a total of five horses) whereas the table made up of e_1, e_4 and e_5 corresponds to 'At most three horses jumped over the fence', Table 4 (right).

Table 4. Teams for modified bare numerals

'exactly 3':			'at least 3'			'at most 3'		
	path	actor		path	actor		path	actor
e_1	f	$h_1 \oplus h_2 \oplus h_3$	e_1	f	$h_1 \oplus h_2 \oplus h_3$	e_1	f	$h_1 \oplus h_2 \oplus h_3$
			e_2	f	$h_1 \oplus h_2 \oplus h_3 \oplus h_4$	e_4	f	$h_1 \oplus h_2$
			e_3	f	$h_1 \oplus h_2 \oplus h_3 \oplus h_4 \oplus h_5$	e_5	f	h_1

Each situation represented by one of the three tables is epistemically indistinguishable for the agent because he does not know which reading applies, given only the information 'three horses'.

4   Strategies, Teams, Sequential Composition and Dynamic Updates

As shown by the data in Sect. 2.2, one major problem that has to be solved in analyzing scalar modifiers is the fact that their meaning cannot be reduced to a set-theoretical condition. We will use strategies to solve this problem. Intuitively, a strategy is a plan to reach a goal. In the linguistic case, a goal is determined by the truth conditions of an expression, for example the set-theoretic condition imposed by a scalar modifier. In general there can be different ways to reach a goal. For example, a superlative scalar modifiers like 'at least n' is analyzed as a strategy that allows to choose between two branches. The two branches correspond to splitting the set-theoretic condition in a deterministic ('=n') and a non-deterministic component ('>n'). By contrast, for the comparative modifier 'more than n-1' one only gets the non-deterministic component and has thus no choice between different branches in the strategy. The motivation behind this splitting is based both on cognitive and complexity considerations (see Sect. 5.2). In the case of bare numerals and scalar modifiers, choices in a strategy express a condition on the cardinality attribute on the NP of which they are part. Thus, they correspond to the available readings of those expressions. For example, an 'exactly'-reading requires a particular value of the cardinality attribute whereas for an 'at least'-reading no particular cardinality is determined although the set of admissible values of the cardinality attribute has to satisfy a specific condition: it has to be a filter. Strategies are introduced in Sect. 4.1.

In our framework, such constraints on the cardinality attribute are modeled using techniques from Dependence Logic ([Vää07]). A central notion in Dependence Logic is that of a *team*, i.e. a set of assignments. A team represents one possible way the world could be according to the beliefs of an agent. Since formulas are interpreted in Dependence Logic not as sets of assignments but as *sets of sets of assignments*, it is possible to impose dependence relations on a team which must hold globally for the whole domain of the model. For example, a limiting case of functional dependence, namely constancy, is expressed by the formula $=(x)$, which says that the value of the attribute x is constant in a team. This formula will be used for 'exactly'-readings. When taken together, the meaning of a bare numeral or a scalar modifier is a pair consisting of a strategy and a set of teams with each team corresponding to one of the choices (branches). Together with structures formalizing such pairs, Dependence Logic is introduced in Sects. 4.2 and 4.3.

Combining two strategies is defined as sequential composition: each possible choice of the strategy corresponding to the modifying expression (say 'at least') is extended with every choice of the strategy denoted by the modified expression (say 'two'). Combining the set of teams corresponding to the different choices in a (branching) strategy are modeled as an update operation based on the notion of a supplement of a team (Sects. 4.4 and 4.5). The interaction of sequential composing and updating team decorated trees is illustrates in Sect. 4.6.

4.1 Strategies for Modeling Different Readings

Our definition of a strategy closely follows [PS11]. [PS11] distinguish basic and complex strategies. Complex strategies are built from basic ones using regular operations from Propositional Dynamic Logic (PDL) like sequencing ';', choice '∪' and iteration '*'. Basic strategies can be branched. Branching is used to model the possibility for an expression of having more than one interpretation, like bare numerals for instance. Complex strategies are used to interpret modifiers like 'at least', which apply to bare numerals denoting basic strategies. The most important reason for using strategies is the following. Recall that 'at least n' and 'more than n-1' define the same set-theoretical relation although both expressions differ in meaning, as shown by the data in Sect. 2.2. Using strategies, this difference can be explained as follows. Each strategy defines a set of states which can be reached by following it. Two strategies can differ although they determine the same set of states.

Strategies are defined in terms of finite labeled trees:

Definition 1 (Finite Labeled Tree). *Let Σ be a (non-empty) finite set of labels. A Σ-labeled finite tree T is a tuple $\langle S, \{\Rightarrow_a\}_{a\in\Sigma}, s^0 \rangle$ where (i) S is a (non-empty) finite set of nodes, (ii) $s^0 \in S$ is the root of T and (iii) for each $a \in \Sigma$, $\Rightarrow_a \subseteq S \times S$ is the edge relation satisfying the usual properties of being irreflexive, antisymmetric and having a unique predecessor, i.e. if $s_1 \Rightarrow_a s$ and $s_2 \Rightarrow_b s$ then $s_1 = s_2$ and $a = b$.*

For a given node $s \in S$, the set $A(s) = \{a \in \Sigma \mid \exists s' \in S : s \Rightarrow_a s'\}$ is the set of *actions available (or executable) at s.* A *leaf node* is an element $s \in S$ s.t. $A(s) = \emptyset$. The set of all leaf nodes in a tree is denoted by $frontier(T)$. The root of a tree T is denoted by $root(T)$.

Definition 2 (Strategy Tree). *A finite tree $T = \langle S, \{\Rightarrow_a\}_{a\in\Sigma}, s^0 \rangle$ over a label set Σ is a (basic) strategy tree if its branching labeling is functional: for each $s, s', s'' \in S$ and $a \in \Sigma$, if $s \Rightarrow_a s'$ and $s \Rightarrow_a s''$ then $s' = s''$ ([PS11, 417]).*

Basic strategies are pairs consisting of a strategy tree and a global team, where the global team is a set of teams and each team is assigned to one leaf of the tree and vice versa (see Sect. 4.2). The idea behind this definition can be explained as follows. The root node s^0 of a basic strategy tree is taken as a kind of *epistemic input* that triggers a particular plan to which an agent is committed if he has agreed to follow this strategy. Epistemic inputs can be observations by the agent (e.g. seeing a particular situation) or utterances by others. The global team assigned to $frontier(T)$ of an event model constitutes the new information with which the agent has to update his current information state (cf. [PS11]).

So far, we introduced strategy trees to model the different readings of bare numerals and scalar modifiers. However, if strategies are to be used as defining operations to update information states, the information associated with the leaf nodes of the tree cannot simply be taken to be 'indivisible'. Rather, the information given at those nodes must be such that it is possible to impose the cardinality constraints expressed by a choice in a strategy tree. Thus, two problems have to be solved: (i) which structures can be used to impose *global*, as opposed to *local*, constraints? and (ii) how can strategies as labeled trees be combined with such structures? The answer to the first problem is: (underspecified) teams from Dependence Logic. The second problem is solved by making use of the notion of a *team decorated tree*.

4.2   Dependence Logic

The basic semantic notion used in Dependence Logic is that of a team, i.e. a set of assignments which map attributes (or variables) to elements of the domain of a first-order model.

Definition 3 (Team). *Let M be a first-order model, and let $\boldsymbol{v} = \langle v_1, \ldots, v_n \rangle$ be a tuple of variables. A team X for M with domain $\boldsymbol{v}$ is a set of assignments with domain $\boldsymbol{v}$ over M.*

In contrast to first-order logic, formulas are interpreted as sets of sets of assignments and, therefore, as sets of teams. Functional dependence between a sequence of attributes $x_1, \ldots, x_n$ and an attribute y is denoted by $=(x_1, \ldots, x_n, y)$. In addition to this dependence atom, the following two operators are defined which are similar to dependence atoms in being true of a team as a whole. $\uparrow x_n$ requires the values of the attribute x_n to be a filter and $\downarrow x_n$ requires the values to be an ideal.

(20) $M \models_X =(x_1 \ldots x_n, y)$ iff for all assignments $s, s' \in X$ with $s(x_i) = s'(x_i)$
        for $i = 1, \ldots, n$, one has $s(y) = s'(y)$
        $M \models_X \uparrow x_n$ iff $\forall s \in X : s(x_n) = \alpha \to \forall \beta (\alpha \sqsubseteq \beta \to \exists s' \in X : s'(x_n) = \beta)$
        $M \models_X \downarrow x_n$ iff $\forall s \in X : s(x_n) = \alpha \to \forall \beta (\beta \sqsubseteq \alpha \to \exists s' \in X : s'(x_n) = \beta)$
        ($\sqsubseteq$ is the part-of relation in a Link-style representation of plural objects)

For formulas of First-Order Logic which do not contain a dependence atom, satisfaction with respect to a team X reduces to the usual Tarskian semantics in the sense that a formula is satisfiable just in case it is satisfiable with respect to each assignment in the team. For example, one has (21).

(21) $M \models_X \phi \wedge \psi$ iff $M \models_X \phi$ and $M \models_X \psi$.

Disjunction ($\otimes$) is defined on the basis of a split team:

(22) $M \models_X \phi \otimes \psi$ iff there exist Y and Z with $X = Y \cup Z$ such that $M \models_Y \phi$
         and $M \models_Z \psi$.

Furthermore, we need two operators comparing the values of attributes:

(23) $M \models_X (x_1 = x_2)$ iff $\forall s \in X : s(x_1) = s(x_2)$
         $M \models_X (x_1 < x_2)$ iff $\forall s \in X : s(x_1) \sqsubseteq s(x_2)$

So far we have shown that in Dependence Logic it is possible to impose global constraints on a team such as they are expressed by the various branches of a strategy. What is missing is a combination between strategies as labeled trees and teams. This link is defined in terms of team decorated trees which are a variant of feature decorated trees ([BGWV93]).

Definition 4 (Team Decorated Finite Labeled Tree; [BGWV93, 24]). *A finite team decorated tree is a pair $\langle T, D \rangle$ where T is a finite labeled tree and D is a function that assigns to each element of $frontier(T)$ a team.*

Definition 5 (Basic Strategy). *A basic strategy is a finite team decorated tree $\langle T, D \rangle$ where T is a strategy tree.*

Thus, each reading of an expression, represented by a choice in the corresponding strategy, is related to a team. If $frontier(T)$ consists of n elements, one gets a total of n teams. Each team in this set represents one possible way the world (context, situation) could be according to the beliefs (knowledge) of an agent, i.e. it is a (partial) description of how the world (context, situation) could possibly be according to the agent.[4] When taken together, the union of these teams represents the agent's epistemic or doxastic uncertainty. Such sets modeling the information state of an agent are called *global teams* and are denoted by $\mathcal{X}$.

Definition 6 (Global Team). *A global team based on a first-order model M is a set $\mathcal{X} = \{X_1, X_2, \ldots\}$ of teams based on M over the same signature.*

In the next section the team decorated trees for bare numerals, scalar modifiers, common nouns and observations will be defined. In addition, it will be shown how the relation between the labels on branches of strategies and teams can be formally defined.

4.3   Basic Strategies for Bare Numerals, Scalar Modifiers, Common Nouns and Observations

We start by defining the basic strategy for bare numerals (see also Fig. 2).

---

[4] Note that single teams can express uncertainty too. This is the case whenever the values of an attribute form a filter or an ideal. However, this uncertainty is due to the interpretation of the expression and need not arise from epistemic uncertainty.

Definition 7 (Basic Strategy for a Bare Numeral). *A strategy for a bare numeral is a team decorated finite labeled tree of height 2 which is based on the label set* $\Sigma = \{\pi^n, \pi^=, \pi^\geq, \pi^\leq\}$ *with path set* $Path = \{\pi^n\pi^=, \pi^n\pi^\geq, \pi^n\pi^\leq\}$. *The root node of the tree is the expression whose meaning is determined by the strategy.*

The path prefix π^n of all paths expresses that an agent first fixes the base cardinality n. Each $a \in \{\pi^=, \pi^\geq, \pi^\leq\}$ corresponds to an option (or choice) an agent has when processing or interpreting the expression: $\pi^=$ is the operation that adds the constraint $=(card)$ (leading to an 'exactly'-reading), $\pi^\geq$ adds $\uparrow card$ ('at least'-reading) and $\pi^\leq$ adds $\downarrow card$ ('at most'-reading). The satisfaction clauses for the strategy labels are given in (24).

(24)

$$\pi^n : M \models_X base = \bigoplus_{i=1}^{n} type \qquad \pi^= : M \models_X =(card)$$

$$\pi^\geq : M \models_X \uparrow card \qquad\qquad \pi^\leq : M \models_X \downarrow card$$

$$\pi^> : M \models_X \uparrow card \wedge (base < card) \qquad \pi^< : M \models_X \downarrow card \wedge (card < base)$$

The strategy for a bare numeral is depicted in Fig. 2. The teams at the leaf nodes are underspecified: First, the value can be the most general one. This is the case for the *type* attribute which is assigned the top element $\top$. Second, the value of the *base* attribute fixes the base cardinality ($\pi^n : M \models_X base = \bigoplus_{i=1}^{n} type$), that is an underspecified sum object of length n consisting of n 'things' dependent on the value of *type* (a similar argument applies to the *card* attribute, which is a complex attribute whose value is computed by the value of the *base* attribute).[5]

The strategies for 'at least' and 'more than' are given in Fig. 3. The basic strategy interpreting the superlative scalar modifier 'at least' is branching, i.e. it allows two different choices (or options). Either the cardinality information in the team is constant and therefore satisfies the constancy dependence atom $=(card)$, or the value of this attribute can vary and forms a filter, $\uparrow card$. By contrast, for 'more than', there is only the filter condition but no constancy requirement. If a bare numeral is combined with such a modifier, this is interpreted as a non-deterministic supplement operation (similar to the existential and the universal quantifier). Each choice that is possible for the modifier is combined with each choice that is admissible for the bare numeral (see Sect. 4.4 below for details).

The meaning of common nouns like 'horse' are non-branching strategies of height 1. The label set Σ is a singleton and the only label *type* corresponds to the operation which fixes the value of the *type* attribute. The tree is given in Fig. 4.

In contrast to the strategy for a bare numeral or another linguistic expression, the strategy for an observation is a tree of height 0. Thus, it has no labeled

---

[5] Here, we implicitly assumed the initialization assumption which will be introduced in (25) in Sect. 4.4.

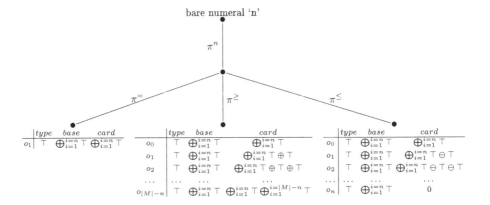

Fig. 2. Strategy for a bare numeral

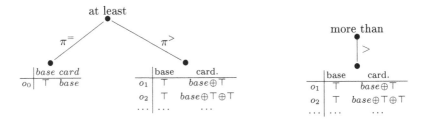

Fig. 3. Strategies for 'at least'(left) and 'more than' (right)

Fig. 4. Strategy for the common noun 'horse'

branches at all. Rather, the only node of the tree is assigned a formula (or a 1-element team) which expresses the content of the observation. In contrast to a strategy representing the meaning of a linguistic expression, a strategy corresponding to an observation admits of only one corresponding team which, furthermore, consists of only one assignment since its meaning is not underspecified.[6]

---

[6] This does *not* mean that the observation is specific in the sense that an attribute is assigned a unique value. For example, without counting the number of horses that one sees one can say that one is seeing at most / at least n horses.

Definition 8 (Strategy for an Observation). *A strategy for an observation P is a finite tree of height 0 with $\Sigma = \emptyset$. The associated team consists of one assignment which specifies the content of the observation.*

In the present context, P is a formula of Dependence Logic which expresses a *global* property of a team, i.e. its truth cannot be reduced to its truth at single elements of the team.

Taking stock, we have shown how the meanings of bare numerals, scalar modifiers and common nouns can be modeled as team decorated trees consisting of a strategy the choices (branches) of which represent the different readings and the global team constituting the 'decorations' of the leaves modeling the object as a team satisfying the cardinality constraint imposed by the corresponding branch. What is missing so far is a mechanism of how such structures can be combined. Since those structures consist of a strategy and a global team, both components must be combined. Composing strategies is defined as a form of sequencing (Sect. 4.4) whereas the combination of the global teams is defined as an update operation that is based on the notion of a supplement of a team (Sect. 4.5).

4.4 Sequencing of Two Strategies

A scalar modifier combines with a bare numeral to form a more complex expression. In our framework, this operation is modeled by sequential composition.

Definition 9 (Sequential Composition of Finite Labeled Trees). *Let $T_1 = \langle S_1, \{\Rightarrow_a^1\}_{a\in\Sigma_1}, s_1^0\rangle$ and $T_2 = \langle S_2, \{\Rightarrow_a^2\}_{a\in\Sigma_2}, s_2^0\rangle$ be two finite labeled trees with $S_1 \cap S_2 = \emptyset$. The sequential composition of T_1 and T_2, denoted by $T_1; T_2$, is the tree T in which each leaf of T_1 is replaced by a copy of T_2. Let $frontier(T_1) = \{f_1, f_2, \ldots, f_n\}$. Then $T = \langle S, \{\Rightarrow_a\}_{a\in\Sigma}, s^0\rangle$ where*

(i) $S = S_1' \cup S_2'$ *with* $S_1' = \{(s,0)|s \in S_1\}$ *and* $S_2' = \bigcup_{1\leq i\leq n}\{(s,i)|s \in S_2 \setminus \{s_2^0\}\}$
that is S_2' *is the n-fold disjoint union of* $S_2 \setminus \{s_2^0\}$ *with* $n = |frontier(T_1)|$,
(ii) $s^0 = (s_1^0, 0)$,
(iii) $(s,i) \Rightarrow_a (s',j)$ *iff*
(a) $i = j$ *and* $s \Rightarrow_a^1 s'$ *or* $s \Rightarrow_a^2 s'$ *or*
(b) $i = 0$ *and* $j \neq 0$ *and* $s = f_j$ *and* $s_2^0 \Rightarrow_a^2 s'$.

According to Definition 9, the sequential composition of two trees T_1 and T_2 is construed by pasting (a copy of) the tree T_2 at all leaf nodes of T_1.

Let us first consider combining 'at least' with 'two'. In this case copies of the tree of the strategy representing 'two' are glued at the leaves of the strategy for 'at least'. The result of this sequential composition yields the tree in Fig. 5(bottom left) of height 3 with six leaves, that is with a total of six theoretical choices.

In general, not all combinations of strategy labels along a path in a sequential composition tree yield satisfiable satisfaction clauses. Thus, in the case of a modified bare numeral not all strategies of the numeral may be admissible

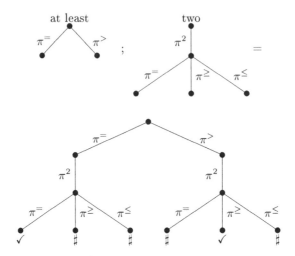

Fig. 5. Sequential composition of 'at least' and 'two'

because they have to satisfy the constraint on the cardinality attribute imposed by the modifier. The following constraint relates the *cardinality* attribute to the *base* attribute if it is not initialized otherwise:

(25)   **Initialization assumption:** If the *card* attribute is not initialized (as in the case of scalar modifiers) then

$$(card = base) \otimes =()$$

holds, i.e. there is at least one assignment in the team such that *card = base* is satisfied. This condition is called the *initialization assumption*.

The satisfaction clauses along a path in a tree resulting from a sequential composition of two strategy trees is the conjunction of the clauses for the individual strategy labels in (24) plus the initialization assumption if it is necessary. Thus, the admissibility conditions for 'at least two' are calculated as follows (the initialization assumption is given in square brackets and contradictions are marked by #).

(26)   a.   ($\checkmark$) $\pi^= \pi^2 \pi^= : M \models_X =(card) \wedge (base = \top \oplus \top)$
              $[\wedge (card = base) \otimes =()]$
         b.   (#) $\pi^= \pi^2 \pi^\geq : M \models_X =(card) \wedge \uparrow card \wedge \ldots$
         c.   (#) $\pi^= \pi^2 \pi^\leq : M \models_X =(card) \wedge \downarrow card \wedge \ldots$
         d.   (#) $\pi^> \pi^2 \pi^= : M \models_X \uparrow card \wedge (card > base) \wedge =(card) \wedge \ldots$
         e.   ($\checkmark$) $\pi^> \pi^2 \pi^\geq : M \models_X \uparrow card \wedge (base = \top \oplus \top) \wedge (card > base)$
         f.   (#) $\pi^> \pi^2 \pi^\leq : M \models_X \uparrow card \wedge (card > base) \wedge \downarrow card \wedge \ldots$

Consider first 'at least'. The left choice imposes a constancy condition. This condition is satisfied on an 'exactly'-reading of the bare numeral (leftmost choice,

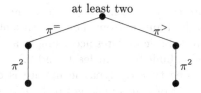

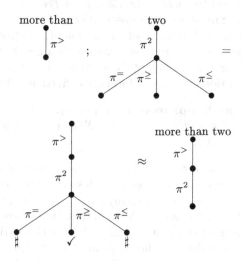

Fig. 6. Strategy for 'at least two'

Fig. 7. Sequential composition of 'more than' and 'two'

$\pi^{=}$) but not by the other two choices which impose either a filter ($\pi^{\geq}$) or an ideal ($\pi^{\leq}$) condition both of which violate constancy. If instead the other choice of the strategy for 'at least' is chosen ($\pi^{>}$), this filter condition excludes both the constancy and the ideal condition of the bare numeral. Non-satisfiable conditions yield strategies that can be removed from a strategy tree. Thus, in the example of 'at least two', the two remaining strategies together yield the strategy represented in Fig. 6.

For 'more than two', the argument goes as follows. The modifier 'more than' requires a filter condition for its cardinality attribute. Sequential composition with the bare numeral 'two' yields a tree with three leafs and thus three options which are shown in Fig. 7 (below left). Two of these options are not admissible because the filter condition imposed by the modifier is violated. Figure 7 (below right) shows the simplified resulting strategy for 'more than two'.

Given these constraints, it follows that an agent only needs to initialize the attribute *base* if a scalar modifier is combined with a bare numeral.

4.5   Dynamic Updates

The processing of utterances changes the input state of an agent. Let $\mathcal{X}$ be such an information state, i.e. a global team. Then an utterance α transforms

$\mathcal{X}$ into $\mathcal{X}'$. If the update corresponding to α is $[\alpha]$, one gets $[\alpha]\mathcal{X} = \mathcal{X}'$. Since utterances are syntactically built up from their constituents, the update α must be defined in terms of more basic updates according to a finite set of operations. For example, 'at least n' is built from 'at least' and 'n'.

In this article, only one type of dynamic update is considered: expansive update. It applies to the set of teams making up the leaves of a team decorated tree. The basic idea is that each element of this global team must be updated by each element assigned to a leaf node (element of $frontier(T)$) of the strategy denoting a linguistic expression or an observation.

Formally, this is defined in terms of the notion of *supplementation of teams* ([Vää07]). The supplement operation on teams adds a new feature to the agents (or events) in a team, or alternatively, it changes the value of an existing attribute. The supplement operation on teams is formally defined as follows.

Definition 10 (Strict Supplement of a Team). *If M is a set, X is a team with M as its codomain and $F : X \rightarrow M$, $X(F/x_n)$ denotes the supplement team $\{s(F(s)/x_n) : s \in X\}$.*

$s(F(s)/x_n)$ is based on the notion of a modified assignment. If s is an assignment, then $s(a/x)$ is the assignment which agrees with s everywhere except that it maps x to a: $dom(s(a/x)) = dom(s) \cup \{x\}$, $s(a/x)(x) = a$ and $s(a/x)(x') = s(x')$ if $x' \neq x$ for $x' \in dom(s)$. In a strict supplementation, the current team is expanded by assigning to each agent or event a single value for the attribute x_n.

An alternative way of defining the supplement operation consists in allowing that an agent or event can be assigned different values for the attribute x_n. This is the case whenever an element of $frontier(T)$ is not a singleton.[7]

Definition 11 (Lax Supplement of a Team). *If M is a set, X is a team with M as its codomain and $F : X \rightarrow \wp(M) \setminus \emptyset$, $X[x_n \mapsto F]$ denotes the supplement team of all assignments $s(a/x_n)$ with $a \in F(s)$.*

The following definition extends the previous one by allowing the supplementation of more than one attribute. The supplement of a team X' by a team X results in a team the domain of which is the union of the domains of X' and X. The supplement team keeps all information of X' and extends it with information about attributes which belong to the domain of team X but not of team X'. The latter attributes are successively supplemented to team X':

Definition 12 (Supplement of a Team by a Team). *Let X, X' be two teams. For $x_n \in dom(X)$ let F_{X,x_n} be the constant function that maps each $s \in X$ to $\{s(x_n) : s \in X\}$. Furthermore let $dom(X)$ be the domain of X and $infdom(X) = \{x \in dom(X) \,|\, \exists s \in X : s(x) \neq \top\}$ be the set of informative attributes of X. If $dom(X) \setminus infdom(X') = \{x_1, \ldots, x_n\}$, the supplement of a team X' by a team X is denoted as $\Delta_X(X')$ and defined as follows: $\Delta_X(X') = (\ldots((X'[x_1 \mapsto F_{X,x_1}])[x_2 \mapsto F_{X,x_2}])\ldots)[x_n \mapsto F_{X,x_n}]$*

---

[7] For details on the distinction between strict and lax semantics in Dependence Logic, see [Gal12].

Note that the former definition could be also read as an update of team X by team X': All attributes which are only defined in X are kept and extended by attributes which are unique for X'. For attributes which occur in the domain of both teams the information about admissible values given in the updated team X is overwritten by the updating team X' if the attribute is informative in X' (that is not constantly of the unspecific value $\top$).

A small example will illustrate the supplement operation and demonstrate that it is an operation which leads to an immense information loss. Consider the following two teams:

$$X = \begin{array}{c|ccc} & \text{type} & \text{color} & \text{form} \\ \hline s_1 & \text{apple} & \text{red} & \text{round} \\ s_2 & \text{peach} & \text{orange} & \text{round} \end{array} \quad \text{and} \quad X' = \begin{array}{c|ccc} & \text{type} & \text{color} & \text{taste} \\ \hline s_1 & \top & \text{red} & \text{sweet} \\ s_2 & \top & \text{green} & \text{sour} \end{array}$$

The former could result from the observation of some round fruit that is either a red apple or an orange peach the latter from the thumb rule that the color of something is an indicator of its taste. If team X' is supplemented by team X (or alternatively X is updated by X') one gets:

$$\Delta_X(X') = \begin{array}{c|cccc} & \text{type} & \text{color} & \text{taste} & \text{form} \\ \hline s_1 & \text{apple} & \text{red} & \text{sweet} & \text{round} \\ s_2 & \text{peach} & \text{red} & \text{sweet} & \text{round} \\ s_3 & \text{apple} & \text{green} & \text{sour} & \text{round} \\ s_4 & \text{peach} & \text{green} & \text{sour} & \text{round} \end{array}$$

We have lost the information about the dependency between the attributes *color* and *type* in team X and the admissible value *orange* for the attribute *color*. Thus, as a general update operations on teams in a team-based semantics, Definition 12 needs a careful revision. However, for our purpose here of combining strategies this rather coarse-grained update operation is sufficient if we filter the resulting teams by the satisfaction clauses resulting from the sequential combination of the strategies.[8] This will be the topic of the following section.

4.6   Putting Update and Sequencing Together

We start by explaining how sequential composition works in parallel with an expansive update of the teams decorating the leaves. Suppose we have two strategy trees T_1 and T_2 which are sequentially combined $(T_1; T_2)$. Since each leaf node k of T_1 is replaced by a copy of the tree T_2, k is in effect replaced by $n = card(frontier(T_2))$ new leaves. Let $\Psi(k)$ denote the set of all teams decorating one of the n leaves which replace k. Let $X_{k,j}$ be the element of $\Psi(k)$ decorating the jth leaf of the tree T_2 and X_k be the team assigned to k in T_1. Furthermore let $C_{k,j}$ be the combined satisfaction clause resulting from the

---

[8] A more fine-grained update or supplement operation can be defined if one uses a sort hierarchy on the values of an attribute. Using such a hierarchy, the value of the *type* attribute in the above example would be calculated as the greatest lower bound of the values in the corresponding elements of the teams.

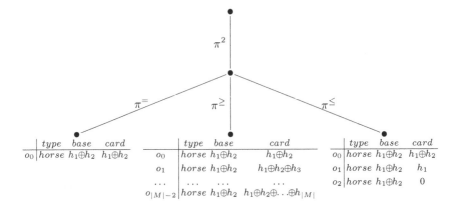

Fig. 8. Combined strategy for 'two horses'

strategy labels along the path from the root node of the sequentially combined tree $T_1; T_2$ to the jth leaf of the copy of T_2 replacing k. Recall from Sect. 4.4 that the strategy labels given in (24) are combined by conjunction plus the initialization assumption if necessary (see Fig. 6 for an example). The team $X_{k,j}$ is transformed to a team X by supplementing it by team X_k (or alternatively, X_k is updated by $X_{k,j}$). The resulting team is only kept if it passes the filter imposed on it by the satisfaction condition $C_{k,j}$.

Let us first illustrate this construction by an example in which a bare numeral is combined with a common noun. An agent first fixes the base cardinality ($\pi^n : M \models_X base = \bigoplus_{i=1}^{n} type$), that is an underspecified sum object of length n consisting of n underspecified 'things' described by $type$ (say π^2 in the case of 'two'). There are three choices: 'exactly', 'at least' and 'more than' with the corresponding teams satisfying the condition imposed on the cardinality attribute. Next sequential composition is applied. Since the strategy for a common noun is non-branching (see Fig. 4), each leaf node k of T_1, the strategy tree for the bare numeral, is replaced by exactly one leaf so that $\Psi(k)$ is a singleton for $1 \leq k \leq 3$. One therefore has three teams X_1, X_2 and X_3, resulting from T_1 and three teams $X_{1,1}$, $X_{2,1}$ and $X_{3,1}$ resulting from T_2. The team $X_{k,1}$ is transformed to a team X by supplementing it by team X_k. In this case there is no loss of information because in X_k the value of this attribute is $\top$, i.e. the most general information which is subsumed by the information provided by the common noun. Since $X_{k,1}$ does not impose any further satisfaction constraint, no team resulting from the supplement operation is discarded. For 'two horses', the resulting team decorated tree is given in Fig. 8.[9]

Table 5 shows the information state of an agent after processing the expression 'two horses' and choosing the 'at least'-reading strategy.

---

[9] The indices at *horse* are used for better readability. Actually, *horse* has to be used without indices because the value of the *base* attribute is a Link-sum object over the values of the *type* attribute.

Table 5. Information state after processing 'two horses' by choosing the 'at least'-reading

	type base	card
o_0	horse $h_1 \oplus h_2$	$h_1 \oplus h_2$
o_1	horse $h_1 \oplus h_2$	$h_1 \oplus h_2 \oplus h_3$
...	... ...	...
$o_{|M|-2}$	horse $h_1 \oplus h_2$	$h_1 \oplus h_2 \oplus \ldots \oplus h_{|M|}$

Consider next the combination of 'at least' with 'two'. In this case $k = 2$ for the strategy tree corresponding to 'at least' (see Fig. 3(left)). Applying sequential composition, yields a total of six branches since the strategy tree for 'two' has three leaves. Consequently, $\Psi(k)$ consists of three teams $X_{k,j}$ with $1 \leq k \leq 2$ and $1 \leq j \leq 3$. Since both strategy trees impose a satisfaction condition, $C_{k,j}$ is the combined satisfaction clause resulting from the strategy labels along the path from the root node of the sequentially combined tree $T_1; T_2$ to the jth leaf of the copy of T_2 replacing k. As was already shown in Sect. 4.4, from the six paths of $T_1; T_2$ four are pruned because the corresponding satisfaction clause cannot be satisfied. Next the $X_{k,j}$ are transformed to a team X by supplementing them with team X_k. Since the attributes $base$ and $cardinality$ are common to $X_{k,j}$ and X_k, the values of these attributes in $X_{k,j}$ are kept. This does not result in a loss of information because, first, the value of the $base$ attribute of the bare numeral is always more specific than the value of this attribute in X_k, where it is $\top$. Second, for 'at least', the value of the $cardinality$ attribute is determined in terms of the value of the (completely underspecified) value of the $base$ attribute. E.g., for the path $\pi^>$ its value for o_1 is $base \oplus \top$. For 'two', the corresponding value is $\bigoplus_{i=1}^{i=2} \oplus \top$. Since $\bigoplus_{i=1}^{i=2} \top$ is more specific than $base = \top$, there is again no loss of information.

The teams at the leaves of the remaining two non-pruned paths are computed as follows. The first one is the result of supplementing the team at the left leaf in Fig. 2 ($\pi^2\pi^=$ strategy for 'two') with the team at the left leaf in Fig. 3 ($\pi^=$ strategy for 'at least'):

	type	base	card
o_1	$\top$	$\top \oplus \top$	$\top \oplus \top$

The second one is the result of supplementing the team at the middle leaf in Fig. 2 ($\pi^2\pi^{\geq}$ strategy for 'two') with the team at the right leaf in Fig. 3 ($\pi^>$ strategy for 'at least'):

	type	base	card
o_1	$\top$	$\top \oplus \top$	$\top \oplus \top \oplus \top$
o_2	$\top$	$\top \oplus \top$	$\top \oplus \top \oplus \top \oplus \top$
...	...	...	...

If the expression 'at least two' is combined with a common noun like 'horse', the *type* attribute and consequently the dependent *base* and *card* attributes will be further specified as described above.

5 Explaining the Empirical Data from Sect. 2.2

5.1 Referential Anaphora

Recall from Sect. 2.2 the following difference between superlative and comparative scalar modifiers.

(27)   a.   I will invite at least two people, namely Jack and Jill.
         b.   ?I will invite more than one person, namely Jack and Jill.

Whereas superlative scalar modifiers allow a reference to specific objects using the 'namely'-construction, this is not the case for the corresponding comparative scalar modifier. This difference is explained in terms of differences in the strategies for superlative and comparative modifiers. Recall that the strategy for the superlative scalar modifier 'at least' allows two different choices. Either the cardinality information in the team is constant and therefore satisfies the constancy dependence atom $=(card)$, or the value of this attribute can vary and forms a filter, $\uparrow card$. By contrast, for 'more than', there is only the filter condition but no constancy requirement. Thus, in contrast to the strategy for a comparative scalar modifier, the strategy for a superlative scalar modifier contains a *deterministic* element: $\pi^=$. Deterministic means that for any given state in a strategy exactly one transition applies (is possible). In PDL, the use of iteration (*) and choice ($\cup$) leads to non-determinism, if no restrictions are imposed. Restricting their use to contexts which yield deterministic programs (while-loops and the 'if then else' construct) is called *Strict Deterministic PDL* (SDPDL) ([HR83]). SDPDL is less complex than PDL. Its decision problem is in polynomial space whereas that of PDL is complete in deterministic exponential time. This leads to the following thesis: The 'namely'-construction requires a deterministic substrategy. In addition, the above way of defining the meaning of bare numerals and scalar modifiers explains their difference in cognitive complexity as follows: (i) bare numerals are simplest because they do not involve the composition of two strategies; (ii) 'At least' is more complex than 'more than' because it involves two different operations in a particular order: sequencing plus choice as opposed to only choice.

5.2 Explaining the Acquisition Data: 5-year-olds Vs. Adults

Similar to adults, 5-year-old children who are preschoolers already have implicit semantic knowledge of the non-deterministic interpretation of bare numerals. That is, they know that the interpretation of these expressions depends on the context and they are able to match these different interpretations successfully in the sense that they are able to perform observation updates after processing a sentence with a bare numeral. By contrast, their application skills do not yet match the accuracy of those shown by adults.

We conjecture that there are the following differences in the semantic knowledge of those children and adults. First, children aged 5 only master simple updates that are given by strategies. Although they already know that a bare numeral allows different readings, they need a context in order to decide which reading applies. They do *not* yet master complex strategies like those imposed by comparative and superlative scalar modifiers. The experiment of [GKC+10], see Sect. 2 above, shows that by the age of eleven, children know that comparative and superlative scalar modifiers impose strategies on the interpretation provided by bare numerals. However, their semantic knowledge shows a clear difference between monotone increasing scalar modifiers like 'at least' and monotone decreasing ones like 'at most' and 'fewer than'. This difference can be explained as follows. Consider the examples in (28) taken from [Sza10, 56].

(28)   a.   *At least two men walk* = There is a set of men with cardinality at least two such that all its elements walk.
        b.   *At most two men walk* $\neq$ There is a set of men with cardinality at most two such that all its elements walk.

If in a given situation two men walk, (28a) is true even if there is a larger situation in which further men walk. The same does not hold for (28b). If someone sees Bill and John walking, (28b) is false if there are other men who are walking too. One way of solving this problem consists in imposing a *maximality* condition on monotone decreasing expressions. In Dependence Logic this difference between monotone increasing and monotone decreasing quantifiers is captured by explicitly introducing a maximality condition (see [Eng12] for details).

(29)   a. $M \models_X Qx\phi$ iff there exists $F : X \to \wp(M)$ such that $M \models_{X(F/x)} \phi$.
        b.   for each $F' \geq F$ s.t. $F' : X \to \wp(M)$, if $M \models_{X(F'/x)} \phi$, then for all $s \in X : F(s) \in Q$ where $F' \geq F$ iff for every $s \in X : F(s) \subseteq F'(s)$.

In (29a) Q is a generalized quantifier (of type $\langle 1 \rangle$) and $X[F/x]$ is the supplement operation. In order to also apply to monotone decreasing quantifiers, it is not sufficient to only require that there is a function F such that $M \models_{X[F/x]\phi}$. Rather, the maximality condition in (29b) must be added.

The poor performance on monotone decreasing modifiers shows that children at the age of eleven still do not master the maximality condition which is imposed by this type of modifier. Finally, the differences in processing load between this type of modifier and the upward entailing ones shows that even for adults the semantic interpretation of the former is more costly than that of the latter. The differences are summarized in Table 6.

Generalizing the above discussion, one arrives at the following tentative hypotheses: (i) sequential composition is costly if it involves pruning, i.e. if admissibility conditions have to be applied. Note that this additional mechanism need not be applied if a bare numeral is combined with a common noun; (ii) the maximality condition, too, can be said to involve an admissibility condition:

Table 6. Comparison of semantic knowledge

	5-year-old	11-year-old	adult
basic strategy for bare numerals	yes	yes	yes
composition operation for scalar modifiers	no	yes	yes
maximality condition for monotone decreasing expressions	no	no	yes

only those supplement operations are admissible which are maximal among all supplement operations. (i) and (ii) together yield thesis (iii): whenever a composition or an update operation involves an admissibility condition which restricts the operation, a higher processing load is triggered.

6   Summary

In this article we developed a formal theory of the Löbner-Barsalou frame hypothesis. The meaning of an expression is a team decorated tree, i.e. a pair consisting of a strategy tree and a set of teams. Each team represents a possible reading of an expression and therefore models one epistemic alternative of an agent. Combining frames is defined in terms of two operations, one for each of the two components of a frame. This framework therefore accounts for two interrelated issues in a formal theory of frames: (i) How can frames be formally modeled? and (ii) How can updates of frames be explicitly modeled?

References

[BGWV93] Blackburn, P., Gardent, C., Meyer-Viol, W.: Talking about trees. In: EACL, pp. 21–29 (1993)

[Car98] Carston, R.: Informativeness, relevance, and scalar implicature. In: Carston, R., Uchida, S. (eds.) Relevance Theory: Applications and Implications, pp. 179–236. John Benjamins Publishing Co., Amsterdam (1998)

[Eng12] Engström, F.: Generalized quantifiers in dependence logic. J. Logic Lang. Inform. **21**, 299–324 (2012)

[Gal12] Galliani, P.: Inclusion and exclusion dependencies in team semantics - on some logics of imperfect information. Ann. Pure Appl. Log. **163**(1), 68–84 (2012)

[GKC+10] Geurts, B., Katsos, N., Cummins, C., Moons, J., Noordman, L.: Scalar quantifiers: logic, acquisition, and processing. Lang. Cogn. Process. **25**(1), 130–148 (2010)

[GN07] Geurts, B., Nouwen, R.: At least et al.: the semantics of scalar modifiers. Language **83**, 533–559 (2007)

[Hor89] Horn, L.R.: A Natural History of Negation. Chicago UP, Chicago (1989)

[HR83] Halpern, J.Y., Reif, J.H.: The propositional dynamic logic of deterministic, well-structured programs. Theor. Comput. Sci. **27**, 127–165 (1983)

[Mus04] Musolino, J.: The semantics and acquisition of number words: integrating linguistic and developmental perspectives. Cognition **93**(1), 1–41 (2004)

[Pet07] Petersen, W.: Representation of concepts as frames. In: Skilters, J., Toccafondi, F., Stemberger, G. (eds.) Complex Cognition and Qualitative Science. The Baltic International Yearbook of Cognition, Logic and Communication, vol. 2, pp. 151–170. University of Latvia, Riga (2007)

[PM03] Papafragou, A., Musolino, J.: Scalar implicatures: experiments at the semantics-pragmatics interface. Cognition 86(3), 253–282 (2003)

[PS11] Pacuit, E., Simon, S.: Reasoning wih protocols under imperfect information. Rev. Symb. Log. 4, 412–444 (2011)

[Sza10] Szabolsci, A.: Quantification. CUP, Cambridge (2010)

[Vää07] Väänänen, J.: Dependence Logic. CUP, Cambrige (2007)

[vB11] van Benthem, J.: Logical Dynamics of Information and Interaction. Cambridge University Press, Cambridge (2011)

Uniqueness and Possession: Typological Evidence for Type Shifts in Nominal Determination

Albert Ortmann[✉]

University of Düsseldorf, Düsseldorf, Germany
ortmann@phil-fak.uni-duesseldorf.de

Abstract. This paper highlights the analogy of definiteness and possession by utilising the distinction between semantic and pragmatic uniqueness as outlined in Löbner's (2011) Concept Type and Determination approach. Assuming, on the basis of the features [± unique] and [± relational], a classification into the four logical types sortal, relational, individual, and functional concept, nouns will be used either in congruence with or deviating from their underlying type. I present evidence from Germanic and Mayan languages for the following claims: (1) noun uses that deviate from the underlying type tend to be reflected by overt morphology; (2) in article split languages, phonologically 'strong' forms indicate pragmatic uniqueness, thus, denote a function from [− unique] to [+ unique], whereas 'weak' forms tend to be semantically redundant. Regarding possession, 'alienable' morphology denotes a function from non-relational to relational (pragmatic possession), whereas 'inalienable' morphology is restricted to semantic possession. Overall, split systems imply a strong correlation between conceptual markedness and morphosyntactic markedness.

Keywords: Type shift · Definiteness · Possession · Alienability · Definite articles · Typology · Compositional semantics

1 Introduction

In this paper I highlight the analogy of two types of nominal determination, namely definiteness and possession, and their cross-linguistic manifestation. I utilise the distinction between semantic and pragmatic uniqueness as outlined

The work reported here was carried out in the research Unit FOR 600 Functional concepts and frames, and subsequently in the Collaborative Research Centre SFB 991 The Structure of Representation in Language, Cognition and Science, both sponsored by the German Research Foundation (DFG). For comments and discussion I would like to thank Adrian Czardybon, Thomas Gamerschlag, Corinna Handschuh, Lisa Hofmann, Sebastian Löbner, and Chris Lucas. Special thanks go to Doris Gerland and Jenny Kohls for their careful and critical reading of an earlier version, and to two anonymous referees for their extremely valuable and detailed comments.

M. Aher et al. (Eds.): TbiLLC 2013, LNCS 8984, pp. 234–256, 2015.
DOI: 10.1007/978-3-662-46906-4_14

in the Concept Type and Determination (CTD) approach to definiteness in Löbner (1985, 2011; cf. also Ortmann 2014). This perspective on determination will be pursued in case-studies from, among others, Mayan and Germanic languages.

With respect to definiteness, the major assumptions of this approach are the following. Unique reference comes about in two different manners. Semantic uniqueness entails that the noun (or the noun phrase, in case of non-lexical functional concepts) denotes an individual, and it exhibits unique reference because of its lexical (or compositional) semantics. Pragmatic uniqueness, in contrast, refers to those uses of nouns whose unique reference only comes about due to the discourse context or context of utterance, which is the case with anaphoric and deictic uses. The present paper underpins this approach by presenting typological evidence that shows that noun uses that are not congruent with the underlying type are indicated by overt morphology. I argue that the morphosyntactic data speak in favour of the following generalisations: in languages that display a definite article split, the phonologically 'strong' definite article denotes a function of the kind $\langle\langle e, t\rangle, e\rangle$, while 'weak' forms tend to be semantically redundant. As far as the category of possession is concerned, so-called 'alienable' morphology (such as relator affix, classifier, and genitive case) denotes a function of the kind $\langle\langle e, t\rangle, \langle e, \langle e, t\rangle\rangle\rangle$. Overall, split systems display a greater correlation of semantics and morphosyntactic markedness.

The paper is structured as follows: In Sect. 2, I outline the CTD approach. In Sect. 3 I offer a small typology of adnominal possession and analyse alienability splits in terms of the distinction between semantic and pragmatic possession, and of type shifts from non-relational to relational noun concepts. Correspondingly, Sect. 4 offers a small typology of definite article splits and provides an analysis in terms of the distinction between semantic and pragmatic uniqueness, and of type shifts from non-unique to unique noun concepts. Section 5 summarises the major theses advocated in this paper.

2   Setting the Stage: The Theory of Concept Types and Determination (CTD)

Löbner 1985 proposes a three-way distinction of nominal concept types that distinguishes sortal, relational and functional concepts. The initial distinction is further elaborated in Löbner (2011) in which he introduces a classification that is based on two dimensions: arity and reference. More specifically, the contrasts that underlie these concept types are monadic vs. polyadic, and inherently unique vs. not inherently unique. The resulting classification is illustrated in the following table.

Thus the cross-classification of the properties 'relational' and 'unique reference' gives rise to the following noun types: SNs are one-place predicates; for example, *dog* delimits the set of individuals that are dogs, hence its logical type is $\langle e, t\rangle$. RNs do the same in relation to some possessor, thus characterising, for example, the set of Hannah's sisters, hence their type is $\langle e, \langle e, t\rangle\rangle$. INs unambiguously single out individuals (often depending on a given time/world coordinate,

	not inherently unique	inherently unique
not inherently relational	sortal nouns (**SN**) $\langle e, t \rangle$ *dog, tree, adjective, water*	individual nouns (**IN**) e *sun, weather, Mary, prime minister*
inherently relational	relational nouns (**RN**) $\langle e, \langle e, t \rangle \rangle$ *sister, leg, friend, blood*	functional nouns (**FN**) $\langle e, e \rangle$ *mother, surface, head, begin*

as with *weather, temperature, prime minister*, to be specified in terms of a situational argument in the sense of Löbner 1985). FNs do the same in relation to a possessor argument; an example is *the beginning of the 21st century*. In this way, INs and FNs are unambiguously assigned exactly one referent, so their logical types are e and $\langle e, e \rangle$, respectively.

There are two different manners in which unique reference (or, in fact, 'non-ambiguous reference', as Löbner 1985 calls it) can emerge. Semantic uniqueness results from the meaning of the noun: underlying INs and FNs warrant the unambiguity of reference, as in *the pope* and *John's mother*. By contrast, the unique reference of underlying SNs and RNs as in *the table, the man at the corner* and *the daughter of John*, respectively, does not come about because of the lexical meaning of the nouns *table, man and sister*, but rather because of the discourse and/or utterance context. For example, one of Hannah's sisters has been already mentioned, or Hannah happens to have exactly one sister. Accordingly, Löbner (1985, 2011) speaks of pragmatic uniqueness.

Since all definite descriptions exhibit unique reference[1], any occurrence of an underlyingly SN or RN as a definite description implies its use as an individual concept or functional concept, respectively. Consequently, the CTD notation differentiates between a noun's underlying type, such as SN, RN, IN, FN, and its actual use, such as SC, RC, IC, FC. A major objective of the CTD approach is to account for the flexibility in the usage of nouns. Virtually any noun can be used as any one of the four concept types. In other words, type shifts (in the sense of Partee 1986) into all directions are possible, from each concept type to any other. As a consequence, a noun can be used either in congruence with or deviating from its underlying concept type. In the case of *the table* we are dealing with a type shift from [− unique] to [+ unique] (SN → IC). This shift is indicated by a definite article in many languages. Moreover, in languages with generalised article use such as English the definite article is also obligatory with INs and FNs, that is, in cases of semantic uniqueness. In these cases it applies vacuously. Indefinite uses of INs and FNs as in *a sun* and *a mother of five* involve the opposite shift, thus, from IN and FN to SC and RC.

---

[1] For controversial cases such as 'configurational uses' see Löbner (2011: 298) and references there. See also Carlson & Sussman (2005) on 'weak definites' such as *(go to) the store*, as well as Coppock & Beaver (2012) on anti-uniqueness effects of predicative definites and also argumental definites under negation.

Fully along the lines of the opposition of semantic and pragmatic uniqueness, I propose that the contrast of inalienable and alienable possession should be re-interpreted as semantic and pragmatic possession. Semantic possession is called so because some relation of affiliation is inherent to the lexical meaning of the possessum. Pragmatic possession is called so because the POSS relation is established by the context rather than by the lexical meaning of the possessum. In the remainder of the paper I argue in favour of the following analogy: the operation that converts [− relational] to [+ relational] (SN → RC, IN → FC) is denoted by what is traditionally called alienable possession, in exactly the same way as the change from [− unique] to [+ unique] is denoted by a strong definite article in case of pragmatic uniqueness.

3   The Typology of Adnominal Possession: The Role of Semantic vs. Pragmatic Possession

3.1   Alienability Splits

In the typological literature, the contrast pair of alienable vs. inalienable is used to distinguish two (not necessarily mutually exclusive) classes of nouns with respect to their morphosyntactic behaviour in possessive contexts. Looking at alienability splits across languages inevitably brings about the question as to their conceptual basis:

Inalienable possession (which corresponds to semantic possession) is characterised by inherent affiliation and by relations that are not subject to the possessor's choice or control: First and foremost among these are kinship, body parts, part-whole, and location.

The major characteristics of alienable possession (which corresponds to pragmatic possession) is temporary affiliation, where the possessor typically has control over the possessum. Accordingly, the function of the possessum (eating, drinking, growing, tool, etc.) for the possessor is of relevance. It is precisely in this area that the notion 'possession' can be understood in the literal sense, like that of legal ownership. Often the relation between the two individuals is conceptualised as a contextually instantiated relation, dependent on the speech situation, as in *my chair*, which can denote the chair that I am sitting on at the moment.

In order to relate this conceptual contrast to the morphology and syntax of natural languages, I give a brief overview of some major modes of expressing an (in)alienability distinction in possession. The nouns on the left in the following examples (1a), (2a) and (3a) are semantically relational, FNs in terms of the classification above. Being FNs, they are inherently possessed, and therefore directly combine with a possessor affix or a possessor phrase. This corresponds to the typological notion of inalienable possession. By contrast, the nouns in (1b) to (3b) are sortal and can therefore be combined with a possessor only after they are overtly morphologically extended:

- Possessor agreement is directly attached to the noun rather than mediated by a connective: In contrast to the FN stem ǝtal^y 'mother', the SN stem ewa: 'house' must be morphologically extended by the connective prefix -ǝ^n in order to be possessed.[2]

(1)   Diegueño (Yuman < Hokan; Mexico; after Nichols 1992: 117):
   a. ʔ-ǝtaly   b. ʔ-ǝ^n-ewa
       1SG-mother   1SG-POSS-house
       'my mother'   'my house'

The term 'connective' (or 'relator') is merely an informal label. I will argue in the following subsection that these markers establish the relation of possession, hence my annotation 'POSS'.

- Possessor agreement is directly attached to the noun rather than attached to a classifier:

(2)   Paamese (Oceanic < Austronesian, Vanuatu; Crowley 1996: 384ff)
   a. yati-n   ēhon   b. ani   emo-n   ēhon
       head-3SG child   coconut   POSSCL(potable)-3SG   child
       'the child's head'   'child's drinking coconut'

Possessive classifiers like that in (2b) can be analysed as encompassing the function of a relator plus some additional, more specific information concerning the sortal properties of the possessum (for example, edibles, domestic animal). Sometimes possessive classifiers specify the relation POSS as being conceived as permanent or temporary, or characterising the utility of the possessum for the possessor. As a widespread typological strategy, possessive classifiers serve as the morphological base to which the possessor agreement is attached Seiler (1983).

- The possessor is realised as a prefix rather than as a free (possessive or personal) pronoun:

(3)   Eastern Pomo (< Hokan; California), after Nichols 1992: 118)
   a. wí-bayle   b. wáx   šári
       1SG-husband   1SG.GEN   basket
       'my husband'   'my basket'

---

[2] In the glosses, I use the following abbreviations of grammatical categories: ACC 'accusative', AUX 'auxiliary', COMP 'complementiser', COP 'copula', DAT 'dative', DEF 'definite article', DEM 'demonstrative pronoun', DEREL 'de-relativisation', DI 'distal determination', E 'ergative', EP 'epenthetic consonant', F 'feminine', GEN 'genitive', IMP 'imperative', INF 'infinitive', LOC 'locative', M 'masculine', N 'neuter', NEG 'negation', NOM 'nominative', NON3RD, '1st or 2nd person', PART 'participle', PAST 'past tense', PL 'plural', POSS 'relation of possession', POSSCL 'possessive classifier', PRES 'present tense', REFL 'reflexive pronoun', REL 'relative clause marker', SG 'singular', STR 'strong article form', SUPERL 'superlative', WK 'weak article form' ; 1, 2 and 3 represent first, second and third person, respectively.

Significantly, all of the illustrated contrasts are attained by straight affixation or juxtaposition of the possessor on the inalienable side, and 'mediation' by a classifier, a connective, a free (possessive) pronoun, or a case marker on the possessor on the alienable side. As a result, the generalisation is that less conceptual distance is mirrored by less morphosyntactic complexity (see the introduction to Chappell & McGregor (1996) and references there).

Obviously, one and the same concept need not be treated alike in all languages with an alienability split. There is in fact considerable cross-linguistic variation as to the class of nouns that may enter inalienable possession. Aspects of language-specific demarcations are discussed, among others, in Seiler (1983), in Nichols (1988: 572) regarding North American languages, as well as in the contributions of Chappell & McGregor (1996). A theoretical implication is that the propensity of [+ relational] nouns to undergo the inalienable construction is a default that may be overwritten by idiosyncratic specification.

3.2   Type Shifts in Possession

In this section I show that the distinction of semantic vs. pragmatic possession largely accounts for what is known as the alienability contrast: Semantic possession implies that the relation between the noun's referential argument (the possessum) and the possessor argument is inherent to the noun's lexical semantics. Pragmatic possession implies that the POSS relation is only contextually established, and often depends on the utterance situation.[3] I argue that morphological markers of alienable possession such as connectives and classifiers should be interpreted as establishing a non-inherent, hence pragmatic POSS relation. Specifically, the goal is to motivate the following claim:

(4)   **Claim:** Pragmatic possession involves the type shift from [− relational] to [+ relational].

This programmatic analysis, which follows the programme outlined in Löbner 2011, will be pursued more radically here, in that the assumed shift operation will be paired with morphosyntactic material that has the function of denoting the operation.

The type shift mentioned, the effect of its application to a SN, and finally the discharging of the possessor argument is schematically and successively sketched in (5).

(5)
   a. sortal noun, e.g. *house*: $\lambda x.\text{HOUSE}(x)$
   b. template of POSS shift SC → RC: $\lambda N.\lambda y.\lambda x.[N(x) \wedge \text{POSS}(y, x)]$
   c. (b) applied to (a) $\lambda y.\lambda x.[\text{HOUSE}(x) \wedge \text{POSS}(y, x)]$
   d. (c) applied to possessor *John*: $\lambda x.[\text{HOUSE}(x) \wedge \text{POSS}(\text{John}', x)]$

---

[3] In Barker (2011: 1113) this distinction is labelled lexical vs. pragmatic interpretation; see also Vikner & Jensen (2002: 194–216) for a similar though not identical distinction.

Note that a template that is equivalent to the POSS type shift (b) is also assumed by Barker (1995; 2011: 1114) for English, based on compositional semantic grounds rather than on typological evidence; cf. also Vikner & Jensen (2002) and Partee & Borshev (2003). I will now look closer at the relevant data in terms of a case study from two Mayan languages.

3.3 'Alienable' Morphology Indicates Pragmatic Possession ([−relational]→[+relational])

In this and the following subsection, I provide a case study which builds on earlier joint work with Corinna Handschuh (cf. Ortmann 2004). It will be shown that Mayan languages are especially explicit in the morphological encoding of noun type shifts, in both directions. Let me first illustrate how non-relational nouns (SNs) are transformed into RCs by means of suffixation of -*il*, and by vowel lengthening, respectively.

Yucatec: (6a,c) displays the SNs *nah* 'house' and *ha* 'water', without a possessor, in contrast to the possessive use in (6b,d), which requires the suffix -*il*.[4]

(6) Yucatec Mayan (Lehmann 1998: 56; Tozzer 1921: 50)

a. *le* *nah-o'*   b. *in* *nah-il*   c. *ha*   d. *u*   *ha-il*   *tš' en*
   DEF house-DI   1SG.E house.POSS   water   3SG.E water-POSS well
   'the house'   'my house'   'water'   'the water of the well'

Crucially, alienably possessed nouns require the suffix -*il* irrespective of whether they are only combined with a possessor agreement clitic (*in* in (6a)), or with a lexical possessor *tš'en* in addition to *u* as in (6d). The class of nouns that follows this pattern is according to Lehmann (1998: 61) the largest and most productive; for inalienably possessed nouns see Subsect. 3.4.

Mam: Mam resembles Yucatec in that a large group of sortal nouns obligatorily undergo an overt change in order to be able to combine with a possessor. Consider the examples in (7).[5]

(7) Mam (Mayan; England 1983: 67)

a. *xaq*   b. *n-xaaq=ai*   c. *ne'l*   d. *n-nee'l=a*
   rock   1SG.E-rock-POSS-NON3   sheep   1SG.E-sheep.POSS-NON3
   'rock'   'my rock'   'sheep'   'my sheep'

In contrast to the Yucatec strategy of employing an affix, Mam uses a prosodic strategy, namely that of vowel lengthening. Cross-linguistically it is not unusual for grammatical features to be marked supra- or subsegmentally; for example, by grammatical tone in African languages, or quantitative ablaut in Germanic. In

---

[4] See Bricker et al. & Po'ot (1998: 358f) for other suffixes with essentially the same function, as well as for further details concerning possession in Yucatec.

[5] As in Yucatec, the possessor clitics belong to the ergative paradigm ('set A' in the Mayanist tradition).

the case of Mam, the category of POSS is prosodically realised, more precisely, by a vowel weight unit, that is, a mora.[6] As in the case of Yucatec, it is obvious from the examples in (7) that the morphological operation that makes nouns 'possessable' is clearly separated, morpho(phono)logically as well as semantically, from possessor agreement. In the same way that -*il* is distinct from *in* in Yucatec, lengthening is distinct from *n*- in Mam in that the first establishes the POSS relation, and the latter specifies the possessor.

There are nouns for which the alternation is less transparent because of phonological irregularity; for example, the vowel following the stressed syllable may be deleted, as in *tz'lom* – *n-tz'áalm-a=ya* 'my plank'. Sometimes the alternation is even entirely blurred by prosodic factors. Mam does not allow for more than one long vowel per word. Since it does not allow for super-long vowels either, there is no possibility of lengthening for a stem with an underlying long vowel: *b'ee* – *n-b'ee=ya* 'my road', *jaa* – *t-jaa-t=a xu'j* 'the woman's house' (England 1983: 34, 143). In this (apparently frequent) pattern, the possessed stem of a noun does not differ from the unpossessed variant. However, the fact that Yucatec and its relative Mam behave analogously in essential regards lends further support for my analysis of the POSS shift as being overtly realised.

Overall, the generalisation is that in the possessed use, alienable nouns in Mam are subject to vowel lengthening unless they already contain an underlying long vowel. Thus, the POSS shift is realised by filling an abstract vowel position.

Representations: In order to account for the above data I pursue a compositional analysis that pairs the involved semantic type shift operations with the involved morphological exponents. In particular, the relator morpheme is analysed as the morphological exponent of establishing the relation POSS for alienable nouns as in (5b), thus, denoting the function from [− relational] to [+ relational].

For the state of affairs in Yucatec, we can assume the following composition:

(8)
   a. sortal noun: *nah*: $\lambda x.\text{HOUSE}(x)$
   b. overt POSS shift: -*il*: $\lambda N.\lambda y.\lambda x.[N(x) \wedge \text{POSS}(y,x)]$
   c. result of POSS shift: *nah-il*: $\lambda y.\lambda x.[\text{HOUSE}(x) \wedge \text{POSS}(y,x)]$
   d. discharge of possessor: *in nah-il*: $\lambda x.[\text{HOUSE}(x) \wedge \text{POSS}(\text{SPEAKER},x)]$

As regards the Mam data, we can assume that the exponent of the POSS-operation is a prosodic element (much like tense is marked by grammatical tone in some Bantu languages). The lengthening, then, is the prosodic effect of adding a morpheme that merely consists of a syllable weight position, devoid of any segment. In prosodic phonology, syllable weight positions are referred to as moras. Consequently, the exponent of the POSS shift in Mam is a mora (μ).

---

[6] In addition to vowel lengthening, some nouns undergo further regular vowel-related processes when they are possessed (cf. England 1983: 44). For example, the processes involved in *n-paatzán=a* 'my sugarcane' (with the unpossessed variant *ptz'on*) are stress assignment, prevocalic glottalisation, and reduction of unstressed vowels, hence the phonetic form [mpá:tz'ənə].

(9)
   a. sortal noun: $ne\,'l$: $\lambda x.\mathrm{SHEEP}(x)$
   b. overt POSS shift: μ: $\lambda N.\lambda y.\lambda x.[N(x) \wedge \mathrm{POSS}(y,x)]$
   c. result of POSS shift: $nee\,'l$: $\lambda y.\lambda x.[\mathrm{SHEEP}(x) \wedge \mathrm{POSS}(y,x)]$
   d. discharge of possessor: $nee\,'l{=}la$: $\lambda x.[\mathrm{SHEEP}(x) \wedge \mathrm{POSS}(\mathrm{SPEAKER},x)]$

What I propose, then, is a compositional solution under which a semantic operation is paired with morphological material. With respect to the semantic status of the possessor this solution simply entails that all possessors, including markers of possessor agreement, are logically treated as individuals, devoid of any relationality of their own. Thus, possessor agreement markers have the same semantics as personal pronouns (where the subscript '$_\mathrm{U}$' represents the utterance parameter relative to which the extension of the pronoun is determined).

(10)   possessor clitic as entity: in: $\iota z[z = \mathrm{SPEAKER}_\mathrm{U}]$

In this way, the representation can be kept as simple as possible. Whatever is assumed as the semantics of personal pronouns, it will sufficiently characterise the clitics at issue. This is a consequence of the POSS shift, and it has two further advantages.

First, it correctly predicts that in the default case [+ relational] nouns such as 'mouth' take a possessor clitic without prior application of the POSS shift due to the relational semantics of the noun; see (14a). Second, it accounts for the fact that the same set of clitic agreement markers occurs with transitive verbs, specifying the ergative argument and also having pronominal status (the Mayan language generally exhibiting the pro-drop property).

Both of these facts would be unexplained if one were to assume a special semantics for these markers that would make reference to possession. This distinctive POSS semantics would have to be 'turned off' for inalienable possession and for the subject (or object, according to the language), which involve the same markers. It is obvious that this would result in undesirable polysemy.

Under the present approach, possessive classifiers are also accounted for straightforwardly. For a fairly large set of SNs in Yucatec, the operation for pragmatic possession is achieved by possessive classifiers, especially by those for domestic animals and for food; consider (11).

(11)   Yucatec Mayan (Lehmann 1998: 62f., 38)

   a. *in*   *w-o'ch*   *ha's*   b. *in*   *w-àlak'*   *k'ée'n-o'b*
      1SG.E EP-POSSCL banana   1SG.E EP-POSSCL pig-PL
      'my banana'   'my pigs'

These classifiers can be represented as in (12). In addition to contributing the POSS operation as in (8) and (9), each classifier imposes its sortal restrictions on the possessum.

(12)   *àalak'*: $\lambda N.\lambda y.\lambda x.[N(x) \wedge \mathrm{DOMESTIC\_ANIMAL}(x) \wedge \mathrm{POSS}(y,x)]$
        o'ch: $\lambda N.\lambda y.\lambda x.[N(x) \wedge \mathrm{FOOD}(x) \wedge \mathrm{POSS}(y,x)]$

3.4 'Inalienable' Morphology Indicates Semantic Possession

In the previous I have analysed the morphological strategies of changing SNs into RCs. Let us now turn to the converse operation. Recall from the (a) examples of (1) to (3) above that the notion of semantic possession entails that the POSS relation is inherent to the lexical meaning. This corresponds to the fact that inalienable possession is morphologically unmarked. But this in turn brings about the question of markedness in non-possessed uses of relational nouns.

In numerous genetically unrelated languages of the Americas and of Melanesia, an overt morphological marker is required if underlying [+ relational] nouns (RNs and FNs) are used as SCs and ICs, that is, without a possessor argument. While this operation is occasionally referred to as 'absolutivisation', Seiler (1983) proposes the term 'de-relationisation', hence I gloss the marker at issue as derel in the following. Again, the Mayan languages prove to be particularly explicit in encoding the operation.

(13)   Mam (Mayan, Guatemala; England 1983: 69)

    a. *n-yaa'=ya*
       1SG.E-grandmother=NON3RD
       'my grandmother'

    b. *yaa-b'aj*
       grandmother-DEREL
       'grandmother'

Being relational, the nouns of this class enter the possessive construction as inalienable, that is, without a POSS suffix or vowel lengthening. In order to use such a noun without a possessor, a suffix must be attached that changes the noun into an absolute (that is, sortal) noun. There are two suffixes that fulfil this function: *-b'aj* is used with body part and kinship terms, and *-j* with nouns denoting clothing; cf. *w-aam-a* 'my skirt' vs. *aam-j* 'skirt'. As far as terms for nourishment are concerned, some take *-b'aj*, while others take *-j*.

Likewise, Yucatec employs the suffix *-tsil* for licensing the non-possessed use of a relational noun:

(14)   Yucatec Mayan (after Lehmann 1998: 70ff)

    a. *in   chi'*
       1SG.E mouth
       'my mouth'

    b. *le   chi'-tsil-o'*
       DEF mouth-DEREL-DI
       'the mouth'

According to the perspective taken here, we are dealing with a morphologically overt operation that reduces the argument structure of the noun, much in the same way as passive and antipassive morphology. The variant with reduced argument structure is morphologically marked, which corresponds to the fact that it is derived from the variant with the full argument structure.[7]

---

[7] Another instance of de-relationisation comes from Teop (Western-Oceanic, Papua New Guinea). Ulrike Mosel (p.c.) informs me that the suffix *-na* serves the same function, as in *sina-na* mother-DEREL '(a) mother'. One more case in question is Cahuilla (Uto-Aztecan; Seiler 1983).

In terms of concept types, then, de-relativising suffixes can be conceived of as denoting a shift from [+ relational] nouns to [− relational] concepts. This is represented in (15).[8]

(15)   'derelative' affixes: *-b'aj, -j, -tsil*: $\lambda R.\lambda x.\exists y R(x, y)$

The operation corresponds to what is called a 'detransitivization type-shifter' by Barker (2011: 1114f), conceived of as a silent operator. In some languages, a de-relativising shift can be followed by the reverse, thus, [+ relational] → [− relational] → [+ relational]. The result of this sequence of operations is that the possessum is provided with a contextual (rather than inherent) relation of possession. Consider the difference that Koyukon makes for one and the same noun between inalienable use, which bears on the inherent part-whole affiliation, and alienable use, which bears on a contextual association with the possessor ((16b) vs. (16c)).

(16)   Koyukon (Athapaskan < Na-Dene; Thompson 1996: 666f)

a. *nelaane*	b. *be-nelaane*	c. *se-k'e-nelaane*
meat	3SG-meat	1SG-POSS-meat
'meat, flesh'	'his/her (own) flesh'	'my (animal's) meat'

In (16c), in order for the inalienable possessor to be unrealised, a shift RN → SC as represented in (15) must apply, albeit in a 'silent' fashion like in English. Subsequently, the prefix *k'e-* is applied, which denotes the function SC → RC and establishes the relation POSS for alienable nouns just like the Mayan markers represented in (9b) and (10b), and the alienable possessor is saturated in terms of the pronominal prefix specifying first singular. The theoretical implication is that alienability distinctions may interact with further type shifts.

This leads to the important issue of 'temporary' (in)alienability assignments. Commonly, nouns are not invariably assigned to one of the two classes; that is, one often encounters so-called temporary (or 'fluid') (in)alienability assignments (not to be confused with temporary possession, as opposed to permanent possession) that come about by different conceptualisations. Consider the following contrast pair, in which the alienably possessed variants are marked by a free pronoun and a preposition, respectively:

(17)   Patpatar (Oceanic < Malayo-Polynesian; Chappell & McGregor 1996: 3)

a. *a kat-igu*	b. *agu kat*
DEF liver-1SG	1SG liver
'my liver'	'my liver (that I am going to eat)'

In order to illustrate how the present approach captures temporary possession, I offer the representation in (18). The operation (18c) existentially binds the

---

[8] Strictly speaking, in the case of FNs (as opposed to RNs) it takes the combination of two shifts to arrive at an SC. One is de-relativisation as in (15), the other is [+ unique] → [− unique] ('de-functionalisation', as it were) and will be briefly touched in 4.2. The effect of the two shifts is represented below in (18).

argument that is originally related to the possessum, and at the same time provides a different relation between which is contextually instantiated (hence the subscript 'context'), thus introducing an alienable possessor.

(18) Representation of temporary possession in Patpatar
    a. scheme for FNs:
        $\lambda y.\iota x[(\text{SortalComponent}(x))\ldots \wedge (\text{RelationalComponent}(x,y))]$
    b. instantiation by *kat* 'liver':
        $\lambda y.\iota x[\text{LIVER}(x)\ldots \wedge \text{PART-OF}(x,y)]$
    c. shift FN → SC plus contextual relation (thus, FN → SC → RC):
        $\lambda FN.\lambda z.\lambda x.\exists y[FN(x,y) \wedge \text{POSS}_{\text{context}}(z,x)]$
    d. (18c) applied to (18b):
        $\lambda z.\lambda x.\exists y[\text{LIVER}(x) \wedge \text{PART-OF}(x,y) \wedge \text{POSS}_{\text{context}}(z,x)]$

The result (18d) can be applied so as to discharge the possessor in exactly the same way as (9d).

Summing up, the essence of this section is that the distinction of semantic vs. pragmatic accounts for what is known as the alienability contrast: 'alienable' morphology (esp. connectives, classifiers) denotes a function from SN to RC. 'Inalienable' is morphologically unmarked because the relation of affiliation is inherent. In this respect, the inalienable construction corresponds to either weak or absent definite articles, which will be the object of the following section.

4 The Typology of Definite Article Splits: The Role of Semantic vs. Pragmatic Uniqueness

The major tenet of the uniqueness approach to definiteness (Löbner 1985, 2011) is that any definite noun phrase indicates unique reference, meaning that its head noun is used as a functional concept (more precisely, IC or FC). It has already been pointed out above that, in the same way as possession comes about in two ways, this also holds true of unique reference: on the one hand, uniqueness may result from the meaning of the noun itself. This is the case with FNs and INs, as in *the temperature (in Tbilisi at noon)*. On the other hand, uniqueness can result from the linguistic or extra-linguistic context; that is, in cases of anaphoric uses of SNs or of situational definiteness (the man at the corner). This distinction, referred to as semantic uniqueness versus pragmatic uniqueness, motivates the asymmetries with regard to the distribution of definite articles that are found cross-linguistically.

4.1 Article Splits

Based on the distinction between semantic and pragmatic uniqueness, Löbner (2011) posits a scale whose elements are arranged according to the restriction in the choice of possible referents. In (19) I render the scale in the slightly revised version established in Ortmann (2014).[9]

(19) Scale of uniqueness (Ortmann 2014: 314, adapted from Löbner 2011): deictic with SN < anaphoric with SN < SN with establishing relative clause < relational DAA < part-whole DAA < non-lexical FC < lexical IN/FN < proper name < personal pronoun

The steps on the scale of uniqueness depict the degree of restriction in the potential of noun referents. The choice among possible referents of the head noun is necessarily limited towards the right end, where semantic uniqueness is located. The choice of referents gets increasingly broader from right to left, in line with the fact that for SNs to refer uniquely, the dependence on the context is high (hence the notion pragmatic uniqueness). The basic hypothesis of the CTD theory is that the distinction between semantic and pragmatic uniqueness, arranged in a more graded fashion on the scale in (19), is the basis of all conceptually governed article splits. Concretely, the scale is connected with the following empirical predictions:

(20) Predictions entailed by the scale of uniqueness:
      1. A decrease of obligatoriness in the use of articles as one moves from the left end to the right. This decrease correlates with a decrease of functional load.

      2. Diachronically, the use of the article spreads from left to right along the scale, thus eventually covering also those areas where it is functionally redundant.

An instance of Prediction 2 is the use of articles with proper names for persons in, for example, Modern Greek and colloquial German. It is a statement with respect to the grammaticalisation of definiteness, in harmony with and corroborated by the generalisations in Himmelmann (1997) and Lyons (1999: 275ff). As regards the implicational statement of Prediction 1, I refer to those languages in which definiteness markers systematically occur in some contexts and not in others as exhibiting a split article system. The contexts of pragmatic uniqueness will be among those in which definite articles occur. Since articles denote a function $\langle\langle e, t\rangle, e\rangle$ from SN/RN to IC/FC in these contexts, their 'functional load' (i.e., their importance) is highest here. Accordingly, the diachronic expectations expressed by the scale are that the use of articles spreads from left to right. This is the typical development of any language in which articles emerged from erstwhile demonstratives, and German is no exception. In Old High German, definite articles are only obligatory with anaphoric NPs, but typically missing

---

[9] The notion 'establishing relative clause' goes back to Hawkins (1978, 138ff.) and will become relevant in 4.4.1. 'DAA' represents 'definite associative anaphora' (also known as 'bridging'). Like other anaphora, DAAs are anchored by the referent of a previously mentioned NP; e.g. ... *a house* ... *the door* .... Non-lexical FCs come about by combining nouns (of any type) with ordinals or superlative adjectives and will be discussed in 4.3.1.

with FNs as in example (21a), in fact even with an FC that results from an establishing relative clause as in (21b) (so-called autophoric reference).

(21)   Old High German (Luke, 2, 46; translation from 8th century)

    a.   ... *her uuas fon* <u>*huse*</u> *inti fon* <u>*hiuuiske*</u> *Dauides.*
         he   was   from house and from line   David's   FCs

    b.   ... *wurðun* <u>*taga*</u> *gifulte   thaz siu bari.*
         were   days fulfilled that she gave_birth   AUTOPHORIC

The passage confirms the central point of this section, namely that semantic uniqueness is unmarked in the sense of not being overtly indicated by a determiner, in harmony with the uniqueness scale and the predictions in (20).

As far as the right edge of the scale is concerned, it is fairly rare for personal pronouns to be accompanied by articles. In Maori, the article variant *a* is used with proper names and personal pronouns of all persons: *ki a au* PREP DEF PRON1SG 'to me', *a koutou* DEF PRON2PL 'you', *i a raatou* OBJ DEF PRON3PL 'them' (Bauer 1993, 4, 371, 368; cf. also note 12). On the other hand, it is quite common for languages not to have definite articles at all. This is the case if demonstratives do not obligatorily occur with anaphoric nouns and, especially, if they are not used with definite associative anaphora either.[10]

The fact that there is considerable variation, and that languages extend the distribution of articles to environments where they are redundant, suggests a tension of competing factors. These factors are economy on the one hand (to be stated as "Avoid overt operators where they are vacuous"), and the uniform syntactic behaviour of nouns on the other hand, roughly: All NPs with unique reference should receive the same determiner. Since any language with articles has to balance these conditions it is not surprising that virtually all article languages show some split.

The fundamental claim of Ortmann (2014) is that language-specific article asymmetries are of one of the two sorts mentioned in (22).

(22)   **Split I:** A leftmost segment of the scale is marked by the definite article, the rest remains unmarked.
       Split II: Two segments of the scale (normally pragmatic and semantic uniqueness) are morphosyntactically distinguished in terms of different article forms, each of which will be subject to the Predictions 1 and 2 of (20).

Examples of Split I systems are Old High German (as well as the previous stages of all other languages with subsequent generalised article use), Old Georgian (cf. Boeder 2010, Ortmann 2014: 315–318) and West Slavic (more on which below).

The Romance language Catalan is an instance of Split II. According to Hualde (1992), Catalan, especially the variety of the Balearic Islands, exhibits the following sets of articles: the forms *(e)l, la, els, les,* thus, l-forms as in other Romance languages. They occur with "nouns that have a unique referent" (Hualde 1992: 281). By contrast, in anaphoric contexts the forms *es, sa,*

---

[10] For these and other criteria see Himmelmann (1997).

ses, which like French *ce* derive from Latin *ipse,* are used. A minimal pair is *l'Església* 'the (Catholic) Church', which is semantically unique, and the pragmatically unique *s'església* 'the church (building)'. Incidentally, we are actually dealing with a three-way split, since in the variety of the Balearic Islands proper names are preceded by particular article forms, *en, na,* that is, by a preproprial article, e.g. *en Joan.* Another case in point is Maori, as described by Bauer (1993), which features *te/ngaa* as the more widely used article, obligatory in cases of semantic uniqueness (INs, FNs, superlative FCs), moreover optional in anaphoric contexts. The forms *taua/aua* are confined to anaphoric and autophoric noun phrases.[11]

As we will see, the grammaticalised distinction between semantic and pragmatic uniqueness in terms of a split II system is especially common in West-Germanic languages.

4.2   Type Shifts in Definiteness

The analysis for definiteness splits is fully parallel to the analysis of possession in Sect. 2. Consequently, the claim I will defend is the following:

(23)   **Claim:** Pragmatic uniqueness involves a shift from $[-$ unique$]$ to $[+$ unique$]$. 'Strong' articles overtly denote this operation, their logical type thus being $\langle\langle e, t\rangle, e\rangle$. 'Weak' articles indicate semantic uniqueness. They signify an identity mapping $\langle e, e\rangle$.

Notice that since the logical type $\langle e, t\rangle$ subsumes SNs as well as RNs whose argument has been saturated, the 'strong' article operation mentioned in (23) captures both subtypes of $[-$ unique$]$. Furthermore, note that analogously to de-relativisation as analysed in 3.4, we can conceive indefinite uses of INs and FNs (e.g., *a sun, many fathers of this success, a mother*) as 'de-functionalisation'. In other words, these uses involve a shift in the opposite direction, that is, IN $\rightarrow$ SC, FN $\rightarrow$ RC, and FN $\rightarrow$ SC, respectively ($\langle e, \langle e, t\rangle\rangle$, and $\langle\langle e, e\rangle, \langle e, \langle e, t\rangle\rangle\rangle$, and $\langle\langle e, e\rangle, \langle e, t\rangle\rangle$).[12]

---

[11] Besides, there is a special article form that is found with proper names (like in Catalan), and moreover with pronouns. Note that Catalan and Maori are not unusual in featuring so-called preproprial articles. One source of the latter, e.g., in dialects of Norwegian, are third person forms of personal pronouns; cf. Matushansky (2008).

[12] An anonymous reviewer (Reviewer 1) raises the question as to the exact nature of such a shift from e to $\langle e, t\rangle$; specifically, if one should exclusively think of it as Partee's (1986) IDENT, in which case there would be a problem with respect to a presupposition of existence (cf. Coppock & Beaver 2012: 533f). Essentially, we are dealing with a variety of shifts of which IDENT is only one. As a matter of fact, Partee (1986: 122) herself proposes another e to $\langle e, t\rangle$ shift, labelled PRED, which returns properties from their entity-correlates. One other is, following Löbner (2011: 284f), a shift that is operative with proper names in predicative or indefinite use, as in *He's an Einstein.* Yet another instance is a shift from an individual constant into a predicate, by way of making use of its descriptive contents, as it seems to be necessary, e.g., for *a moon.*

In the following subsections, the goal is to provide evidence for the claim in (23). Further instances are discussed and analysed in Ortmann (2014).

4.3 'Zero' and Weak Articles Indicate Semantic Uniqueness

4.3.1 The 'Zero' Article Implies Semantic Uniqueness: Split I

A paradigm case of a Split I system (that is, article as opposed to no/zero article) is that of Colloquial Upper Sorbian (Obersorbische Umgangssprache) as analysed by Breu (2004). The definite article was grammaticalised from the former demonstrative pronoun tón, ta, to. In present-day use it is found in many environments (even including some environments of semantic uniqueness) but not all. Crucially, the article does not occur with lexical INs or FNs such as unicums and typical institutions:

(24) Upper Sorbian (< West Slavic; Breu 2004: 30)
    a. *slónco*   b. *Tame jo* <u>*dwórnišćo.*</u>   c. *Tame jo* <u>*cyrkej.*</u>
       sun   there AUX station   there AUX church
       'the sun'   'There's the station.'   'There's the church.'

This behaviour is shared by another West Slavic language, viz. the Upper Silesian variety of Polish, as analysed by Czardybon (2010). In Upper Silesian, the definite article, grammaticalised from the demonstrative *tyn, ta, te,* is also excluded with lexical INs and FNs:

(25) Upper Silesian (< West Slavic; Breu 2010: 37)
    To   *jest*   *chyba*   *koniec tego*   *film-u.*
    DEF.N COP.3SG.PRES probably end   DEF.GEN.M film-GEN

    'This is probably the end of the film.'

For all contexts further left on the scale of uniqueness, articles are either optional or even obligatory. For example, Czardybon (2010: 35) states that articles are commonly missing with non-lexical ICs and FCs, as in *Nojlepszo zoza jes moja* 'The best sauce is mine'; however, Adrian Czardybon (p.c.) informs me that at closer inspection it turned out that in most cases articles can in fact optionally be used. That the article is realised with all steps still further to the left of the scale will be illustrated in the following subsection.

4.3.2 The Weak Article Implies Semantic Uniqueness: Split II

Split II pertains to a morphological opposition of two (paradigms of) definite articles. Often one is a phonologically reduced form of the other. For this reason, the contrast is commonly referred to as 'strong' vs. 'weak'. In fact many, if not most, spoken varieties of German have developed weak article forms, which indicate the presence of an IN or an FN.

Consider the definite articles of the Rhineland, here represented by the Ripuarian dialect of Central Franconian.

(26)   Definite articles of Kölsch (Ripuarian); after Tiling-Herrwegen (2002: 150)

		masc	fem	neuter	plural
strong	NOM/ACC:	*dä*	*die*	*dat*	*die*
	DAT:	*dä*	*dä*	*däm*	*dä (/denne)*
weak	NOM/ACC:	*der*	*de*	*et*	*de*
	DAT:	*dem*	*der*	*dem*	*de*

The weak article occurs with all subtypes of semantically unique concepts (INs or FNs) such as proper names (*der Pitter, et Marie*) and abstract nouns (*et Levve* 'life'). (27) provides a so-called 'weak definite' noun use (that is, not showing particular reference; cf. Carlson & Sussman 2005):[13]

(27)   Kölsch (< C. Franconian < West Germanic; Tiling-Herrwegen 2002: 142):
       Nemm der   Schirm   met, et   es   am rähne!
       take DEF.M.WK umbrella with 3SG.N BE.3SG at rain.INF
       'Take your (*lit.*: the) umbrella, it is raining.'

A very similar distribution is found for Alemannic, the dialect group that comprises Swiss German as well as the dialects of south-western Germany and the westernmost part of Austria. Studler 2014 speaks of the opposition as 'full' and 'reduced' article forms. The reduced forms de, d, s occur in contexts of inherent uniqueness. This is illustrated in (28) by a (non-lexical) FN and an IN.

(28)   Swiss German (Alemannic < West Germanic; Studler 2014: 155)

a. *s   grööscht Schtück Chueche*   b. *de   Mond schiint*
   DEF.N.WK largest   piece   cake   DEF.M.WK moon shine.3SG
   'the largest piece of cake'   'the moon is shining'

In accordance with our expectations, then, [+ unique] nominals take weak article forms in the dialects under consideration.

---

[13] An anonymous reviewer (Reviewer 2) rightly points out that underlying SNs such as 'umbrella' and 'dog ' must be turned into an IC in order for the weak article to be available in cases such as (27). The reviewer asks why this shift is not associated with morphological marking. As a matter of fact, many, if not most, shifting operations are silent rather than overtly marked. Typically, they are lexically restricted and depend on world knowledge, as in the case of 'weak definites' ; other instances are IN → SC shifts as discussed in note 13 and cases of polysemy. It appears that with regar to operations among nominal concept types, only the most productive ones tend to be overt. Note that these are mainly the ones that rely on contextual rather than lexical information: the appropriate context to identify the antecedent of an anaphoric NP (SC → IC) or a non-lexical POSS relation (SN → RC). Similarly, existential binding, which is involved in the operation [+relational] → [-relational], does not require lexical information either. More discussion of the shifting operations in detail is found in Löbner (2011: 310–312).

4.4   (Strong) Articles Indicate Pragmatic Uniqueness ([− Unique] → [+ Unique])

4.4.1   Article as Opposed to No Article: Split I

While in Upper Silesian *tyn, ta, te* were shown to be rejected in contexts of semantic uniqueness, in anaphoric and autophoric contexts the occurrence of these forms is obligatory (and they can therefore be said to function as definite articles). The notion of autophoricity implies that unique reference is established by restricting the noun's potential referents in terms of a relative clause as in (29), hence the notion of an 'establishing relative clause'.

(29)   Upper Silesian (< West Slavic; Czardybon 2010: 34)

*Jak sie   nazywo **tyn**   ptok, co kradnie?*
how REFL call.3SG DEF.ACC.M.SG bird REL steal.3SG

'What is the name of the bird that steals?'

In Upper Sorbian, contexts of anaphoricity and autophoricity also require the article, as shown in (30a) and (30b), respectively.[14]

(30)   Upper Sorbian (< West Slavic; Breu 2004: 39, 22)

a. *Papa jo   s   woza panoł   ha ji   sej ruku złamał.*
Papa AUX from car   fall.PRET and 3SG REFL hand break.PRET

   ***Ta**   ruka dyrbi   něk dwě nězli we gipsu wostać.*
DEF.F.SG hand must.3SG now two weeks in cast stay

   'Daddy fell from the cart and broke his hand. The hand now has to stay in the cast for two weeks.'

b. *Kóždy   dóstane **tón**   žonu, kiž   sej wón   zasłuži.*
everyone get.3SG DEF.ACC.F wife REL.F REFL 3SG.M deserve.3SG

   'Every man gets the wife that he deserves.'

Notice that *žonu,*'wife' in (30b) must have previously undergone a silent shift from FN to SC, to be combinable with an establishing relative clause with the function of contrasting different sorts of wives.

In summary, where Split I articles occur they indicate pragmatic uniqueness, hence formally denoting a function that takes SN to IC.[15]

---

[14] Thanks to Adrian Czardybon for providing the glosses for the examples from Sorbian.

[15] In contrast to Upper Silesian, in Upper Sorbian the article is also obligatory with non-lexical functional concepts (i.e., ICs and FCs that come about by ordinal numbers and superlatives, which comprises a function over the domain that is characterised by the noun predicate), provided the NP is the comment rather than the topic of the clause. Similarly, associative anaphora (DAAs) tend to be generally preceded by the article in Upper Sorbian (Breu 2004: 20, 41), whereas in Upper Silesian this tends to be restricted to part-whole DAAs Czardybon (2010: 30ff, 2014: 309ff). What this shows with respect to the language-specific cut-off points on the scale (19) is that for Upper Sorbian the obligatory use of articles is two steps further advanced than in Upper Silesian.

4.4.2   The Strong Article Indicates Pragmatic Uniqueness: Split II

As mentioned in 4.3.2, numerous spoken varieties of German such as Alemannic, Bavarian, and dialects of the Rhineland show this split. Notice that for all variants at issue the definite articles are at least prosodically distinct from the demonstrative pronouns in that the latter are stressed and often lengthened. First, let me return to Rhinelandic as mentioned in 4.3. Recall that the weak article occurs with semantically unique concepts (INs or FNs). The strong article, by contrast, occurs in contexts of deictic, anaphoric and autophoric reference, hence pragmatic uniqueness (see also Schroeder 2006: 560f and references there). This can be nicely illustrated by an example from Rheydter Platt, a variety of the lower Rhine:[16]

(31)   Rheydter Platt (< Low Franconian < West Germanic)

    in   dä   Pott jeschutt, dat mit   die   Karr
    into DEF.M.STR pot   poured   3SG with DEF.F.STR cart

    narem   Veld jefahre
    to_DEF.DAT.WK field driven

    '(was) poured into the pot and carried to the field with the cart'

The noun phrase *dä Pott*'the pot' is coreferent with the previously introduced *e Vaat*'a barrel', and *die Karr* with *enne Warel*'a cart', respectively.

Another instance of a Split II is the opposition in Swiss German. It was shown above that weak forms are found with INs and FNs. The full forms in (32) signal anaphoric and autophoric use, that is, pragmatic uniqueness.

(32)   Swiss German (Alemannic < West Germanic; Studler 2014: 156)

    a. *Uf em   Tesch liit   es   Buech. Das   Buech*
        on DEF.DAT.WK table lie.3SG INDEF.N book   DEF.N.STR book

        wot   i lääse.
        want I read

        'There is a book on the table. I want to read the book.'

    b. *Das   Buech, wo-n-i   geschter gchouft   ha*
        DEF.N.STR book   REL-EP-1SG yesterday buy.PART have

        'the book that I bought yesterday'

The opposition in the article forms in Alemannic, then, renders the conceptual difference of semantic and pragmatic uniqueness, where the latter requires a strong article. Like in Ripuarian and elsewhere, the strong forms indicate an operation that turns [− unique] to [+ unique].

Particularly revealing in this connection is an observation with respect to the distribution of definite articles in Fering, a variety of Northern Frisian spoken on the islands of Föhr and Amrum. Basically, the so-called D-forms *di, det, don* are

---

[16] The example (31) is an excerpt from spontaneous conversation among two elderly dialect speakers, recorded and transcribed by Jennifer Kohls. I would like to thank her for permitting me to quote her data.

unstressed variants of the demonstrative pronoun, and confined to pragmatic uniqueness, hence indicate the operation SN → IC. The so-called A-forms *a,* *at* cover the contexts of semantic uniqueness; see Ebert 1971 and 1985. The additional observation by Keenan & Ebert (1973) concerns the contrast found in autophoric context in the scope of matrix verbs that give rise to referential ambiguities. Consider the following example pair:

(33)   Fering (Northern Frisian < West Germanic; Keenan & Ebert 1973: 422f)
       John wonnert ham,   dat   a   / di   maan wat woon
       John wonder 3SG.ACC.M COMP DEF.WK / DEF.STR man REL won
       bisööpen wiar.
       drunk   was
       'John was surprised that the man who won was drunk.'

Crucially, the A-form in (33) is tied to a de dicto reading, that is, an opaque reading with the concept of 'winner' as such. The de re reading, that is, the transparent interpretation involving the extensional meaning of winner, is not available; it would instead require the D-form, which is ambiguous between both readings. This piece of data strongly confirms the thesis that split article systems serve to mark the functional distinction of semantic and pragmatic uniqueness. The weak article indicates that the uniqueness comes about independently of the situation and does not require any shift induced by the context, as it would be needed in order to determine who the winner is.

    Keenan & Ebert (1973: 423f) furthermore argue that the de dicto vs. de re contrast also accounts for the distribution of articles in Malagasy.

(34)   Malagasy (Austronesian; Keenan & Ebert 1973: 423f)
       Gaga   Rakoto fa   mamo ny   / ilay   mpandresy.
       surprised Rakoto COMP drunk DEF.WK / DEF.STR winner
       'Rakoto was surprised that the winner was drunk.'

Of the two forms at issue, *ny* and *ilay*, the former is the general definite article that occurs in contexts of semantic as well as pragmatic uniqueness. Accordingly, it allows for both the opaque and the transparent reading in contexts analogous to (34). This is in contrast with the form *ilay*, "whose use is narrowly restricted to objects that the hearer has specifically identified prior to the utterance" (l.c.: 423). In other words, *ilay* covers a certain section of pragmatic uniqueness, hence it only allows for the de re reading. Note that this does not imply that every article split language will exhibit a de dicto vs. de re contrast comparable to those of Fering and Malagasy; for example, German does not, as an anonymous reviewer points out. Rather, as with the other asymmetries analysed in this section, the implication is that if there is such a contrast, the distribution will always be along these lines, and cannot be the reverse.

    In sum, the generalisation for the various instances of Split II can be represented along the following lines: weak articles merely redundantly display unique reference. Being otherwise vacuous, they denote an identity mapping of the type $\langle e, e \rangle$. Strong articles indicate that uniqueness comes about by reference to the context or discourse. They denote a semantic operation from [− unique] to [+ unique], thus, SN → IC.

5 Conclusion

I have argued in this paper that the distinction between semantic and pragmatic uniqueness and possession is successful in explaining morphosyntactic splits regarding two essential categories of nominal determination, namely uniqueness and possession. The goal was to provide evidence for the adequacy of conceptual noun types and of shifts among them. The results also show that type shift operations are not merely a construct in order to remedy the composition as conceived by the theoretician. Rather, in many languages there are morphological markers that do overtly what has been thought to be the job of covert operations, and in fact is the job of type shifts in other languages. They should therefore be regarded as fundamental ingredients of the human language capacity, substantiated by the overt lexical inventory of natural languages.

Let me sum up the major theses I have advocated above:

1. As for definiteness, semantic uniqueness implies that the reference of a noun is unique because of its lexical semantics. Pragmatic uniqueness characterises those uses of a noun in which a unique determination of its referent only comes about by the discourse or utterance context. Anaphoric or deictic reference, hence pragmatic uniqueness, implies a type shift $\langle\langle e, t\rangle, e\rangle$ from sortal to individual (SN → IC).
2. This distinction is reflected by two different sorts of splits: Split I: Pragmatic uniqueness is marked by the definite article, whereas semantic uniqueness is unmarked (e.g., in West Slavic). Split II: Pragmatic and semantic uniqueness is morphosyntactically separated by different article forms (e.g., in West Germanic and Catalan).
3. 'Weak' articles are semantically redundant, merely signalling the presence of an IN or FN. 'Strong' articles, as well as the articles of Split I languages, denote a function SN → IC ($\langle\langle\langle et\rangle, e\rangle$). This holds, among others, for *dä, die, dat* (as opposed to *d(e)r, de, et*) as they are found in various versions in most spoken varieties of German.
4. Indefinite uses of underlying [+ unique] nouns (e.g., *a sun*) implicate a shift in the opposite direction (IN → SC, FN → RC), thus, $\langle e, \langle e, t\rangle\rangle$ and $\langle\langle e, e\rangle, \langle e, \langle e, t\rangle\rangle\rangle$, respectively.
5. As for possession, semantic possession implies that the relation between possessum and possessor is inherent to the lexical semantics of the possessum noun. Pragmatic possession implies that the POSS relation is contextually established.
6. The distinction of semantic vs. pragmatic possession largely accounts for what is known as alienability contrast. In many languages sortal nouns must be endowed with a connective or classifier when combined with a possessor. Thus, 'alienable' morphology overtly denotes a function taking [− relational] to [+ relational], thus, $\langle\langle e, t\rangle, \langle e, \langle e, t\rangle\rangle\rangle$.

7. Conversely, 'inalienable' morphology merely signals the inherence of a relation of affiliation. Thus, for relative nouns the possessed use is canonical and unmarked, while the omission of a possessor in some languages requires a de-relativizing marker, thus, an overt exponent of an $\langle\langle e, \langle e, t\rangle\rangle, \langle e, t\rangle\rangle$ operation converting [+ relational] to [− relational].

8. The two categories of nominal determination, definiteness and possession, have been shown to be parallel in the following regards: 1.) the distinction of semantic vs. pragmatic determination; 2.) the type shifts and overt operations from underlying concept type to actual use; 3.) the close correlation of semantic and morphosyntactic markedness.

References

Barker, C.: Possessive Descriptions. CSLI Publications, Stanford (1995)

Barker, C.: Possessives and relational nouns. In: Maienborn, C., von Heusinger, K., Portner, P. (eds.) Semantics: An International Handbook Of Natural Language Meaning, pp. 1109–1130. De Gruyter, Berlin (2011)

Bauer, W.: Maori. Routledge, London (1993)

Boeder, W.: Klassizistische Sprachkompetenz: Der altgeorgische Artikel bei Sulchan-Saba Orbeliani. (Klasicisṭuri enobrivi kompeṭenturoba: ȝveli Karṭuli naçevari Sulxan-Saba Orbelianis "Sibrȝne sicruisaši"). Enatmecnirebis sakitxebi / Linguistic Issues **2009**(12), 140–163 (2010)

Breu, W.: Der definite Artikel in der obersorbischen Umgangssprache. In: Krause, M., Sappok, C. (eds.) Slavistische Linguistik 2002. Referate des XXVIII. Konstanzer Slavistischen Arbeitstreffens. Sagner, München (2004)

Bricker, V.R., Po'ot Yah, E., Dzul Po'ot, O.: A Dictionary of the Maya Language as Spoken in Hocabá, Yucatán. University of Utah Press, Salt Lake City (1998)

Carlson, G.N., Sussman, R.: Seemingly indefinite definites. In: Kepser, S., Reis, M. (eds.) Linguistic Evidence: Empirical, Theoretical and Computational Perspectives, pp. 71–86. Mouton de Gruyter, Berlin (2005)

Chappell, H., McGregor, W.: The Grammar of Inalienability: A Typological Perspective on Body Part Terms and the Part Whole Relation. Mouton de Gruyter, Berlin (1996)

Coppock, E., David, B.: Weak Uniqueness: the only difference between definites and indefinites. In: Proceedings of SALT, vol. 22, pp. 527–544 (2012)

Crowley, T.: Inalienable possession in paamese grammar. In: Chappell, H., McGregor, W. (eds.) The Grammar of Inalienability: A Typological Perspective on Body Part Terms and the Part Whole Relation, pp. 383–432. Mouton de Gruyter, Berlin (1996)

Czardybon, A.: Die Verwendung des definiten Artikels im Oberschlesischen im Sprachvergleich. Master thesis, University of Düsseldorf (2010)

Ebert, K.H.: Referenz, Sprechsituation und die bestimmten Artikel in einem nordfriesischen Dialekt (Fering). Nordfriisk Instituut, Bredstedt (1971)

England, N.C.: A Grammar of Mam, a Mayan Language. University of Texas Press, Austin (1983)

Hawkins, J.A.: Definiteness and Indefiniteness. A Study In Reference And Grammaticality Prediction. Croom Helm, London (1978)

Himmelmann, N.: Deiktikon, Artikel, Nominalphrase: Zur Emergenz syntaktischer Struktur. Niemeyer, Tübingen (1997)

Hualde, J.: Ignacio: Catalan. Routledge, London (1992)

Keenan, E.L., Ebert, K.H.: A note on marking transparency and opacity. Linguist. Inquiry 4, 412–424 (1973)

Lehmann, C.: Possession in Yucatec Maya. Lincom Europa, Munich (1998)

Löbner, S.: Concept types and determination. J. Semantics 4, 279–326 (1985)

Löbner, S.: Concept types and determination. J. Seman. 28, 279–333 (2011)

Lyons, C.: Definiteness. Cambridge University Press, Cambridge (1999)

Matushansky, O.: On the linguistic complexity of proper names. Linguist. Philos. 31, 573–627 (2008)

Nichols, J.: On alienable and inalienable possession. In: Shipley, W. (ed.) In Honor of Mary Haas. Haas Festival Conference on Native American Linguistics, pp. 557–609. Mouton de Gruyter, Berlin (1988)

Nichols, J.: Linguistic Diversity in Space and Time. The University of Chicago Press, Chicago (1992)

Ortmann, A.: Definite Article Asymmetries and Concept Types: semantic and pragmatic uniqueness. In: Gamerschlag, T., Gerland, D., Osswald, R., Petersen, W. (eds.) Frames and Concept Types: Applications in Language and Philosophy, pp. 293–321. Springer, Dordrecht (2014)

Ortmann, A., Corinna H.: Semantic Factors of Valence-Changing Processes with Nouns: Possession in the Mayan Languages. DGfS-Jahrestagung Mainz, (2004)

Partee, B.H.: Noun phrase interpretation and type-shifting principles. In: Groenendijk, J., de Jongh, D., Stokhof, M. (eds.) Foundations of pragmatics and lexical semantics, pp. 115–143. Foris, Dordrecht (1986)

Partee, B.H.: Borshev, Vladimir: Genitives, Relational Nouns, and Argument-Modifier Ambiguity. In: Lang, E., Maienborn, C., Fabricius-Hansen, C. (eds.) Modifying Adjuncts, pp. 67–112. Mouton de Gruyter, Berlin (2003)

Seiler, H.: Possession as an Operational Dimension of Language. Narr, Tübingen (1983)

Studler, R.: The morphology, syntax and semantics of definite determiners in Swiss German. In: Hofherr, P.C., Zribi-Hertz, A. (eds.) Crosslinguistic Studies on Noun Phrase Structure and Reference, pp. 143–171. Leiden, Brill (2014)

Thompson, C.: On the grammar of body parts in koyukon athabaskan. In: Chappell, H., McGregor, W. (eds.) The Grammar of Inalienability: A Typological Perspective on Body Part Terms and the Part Whole Relation, 551–676. Mouton de Gruyter, Berlin (1996)

Tiling-Herrwegen, A.: De kölsche Sproch. Kurzgrammatik Kölsch - Deutsch. Cologne, Bachem (2002)

Tozzer, A. M.: A Maya Grammar. With Bibliography and Appraisement of the Works Noted. Cambridge, MA. Reprinted 1974 by Kraus Reprint. Millwood, N.Y. (1921)

Vikner, C., Jensen, P.A.: A semantic analysis of the english genitive. interaction of lexical and formal semantics. Studia Linguistica 56, 191–226 (2002)

Alternative Semantics for Visser's Propositional Logics

Katsuhiko Sano[1]($\boxtimes$) and Minghui Ma[2]

[1] School of Information Science, Japan Advanced Institute of Science
and Technology, 1-1, Asahidai, Nomi, Ishikawa 923-1292, Japan
v-sano@jaist.ac.jp
[2] Institute for Logic and Intelligence, Southwest University, Beibei District,
Chongqing 400715, China
mmh.thu@gmail.com

Abstract. Visser's basic propositional logic **BPL** is the subintuitionistic logic determined by the class of all transitive Kripke frames, and his formal provability logic **FPL**, an extension of **BPL**, is determined by the class of all irreflexive and transitive finite Kripke frames. While Visser showed that **FPL** is embeddable into the modal logic **GL**, we first show that **BPL** is embeddable into the modal logic **wK4**, which is determined by the class of all weakly transitive Kripke frames, and we also show that **BPL** is characterized by the same frame class. Second, we introduce the *proper successor* semantics under which we prove that **BPL** is characterized by the class of weakly transitive frames, transitive frames, pre-ordered frames, and partially ordered frames. Third, we introduce topological semantics by interpreting implication in terms of the co-derived set operator and prove that **BPL** is characterized by the class of all topological spaces, T_0-spaces and T_d-spaces. Finally, we establish the topological completeness of **FPL** with respect to the class of scattered spaces.

1 Introduction

Visser [18] introduced a natural deduction for the logic called basic propositional logic (**BPL**), and the formal provability logic **FPL** for interpreting formal provability in Peano Arithmetic is obtained from **BPL** by adding Löb's rule. Visser proved that **BPL** is characterized by the class of all transitive Kripke frames, and **FPL** by the class of all finite irreflexive transitive frames. Intuitionistic logic (**Int**) is also shown by Visser [18] to be an extension of **BPL** which is incomparable with **FPL**. These propositional logics are related with modal logics by Gödel-Mckinsey-Tarski style translations. It is well-known that the Gödel-Mckinsey-Tarski translation [10,13] faithfully embeds **Int** into the modal logic **S4**. Visser [18, p.179] considered two variants, G_0 and G_1 (in our terminology), of Gödel-Mckinsey-Tarski translation and showed that both of them faithfully embed **FPL** into modal provability (Gödel-Löb) logic **GL**. The translation G_0 from the language for **BPL** to modal logic is defined recursively as follows:

© Springer-Verlag Berlin Heidelberg 2015
M. Aher et al. (Eds.): TbiLLC 2013, LNCS 8984, pp. 257–275, 2015.
DOI: 10.1007/978-3-662-46906-4_15

$$G_0(p) = \Box p \qquad\qquad G_0(\varphi \vee \psi) = G_0(\varphi) \vee G_0(\psi)$$
$$G_0(\bot) = \bot \qquad\qquad G_0(\varphi \wedge \psi) = G_0(\varphi) \wedge G_0(\psi)$$
$$G_0(\varphi \to \psi) = \Box(G_0(\varphi) \to G_0(\psi)).$$

The difference between G_0 and G_1 is in the atomic clause: while G_0 sends a variable p to $\Box p$, G_1 sends p to $p \wedge \Box p$. It is already known that G_0 embeds **BPL** into modal logic **K4**. For example, in [17], a Gödel-Mckinsey-Tarski translation is studied in an extension of **BPL** with a new implication symbol. As far as we know, no one has investigated which modal logics we can embed **BPL** into via the translation G_1. In this paper, we give an answer to this question in a generalized form (Theorem 1): G_1 embeds **BPL** into **wK4**, where **wK4** was shown by Esakia [8] to be the modal logic of *weakly transitive* Kripke frames.

Another observation about G_1 is the following: the modal formula $p \wedge \Box p$ is logically equivalent to $\Box p$ over reflexive Kripke frames, but they are not logically equivalent over non-reflexive Kripke frames. Thus, if we use a sort of proper successor semantics, i.e., the semantics that interpreting implication with proper successors even in reflexive transitive frames, we can characterize the logic **BPL**. In the proper successor semantics, the current evaluation point is disregarded, and so reflexivity of pre-ordered or partially ordered frames is also disregarded. Thus we can give various Kripke-type semantics for **BPL** (Theorem 2).

The third observation about the embedding of **BPL** into **wK4** is that we can provide a *topological* semantics for **BPL**, since **wK4** is the logic of all topological spaces if the diamond $\Diamond$ is interpreted as the *derivative operator* or the *limit operator* [3,9]. In finding the corresponding notion to proper successor semantics for the topological setting, we naturally introduce the co-derivative operator, i.e., the dual of the derivative operator, and use this to interpret implication. With the help of the result of translation, we also establish several new topological completeness results of **BPL** (Theorem 3). Although *modal* logics of all the topological spaces, all T_0-spaces and all T_d-spaces are distinct from each other [3,8], we show that the propositional logics (in the language of **BPL**) of all topological spaces, all T_0-spaces and all T_d-spaces are all the same as **BPL**, provided we interpret the implication symbol in terms of the co-derivative operator. Finally, under the same topological interpretation of implication, we also show that Visser's formal provability logic **FPL** is characterized by the class of all scattered spaces (Theorem 4), as a corollary of the embedding of **FPL** into **GL** and the topological completeness of **GL** with respect to the same class of spaces.

2   Visser's Basic Propositional Logic

The language $\mathcal{L}$ of **BPL** is the same as the language of intuitionistic propositional logic, consisting of a countable set Prop of propositional variables, and propositional connectives $\bot, \wedge, \vee, \to$. The set $\mathsf{Form}_{\mathcal{L}}$ of all $\mathcal{L}$-formulas is defined by the following inductive rule:

$$\varphi ::= \bot \mid p \mid \varphi \wedge \psi \mid \varphi \vee \psi \mid \varphi \to \psi \qquad (p \in \mathsf{Prop}).$$

We will now introduce Kripke semantics for Visser's **BPL**. A *Kripke frame* is a pair $\mathfrak{F} = (W, R)$ where W is a nonempty set and $R \subseteq W \times W$ is a binary relation. A *Kripke model* $\mathfrak{M}$ is a pair of a Kripke frame $\mathfrak{F} = (W, R)$ and a valuation mapping $V : \mathsf{Prop} \to \mathcal{P}(W)$. A Kripke frame $\mathfrak{F} = (W, R)$ (or a model $\mathfrak{M}$) is said to be

(i) *transitive*, if wRv and vRu imply wRu for all $w, v, u \in W$.

(ii) *weakly-transitive*, if wRv and vRu and $w \neq u$ imply wRu for all $w, v, u \in W$.

(iii) *pre-ordered*, if it is transitive and *reflexive*, i.e., wRw for all $w \in W$.

(iv) *partially ordered*, if it is pre-ordered and *anti-symmetric*, i.e., wRv and vRw jointly imply $w = v$ for all $w, v \in W$.

The reader can find the names for several classes of Kripke frames in the following table:

WT	the class of all weakly-transitive Kripke frames
TR	the class of all transitive Kripke frames
ITR$_{\mathrm{fin}}$	the class of all finite irreflexive and transitive frames
PRE	the class of all pre-ordered frames
PO	the class of all partially ordered frames

Definition 1. *Given a Kripke frame* $\mathfrak{F} = (W, R)$, *we say that a valuation* V : $\mathsf{Prop} \to \mathcal{P}(W)$ *in* $\mathfrak{F}$ *is persistent, if* $w \in V(p)$ *and* wRu *imply* $u \in V(p)$ *for all* $w, u \in W$ *and* $p \in \mathsf{Prop}$. *We say that a Kripke model* $\mathfrak{M} = (W, R, V)$ *is persistent, if the valuation* V *is persistent.*

Given any persistent Kripke model $\mathfrak{M} = (W, R, V)$, the satisfaction relation $\mathfrak{M}, w \models \varphi$ (note that we use '$\models$' here, this is different from '$\Vdash$' for our modal syntax below) is defined as follows:

$\mathfrak{M}, w \models p$ iff $w \in V(p)$,

$\mathfrak{M}, w \models \bot$ Never,

$\mathfrak{M}, w \models \varphi \wedge \psi$ iff $\mathfrak{M}, w \models \varphi$ and $\mathfrak{M}, w \models \psi$,

$\mathfrak{M}, w \models \varphi \vee \psi$ iff $\mathfrak{M}, w \models \varphi$ or $\mathfrak{M}, w \models \psi$,

$\mathfrak{M}, w \models \varphi \to \psi$ iff (wRu and $\mathfrak{M}, u \models \varphi$) imply $\mathfrak{M}, u \models \psi$, for all $u \in W$.

We do not require any condition on R here. It is known that transitivity of R and the persistency condition for all propositional variables imply the persistency for all formulas. We can also weaken the transitivity condition on R as follows:

Proposition 1. *Let* $\mathfrak{M} = (W, R, V)$ *be a persistent and weakly-transitive model. For all* $w, u \in W$ *and all* $\varphi \in \mathsf{Form}_{\mathcal{L}}$, *if* $\mathfrak{M}, w \models \varphi$ *and* wRu, *then* $\mathfrak{M}, u \models \varphi$.

Proof. By induction on φ. We show only the case $\varphi \equiv \psi \to \chi$. Assume that wRu and $\mathfrak{M}, w \models \psi \to \chi$. We need to show $\mathfrak{M}, u \models \psi \to \chi$. Suppose that uRv and $\mathfrak{M}, v \models \psi$. It suffices to show $\mathfrak{M}, v \models \chi$. We divide our argument into two cases: (1) $w \neq v$ and (2) $w = v$. For case (1), by the weak-transitivity of R, we obtain wRv. Since $\mathfrak{M}, w \models \psi \to \chi$ and $\mathfrak{M}, v \models \psi$, we get $\mathfrak{M}, v \models \chi$. For case (2), since $\mathfrak{M}, v \models \psi$, we get $\mathfrak{M}, w \models \psi$. By the inductive hypothesis $[\![\rho]\!]^\bullet \subseteq \mathbf{t}_\tau([\![\rho]\!]^\bullet)$ and monotonicity of $\mathbf{t}_\tau$, $\mathbf{t}_\tau([\![\rho]\!]^\bullet) \subseteq \mathbf{t}_\tau(\mathbf{t}_\tau([\![\rho]\!]^\bullet))$. Therefore, we obtain $w \in \mathbf{t}_\tau(\mathbf{t}_\tau([\![\rho]\!]^\bullet))$.

Given a class $\mathbb{F}$ of Kripke frames, we say that $\varphi \in \mathsf{Form}_\mathcal{L}$ is *valid* in $\mathbb{F}$ (notation: $\mathbb{F} \models \varphi$) if $(\mathfrak{F}, V), w \models \varphi$ for all $\mathfrak{F} \in \mathbb{F}$, all persistent valuations V in $\mathfrak{F}$ and all $w \in W$. Define the propositional logic of $\mathbb{F}$ by:

$$\mathrm{Log}(\mathbb{F}) := \{\, \varphi \in \mathsf{Form}_\mathcal{L} : \mathbb{F} \models \varphi \,\}.$$

It is well-known that $\mathrm{Log}(\mathbb{PO}) = \mathrm{Log}(\mathbb{PRE})$ is the same as the set of all theorems of intuitionistic logic **Int**. Since $\mathbb{PRE} \subseteq \mathbb{TR}$, we have $\mathrm{Log}(\mathbb{TR}) \subseteq \mathrm{Log}(\mathbb{PRE}) = \mathbf{Int}$. The following fact demonstrates that $\mathrm{Log}(\mathbb{TR}) \neq \mathbf{Int}$.

Fact 1. *Both* $(p \wedge (p \to q)) \to q$ *and* $(p \to (p \to q)) \to (p \to q)$ *are theorems of* **Int** *but they are not in* $\mathrm{Log}(\mathbb{TR})$.

Proof. For the first, it suffices to take the following Kripke model (W, R, V) where $W = \{0, 1\}$, $R = \{(0, 1)\}$ and $V(p) = \{0, 1\}$, $V(q) = \{1\}$. Then, the given formula is false at 0. For the second, we change the valuation into V' such that $V'(p) = \{1\}$ and $V'(q) = \varnothing$. The formula is false at 0.   □

Remark 1. We can define the *local consequence relation* as follows: Given a set $\Gamma \cup \{\varphi\}$, φ is a *semantic consequence* from Γ (notation: $\Gamma \models \varphi$), if for all transitive and persistent Kripke models $\mathfrak{M} = (W, R, V)$ and all $w \in W$, $\mathfrak{M}, w \models \gamma$ for all $\gamma \in \Gamma$ implies $\mathfrak{M}, w \models \varphi$. One can easily verify that $\{\varphi_1, \ldots, \varphi_{n-1}, \varphi_n\} \models \psi$ implies $\{\varphi_1, \ldots, \varphi_{n-1}\} \models \varphi_n \to \psi$. However, the converse does not hold in general. For example, $\{p \to q\} \models p \to q$ but $\{p \to q, p\} \not\models q$. The reflexivity condition on R is sufficient for the converse direction. Moreover, we observe from [15] that $\{\varphi_1, \ldots, \varphi_{n-1}, \varphi_n\} \models \psi$ iff $\bigwedge_{1 \leq i \leq n} \varphi_i \models \psi$.

We will now move to the axiomatization of **BPL**. Visser introduced the natural deduction for **BPL**. Here we present Suzuki and Ono's Hilbert-style axiomatization of **BPL** [16]. Their axiomatization is an extension of Corsi [6]'s axiomatization of the logic **F** of strict implication.

Fact 2 ([16]). **BPL** *is completely axiomatized by the following axioms and inference rules:*

(A1) $p \to p$

(A2) $p \to (q \to p)$

(A3) $(p \to q) \wedge (q \to r) \to (p \to r)$

(A4) $p \wedge q \to p$

(A5) $p \wedge q \to q$

(A6) $(p \to q) \wedge (p \to r) \to (p \to q \wedge r)$

(A7) $p \to (q \to p \wedge q)$

(A8) $p \to p \vee q$

(A9) $q \to p \vee q$

(A10) $(p \to r) \wedge (q \to r) \to (p \vee q \to r)$

(A11) $p \wedge (q \vee r) \to (p \wedge q) \vee (p \wedge r)$

(A12) $\bot \to p$

(MP) *From* φ *and* $\varphi \to \psi$, *infer* ψ

(Sub) *From* φ, *infer any uniform substitution instance of* φ.

Fact 3 ([16,18]). **BPL** = Log($\mathbb{TR}$).

It is known from [12] and [6] that **Int** is an extension of **BPL**, obtained by adding the axiom $(p \land (p \to q)) \to q$ (recall Fact 1). It is also easy to show from [18] that Visser's logic **FPL** is also an extension of **BPL**, obtained by adding the Löb axiom $((\top \to p) \to p) \to (\top \to p)$. Moreover, **FPL** is characterized by the class $\mathbb{ITR}_{fin}$ of all finite irreflexive transitive Kripke frames [18].

Fact 4 ([18]). **FPL** = Log($\mathbb{ITR}_{fin}$).

In order to capture these logics uniformly, we will introduce the concept of *superbasic logics*.

Definition 2. *A set $\Gamma \subseteq$ Form$_\mathcal{L}$ is a* superbasic *logic if Γ contains all the axioms of Fact 2 and closed under modus ponens* (MP) *and uniform substitution* (Sub). *Given a set $\Sigma \subseteq$ Form$_\mathcal{L}$, we use* **BPL** $\oplus \Sigma$ *to mean the smallest superbasic logic containing Σ.*

We note that both **FPL** and **Int** are superbasic logics. However, since the formula $((\top \to p) \to p) \to (\top \to p)$ is not a tautology, it is not a theorem of **Int**. This implies that **Int** and **FPL** are incomparable.

For any classes of frames $\mathbb{F}$ and $\mathbb{G}$, notice that $\mathbb{F} \subseteq \mathbb{G}$ implies Log($\mathbb{G}$) $\subseteq$ Log($\mathbb{F}$). Since $\mathbb{TR} \subseteq \mathbb{WT}$ clearly holds, we obtain Log($\mathbb{WT}$) $\subseteq$ Log($\mathbb{TR}$). Fact 3 enables us to derive the following Proposition 2 immediately.

Proposition 2. Log($\mathbb{WT}$) $\subseteq$ **BPL**.

The converse direction of this proposition also holds.

Proposition 3. **BPL** $\subseteq$ Log($\mathbb{WT}$).

Proof. The axioms of **BPL**, except (A2) and (A7), are valid on all (possibly non-weakly transitive and non-persistent) Kripke models. The axioms (A2) and (A7) are valid on $\mathbb{WT}$ by Proposition 1. It is easy to show that (Sub) preserves the validity on $\mathbb{WT}$. We will focus on (MP) here. Suppose that $\mathbb{WT} \models \varphi$ and $\mathbb{WT} \models \varphi \to \psi$. Our goal is to show $\mathbb{WT} \models \psi$. Fix any persistent Kripke model $\mathfrak{M}$ = (W, R, V) such that $(W, R) \in \mathbb{WT}$, and any state $w \in W$. We show $\mathfrak{M}, w \models \psi$. Take a state $* \notin W$. We construct the Kripke model $\mathfrak{M}^* = (W^*, R^*, V^*)$ by putting $W^* = W \cup \{*\}$, $R^* = R \cup \{(*, x) : x \in W\}$ and $V^*(p) = V(p)$ for all $p \in$ Prop. That is, we add a new point to $\mathfrak{M}$ as a root. It is trivial to see that R^* is weakly transitive and V^* is persistent. It is easy to show by induction on the construction of formulas that $\mathfrak{M}, x \models \chi$ iff $\mathfrak{M}^*, x \models \chi$ for all $x \in W$ and all $\chi \in$ Form$_\mathcal{L}$. Since $\mathbb{WT} \models \varphi$ and $\mathbb{WT} \models \varphi \to \psi$, we obtain $\mathfrak{M}^*, * \models \varphi \to \psi$ and $\mathfrak{M}^*, w \models \varphi$. By construction of $\mathfrak{M}^*$, we have $\mathfrak{M}^*, w \models \psi$. Hence $\mathfrak{M}, w \models \psi$. □

Remark 2. While the inference rule (MP) does *not* preserve truth on a fixed persistent Kripke model, it preserves validity on the *class* of persistent Kripke models or frames.

By Propositions 2 and 3, we obtain the following, i.e., **BPL** is sound and (weakly) complete with respect to $\mathbb{WT}$.

Corollary 1. **BPL** = Log($\mathbb{WT}$).

3   Embedding of Extensions of BPL into Modal Logics

In this section, we prove that **BPL** is embeddable into the modal logic **wK4** of the class $\mathbb{WT}$ of all weakly transitive frames. We introduce some basic notions of modal logic first. The syntax $\mathcal{ML}$ of modal logic consists of a set Prop of propositional variables, $\wedge$, $\vee$, $\bot$, $\to$ and a modal operator $\Box$. The set $\mathsf{Form}_{\mathcal{ML}}$ of all $\mathcal{ML}$-formulas is generated by the following grammar:

$$\alpha ::= \bot \mid p \mid \alpha \wedge \beta \mid \alpha \vee \beta \mid \alpha \to \beta \mid \Box \alpha \quad (p \in \mathsf{Prop}).$$

Given any Kripke model $\mathfrak{M}$ and a state w, the notion of truth or satisfaction $\mathfrak{M}, w \Vdash \alpha$ is defined as usual [4]. Given a class $\mathbb{F}$ of frames, we say that a modal formula α is *valid* in $\mathbb{F}$ (notation: $\mathbb{F} \Vdash \alpha$) if $(\mathfrak{F}, V), w \Vdash \alpha$ for all $\mathfrak{F} \in \mathbb{F}$, all valuations V in $\mathfrak{F}$ and all $w \in W$. Define

$$\mathrm{MLog}(\mathbb{F}) := \{\, \alpha \in \mathsf{Form}_{\mathcal{ML}} : \mathbb{F} \Vdash \alpha \,\}.$$

We say that a set $\Lambda \subseteq \mathsf{Form}_{\mathcal{ML}}$ of modal formulas is a *normal modal logic*, if it contains all instances of propositional tautologies, the axiom (K) $\Box(p \to q) \to (\Box p \to \Box q)$, and is closed under modus ponens (MP), uniform substitution (US), and $\Box$-necessitation (from φ infer $\Box\varphi$). It is well-known that the modal operator $\Box$ is *monotone* in any normal modal logic Λ: if $\alpha \to \beta \in \Lambda$, then $\Box\alpha \to \Box\beta \in \Lambda$. Let **K** be the minimal normal modal logic. Given a set Σ of modal formulas, we use $\mathbf{K} \oplus \Sigma$ to mean the smallest normal modal logic containing Σ.

Let **NExt(wK4)** be the class of all normal modal logics that contain the modal axiom $(w4)$ $p \wedge \Box p \to \Box\Box p$, which defines weak-transitivity of R. In what follows, we use the following standard names for normal modal logics.

- $\mathbf{wK4} := \mathbf{K} \oplus p \wedge \Box p \to \Box\Box p$.
- $\mathbf{K4} := \mathbf{K} \oplus \Box p \to \Box\Box p$.
- $\mathbf{S4} := \mathbf{K} \oplus \{\, \Box p \to \Box\Box p, \Box p \to p \,\}$.
- $\mathbf{GL} := \mathbf{K} \oplus \Box(\Box p \to p) \to \Box p$.

It is well-known that $\mathbf{K4} = \mathrm{MLog}(\mathbb{TR})$. Moreover, Esakia [8] proved the following result.

Fact 5 ([8]). $\mathbf{wK4} = \mathrm{MLog}(\mathbb{WT})$.

It is easy to see that the modal logic **wK4** is a proper sublogic of **K4**. However, if we add the modal axiom (T) $\Box p \to p$ for reflexivity to both logics, we get the same modal logic **S4**.

In the introduction of this paper, we mentioned Visser's embedding of **BPL** into **K4** by G_0, and **FPL** into **GL** by G_1. Inspired by Easkia's result on **wK4**, we will prove that Visser's translation G_1 faithfully embeds **BPL** into **wK4**.

Definition 3. *The translation* $G_1 : \mathsf{Form}_{\mathcal{L}} \to \mathsf{Form}_{\mathcal{ML}}$ *is defined recursively as follows:*

$$G_1(p) = p \wedge \Box p \qquad\qquad G_1(\varphi \vee \psi) = G_1(\varphi) \vee G_1(\psi)$$
$$G_1(\bot) = \bot \qquad\qquad G_1(\varphi \wedge \psi) = G_1(\varphi) \wedge G_1(\psi)$$
$$G_1(\varphi \to \psi) = \Box(G_1(\varphi) \to G_1(\psi)).$$

Proposition 4. *For any normal modal logic* $\Lambda \in \mathbf{NExt}(\mathbf{wK4})$, *and any formula* $\varphi \in \mathsf{Form}_{\mathcal{L}}$, $\vdash_\Lambda G_1(\varphi) \to \Box G_1(\varphi)$.

Proof. By induction on φ. We show only the atomic case and the case for implication. Other cases are easily shown by the inductive hypothesis. For $\varphi \equiv p$, we have $G_1(p) = p \wedge \Box p$. By $(w4) \in \Lambda$, we have $p \wedge \Box p \to \Box p \wedge \Box\Box p \in \Lambda$. Since $\Box p \wedge \Box\Box p \leftrightarrow \Box(p \wedge \Box p) \in \Lambda$, we have $p \wedge \Box p \to \Box(p \wedge \Box p) \in \Lambda$. For $\varphi \equiv \psi \to \chi$, we want to show $\Box(G_1(\psi) \to G_1(\chi)) \to \Box\Box(G_1(\psi) \to G_1(\chi)) \in \Lambda$. Let $\alpha := G_1(\psi)$ and $\beta := G_1(\chi)$. By the inductive hypothesis, we have $\alpha \to \Box\alpha \in \Lambda$ and $\beta \to \Box\beta \in \Lambda$. It suffices to show the following:

(1) $\neg\alpha \to (\Box(\alpha \to \beta) \to \Box\Box(\alpha \to \beta)) \in \Lambda$; and
(2) $\alpha \to (\Box(\alpha \to \beta) \to \Box\Box(\alpha \to \beta)) \in \Lambda$.

For (1), since $\neg\alpha \wedge \Box(\alpha \to \beta) \to \neg\alpha \wedge (\alpha \to \beta) \wedge \Box(\alpha \to \beta) \in \Lambda$, by the axiom $(w4)$, we obtain $\neg\alpha \to (\Box(\alpha \to \beta) \to \Box\Box(\alpha \to \beta)) \in \Lambda$. For (2), since $\Box\alpha \wedge \Box(\alpha \to \beta) \to \Box\beta \in \mathbf{wK4}$, by the inductive hypothesis $\beta \to \Box\beta \in \Lambda$, we have $\Box\alpha \wedge \Box(\alpha \to \beta) \to \Box\Box\beta \in \Lambda$. As $\beta \to (\alpha \to \beta)$ is a tautology, and by the monotonicity of $\Box$, we get $\Box\alpha \wedge \Box(\alpha \to \beta) \to \Box\Box(\alpha \to \beta) \in \Lambda$. Finally, by the inductive hypothesis $\alpha \to \Box\alpha \in \Lambda$, we get $\alpha \wedge \Box(\alpha \to \beta) \to \Box\Box(\alpha \to \beta) \in \Lambda$. $\square$

Now we consider the following inference rule and provide a sufficient condition for that **BPL** is embeddable into a normal modal logic Λ:

$$(\mathrm{MP}_\Box) \text{ from } p \text{ and } \Box(p \to q) \text{ infer } q.$$

We say that $(\mathrm{MP}_\Box)$ is *admissible* in a normal modal logic Λ if, for any uniform substitution σ in $\mathsf{Form}_{\mathcal{ML}}$, $p^\sigma \in \Lambda$ and $\Box(p^\sigma \to q^\sigma) \in \Lambda$ imply $q^\sigma \in \Lambda$. Note that the addition of the admissible rule to Λ does not change the set of all theorems in Λ. We need this admissibility because of (MP) in **BPL** (recall Remark 2).

Lemma 1. *Let* $\Sigma \subseteq \mathsf{Form}_{\mathcal{L}}$ *and* Λ *a normal modal logic such that* $(\mathrm{MP}_\Box)$ *is admissible in* Λ *and* $G_1[\Sigma] \cup \{(w4)\} \subseteq \Lambda$. *Then, for all* $\varphi \in \mathsf{Form}_{\mathcal{L}}$,

$$\vdash_{\mathbf{BPL} \oplus \Sigma} \varphi \text{ implies } \vdash_\Lambda G_1(\varphi).$$

Proof. Assume $\vdash_{\mathbf{BPL} \oplus \Sigma} \varphi$. We show $\vdash_\Lambda G_1(\varphi)$ by induction on the derivation of φ in $\mathbf{BPL} \oplus \Sigma$, where we treat elements of Σ as new axioms. It suffices to show that the translation G_1 converts all axioms in **BPL** into theorems in Λ, and that inferences rules (MP) and (Sub) are preserved under G_1. We check only the axiom (A2) $p \to (q \to p)$ and (MP). Other axioms and rules can be checked similarly.

For (A2), we need to show $\Box(G_1(p) \to \Box(G_1(q) \to G_1(p)) \in \Lambda$. By Proposition 4 (we need the axiom $(w4)$ here), $G_1(p) \to \Box\, G_1(p) \in \Lambda$, which implies $G_1(p) \to \Box(G_1(q) \to G_1(p)) \in \Lambda$. By $\Box$-necessitation, we obtain our goal.

For (MP), assume that χ is obtain from ψ and $\psi \to \chi$ in $\mathbf{BPL} \oplus \Sigma$. By the inductive hypothesis, we have $G_1(\psi) \in \Lambda$ and $G_1(\psi \to \chi) \in \Lambda$. By Proposition 4, $\Box(G_1(\psi) \to G_1(\chi)) \in \Lambda$. Since $(\mathrm{MP}_\Box)$ is admissible in Λ, we obtain $G_1(\psi) \in \Lambda$. $\Box$

Lemma 2. *Let $\Sigma \subseteq \mathsf{Form}_\mathcal{L}$, Λ a normal modal logic and $\mathbb{F}$ be a class of frames such that $\Lambda \subseteq \mathrm{MLog}(\mathbb{F})$ and $\mathrm{Log}(\mathbb{F}) \subseteq \mathbf{BPL} \oplus \Sigma$. Then, for all $\varphi \in \mathsf{Form}_\mathcal{L}$,*

$$\vdash_\Lambda G_1(\varphi) \text{ implies } \vdash_{\mathbf{BPL} \oplus \Sigma} \varphi.$$

Proof. Assume $\varphi \notin \mathbf{BPL} \oplus \Sigma$. By the assumption $\mathrm{Log}(\mathbb{F}) \subseteq \mathbf{BPL} \oplus \Sigma$, there exists a frame $\mathfrak{F} \in \mathbb{F}$ such that $\mathfrak{F} \nVdash \varphi$. Let $\mathfrak{M}$ be a model based on $\mathfrak{F}$ with a persistent valuation and w a state in $\mathfrak{M}$ such that $\mathfrak{M}, w \nVdash \varphi$. By assumption $\Lambda \subseteq \mathrm{MLog}(\mathbb{F})$, it suffices to show $\mathfrak{M}, w \nVdash G_1(\varphi)$. By induction on $\psi \in \mathsf{Form}_\mathcal{L}$, we show that, for all x in $\mathfrak{M}$,

$$\mathfrak{M}, x \models \psi \text{ iff } \mathfrak{M}, x \Vdash G_1(\psi),$$

Then we conclude from $\mathfrak{M}, w \nvDash \varphi$ that $\mathfrak{M}, w \nVdash G_1(\varphi)$. Our inductive proof proceed as follows: The atomic case is done by persistency. We show only the case of implication. Let $\psi = \xi \to \chi$. By definition of $\mathfrak{M}, x \models \xi \to \chi$, we obtain $\mathfrak{M}, y \models \xi$ implies $\mathfrak{M}, y \models \chi$ for all y in $\mathfrak{M}$ such that xRy. By the inductive hypothesis, this is equivalent to: $\mathfrak{M}, y \Vdash G(\xi)$ implies $\mathfrak{M}, y \Vdash G(\chi)$ for all y in $\mathfrak{M}$ such that xRy, hence $\mathfrak{M}, x \Vdash \Box(G_1(\xi) \to G_1(\chi))$. $\Box$

By Lemmas 1 and 2, we conclude the following theorem.

Theorem 1. *Let $\Sigma \subseteq \mathsf{Form}_\mathcal{L}$ and Λ a normal modal logic such that $(\mathrm{MP}_\Box)$ is admissible in Λ and $G_1[\Sigma] \cup \{(w4)\} \subseteq \Lambda$. Let $\mathbb{F}$ be a class of frames such that $\Lambda \subseteq \mathrm{MLog}(\mathbb{F})$ and $\mathrm{Log}(\mathbb{F}) \subseteq \mathbf{BPL} \oplus \Sigma$. Then, $\mathbf{BPL} \oplus \Sigma$ is embeddable into Λ via G_1, i.e., for all $\varphi \in \mathsf{Form}_\mathcal{L}$,*

$$\vdash_{\mathbf{BPL} \oplus \Sigma} \varphi \text{ iff } \vdash_\Lambda G_1(\varphi).$$

Proposition 5. *The rule $(\mathrm{MP}_\Box)$ is admissible in $\Lambda \in \{\mathbf{wK4}, \mathbf{K4}, \mathbf{S4}, \mathbf{GL}\}$.*

Proof. Let $\Lambda \in \{\mathbf{wK4}, \mathbf{K4}, \mathbf{S4}, \mathbf{GL}\}$. Suppose that $\alpha, \Box(\alpha \to \beta) \in \Lambda$. Recall that $\Lambda = \mathrm{MLog}(\mathbb{F})$, where $(\Lambda, \mathbb{F}) = (\mathbf{wK4}, \mathbb{WT})$, $(\mathbf{K4}, \mathbb{TR})$, $(\mathbf{S4}, \mathbb{PRE})$, or $(\mathbf{GL}, \mathbb{ITR}_{\mathrm{fin}})$. In order to show $\beta \in \Lambda$, it suffices to show that β is valid on all frames $\mathfrak{F} \in \mathbb{F}$ by $\Lambda = \mathrm{MLog}(\mathbb{F})$. Take any Λ-frame $\mathfrak{F} = (W, R)$, and any valuation V in $\mathfrak{F}$ and any $w \in W$. Let $\mathfrak{M} = (\mathfrak{F}, V)$. It suffices to show $\mathfrak{M}, w \Vdash \beta$. By the same construction as in the proof of Proposition 3, we construct $\mathfrak{M}^*$, i.e., we add a new state $*$ down to $\mathfrak{F}$ and get a new Λ-frame and a model $\mathfrak{M}^*$ in which the valuation of propositional variables is the same as that in $\mathfrak{M}$. Then it is easy to check that $(\mathfrak{M}^*, x)$ and $(\mathfrak{M}, x)$ satisfy the same modal formulas for all $x \in W$. By assumption, we obtain $\mathfrak{M}^*, * \Vdash \Box(\alpha \to \beta)$ and $\mathfrak{M}^*, w \Vdash \alpha$ (note that the frame part of $\mathfrak{M}^*$ is still in $\mathbb{F}$ for our choice of Λ). By the construction of $\mathfrak{M}^*$, we have $\mathfrak{M}^*, w \Vdash \beta$. Hence $\mathfrak{M}, w \Vdash \beta$. $\Box$

Corollary 2. *For all $\varphi \in \mathsf{Form}_\mathcal{L}$, $\vdash_{\mathbf{BPL}} \varphi$ iff $\vdash_{\mathbf{wK4}} G_1(\varphi)$.*

Proof. By Fact 3, Propositions 2, 5 and Theorem 1.   □

Corollary 3. *For all $\varphi \in \mathsf{Form}_\mathcal{L}$, $\vdash_{\mathbf{BPL}} \varphi$ iff $\vdash_{\mathbf{K4}} G_1(\varphi)$.*

Proof. By $\mathbf{K4} = \mathrm{MLog}(\mathbb{TR})$, Fact 3, Proposition 5 and Theorem 1.   □

Corollary 4. *For all $\varphi \in \mathsf{Form}_\mathcal{L}$, $\vdash_{\mathbf{Int}} \varphi$ iff $\vdash_{\mathbf{S4}} G_1(\varphi)$.*

Proof. By $\mathbf{S4} = \mathrm{MLog}(\mathbb{PRE})$, $\mathbf{Int} = \mathrm{Log}(\mathbb{PRE})$, Proposition 5, Theorem 1.   □

Corollary 5. *For all $\varphi \in \mathsf{Form}_\mathcal{L}$, $\vdash_{\mathbf{FPL}} \varphi$ iff $\vdash_{\mathbf{GL}} G_1(\varphi)$.*

Proof. By $\mathbf{GL} = \mathrm{MLog}(\mathbb{ITR}_{\mathrm{fin}})$, Fact 4 (i.e., $\mathbf{FPL} = \mathrm{Log}(\mathbb{ITR}_{\mathrm{fin}})$), Proposition 5 and Theorem 1. Notice also that $G_1((((\top \to p) \to p) \to (\top \to p))$ is equivalent with $\Box(\Box(\Box G_1(p) \to G_1(p)) \to \Box G_1(p))$, which is provable in $\mathbf{GL}$.   □

4   Alternative Kripke Semantics for Visser's BPL

Recall that $\mathbb{PRE}$ is the class of all pre-ordered frames and $\mathbb{PO}$ is the class of all partially ordered frames. We already know that $\mathbf{BPL} = \mathrm{Log}(\mathbb{TR}) \subsetneq \mathrm{Log}(\mathbb{PRE}) = \mathrm{Log}(\mathbb{PO}) = \mathbf{Int}$. Moreover, we have shown $\mathbf{BPL} = \mathrm{Log}(\mathbb{WT})$ in Corollary 1. Visser's motivation in [18] for obtaining $\mathbf{BPL}$ is to drop the requirement of reflexivity in Kripke frames for intuitionistic logic. Here we present an alternative way for obtaining $\mathbf{BPL}$ where we can keep the requirement of reflexivity in Kripke frames.

Given a persistent Kripke model $\mathfrak{M} = (W, R, V)$ and $\varphi \in \mathsf{Form}_\mathcal{L}$, we define the alternative satisfaction relation $\mathfrak{M}, w \models^{\bullet} \varphi$ by replacing the truth clause of $\varphi \to \psi$ with the following clause:

$$\mathfrak{M}, w \models^{\bullet} \varphi \to \psi \text{ iff } wRu \ \& \ w \neq u \ \& \ \mathfrak{M}, u \models^{\bullet} \varphi \text{ imply } \mathfrak{M}, u \models^{\bullet} \psi.$$

The underlying idea of this new clause is to disregard the current evaluation point w by adding the condition of '$w \neq u$'. In other words, we restrict our attention to the *proper* future or successor points. We will call the new semantics the *proper-successor semantics*. It allows us to characterize Visser's $\mathbf{BPL}$ in various ways. First, we obtain the following persistency result by induction on the construction of formulas.

Proposition 6. *Let $\mathfrak{M} = (W, R, V)$ be persistent and weakly-transitive. For all $w, u \in W$ and $\varphi \in \mathsf{Form}_\mathcal{L}$, if $\mathfrak{M}, w \models^{\bullet} \varphi$ and wRu, then $\mathfrak{M}, u \models^{\bullet} \varphi$,*

By $\mathbb{F} \models^{\bullet} \varphi$ we mean that $(\mathfrak{F}, V), w \models^{\bullet} \varphi$ for all $\mathfrak{F} \in \mathbb{F}$, all persistent valuations V and all points w in $\mathfrak{F}$. Given any class of frames $\mathbb{F}$, define

$$\mathrm{Log}^{\bullet}(\mathbb{F}) = \{\, \varphi \in \mathsf{Form}_\mathcal{L} : \mathbb{F} \models^{\bullet} \varphi \,\}.$$

Thus we get the following lemma immediately by the fact that $\mathbb{PO} \subseteq \mathbb{PRE} \subseteq \mathbb{TR} \subseteq \mathbb{WT}$.

Lemma 3. $\mathrm{Log}^{\bullet}(\mathbb{WT}) \subseteq \mathrm{Log}^{\bullet}(\mathbb{TR}) \subseteq \mathrm{Log}^{\bullet}(\mathbb{PRE}) \subseteq \mathrm{Log}^{\bullet}(\mathbb{PO})$.

In what remains of this section, we will show that all the logics in Lemma 3 are equal to **BPL**. First, by induction on the proof in **BPL** and Proposition 6, we can easily establish the soundness of **BPL** with respect to the class of frames $\mathbb{WT}$ under the proper successor semantics.

Lemma 4. $\mathbf{BPL} \subseteq \mathrm{Log}^{\bullet}(\mathbb{WT})$.

In order to show completeness, Lemmas 3 and 4 tell us that it suffices to show $\mathrm{Log}^{\bullet}(\mathbb{PO}) \subseteq \mathbf{BPL}$. Our proof is divided into to two parts: $\mathrm{Log}^{\bullet}(\mathbb{PO}) \subseteq \mathrm{Log}^{\bullet}(\mathbb{TR})$ (cf. Lemma 6) and $\mathrm{Log}^{\bullet}(\mathbb{TR}) \subseteq \mathrm{Log}(\mathbb{TR}) = \mathbf{BPL}$ (cf. Lemma 5). First, we concentrate on the latter part. Our tool for proving it is the notion of *duplication* of a weakly transitive Kripke model, defined as follows:

Definition 4. *Let* $\mathfrak{M} = (W, R, V)$ *be a persistent Kripke model. Define the* duplication *of* $\mathfrak{M}$ *as the model* $\mathfrak{M}' = (W', R', V')$ *where*

(i) $W' = (W - C) \uplus (C \times \{0,1\})$, *where* $C = \{w \in W : wRw\}$ *and* $\uplus$ *means the disjoint union;*
(ii) *Define a surjective function* $f : W' \to W$ *by*

$$f(x) = \begin{cases} c, & \text{if } x = (c, i) \text{ for some } (c, i) \in C \times \{0,1\}. \\ x, & \text{otherwise.} \end{cases}$$

Define $R' \subseteq W' \times W'$ *as follows: for all* $x, y \in W'$,

$$xR'y \text{ iff } f(x)Rf(y).$$

(iii) $V'(p) = f^{-1}[V(p)]$ *for each propositional variable* p.

In the duplication of a model, each reflexive point (possibly without proper successors) is replaced by a proper cluster of two copies, e.g.

Thus, each reflexive point in $\mathfrak{M}$ has a proper successor in the duplication $\mathfrak{M}'$.

Proposition 7. *For any persistent model* $\mathfrak{M} = (W, R, V)$, *let* $\mathfrak{M}' = (W', R', V')$ *be its duplication. Then the following hold:*

(1) V' *is persistent.*
(2) *If* R *is transitive, then* R' *is also transitive.*
(3) $\mathfrak{M}, f(x) \models \varphi$ *iff* $\mathfrak{M}', x \models^{\bullet} \varphi$, *for all* $x \in W'$ *and* $\varphi \in \mathsf{Form}_{\mathcal{L}}$.

Proof. For (1), assume $x \in V'(p)$ and $xR'y$. Then by definition of duplication, we get $f(x)Rf(y)$ and $f(x) \in V(p)$. Since $\mathfrak{M}$ is persistent, we have $f(y) \in V(p)$, and so $y \in V'(p)$. For (2), assume that R is transitive. Suppose that $xR'y$ and $yR'z$. By the definition of R', we have $f(x)Rf(y)$ and $f(y)Rf(z)$. By the transitivity of R, we have $f(x)Rf(z)$. Hence $xR'z$.

We show (3) by induction on φ. We check only the case of implication. Other cases are shown easily by using inductive hypothesis. Let $\varphi \equiv \psi \to \chi$. Assume $\mathfrak{M}, f(x) \models \psi \to \chi$. Consider any point $y \in W'$ such that $xR'y$, $x \neq y$ and $\mathfrak{M}', y \models^\bullet \psi$. By the inductive hypothesis, $\mathfrak{M}, f(y) \models \psi$. By $xR'y$, we have $f(x)Rf(y)$. Then $\mathfrak{M}, f(y) \models \chi$. By the inductive hypothesis, $\mathfrak{M}', y \models^\bullet \chi$.

Conversely, assume $\mathfrak{M}', x \models^\bullet \psi \to \chi$. Let w be any state in W such that $f(x)Rw$ and $\mathfrak{M}, w \models \psi$. We divide our argument into the following two cases:

Case 1. $f(x) = w$. Then wRw and so there exists $y \in W'$ such that $f(y) = w$ and $x \neq y$. By the inductive hypothesis, $\mathfrak{M}', y \models^\bullet \psi$. Since $xR'y$ and $x \neq y$, we have $\mathfrak{M}', y \models^\bullet \chi$. By $f(y) = w$ and inductive hypothesis, $\mathfrak{M}, w \models \chi$.

Case 2. $f(x) \neq w$. Since f is surjective, we find a $y \in W'$ such that $f(y) = w$ and $x \neq y$. It follows from $f(x)Rw$ and $\mathfrak{M}, w \models \psi$ that $xR'y$ and $\mathfrak{M}', y \models^\bullet \psi$ by the inductive hypothesis. By assumption, $\mathfrak{M}', y \models^\bullet \chi$. Hence by the inductive hypothesis, we get $\mathfrak{M}, f(y) \models \chi$. □

Lemma 5. $\mathrm{Log}^\bullet(\mathbb{TR}) \subseteq \mathrm{Log}(\mathbb{TR})$.

Proof. Assume $\varphi \notin \mathrm{Log}(\mathbb{TR})$. Then there exists a $\mathfrak{F} \in \mathbb{TR}$ and a persistent valuation V such that $(\mathfrak{F}, V), w \not\models \varphi$ for some state w in $\mathfrak{F}$. Let $\mathfrak{M} = (\mathfrak{F}, V)$ and $\mathfrak{M}' = (\mathfrak{F}', V')$ be its duplication. Since f is surjective, there exists an $x \in W'$ such that $f(x) = w$ and $\mathfrak{M}', x \not\models^\bullet \varphi$ by Proposition 7. By $\mathfrak{F}' \in \mathbb{TR}$, we get $\varphi \notin \mathrm{Log}^\bullet(\mathbb{TR})$. □

In order to show $\mathrm{Log}^\bullet(\mathbb{PO}) \subseteq \mathbf{BPL}$, we now show that $\mathrm{Log}^\bullet(\mathbb{PO}) \subseteq \mathrm{Log}^\bullet(\mathbb{TR})$ by employing the tree-unravelling technique.

Lemma 6. $\mathrm{Log}^\bullet(\mathbb{PO}) \subseteq \mathrm{Log}^\bullet(\mathbb{TR})$.

Proof. Assume $\varphi \notin \mathrm{Log}^\bullet(\mathbb{TR})$. Then there exists an $\mathfrak{F} = (W, R) \in \mathbb{TR}$ and a persistent valuation V and a point $w \in W$ such that $(\mathfrak{F}, V), w \not\models^\bullet \varphi$. Let $\mathfrak{M} = (\mathfrak{F}, V)$. Define the following tree-unraveling $\overrightarrow{\mathfrak{M}}[w] = (\overrightarrow{W}, \overrightarrow{R}, \overrightarrow{V})$ of $\mathfrak{M}$ from w as follows:

- $\overrightarrow{W} = \{(w_0, w_1, \ldots, w_n) : w_0 = w \text{ and } w_i R w_{i+1} \text{ and } w_i \neq w_{i+1} \text{ for all } i < n\}$;
- $(w_0, w_1, \ldots, w_n) \overrightarrow{R} (w_0, v_1, \ldots, v_m)$ iff $n \leq m$ and $w_i = v_i$ for all $0 < i \leq n$.
- $\overrightarrow{V}(p) = \{(w_0, w_1, \ldots, w_n) : w_n \in V(p)\}$ for each propositional variable p.

It is easy to check that $\overrightarrow{V}$ is persistent and $(\overrightarrow{W}, \overrightarrow{R})$ is a transitive and reflexive tree and, thus, a partial order. It suffices to show the following by induction on $\psi \in \mathsf{Form}_{\mathcal{L}}$,

$$\overrightarrow{\mathfrak{M}}[w], (w_0, w_1, \ldots, w_n) \models^\bullet \psi \text{ iff } \mathfrak{M}, w_n \models^\bullet \psi.$$

We check only the case for implication. Other cases are easy by the inductive hypothesis. Let $\psi \equiv \xi \to \chi$. Assume that $\overrightarrow{\mathfrak{M}}[w], (w_0, w_1, \ldots, w_n) \models^\bullet \xi \to \chi$. Let $w_n R w_{n+1}$, $w_n \neq w_{n+1}$ and $\mathfrak{M}, w_{n+1} \models^\bullet \xi$. By the inductive hypothesis, we obtain $\overrightarrow{\mathfrak{M}}[w], (w_0, \ldots, w_n, w_{n+1}) \models^\bullet \xi$. By $(w_0, \ldots, w_n) \neq (w_0, \ldots, w_n, w_{n+1})$, we obtain $\overrightarrow{\mathfrak{M}}[w], (w_0, \ldots, w_n, w_{n+1}) \models^\bullet \chi$. By the inductive hypothesis, $\mathfrak{M}, w_{n+1} \models^\bullet \chi$. Conversely, assume that $\mathfrak{M}, w_n \models^\bullet \xi \to \chi$. Suppose that $(w_0, w_1, \ldots, w_n) \neq (w_0, w_1, \ldots, w_{n+m})$ $(m > 0)$ and $\overrightarrow{\mathfrak{M}}[w], (w_0, w_1, \ldots, w_{n+m}) \models^\bullet \xi$. We may focus on the case $w_n \neq w_{n+m}$ (otherwise, we can use the argument by persistency to obtain our goal). By the inductive hypothesis, we have $\mathfrak{M}, w_{n+m} \models^\bullet \xi$ and so $\mathfrak{M}, w_{n+m} \models^\bullet \chi$, and hence $\overrightarrow{\mathfrak{M}}[w], (w_0, w_1, \ldots, w_{n+m}) \models^\bullet \chi$. $\qquad \square$

Putting Fact 3 and Lemmas 3, 4, 5 and 6 together, we get the following main theorem of this section:

Theorem 2. BPL $= \mathrm{Log}^\bullet(\mathbb{WT}) = \mathrm{Log}^\bullet(\mathbb{TR}) = \mathrm{Log}^\bullet(\mathbb{PRE}) = \mathrm{Log}^\bullet(\mathbb{PO})$.

5 Topological Semantics for Visser's Propositional Logics

5.1 Topological Semantics for BPL

Since **wK4** is the modal logic of all topological spaces, if the diamond $\Diamond$ is interpreted as the *derivative operator* [9], it is quite natural to ask if we can also provide a topological semantics for **BPL**. In this section, we give a positive answer to this question. The key to finding a topological semantics for **BPL** lies in the answer to the following question: what is the corresponding notion in the topological setting to the proper-successor semantics over Kripke models? Our answer will be given in terms of the co-derivative operator, i.e., the dual of the derivative operator. First, we will introduce some basic concepts.

Definition 5. *We say that (W, τ) is a* topological space, *if W is a non-empty set and $\tau : W \to \mathcal{PP}(W)$ satisfies the following conditions:*

(i) *for each $w \in W$, $\tau(w)$ is non-empty, upward-closed and closed under binary intersections.*
(ii) *$X \in \tau(w)$ implies $w \in X$, for all $X \subseteq W$ and $w \in W$.*
(iii) *$\Box_\tau(X) \subseteq \Box_\tau(\Box_\tau(X))$ for all $X \subseteq W$, where $\Box_\tau(X) := \{ w \in W : X \in \tau(w) \}$, i.e., the interior of X.*

When a set $X \subseteq W$ is a fixed point of the operation $\Box_\tau$, i.e., $\Box_\tau(X) = X$, we say that X is an open set *in (W, τ). Given a topological space (W, τ), a valuation $V : \mathsf{Prop} \to \mathcal{P}(W)$ is τ-persistent, if $V(p) \subseteq \Box_\tau(V(p))$. We say that $\mathfrak{M} = (W, \tau, V)$ is τ-persistent, if V is τ-persistent.*

Notice that condition (ii) of the definition of a topological space can be reformulated as: $\Box_\tau(X) \subseteq X$ for all $X \subseteq W$. Then, it is easy to see that a valuation $V : \mathsf{Prop} \to \mathcal{P}(W)$ is τ-persistent iff $V(p) = \Box_\tau(V(p))$, i.e., $V(p)$ is an open set in (W, τ).

Definition 6. *Let* $X, Y \subseteq W$. $X \Rightarrow Y := (W \setminus X) \cup Y$.

We will introduce two kinds of topological semantics for the propositional language $\mathcal{L}$: ordinary and proper-successor topological semantics. Let $\mathfrak{M} = (W, \tau, V)$ be a τ-persistent model. Define the ordinary topological semantics $\models$ for $\mathcal{L}$ similarly to Kripke semantics except the following interpretation for implication:

$$\mathfrak{M}, w \models \varphi \rightarrow \psi \text{ iff } X \cap \llbracket \varphi \rrbracket \subseteq \llbracket \psi \rrbracket \text{ for some } X \in \tau(w),$$

where $\llbracket \varphi \rrbracket := \{ w \in W : \mathfrak{M}, w \models \varphi \}$. As is well-known, we can reformulate this semantic clause in terms of the interior operation as follows:

$$\mathfrak{M}, w \models \varphi \rightarrow \psi \text{ iff } w \in \Box_\tau((W \setminus \llbracket \varphi \rrbracket) \subseteq \llbracket \psi \rrbracket)$$
$$\text{iff } w \in \Box_\tau(\llbracket \varphi \rrbracket \Rightarrow \llbracket \psi \rrbracket).$$

Theorems of **Int** coincide with the valid formulas on all topological spaces, in this semantics.

For the proper-successor semantics $\models^\bullet$ for $\mathcal{L}$, the semantic clause for implication is:

$$\mathfrak{M}, w \models^\bullet \varphi \rightarrow \psi \text{ iff } (X \setminus \{ w \}) \cap \llbracket \varphi \rrbracket^\bullet \subseteq \llbracket \psi \rrbracket^\bullet \text{ for some } X \in \tau(w),$$

where $\llbracket \varphi \rrbracket^\bullet := \{ w \in W : \mathfrak{M}, w \models^\bullet \varphi \}$.

Definition 7. *Given a topological space* (W, τ), *the* closure operator $\Diamond_\tau$ *is defined by:*

$$\Diamond_\tau(X) := W \setminus \Box_\tau(W \setminus X).$$

We define the derivative operator $\mathbf{d}_\tau$ *by putting*

$$\mathbf{d}_\tau(X) := \{ w \in W : w \in \Diamond_\tau(X \setminus \{ w \}) \}.$$

The co-derivative operator $\mathbf{t}_\tau$ *is the dual of the derivative operator and defined by putting*

$$\mathbf{t}_\tau(X) = W \setminus \mathbf{d}_\tau(W \setminus X).$$

By definition, we obtain the following equivalences:

$$w \in \Diamond_\tau(X) \text{ iff } Y \cap X \neq \emptyset \text{ for all } Y \in \tau(w),$$
$$w \in \mathbf{d}_\tau(X) \text{ iff } (Y \setminus \{ w \}) \cap X \neq \emptyset \text{ for all } Y \in \tau(w),$$
$$w \in \mathbf{t}_\tau(X) \text{ iff } (Y \setminus \{ w \}) \subseteq X \text{ for some } Y \in \tau(w).$$

Since $(Y \setminus \{ w \}) \subseteq X$ is equivalent to $Y \subseteq X \cup \{ w \}$, we get:

$$w \in \mathbf{t}_\tau(X) \text{ iff } X \cup \{ w \} \in \tau(w).$$

The proper-successor semantics $\models^\bullet$ for the implication is reformulated as:

$$\mathfrak{M}, w \models^\bullet \varphi \rightarrow \psi \text{ iff } w \in \mathbf{t}_\tau((W \setminus \llbracket \varphi \rrbracket^\bullet) \cup \llbracket \psi \rrbracket^\bullet)$$
$$\text{iff } w \in \mathbf{t}_\tau(\llbracket \varphi \rrbracket^\bullet \Rightarrow \llbracket \psi \rrbracket^\bullet).$$

The following proposition states well-known properties of the operator $\mathbf{t}_\tau$ (cf. [2, pp. 246-7]).

Proposition 8. *Given a topological space (W, τ), $\square_\tau X = X \cap \mathbf{t}_\tau(X)$ for all $X \subseteq W$. Therefore, X is an open set in (W, τ) iff $X \subseteq \mathbf{t}_\tau(X)$. Moreover, $X \cap \mathbf{t}_\tau(X) \subseteq \mathbf{t}_\tau\mathbf{t}_\tau(X)$ holds for all $X \subseteq W$.*

Proposition 9. *For any τ-persistent topological model $\mathfrak{M} = (W, \tau, V)$, both $[\![\varphi]\!] \subseteq \square_\tau([\![\varphi]\!])$ and $[\![\varphi]\!]^\bullet \subseteq \square_\tau([\![\varphi]\!]^\bullet)$ hold for all $\varphi \in \mathsf{Form}_\mathcal{L}$.*

Proof. Fix any τ-persistent topological model $\mathfrak{M} = (W, \tau, V)$. Here we check only the latter statement, i.e., $[\![\varphi]\!]^\bullet \subseteq \square_\tau([\![\varphi]\!]^\bullet)$ holds for all $\varphi \in \mathsf{Form}_\mathcal{L}$. The former is shown quite similarly. By Proposition 8, it suffices to show that $[\![\varphi]\!]^\bullet \subseteq \mathbf{t}_\tau([\![\varphi]\!]^\bullet)$ holds for all $\varphi \in \mathsf{Form}_\mathcal{L}$. We only check the case where φ is of the form $\psi \to \rho$. Other cases are quite easy. We need to show $\mathbf{t}_\tau([\![\psi]\!]^\bullet \Rightarrow [\![\rho]\!]^\bullet) \subseteq \mathbf{t}_\tau(\mathbf{t}_\tau([\![\psi]\!]^\bullet \Rightarrow [\![\rho]\!]^\bullet))$. Assume that $w \in \mathbf{t}_\tau([\![\psi]\!]^\bullet \Rightarrow [\![\rho]\!]^\bullet)$. We divide our argument into two cases: (i) $w \notin [\![\psi]\!]^\bullet$ and (ii) $w \in [\![\psi]\!]^\bullet$. For case (i), first we see that $w \in [\![\psi]\!]^\bullet \Rightarrow [\![\rho]\!]^\bullet$. By Proposition 8 and the assumption $w \in \mathbf{t}_\tau([\![\psi]\!]^\bullet \Rightarrow [\![\rho]\!]^\bullet)$, we have $w \in \mathbf{t}_\tau(\mathbf{t}_\tau([\![\psi]\!]^\bullet \Rightarrow [\![\rho]\!]^\bullet))$. For case (ii), assume $w \in [\![\psi]\!]^\bullet \subseteq \mathbf{t}_\tau([\![\psi]\!]^\bullet)$. By $w \in \mathbf{t}_\tau([\![\psi]\!]^\bullet \Rightarrow [\![\rho]\!]^\bullet)$, we obtain $w \in \mathbf{t}_\tau([\![\rho]\!]^\bullet)$. By the inductive hypothesis $[\![\rho]\!]^\bullet \subseteq \mathbf{t}_\tau([\![\rho]\!]^\bullet)$ and monotonicity of $\mathbf{t}_\tau$, $\mathbf{t}_\tau([\![\rho]\!]^\bullet) \subseteq \mathbf{t}_\tau(\mathbf{t}_\tau([\![\rho]\!]^\bullet))$. Therefore, we obtain $w \in \mathbf{t}_\tau(\mathbf{t}_\tau([\![\rho]\!]^\bullet))$. $\square$

Given a class $\mathbb{S}$ of topological spaces, we define the logic $\mathrm{Log}(\mathbb{S})$ of $\mathbb{S}$ with respect to the ordinary semantics and the logic $\mathrm{Log}^\bullet(\mathbb{S})$ of $\mathbb{S}$ with respect to the proper-successor semantics similarly to the case of Kripke semantics.

Let (W, τ) be a topological space. (W, τ) is T_0 if, whenever $x \neq y$, there is an $X \in \tau(x)$ such that $y \notin X$ or there is a $Y \in \tau(y)$ such that $x \notin Y$. (W, τ) is T_d if $\mathbf{t}_\tau(X) \subseteq \mathbf{t}_\tau(\mathbf{t}_\tau(X))$ for all $X \subseteq W$. We denote the class of all topological spaces by $\mathbb{TOP}$. By $T_0\mathbb{SP}$ and $T_d\mathbb{SP}$ we mean the class of all T_0-spaces and the class of all T_d-spaces, respectively. We immediately obtain the following lemma.

Lemma 7. $\mathrm{Log}^\bullet(\mathbb{TOP}) \subseteq \mathrm{Log}^\bullet(T_0\mathbb{SP}) \subseteq \mathrm{Log}^\bullet(T_d\mathbb{SP})$.

Proof. By the fact that $T_d\mathbb{SP} \subseteq T_0\mathbb{SP} \subseteq \mathbb{TOP}$. $\square$

Lemma 8. $\mathbf{BPL} \subseteq \mathrm{Log}^\bullet(\mathbb{TOP})$.

Proof. By induction on the length of proof in **BPL**. We only show that the axiom (A2) is valid and that the rule (MP) preserves validity in $\mathbb{TOP}$ under the proper successor topological semantics. Other axioms and rules are shown easily. For the validity of (A2), we need to use τ-persistency. Fix any topological model $\mathfrak{M} = (W, \tau, V)$. By τ-persistency, we have $[\![p]\!]^\bullet \subseteq \mathbf{t}_\tau([\![p]\!]^\bullet)$. Since $\mathbf{t}_\tau([\![p]\!]^\bullet) \subseteq \mathbf{t}_\tau([\![q \to p]\!]^\bullet)$, we obtain $[\![p]\!]^\bullet \subseteq \mathbf{t}_\tau([\![q \to p]\!]^\bullet)$. Then, $[\![p]\!]^\bullet \Rightarrow \mathbf{t}_\tau([\![q \to p]\!]^\bullet) = W$. It follows that $\mathbf{t}_\tau([\![p]\!]^\bullet \Rightarrow \mathbf{t}_\tau([\![q \to p]\!]^\bullet)) = \mathbf{t}_\tau(W) = W$. This means that $[\![p \to (q \to p)]\!]^\bullet = W$.

For (MP), assume that $\mathbb{TOP} \models^\bullet \varphi$ and $\mathbb{TOP} \models^\bullet \varphi \to \psi$. In order to show $\mathbb{TOP} \models^\bullet \psi$, take any topological model $\mathfrak{M} = (W, \tau, V)$ with τ-persistent valuation V and state $w \in W$. We show $\mathfrak{M}, w \models^\bullet \psi$. Fix some $* \notin W$. Define

$\mathfrak{M}^* = (W^*, \tau^*, V^*)$ as follows: $W^* := W \cup \{*\}$; $\tau^* : W^* \to \mathcal{PP}(W^*)$ is defined by:

$$\tau^*(x) := \begin{cases} \{W^*\}, & \text{if } x = *. \\ \{Y \subseteq W^* : X \subseteq Y \text{ for some } X \in \tau(x)\}, & \text{otherwise.} \end{cases}$$

$V^* : \mathsf{Prop} \to \mathcal{P}(W)$ is defined by putting $V^*(p) = V(p)$ for all $p \in \mathsf{Prop}$. Note that $\tau(x) \subseteq \tau^*(x)$ for all $x \in W$. Now we need to show that (W^*, τ^*) is a topological space and V^* is τ^*-persistent. First, let us show the τ^*-persistency of V^*. Let $x \in V^*(p) = V(p)$. Then $x \neq *$. Hence by τ-persistency of $V(p)$, we obtain $V(p) \in \tau(x) \subseteq \tau^*(x)$. Hence $V^*(p) \in \tau^*(x)$.

Second, let us show that (W^*, τ^*) is a topological space. It is easy to see that (W^*, τ^*) satisfies conditions (i) and (ii) of Definition 5. For clause (iii) of Definition 5, let $Z \subseteq W^*$. Assume $x \in \Box_{\tau^*}(Z)$, i.e., $Z \in \tau^*(x)$. We need to show $\Box_{\tau^*}(Z) \in \tau^*(x)$, i.e., $x \in \Box_{\tau^*}(\Box_{\tau^*}(Z))$. If $x = *$, then $Z = W^*$. Hence $\Box_{\tau^*}(W^*) \in \tau^*(x)$ by $\Box_{\tau^*}(W^*) = W^*$. Assume $x \neq *$. By the definition of τ^* and $Z \in \tau^*(x)$, we can find a $Y \in \tau(x)$ such that $Y \subseteq Z$. Since (W, τ) is a topological space, $Y \in \tau(x)$ implies $\Box_\tau(Y) \in \tau(x)$. Now it suffices to show $\Box_\tau(Y) \subseteq \Box_{\tau^*}(Z)$ by the definition of τ^*. By $Y \subseteq Z$, we obtain $\Box_\tau(Y) \subseteq \Box_\tau(Z \setminus \{*\})$. In what follows, we show $\Box_\tau(Z \setminus \{*\}) \subseteq \Box_{\tau^*}(Z)$. Fix any $y \in \Box_\tau(Z \setminus \{*\})$, i.e., $Z \setminus \{*\} \in \tau(y)$. It follows from $Z \setminus \{*\} \subseteq Z$ that $Z \in \tau^*(y)$. Hence $y \in \Box_{\tau^*}(Z)$.

It is easy to show by induction on formulas that $\mathfrak{M}^*, x \models^\bullet \rho$ iff $\mathfrak{M}, x \models^\bullet \rho$ for all $x \in W$ and $\rho \in \mathsf{Form}_\mathcal{L}$. Then by $\mathbb{TOP} \models^\bullet \varphi \to \psi$, we obtain $\mathfrak{M}^*, * \models^\bullet \varphi \to \psi$, which implies $[\![\varphi]\!]^\bullet \subseteq [\![\psi]\!]^\bullet$. Since $\mathbb{TOP} \models^\bullet \varphi$, we have $\mathfrak{M}^*, w \models^\bullet \varphi$. By $[\![\varphi]\!]^\bullet \subseteq [\![\psi]\!]^\bullet$, we get $\mathfrak{M}^*, w \models^\bullet \psi$. Hence $\mathfrak{M}, w \models^\bullet \psi$. $\qquad\square$

Given a partially ordered frame (W, R), define $\tau_R : W \to \mathcal{PP}(W)$ by putting $\tau_R(x) := \{X \subseteq W : R(x) \subseteq X\}$, where $R(x) := \{y \in W : xRy\}$. It is easy to check that (W, τ_R) is a topological space. We say that (W, τ_R) is the derived topological space from (W, R).

Proposition 10. *Let (W, R) be a partially ordered Kripke frame. Then, its derived topological space (W, τ_R) is a T_d-space.*

Proof. Define the binary relation $\underline{R}$ over W by: $u\underline{R}v$ iff uRv and $u \neq v$ for all $u, v \in W$. We need to show that $\mathbf{t}_{\tau_R}(X) \subseteq \mathbf{t}_{\tau_R}(\mathbf{t}_{\tau_R}(X))$ for all $X \subseteq W$. Let $X \subseteq W$ and $x \in \mathbf{t}_{\tau_R}(X)$. Then $\{x\} \cup X \in \tau_R(x)$. It follows that $\underline{R}(x) \subseteq X$. Thus, $R(x) \setminus \{x\} \subseteq X$. Now we show that $x \in \mathbf{t}_{\tau_R}(\mathbf{t}_{\tau_R}(X))$, i.e., $\{x\} \cup \mathbf{t}_{\tau_R}(X) \in \tau_R(x)$, which is equivalent to $\underline{R}(x) \subseteq \mathbf{t}_{\tau_R}(X)$. Take any $y \in R(x) \setminus \{x\}$. We need to show $\{y\} \cup X \in \tau_R(y)$, i.e., $\underline{R}(y) \subseteq X$. Consider any $z \in \underline{R}(y)$. We will show $z \in X$. Since (W, R) is a partial ordering, $(W, \underline{R})$ is a strict partial ordering, i.e., $\underline{R}$ is irreflexive and transitive. Note that we already have $x\underline{R}y$ and $y\underline{R}z$. These implies $x\underline{R}z$ by transitivity of $\underline{R}$. Since $\underline{R}(x) \subseteq X$, $x\underline{R}z$ implies $z \in X$. $\square$

Lemma 9. $\mathrm{Log}^\bullet(T_d\mathbb{SP}) \subseteq \mathbf{BPL}$.

Proof. Let $\varphi \notin \mathbf{BPL}$. By $\mathrm{Log}^\bullet(\mathbb{PO}) \subseteq \mathbf{BPL}$, there exists a Kripke frame $(W, R) \in \mathbb{PO}$ and a persistent valuation V and $w \in W$ such that $\mathfrak{M}, w \not\models^\bullet \varphi$

where $\mathfrak{M} = (W, R, V)$. Since (W, R) is partially ordered, it follows from Proposition 10 that (W, τ_R) is a T_d-space. It is also easy to show that V is τ_R-persistent. Moreover, by induction on formulas, it is easy to show that $\mathfrak{M}, x \models^\bullet \psi$ iff $(W, \tau_R, V), x \models^\bullet \psi$ for all $x \in W$ and $\psi \in \mathsf{Form}_\mathcal{L}$. Hence $(W, \tau_R, V), w \not\models^\bullet \varphi$, which implies $\varphi \notin \mathrm{Log}^\bullet(T_d \mathbb{SP})$.   □

By Lemmas 7, 8, and 9, we conclude the following main theorem of this section.

Theorem 3. $\mathrm{Log}^\bullet(\mathbb{TOP}) = \mathrm{Log}^\bullet(T_0 \mathbb{SP}) = \mathrm{Log}^\bullet(T_d \mathbb{SP}) = \mathbf{BPL}$.

5.2 Topological Semantics for FPL

Definition 8. *Let (W, τ) be a topological space. $X \subseteq W$ is* dense-in-itself *if $\mathbf{d}_\tau(X) = X$. (W, τ) is* scattered *if it contains no non-empty subset X such that X is dense-in-itself. Let us denote the class of scattered spaces by $\mathbb{SCA}$.*

Let us define the following topological semantics for modal formulas, where we interpret $\square$ by the co-derivative operator. This semantics is usually called *d-semantics* because we interpret $\Diamond$ by the derivative operator. Given a topological space (W, τ) and a valuation V, we write $\mathfrak{M} = (\mathfrak{F}, V)$ and define the satisfaction relation $\mathfrak{M}, w \Vdash^\bullet \varphi$ as follows:

$$
\begin{array}{lll}
\mathfrak{M}, w \Vdash^\bullet p & \text{iff } w \in V(p), \\
\mathfrak{M}, w \Vdash^\bullet \bot & \text{Never}, \\
\mathfrak{M}, w \Vdash^\bullet \alpha \wedge \beta & \text{iff } \mathfrak{M}, w \Vdash^\bullet \alpha \text{ and } \mathfrak{M}, w \Vdash^\bullet \beta, \\
\mathfrak{M}, w \Vdash^\bullet \alpha \vee \beta & \text{iff } \mathfrak{M}, w \Vdash^\bullet \alpha \text{ or } \mathfrak{M}, w \Vdash^\bullet \beta, \\
\mathfrak{M}, w \Vdash^\bullet \alpha \to \beta & \text{iff } \mathfrak{M}, w \Vdash^\bullet \alpha \text{ implies } \mathfrak{M}, w \Vdash^\bullet \beta, \\
\mathfrak{M}, w \Vdash^\bullet \square \alpha & \text{iff } w \in \mathbf{t}_\tau(\{ v \in W : \mathfrak{M}, v \Vdash^\bullet \alpha \}).
\end{array}
$$

Given a class $\mathbb{S}$ of topological spaces, we say that α is *d-valid* on $\mathbb{S}$ (notation: $\mathbb{S} \Vdash^\bullet \alpha$) if, for each $(W, \tau) \in \mathbb{S}$, each valuation V and each $w \in W$, $\mathfrak{M}, w \Vdash^\bullet \alpha$. Given a class $\mathbb{S}$ of topological spaces, we introduce the following notation for all the *d-valid* modal formulas on $\mathbb{S}$:

$$
\mathrm{MLog}^\bullet(\mathbb{S}) = \{ \alpha \in \mathsf{Form}_{\mathcal{ML}} : \mathbb{S} \Vdash^\bullet \alpha \}
$$

Esakia [7] showed that the modal axiom $\square(\square p \to p) \to \square p$ defines the class of scattered spaces in terms of topological *d-semantics* above (cf. [2, p.262]). Moreover, Abashidze and Blass showed that $\mathbf{GL}$ coincides with all the *d-valid* modal formulas on $\mathbb{SCA}$.

Fact 6 ([1,5]). $\mathbf{GL} = \mathrm{MLog}^\bullet(\mathbb{SCA})$.

Since the translation G_1 embeds $\mathbf{FPL}$ into the modal logic $\mathbf{GL}$, we can also establish a completeness result of $\mathbf{FPL}$ with respect to the class $\mathbb{SCA}$, as follows:

Theorem 4. $\mathrm{Log}^\bullet(\mathbb{SCA}) = \mathbf{FPL}$.

Proof. First we show $\text{Log}^\bullet(\mathbb{SCA}) \subseteq \textbf{FPL}$. Assume $\varphi \notin \textbf{FPL}$. By the translation G_1, $G_1(\varphi) \notin \textbf{GL}$. By Fact 6, we can find a scattered space (W, τ) and a valuation V and a point $w \in W$ such that $(W, \tau, V), w \not\Vdash^\bullet G_1(\varphi)$. Define a new ($\tau$-persistent) valuation V' by $V'(p) = \Box_\tau(V(p))$, i.e., the interior of $V(p)$. Then, we can show that $(W, \tau, V), v \Vdash^\bullet G_1(\psi)$ iff $(W, \tau, V'), v \models^\bullet \psi$ for all $v \in W$ and all $\psi \in \textsf{Form}_\mathcal{L}$. It follows that $(W, \tau, V'), w \not\models^\bullet \varphi$ hence $\varphi \notin \text{Log}^\bullet(\mathbb{SCA})$.

Now we establish $\textbf{FPL} \subseteq \text{Log}^\bullet(\mathbb{SCA})$. Take any $\varphi \in \textbf{FPL}$ and consider any scattered space (W, τ). Fix a τ-persistent valuation V and a point $w \in W$. Let $\mathfrak{M} = (W, \tau, V)$. Our goal is to show $\mathfrak{M}, w \models^\bullet \varphi$. By induction on ψ, we can show that $\mathfrak{M}, v \models^\bullet \psi$ iff $\mathfrak{M}, v \Vdash^\bullet G_1(\psi)$ for all $v \in W$. It suffices to show $\mathfrak{M}, w \Vdash^\bullet G_1(\psi)$. Since $\varphi \in \textbf{FPL}$, our translation G_1 tells us that $G_1(\varphi) \in \textbf{GL}$. By Fact 6, we conclude $\mathfrak{M}, w \Vdash^\bullet G_1(\psi)$.   □

6   Conclusion

This paper has shown that Visser's basic propositional logic $\textbf{BPL}$ can be characterized in different ways. First, it can be embedded into the modal logic $\textbf{wK4}$ as a corollary of our embedding theorem for extensions of $\textbf{BPL}$ into modal logics (Theorem 1). Second, it can be characterized by several different Kripke semantics. This is summarized in the following table (Theorem 2):

Weakly-transitive	Transitive	Pre-order	Partial order
$\text{Log}(\mathbb{WT}) = \textbf{BPL}$	$\text{Log}(\mathbb{TR}) = \textbf{BPL}$ [18]	$\text{Log}(\mathbb{PRE}) = \textbf{Int}$	$\text{Log}(\mathbb{PO}) = \textbf{Int}$
$\text{Log}^\bullet(\mathbb{WT}) = \textbf{BPL}$	$\text{Log}^\bullet(\mathbb{TR}) = \textbf{BPL}$	$\text{Log}^\bullet(\mathbb{PRE}) = \textbf{BPL}$	$\text{Log}^\bullet(\mathbb{PO}) = \textbf{BPL}$

Moreover, we developed topological semantics for $\textbf{BPL}$, which is summarized in the following table (Theorem 3):

Topological spaces	T_0-spaces	T_d-spaces
$\text{Log}(\mathbb{TOP}) = \textbf{Int}$	$\text{Log}(T_0\mathbb{SP}) = \textbf{Int}$	$\text{Log}(T_d\mathbb{SP}) = \textbf{Int}$
$\text{Log}^\bullet(\mathbb{TOP}) = \textbf{BPL}$	$\text{Log}^\bullet(T_0\mathbb{SP}) = \textbf{BPL}$	$\text{Log}^\bullet(T_d\mathbb{SP}) = \textbf{BPL}$

Finally, we also showed that $\textbf{FPL}$ can be characterized as the logic of scattered spaces with the help of the embedding of $\textbf{FPL}$ into $\textbf{GL}$ (Theorem 4).

There are several directions for further research. First, we may investigate the logic of the rational numbers $\mathbb{Q}$, the real line $\mathbb{R}$ or Eucledean space $\mathbb{R}^n$ in the syntax of $\textbf{BPL}$. Second, we may consider the dual version of $\textbf{BPL}$ similarly to the dual-intuitionistic logic where propositions are interpreted by closed sets. In the dual version of $\textbf{BPL}$, the derived set operator will play a more direct role than in $\textbf{BPL}$. Finally, there are several studies of first-order extension of $\textbf{BPL}$

over Kripke semantics [11,14], and it would be interesting to consider if it is possible to provide a *topological semantics* for the first-order extension of **BPL** or **FPL**.

Acknowledgement. We would like to thank the anonymous reviewers for helpful corrections and comments. We also would like to thank the audience of the presentation at Tenth International Tbilisi Symposium on Language, Logic and Computation. The work of the first author was supported by JSPS KAKENHI, Grant-in-Aid for Young Scientists (B) 24700146, and the work of the second author was supported by China National Fund for Social Sciences (grant no. 12CZX054). Finally, the first author wishes to thank Corad Asmus for his correcting English of our paper.

References

1. Abashidze, M.: Algebraic analysis of the Gödel-Löb modal system. Ph.D. thesis, Tbilisi State University (1987)
2. van Benthem, J., Bezhanishvili, G.: Modal logics of space. In: Aiello, M., Pratt-Hartmann, I., Van Benthem, J. (eds.) Handbook of Spatial Logics, Chap. 1, pp. 217–298. Springer, Heidelberg (2007)
3. Bezhanishvili, G., Esakia, L., Gabelaia, D.: Spectral and T_0-spaces in d-Semantics. In: Bezhanishvili, N., Löbner, S., Schwabe, K., Spada, L. (eds.) TbiLLC 2009. LNCS, vol. 6618, pp. 16–29. Springer, Heidelberg (2011)
4. Blackburn, P., de Rijke, M., Venema, Y.: Modal Logic. Cambridge University Press, New York (2001)
5. Blass, A.: Infinitary combinatorics and modal logic. J. Symbolic Logic **55**(2), 761–778 (1990)
6. Corsi, G.: Weak logics with strict implication. Math. Logic Q. **33**(5), 389–406 (1987)
7. Esakia, L.: Diagonal constructions, Löb's formula and Cantor's scattered spaces. In: Mikeladze, Z. (ed.) Studies in Logic and Semantics, pp. 128–143. Metsniereba, Tbilisi (1981). In Russian
8. Esakia, L.: Weak transitivity - a restitution. Logical Investigation, pp. 244–245. Nauka Press, Moscow (2001). In Russian
9. Esakia, L.: Intuitionistic logic and modality via topology. Ann. Pure Appl. Logic **127**(1–3), 155–170 (2004)
10. Gödel, K.: Eine interpretation des intuitionistischen Aussagenkalküls. Ergebn. Eines Mathematischen Kolloquiums **4**, 39–40 (1933)
11. Ishigaki, R., Kikuchi, K.: A tree-sequent calculus for a natural predicate extension of Visser's propositional logic. Logic J. IGPL **15**(2), 149–164 (2007)
12. Ishigaki, R., Kikuchi, K.: Tree-sequent methods for subintuitionistic predicate logics. In: Olivetti, N. (ed.) TABLEAUX 2007. LNCS (LNAI), vol. 4548, pp. 149–164. Springer, Heidelberg (2007)
13. Mckinsey, J.C.C., Tarski, A.: Some theorems about the sentential calculi of Lewis and Heyting. J. Symbolic Logic **13**, 1–15 (1948)
14. Ruitenburg, W.: Basic predicate calculus. Notre Dame J. Formal Logic **39**, 18–46 (1998)
15. Sasaki, K.: Formalizations for the consequence relation of Visser's propositional logic. Rep. Math. Logic **33**, 65–78 (1999)

16. Suzuki, Y., Ono, H.: Hilbert-style proof system for BPL. Technical report, IS-RR-97-0040F Japan Advanced Institute of Science and Technology (1997)
17. Suzuki, Y., Wolter, F., Zakharyaschev, M.: Speaking about transitive frames in propositional languages. J. Logic Lang. Inform. **7**, 317–339 (1998)
18. Visser, A.: A propositional logic with explicit fixed points. Studia Logica **40**, 155–175 (1981)

Between-Noun Comparisons

Galit W. Sassoon[(✉)]

Bar Ilan University, Ramat Gan, Israel
galitadar@gmail.com

Abstract. Adjectives are typically felicitous in within-predicate comparisons—constructions of the form 'X is more A than y', as in *This is bigger than that*, but are often infelicitous in between-predicate comparisons—'X is more A than (y is) B', as in **Tweety is bigger than (it is) heavy*. Nouns, by contrast, exhibit the inverse pattern. The challenge is to account for the felicity of between-noun comparisons, such as *more a duck than a goose*, while capturing the infelicity of within-noun comparisons, such as *#This bird is more a duck than that one*. Postulating even only ad hoc, meta-linguistic gradable interpretations for noun to capture the meaning of between-noun comparisons results in wrong predictions for within-noun comparisons and other gradable constructions (*#very duck*; *too duck*). To address this challenge, the paper exploits the psychological notion of a contrast-set. The solution correctly predicts inference patterns and truth value judgments.

Keywords: Gradability · Noun · Adjective · Dimension · Comparison · Contrast set

1 Comparison Constructions with Adjectives vs. Nouns

Within-predicate comparisons are constructions such as (1a), whose interpretation involves a comparison of two entities along the ordering dimension of a single predicate. By contrast, *between-predicate comparisons*—the main focus of this paper—are constructions such as (1b) that involve a comparison of either one or two entities along the dimensions of two different predicates. Many adjective pairs exhibit incommensurability in that they cannot felicitously co-occur in a between-predicate comparison (Kennedy 1999), as illustrated in (2).

(1)   a.   The sofa is (2 centimeters) longer than the table (is).
        b.   The sofa is (2 centimeters) longer than {it, the table} is wide.
(2)   a.   #The table is longer than the sofa is heavy.

Nouns behave differently. First, most of the degree morphemes which classically combine with adjectives are incompatible with nouns (*#Ducker, #Duckest, #duck*

This paper has been dedicated to Frank Veltman upon his retirement, as part of the Festschrift for Jeroen Groenendijk, Martin Stokhof and Frank Veltman, edited in 2013 by Aloni, Franke, and Roelofsen.

© Springer-Verlag Berlin Heidelberg 2015
M. Aher et al. (Eds.): TbiLLC 2013, LNCS 8984, pp. 276–289, 2015.
DOI: 10.1007/978-3-662-46906-4_16

enough, #too duck, #very duck). The situation persists across languages (see Baker 2003 for a review). In particular, within noun comparisons such as (3a) and its Hebrew equivalent (3b) are infelicitous. In English, for a within-noun comparison to be felicitous, the noun must be the complement of a preposition such as *of* in (3c). Languages like Hebrew do not allow this possibility.

(3) a. #The rightmost bird is more a duck than the leftmost bird.
     b. #Ha-cipor ha-yemanit hi yoter barvaz me-ha-cipor ha-smalit
         'the-bird the-rightmost is more duck from-the-bird the-leftmost',
         The rightmost bird is more a duck than the leftmost bird.
     c. The rightmost bird is more **of** a duck than the leftmost bird.

Interestingly, the felicity of within noun comparisons such as those in (3), namely comparisons with bare nouns (i.e., nouns not modified by *of, typical of, much of,* or the like), improves significantly in contexts that trigger a shift away from the literal interpretation of the noun.

Fig. 1. Literal and nonliteral ('duck-like') readings of *duck*

Thus, an utterance of (3a), which is odd in the context of real ducks, as in the picture in the left side of Fig. 1, significantly improves in the context of toy ducks, as in the picture in the right side of Fig. 1 (many thanks to Moria Ronen for this example and picture). The Hebrew (3b) becomes completely felicitous. The status of the noun *barvaz* ('duck') with other degree morphemes improves as well. However, once a literal interpretation is enforced, comparison and degree morphology more generally becomes clearly infelicitous again, as in the use of (4) in the context of the toy ducks in Fig. 1. This fact strengthens the generalization: Default literal interpretations of nouns are incompatible with the semantics of within-predicate comparison morphemes and morphemes with similar distributional constraints.

(4) #The rightmost bird is more a **toy** duck than the leftmost bird.

At the same time, nouns do occur freely, even more freely than dimensional adjectives do, in between-predicate comparisons. This is illustrated with the examples in (5).

(5) a. Tweety is more **a duck** than **a goose**.
     b. Chevy is more **a car** than **a truck**.
     c. This is more a chair than a table.
     d. This drink is more **water** than **wine**.
     e. The ostrich is more **a bird** than (the platypus is) **a mammal**.

In sum, adjectives are typically more felicitous in within- than in between-predicate comparisons, while in nouns, typically, the situation is reversed. This poses a problem which this paper sets out to address. The problem is how to account for the felicity of nouns in between-predicate comparisons, while capturing their infelicity in within-predicate comparisons. A postulation of even only ad hoc, contextual, meta-linguistic, last resort gradability to capture, for instance, (6c) or its Hebrew equivalent (6d), results in wrong predictions for (6a) and its Hebrew equivalent (6b).

(6)   a.   #Rubinstein is more a pianist than my son.
       b.   #Rubinstein yoter psantran me-ha-ben sheli
             'Rubinstein is more pianist from the-son mine'
             'Rubinstein is more a pianist than my son'.
       c.   Rubinstein is more a pianist than a conductor.
       d.   Rubinstein yoter psantran me-menacea'x
             'Rubinstein is more pianist from conductor'
             'Rubinstein is more a pianist than a conductor'.

Although noun comparisons are the main focus of this paper, a short inspection of the interpretation of adjectival comparisons may help track the way the interpretation of noun comparisons diverges. The orderings associated with the adjectives in the felicitous between-predicate comparison (1a), *The sofa is (2 centimeters) longer than {it, the table} is wide*, are based on measurements of length and width. The degrees of these two measurement scales align by virtue of a common unit, namely the length of a conventional object (such as any centimeter or inch ruler). The ratio between the length of the meter and the length of an entity is a number that can be meaningfully compared to the ratio between the length of the meter and the width of an entity.

Similarly, in (7a), the degree to which a ladder is (not) tall compares to the degree to which a house is (not) high (Büring 2007; Heim 2008), for *tall* and *high* share a unit. In (7b), again, common units, for example, seconds or minutes, allow for comparison of the degree to which a clock is fast and the degree to which it is slow with respect to the actual time, comparison of deviations from a midpoint, the correct time, in different directions (Kennedy 1999).

(7)   a.   The ladder is shorter than the house is high.
       b.   My clock is faster than yours is slow.

By contrast, the orderings of the adjectives in the infelicitous (2a), *#The table is longer than the sofa is heavy*, are based on measurements that do not share a standard unit. Therefore, a unit-based comparison is impossible.

All of these examples reveal the importance of the notion of *degree differences* (or intervals) in the interpretation of statements with adjectives. Our conceptualization of entities in the world is sensitive not only to the ordering determined by their length, but also to the differences between their lengths, as well as the ratios between these differences. This fact renders adjectives compatible with gradability morphemes whose interpretation is mediated by degree-difference operations. For example, on a widespread view,[1] the truth conditions of, e.g., (1a), *The sofa is two centimeters longer than the table* yield truth iff the *difference* between the length of the table and of the sofa equals twice the length of a centimeter unit object. Other adjectival morphemes whose semantics relates to length intervals include *slightly* and *very* (as in *The table is slightly longer than the sofa is wide*).

One explanation for the incompatibility of nouns with this type of gradable morphemes is, therefore, that they denote ordinal properties, namely properties that encode entity orderings, but do not reliably reflect differences and ratios between entities (Sassoon 2010). Accordingly, gradability and comparison in nouns is not unit-based. In fact, except for adjective nominalizations, such as *height* and *length*, no noun or noun comparison reported in the literature is associated with unit-based measure phrases. Combinations like **two degrees (a) bird* and **two bits more (of) a bird* are infelicitous. Ordinal interpretations also explain the infelicity of nouns with difference morphemes, including within-predicate comparison morphemes, as in (3)–(4). Even vague difference modifiers, which do not refer to conventional units explicitly, cannot naturally modify nominal comparisons, e.g., *#slightly more (of) a car than a truck* is judged infelicitous.

Thus, between-noun comparisons are not based on a common unit. Nor are they based on deviations from a midpoint, as in (7b), *My clock is faster than your clock is slow*, which entails the positive forms *My clock is fast* and *Your clock is slow*. An entity a, which is not a car, can be *more a car than a truck*, and an entity b, which is not a truck, can be such that *a is more a car than b is a truck*. A semantic representation should allow between noun comparisons but not within-noun comparisons or between-noun comparisons based on units or degree differences.

The analysis of between-noun comparisons should capture several additional challenging properties. The first one is a preference for single arguments. Speakers clearly prefer the construction in (8a) to the one in (8b).

(8)　a.　　Tweety is more a bird than a mammal.
　　　b.　　?Tweety is more a bird than Mister Ed is a mammal.

A second property is the strong metalinguistic inference speakers derive from such comparisons. From (8a) it follows that the speaker prefers to call Tweety a bird than to call him a mammal, at least if these are the only available options.

Third is the negative flavor of such comparisons. Upon an utterance of a between-noun comparison, it is understood that the two nominal labels are not optimal options, for otherwise the speaker would have asserted simpler categorization statements with the given nouns, such as those in (9).

(9)　a.　　Tweety is a bird.
　　　b.　　Tweety is not a mammal.
　　　c.　　Mister Ed is not a mammal.

---

[1] Cf. von Stechow (1984), Schwarzschild and Wilkinson (2002), and Sassoon (2010).

The fourth and last property relates to the fact that the metalinguistic implications of comparisons of two different entities, as in (9b), seems to be considerably weaker. Examples such as (9b) are felt to be less useful or informative, for it is not clear what can be inferred from them (if (9b), then what?). Once the analysis is presented, this observation will be cashed out by showing that inferences from single entity between-noun comparisons such as (8a) are lost in two entity comparisons such as (8b).

To be sure, these types of comparison are not exclusively restricted to nouns. For instance, the examples in (10) resemble the between-noun comparisons in (8) more than they resemble the between-adjective comparisons in (1b) and (7).

(10)   a.   ?Dan is more tall than Ram is intelligent.
        b.   Your problems are more legal than financial.
        c.   Dan is more hungry than tired, while Bill is more tired than hungry.

Existing analyses classify such examples as metalinguistic or indirect comparisons. Giannakidou and Yoon (2011) describe such examples as comparisons of appropriateness or subjective preference of propositions according to speakers. Morzycki (2011) describes them as comparisons along degrees of imprecision of propositions. For example, (11a), on this analysis, conveys that the degree of precision required to render Ram intelligent is lower than the one required to render Dan tall. Bale (2011) argues that these are comparisons of ranks. Thus, (11a) is true iff the number of entities at least as tall as Dan is greater than the number of entities at least as intelligent as Ram. Similarly, McConnel Ginnet (1973), Klein (1980) and van Rooij (2011) argue that (11a) is true iff for some modifier M (e.g., *slightly, pretty, very, very very, very very very*), *Dan is M tall* is true, but *Ram is M intelligent* is not true.

All these analyses capture the metalinguistic flavor of between-noun comparisons. However, they fail to explain the fact that in languages with two different morphemes for ordinary and metalinguistic comparisons, such as, e.g., Greek, both types of morpheme license between-noun comparisons (Giannakidou and Yoon 2011). This suggests that noun comparisons and similar adjectival comparisons can be more than merely metalinguistic in nature.

Moreover, none of these analyses is restricted enough. The imprecision analysis is the most restricted (Morzycki 2011). However, if gradable interpretations based on imprecision are generally available for nouns, within-noun comparisons of the form 'X is more A than Y (is A)' are predicted to be licensed as well, namely, between-predicate comparisons with a single noun hosting both of the nominal positions (such a noun would not be seen overtly in the than-clause due to its recoverability). This prediction is not borne out; for instance, there is a notorious felicity contrast between *This creature is more a crab than a lobster* and #*This creature is more a crab than that creature is*. The latter is judged less natural despite the fact that the propositions *This is a crab* and *That is a crab* may differ in terms of their distance from the truth at least as much as the propositions *This is a crab* and *This is a lobster* may. In the same way, the ranks of each two entities with respect to being *a crab* may differ as much as their ranks with respect to being a *crab* and being a *lobster* may. And if gradable interpretations based on speaker preferences are available for nouns (Giannakidou and Yoon 2011), again, within-noun comparisons are predicted to be licensed, contra to fact.

This argument can be generalized. Analyses that assign gradable interpretations for nouns wrongly predict that they be freely licensed in gradable constructions, contra to fact (e.g., #the most bird; #too bird; #very bird).

In conclusion, we need an analysis of between-noun comparisons that will explain why the distribution of nouns is restricted to this and no other gradable constructions. To uncover the semantics of this construction, we need to look deeper at the type of conceptual gradability underlying categorization in nouns.

2 Toward a Solution

An important observation arises from the preceding discussion. The analysis of between-noun comparisons such as *Chevy is more a car than a truck* must involve orderings based on at least two nominal predicates. Such a solution would elegantly block the possibility of felicitous usage of within-noun comparisons, such as *#This Chevy is more a car than that Chevy,* for the latter only has one predicative argument.

The next section develops an implementation of this idea, making crucial use of the psychological notion of *contrast-based categorization* presented in Sect. 2.1. This type of categorization rests on competition between linguistic concepts that are perceived as *contrasting*, namely as denoting non-overlapping categories. Following the presentation of a contrast-based analysis in Sect. 2.2, a generalization is proposed for the case of comparisons involving linguistic concepts that are perceived as denoting overlapping categories. Distinctions in inference patterns are discussed.

2.1 Contrast-Based Categorization

Consider the following between predicate-comparisons. The common denominator between these three examples is that the predicate pairs occurring in them are perceived as contrasting. Contrasting concepts easily compare.

(11) a.   Tweety is more **a bird** than **a mammal**.
      b.   This Thai dish is more **sour** than **sweet**.
      c.   This ball is more **red** than **blue**.

The nouns in (11a) denote taxonomical categories, the borders between which ought to be fully discriminated. As for the adjectives in (11b, c), instead of a unique antonym, a set of contrasting categories K_P plays a role in their interpretation as well:

(12) a. K_{bird} = {mammal, bird, reptile, insect, fish ...}.
      b. K_{sweet} = {sweet, sour, salty, ...}.
      c. K_{red} = {pink, white, orange, yellow...}.

The idea that contrasting categories affect categorization was introduced within dimension-based categorization theories (see Tversky 1977; Hampton 1995; Smith and Minda 2002, among others). On these analyses, entities classify under nouns iff their values on multiple dimensions sufficiently match the ideal values for the noun. The degree of an entity in a given noun is built by addition or multiplication of its degrees of similarity to the ideal in multiple dimensions. The resulting weighted sum or product should exceed a threshold—a membership standard—for the entity to classify under the noun.

This standard-based categorization principle predicts many offline and online typicality effects. Importantly, it predicts the monotonic relation between likelihood of categorization of an entity and its similarity to the prototype; e.g., Hampton (1998) found a very strong coupling between the mean typicality ratings of items and the probability that they were categorized positively in about 500 items of 18 categories. Thus, this theory captures the fact that we can determine membership of infinitely many new instances, on the basis of a finite set of known facts about dimensions and category members. Newly encountered entities whose mean similarity is higher than that of known members can be automatically regarded as members.

However, in Hampton's (1998) data, there were also systematic dissociations between typicality and membership present. One of the three main reasons for them was the existence of *contrast concepts*. For example, both *kitchen utensil* and *furniture* were part of the stimuli. This reduced the likelihood of classification, but not the typicality of items like a *refrigerator* in the category *furniture*. To account for this, concepts P are often assumed to belong to a contrast set, K_P, of at least two disjoint categories that cover a local domain, D_{Kp}:

(13)   The contrast set: $\forall K_P \subseteq$ CONCEPT, $|K_P| > 1$:
      a.   Mutual exclusivity: $\forall Q_1, Q_2 \in K_P$, $([\![Q_1]\!] \cap [\![Q_2]\!]) = \varnothing$.
      b.   Domain cover: $D_{Kp} = \{d \in [\![Q]\!] \mid Q \in K_P \}$.

Contrast-based categorization is defined as follows. First, as stated in (14a), the similarity degree of d in P, Deg(d,P), is normalized relative to the sum of d's degrees in the concepts of K_P. The resulting degree—the ratio between d's similarity to P and d's similarity to the contrast categories—represents the extent to which d is P and not anything else. Second, as stated in (14b), an entity is classified in the contrast concept it resembles most, namely in the concept that yields the highest normalized degree.

(14)   a.   The similarity of d to P normalized relative to K_P:
          Norm(d,P,K_P) = Deg(d,P) / $\Sigma_{Q \in K_P}$Deg(d,Q).
      b.   An entity is classified in the contrast category it resembles most:
          $[\![P]\!]_{KP} = \{d \in D_P \mid \forall Q \in K_P$, Norm(d,P,$K_P$) > Norm(d,Q,$K_P$) $\}$.

For example, assume that the contrast set is the triple K = {P, Q, Z}, and consider two items d_1 and d_2 whose degrees are listed in Table 1. Because the sum of degrees of each entity is 1, the normalized degrees are identical to the original similarity degrees. In each predicate P, Norm(d,P,K) = Deg(d,P)/1. As the table indicates, d_2 is more similar to Z than d_1 **(0.40 > 0.34)**, but d_1 is Z, the category which d_1 resembles most, (0.34 > 0.33 = 0.33) and d_2 is P, the category d_2 resembles most (0.42 > 0.40 > 0.18). Thus, membership likelihood *may not* be monotonically related to normalized similarity: d_2 is more of a Z than d_1, but is not classified under Z.

Table 1. Degrees and normalized degrees in contrast categories

Degrees:	P	Q	Z	Sum	Normalized degrees:	P	Q	Z
d_1	0.33	0.33	**0.34**	1		0.33	0.33	**0.34**
d_2	**0.42**	0.18	**0.40**	1		**0.42**	0.18	**0.40**

Table 2. Degrees and normalized degrees in binary contrast categories

Degrees:	P	Z	Sum	Normalized degrees:	P	Z	Sum
d_1	0.49	**0.51**	1		0.49	0.51	1
d_2	**1**	0.66	1.66		0.60	0.40	1

The situation is different, however, with binary contrast sets K = {P, Z}, as in Table 2. Recall that the normalized degree of an entity in a predicate equals its degree of similarity to that predicate divided by the sum of its degrees of similarity to the contrast concepts, e.g., for d_2, **Norm(d_2,P,K_P)** = deg(d_2,P)/(deg(d_2,P) + deg(d_2,Z)) = 1/ (1 + 0.66) = 0.60. Thus, as Table 2 indicates, d_1 is Z, the category d_1 resembles most in K, and d_2 is P, the category d_2 resembles most in K. Before normalization d_2 is more similar to Z than d_1, but with respect to K, d_2 is less so. For example, a refrigerator better exemplifies the noun *furniture* than a lamp (cf., d_2 vs. d_1's degrees in Z at the right side of Table 2), but relative to a contrast set K comprising of the nouns *furniture* and *kitchen utensil*, the refrigerator classifies as a kitchen utensil, while the lamp classifies as a piece of furniture (cf., d_2 vs. d_1's normalized degrees in Z at the left side of the table).

Importantly, in a binary contrast set, by definition, the normalized degree of an entity in one concept equals 1 minus its degree in the contrast concept. For any d, Norm(d,Z, {P,Z}) = 1 − Norm(d,P,{P,Z}). Thus, if d_1's normalized degree in P is bigger than d_2's, then d_1's normalized degree in Z is smaller than d_2's. For instance, if the entities' degrees in P are a and b such that 1 ≥ a > b ≥ 0, then their degrees in Z are 1 − a and 1 − b, respectively, where 1 − a < 1 − b. Together with the fact that entities classify in the category to which they resemble most, this means that d_2 being more Z than d_1 relative to {P,Z} is incompatible with classification of d_1, but not d_2, under Z. The reason is that if Z is the category to which d_1 resembles most, then Norm(d_1,Z,{P,Z}) > ½. Hence, Norm(d_2,Z,{P,Z}) which is a higher degree, is definitely bigger than ½, meaning that it as well should classify under Z relative to {P,Z}.

In conclusion, in binary contrast-sets, membership *is* coupled with *normalized* similarity. If |K_P| = 2, new entities, which are more P relative to K_P than known Ps, can be automatically regarded as P relative to K_P.

2.2 Contrast-Based Comparisons

Most of the predicates with more than one contrasting category seem to be nouns or noun phrases of taxonomic categories, for instance, animals and plants, but other nouns as well as adjectives can also be regarded as contrasting within a suitable context. Many between-noun comparisons, and some between-adjective comparisons, appear intuitively to involve concepts of the same contrast set. The following semantics reflects this intuition, by taking between-noun comparisons, and similar adjectival comparisons, to be comparisons of degrees normalized relative to a contrast set K consisting of the predicative arguments of *more* (cf., Sassoon 2013).[2]

(15)   a.   Contrast-set comparisons:
$[\![X \text{ is more } \mathbf{A} \text{ than } Y \text{ is } \mathbf{B}]\!]_{w,g} = 1$ iff
For $\mathbf{K} = \{\mathbf{A},\mathbf{B}\}$: $\text{Norm}([\![X]\!]_{w,g},\mathbf{A},K,w,g) > \text{Norm}([\![Y]\!]_{w,g},\mathbf{B},K,w,g)$.
        b. $\text{Norm}(d,P,K_P,w,g) = \text{Deg}(d,P,w,g) / \Sigma_{Q \in K_P}\text{Deg}(d,Q,w,g)$.

For example, in deciding whether Tweety is more a bird than Mister Ed is a mammal, the contrast set K consists of the predicative arguments of *more*, *bird* and *mammal*, as in (16a). As contrastive categories, they ought to be treated as contextually disjoint and the only alternatives covering a local domain of discourse. The similarity of an entity to a contrast concept is normalized relative to K. As shown in (16b–c), an entity's normalized degree is the ratio between its similarity to the category applied to it and its similarity to the contrast category – the one applied to the compared entity.

(16)   a. $[\![\text{Tweety is more a bird than a mammal}]\!]_{w,g} = 1$ iff
for K = {bird, mammal},
$\text{Norm}([\![\text{Tweety}]\!]_{w,g},\text{bird},K,w,g) >$
$\text{Norm}([\![\text{Tweety}]\!]_{w,g},\text{mammal},K,w,g)$.
        b. $\text{Norm}([\![\text{Tweety}]\!]_{w,g},\text{bird},K,w,g) = \text{deg}([\![\text{Tweety}]\!]_{w,g},\text{bird},w,g) /$
$(\text{deg}([\![\text{Tweety}]\!]_{w,g},\text{bird},w,g) + \text{deg}([\![\text{Tweety}]\!]_{w,g},\text{mammal},w,g))$
        c. $\text{Norm}([\![\text{Tweety}]\!]_{w,g},\text{mammal},K,w,g) =$
$\text{deg}([\![\text{Tweety}]\!]_{w,g},\text{mammal},w,g) /$
$(\text{deg}([\![\text{Tweety}]\!]_{w,g},\text{bird},w,g) + \text{deg}([\![\text{Tweety}]\!]_{w,g},\text{mammal},w,g))$.

The normalized degrees of the entity-arguments compare. Thus, the given sentence is true in w and g iff Tweety is closer to the prototype of *bird* than Mister Ed is close to the prototype of *mammal*, when taking only these two prototypes into account.

This account captures the special features of between-noun comparisons. First, recall that these type of comparisons has a strong metalinguistic flavor; e.g., from *Tweety is more a bird than a mammal*, it follows that the speaker prefers to call Tweety a bird than to call him a mammal, at least if these are the only available options. Recall that in binary contrast sets, categorization is always monotonic to similarity. Thus, *Tweety is more a bird than a mammal* implies that *Tweety is a bird*, given the contrast set. This gives rise to the implication that the speaker prefers to call Tweety a *bird* than to call him a *mammal*.

---

[2] For generality, this semantic definition is formulated for the two-subject case. The preference for a single subject is explained below.

Second, this type of comparison has a negative flavor. It is implied that *mammal* and *bird* are not optimal labels for Tweety, for otherwise the speaker would have stated that *Tweety is a bird, not a mammal*. The comparison construction does not entail this alternative statement. If the contrast set is bigger, or if categorization is not based on a contrast set, Tweety may not classify as a bird. In fact, the message that the speaker prefers to call Tweety a *bird* than to call him a *mammal* is likely to be informative precisely when **the default setting of parameters for categorization** – the dimensions, their weights, and the set of contrast categories, if such a set is involved as a default – **do not render Tweety a bird**. Only the setting of parameters with $K = \{\text{bird, mammal}\}$ does so.

Third, for many speakers the construction in (16a) is preferred to the one in (17a).

(17)　a.　$[\![$ Tweety is more a bird than Mr. Ed is a mammal $]\!]_{w,g} = 1$

　　　　　iff for $K = \{\text{bird, mammal}\}$, $\text{Norm}([\![\text{Tweety}]\!]_{w,g}, \text{bird}, K, w, g) >$
　　　　　$\text{Norm}([\![\text{Mr. Ed}]\!]_{w,g}, \text{mammal}, K, w, g)$.

　　　b.　$\text{Norm}([\![\text{Tweety}]\!]_{w,g}, \text{bird}, K, w, g) = \text{deg}([\![\text{Tweety}]\!]_{w,g}, \text{bird}, w, g) /$
　　　　　$(\text{deg}([\![\text{Tweety}]\!]_{w,g}, \text{bird}, w, g) + \text{deg}([\![\text{Tweety}]\!]_{w,g}, \text{mammal}, w, g))$

　　　c.　$\text{Norm}([\![\text{Mister Ed}]\!]_{w,g}, \text{mammal}, K, w, g) =$
　　　　　$\text{deg}([\![\text{Tweety}]\!]_{w,g}, \text{mammal}, w, g) / (\text{deg}([\![\text{Mister Ed}]\!]_{w,g}, \text{bird}, w, g) +$
　　　　　$\text{deg}([\![\text{Mister Ed}]\!]_{w,g}, \text{mammal}, w, g))$.

The problem with (17a) is a low potential for inference. *Tweety is more a bird than Mr. Ed is a mammal* implies very little about their categorization. They may both be birds or both be mammals relative to {bird, mammal}. Only single-entity comparisons have categorization entailments; e.g., (16a) entails that Tweety is a bird relative to K, but the two entity comparison in (17a) is consistent with Tweety not being a bird relative to K. The normalized degrees of a single entity are complementary in the sense that they sum up to 1. This is the source of the metalinguistic inference – the bigger normalized degree of an entity is also the biggest one for that entity. This is also the reason for the absence of inference in two entity comparisons. The compared degrees in such comparisons need not be the highest ones for any of the entities.

For the two entity comparison in (17a), we only derive weaker entailments, such as the trivial (18a–c).

(18)　Tweety is more a bird than Mister Ed is a mammal $\Rightarrow$
　　　a.　Mr. Ed is less a mammal than Tweety is a bird.
　　　b.　Tweety is less a mammal than Mr. Ed is a bird.
　　　c.　Mr. Ed is more a bird than Tweety is a mammal.

To see this consider again the context given in Table 2. In this context, (17a) is true because for $K = \{\text{bird, mammal}\}$, $\text{Norm}([\![\text{Tweety}]\!]_{w,g}, \text{bird}, K, w, g) = 0.60$, which is bigger than $\text{Norm}([\![\text{Mr. Ed}]\!]_{w,g}, \text{mammal}, K, w, g) = 0.51$. (18a) is also true for the exact same reason. At the same time, (18c) is true, and so is (18b), because $\text{Norm}([\![\text{Mr. Ed}]\!]_{w,g}, \text{bird}, K, w, g) = 0.49$, which is bigger than $\text{Norm}([\![\text{Tweety}]\!]_{w,g}, \text{mammal}, K, w, g) = 0.40$. This result follows from the fact that the two normalized degrees of each entity in a binary contrast set sum up to 1, as explained above. Thus, 'X is more A than Y is B' entails that 'Y is more A than X is B' as well. This shows how little informative value such statements carry. Examples of the form 'X is more A than Y is B' appear to only contradict examples of the form 'X is more B than Y is A' (but see the discussion of overlapping categories below). Finally, despite the fact that Mr. Ed is more a bird than Tweety is a mammal, Mr. Ed is not a bird relative to K, for the contrast concept it resembles most is *mammal* (0.51 > 0.49). This illustrates that in two entity comparisons the metalinguistic flavor is lost.

To illustrate the intuitive basis of these inferences consider (19a). It is intuitively true because the dolphin resembles a fish not a bird, while the platypus resembles both. This truth value judgment is captured by the proposed analysis, for both of the degrees of the platypus in these circumstances appear close to 0.50, as opposed to the dolphin's two less balanced degrees. Also, intuitively, it holds true, as predicted, that the Platypus is more a fish than the dolphin is a bird, merely because the dolphin does not resemble a bird in any way, while the platypus does resemble a fish in some ways. This is an illustration of the pattern of inference from 'X is more A than Y is B' to 'Y is more A than X is B'. Finally, (19a) does not imply that the dolphin is a fish relative to K = {fish, bird}. Thus, this construction is more marked for lack of inferential power.

(19)   a.   ?The Dolphin is more a fish than the platypus is a bird
         b.   ?The Dolphin is more a mammal than the platypus is a bird.

We accept usages of this construction mainly in trivial cases such as those illustrated in (19b). (19b) is clearly true merely because the dolphin is a mammal, and the platypus, which is a mammal too, is not a bird. But precisely because the dolphin is a mammal, (19b) sounds odd (it is too weak).

Notice also that different entities may render salient different contrast categories. We have world knowledge telling us that the platypus and dolphin are mammals, or borderline between *mammal* and *bird* and between *mammal* and *fish*, respectively. Thus, we may be disposed to add the contrast concept *mammal*, or even accommodate different contrast sets when relating to these species as in (19a). But this creates a clash with the semantics that strictly defines the contrast set as the two compared nouns. In addition, such a move only decreases the inferential power. Recall that for a binary set such as {bird, mammal}, (17a) is predicted to entail (18b), because the normalized degrees of each entity sum up to 1. For a bigger contrast set, even this inference is lost. Table 3 illustrates this case. Tweety is more a bird than Mr Ed is a mammal, because 0.3 > 0. However, it is not the case that Tweety is less a mammal than Mr. Ed is a bird, Tweety is more so, because 0.2 > 0.[3]

It is now the time to give a solution to the main problem this paper set out to address. A clear advantage of the contrast-based analysis over existing alternatives is that contrast-based *more* in statements of the form 'X is more P than (y is) Q' cannot be licensed when P and Q are one and the same predicate.

---

[3] Notice that the television figure called Mr. Ed is actually a talking horse, not a fish.

Table 3. Degrees and normalized degrees in nonbinary contrast categories

Normalized degrees:	Fish	Bird	Mammal	Sum
Mr. Ed	1	0	0	1
Tweety	0.5	0.3	0.2	1

The notion of a contrast set K presupposes the existence of at least two different contrast concepts, $|K| > 1$, namely, $P \neq Q$. This is so for a reason. All entities are predicted to always be equally A relative to the singleton contrast set $\{A\}$. The reason for this is that a degree normalized relative to one and the same predicate always equals 1, for $Norm(d,A,w,g) = deg(d,A,g,w)/deg(d,A,g,w)$. The only exception to this generalization is the undefined case, 0/0. These results explain the fact that a statement of the form 'X is more a bird than Y' is intuitively considered false. This judgment emerges precisely because all birds are judged to be equally so. This judgment persists despite of the fact that speakers are willing to admit graded exemplariness judgments when interpreting statements of the form 'X is more (typical) of a bird than Y'.[4]

Last, but not least, an analysis in terms of a contrast set has to be generalized to apply to comparisons with nouns that refer to potentially overlapping categories. Examples include the nouns in (20a), *pianist* and *composer*, among many other nouns that name human traits, dispositions, habits or professions. Importantly, comparisons of overlapping categories exhibit systematically different inference patterns. In particular, we may hold both (20b) and (20c) true together.

(20) a.   Mary is more a pianist than Bill is a conductor.
      b.   Bill is more a philosopher than Mary is a linguist

---

[4] Contrast based comparisons differ significantly from typical within-adjective comparisons. Degree modifiers such as the ones in (a) below can modify adjectival comparisons and contribute an evaluation of the size of difference between the degrees of the compared entities. Adjectives denote mappings to degrees for which a difference or ratio operation can meaningfully apply. By contrast, categorization under nouns is not mediated by degrees for which differences or ratios are meaningful. The nominal degrees are based on context sensitive dimensional weights and on various transformations such as inversion and normalization that leave little chance for any degree differences or ratios to be preserved. Hence, it is not surprising that difference and ratio modifiers are ungrammatical within contrast-based comparisons that exploit the nominal type of degree calculation, whether they contain nouns or adjectives, as (b–e) illustrate (Morzycki 2011).

a. George is {much, slightly, somewhat, a lot, no, three times} taller than Bill.
b. George is {much, ?slightly, ??somewhat, ??a lot, ?no, ?? three times} more dumb than crazy.
c. George is dumb {much, *?slightly, *?somewhat, *?a lot, *?no, ?? three times} more than crazy.
d. Tweety is {much, ?slightly, ??somewhat, ??a lot, ?no, ?? three times} more a bird than a mammal.
e. Tweety is a bird {much, *?slightly, *?somewhat, *?a lot, *?no, ?? three times} more than a mammal.

Notice also the oddity of contrast based comparisons such as *more a duck than {a tree, a table, a cloud}*. The reason on the rationale of the present analysis is triviality. It makes little sense to compare ducks and trees unless some entity exists which is half way between a duck and a tree. Indeed, in the context of such an entity, the example appears to become acceptable. This suggest that it is ruled not by a grammatical constraint, but only by a pragmatic ban on triviality.

Table 4. Degrees and normalized degrees in overlapping categories

Degrees: %	P&¬L	L& ¬P	L&P	Normalized degrees:	Norm(P) deg(P&¬L) +deg(P&L)	Norm(L) deg(L&¬P) +deg(P&L)	Sum
Frank	0	**0**	100		100/100 = **1**	100/100 = 1	**2**
Galit	10	80	10		10 + 10/ 100 = **.2**	90/100 = .9	**1.1**

We may aim to treat the compared nouns in (20b, c) as contrasting, but this would rule out the possibility that both (20b) and (20c) be simultaneously true. Thus, let us conclude the discussion with a generalized definition of normalized degrees which will be of use in such cases. The problem parallels that of the calculation of probabilities of overlapping events e_1 and e_2. The solution requires resort to the set of disjoint sub events e_3, e_4 and e_5, such that $e_1 = e_3 + e_4$ and $e_2 = e_3$ and e_5. Similarly, the generalized definition of contrast comparisons uses for, e.g., (20b,c), the set of disjoint contrast categories *philosopher who is not a linguist* (P&¬L), *linguist who is not a philosopher* (L&¬P) and *one who's both a linguist and a philosopher* (L&P). The degree of each entity in *linguist* and *philosopher* is normalized relative to these disjoint categories.

(21)   a.   Contrast-set comparisons, a generalized definition:
⟦ X is more A than Y is B ⟧$_{w,g}$ = 1 iff for K = {A,B},
Norm^o(⟦X⟧$_{w,g}$,A,K,w,g) > Norm^o(⟦Y⟧$_{w,g}$,B,K,w,g).
b.   Norm^o(d,A,{A,B},w,g) =
(Deg(d,A & ¬B,w,g) + (Deg(d,A & B,w,g)) /
(Deg(d,A & ¬B,w,g) + (Deg(d,A & B,w,g) + (Deg(d, ¬A & B,w,g)).

In non overlapping categories, the value (Deg(d,A & B,w,g) equals zero. Thus, the generalized definition reduces to the one presented earlier. Table 4 illustrates the utility of a generalized notion of a contrast set for the case of overlapping categories.

A suitable context for this table is one in which Bill's work is truly interdisciplinary; his work is distinguished relative to the work of specialists both in linguistics and philosophy. Mary, by comparison, is an ordinary linguist. She does linguistics research reasonably well, but only rarely does her work have any philosophical significance, and she never asks purely philosophical questions. The shift to the disjoint contrast-set allows for an assignment of normalized degrees for each entity that sum up to more than just 1; e.g., the sum of normalized degrees is 1.1 in Mary's case, and it is 2 in Bill's case. This reflects the potentially overlapping nature of the concepts in question, and the degree to which each entity exemplifies each concept separately or both concepts together.

In conclusion, for entities to compare relative to a nominal concept A either a designated morpheme ought to mediate the interpretation such as *typical* or the bare particle *of*, or another concept B ought to occur and license a contrast-based comparison. In that case, a tendency toward interpretations relative to binary contrast sets and single entities emerges so as to increase the inferential power, which is reduced in more than two-category or two-entity comparisons. Moreover, comparisons with non-disjoint categories support a generalized definition of normalized degrees. The resulting analysis of contrast comparisons captures intuitive truth value judgments and inference patterns in disjoint vs. overlapping categories. Future research should determine whether it extends to between-adjective comparisons that are typically analyzed as metalinguistic or indirect.

The theory of contrast based categorization was developed based on experimental research. Its linguistic significance has yet to be pinned down, including its connection to other alternative-based mechanisms such as those used in Aloni et al. (2013) or for implicature calculation.

References

Aloni, M., Franke, M., Roelofsen F. (eds.): Festschrift for Jeroen Groenendijk, Martin Stokhof and Frank Veltman. Pumbo, The Netherlands (2013)

Baker, M.C.: Lexical Categories: Verbs, Nouns, and Adjectives. Cambridge University Press, Cambridge (2003)

Bale, A.: Scales and comparison classes. Nat. Lang. Seman. **19**(2), 169–190 (2011)

Büring, D.: Cross-polar nomalies. In: Proceedings of Semantics and Linguistic Theory, vol. 17. CLC Publications, Ithaca (2007)

Giannakidou, A., Yoon, S.: The subjective mode of comparison: metalinguistic comparatives in Greek and Korean. Nat. Lang. Linguist. Theor. **29**(3), 621–655 (2011)

Hampton, J.: Testing the prototype theory of concepts. J. Mem. Lang. **34**, 686–708 (1995)

Hampton, J.: Similarity based categorization and fuzziness of natural categories. Cognition **65**, 137–165 (1998)

Heim, I.: Decomposing antonyms? In: Grønn, A. (ed.) Proceedings of Sinn und Bedeutung, vol. 12, pp. 212–225. University of Oslo, Oslo (2008)

Kennedy, C.: Projecting the Adjective: The Syntax and Semantics of Gradability and Comparison. Garland, New York (1999)

Klein, E.: A semantics for positive and comparative adjectives. Linguist. Philos. **4**(1), 1–45 (1980)

McConnell-Ginet, S.: Comparative constructions in english: a syntactic and semantic analysis. Doctoral dissertation, University of Rochester (1973)

Morzycki, M.: Metalinguistic comparison in an alternative semantics for imprecision. Nat. Lang. Seman. **19**(1), 39–86 (2011)

van Rooij, R.: Measurment and interadjective comparisons. J. Seman. **28**, 335–358 (2011)

Sassoon, G.W.: Measurement theory in linguistics. Synthese **174**(1), 151–180 (2010)

Sassoon, G.W.: Vagueness, Gradability, and Typicality, The Interpretation of Adjectives and Nouns. CRiSPI, Brill, Leiden (2013)

Schwarzschild, R., Wilkinson, K.: Quantifiers in comparatives: a semantics of degree based on intervals. Nat. Lang. Seman. **10**(1), 1–41 (2002)

Smith, D.J., Minda, J.P.: Distinguishing prototype-based and exemplar-based processes in category learning. J. Exp. Psychol. Learn. Mem. Cogn. **28**, 800–811 (2002)

Tversky, A.: Features of similarity. Psychol. Rev. **84**, 327–352 (1977)

von Stechow, A.: Comparing semantic theories of comparison. J. Seman. **3**, 1–77 (1984)

On the Licensing of Argument Conditionals

Kerstin Schwabe[(✉)]

Zentrum für Allgemeine Sprachwissenschaft Berlin, Schützenstraße 18,
10117 Berlin, Germany
schwabe@zas.gwz-berlin.de

Abstract. The paper focusses on the syntactic and semantic licensing conditions of constructions like *Max akzeptiert es, wenn Lea Geige spielt.* 'Max accepts it if Lea plays the violin'. The clause introduced by *wenn* 'if' has a double function in that it is an adverbial that provides the protasis of an implication as well as the propositional argument of a matrix predicate. The paper argues against Pullum [15], Pesetsky [14], and Hinterwimmer [8], suggesting that the conditional conjunction *wenn* encodes two implication types: the *classic type*: if p is contingent and true, then $q(p)$ and the *preference type*: if p is contingent, then $q(p)$. Additionally, the paper focusses on the characteristic properties of the matrix predicates that license argument conditionals.

Keywords: Conditionals · Sentential proform · m-command · Potentially factive predicates · Preference predicates

1 The Phenomenon

This paper discusses German constructions in which the propositional argument of a clause-embedding verb is provided by a clause having the form of a conditional – cf. (1a-c).[1] Here the latter are called *argument conditionals*. In German, an argument conditional can be introduced by either *falls* in case' or *wenn* 'if' or it can occur as a V1-conditional.

(1) a. *Wir bedauern (es), wenn er nicht bereit ist zu kommen.*
         we regret   it   if   he not willing is to come
    b. *Wir bedauern (es), falls er nicht bereit ist zu kommen.*
    c. *Ist er nicht bereit zu kommen, bedauern wir es.*
    d. *Wir bedauern (es), dass er nicht bereit ist zu kommen.*

Fabricius-Hansen [5], Zifonun et al. [28] and Kaiaty [9] call German argument conditionals "Ergänzende *wenn*-Sätze" 'complementary *wenn*-clauses' since they

---

The author gratefully acknowledges the helpful discussions with Robert Fittler and Hubert Truckenbrodt, as well as the comments of the anonymous reviewers.

---

[1] Each construction type shown here can be exemplified by a corpus example provided by the ZAS-Database on clause-embedding predicates.

© Springer-Verlag Berlin Heidelberg 2015
M. Aher et al. (Eds.): TbiLLC 2013, LNCS 8984, pp. 290–309, 2015.
DOI: 10.1007/978-3-662-46906-4_17

somehow provide the propositional argument for a matrix predicate. As for English constructions like (2), they are called "non-logical *if*-clauses" by Pesetsky [14], "complement *if*-clauses" by Pullum [15], "irrealis *if*-clauses" by Rocchi [17] or "protasis-referring conditionals" by Thompson [27].

(2)   *John would like it if Mary knew French.*

Argument conditionals also occur in many other languages as for instance in Polish (3a), Italian (3b) and even in creole languages such as, for instance, the English based creole language Kamtok (3c) – cf. Schwabe et al. [24] and Rocchi [17].

(3)   a.   *Słyszałam,   że duchy uwielbiają jeśli się   je   czci*
              hear.1SG.PST that spirits adore.3PL if   REFL they.ACC worship.3SG
              'I heard that spirits adore being worshiped.' *NKJP*, 1991/10/1

       b.   *Mi   piace   se la gente   mi sorride*
              me   please.3SG if the people me smile.3SG.IND
              'I like it if people smile at me.'

       c.   *E fo   beta fo yi   if dem no fo   born yi*
              it COND better for 3SG if 3PL NEG COND bear 3SG
              'It would be better for him if he had not been born.' *Gud Nyus*, 14/3

As to the syntactic status of the argument *wenn*-clause, the paper regards it as an adverbial. This view is not uncontroversial. Thus, Schmid [19], Eisenberg [4], Breindl [2], and Pasch et al. [13] regard such clauses primarily as complements, more precisely, as complements with an adverbial function. Similar to Fabricius-Hansen [5], Kaiaty [9], Rothstein [18] and Thompson [27], Schwabe [22] suggests that argument conditionals are pure adverbials. Thus, this paper will focus on a discussion of Pullum [15], Pesetsky [14] and Hinterwimmer [8], who consider argument conditionals as originating in a complement position and moving to an adverbial position. Furthermore, the paper will focus on the classes of matrix predicates licensing argument conditionals. It will show that factivity is neither a necessary nor a sufficient condition.

2 Syntactic Analysis of German Argument Conditionals

2.1 Syntactic Data to be Explained

As for German, there is a fundamental difference between constructions with a canonical declarative complement *dass*-clause and constructions with an argument conditional. If a *dass*-clause is in the left periphery, an *es*-correlate or prepositional proform (ProPP) is forbidden in the subject or object position – cf. (4a) to (6a). If the *dass*-clause is linked to the predicate by a preposition, it only moves with its PP-shell to the left periphery – cf. (6a'). If, however, an argument conditional is in the left periphery and the propositional argument is obligatory, the latter must be expressed by an *es*-correlate or by a ProPP – cf. (4b) to (6b). In other words, the complement position must not be empty.

(4) *Subject*
    a.   **Dass Lea Violine spielt, langweilt es/das Max.*
          if   Lea violin plays bores   it/das   Max
    a'.   *Dass Lea Violine spielt, langweilt Ø Max.*
    b.   *Wenn Lea Violine spielt, langweilt es/das Max.*
          when Lea violin plays bores   it/das   Max
    b'.   **Wenn Lea Violine spielt, langweilt Ø Max.*

(5) *Direct object*
    a.   **Dass Lea Violine spielt, akzeptiert es/das Max.*
          that   Lea violin plays accepts   it/this   Max
    a'.   *Dass Lea Violine spielt, akzeptiert Ø Max.*
    b.   *Wenn Lea Violine spielt, akzeptiert es/das Max*
          if   Lea violin plays accepts   it/das   Max
    b'.   **Wenn Lea Violine spielt, akzeptiert Ø Max.*

(6) *Prepositional object*
    a.   **Dass Lea Geige spielte, hat Max Leo darauf aufmerksam gemacht.*
          that   Lea violin played has Max Leo PP[of]   advised
    a'.   *Darauf, dass Lea Geige spielte, hat Max Leo aufmerksam gemacht.*
    b.   *Wenn Lea Geige spielte, hat Max Leo darauf aufmerksam gemacht.*
          if   Lea violin played has Max Leo PP[of]   alerted
    b'.   **Wenn Lea Geige spielte, hat Max Leo Ø aufmerksam gemacht.*

The picture changes slightly when the *wenn*-clause is post-sentential. As is the case with a *dass*-clause, an *es*-correlate is optional – cf. (7b) and (8b). There are also a few matrix predicates that subcategorize obligatory propositional complements where the ProPP is optional, e.g. *sich (damit) begnügen* 'content oneself with sth.' or *jm. (darauf) aufmerksam machen* 'bring sth. to someone's attention' – cf. (9b). Recall that the *es*-correlate or the ProPP is obligatory if the *wenn*-clause is in the left periphery and the propositional complement is obligatory – cf. (4) to (6).[2]

---

[2] Note that Eisenberg [4] regards *es*-correlates as obligatory and that Fabricius-Hansen [5] considers constructions without them as very marked. However, it can be shown that constructions without an *es*-correlate are quite frequent.

(7) a. *Max langweilt es, wenn/dass Lea Geige spielt.*
         Max bores   it   if/that   Lea violin plays
     b. *Max langweilt ∅, wenn/dass Lea Geige spielt.*

(8) a. *Max akzeptiert es, wenn/dass Lea Geige spielt.*
         Max accepts   it   if/that   Lea the violin plays
     b. *Max akzeptiert ∅, wenn/dass Lea Geige spielt.*

(9) a. *Max macht Leo darauf aufmerksam, wenn/dass Lea Geige spielt.*
         Max alerts Leo PP[to]   if /that Lea violin plays
     b. *Max macht Leo ∅ aufmerksam, wenn Lea Geige spielt.*

If, however, a ProPP is obligatory, it may not be omitted even if the *dass-* or *wenn-*clause is post-sentential – cf. (10b).

(10) a. *Max stört sich daran, wenn/dass Lea Geige   spielt*
         Max is bothered PP if /that   Lea violin plays
     b. **Max stört sich ∅, wenn Lea Geige spielt.*

As far as the relationship between the *es*-correlate and its correspondent clause is concerned, subject clauses like (4) and (7) behave in almost the same manner as object clauses do. Therefore we can neglect them in the following.

The next section discusses approaches that have mainly been designed for English. Let's try to find out whether they are appropriate for explaining the German data.

2.2 Accounts of English Argument Conditionals

As for a purely syntactic account, Pullum [15] advocates that the conditional undergoes rightward movement from a complement position to a higher adjunct position, leaving behind a trace which is spelled out as the expletive pronominal *it*. Pullum's approach seems to provide an account of the analysis of German post-sentential argument *wenn-*clauses as given in (8a). However it fails with respect to the proposed expletive status of the sentential proform *it*. Following Thompson [27], one could object this claim as follows.

French, which clearly distinguishes between expletive and referential proforms – *il* is expletive and *ce* is referential – only allows the referential *ce* to be in the matrix clause of a construction with an argument *if*-clause – cf. (11a, b). It would be fallacious to assume that English exhibits an expletive where French uses a referential proform.

(11)   a.   *Ce serait tragique si elle était partie.*   [= (20b) in Thompson]
             'It would be tragic if she left.'
       b.   **Il serait tragique si elle était partie.*   [= (20a) in Thompson]

Moreover, the English *it* as well as the German *es* can be replaced by a referential demonstrative, as shown in (12a, b).

(12)   a.   *If we had a cheese plate in the room right now, that would be awesome.*
             [= (21a) in Thompson]
       b.   *Wenn sie kommt, schätzt   er das ungemein.*
             if   she comes appreciates he this immensely

Furthermore, a German ProPP as in (9a) can hardly be regarded as a spell-out of a clause which is moved to the right. If this were the case, the post-sentential clause would be a PP, which obviously is not the case.

Additionally, as shown in (7b) to (9b) for German, it is possible for the matrix clause to lack an overt propositional proform. Are we dealing here with a trace that is not spelled out? The answer is no since the syntactic category of the trace in (9b), which should be PP, would be inconsistent with the syntactic category of the relating clause. As for (8b), the answer could be yes. But then, one would have to explain when a trace is spelled out by an expletive and when it is not. If a proform is lacking, it is more reasonable to assume a null proform – a null complement anaphor (NCA) in Thompson's [27] terms. We will return to this issue in Sect. 2.3.

Following Kratzer [10], Pesetsky [14] considers an English argument *if*-clause to be the restrictor of a quantifier which quantifies over the nuclear scope, the IP in his terms. In order to function as a restricting term, the *if*-clause must be in an A-bar-position external to IP – cf. (249) in Pesetsky. If the argument clause is pre-sentential as in (13), it is a base-generated left IP-adjunct and the sentential proform *it* is referential – cf. Pesetsky (p. 72 f.).

(13)   If he played the violin right now, I would like it.

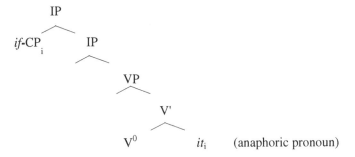

The referential *it* must be locally m-bound by the *if*-clause – cf. Pestsky's (270) to (273) and his (290) to (292) repeated here in (14).

(14)   *Local Binding Requirement on A-bar-chains*
        For C a chain and α an A-bar position, $*C = (\dots \alpha, \beta \dots)$, unless α locally m-binds β.

   a. α *locally m-binds* β iff α m-binds β and there is no γ such that α m-binds γ and γ m-binds β.
   b. α *m-binds* β iff α is coindexed with β and α m-commands β.
   c. α m-commands β if α does not dominate β and no maximal projection γ that dominates α excludes β^3.
   d. α is *dominated* by β iff it is dominated by every segment of β.
   e. α *excludes* β iff no segment of α dominates β.

Pesetsky regards a post-sentential *if*-clause as a right VP-adjunct – cf. (15). Because of its restrictor function the *if*-clause must move to an IP-external A-bar-position at LF. But this will be impossible if the sentential proform is regarded as a referential proform. If it were a referential proform, it should be locally m-bound by the *if*-clause. This is prevented by the intervening trace t_i – cf. Pesetsky (p. 73).

(15) *I would like it better if he played the violin right now.*   [= Pesetsky's (263b)]

What could be seen as a way out of this dilemma would be to not regard *it* as referential. And this is what Pesetsky proposes. According to him, a proform of a post-sentential argument conditional is neither a referential nor an expletive. It is not an expletive because it is theta-marked by V^0. It serves as a device to copy the content of the *if*-clause into the complement position – cf. (16), which corresponds to (338) in Pesetsky.

---

^{3} As to m-command, Pesetsky proposes two versions, m_e- and m_d-command. Since the difference between them is not relevant for our purposes, we neglect it at this place.

(16)   *If-Copying Rule (IC)*
    a.   Take a clause k of the form [IF IP], where k modifies a sentence Σ.
    b.   Copy k as k', substituting *that* for *IF*, making appropriate changes to mood so as to replace irrealis with realis mood marking.
    c.   Place k' in an argument position of Σ. Leave k as an adjunct modifier. (It gets interpreted as a restrictive clause, with S the nuclear scope.)
    d.   k' is factive.

IC applies if the "copy" *it* is related to the *if*-clause by *m-command* – cf. (14). Thus, the post-sentential *if*-clause has a double function. It is the restrictor of a quantifier as well as a complement of V^0. But Pesetsky's approach evokes a few objections. One is already known from the discussion of Pullum [15]. In French, a proform must be referential if it is related to an argument conditional – cf. (11). Furthermore, Pesetsky's IC Rule does not account for constructions with preference predicates – cf. (17) and Fabricius-Hansen [5]. Preference predicates do not presuppose factivity of an embedded *that*-clause – see Sect. 3 below.

(17)   *Frank zieht   es vor, wenn Maria Geige spielt.*
    Frank prefers it   if   Maria violin plays
    *If Maria plays the violin, Frank prefers that she plays the violin.

Like Pullum's analysis, Pesetsky's does not account for constructions where the *if*-clause is a complex construction. As shown in (18b), it is not the *if*-clause which is copied into the complement position but the complement clause embedded in the *if*-clause – cf. Fabricius-Hansen [5:83] for corresponding German constructionss.

(18)   *John would hate it if he realized that his colleague snored.*
    a.   #John would hate that he realized that his colleague snored if his colleague snored.
    b.   John would hate that his colleague snored if his colleague snored.

Like Pesetsky, Hinterwimmer [8] also stipulates a double function for English *if*- as well as *when*-clauses – cf. (19a, b).[4] He suggests that the *when*-clause is base-generated as a complement of a silent determiner in a DP-shell, which itself renders the argument of V^0.[5] From there, it moves to a right adjunct-position in order to serve there as a restrictor of a quantifier. The *if*-clause, Hinterwimmer proposes, is base-generated as a left or right TP-adjunct with a copy in the DP-shell. As to the *it*-correlate, Hinterwimmer regards it as the spell-out of the silent determiner. He suggests two silent determiners: DET_{fact} and DET_{event}. DET_{fact} turns a proposition which is denoted by the *that*- or *if*-clause into a fact, the latter being an abstract entity which makes the proposition true – cf. ②. DET_{event} converts a *when*-clause into an abstract event entity – cf. ②'. Thus, Hinterwimmer explains, the

---

[4] (19a) corresponds to Hinterwimmer's [8] (31a) and (19b) corresponds to his (24a).
[5] Sudhoff [26] provides a similar proposal for embedded *dass*-clauses in German.

proform *it* spells out two covert determiners that denote in different domains: the domain of facts and the domain of events. This means that predicates such as *like* or *hate* subcategorize for fact- or event-arguments.

(19) a. *Paul would hate it if Lea played the violin right now.*
      b. *Paul hates it when Lea snores.*

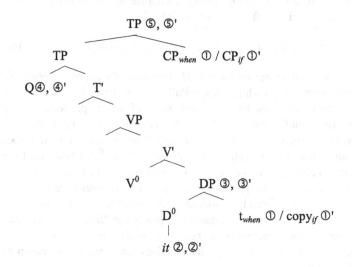

a.

① $\lambda w''\ \exists e\ [play\_violin\ (e,\ g(x_1))\ (w'')]$

② $[\![DET_{fact}]\!] = \lambda p_{<s,\ t>}.\ \iota x\ [\Re(x,\ p)\ (w_0)]$, where $\Re(x,\ p)\ (w_0)$ means x makes p true in w_0.

③ $\iota x\ [\Re(x,\ \lambda w''\ \exists e\ [play\_violine\ (e,\ g(x_1))\ (w'')])\ (w')]$

④ $\lambda p\ \lambda q\ \forall w'\ \{[R(w_0,\ w') \wedge q(w')] \Rightarrow \exists e'\ [p(e')]\}$

⑤ $\forall w'\ \{[R(w_0,\ w') \wedge \exists e\ [play\_violin\ (e,\ g(x_1))\ (w')]] \Rightarrow$
$\exists e'\ [like\ (e',\ paul,\ \iota x\ [\Re(x,\ \lambda w''\ \exists e\ [play\_violin\ (e,\ g(x_1))\ (w'')])\ (w')])$
$(w')]\}$

b.

①' $\lambda e'''\ [snore\ (e''',\ colleague)\ (w_0)]$

②' $[\![DET_{event}\ e_n]\!]^g = \lambda P.\ \iota e'\ [P(e)(w_0) \wedge o(e,\ g(e_n))\ (w_0))]$,
where $o(e,\ g(e_n))\ (w_0)$ means that the running times of e and $g(e_n)$ overlap in w_0.

③' $\iota e\ [snore\ (e,\ colleague)\ (w_0) \wedge o(e,\ g(e_n))\ (w_0)]$

④' $\lambda P.\ \lambda Q.\ \forall e\ [Q(e) \Rightarrow \exists e''\ [(e \leq e'') \wedge (P(e''))]]$

⑤' $\forall e\ [snore\ (e,\ colleague)\ (w_0) \Rightarrow \exists e''\ [(e \leq e'') \wedge (\ hate\ (e'',\ paul,\ \iota e\ [snore$
$(e,\ colleague)\ (w_0) \wedge o(e,\ e'')\ (w_0))])(w_0))]]$

Hinterwimmer's analysis accounts for the observation that a *that*- or *when*-clause can be extraposed but must not move to the left periphery – cf. (20a, b). Movement from a right-adjunct position of a DP-shell to the left periphery would result in a violation of the *Principle of Unambiguous Binding* (PUB) – cf. Müller & Sternefeld [12], Müller [11] and Sternefeld [25].

(20)   a.   *That his colleague always snores, Paul hates it.*
       b.   *? When his colleague snores, Paul hates it.*

According to Hinterwimmer, English *if*-clauses can appear in the left periphery because they can be base-generated as left TP-adjuncts – cf. (21).

(21)   *If he played the violin right now, I would like it.* [= (263b) in Pesetsky [14]]

The objections which can be raised against Hinterwimmer's approach resemble the ones we've already mentioned with respect to Pullum's and Pesetsky's accounts. First, French sentential proforms must be expressed by a referential pronoun if they are related to an argument conditional – cf. (11a). They can hardly be seen as spell-outs of an empty determiner. Second, Hinterwimmer also faces problems with respect to constructions with preference predicates – cf. (17) and (19)②, ②'. Third, constructions where the conditional clause itself is complex are problematic for his account – cf. (18). An alternative way to obtain the desired representation is to regard the proform *it* as referential proform that is referentially linked to the embedded clause of the *when*-clause. Even if one could succeed in somehow copying the "fact" argument into the DP-shell argument of *hate*, the problem becomes insolvable if there is a *believe* predicate in the consequence as in (22). Here, it does not seem to be reasonable to regard *it* as a determiner.

(22)   *Leo would believe it if Lea promised him to come.*

As far as German is concerned, ProPPs turn out to be a further problem for Hinterwimmer's analysis since it is hardly possible to gain access to the pronominal *d*–part within the morphologically closed PP in order to get a determiner for the *wenn*-clause – cf. (9a).

    Rothstein [18] and Thompson [27] present a quantificational analysis that does without the movement of the argument conditional. They regard the proform *it* as a variable which is bound by an operator OP which is adjoined to IP – cf. Rothstein's proposal, which is taken from Hinterwimmer [8] and reproduced in (23).

(23)   *Paul hates it when his colleague snores.*
       Gen e [[snore (e, colleague)] $\Rightarrow$ $\exists e'$[o (e, e')$\wedge$ (hate (e', paul, e)]].
       where o(e, e') means that the running times of e and e' overlap.

Here again, the analysis does not account for constructions with preference predicates like (17). Nor does it account for constructions like (18) where the protasis itself is a complex construction either.

2.3 A Further Account for German Argument Conditionals

Regarding constructions like (4b) to (6b) and (24a) with a pre-sentential argument *wenn*-clause and a correlate in the matrix clause, their argument *wenn*-clause is base-generated as a left TP-adjunct.

(24) a. *Wenn Lea krank ist, bedauert es Max*
          if   Lea ill   is   regrets it Max
      b. *Max bedauert es, wenn Lea krank ist* .
          Max regrets   it   it   Lea ill   is

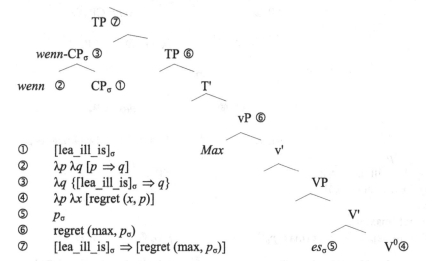

①	$[\text{lea\_ill\_is}]_\sigma$
②	$\lambda p\, \lambda q\, [p \Rightarrow q]$
③	$\lambda q\, \{[\text{lea\_ill\_is}]_\sigma \Rightarrow q\}$
④	$\lambda p\, \lambda x\, [\text{regret}\,(x, p)]$
⑤	p_σ
⑥	$\text{regret}\,(\text{max}, p_\sigma)$
⑦	$[\text{lea\_ill\_is}]_\sigma \Rightarrow [\text{regret}\,(\text{max}, p_\sigma)]$

If the argument *wenn*-clause is post-sentential as in (7a) to (9a) and (24b), it is base-generated as right TP-adjunct. Both the left- and the right-adjoined *wenn*-clause locally m-bind a sentential correlate in a complement position – cf. (14). Depending on the matrix predicate, the correlate is an *es*-correlate in the direct object or subject position. A prepositional correlate is regarded as a V^0-adjunct because it can co-occur with a direct object. Similar to Fabricius-Hansen [5:185], *es*-correlates as well as prepositional correlates are regarded here as referential proforms. They are theta-marked by V^0 and locally m-bound by the *wenn*-clause.

The reason why a pre-sentential *dass*-clause cannot co-occur with an *es*-correlate is that it is base-generated as a V^0-complement. When it moves to the left periphery, it leaves a trace which prevents the correlate – cf. (4a) and (5a).[6] A *dass*-clause that relates to a ProPP is part of a PP-shell. It cannot leave this shell in order to move to the left periphery.

It is attested by the ZAS-database that an *es*-correlate or a ProPP can be missing in a construction with a post-sentential argument *wenn*-clause like (7b) to (9b). As shown in (25), the missing correlate is represented as the proform *pro* which is located in the

---

[6] This view differs from Sudhoff's [26]. He assumes that the *es*-correlate is a part of a DP-shell so that it cannot leave the shell when moving to the left – see the arguments against this analysis in Schwabe [21].

canonical complement position and theta-marked there by V^0. Like an *es*-correlate or a ProPP, it is referential, but unlike them, it cannot be anaphoric. The reason for this is that its relating clause has to be in its local environment. In other words, *pro* must be locally m-bound by its relating clause – cf. (14). The relating clause is regarded as a *dass*-clause which is a base-generated vP-adjunct – cf. Haider [7]. It can be deleted under conditions that are presented below.[7]

(25)   *Max bedauert, wenn Lea krank ist.*
       Max regrets   it   Lea ill   is

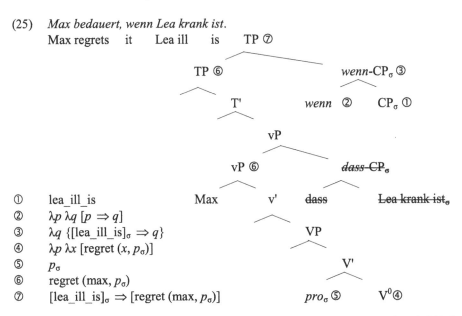

① lea_ill_is
② $\lambda p \, \lambda q \, [p \Rightarrow q]$
③ $\lambda q \, \{[\text{lea\_ill\_is}]_\sigma \Rightarrow q\}$
④ $\lambda p \, \lambda x \, [\text{regret} \, (x, p_\sigma)]$
⑤ p_σ
⑥ regret (max, p_σ)
⑦ $[\text{lea\_ill\_is}]_\sigma \Rightarrow [\text{regret} \, (\text{max}, p_\sigma)]$

As for a 'silent' ProPP, it is additionally necessary that the ProPP is optional. This is the case with respect to verbs like *sich (damit) begnügen* 'to content oneself with sth.' or *jm. (darauf) aufmerksam machen* 'bring sth. to someone's attention' – see also Sect. 2.1.

The *dass*-clause can be deleted if it is locally m-bound by the *wenn*-clause. This implies that both are coreferential and thus alike with respect to their information structure – cf. (26) and (27).

(26) Q: *Unter welcher Bedingung akzeptierte Max, dass Lea sang?*
             under which   condition   accepted   Max   that Lea sang

      A1:   **Er akzeptierte pro$_\sigma$ (dass Lea sang)$_\sigma$ [wenn Lea sang]$_{\sigma, \text{FOC}}$.*
             he accepted   that Lea sang   if   Lea sang
      A2:   *Er akzeptierte pro$_\sigma$ (dass Lea sang)$_\sigma$ [wenn Lea sang]$_{\sigma, \text{FOC}}$.*
      A3:   *Er akzeptierte es$_\sigma$ [wenn Lea sang]$_{\sigma, \text{FOC}}$.*

(27) Q: *Was akzeptierte Max?*
             what accepted   Max
      A: *Er akzeptierte pro$_{\sigma, \text{FOC}}$ (dass Lea sang)$_{\sigma, \text{FOC}}$ [wenn Lea sang]$_{\sigma, \text{FOC}}$.*
             he accepted   that Lea sang   if   Lea sang

---

[7] The motivation for assuming ellipsis is due to Hubert Truckenbrodt (p.c.).

A further deletion condition demands that the *dass-* and *wenn-*clauses have to be identical, with the exception of their complementizer. In (28a), the *wenn-*clause contains a negative polarity item which is not licensed in the *dass-*clause.[8] An *es*-correlate in the matrix clause need not be locally m-bound by a *dass-*clause – cf. (28b).

(28) a.   *Max bedauert pro$_\sigma$ (~~dass Lea einen Fehler gemacht hat~~)$_\sigma$,
             Max regrets   that Lea a   mistake made   has
             [wenn Lea auch nur einen Fehler gemacht hat]$_1$.
             if   Lea even only any   mistake made

      b.   Max bedauert es$_\sigma$ [wenn Lea auch nur einen Fehler   gemacht hat]$_\sigma$
             Max regrets   it   if   Lea even only any   mistake made   has
             'Max regrets it if Lea even only any mistake has made.'

The next condition on *dass-*clause deletion prevents structures with pre-sentential *wenn-*clauses and *pro* (4b') to (6b') and (29). It says that the *dass-* and *wenn-*clause must be adjacent.

(29)   *[Wenn Lea krank ist]$_\sigma$, bedauert Max pro$_\sigma$ (~~dass Lea krank ist~~)$_\sigma$.
        if   Lea ill   is   regrets Max   that Lea ill   is

If the propositional argument is optional as is the case with respect to predicates like *schreiben* 'write' or *glücklich sein* 'be happy', *pro* is not necessary – cf. (30). The propositional variable *p* given by the argument structure of the matrix predicate ④ receives the index of the *wenn-*clause that m-binds TP.

(30)   *Max ist glücklich, wenn Lea singt.*
        Max is happy   if   Lea sings

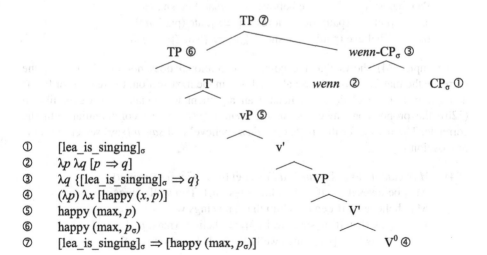

① [lea_is_singing]$_\sigma$
② $\lambda p \lambda q [p \Rightarrow q]$
③ $\lambda q \{[\text{lea\_is\_singing}]_\sigma \Rightarrow q\}$
④ $(\lambda p) \lambda x [\text{happy}(x, p)]$
⑤ happy (max, p)
⑥ happy (max, p_σ)
⑦ [lea_is_singing]$_\sigma \Rightarrow$ [happy (max, p_σ)]

---

[8] Regarding German NPI-elements see Richter & Soehn [16].

If the variable is not bound within the sentence, it gets existentially bound – cf. (31A). That is, (30) is ambiguous in that it can have the representation as given with (30) ⑦ or it is represented as in (31A) where the reason for Max' happiness is not expressed.

(31) Q: *Wann ist Max glücklich?*
             when is Max happy
       A: Max ist glücklich, wenn Lea singt.
             Max is happy   if   Lea sings
             $\exists p$ {[lea_is_singing] $\Rightarrow$ [happy (max, p)]}

A complex argument *wenn*-clause like (32) is also a right or left TP-adjunct. It locally m-binds the correlate in the matrix clause so that it is coreferential with the correlate – cf. (32a). However the variable the correlate represents can also be coreferential with the clause embedded in the conditional – cf. (32b). This is possible because the matrix predicates *hassen* 'hate' and *merken* 'realize' both select a clause denoting a fact. In (33b), the proposition embedded by *glauben* 'believe' does not represent a fact. Therefore, it cannot be coindexed with the correlate embedded by *hassen* 'hate'.

(32) *Paul hasst es$_{\sigma/t}$ [wenn er merkt, [dass Leo schnarcht]$_\sigma$]$_t$*
       Paul hates it   if   he realizes   that Leo snores.
       'Paul hates it if he realizes that Leo is snoring.'
       a.   [realize (paul, [leo_snores]$_\sigma$)]$_\tau$ $\Rightarrow$ [hate (paul, p_t)]
       b.   [realize (paul, [leo_snores]$_\sigma$)]$_\tau$ $\Rightarrow$ [hate (paul, p_σ)]

(33) *Paul hasst es$_{*\sigma/\tau}$ [wenn er glaubt, [dass Leo schnarcht]$_\sigma$]$_\tau$*
       Paul hates it   if   he believes   that Leo snores.
       a.   [believe (paul, [leo_snores]$_\sigma$)]$_\tau$ $\Rightarrow$ [hate (paul, p_t)]
       b.   *[believe (paul, [leo_snores]$_\sigma$)]$_\tau$ $\Rightarrow$ [hate (paul, p_σ)]

Example (34) shows that the complex conditional does not locally m-bind the correlate the matrix clause. As we also will see in the next section, the reason for this is that *glauben* 'believe' does not license an argument *wenn*-clause. However like in (32b), the proposition embedded in the *wenn*-clause can be coreferential with the correlate. The reason for this is that *glauben* 'believe' and *sagen* 'say' select the same proposition type.

(34) *Max glaubt   es$_{\sigma/*t}$ [wenn Lea ihm sagt [dass Tim schön singt]$_\sigma$]$_\tau$*
       Max believes it   if   Lea him says that Tim well sings
       'Max believes it if Lea tells him that Tim sings well.'
       a.   [say (lea, [tim_sings well]$_\sigma$)]$_\tau$ $\Rightarrow$ [believe (max, p_σ)]
       b.   *[say (lea, [tim_sings well]$_\sigma$)]$_\tau$ $\Rightarrow$ [believe (max, p_τ)]

Note that the clause embedded in the *wenn*-clause in (35a) and (35b) cannot be represented by *pro*. We already know the reason for this from the simple cases (7b) to (9b) and (25). *Pro* must be m-bound by a *dass*-clause which can only be deleted if it is adjacent to the clause that m-binds it.

(35) a.   *Paul hasst pro$_\sigma$ [~~dass Leo schnarcht~~]$_\sigma$ [wenn er merkt, [dass Leo
            Paul hates   that Leo snores   if   he realizes that Leo
            schnarcht]$_\sigma$]$_t$
            snores

      b.   *Max glaubt pro$_\sigma$ [~~dass Tim schön singt~~]$_\sigma$ [wenn Lea ihm sagt [dass
            Max believes   that Tim well   sings   if   Lea him says   that
            Tim schön singt]$_\sigma$]$_\tau$
            Tim well   sings

To conclude, argument *wenn*-clauses are adverbials that are either left- or right-adjoined to TP. They locally m-bind an overt correlate which is in the complement position of V^0. The correlates they bind are referential proforms that are theta-marked by V^0. Depending on the matrix predicate, the correlate can be *es* or ProPP. A correlate can be non-overt, that is, *pro*. Like the overt correlates it is theta-marked by V^0. But unlike them, it must be locally m-bound by a *dass*-clause which is a base-generated vP-adjunct [7]. The *dass*-clause can be deleted if it is locally m-bound by the *wenn*-clause. This implies that the *wenn*- and *dass*-clauses must be coreferential and alike with respect to their information structure and that they have to be identical with the exception of their complementizer. It is a further deletion condition that the *dass*- and the *wenn*-clauses are adjacent. Besides argument *wenn*-clauses, there are complex conditionals containing an embedded clause which provides the argument of the matrix predicate.

With the analysis as given in this section we have found answers to the questions raised above: Why do pre-sentential argument conditionals allow sentential correlates, but pre-sentential *dass*-clauses do not – cf. (4) to (6) and (7) to (9), and why do post-sentential *wenn*-clauses allow *pro*, whereas pre-sentential *wenn*-clauses do not – cf. (10b) to (12b) and (4b) to (6b)? What is still lacking is an answer to the question as to which clause-embedding predicates allow argument conditionals; in other words, which semantic properties enable them to construe constructions with an argument *wenn*-clause?

3   Predicates Licensing Argument Conditionals[9]

According to Asher [1], Pesetsky [14] and Schwabe [20], a proposition is regarded as an abstract object in a particular context. Its context-givenness is represented here by a propositional index at the clause that represents it – cf. (24①). The proforms *es*, ProPP

---

[9] This section only analyses constructions with simple argument *wenn*-clauses. Complex ones like those in (32) to (34) are neglected here.

and *pro* are considered to be variables that refer to propositions. Their context-givenness is again represented by an index – cf. (24⑤). As to the *es*-correlate or ProPP, the propositions they refer to can be given anaphorically as in (4b) to (6b) and (24) as well as cataphorically as in (7a) to (9a). As we have seen in the previous section, correlates of a simple argument *wenn*-clause are m-bound by the *wenn*-clause and thus coindexed with it. A non-overt correlate must be m-bound by a *dass*-clause which itself is m-bound by the *wenn*-clause. Thus *pro*, the *dass*-clause and the *wenn*-clause are coreferent.

The conjunction *wenn* relates two propositions in that it creates an implication where the argument *wenn*-clause provides the protasis as well as the specification of the argument variable of the matrix predicate. Depending on the matrix predicate, the conjunction constructs two implication types. The first one concerns the classic implication type. Here, the *wenn*-clause focusses on a semantic condition of the matrix predicate τ in the consequence. The condition is that τ is true if the clause σ, which is embedded by τ, is contingent and true. As for (36), this means that the clause *Max accepts it that Lea sings* is true if *Lea sings* is contingent and true – cf. (36a, b).[10]

(36)   *Max akzeptiert es wenn [Lea singt]$_\sigma$*
        Max accepts it if   Lea sings
        a.   If Lea sings is contingent and true, Max accepts it that Lea sings
        b.   [[lea_sings]$_\sigma$ is contingent and true] $\Rightarrow$ [accept (max, p_σ)]$_\tau$

Predicates like (*es*) *akzeptieren* 'accept', (*es*) *ignorieren* 'ignore' and *sich darüber freuen* 'be glad about', belong to the class of matrix predicates that are compatible with the semantic condition that the clause they embed is contingent and true. They are veridical and even factive when used with a correlate – cf. Schwabe [21], Schwabe & Fittler [23] and Sudhoff [26].[11] Predicates like *merken* 'realize', *wissen* 'know' and *hören* 'hear', which are also factive with an *es*-correlate, also allow argument condi-tionals. But does this mean that factivity is a sufficient and necessary condition for a matrix predicate to select an argument conditional as claimed by various authors?

Factivity is not sufficient because a predicate like *bedenken dass* 'consider' is factive with a correlate, but does not allow an argument conditional. Unlike *hören* 'hear', *sich darüber freuen* 'be glad' and *akzeptieren* 'accept', *bedenken* construes the "non-reducible *ob*-form" [23]: [A *verb* ($\sigma \vee \sigma$)].[12] Verbs like *hören* 'hear' and *ig-norieren* 'ignore' allow a "reducible *ob*-form" [23]: [(A *verb dass* σ) $\vee$ (A *verb dass* σ)]. Except for *zweifeln* 'doubt', a matrix verb that allows a reducible *ob*-form also

---

[10]   Contingent propositions are neither tautological nor contradictory. The fact that the proposition has to be true lead some authors, as for instance Pesetsky [14], Hinterwimmer [8] and Kaiaty [9], to regard ``factivity' as a necessary condition for licensors of argument conditionals.

[11]   According to Égré [3], a predicate is veridical if *A predicate dass* $\sigma \Rightarrow \sigma$ and a predicate is factive if *A (non) predicate dass* $\sigma \Rightarrow \sigma$.

[12]   Predicates licensing a non-reducible *ob*-form correspond to Groenendijk & Stokhof's [6] question intension embedding predicates, and predicates allowing a reducible *ob*-form are consistent with Groenendijk and Stokhof 's question extension embedding predicates.

allows an argument conditional.[13] Characteristic properties of question embedding matrix predicates are described in Schwabe & Fittler [23].

Factivity is not a necessary condition either. Factivity distinguishes a predicate like *es akzeptieren* 'accept' or *bedauern* 'regret', which license constructions with an argument *wenn*-clause, from a veridical predicate like *es beweisen* 'prove', which does not do so. Predicates like *davon hören* 'hear about' and *sich darauf stützen* 'rely on sth.' are not factive, but allow argument conditionals. *Davon hören*, which, without its correlate, allows the reducible *ob*-form, licenses the "neutral *ob*-form" [23]. *Sich darauf stützen*, which does not embed any *ob*-question, is *cognitent* in terms of Schwabe & Fittler. According to them, an embedding predicate *pred* is cognitent if *A pred σ* implies that *σ* follows from what *A* knows. But it turns out that cognitence is not sufficient either. *Sich danach richten* 'comply with' as well as *darüber nachdenken* 'cogitate' are cognitent, but only *sich danach richten* licenses an argument conditional. Both predicates differ in that *sich danach richten* licenses the reducible *ob*-form while *darüber nachdenken* does not.

As for predicates licensing argument conditionals, one can now summarize:

(37) A predicate *verb dass τ* licenses a construction with an argument *wenn*-clause with the paraphrase: If *σ* is contingent and true, then *A verb dass σ* is true iff

    i.   *verb dass* is distinct from *zweifeln dass* 'doubt' and licenses the reducible *ob*-form
        [e.g. (*es*) *hören* 'hear about', (*es*) *ignorieren* 'ignore', *sich danach richten* 'comply with'] or

    ii.   *verb ProPP dass* licenses without the ProPP the reducible *ob*-form
        [(*davon*) *hören* 'hear about', (*darüber*) *schreiben* 'write about'] or

    iii. *verb dass* does not license any *ob*-form and is either factive with the *es*-correlate or cognitent with its ProPP
        [e.g. (*es*) *akzeptieren* 'accept', *sich darüber freuen* 'be glad about', *sich darauf stützen* 'rely on'].

Obviously, sentences with an argument *wenn*-clause like (38) and corresponding ones with a *dass*-clause like (39) have the same truth values if Lea sings off-key. But, they are not equivalent. Their truth values differ if Lea does not sing off-key.

(38) *Max merkt   es$_σ$ wenn [Lea falsch singt]$_σ$*
      Max realizes it   if   Lea sings off-key

(39) *Max merkt   es$_σ$ dass [Lea falsch singt]$_σ$*
      Max realizes it   that   Lea sings off-key

---

[13] *Zweifeln dass σ* is consistent with *zweifeln dass ¬σ*. Thus, *zweifeln ob* construes the reducible *ob*-form [A *zweifelt dass σ*] [A *zweifelt dass ¬σ*], but is not related to question extensions – cf. Schwabe & Fittler [23].

If Lea does not sing off-key, the sentence with the *dass*-clause is false whereas the sentence with the *wenn*-clause is still true. If one uses a sentence with a *wenn*-clause, one does not commit oneself to the truth of the propositional argument. However, if the argument is true, one has indirectly expressed that it is true.

A sentence with an argument *ob*-clause like (40) is also true if the embedded clause is true.

(40)   *Max merkt   es_σ,   ob   [Lea falsch singt]_σ*
        Max finds out it   if/whether Lea sings off-key
        'Max finds it out if/whether Lea sings off-key.'
        (Max finds it out that Lea sing off-key) or (Max finds it out that Lea does not sing off-key)

Examples (38), (39) and (40) are true if Lea sings off-key and Max finds out that she sings off-key. Whereas (39) is false if Lea does not sing off-key, (38) and (40) are still true in such a situation. But this does not mean that (38) and (40) are equivalent. If Lea does not sing off-key and Max does not find out that she does not sing off-key, sentence (38) with the argument *wenn*-clause is true whereas sentence (40) with the *ob*-clause is false.

As to constructions like (41) exhibiting a preference predicate like *vorziehen* 'prefer', they cannot be paraphrased in the same way as a construction like (36) with a predicate like *akzeptieren* 'accept'. This becomes apparent in the faulty paraphrase (41a), which is rendered more precisely by (41a'). Fabricius-Hansen [5], who has observed this problem, concedes that she does not have an appropriate paraphrase for a construction with a preference predicate.

As shown in the paraphrase (41b), the *wenn*-clause restricts σ to being contingent, but not to being true. In this way, the *wenn*-clause is a faultless protasis for the matrix clause.

(41)   *Max zieht es_σ vor wenn [Lea singt]_σ*
        Max prefers it   if   Lea sings
    a.   * If Lea sings Max prefers that Lea sings.
    a'.   *[σ is contingent and true $\Rightarrow \tau(\sigma)$]
    b.   If *Lea sings* is contingent, Max prefers that *Lea sings*.
    b'   [σ is contingent $\Rightarrow \tau(\sigma)$]

The protasis implies that both σ and $\neg \sigma$ are possible. They are alternatives. It is characteristic for preference predicates that their subject decides on the alternative expressed in the protasis. So, preference predicates are only compatible with contingent embedded propositions.

A sentence like (41) is equivalent to a corresponding construction with a *dass*-clause provided contradictory and tautological propositions are ignored – cf. (42).

(42)   *Max zieht   es_σ vor dass [Lea singt]_σ*
        Max prefers it   that Lea sings

It follows that the conjunction *wenn* 'if' in constructions with an argument *wenn*-clause has two functions: It indicates an implication where the protasis provides the argument of the matrix predicate. Depending on the matrix predicate, the protasis either expresses that the argument of the matrix predicate is contingent and true or it expresses that the argument of the matrix predicate is contingent. It follows that there are two conjunctions *wenn*:

(43) a.   *wenn*$_{truth}$: p is contingent and true $\Rightarrow q(p)$
       b.   *wenn*$_{contingence}$: q is contingent $\Rightarrow p(q)$

It depends on the semantic properties of the matrix predicate whether the veridical *wenn* or the contingent one is appropriate. Predicates fulfilling (37) select clauses with *wenn*$_{truth}$ and preference predicates, that is, predicates that select contingent statements, select clauses with *wenn*$_{contingence}$.

4 Conclusion

Similar to Fabricius-Hansen [5], Pesetsky [14], and Hinterwimmer [8], this paper argues that a *wenn*-clause in a construction with an argument *wenn*-clause has a double function in that it is primarily an adverbial that provides the protasis of an implication and that it additionally contributes the propositional argument for the matrix predicate. Unlike Pesetsky [14] and Hinterwimmer [8], who regard the conjunctions *if* or *when* as "instructions" for the adverbial to move to an A-bar-position in order to become the restrictor of a quantifier, this paper suggests that the conditional conjunction *wenn* encodes an implication. It encodes wo implication types, the classic type: [(σ is contingent and true) $\Rightarrow \tau(\sigma)$] and the preference type: [(σ is contingent) $\Rightarrow \tau(\sigma)$]. The adverbial function of the *wenn*-clause is indicated by the conjunction *wenn* and by the syntactic position of the *wenn*-clause as left or right TP-adjunct. Its argument function becomes apparent by its locally m-binding [4] a correlate in a canonical complement position. In this position, the correlate is theta-marked by V^0. Depending on the matrix predicate the correlate is either *es* or ProPP. It can be non-overt, that is, *pro*, if it locally m-binds a *dass*-clause which is a right vP-adjunct [7]. The *dass*-clause can be deleted if it is locally m-bound by a *wenn*-clause. The deletion requires that the *wenn*- and *dass*-clauses are coreferential and alike with respect to their information structure and that both are identical with the exception of their complementizer. Furthermore, the *dass*- and the *wenn*-clause must be adjacent. It has been shown that besides argument *wenn*-clauses, there are complex conditionals containing an embedded clause which provides the argument of the matrix predicate – cf. (32) and (34).

The syntactic analysis has provided answers to the questions raised in the beginning: Why do pre-sentential argument conditionals allow sentential correlates, while pre-sentential *dass*-clauses do not – cf. (4) to (6) and (7) to (9)? And why do post-sentential *wenn*-clauses allow the non-overt correlate *pro*, while pre-sentential *wenn*-clauses do not – cf. (10b) to (12b) and (4b) to (6b)?

The paper has shown that the classic implication type [(σ is contingent and true) $\Rightarrow (\tau(\sigma))$] is allowed *i.* by predicates that license the reducible *ob*-form with the exception of *zweifeln* 'doubt' [e.g. (*es/davon*) *hören* 'realize', (*es*) *ignorieren* 'ignore', *sich danach richten* 'comply with'], *ii.* by predicates with a ProPP that license without the ProPP the reducible *ob*-form [(*davon*) *hören* 'hear about', (*darüber*) *schreiben* 'write about'] and *iii.* by predicates that do not license any *ob*-form and are either factive with the *es*-correlate or cognitent with the ProPP [(*es*) *akzeptierern* 'accept', *sich darüber freuen* 'be glad about'].

The preference type [(σ is contingent and true) $\Rightarrow$ ($\tau(\sigma)$)] is licensed by predicates that are compatible only with contingent propositions (*es*) *vorziehen* 'prefer'.

References

1. Nicholas, A.: Reference to Abstract Objects in Discourse. Kluwer, Dordrecht (1993)
2. Breindl, E.: Präpositionalobjekte und Präpositionalobjektsätze im Deutschen. Niemeyer, Berlin (1989)
3. Égré, P.: Question-embedding and factivity. Grazer Philosophische Studien **77**, 85–125 (2008)
4. Eisenberg, P.: Grundriß der deutschen Grammatik. In: 2., überarbeitete und erweiterte Auflage. J.B: Metzlersche Verlagsbuchhandlung, Stuttgart (1989)
5. Fabricius-Hansen, C.: Sogenannte ergänzende wenn-Sätze. Ein Beispiel syntaktisch-semantischer integration. In: Bech, G., Dyhr, M., Hyldgaard-Jensen, K., Olsen, J. (eds.) Festschrift für Gunnar Bech: zum 60. Geburtstag am 23. März, (Kopenhagener Beiträge zur germanistischen Linguistik, Sonderband 1), pp. 61–83. København, Institut for germansk filologi (1980)
6. Groenendijk, J., Stokhof, M.: Martin: Question. In: van Benthem, J., ter Meulen, A. (eds.) Handbook of Logic and Language, pp. 1055–1124. Elsevier, Amsterdam (1997)
7. Haider, H.: The Syntax of German. Cambridge University Press, Cambridge (2010)
8. Hinterwimmer, S.: When-clauses, factive verbs and correlates. In: Fanselow, G., Hanneforth, T. (eds.) Language and Logos: Festschrift for Peter Staudacher on his 70th Birthday (Studia Grammatica 72), pp. 176–189. Akademie Verlag, Berlin (2010)
9. Kaiaty, M.: Überlegungen zu sog. ergänzenden wenn-Sätzen im Deutschen. Deutsche Sprache **4/10**, 287–308 (2010)
10. Kratzer, A.: Conditionals. In: Farley, A.M., Farley, P., McCollough, K.E. (eds.) Papers From the Parasession on Pragmatics and Grammatical Theory, pp. 115–135. Chicago Linguistics Society, Chicago (1986)
11. Müller, G.: On extraposition & successive cyclicity. In: Lutz, U., Pafel, J. (eds.) On Extraction and Extraposition in German, pp. 213–243. Benjamins, Amsterdam (1995)
12. Müller, G., Sternefeld, W.: Improper movement and unambiguous binding. Linguistic Inquiry **24**, 461–507 (1993)
13. Pasch, R., Brauße, U., Breindl, E., Waßner, U.H.: Handbuch der Deutschen Konnektoren. Walter de Gruyter, Berlin (2003)
14. Pesetsky, D.: Zero Syntax, Part II. MIT (1991) (Unpublished manuscript). http://web.mit. edu/linguistics/people/faculty/pesetsky/publications.html
15. Pullum, G.: Implications of english extraposed irrealis clauses. In: Miller, A., Powers, J. (eds.) ESCOL 1987: Proceedings of the Fourth Eastern States Conference on Linguistics, pp. 260–270. The Ohio State University, Columbus (1987)

16. Richter, F., Soehn, J.-P.: Braucht niemanden zu scheren: A survey of NPI licensing in German. In: Müller, S. (ed.) Proceedings of the 13th International conference on Head-Driven Phrase Structure Grammar, pp. 421–440. CSLI Publications, Stanford (2006)
17. Rocchi, M.: A Third If? Master's thesis, University of Edinburgh (2010). http://hdl.handle.net/1842/5350 (Accessed: 28 March 2012)
18. Rothstein, S.: Adverbial quantification over events. Nat. Lang. Seman. 3, 1–31 (1995)
19. Schmid, H.U.: Überlegungen zu Syntax und Semantik ergänzender wenn-Sätze. Sprachwissenschaft 12, 265–292 (1987)
20. Schwabe, K.: Old and new propositions. In: Späth, A. (ed.) Language, Context and Cognition, pp. 97–114. Mouton de Gruyter, Berlin (2007)
21. Schwabe, K.: Eine uniforme Analyse sententialer Proformen im Deutschen. Deutsche Sprache 41, 142–164 (2013)
22. Schwabe, K.: Sentential Proforms and Argument Conditionals. ZAS, Berlin (2014)
23. Schwabe, K., Fittler, R.: Über semantische Konsistenzbedingungen deutscher Matrixprädikate. Teil 1. Sprachtheorie und germanistische Linguistik 24.1, 45–75. Teil 2. Sprachtheorie und germanistische Linguistik 24.2, 123–150 (2014)
24. Schwabe, K., Jędrzejowski, Ł., Kellner, E.: A cross-linguistic perspective on complement-like if-clauses. In: Workshop (Mis-) Matches in Clause Linkage, 13–14 April. ZAS, Berlin (2012)
25. Sternefeld, W.: Syntax. Eine morphologisch motivierte generative Beschreibung des Deutschen. Stauffenburg, Tübingen (2006)
26. Sudhoff, S.: Argumentsätze und es-Korrelate – zur syntaktischen Struktur von Nebensatzeinbettungen im Deutschen. Wissenschaftlicher Verlag, Berlin (2003)
27. Thompson, A.: Deriving Some Properties of Protasis-Referring Conditionals. In: Choi, J., Hogue, E.A., Punske, J., Tat, D., Schertz, J., Trueman, A. (eds.) Proceedings of the 29th West Coast Conference on Formal Linguistics, pp. 250–258 (2011)
28. Zifonun, G., Hoffmann, L., Strecker, B.: Grammatik der Deutschen Sprache, vol. II. Walter de Gruyter, Berlin (1997)

Biaspectual Verbs: A Marginal Category?

Yulia Zinova and Hana Filip[✉]

Heinrich-Heine Universität Düsseldorf, Düsseldorf, Germany
hana.filip@gmail.com

Abstract. The hallmark property of the Russian verbal system is taken to be the bipartite perfective/imperfective distinction in the domain of grammatical aspect. In this paper we show that there is a substantial and productive class of morphologically complex verbs that do not clearly pattern as either perfective or imperfective on standard formal (distributional) tests for perfectivity versus imperfectivity. Such verbs also pose problems for contemporary syntactic approaches to Russian complex verbs. The main innovation we propose is a new positive test for perfectivity which, along with the standard formal (distributional) tests, allows us to provide empirical evidence for the existence of a class of verbs that exhibit a variable grammatical aspect behavior, i.e., behave like perfective or imperfective verbs in dependence on context. Apart from shedding a new light on the standard tests for the aspectual membership of Russian verbs, the main empirical outcome seems to suggest that a third–biaspectual–class of verbs which cannot be neatly aligned with either the perfective or imperfective class must be recognized. This immediately raises the question about its status with respect to the traditional bipartite perfective/imperfective distinction.

1 Introduction

The main goal of this paper is to provide evidence for the existence of a productive class of verbs in Russian that are morphologically complex and behave in the same way as those verbs that are traditionally considered biaspectual. This class of verbs poses challenges to both traditional and contemporary syntactic accounts of Russian verbal aspect. First, they cannot be identified by means of the standard formal (distributional) tests for determining whether a given verb form is imperfective or perfective, because such tests are formulated as negative diagnostics for perfectivity, i.e., the possibility they exclude is that a given verb form is perfective. Consequently, such tests fail to distinguish biaspectual verbs from imperfective ones. Second, current syntactic approaches that make the most explicit claims about the formal properties of Russian complex verbs make wrong or inconsistent predictions about the aspectual membership of such verbs.

We would like to thank the organizers, audiences and anonymous reviewers of the Tenth International Tbilisi Symposium on Language, Logic and Computation and the 10th European Conference on Formal Description of Slavic Languages. Separate thanks to Daniel Altshuler and Stephen Dickey for personal discussions of the topic.

M. Aher et al. (Eds.): TbiLLC 2013, LNCS 8984, pp. 310–332, 2015.
DOI: 10.1007/978-3-662-46906-4_18

We suggest a new positive test for perfectivity that allows us to provide evidence for a class of biaspectual verbs: namely, this class satisfies our new positive test for perfectivity, which true imperfectives fail, while at the same time, it fails to be aligned with true perfectives, according to the traditional negative tests for perfectivity. If it is correct that there is a productive class of biaspectual verbs with formal (distributional) and semantic properties that clearly set it apart from true perfectives and true imperfectives, then this would raise the question about its status with respect to the traditional binary aspectual opposition between perfectivity and imperfectivity, and whether the possibility of a tripartite division should be considered.

The paper is structured as follows. Section 2 provides the main data. Section 3 focuses on prefixed biaspectual verbs. We first provide a survey of the approaches to Russian prefixation and then show that none of the existing accounts is able to capture the existence of prefixed biaspectual verbs. In Sect. 4.1 we discuss the existing tests for verbal aspect and show that none of them is suitable for distinguishing between biaspectual and imperfective verbs. Section 4.2 is dedicated to the new test that is positive for perfectivity. Section 5 is a discussion of the consequences of the integration of the productive group of biaspectual verbs into the theory of Russian aspect and prefixation.

2 Main Data: Biaspectual Verbs

Biaspectual verbs have received constant attention in the studies of Russian verbal and aspectual systems (see, e.g., Isačenko 1960; Avilova 1968; Skott 1979; Gladney 1982; Čertkova 1998; Jászay 1999; Anderson 2002; Timberlake 2004; Janda 2007). Two classes are commonly distinguished: a relatively small group of verbs with historically Slavic roots, such as *kaznit'*$^{PF/IPF}$ 'to execute' and foreign borrowings ending in *ovat'*, such as *reformirovat'*$^{PF/IPF}$ 'to reform'. According to Čertkova and Čang 1998, the second group constitutes more than 90 % of the biaspectual verbs (their statistical study uses the data from the Ožegov 1990, dictionary) and according to Anderson 2002, – about 95 % (data taken from Zaliznjak 1977). All of the studies listed above are concerned exclusively with nonprefixed biaspectual verbs listed in the dictionaries.

However, there are also prefixed (and suffixed) biaspectual verbs, as is clearly evident from corpus-based studies (see e.g., Borik and Janssen 2012). Such verbs constitute an open class of lexical items with subgroups that follow productive patterns. Let us examine one such group: namely, the biaspectual verbs that are formed with the formant *-iva-/-yva-* and two or more prefixes, where the outermost is the completive *do-*[1]:

---

[1] In this scheme all the components are crucial: those verbs that contain *do-* as the outermost prefix, but do not contain the imperfective suffix, are clearly perfective and those verbs where the only prefix is *do-* and the imperfective suffix is present are imperfective.

(1)   do$_{COMP}$-PREF$^+$-ROOT-yva-t'^{2}

Some illustrative examples (among many others) are:

(2)   a.   *do-pere-za-pis-yva-t'* 'to finish writing down again',
       b.   *do-pere-stra-iva-t'* 'to finish rebuilding',
       c.   *do-vy-š-iva-t'* 'to finish embroidering',
       d.   *do-za-pis-yva-t'* 'to finish writing down',
       e.   *do-pere-pis-yva-t'* 'to finish rewriting/copying',
       f.   *do-za-kaz-yva-t'* 'to finish ordering'.

Depending on the context, these verbs are assigned to either the imperfective aspect (examples (3-a) and (4-a)) or the perfective aspect (examples (3-b) and (4-b)).

(3)   a.   V dannyj moment doperezapisyvaju   ešče 2 pesni.
             in given   moment do.pere.za.write.imp.1sg also 2 songs
             'I'm currently finishing rerecording two more songs.'
       b.   Doperevela   "Talisman" Šandmaulej   i
             do.translate.pst.sg.f "Talisman" Šandmaul.gen and
             doperezapisyvala   sobstvennye pesni.
             do.pere.za.write.imp.pst.f.sg own   songs.
             'I finished translating "Talisman" by the group "Šandmaul" and fin-
             ished rerecording my own songs.'^{3}

(4)   a.   Ja skol'ko   ni   doperestraival,   ljudi v itoge tratili
             I   how.much ever do.pere.build.pst.sg.m, people in total spent
             bol'še, čem na novuyu postrojku.
             more then on new bulding.
             'Every time I was rebuilding something, in the end the clients spent
             more than they would have paid for the new building.'
       b.   Vot tol'ko traktir doperestraivaju,   proekt
             here only tavern do.pere.build.imp.pres.1sg, project
             sdam,   diplom poluču...
             hand.in.pres.1sg, diploma receive.pres.1sg
             'I will just first finish rebuilding the tavern, then hand in the project
             and receive the diploma...'

---

^{2} The superscripts 'IPF' and 'PF' on a verb stand for the imperfective and perfective aspect. The following abbreviations are used in the glosses: NOM = nominative, GEN = genitive, DAT = dative, ACC = accusative, SG = singular, PL = plural, F = feminine, M = masculine, N = neuter, PRES = present tense, PAST = past tense, INCEP = inceptive, COMP = completive, IMP = imperfective suffix, PREF = lexical prefix.

^{3} The past tense verbal form itself does not specify the person, only gender and number, so the information about the person comes from the context.

In (3-a) the verb *doperezapisyvaju* 'I am finishing rewriting' behaves like an imperfective verb, because it has a progressive interpretation triggered by the adverbial *v dannyj moment* 'currently' (see also below), while *doperezapisyvala* 'I finished rerecording' in (3-b) behaves like a perfective verb, because of the conjunction with the perfective verb *doperevela* 'finished translating' (see the more detailed explanation in Sect. 4.2).

In (4-a) the verb *doperestraival* 'was finishing rebuilding' is used as an imperfective verb with an iterative meaning and in (4-b) the same verb *doperestraivaju* 'I will finish rebuilding' can only be assigned the perfective aspect because it has future reference in the nonpast tense.

The variability of the perfective and imperfective uses of biaspectual verbs is a matter of some disagreement, not all the speakers can access both the perfective and imperfective variant. For instance, according to some speakers, *dozapisyvat'* 'to be finishing/finish writing down' cannot be used as a perfective verb, i.e., it is not biaspectual at all. However, such speakers would also agree that the structurally similar verb *dovyšivat'* 'to be finishing/finish embroidering' can, indeed, be used as a perfective verb, as in (5).

(5)   Planiruyu   pristupit' k rabote čerez dve nedeli, kak tol'ko
       Plan.pres.1sg start.inf to work over two weeks, as   only
       dovyšivayu   "Lesnuju zarju".
       do.vy.sew.imp.pres.1sg "Forest   dawn"
       'I plan to start the work in two weeks' time; as soon as I will have finished
       embroidering "Dawn in the forest".'

3 Russian Prefixation System

3.1 An Overview of the Existing Syntactic Approaches

As is well-known, the Russian grammatical aspect provides formidable challenges to any theory of aspect. One of the main reasons for this is the system of verbal prefixation, which is highly idiosyncratic. The difficulties start with the fact that even standard Russian grammars do not agree on the number of verbal prefixes and their meanings. Traditionally, the number of prefixes is claimed to be 18 (Isačenko 1960; 1968; Russian Grammar 1952), but Krongauz (1998, pp. 131–141) lists 19, proposing to split *o-/ob-* in two separate entries and Barykina et al. (1989) gives 21 prefixes. The largest number of prefixes is listed in Švedova (1982), who claims that the total number is 28. Her list includes 23 prefixes that she takes to be productive: *v-/vo-, vz-/vzo-, voz-/vozo-, vy-, dis-* (productive in scientific speech), *do-, za-, iz-/izo-, na-, nad-/nado-, nedo-, o-, ob-/obo-, ot-/oto-, pere-, po-, pod-/podo-, pred-/predo-, pri-, pro-, raz-/razo-, s-/so1-*. The other five are nonproductive (*niz-* and *pre-*) or loaned and productive only in literary language (*re-, de-* and *so2-*). In her list of the productive prefixes, the median number of their different uses/senses is 5.

Traditional, descriptive grammars (e.g., Russian Grammar 1952; Ušakov 1940; Švedova 1982) provide a number of valuable intuitive and descriptive observations, but they do not offer any systematic theory of prefixation. It is crucial to note that they either do not mention the possibility of prefix stacking (as illustrated by examples in (2)) at all (see e.g., Švedova 1982) or if they do, they tend to list certain prefix combinations without motivating why exactly such combinations should occur[4].

One of the possible reasons for this omission is the widespread view that the main function of Russian (and, in general, Slavic) prefixes is to be added to imperfective simplex verbs and form perfective verbs. With certain restrictions, the imperfective suffix is added to prefixed perfective stems and derives secondary imperfective verbs. While this captures two of the most common formation processes of complex verbs, it must also be acknowledged that there are others that are traditionally barely mentioned. In particular, the stacking of prefixes has escaped any systematic treatment.

Filip (2000, 2003) attempts at providing systematic semantic motivation for at least some of the cases of stacked prefixes (based on Czech examples), and in this connection calls into question the common view of Slavic prefixes, according to which prefixes are only attached to imperfective verbs and form perfective verbs, showing that prefixes can also be attached directly to perfective verbs, both basic and prefixed.

Another important strand of research that addresses the phenomenon of Russian verbal prefixation, is syntactically based and has been developed in the past ten years or so. It has its origins in the long-standing tradition of distinguishing between two types of prefixes (Forsyth 1970; Isačenko 1960; Townsend 1975): lexical prefixes (also called internal prefixes) vs. those prefixes that derive Aktionsart verbs (later in the literature called superlexical or external).

The division of the prefixes into lexical/internal and superlexical/external is a key component in contemporary (mostly syntactically-based) approaches to Russian prefixation: Babko-Malaya (1999); Borik (2002); Gehrke (2004); Ramchand (2004); Schoorlemmer (1995); Romanova (2004, 2006); Svenonius (2004a, 2004b); Di Sciullo and Slabakova (2005). Following Svenonius (2004b, p. 229) who builds on the discussion of Russian in Schoorlemmer (1995), these two groups are distinguished according to the following diagnostics: superlexical prefixes (i) do not allow the formation of secondary imperfectives (invalid in Bulgarian), (ii) can occasionally stack outside lexical prefixes, never inside, (iii) select for imperfective stems, (iv) attach to the non-directed form of a motion verb, (v) have systematic, temporal or quantizing meanings, rather than spatial or resultative ones.

Babko-Malaya (1999) was the first to propose that the internal structure of complex verbs is represented by means of syntactic trees and lexical and superlexical prefixes occupy different syntactic positions in it. More precisely, lexical prefixes are adjoined to a lexical head, while superlexical prefixes are adjoined instead to a functional category. She predicts that "lexical prefixes modify the meaning of the verb, whereas superlexical prefixes are modifiers of verbal phrases

---

[4] For example, in Russian Grammar (1952) it is only stated that *na-, pere-, pod-, pri-* and *po-* are productive as second verbal prefixes and that *po-* can also be used as a third prefix.

or whole sentences" (Babko-Malaya 1999, p. 76). The (im)perfective aspect of a given complex verb is then determined by the properties of the highest affix in a structure. In what follows, let us have a look at a couple of proposals that follow this research program.

Romanova (2004) proposes the structure for Russian verbs that is represented in Fig. 1. Romanova (2004, p. 272) assumes "the presence of AspP in between VP and vP," that "is a possible place for merge of the secondary imperfective suffix or purely perfectivizing prefixes", and that lexical prefixes are located below AspP, while "superlexical prefixes originate – or at least end up – above the AspP domain" (p. 271). Throughout the paper, a lot of questions regarding the behavior of prefixes are posed and the author arrives at the conclusion that "there is no uniform distribution of all superlexicals".

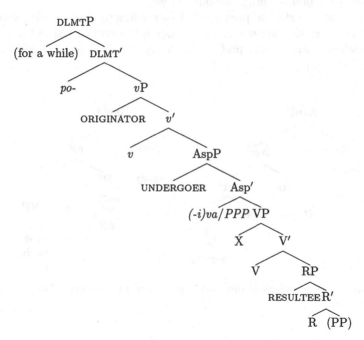

Fig. 1. Verbal structure according to Romanova (2004, p. 272)

While Babko-Malaya (1999) and Schoorlemmer (1995), among others, assume that superlexical prefixes form a homogeneous class, Svenonius (2004b) argues that there is a tripartite division among superlexical prefixes based on their ability to form secondary imperfectives.

According to Svenonius (2004b), certain superlexical prefixes (*za-* with inceptive meaning, *ot-* with terminative meaning and *pere-* with distributive meaning[5]) may be attached higher than the structural position of the imperfective

---

[5] *Pere-* has a variety of meanings (e.g. Švedova 1982 distinguishes between 10 different meanings) including spatial, temporal, comparative, iterative, crossing the boundary, distributive and *pere-* of excess.

suffix, which is *Asp*, the head of *AspP*. Such prefixes disallow the formation of secondary imperfectives, (e.g., *za-* in its inceptive use, as in Fig. 2). That is, the imperfective suffix cannot be directly attached to an imperfective stem and the result is an invalid structure (see Fig. 2).

There are also mixed cases like cumulative *na-*, excessive *pere-*, and attenuative *po-*. The normal point of attachment of such prefixes is outside the scope of the secondary imperfective, however under certain exceptional conditions they allow a lower point of attachment (p. 231).

Svenonius' main generalizations can be stated as follows (see also the summary in Svenonius 2012):

(i) lexical prefixes originate inside *v*P;
(ii) superlexical prefixes originate outside *v*P;
(iii) lexical and superlexical prefixes that (according to him) disallow secondary imperfectivization are separated by Asp in the syntactic structure;
(iv) exceptional superlexical prefixes are merged (sometimes) outside *v*P, but below the Asp.

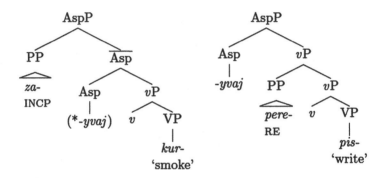

Fig. 2. Structural positions of different superlexical prefixes according to Svenonius (2004b, p. 231)

Ramchand (2004) proposes the following 'bottom-up' order:

(i) lexical prefixes;
(ii) aspectual head that may contain either the imperfective suffix or a superlexical prefix;
(iii) a DP projection for superlexical distributional prefixes (she cites *pere-* and *po-*).

While the motivation for this hierarchical order is not entirely clear, it would seem to derive from the following assumptions made by Ramchand (2004):

1. lexical prefixes appear low in the syntactic structure, due to which a "presuppositional structure to the aspectual head" is introduced "to the effect that it creates a definite rather than an indefinite time moment in Asp" (p. 349);

2. most superlexical prefixes are in Asp and "impose a specific reference time on the relation between event and temporal anchoring" (p. 351);

3. a position that superlexical prefixes that are distributional (*pere-* and distributive *po-*) occupy is higher in the hierarchy than the Asp head (p. 352); such prefixes can be attached directly to the root or to the secondary imperfective verb.

The fundamental two-way distinction is of key importance for Romanova (2004); Svenonius (2004b); Ramchand (2004) despite the fact that they split the class of superlexicals into subclasses and acknowledge that "there is no uniform distribution of all superlexicals" (Romanova 2004, p. 271).

In further developments we see a shift of focus from the bipartite distinction to the split of the whole class of prefixes into more than just two main classes. A good example is the work by Tatevosov (2007), who proposes a three-way classification of verbal prefixes, arguing for the existence of intermediate prefixes, in addition to lexical and superlexical ones. The group of the intermediate prefixes is constituted by completive *do-* and repetitive *pere-*.

This division is motivated by examples like (6-a) and (6-b). For the analysis that assumes the two-way distinctions, the verbs in (6-a) and (6-b) have identical internal structure: a superlexical prefix, a lexical prefix, a stem and the imperfective suffix. Nevertheless, these verbs are assigned to a different aspect: *nazapisyvat'* 'to write down a lot' is perfective while *perezapisyvat'* 'to be rewriting/to rewrite' is imperfective. For Tatevosov (2007), there is a structural difference between the two verbs, because *pere-* is classified as an intermediate prefix and is positioned between lexical prefixes and the imperfective suffix. As a result, the verb in (6-b) gets assigned the imperfective aspect. At the same time, *na-* remains a superlexical prefix and thus the verb *nazapisyvat'* 'to write down a lot' gets assigned the perfective aspect.

(6)   a.   nazapisyvat'^{PF}
            na.za.write.imp.inf
            'to write down a lot'
       b.   perezapisyvat'^{IPF}
            pere.za.write.imp.inf
            'to be rewriting/to rewrite'

A more elaborate classification is proposed in Tatevosov (2009) that is mainly dedicated to the problem of prefix stacking. However, in order to account for the relevant stacking constraints, the proposal amounts to a list of postulations about the position of prefixes in the syntactic tree. Tatevosov (2009) abandons the previous tripartite distinction among all the prefixes proposed in Tatevosov (2007) and instead argues for a classical division of all the prefixes into lexical and superlexical ones, enriching it with a three-way classification of superlexical prefixes in order to account for the relevant facts: left periphery prefixes, selectionally limited prefixes and positionally limited prefixes.

The group of left periphery prefixes is constituted by only one prefix: distributional *po-* (*pobrosat'* 'to spend some time throwing'). It occupies the left periphery of the verbal structure. Selectionally limited prefixes can be added only to a formally imperfective verb. The group includes delimitative *po-* (*posidet'* 'to sit for some time'), cumulative *na-* (*navarit'* 'to cook a considerable amount of something'), distributional *pere-* (*perelovit'* X 'to catch all of X') and inchoative *za-* (*zabegat'* 'to start running about').

The last group of positionally limited prefixes is constituted by the completive *do-* (*dodelat'* 'to finish doing'), repetitive *pere-* (*perepisat'* 'to rewrite') and attenuative *pod-* (*podustat'* 'to become a little bit tired'). These prefixes, according to Tatevosov (2009), can be added only before the secondary imperfective suffix *-yva-/-iva-* and end up in the same structural position as intermediate prefixes in Tatevosov (2007), the group being extended by one prefix.

The net advantage of Tatevosov (2009) over Tatevosov (2007) seems to be that only the former can motivate the difference between (7-a) and (7-b), but it also requires the stipulation that distributive *po-* forms a singleton group. On Tatevosov's (2009) account, distributive *po-* must be situated on the left periphery of the verb, thus there can be no derivation for (7-b).

(7)   a.   ponazapisyvat'
             distr.cum.za.write.imp.inf
             'to write down a lot one after another'
       b.   *nápozapisyvat'
             cum.distr.za.write.imp.inf

3.2   Summary and Criticism of the Existing Syntactic Approaches: Predictions and Counterexamples

Although the approaches summarized above vary in many details, they all share the idea that prefixes fall into distinct groups characterized by different syntactic properties from which their semantic behavior is assumed to follow: superlexical prefixes have transparent meaning and behave compositionally, while the result of the combinations of verbal stems with lexical prefixes is lexicalized.

One problem is that the class of superlexical prefixes is not clearly delimited. There are substantial differences among the researchers on which prefixes belong to the superlexical class. The longest list can be found in Svenonius (2004a, p. 195, (28)): inceptive *za-*, terminative *ot-*, completive *do-* and *iz-*, perdurative *pro-*, delimitative, attenuative and distributive *po-*, repetitive, excessive and repetitive *pere-* and cumulative and saturative *na-*. While the list by Romanova (2004) is shorter, it also includes attenuative *pod-* and *pri-*.

As far as determining the aspect of a complex verb is concerned, what implicitly emerges from Ramchand (2004); Romanova (2004); Svenonius (2004b), can be summarized by the schema in (8), given in Borer (2013):

(8)   a.   V → *imperfective*[6]
       b.   Prefix + V → *perfective*
       c.   V + Semelfactive → *perfective*

---

[6] Plus a list of biaspectual and perfective underived verbs.

    d.   Prefix + V + S-imperfective/Hab → *imperfective*
    e.   Prefix + (Prefix + V + S-imperfective/Hab) → *perfective*

Taking into account also the proposals by Tatevosov (2007, 2009), the schema in (8) may be completed with the following rule (f), where (f) must be applied instead of (e) in case of intermediate/positionally limited prefixes (completive *do-*, repetitive *pere-*, attenuative *pod-*).

    f.   (PosLim/ItmPrefix + Prefix* + V) + S-imperfective/Hab → *imperfective*

Examples (9-a)-(9-f) illustrate the application of the corresponding rules (8-a)-(8-f).

(9)   a.   pisat'^{IPF}
            write.inf
            'to write'

        d.   zapisyvat'^{IPF}
            za.write.imp.inf
            'to be writing down/to write down'

    b.   zapisat'^{PF}
            za.write.inf
            'to write down'

        e.   nazapisyvat'^{PF}
            cum.za.write.imp.inf
            'to write down a lot'

    c.   prygnut'^{PF}
            jump.semelf.inf
            'to jump once'

        f.   perezapisyvat'^{IPF}
            iter.za.write.imp.inf
            'to be rewriting/to rewrite'

From the schema in (8) it follows that all the existing syntactic approaches implicitly postulate that there is exactly one syntactic structure allowable for any given single verb token with a given interpretation. The structural position for each prefix use in the syntactic structure is fixed. To illustrate this point, which is key for our purposes, let us take as an example the biaspectual verb *dozapisyvat'* 'to finish writing/to be finishing writing' that follows the pattern in (1). Given the syntactic assumptions, summarized in the schema (8), it can be shown that the biaspectual nature of the verb cannot be predicted.

    The verb in question contains the following derivational morphemes: the superlexical prefix *do-* with the completive meaning (see, e.g., Svenonius 2004a), the lexical prefix *za-* with non-compositional semantic contribution, the stem *-pis-* and the imperfective suffix *-yva-*.

    Following Svenonius (2004b) and rule (e) in schema (8), we obtain the tree in Fig. 3 for the verb *dozapisyvat'*. The completive prefix *do-* scopes over the imperfective suffix, so the verb must be assigned the perfective aspect. Note that Svenonius (2004b) does not explicitly discuss the characteristics of the prefix *do-*. However, in Svenonius (2004a) this prefix is assigned to the superlexical class and in Svenonius (2004b) general statements about the properties of the superlexical prefixes are made. In sum, this allows us to conclude that the verb *dozapisyvat'* should be analyzed in the way illustrated in Fig. 3. Ramchand (2004, p. 357) makes the same predictions.

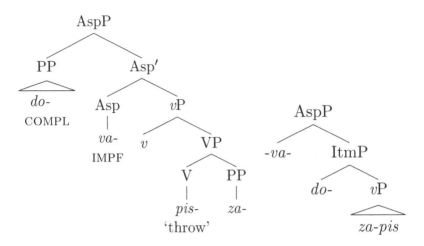

Fig. 3. Tree for *dozapisyvat'* following Svenonius (2004b)

Fig. 4. Tree for *dozapisyvat'* following Tatevosov (2007)

Contrary to both Svenonius (2004b) and Ramchand (2004), Tatevosov (2007) arrives at a different aspectual classification of the same verb. This is because according to Tatevosov (2007), *do-* occupies a special projection for intermediate prefixes so that the resultant syntactic structure is as in Fig. 4. As we see, the imperfective suffix is in the highest position and the aspect of the whole verb must be imperfective. The analysis in Tatevosov (2009) amounts to the same prediction.

As is evident from the examples above, each theory predicts exactly one syntactic structure for the verb *dozapisyvat'*, as well as for any other verb. This holds true even for the most detailed account by Tatevosov (2009). Here the existence of an exceptional group of superlexical prefix uses is postulated. This group is the group of selectionally limited prefixes and includes delimitative *po-*, cumulative *na-*, distributional *pere-* and inchoative *za-*. These prefixes, according to Tatevosov (2009), can assume a position "above" or "below" the imperfective suffix (which is not allowed in other approaches). However, this fact does not affect the overall prediction that there is a unique syntactic structure assigned to each given complex verb due to the selectional restriction.

The impossibility of having syntactic ambiguity for a given verb with a fixed interpretation should not be confused with the situation in which the verb has two meanings, i.e., the case of a genuine lexical ambiguity. In such case, all the approaches discussed predict for each meaning to be associated with a different syntactic tree.

In sum, the notion of a structural position is helpful in motivating at least certain facts about the formation of complex verbs (see example (9)). For this reason syntactic approaches were a necessary step in the process of understanding the system of Russian prefixation. However, the problematic part of these approaches is that they, as we have shown, exclude the existence of biaspectual affixed verbs. The reason for this is that the structural assumptions that are postulated enforce a given complex verb to be unambiguously assigned to either the perfective or the imperfective aspect category independently of any other factors[7].

4 Identifying Biaspectual Verbs

4.1 Standard Diagnostics for Distinguishing Between Perfectives and Imperfectives

In Russian, the tests for determining the aspectual membership of a given verb form typically aim at excluding the possibility that a given verb form is perfective. Hence, they focus on the negative formal properties of perfective verbs. One good example of such a test set is given by Schoorlemmer (1995):

(10) (i) perfective verbs do not get an "ongoing" interpretation in nonpast tense;

 (ii) perfective verbs cannot be used as complements of phasal verbs (e.g., *načat'* 'to begin');

 (iii) perfective verbs cannot form present participles.

Notice that all of these tests are negative in so far as they specify the properties that perfectives fail to have. While these tests delimit perfective verbs, they cannot distinguish between imperfective and biaspectual verbs. Based on the previous aspect studies, there seem to be two possible candidate tests for perfectivity: one relies on past passive participle formation and the other makes use of the properties of the narrative sequence. We will ultimately show that neither of them works.

According to the first test, past passive participles (PPPs) can only be formed from perfective verbs. For example, in the aspectual pair in (11) only the perfective member sanctions the derivation of a PPP (12-b), but not the imperfective one (12-a).

(11) gruzit'^{IPF} → zagruzit'^{PF}

(12) a. gruzit'^{IPF} ↛ *gružennyj

 b. zagruzit'^{PF} → zagružennyj

---

[7] One exception is a modification of Tatevosov (2009) proposed in Tatevosov (2013) that seems to implicitly react on problematic examples first mentioned in the work by Zinova (2012). Tatevosov (2013) proposes that the completive prefix *do-* (for a certain group of Russian speakers) does not have any restrictions on its attachment. If, however, such modification is adopted without further restrictions, the class of biaspectual verbs turns out to be too large. This problem seems to be solvable, although no solution is offered by the author. For a bit more details on this point and the data that remains problematic after such modification see Zinova and Filip (2014). Another conceptual problem is that the class of superlexical prefixes then contains 4 subclasses, two of which are inhabited by only one prefix.

However, matters are not as simple as that. As was pointed out by Schoorlemmer (1995), this test is applicable only to transitive and aspectually paired verbs. Specifically, according to Schoorlemmer, no perfective verbs with superlexical prefixes form aspectual pairs, which makes the test of little help for our purposes. Second, Romanova (2006) provides a number of counterexamples of past passive participles derived from imperfective verbs, among others (13).

(13)   ...kolonna   avtomašin, gružennyx   bumažnymi   paketami...
         column.nom cars.pl.nom loaded^{IPF}.pl.gen paper.pl.instr bags.instr
         '...a string of cars, loaded with paper bags...'

This suffices to show that the PPP formation test is neither reliable nor general enough.

The second possible positive test is connected to the phenomenon of aspectual pairs and to the contribution of the verbal aspect to the narrative sequence. Both are evoked in connection with what is referred to as the 'Maslov criterion' that first appears in the following formulation: "Pri perevode povestvovanija iz ploskosti prošedšego vremeni v ploskost' istoričeskogo nastojaščego vse glagoly kak SV, tak i NSV, okazyvajutsja uravnennymi v formax nastojaščego vremeni NSV" [When the narrative is transformed from the past into the historical present, all the verbs, both perfective and imperfective, result in forms of imperfective verbs in present tense] (Maslov 2004, pp. 76–77). However, the specific reference to Maslov's work is typically not given when the criterion is applied. We cite Mikaelian et al. (2007) as one of the clearest formulations found in the literature. The 'Maslov criterion' is formulated as follows in Mikaeljan et al. (Mikaelian et al. (2007), p. 1):

"A perfective and an imperfective verb can be considered an aspectual pair if and only if the imperfective verb can be substituted for the perfective verb in situations (such as descriptions of reiterated events or narration in historical present) where the latter is not allowed."

Mikaelian et al. (2007) illustrate the above with the following contrast:

(14)   a.   Prišel^{PF},   uvidel^{PF},   pobedil^{PF}
               Come.past.sg.m, see.pst.sg.m, conquer.pst.sg.m
               'I came, I saw, I conquered'
         b.   Prixožu^{IPF},   vižu^{IPF},   pobeždaju^{IPF}
               Come.pres.1sg, see.pres.1sg, conquer.pres.1sg
               'I come, I see, I conquer'

The sentence in (14-a) describes a sequence of events in the past, suggesting that each event was completed before the next started. Now, if the speaker wants to represent the same state of affairs in the historical present or as a habitual situation (their "reiterated event"), due to independently motivated constraints on the Russian aspectual system, only the corresponding[8] imperfective verbs can be used, as in (14-b).

---

[8] 'Corresponding' is understood as the imperfective verb that constitutes the aspectual pair with the original perfective verb.

It is plausible to approach biaspectual verbs by considering them as a kind of a covert aspectual pair and apply the 'Maslov criterion' in order to find them. One of the verbs that are often cited as paradigm examples of native biaspectual verbs is *kaznit'* 'to execute'. If the verbs in (15-a) and (15-b) can be thought of as constituting an aspectual pair, then the verb *kaznit'* in two different aspects in (15-c) might be thought of along the same lines, but of course in (15-c) the alleged members of the aspectual pair just happen to be not phonologically differentiated.

(15)   a.   pisat'^{IPF} – napisat'^{PF}
          b.   zapisat'^{IPF} – zapisyvat'^{PF}
          c.   kaznit'^{IPF} – kaznit'^{PF}

Applying the test to *kaznit'*, one can see that it can be used in the narrative sequence, which seems to suggest that it behaves like a perfective verb (16-a). The same verb can be used in the historical present or the habitual situation context, strongly suggesting that in (16-b) *kaznit'* behaves like an imperfective verb.

(16)   a.   Prišel^{PF},   uvidel^{PF},   pobedil^{PF},   kaznil^{PF}
              Come.pst.sg.m, see.pst.sg.m, conquer.pst.sg.m, execute.pst.sg.m
              vragov.
              enemies
              'I came, I saw, I conquered, I executed the enemies.'
          b.   Prixožu^{IPF},   vižu^{IPF},   pobeždaju^{IPF},   kaznju^{IPF}
              Come.pres.1sg, see.pres.1sg, conquer.pres.1sg, execute.pres.1sg
              vragov.
              enemies
              'I come, I see, I conquer, I execute the enemies.'

This would seem to be in compliance with the 'Maslov criterion', as formulated by Mikaelian et al. (2007). Therefore, (16) seems to indicate that biaspectual verbs like *kaznit'* could be treated as covert aspectual pairs: in (16-a) the verb is perfective, while in (16-b) it is imperfective.

However, in the same contexts (narrative sequence and historical present/habitual situation) it is also possible to use imperfective verbs like *dumat'* 'to think', as we see in (17).

(17)   a.   Prišel^{PF},   uvidel^{PF},   pobedil^{PF},   dumal^{IPF} o
              come.pst.sg.m, see.pst.sg.m, conquer.pst.sg.m, think.pst.sg.m about
              buduščem.
              future
              'I came, I saw, I conquered, I thought about the future.'
          b.   Prixožu^{IPF},   vižu^{IPF},   pobeždaju^{IPF},   dumaju^{IPF} o
              come.pres.1sg, see.pres.1sg, conquer.pres.1sg, execute.pres.1sg about
              buduščem.
              future
              'I come, I see, I conquer, I think about the future.'

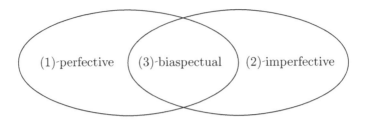

Fig. 5. Aspectual classes

This shows that such contexts cannot be used as diagnostics for perfectivity and imperfectivity. The 'Maslov criterion' requires a perfective verb as an input condition, so it is also negative for perfectivity and does not allow to distinguish between biaspectual and imperfective verbs. In (16) the same verb is used in both sentences due to its biaspectual nature. At the same time the possibility to use the same verb in both sentences in (17) is explained by the imperfective aspect of *dumal* 'thought' in the first sentence. Moreover, there are other problems related to the application of the 'Maslov criterion', which we cannot address given space limitations[9].

The key point to be made here and one that has not yet been emphasized enough in the research on Russian aspect, is that there is no positive test for perfectivity. Figure 5 schematically represents the aspectual classes of Russian verbs. The standard tests are negative for perfectivity, as illustrated by (10). They merely exclude the possibility that a given verb form is a member of Set 1. To separate the subset of biaspectual verbs (Set 3) from true imperfective verbs (Set 2), we need a positive test for perfectivity (Set 1). In the next section we will do just that and propose a new positive method of testing if a given verb is perfective. In combination with the standard tests we can then identify the class of the biaspectual verbs.

4.2   New Positive Test for Perfectivity: Narration Relation

The new positive test for perfectivity capitalizes on the notion of the *Narration relation*, defined as follows by Lascarides and Asher (1993):

Narration(α, β): The event described in β is a consequence of (but not strictly speaking caused by) the event described in α. If *Narration* (α, β) holds, and α and β describe eventualities e_1 and e_2 respectively, then e_1 occurs before e_2.

The *Narration* relation can be illustrated by (18):

(18)   Max woke up. He opened the window.

In English, it is natural to use telic verb phrases in non-progressive tense in the *Narration* relation. A parallel Russian example (19) contains two perfective

---

[9] Mikaeljan et al. (2007, p. 2) write that "rather than a tool for establishing aspectual pairs, the Maslov criterion should be taken as a definition and raison d'être of the aspectual correlation."

verbs. In observing that the main line of a narrative is constituted by sequences of perfective verb forms, which move narrative time forward, we draw on well-known insights in the vast literature on aspect and discourse structure (for Russian, see in particular Padučeva 1996; Padučeva 2004 and elsewhere).

(19) Maksim prosnulsja^{PF}. On otkryl^{PF} okno.
      Maksim woke.up.pst.m.refl he open.pst.m window.acc
      Maksim woke up. He opened the window.

The property that is crucial for us is that if the *Narration* relation holds and the second verb is perfective, the aspect of the first verb must be perfective as well. (20) demonstrates that the combination of an imperfective and a perfective verb is uninterpretable. Under the most normal assumptions about how situations in the world take place, people do not open the windows while sleeping nor is the event of opening a window normally interpreted as result or a continuation of the waking up event. Given that, the only possible relation between the two events is *Narration*.

(20) ??Maksim prosypalsja^{IPF}.   On otkryl^{PF} okno.
      Maksim woke.up.imp.pst.m.refl he open.pst.m window.acc
      ??Maksim was waking up. He opened the window.

Table 1. Verbal aspect and the *Narration* relation

Verbal combination		Acceptance judgment
Perfective verb	*i* 'and' perfective verb	Ok
Imperfective verb	*i* 'and' perfective verb	??
Biaspectual verb	*i* 'and' perfective verb	Ok

The idea of the test is summarized in Table 1. We propose to use sentences like (21) and (22), where the second verb is perfective such that the *Narration* relation is the only possible discourse relation between the events, described by the two clauses (see more details below). In such cases, the aspect of the first verb must be perfective, as well. Example (21) is in the non-past, whereas (22) – in the past tense. This shows that tense is not relevant for our purposes. Note that this is not to deny that the Narration Relation may also hold in sequences with imperfective verbs only, as in (23).

(21) a. Ja s"em^{PF} zavtrak i pojdu^{PF} na rabotu.
          I s.eat.pres.1sg breakfast and pref.go.pres.1sg on work
          'I will finish my breakfast and go to work.'
      b. ??Ja em^{IPF} zavtrak i pojdu^{PF} na rabotu.
          I eat.pres.1sg breakfast and pref.go.pres.1sg to work

(22) a. Ja s"el^{PF} zavtrak i pošel^{PF} na rabotu.
          I pref.eat.pst.sg.m breakfast and pref.go.pres.sg.m on work

'I finished my breakfast and went to work.'
b. $^{??}$Ja el^{IPF} zavtrak   i   pošel^{PF} na rabotu.
    I   eat.pst.sg.m breakfast and pref.go.pst.sg.m to work

(23)   Uže   8:00. Ja em^{IPF} zavtrak   i   idu^{IPF} na rabotu.
    Already 8:00. I   eat.pres.1sg breakfast and go.pres.1sg to work
    It is already 8:00. I eat the breakfast and go to work.

Examples (21-a) and (22-a) illustrate the first line of the table, (21-b) and
(22-b) – the second line of the table. (21-b) and (22-b) are not interpretable,
because neither the *Narration* nor any other coordinating relation, e.g., a *Background* relation, can be construed.

The examples in (24) illustrate the third line of the table above which is
the key to the case of biaspectual verbs. In a given context, *kaznit'* 'to execute'
can behave either as a perfective or an imperfective verb. Given that in the
test context imperfective verbs are odd, biaspectual verbs pattern together with
perfective verbs. Thus, the proposed test context allows to distinguish between
biaspectual and imperfective verbs.

(24)   a.   Palač   kaznit   prestupnika i   pojdët^{PF} domoj.
       Hangman execute.pres.3sg criminal   and po.go.pres.3sg home
       'The hangman will execute the criminal and will go home.'
    b.   Palač   kaznil   prestupnika i   pošel^{PF} domoj.
       Hangman execute.pst.m criminal   and po.go.pst.m home
       'The hangman executed the criminal and went home.'

Now that we have explained the basic workings of the test, let us address the
precise conditions under which it works as a positive test for perfectivity. To
enforce the *Narration* relation, the crucial conditions are required to be met.

1. The main lexical verb in the second clause must have a temporal extent.
2. The event denoted by the main lexical verb in the second clause must not be
   caused or considered a continuation of the event denoted by the main lexical
   verb in the first clause.
3. The clauses must be conjoined using plain conjunction *i* 'and' without any
   temporal or modal (epistemic) adverbial.

The conditions above reveal the workings of the test: when the two verbs denote
such events that all the other coordinating relations such as *Background* or *Cause*
are excluded (conditions 1 and 2), *i* 'and' (condition 3) can only indicate a *Narration* relation between the two clauses (as it is a marker of a coordinating relation
and other coordinating relations are excluded), if it is acceptable; however, if a
Narration relation between the two clauses cannot be established, the discourse
is infelicitous, as in (21-b) and (22-b)).

The reason for the first condition is that verbs denoting punctual events could
be construed as describing events that are temporally located within the time
span of the first event. In such case, it is not the *Narration* (but the *Background*)
relation that holds between the two clauses and thus the rule expressed in the

last line of the table above (Table 1) is not applicable, as illustrated by (25). This condition is relevant if the test is applied in the past tense.

(25)   Ona igrala^{IPF} v futbol i   slomala^{PF} nogu.
        She play.pst.sg.f in football and break.pst.sg.f leg
        'While she was paying football, she broke her leg.'

Examples like (26) reveal the importance of the second condition: if the events denoted by the two main verbs are connected, the discourse relation is not one of Narration. As, according to Txurruka (2003), the natural language conjunction 'and' markes a coordinating relation, which means one of Narration, Background, Result, Continuation, Parallel or Contrast (Asher and Vieu 2005), one has to ensure that the Narration relation is the only possible one between the two events.

(26)   Ona xorošo igrala^{IPF} i   zarabotala^{PF} nagradu.
        She well   play.pst.sg.f and pref.work.pst.sg.f reward
        'She was playing good and earned a reward.'

On the basis of the observation by Txurruka (2003) that Narration is marked by *then*, we propose to use the substitution of *potom* 'then' instead of *i* 'and' to check whether it is in fact Narration that connects the two coordinated clauses. If it is, then the meaning of the two sentences is (nearly) identical (compare (21) with (27-a)). If it is not, the meaning changes significantly after such substitution (compare (25) with (27-b) and (26) with (27-c): the sentences in (27-b) and (27-c) suggest that the second event is not caused or explained by the first one).

(27)   a.   Ja s"em^{PF} zavtrak, potom pojdu^{PF} na rabotu.
             I s.eat.pres.1sg breakfast, then   po.go.pres.1sg on work
             'I will finish my breakfast, then I will go to work.'
        b.   Ona igrala^{IPF} v futbol, potom slomala^{PF} nogu.
             She play.pst.sg.f in football, then   break.pst.sg.f leg
             'She was paying football, then she broke her leg.'
        c.   Ona xorošo igrala^{IPF},   potom zarabotala^{PF} nagradu.
             She well   play.pst.sg.f, then   pref.work.pst.sg.f reward
             'She was playing good, then she earned a reward.'

Examples in (28) and (29) demonstrate why the second condition is important: a sequence of two sentences without a conjunction or any explicit adverbial indicating their connection, as (28-a), is a bit strange (also a pause will be present between the two sentences in such case), but acceptable in an appropriate context (for example if someone is asked about his plans). (28-b), (28-c) are at least much better than (21-b) and (22-b) and (28-d) is completely natural. In those cases the Narration relation between the two clauses holds. In (28-b) and (28-d) it is explicit due to the presence of *potom* 'then' that, as was mentioned above, is a marker of the Narration. As the idea of the test is to exclude all the coordinating relations (the coordinating requirement is imposed by *i* 'and', so it must be present) except for Narration and see whether it can be established given that the verb in the second clause is perfective, it is important to not include an explicit marker of this relation in the test context and thereby force its application.

(28)   a.   Ja jem^{IPF} zavtrak. Pojdu^{PF} na rabotu.
            I   eat.pres.1sg breakfast. pref.go.pres.1sg to work
            'I'm eating breakfast. Will go to work.'
       b. $^?$Ja jem^{IPF} zavtrak i   potom pojdu^{PF} na rabotu.
            I   eat.pres.1sg   breakfast and   afterwards pres.go.pres.1sg to work
            'I'm eating breakfast and will go to work afterwards.'
       c. $^?$Ja jem^{IPF} zavtrak i   obyazatel'no pojdu^{PF} na.
            I   eat.pres.1sg breakfast and necessarily   pres.go.pres.1sg to
            'I'm eating breakfast and I of course will go to work.'
       d.   Ja jem^{IPF} zavtrak. Potom   pojdu^{PF} na rabotu.
            I   eat.pres.1sg breakfast. Afterwards pres.go.pres.1sg to work
            'I'm eating breakfast. Will go to work afterwards.'

Similarly in the past tense, (29-a) is perfectly fine in a context in which the speaker remembers what s/he did on a given occasion, and just in case there is a distinct pause between the two sentences. For (29-b), there do not seem to be any clear judgments and (29-c) is also fine.

(29)   a.   Ja el^{IPF} zavtrak. Pošel^{PF} na rabotu.
            I   eat.pst.sg.m breakfast. pres.go.pst.sg.m to work
            'I was eating breakfast. Went to work.'
       b. $^?$Ja el^{IPF} zavtrak i   potom   pošel^{PF} na rabotu.
            I   eat.pst.sg.m breakfast and afterwards pres.go.pst.sg.m to work
            'I was eating breakfast and went to work afterwards.'
       c.   Ja el^{IPF} zavtrak. Potom   pošel^{PF} na   rabotu.
            I   eat.pst.sg.m breakfast. Afterwards pres.go.pst.sg.m to work
            'I was eating breakfast. I went to work afterwards.'

Such examples should suffice to illustrate the basic intuition behind the test. The main idea of the test is the well-known generalization given by Jespersen (1924) that if the verb is imperfective, it does not trigger narrative progression (in our case it is the verb in the first clause). Theoretically speaking, the relevant background for the workings of the test is best outlined in Altshuler (2012). His account of the discourse properties of the Russian imperfective relies on a multi-coordinate approach to aspect. He proposes interpretations for the NARR operator and for the aspectual operators and explains why only perfective verb is fine in (30-a) (ex. (73-a) in Altshuler 2012), which is an example similar to our test context.

(30)   a.   Lev ko mne {^{OK}priexal^{PF} / $^{\#}$priezžal^{IPF}}
            Lev to me   pref.arrive.pst.3sg / pref.arrive.imp.pst.3sg
       b.   i   srazu   pošel^{PF} kušat'.
            and right.away pref.go.pst.3sg eat
            'Lev arrived at my place and went to go eat right away.'

Now let us apply the test to the verbs *dopisyvat'* 'to finish/be finishing writing' and *dozapisyvat'* 'to finish/be finishing recording'. According to the syntactic theories, summarized in Sect. 3, these verbs are always assigned to one aspect: either perfective (Ramchand 2004; Romanova 2004; Svenonius 2004b) or imperfective (Tatevosov 2009). However, as examples (31) and (32) show, these two verbs pattern differently with respect to the narration relation test.

(31)   a. $^{??}$Ja dopisyvaju   tekst i   pojdu^{PF} domoj.
              I   do.write.imp.pres.1sg text and go.pres.1sg home

        b.   Ja dozapisyvaju   disk i   pojdu^{PF} domoj.
              I   do.za.write.imp.pres.1sg CD and go.pres.1sg home
              I will finish recording the CD and go home.

(32)   a. $^{??}$Ja dopisyval   text i   pošel^{PF} domoj.
              I   do.write.imp.pst.sg.m tekst and go.pst.sg.m home

        b.   Ja dozapisyval   disk i   pošel^{PF} domoj.
               I   do.za.write.imp.pst.sg.m CD and go.pst.sg.m home
              I will finish recording the CD and go home.

Examples (33-b) and (34-b) show that the same results as for *dozapisyvat'* are obtained for other verbs formed following the same pattern for biaspectual verbs (1). A good example is *dovyšivat'* 'to finish embroidering'. Notice that a derivationally related verb with the same root, namely, *došivat'*, to finish/be finishing sewing) is not acceptable in the test context, as shown by the examples (33-a) and (34-a).

(33)   a. $^{??}$Ja došivala   platje i   podarila^{PF} ego sestre.
              I   do.sew.imp.pst.sg.f dress and pref.present.pst.sg.f he sister

        b.   Ja dovyšivala   kartinu i   povesila^{PF} eë.
              I   do.embroid.imp.pst.sg.f picture and pref.hang.pst.sg.f she
              'I finished embroidering the picture and hang it (on the wall).'

(34)   a. $^{??}$Ja došivaju   platje i   podarju^{PF} ego sestre.
              I   do.sew.imp.pres.1sg dress and pref.present.pres.1sg he sister

        b.   Ja dovyšivala   kartinu i   povesila^{PF} eë.
               I   do.embroid.imp.pst.sg.f picture and pref.hang.pst.sg.f she
              'I finished embroidering the picture and hang it (on the wall).'

To summarize, we have shown that the verbs formed according to the pattern in (1), e.g. *dozapisyvat'*, behave like those verbs that are traditionally considered biaspectual (e.g., *kaznit'*) and are intractable in the syntactic theories.

5 Discussion

As we have seen there is no test that allows to positively identify perfective verbs. This problem together with the widespread assumption that Russian verbal aspect is a binary category seems to be the reason why complex biaspectual verbs have remained largely unexplored and tend to be lumped together with imperfective verbs. Traditional descriptive studies tend to mention only simplex biaspectual verbs, rather than complex ones, which are the focus of this paper. As for the recent syntactic theories of Russian prefixation, we aimed to provide evidence that they cannot account for the existence of complex biaspectual verbs without further modifications.

The existence of a non-neglectable class of complex verbs that can behave either as perfective or imperfective verbs, in dependence on context, raises important questions about their status with respect to the bipartite perfective vs. imperfective distinction. In what follows, let us briefly mention the following three. First, are such verbs ambiguous between the perfective and imperfective aspect or are they underspecified for grammatical aspect? The claim that they are ambiguous would imply that there are two different verbs (each with a different internal structure) that just happen to have the same phonological realization.

Second, it is not entirely clear whether there is just one class of complex verbs with variable grammatical aspect behavior or whether its domain needs to be split into subclasses. Third, what also needs to be clarified is the relation of complex verbs with variable grammatical aspect behavior to native simple biaspectual verbs like *kaznit'*, and to borrowed biaspectual verbs, both simple and complex, like *(pod-)amortizirovat'* 'to cushion (slightly).' The latter are claimed to lose their biaspectuality over time (see, e.g., Janda 2007; Korba 2007), in contrast to native biaspectual verbs like *kaznit'*. The answer to such questions must be left for future research.

A large part of the paper is devoted to providing a new positive test for perfectivity. This test relies on discourse structure, and its application requires several conditions to be observed. So far, no other suitable general positive test for perfectivity has been put forth. The fact that syntactic and morphological properties are used for a positive identification of imperfectivity, but the discourse level is needed in order to positively establish perfectivity of a given verb, is in itself an intriguing indication about another difference between imperfective and perfective aspect, which has not yet been noticed.

This paper is a part of a larger research program. In a related paper by (Zinova and Filip 2014) it is shown that there are other prefixed biaspectual verbs (not only prefixed with the completive *do-*, but also with the iterative *pere-* and the attenuative *pri-*). Some motivation why exactly those complex verb forms (with such prefixes) exhibit properties of biaspectuality is also provided. Significantly, the distinction between lexical and superlexical prefixes, and other finer distinctions among prefixes based on syntactic criteria, proves to be irrelevant in motivating their biaspectual behavior.

References

Altshuler, D.: Aspectual meaning meets discourse coherence: a look at the Russian imperfective. J. Semant. **29**(1), 39–108 (2012)

Anderson, C.: Biaspectual verbs in Russian and their implications on the category of aspect. Senior honor dissertation, The University of North Carolina (2002)

Asher, N., Vieu, L.: Subordinating and coordinating discourse relations. Lingua 115(4), 591–610 (2005)

Avilova, N.S.: Dvuvidovye glagoly s zaimstvovannoj osnovoj v russkom literaturnom jazyke novogo vremeni [Biaspectual verbs with loaned stem in contemporary Russian literary language]. Voprosy jazykoznanija, pp. 66–78 (1968)

Babko-Malaya, O.: Zero morphology: A study of aspect, argument structure, and case. Dissertation, Rutgers University (1999)

Barykina, A.N., Dobrovol'skaya, V.V., Merzon, S.N.: Izučenie glagol'nyx pristavok [Study of verbal prefixes]. Russkij yazyk (1989)

Borer, H.: Between function and content - the case of Slavic perfective prefixes [Plenary talk handout, FDSL 2010]. Leipzig, Germany (2013)

Borik, O.: Aspect and reference time. Ph.D. thesis, Universiteit Utrecht (2002)

Borik, O., Janssen, M.: A database of Russian verbal aspect. In: Proceedings of the Conference Russian Verb, St. Petersburg, Russia (2012)

Čertkova, M.J., Čang, P.Č.: Evoljucija dvuvidovyx glagolov v sovremennom russkom jazyke. [Evolution of the biaspectual verbs in contemporary Russian.]. Russian Linguistics 22, 13–34 (1998)

Di Sciullo, A.M., Slabakova, R.: Quantification and aspect. In: Verkeyl, H.J., de Swart, H., van Hout, A. (eds.) Perspectives on Aspect, pp. 61–80. Springer, The Netherlands (2005)

Filip, H.: The Quantization Puzzle. In: Events as Grammatical Objects, pp. 3–60. CSLI Press, Stanford (2000)

Filip, H.: Prefixes and the delimitation of events. J. Slavic Linguist. 1(11), 55–101 (2003)

Forsyth, J.: A Grammar of Aspect: Usage and Meaning in the Russian Verb. Cambridge University Press, Cambridge (1970)

Gehrke, B.: How temporal is telicity? In: Paper presented at the workshop "Argument realization-Conceptual and grammatical factors", Leipzig (2004)

Gladney, F.Y.: Biaspectual verbs and the syntax of aspect in Russian. Slavic East Eur. J. 26, 202–215 (1982)

Isačenko, A.: Grammatičeskij stroj russkogo jazyka v sopostavlenii s slovackim [Grammatical structure of Russian in comparison to Slovak]. Jazyki slavjanskoj kultury (1960)

Isačenko, A.V.: Die Russische Sprache der Gegenwart. M. Hueber, München (1968)

Janda, L.A.: What makes Russian bi-aspectual verbs special. In: Cognitive Paths into the Slavic Domain. Cognitive Linguistics Research, pp. 83–109 (2007)

Jászay, L.: Vidovye korreljaty pri dvuvidovyx glagolax [Aspectual correlates of biaspectual verbs]. Studia Russica 17, 169–177 (1999)

Jespersen, O.: Philosophy of grammar. George Allen and Unwin Ltd, London (1924)

Korba, J.J.: The development of overt aspectual marking among Russian biaspectual verbs. ProQuest (2007)

Krongauz, M.: Pristavki i glagoly v russkom yazyke: Semanticheskaya grammatika [Prefixes and Verbs in Russian Language: A Semantics Grammar], Moscow (1998)

Lascarides, A., Asher, N.: Temporal interpretation, discourse relations and commonsense entailment. Linguist. Philos. 16(5), 437–493 (1993)

Maslov, J.S.: Izbrannye trudy: Aspektologija. Obščee jazykoznanie [Selected Writings: Aspectology. General Linguistics]. Jazyki slavjanskoj kultury. Moscow (2004)

Mikaeljan, I., Šmelev, A., Zaliznjak, A.: Imperfectivization in Russian. In: Proceedings of the 3rd International Conference on Meaning-Text Theory, pp. 20–24 (2007)

Ožegov, S.I.: Slovar' russkogo jazyka [Dictionary of Russian] (1990)

Padučeva, E.V.: Semantičeskie issledovanija: Semantika vremeni i vida v russkom jazyke; Semantika narrativa [Semantic Studies: The Semantics of Tense and Aspect in Russian; The Semantics of Narrative]. Škola "Jazyki Russkoj Kultury". Moscow (1996)

Padučeva, E.V.: O semantičeskom invariante vidovogo značenija glagola v russkom jazyke [About the semantic invariant of the verbal aspect meaning in Russian]. Russkij jazyk v naučnom osveščenii **2**(8), 5–16 (2004)

Ramchand, G.: Time and the event: the semantics of Russian prefixes. Nordlyd **32**(2), 323–361 (2004)

Romanova, E.: Superlexical versus lexical prefixes. Nordlyd **32**(2), 255–278 (2004)

Romanova, E.: Constructing Perfectivity in Russian. Ph.D. thesis, University of Tromsø (2006)

Grammar, R.: Grammatika russkogo jazyka [Grammar of Russian]. Izdatelstvo AN SSSR, Moscow (1952)

Schoorlemmer, M.: Participial passive and aspect in Russian. LEd, Utrecht (1995)

Skott, S.: On biaspectual verbs in Russian. In: Pettersson, T. (ed.) Aspectology, pp. 17–33. Almqvist and Wiksell, Stockholm (1979)

Svenonius, P.: Slavic prefixes and morphology. an introduction to the Nordlyd volume. Nordlyd **32**(2), 177–204 (2004a)

Svenonius, P.: Slavic prefixes inside and outside VP. Nordlyd **32**(2), 205–253 (2004b)

Svenonius, P. : Structural and featural distinctions between germanic and slavic prefixes (2012)

Tatevosov, S.: Intermediate prefixes in Russian. In: Proceedings of the Annual Workshop on Formal Approaches to Slavic linguistics, vol. 16 (2007)

Tatevosov, S.: Množestvennaja prefiksacija i anatomija russkogo glagola [Multiple prefixation and the anatomy of Russian verb]. In: Korpusnye issledovanija po russkoj grammatike, pp. 92–157 (2009)

Tatevosov, S.: Množestvennaja prefiksacija i eë sledstvija (Zametki o fiziologii russkogo glagola) [Multiple prefixation and its consequences (Notes on the physiology of Russian verb)]. Voprosy jazykoznanija **3**, 42–89 (2013)

Timberlake, A.: A Reference Grammar of Russian. Cambridge University Press, Cambridge (2004)

Townsend, C.E.: Russian Word-Formation. Slavica Publishers, Bloomington (1975)

Txurruka, I.G.: The natural language conjunction and. Linguist. Philos. **26**(3), 255–285 (2003)

Ušakov, D., (ed.): Tolkovyj slovar' russkogo jazyka [Explanatory Dictionary of the Russian Language]. State Publishing House of Foreign and National Dictionaries, Moscow (1934–1940)

Švedova, N.J.: Russkaja grammatika [Russian Grammar], vol. 1. Nauka, Moscow (1982)

Zaliznjak, A.A.: Grammatičeskij slovar' russkogo jazyka [Grammatical Dictionary of Russian]. Russkij jazyk, Moscow (1977)

Zinova, Y.: Russian verbal prefixation puzzles. Handout of the talk given at the Graduate Research Seminar at Heinrich-Heine University (2012). https://www.academia.edu/8359697

Zinova, Y., Filip, H.: The role of derivational history in aspect determination. In: Proceedings of 24 FDSL Conference, Leipzig, Germany (2014, to appear)

Author Index

Printed in the United States
By Bookmasters

Printed in the United States
By Bookmasters